D0150368

TRIVIAL CONQUEST

THE SMART
REFERENCE SOURCE FOR
TRIVIAL PURSUIT:
THE BOARD GAME

Avon Books are available at special quantity discounts for bulk purchases for sales promotions, premiums, fund raising or educational use. Special books, or book excerpts, can also be created to fit specific needs.

For details write or telephone the office of the Director of Special Markets, Avon Books, Dept. FP, 1790 Broadway, New York, New York 10019, 212-399-1357.

TRIVIAL CONQUEST

Lisa Merkin & Eric Frankel

THE SMART REFERENCE SOURCE FOR TRIVIAL PURSUIT: THE BOARD GAME

 AVON
PUBLISHERS OF BARD, CAMELOT, DISCUS AND FLARE BOOKS

TRIVIAL CONQUEST The Smart Reference Source for Trivial Pursuit®: The Board Game is an original publication of Avon Books. This work has never before appeared in book form.

TRIVIAL PURSUIT® Is a Registered TRADEMARK OF HORN ABBOT LTD., St. Catharines, Ontario, Canada, for its Board Game and equipment including a playing board, die, rules of play, question and answer cards, card boxes, player tokens and scoring materials. This book does not emanate from and is neither sponsored nor authorized by Horn Abbot Ltd.

AVON BOOKS
A division of
The Hearst Corporation
1790 Broadway
New York, New York 10019

Copyright © 1984 by Grapevine Entertainment, Inc.,
Published by arrangement with the authors
Library of Congress Catalog Card Number: 84-45256
ISBN: 0-380-89492-0

All rights reserved, which includes the right to reproduce this book or portions thereof in any form whatsoever except as provided by the U. S. Copyright Law. For information address The William Morris Agency, 1350 Avenue of the Americas, New York, New York 10019

First Avon Printing, August, 1984

AVON TRADEMARKS REG. U. S. PAT. OFF. AND IN OTHER COUNTRIES, MARCA REGISTRADA, HECHO EN U. S. A.

Printed in the U. S. A.

OP 10 9 8 7 6 5 4 3 2

ACKNOWLEDGMENTS

Pete Adams, Pat Baetens-Adler, Jerry Beck, Jeff Bernstein, Pat Birde, Edward Bleier, Eve Brody, Peter Burton, Kathleen Daley, Rachel Dash, Philippe de La Chapelle, Andrea Dennis, Tim Fichter, Robin Field, Liz Fischer, Beth Fishtein, Dr. Tom Fleming, Arthur Frankel, Ronald & Marjorie Frankel, John Gibson, Lauren Gibson, Mark Greenberg, Mike Greenstein, Robert Gottlieb, Bill Hunnell, Ted Leonsis, Susan Mackin, Dennis Mathis, Bruce Merkin, Natalie & Norman Merkin, Julia Pistor, Andrea & Larry Price, Robina Ramsay, Judith Roberts, Carol Fein-Ross, Janet Sarcia and Leading Edge Products, Inc., for use of their NUTSHELL™ INFORMATION SYSTEM, Stanley Solson, David Spiegelman, Ronald S. Sweet, Helen Wilson, Kihm Winship and Milo Yelesiyevich.

And thanks to the Avon Books staff:
Rose Dreger, David Eisner, Kendall Fousek, Caron Harris, Jerold Kappes, Coleen O'Shea, Jan Parrish, Sharon Shavers, Lynn Strong, Maureen Tracy and Kathryn Vought

NOTE TO READERS

Trivia is fact, and facts change. Therefore, it is possible that by the time you read this book, certain statistics may have changed. It is also possible, due to differing opinions, that some entries may appear to be in error. However, we have tried in every case to use the information most widely accepted by experts.

In order to ease your search, *TRIVIAL CONQUEST* is arranged in an alphabetical configuration. But there are certain rules that we have generally followed to add a consistency to the book:

Real people are listed last name first. For information about John Kennedy, see **KENNEDY, JOHN.**

Fictional characters are listed by the name they are best known as. For information about Huckleberry Hound, see **HUCKLE-BERRY HOUND.** For information about James Bond, see **BOND, JAMES,** as in the 007 movies where Sean Connery or Roger Moore often introduce themselves as "Bond, James Bond."

Actors, actresses and directors, when mentioned in the context of a specific movie, play or television series, are generally listed by the movie, play or series name. For information about Clint Eastwood in *Dirty Harry,* see **DIRTY HARRY.**

Works of literature and art are listed by the author or artist's name. For information about Mario Puzo's novel *The Godfather,* see **PUZO, MARIO.** For information about Michelangelo's *Pietà,* see **MICHELANGELO.**

Rules and terms pertaining to sports are generally listed under the particular sport. For information about hockey pucks, see **HOCKEY.**

Many questions in TRIVIAL PURSUIT® have more than one subject that would appear to serve as a logical "heading." For example, if you're looking for information regarding Adolf Hitler's role in World War II, make sure you check both **HITLER, ADOLF,** and **WORLD WAR II.**

Should you find any discrepancies or wish to contact us, please feel free to write: *TRIVIAL CONQUEST,* c/o Grapevine Entertainment, Inc., P.O. Box 8106, F.D.R. Station, New York, NY 10050.

Now, it's time to PURSUE and CONQUER!

INTRODUCTION

What is part atlas, part dictionary, part encyclopedia, and probably the widest-ranging and most informative, entertaining reference source available?

You're holding it. *TRIVIAL CONQUEST*, The Smart Reference Source for Trivial Pursuit®: The Board Game, filled with fascinating facts about geography, entertainment, history, science, nature, art, literature, sports and more. The reference source for trivia fanatics and also the only single-edition companion to the world's most popular trivia game, guaranteed to satisfy its players and complete the game cycle.

Cultivating a passion for trivia requires persistent curiosity. "Buffs" are never satisfied with a simple answer. Not just the who, but the where, when, how and why—they want MORE. Our offering to trivia buffs, and to those of you who are just learning to enjoy trivia, is MORE.

Dig deeper, there are facts to be learned, trivia beyond trivia, and a good, fun time to be had by all. Enjoy!

FOREWORD

This book was written by two players of TRIVIAL PURSUIT®, Lisa Merkin and Eric Frankel, whose enthusiasm for the game grew, much as yours surely will, into a pure and pleasurable habit. Their enthusiasm, however, unlike that of most players, took an unusual bent. It led them, of all things, to ponder many questions of their own, based on the areas covered by the game, and to seek elaboration.

The elaborations, they soon found, intensified the pleasure of the game, compounding the fun and excitement of play. Soon they began to keep lists of these extended answers—lists that became the genesis of this book, TRIVIAL CONQUEST, The Smart Reference Source for Trivial Pursuit®: The Board Game.

"How can it be?" you ask. "How can more elaborate, more definitive answers act as a catalyst to intensify the enjoyment of the game?" Easily. Let's try a few examples. See if it doesn't work for you. And if it does, you'll be hooked like so many others who have made TRIVIAL CONQUEST their information-filled, fun-filled companion every time they and their friends or family play. It will serve as your personal, definitive reference book, filling the information gap for the most exciting, best-selling game in history.

Here's why. Hypothetical example:

Question: What city hosts an annual Swan upping?
Answer: London, England
Players' question: What is a Swan upping and when does it occur?
TRIVIAL CONQUEST's **answer:** (found under **SWAN UPPING**)

Week-long event held each July on the River Thames. Swans are owned by the monarch, and the Vintners and the Dyers (two of the city's Greater Companies—successors of medieval fraternal guilds). Boats flying the company (Guild) flag sail to Windsor, catch and mark cygnets (young swans) on the bill with the company mark found on the parent swan, whose marks are renewed. Swans with no marks are given the insignia of the monarch.

Sensible and quite a difference, isn't it? Let's try some more.

Question: How many of the movie industry's top 10 box-office hits has Steven Spielberg directed?

Answer: Three

Players' question: What are the top 10 box-office hits and which of them did Spielberg direct?

TRIVIAL CONQUEST's answer: (found under **BOX-OFFICE HITS, MOVIES**)

The movie industry's top-grossing films are:

Title	Director/Producer
E.T.: The Extraterrestrial	S. Spielberg/S. Spielberg
Star Wars	G. Lucas/G. Kurtz
Return of the Jedi	R. Marquand/G. Lucas & H. Kazanjian
The Empire Strikes Back	I. Kershner/G. Lucas & G. Kurtz
Jaws	S. Spielberg/R. Zanuck & D. Brown
Raiders of the Lost Ark	S. Spielberg/G. Lucas, H. Kazanjian & F. Marshall
Grease	R. Kleiser/R. Stigwood & A. Carr
Tootsie	S. Pollack/S. Pollack & D. Richards
The Exorcist	W. Friedkin/W.P. Blatty
The Godfather	F. F. Coppola/A. Ruddy

Question: What are VHF and UHF?

Answer: Radio frequencies

Players' question: What do these abbreviations stand for, and what other radio frequencies are there?

TRIVIAL CONQUEST's answer: (found under **RADIO FREQUENCIES**)

Radio frequencies include:
ELF (extremely low frequency); VF (voice frequency); VLF (very low frequency); LF (low frequency); MF (medium frequency); HF (high frequency); VHF (very high frequency); UHF (ultrahigh frequency); SHF (superhigh frequency); and EHF (extremely high frequency).

Now you can see why *TRIVIAL CONQUEST* is at the right hand of so many players. But there is more, of course, that goes beyond fun and games. It has something to do with brains. A pleasure to read on its own, this book can help you look and sound smarter, earn a wide-ranging reputation for knowledgeability—and become a master of trivia.

—Ron Frankel

A CAPPELLA   Singing done by voices without instrumental accompaniment. Generally associated with rhythm-and-blues singers of late 1950s and early '60s.

A.D.   Abbreviation of Latin *anno Domini*, meaning "in the year of the Lord." Marks dates after birth of Christ.

A.M., P.M.   Abbreviations of Latin phrases *ante meridiem* ("before noon") and *post meridiem* ("after noon"). Twelve o'clock midnight is considered the start of A.M., while P.M. starts at 12 noon.

AARDVARK   Also called antbear, earth pig or cape anteater. Burrowing animal of Africa that eats ants and termites. These stocky animals have foot-long tongues and can fend off lions with their powerful claws.

AARON, HANK (1934–   )   Finished major league baseball career with Milwaukee Brewers (American League) hitting 22 home runs in 1975 and 1976 seasons to finish with career record of 755, 41 more than Babe Ruth. Named to American League All-Star team both years. Remainder of home runs hit with Braves (National League) in Milwaukee and Atlanta. Broke Ruth's record April 8, 1974, vs. Los Angeles Dodgers. Led National League in homers four times.

ABACUS   Type of mechanical calculator still used in China and other Asian countries. Typical abacus has beads arranged in 13 columns, each representing a power of 10. Usually seven beads per column: five to indicate one unit each, two to indicate five units each. A trained operator can use an abacus to add, subtract, multiply, divide and find square and cube roots with remarkable speed.

ABBOTT AND COSTELLO MEET DR. JEKYLL AND MR. HYDE 1953 comedy starring Bud Abbott and Lou Costello as two American police officers studying London police methods. They encounter the famous doctor, portrayed by Boris Karloff.

ABDICATION December 12, 1936, headline of London *Star.* Announced abdication of recently crowned King Edward VIII of England. Abandoned throne to marry American divorcée Wallis Simpson, deemed unacceptable to the royal family.

ABDUL-JABBAR, KAREEM (1947–   ) Born Ferdinand Lewis Alcindor in New York City. Adopted present Muslim name, 1971. Led UCLA to three NCAA basketball championships, 1967–1969. National Basketball Association Rookie of the Year, 1970, with Milwaukee Bucks. Played on NBA championship teams with Milwaukee (1971), Los Angeles Lakers (1980, 1982). Won six Most Valuable Player awards. Became NBA's all-time leading scorer, 1984.

ABEL, RUDOLF I. (1903?–1971) Russian spy. U.S. alias, Emil Goldfus. Arrested for espionage against U.S., June 1957. Found wih coded microfilm message in a coin. Exchanged February 1962 by U.S. for Francis Gary Powers, pilot of U-2 reconnaissance plane shot down over U.S.S.R., 1960.

ABOLITIONISTS Term given to anti-slavery groups of early 19th century. First abolitionist presidential candidate, James G. Birney. Ran on Liberty Party ticket, 1840. Slavery officially abolished 1865, with ratification of 13th Amendment to U.S. Constitution.

ABOMINABLE SNOWMAN, THE Or Himalayas' Yeti. Animal believed by some to live in Himalayan Mountains. Supposed to be large, hairy, apelike creature. No sighting ever verified.

ABORTION Ending of pregnancy before birth. Either spontaneous (natural causes) or induced. Induced abortions first legal in Iceland, 1935. U.S. Supreme Court in 1973 ruled that abortions during first trimester of pregnancy could not be forbidden if doctor approved.

ABRAHAM, MARTIN AND JOHN 1968 hit song by Dion Dimucci, tribute to Abraham Lincoln, Martin Luther King,

John and Bobby Kennedy. Dimucci formed Dion and the Belmonts in 1958 and had hit songs "A Teenager in Love" (1959) and "Where and When" (1960). Went solo with popular songs "Runaround Sue" (1962) and "The Wanderer" (1962).

ABSCAM FBI investigation of political corruption, 1980. FBI agents, later accused of entrapment, posed as Arabs working for fictitious company, Abdul Enterprises. Agents proceeded to bribe seven U.S. congressmen and many officials of Pennsylvania and New Jersey to change immigration legislation and secure building permits and casino licenses.

ABSENT-MINDED PROFESSOR, THE Popular 1961 comedy film from Walt Disney studio. Fred MacMurray stars in title role as science teacher who invents flying rubber, nicknamed "flubber," which causes everything from his Model-T to the entire school basketball team to fly. Sequel *Son of Flubber* released in 1963.

ABSOLUTE ZERO Conceptually, the temperature where there is no heat or molecular motion. Celsius, $-273.15°$ C; Fahrenheit, $-459.67°$ F; Kelvin, $0°$ Kelvin (OK). From scale of Lord Kelvin. Based on second law of thermodynamics.

ABZUG, BELLA (1920–   ) Politician. Admitted to NY State Bar, 1947. Served in U.S. House of Representatives, 1961–1970, representing Manhattan districts. Known for wide-brimmed hats and liberal views.

ACADEMY AWARDS Annual awards given by Academy of Motion Picture Arts and Sciences. First presented at Hollywood's Roosevelt Hotel on May 16, 1927, the only year an award was given for "title writing." The awarded statue, nicknamed Oscar, is of a strong man holding a crusader's sword and standing on a reel of film. The public accounting firm of Price Waterhouse & Company tabulates the ballots of the voting members and places the winners' names in a sealed envelope.

ACAPULCO Seaport on Pacific coast of Mexico, in state of Guerrero. Popular resort area. Visitors enjoy warm climate, deep-sea fishing and famed diving area, 100 ft. (30 m.) above waters containing Quebrada rocks. June–September is rainy season.

ACE As noun: a serve untouched by receiver in tennis, handball or any other racket game; a hole-in-one in golf; or an outstanding player or star in any sport (e.g., the "ace" of the pitching staff). As verb: to score on an unreturned serve (in racket sports) or to sink a hole-in-one in golf.

ACHILLES Hero of Homer's *Iliad*. Greek mythology's most illustrious warrior in Trojan War. Slew Hector. Dipped by mother in river Styx as baby, making him invulnerable except on right heel by which she held him. Fatally wounded when hit there by arrow; hence phrase "Achilles' heel" for point of vulnerability.

AD ARMA Latin phrase, meaning "to arms." From *ad* ("to" or "by") plus *arma* ("weapons" or "arms," especially "shields"). Used as battle cry by the Romans. Another famous call to arms is a bugler blowing "assembly."

ADAM Created by God on sixth day as the "roof and crown" of creation. Name comes from Hebrew *Adamah*, for "ground," from which he was formed. Called Father of Human Race because he had three sons by Eve: Cain, Abel and Seth, who was conceived after Cain slew Abel. Bible implies Adam had additional children.

ADAMS, JOHN (1735–1826) Lawyer and second U.S. president, 1796. Began as vice-president to George Washington, 1789. Said of his job, "[It is] the most insignificant office that ever the invention of man contrived or his imagination conceived."

ADAMS, RICHARD GEORGE (1920–   ) British novelist. Best known for *Watership Down* (1972), allegorical novel about band of rabbits en route to new home. Characters include valiant Bigwig, menacing General Woundwort, psychic Fiver and seagull Kehaar; includes glossary of rabbit language. Also wrote *Shardik* (1974), *The Plague Dogs* (1977) and *The Girl on a Swing* (1980).

ADAMSON, JOY (1911–1980) Naturalist and writer. Wife of game warden in Kenya. Wrote about how she and husband raised three lion cubs. Two sent to zoo, one, Elsa the lioness, stayed with them. Story of raising her and ultimately returning her to the wild told in *Born Free* (1960), *Living Free* (1961) and *Forever Free* (1962). Murdered by fired employee, 1980. (see BORN FREE)

ADDAMS FAMILY, THE Comedy TV series, 1964–1966. Strange, eccentric family consisted of Gomez, the father (played by John Astin); Morticia, his wife (Carolyn Jones); Pugsley, their son (Ken Weatherwax); Wednesday, their daughter (Lisa Loving); and Uncle Fester (Jackie Coogan). Ted Cassidy portrayed Lurch, their butler.

ADDER   Any of many species of snakes classified as genus Heterodon, including: death adder (Australia), dangerous, related to cobra; European viper, also known as adder, only poisonous snake found in Great Britain; hognose snake (U.S.), harmless, also called blowing adder; puff adder (Africa), long fangs, venomous.

ADENAUER, KONRAD (1876–1967)   Chancellor of West Germany, 1949–1963. Imprisoned, World War II, for his political sympathies. Later founded Christian Democratic Union (CDU), a moderate party aiming to rebuild a shattered Germany in the Christian spirit.

ADMIRALTY ARCH   Built by Sir Aston Webb in memory of Queen Victoria. Located in London at eastern end of the Mall, wide tree-lined street leading to Buckingham Palace.

ADOLESCENCE   Transition period between childhood and adulthood. In physiological sense, begins at puberty and ends at maturity in the early 20s. Legally, generally begins at 13 and ends at 18.

ADRIATIC SEA   Named for Adria, a city in northern Italy. Arm of the Mediterranean Sea, separating Italy from Yugoslavia and Albania. About 480 mi. (772 km.) long and 100 mi. (160 km.) wide.

ADVENTURE IN PARADISE   Adventure TV series starring Gardner McKay as Adam Troy. Captain of free-lance schooner named *Tiki*. Stories revolved around schemers and beauties at Miki Hotel and in waters of South Pacific.

AEGEAN SEA   Arm of Mediterranea Sea. Located between Greece and Asia Minor. Southern area called Sea of Crete. Sprinkled throughout the sea are several hundred Grecian islands.

AER LINGUS   Ireland's national airline, owned by Irish government. Founded 1936. Headquartered in Dublin. First transatlantic flight, 1958. Flies 21 aircraft to 11 countries.

AEROFLOT   National airline of Russia. World's largest airline. Links Russia with over 80 countries in North and South America, Europe, Asia and Africa. Established 1923. Headquarters, Moscow. U.S. offices closed when airline was banned from landing in U.S. after Soviets shot down South Korean commercial airplane, 1983.

AESOP (c.620–560 B.C.)   Phrygian slave who allegedly wrote famed fables. Historians doubt he wrote all; some doubt he existed. His fables are tales with morals in which talking animals illustrate human virtues and vices. Moral of his fable "The Milkmaid and Her Pail": Don't count your chickens before they're hatched. Fable of fox and grapes concerns thirsty fox who comes upon grapes hanging from tree, leaves them there after several fruitless attempts to grab them and rationalizes that they were sour. Moral: It's easy to despise what you can't have anyway.

AFRICA Northernmost point: Ras'ben Sekka, near Cape Blanc. Southernmost point: Cape Agulhas. Easternmost point: Ras Hafum, near Cape Guardafui. Westernmost point: Cape Verde. Continent consisting of more countries than any other, with 51 individual countries and several units. Second largest continent in area and third largest in population. Ninety-nine percent of total area lies within tropics, making it the warmest continent. Temperatures may vary more between day and night than between summer and winter. Highest recorded temperature: 136 degrees F (58 degrees C) in the shade, Libya, September 13, 1922.

AFRICAN QUEEN, THE 1951 feature film starring Humphrey Bogart as Charlie Allnut, the drunken skipper who changes his ways for missionary Rosey Sayer (Katharine Hepburn) during their voyage down an African river. Bogart won his only Oscar as Best Actor for his performance.

AGE. See MORTALITY AND LIFE EXPECTANCY

AGNEW, SPIRO THEODORE (1918–) American right-wing politician. Republican governor of Maryland, 1966–1969. Nominated Richard Nixon for president at 1968 Republican Convention. Became Nixon's vice-president, 1969. Rhetorical style and glib comments infuriated critics. As to problems of the urban poor, he said: "If you've seen one slum, you've seen them all." Commenting on the press, he remarked: "Some newspapers dispose of their garbage by printing it." Resigned as vice-president, 1973.

AIRPLANE Largest jet, 747, holds nearly 500 passengers. Wings of aircraft balance plane in flight and absorb most bumps; seats to rear of wings are noisier and may render a bumpier ride. Streamlined design facilitates smoother flying.

AJAX All-purpose liquid cleaner. Manufactured by Colgate-Palmolive Inc., Chicago. Supposed to clean with the fury of a "white tornado," its trademark since 1963.

AKRON, OHIO Located in northeastern part of state. Home

of four of world's largest rubber companies: Firestone, General Tire, Goodrich and Goodyear. Called "Rubber Capital of the World." Rubber industry began there in 1870, when Benjamin F. Goodrich opened his factory.

ALABAMA   Four bordering states: Tennessee to the north; Georgia to the east; Florida to the south; Mississippi to the west.

ALAMO   Franciscan mission, San Antonio, TX. Scene of siege led by Mexican general Santa Anna, killing all Texans present, March 6, 1836. Following the massacre, Texans struggling for freedom from Mexico would rally with "Remember the Alamo." By April 21, 1836, Texas had won independence.

ALASKA   Least populated and largest state. Westernmost point is 51 mi. (82 km.) from Russia. Called Russian America until 1867, when bought from Russia by American Secretary of State William H. Seward for $7,200,000 (two cents per acre). Also called the Last Frontier because so much of its territory has not been settled. Became a U.S. state in 1958. Shares longer border with Canada than any other U.S. state, for a total distance of 1,150 mi. (1,840 km.). State bird: willow ptarmigan. State flower: forget-me-not. State motto: "North to the Future." State tree: sitka spruce. Mount McKinley lodgings include McKinley Village Hotel, Mount McKinley Station Hotel and McKinley Chalets. Sunshine: receives less than any other U.S. state. Cities and their average percent of daytime hours of sunshine per month: Anchorage, 45%; Fairbanks, 44%; Nome, 41%; Juneau, 30%.

ALASKA HIGHWAY   Connects Dawson Creek, British Columbia, with Delta Junction, Alaska, where Richardson Highway leads to Fairbanks. Alaska is linked to other states and Canada by this road only. Runs for 1,422 mi. (2,288 km.). One-quarter is paved; the rest is gravel.

ALBEE, EDWARD FRANKLIN (1928–   )   American playwright. Wrote one-act play *The Zoo Story* (1958) before his first full-length play, *Who's Afraid of Virginia Woolf?* (1962), became critical and popular success. In latter, childless couple George and Martha, college professor and daughter of college president, unveil their relationship during an evening with another couple, biology instructor Nick and his wife Honey.

ALBERTA   Westernmost prairie province of Canada. One of North America's greatest oil producers. Name dates from 1882, when province was named for Princess Louis Caroline Alberta, daughter of Queen Victoria and wife of Canadian governor-general.

ALCATRAZ PRISON Federal prison on Alcatraz Island in San Francisco Bay. In operation, 1933–1963. Closed due to high maintenance costs. Now part of national recreation area. Stands on 12 acres of solid rock. All prisoners who tried to escape drowned or were captured. Called "The Rock."

ALCOHOLISM. See DRUGS

ALCOTT, LOUISA MAY (1832–1888) American novelist whose *Little Women* (1868) sold millions. Subtitled *Meg, Jo, Beth and Amy*, story's heroine is Jo March, most tomboyish and literary of four sisters. Traces their growing up and marriages. Sequels: *Little Men* (1871) and *Jo's Boys* (1886).

ALDRIN, EDWIN E. JR. (BUZZ) (1930–   ) Astronaut. Former Air Force officer. Flew 66 combat missions, Korea. Pilot, Gemini 12, 1966; left spacecraft to "walk" in space for five and one-half hours. After Neil Armstrong, Aldrin was second person to walk on moon's surface, July 20, 1969, Apollo 11.

ALEXANDRIA Chief seaport and second largest city in Egypt. Founded 331 B.C. by Alexander the Great. Lies on Mediterranean Sea. Only 2% inhabitants are foreigners. Economy is strengthened by tourism.

ALGARVE Province in southern Portugal, noted for its resorts. Warm climate, bathing and lush vegetation, such as pomegranate, pear and fig trees, attract visitors. Approximately 124 mi. (200 km.) of coast is developed. Entire province faces Atlantic Ocean. Originally inhabited by Moors.

ALGERIA, MOROCCO, TUNISIA Originally French colonies. In 1830 France began war with Algeria, which fought for independence. Tunisia, Morocco and other French possessions were drawn into the conflict, in which they won independence.

ALHAMBRA PALACE Palace and fortress built by Moors, 1248–1354, Granada, Spain. Considered Europe's best example of Moorish art. Name from Arabic words for "the red," referring to color of outer wall. Captured from Moors by Spanish armies, 1492.

ALI, MUHAMMAD (1942–   ) Three-time world heavyweight boxing champion (1964–1968, 1974–1978, 1978–1980). Born Cassius Marcellus Clay in Louisville, KY. Prefight poetry earned him nickname "Louisville Lip." Changed name upon becoming Black Muslim, 1964. 1960 Olympic light-heavyweight champion in Rome. Won heavyweight crown from Sonny Liston, 1964, with strategy to "float like a butterfly, sting like a bee," according to trainer Drew "Bundini" Brown. Stripped of his title, 1967, for refusing U.S. Army induction on religious grounds. While barred from fighting, preached and lectured at colleges and starred in *Buck White*, 1969 musical about black power group written by Oscar Brown, Jr.; play closed after seven performances. Supreme Court reversed draft evasion conviction, January 1970. Resumed boxing career, losing to Joe Frazier in "Fight of the Century," March 1971. Lost to Ken Norton in 12-round decision, non-title fight, March 31, 1973, in San Diego, after Norton broke his jaw in first round. Regained title, 1974, from George Foreman. Beat Frazier in 1975 "Thrilla in Manila." Lost and regained title from Leon Spinks, 1978. Retired 1979. Lost to champion Larry Holmes in 1980 comeback attempt. Autobiography *The Greatest: My Own Story*, co-written by Richard Dunbar, published 1975; dedicated to his mother and father. Ali was first fighter to be seen worldwide via satellite; claims to be most recognized person in the world.

ALICE. See CARROLL, LEWIS

ALICE'S RESTAURANT Stockbridge, MA, restaurant made famous by folksinger Arlo Guthrie with his 20-minute tall tale recorded in 1967. Made into feature film in 1969 with Guthrie, Pat Quinn as Alice. Directed by Arthur Penn.

ALL ABOUT EVE 1950 drama starring Bette Davis as Margo Channing, an insecure actress who gives counsel to aspiring performer Eve Harrington (Anne Baxter). Joseph L. Mankiewicz wrote and directed this cynical view of theater life. Winner of seven Oscars, including Best Picture.

ALL IN THE FAMILY Top-rated comedy TV series, 1971–1979. Carroll O'Connor portrayed the bigoted Archie Bunker; Jean Stapleton was his "dingbat" wife, Edith. Based on British TV series *Till Death Do Us Part*. Family resided at 704 Hauser Street, Queens, NY.

ALL SAINTS' DAY November 1. Follows Halloween (All Hallows' Eve). Originated in 7th century from conversion of the Pantheon at Rome into a Christian place of worship and its dedication by Pope Boniface IV to the Virgin Mary and all the martyrs.

ALL THAT GLITTERS IS NOT GOLD   Spanish novelist Miguel de Cervantes issued this warning in *Don Quixote* (1615), but was not the first or only writer to do so. Others were: Alain de Lille, 12th century; Chaucer, 15th century; Lydgate, 15th century; Gabriel Biel, 15th century; Shakespeare, 16th century; Spenser, 16th century; Middleton, 17th century; Dryden, 17th century. Common proverb is traced to Aristotle's "Yellow-colored objects appear to be gold." (see CERVANTES, MIGUEL DE)

ALL THE KING'S MEN   Pulitzer Prize-winning novel by Robert Penn Warren became much acclaimed 1949 feature film starring Broderick Crawford. Crawford won an Oscar for Best Actor in this story of a Southern governor who inaugurates a reckless, corrupt administration.

ALL THE PRESIDENT'S MEN   1976 film directed by Alan J. Pakula, based on investigative work of reporters Carl Bernstein and Bob Woodward in exposing the Watergate scandal. Dustin Hoffman and Robert Redford star as Bernstein and Woodward; Jason Robards won Best Supporting Oscar as their editor, Ben Bradlee; Hal Holbrook was "Deep Throat," the mystery informer.

ALADDIN, ALI BABA. See ARABIAN NIGHTS

ALLEN, MEL (1913–   )   "Voice of the Yankees." Radio and TV play-by-play announcer for New York baseball team, 1939 to 1964, when Yankees abruptly "retired" him. Now calls games for Sports Channel and narrates *This Week in Baseball* TV show. Famed for saying, "How about that?" beginning in 1949 when Yankee slugger Joe DiMaggio returned from injury with four homers in three games. Allen and Red Barber first two broadcasters given Ford Frick Award and enshrined in Baseball Hall of Fame, 1978.

ALLEN, STEVE (1921–   )   Popular comedian, musician and author who began his TV career in 1950. Hosted *The Tonight Show*, 1954–1957. Began prime-time series in 1956 with cast including Louis Nye as smug Gordon Hathaway, whose line "Hi-Ho, Steverino" would start the "Man on the Street" interviews.

ALLEN, WOODY (1935–   )   Born Allen Stewart Konigsberg. Comedy writer and nightclub comic turned filmmaker. Also plays clarinet professionally. Films include: *Take the Money and Run* (1969), *Sleeper* (1973) and *Zelig* (1983), among others. Won Academy Award for Best Picture with *Annie Hall* (1977).

ALLENDE, DR. SALVADOR (1908–1973) Marxist president of Chile. Democratically elected. Reformed and nationalized foreign-owned Chilean resources, leading to resentment by the middle class. Killed, 1973, in violent military coup led by an army general.

ALLEY OOP. See HAMLIN, VINCENT T.

ALLEYS. See MARBLES

ALLIGATORS AND CROCODILES Differ in the following ways: crocodiles have narrower snouts and protruding lower teeth, are usually more aggressive, but are slower than the alligator on land. Alligators live in the southeast U.S. and parts of China, while crocodiles are found throughout the tropics.

ALLILUYEVA, SVETLANA (1926–   ) Joseph Stalin's daughter. Defected to U.S., 1967. Chose to use mother's maiden name. Relatively unknown in U.S.S.R.

ALOHA Hawaiian word for "love." Used as both greeting and farewell. Hawaii called Aloha State (50th state, 1959). State anthem is "Aloha 'Oe (Farewell to Thee)."

ALOU BROTHERS Felipe, Matty and Jesus Alou, from Dominican Republic, each started professional baseball career with San Francisco Giants, then played with other teams. Years with Giants (and birthdate) of each: Felipe, 1958–1963 (1935); Matty, 1960–1963 (1938); Jesus, 1963–1968 (1942).

ALPERT, HERB (1937–   ) Trumpet player and record producer. Formed A&M Records with Jerry Moss in 1962. Hit recordings include: "The Lonely Bull" (1962), "A Taste of Honey" (1965) and "This Guy's in Love with You" (1968). Leader of popular 1960s group, Tijuana Brass.

AMARETTO Almond-flavored liqueur said to have been concocted in 1525 by beautiful but impoverished young widow, as present for Bernadino Luini, artist in school of Leonardo da Vinci. Liqueur is 48 to 56 proof. Its flavor comes from apricot pits.

AMATEUR HOUR Weekly showcase of singers, kazoo players and one-man bands judged by audience for top prize. Begun on radio by Major Bowes, who discovered Frank Sinatra on the show in 1937. Ted Mack replaced the Major and brought the show to TV, where it lasted until 1970.

AMAZON RIVER World's widest and second longest river,

after the Nile. Length: 4,000 mi. (6,437 km.). Ranges from 1.5 to 6 mi. (2.4 to 10 km.) wide. Width at mouth of river: 90 mi. (140 km.). America's longest river and world's longest navigable river. Early explorers, attacked by female warriors, named river after Amazons, female warriors in Greek mythology.

AMAZONS, THE   Mythical race of female warriors of Scythia. In Greek legend, burned their right breasts off in order to draw their bows better. Destroyed or sent away any male children they had as result of encounters with neighboring tribes.

AMBASSADOR BRIDGE   Connects U.S. with Canada from Detroit, MI, to Ontario. Completed, 1929. Has two cables and is 1,850 ft. (555 m.) long.

AMBER   Fossilized resin. Produced by species of coniferous tree, now extinct. Mined from sands of tertiary period, 40 million to 60 million years old. Used since ancient Greek and Roman times in jewelry.

AMBROSIA   From Greek *ambrotos*, meaning "immortal." Refers to food of Greek gods thought to bestow immortality. In modern usage, anything that tastes or smells delicious; also a type of ragweed.

AMEN   Literally means "true." Used in sense of swearing acceptance and truthfulness of what has just been said. Custom of saying this word after prayers began in Judaism and was continued by early Christians. In Hebrew, means "So be it." Used by Jews, Christians and Moslems. Last word in Bible. Also, amain.

AMERICA'S CUP   Most revered yachting trophy. International racing began in 1851, when New York Yacht Club won Hundred Guineas Cup (worth about $500) from England with schooner *America*. Renamed America's Cup and deeded to NYYC. Survived 24 challenges until 1983, when *Australia II* beat U.S. boat *Liberty* four races to three to become first foreign winner. While in U.S. possession, Canada, Australia and Britain (including Scotland) were only countries posing competition to U.S. for the cup.

AMERICAN BANDSTAND   Long-running teenage music show, started 1952 on WFIL-TV, Philadelphia. Network debut in 1957 on ABC with Dick Clark as host. Regularly featured dancers on show: Kenny Rossi and Justine Corelli.

AMERICA FIRSTERS   America First Committee. Founded,

1940. Opposed U.S. participation in World War II. Originally endorsed by Henry Ford, historian Charles Beard, Charles A. Lindbergh and others. Began to deteriorate by October 1941.

AMERICAN GOTHIC. See WOOD, GRANT

AMERICAN GRAFFITI   1973 film, written and directed by George Lucas, about 1962 graduation day in the life of a group of teenagers in a small Californian town. Ronny Howard, Charles Martin Smith, Richard Dreyfuss and Cindy Williams star.

AMERICAN IN PARIS, AN   Oscar-winning Best Picture of 1951. Gene Kelly stars in this musical as an ex-G.I. who stays in Paris to pursue his career as an artist. Leslie Caron plays his love. Music by George Gershwin.

AMERICAN REVOLUTION   America's war for independence from Great Britain. From 1776, France (with old grudge against England) sent secret aid to America; was first country to recognize the new nation, 1778. As a French ally, Spain also gave America aid.

AMETHYST   Variety of the quartz, silicon dioxide. Presence of manganese produces purple color. February's birthstone. Also known as the Bishop's Stone.

AMIN, IDI DADA (1925–   )   President of Uganda, 1971–1979. Overthrew Milton Obote in 1971 military coup. Former Ugandan heavyweight boxing champ, 1951–1960. Notorious as Africa's harshest dictator. Blatant racist. Expelled 50,000 Asian bourgeois, 1972. Supported extinction of Israel; praised Hitler's genocidal policies. Sympathized with Nixon's Watergate ordeal. Overthrown by Ugandan rebels backed by Tanzanian troops, 1979. Lives in Saudi Arabia. Named himself "Conqueror of the British Empire."

AMSTERDAM   Capital and largest city of the Netherlands. Name means "dam of Amstel"; refers to dam built here in 1200s on Amstel River. Notable sights: Old Church built in 1200s; former town hall, now a royal palace; Dam Square; Rembrandt's former house.

AMUNDSEN, ROALD (1872–1928)   Norwegian explorer. First to reach South Pole, December 14, 1911. Also discovered Northwest Passage from the Atlantic to the Pacific by sea above Canada, 1906.

ANTARCTICA Continent's three main regions: Queen Maud Land, claimed by Norwegian government, 1939; Wilkes Land, discovered by U.S. Naval Officer Charles Wilkes, 1839; Marie Byrd Land, claimed by Richard E. Byrd for U.S., 1929.

ANASTASIA 1956 film about a Russian rogue (Yul Brynner) who, in an effort to claim a $40 million inheritance, persuades an amnesiac girl to think she is the daughter of the Czar. Ingrid Bergman won Best Actress Oscar for her role as Anna Anderson.

ANASTASIA, PRINCESS OF RUSSIA (1901–?) Daughter of Russia's last czar, Nicholas II. Rumored to have escaped execution by the revolutionaries, 1918. In 1922, a mental patient in Berlin, called Fräulein Unknown, claimed to be the Princess. The claim was never proven.

ANATOMY OF A MURDER 1959 courtroom drama directed by Otto Preminger. James Stewart, Lee Remick, Ben Gazzara, Arthur O'Connell, Eve Arden and George C. Scott star in this controversial film. Duke Ellington wrote the score.

ANCHORAGE Alaska's largest city and main center of commerce and transportation. Situated on Cook Inlet in southern Alaska. Name chosen in 1915 because ships anchored here with supplies for the railroad.

ANCHOR'S AWEIGH Written, 1906, for annual Army-Navy football game. Words by Alfred H. Miles and Royal Lovell; music by Charles A. Zimmerman. Sung exclusively at the game until 1926, when it was published, with additional verses by Lovell, as "Anchor's Aweigh." Became Navy's marching song.

ANCHORS AWEIGH 1945 musical starring Gene Kelly and Frank Sinatra as two sailors, on leave in Hollywood, who help a pretty starlet get her big chance in movies. Highlight of film is Kelly's dance sequence with cartoon Jerry Mouse.

AND Appears 46,227 times in the Bible, according to research of British Bible scholar Dr. Thomas Hartwell Horne (1780–1862). Horne spent three years counting letters and words of King James Version. Concluded there are 774,746 words in Old and New Testaments, containing 3,566,480 letters.

AND GOD CREATED WOMAN 1957 film directed by Roger Vadim, starring Brigitte Bardot as a girl from St. Tropez given a home by a family with three handsome sons who become rivals for her affection.

ANDERSEN, HANS CHRISTIAN (1805–1875) Danish author and storyteller. Born in poverty, came to have King Frederick VI as his patron. Mixed success before turning to children's stories. Wrote 168 between 1835 and 1872, including: "Emperor's New Clothes," about an emperor duped by tailor into parading nude; "The Princess and the Pea"; "The Red Shoes"; and "The Ugly Duckling," about a swan hatched among ducklings and mocked for being different until its identity becomes apparent. Honored by Danish people with Copenhagen harbor statue of Little Mermaid, one of his characters. Known for eccentricities such as traveling with a rope in order to escape fire. Also terrified of being declared dead prematurely and being buried alive. Often left note at bedside: "I only seem dead."

ANDERSON, JOHN BAYARD (1922-   ) American politician. Independent candidate, 1980 presidential race. Finished third in popular vote behind Reagan and Carter. Ten-term Republican congressman representing Illinois, 1960–1980.

ANDERSON, KATHY, JAMES AND BETTY Characters in popular TV series *Father Knows Best* (1954–1960). Father was played by Robert Young; mom was Jane Wyatt. Kathy (Kitten) was portrayed by Lauren Chapin, James (Bud) by Billy Gray and Betty (Princess) by Elinor Donahue.

ANDES MOUNTAINS World's longest chain of mountains, stretching 4,500 mi. (7,240 km.) along South America's west coast. Four railroads run up the mountains in Peru and Bolivia. The Central Railway, the world's highest standard-gauge railroad, reaches over 15,800 ft. (4,816 m.) above sea level.

ANDORRA Tiny country situated in Pyrenees mountains between France and Spain. Ruled by Bishop of Spain and France's president. Treaty signed in 1200s requires Andorra to pay the equivalent of $2 to the president of France once every two years. The Spanish Bishop gets the equivalent of $8, 6 hams, 6 cheeses and 12 hens.

ANDREA DORIA Italian ocean liner, named after great 15th-century Italian statesman and admiral. July 25, 1956, hit broadside in the fog by Swedish ocean liner *Stockholm*. Sunk off coast of Massachusetts. Fifty-two passengers killed.

ANDRETTI, MARIO (1940–   )   American race driver, born in Italy; moved to U.S. in 1955. Switched from Indianapolis-type cars to primarily Grand Prix driving, 1976. Won world championship in 1978, driving a Lotus. Won Indianapolis 500 in 1969.

ANDREWS SISTERS, THE   Popular singing group of 1940s, consisting of sisters Patti, Maxine and LaVerne Andrews. Hit songs include: "Don't Sit Under the Apple Tree" and "Boogie Woogie Bugle Boy of Company B." Appeared on radio and in movies, including *Buck Privates* (1941) with Abbott and Costello.

ANDREWS, JULIE (1934–   )   Born Julia Wells in England. Gained fame as the original Eliza Doolittle in Broadway's *My Fair Lady*. Won Oscar in 1964 for role in *Mary Poppins*. Other notable films include *The Sound of Music* (1965) and *Victor/Victoria* (1982). Married to filmmaker Blake Edwards.

ANDROMEDA   Galaxy. Contains up to 200 billion stars. Closest galaxy to earth's Milky Way; 1,500,000 light-years away. Studies by astronomer Walter Baade, 1950s, found it to be twice as large as originally believed. Led to redefinition of size of universe.

ANDY CAPP   Title character, Reginald Smythe's British comic strip. Capp runs to neighborhood pub, frequently with mate Chalky, to avoid Flo, his long-suffering missus.

ANGEL FALLS   World's highest waterfall. Located within Canaima National Park, Bolivar State, in southeastern Venezuela. Discovered by U.S. explorer and aviator James Angel, 1935; two years later, he had minor plane crash nearby. Greatest uninterrupted drop is 2,640 ft. (800 m.).

ANIMAL GROUPS

Ant	Colony
Bear	Sloth or sleuth
Beaver	Lodge
Cat	Clowder
Crow	Murder
Dog	Kennel
Donkey	Pace
Fox	Skulk
Goose	Gaggle

Kangaroo	Mob
Kitten	Kindle
Lion	Pride
Rabbit	Warren
Seal	Trip
Whale	Pod

ANIMAL NAMES

Animal	*Male*	*Female*
Antelope	Buck	Doe
Bear	Boar	Sow
Donkey	Jackass	Jennet
Fox	Dog	Vixen
Goose	Gander	Goose
Horse	Stud	Mare
Rat	Buck	Doe
Seal	Bull	Cow
Swan	Cob	Pen
Zebra	Stallion	Mare

ANIMAL YOUNG

Cattle	Calf or heifer (female)
Eagle	Eaglet
Elephant	Calf
Fox	Cub or kit
Goat	Kid
Goose	Gosling
Hog	Shoat, farrow or piglet
Horse	Foal, colt (male) or filly (female)
Kangaroo	Joey
Rabbit	Kit
Sheep	Lamb or teg
Swan	Cygnet
Turkey	Poult
Whale	Calf

ANNIVERSARIES

1st - Paper	10th - Tin	35th - Coral
2nd - Cotton	15th - Crystal	40th - Ruby
3rd - Leather	20th - China	45th - Sapphire

TRIVIAL CONQUEST

4th - Linen	25th - Silver	50th - Gold
5th - Wood	30th - Pearl	60th - Diamond
	75th - Gold	

ANTE. See **POKER**

ANTE MORTEM Latin phrase meaning "before death." From *ante*, "before or preceding," and *mort*, "death." Term used in medical and legal professions. Opposite is post mortem, used to refer to medical examination after death; also called autopsy.

ANTHONY, SUSAN BROWNWELL (1820–1906) American suffragist and feminist. Paved way for adoption of 19th Amendment, giving women right to vote, 1920. First woman to appear on national currency, paper or coin; honored on silver dollar, issued January 1979.

ANTHROPOPHAGIST From Greek *anthropos*, meaning "human," and *phagos*, meaning "eating." An eater of humans ("long pig") or cannibal. Cannibalism is still practiced in areas of New Guinea and on some Pacific Islands.

ANTOINETTE, MARIE (1755–1793) Wife of Louis XVI. Her attempts to restore the lost monarchy during the French Revolution led to her being called "the Widow of Capet" (Capet was dynastic name of French kings). Also falsely attributed with having said, in response to French people's lack of bread, ". . . Let them eat cake"; this earned her the title "the Baker's Wife." Guillotined, along with her husband, 1793. Allegedly had same bust size as actress Jayne Mansfield.

AORTA Largest artery of the body. Carries oxygenated blood from the heart to the cells. Many other arteries, including coronary arteries, branch off the aorta. Syphilis and atherosclerosis are most serious diseases affecting the aorta.

APARTHEID From the word meaning "apartness" in Afrikaans. Official policy of white South African ruling minority maintaining separate economic, political and social rights based on race. Country's population roughly 66% Africans, 20% whites, 11% coloreds (mixed descent) and 3% Asians.

APENNINES Mountain range made of marble and limestone, that runs from Gulf of Genoa to the toe of Italy's boot. Among Europe's lowest mountains. Worn down by wind and rain over years. Most famous peak is volcano Vesuvius on Bay of Naples.

APES   Man's closest relatives. Four kinds: chimpanzee and gorilla of Africa and gibbon and orangutan of Asia. Differ from man in the following ways: arms are longer than legs, do not stand erect, have much body hair, have larger teeth and jaw and have smaller brains.

APHRODITE   Greek goddess of love and beauty. Roman equivalent is Venus. Beguiled all gods and men alike. In Homer's *Iliad*, she was daughter of Zeus and Dione, but later poems have her springing out of sea; her name explained as meaning "the foam risen" (*aphros* means "foam" in Greek).

APOLLO MISSIONS   Numbered 1–17. Succeeded in placing man on the moon. Three-man missions lasted 1966–1972. December 1968, the first manned spacecraft to travel around the moon. Captain, Frank Borman. First photographs of near and far side of moon taken by man, from 70 miles away. Read from Genesis during Christmas while in orbit. During Apollo 11, Neil Armstrong took one giant leap for mankind by stepping onto lunar surface on July 20, 1969. Armstrong and Aldrin's lunar module was called the Eagle. Missions 1–10 preceded the moon landing of mission 11. Michael Collins remained in orbit in Command Service Module during Apollo 11 mission while Armstrong and Aldrin landed in Lunar Landing Module, July 20, 1969. First words from moon: "Houston, Tranquility Base here: the Eagle has landed." Apollo missions carried three astronauts, Mercury carried one, Gemini two.

APPALACHIAN MOUNTAINS   North America's oldest and second largest mountain system. Extends 1,500 mi. (2,400 km.) between Quebec's Gulf of St. Lawrence and Birmingham, AL. Formed nearly 230 million years ago. Highest peak Mt. Mitchell (6,684 ft./ 2,037 m.) in Blue Ridge Mountains of North Carolina.

APPELLATION D'ORIGIN CONTROLEE   French government wine laws which regulate production and avoid fraud. Laws control use of vineyard names and set up standards for type of soil and vines, alcoholic content, bouquet and other characteristics.

APPIAN WAY   Ancient paved road. Extended from Rome to Brindisi. Most efficient route between the two cities. Built by statesman Appius Claudius Caecus, 312 B.C. Called *longarum regina viarum*, meaning "the queen of the long roads."

APPLE   Most widely cultivated fruit. Family rosaceae, genus Malus. 7,500 varieties grown worldwide; 2,500 in U.S. including

Red and Golden Delicious, first and second most popular. Mature apples approximately 84% water. France and U.S., leading producers. Other varieties include: The Granny Smith, large, tart, green eating and cooking apple. Named for elderly Australian woman who discovered tree bearing this fruit on her farm in Queensland, Australia. Also grown in New Zealand, Chile, France and U.S.

APPLES, GOLDEN Greek mythology. Given to Earth by Hera in honor of her marriage to Zeus. Guarded by the Hesperides. One of the twelve labors of Hercules was to steal them. Alleged that the apples were in fact apricots. Apricots sometimes called "the golden seed of the sun."

AQUARIUS Constellation, pictured as man pouring water. Also called the Water Bearer, possibly because it lies over Euphrates Valley during rainy season. From Latin *Aquaril* meaning "water carrier." Eleventh zodiac sign.

ARABIAN NIGHTS Formally, *The Arabian Nights' Entertainments*, or *A Thousand and One Nights*, collection of ancient Persian-Indian-Arabian tales, originally in Arabic. Arranged in present form c. 1450. Stories unified by supposed storyteller Scheherezade, who postpones her execution by telling her husband a new story night after night, holding back climax until next morning. Among them: "Aladdin, or the Wonderful Lamp": Story about poor Chinese boy, lazy and mischievous, who comes into possession of magic lamp. By rubbing it, calls up two slaves of the Lamp (genii) to do his bidding. "Ali Baba and the 40 Thieves": Overhearing password "open sesame," poor woodcutter Ali Baba gains access to thieves' cave and treasure. They swear vengeance, but Ali Baba's female slave Morgiana pours boiling oil on them as they lie in ambush. "Sinbad the Sailor": Tale of a Baghdad merchant who acquires great wealth by going on seven voyages. His recollections of them demonstrate how wealth can be obtained by personal enterprise. On third voyage, he meets the Cyclops, monster of Greek mythology with one eye in center of forehead.

ARABIAN NOMADS Traditionally, do not eat with left hand, which is used for all bathing and cleaning. Hence, left hand is seen as impure. Also the practice in India.

ARABIC LANGUAGE Spoken by roughly 120 million people in northern Africa and the Middle East. Official language of 16 countries, including Egypt, Morocco and Tunisia. Has 28 letters, which are all consonants. Marks above and below letters convert them to vowels.

ARAFAT, YASSER (1929–   ) Official spokesman for Palestinian Liberation Organization (PLO), which he founded 1950s. During 1983 address to UN, pistol holder exposed under his shirt.

ARBUTHNOT, MAY HILL (1884–1969) American educator and author of classic learn-to-read series *Fun with Dick and Jane*. Their parents, known as Mother and Father, had another, younger child — Sally. Sister Sally had a teddy bear named Tim. Puff was their cat and Spot was their dog.

ARC DE TRIOMPHE Arch in Paris where twelve major boulevards meet. Located at head of Champs Elysees in the Place Charles de Gaulle. Construction began in 1806 by Napolean in honor of his troops. Completed by Louis Philippe in 1836. Names of Napoleon's 386 generals and 96 of his triumphs are written on its inner walls.

ARCARO, EDDIE (1916–   ) Hall of Fame jockey, 1931–62. Nicknamed "Banana Nose." After losing in first 250 races, rode 4,779 winners, including five Kentucky Derby victors and two Triple Crown winners, Whirlaway (1941) and Citation (1948). Only jockey to ride two Triple Crown champions.

ARCH Curved structure designed to support weight of the material above it. Roman invention. Along with the vault, eliminated the need for columns to support the roof. Center stone, called a keystone, holds other parts in place.

ARCH OF HADRIAN One of many structures in ancient Athens attributed to the patron Hadrian, Emperor of Rome, A.D. 117–138. The arch located near the Olympeum, separated the new and old cities of Athens.

ARCH OF TITUS Built by Emperor Vespasian for his son Titus' victory at Jerusalem. Completed in A.D. 81 in Rome, Italy. Located on the Sacred Way near the Roman Forum. Titus was a Roman emperor known for his kindness.

ARCHERY Standard target (48 in. diameter) has five zones: yellow bullseye (9.6 in. diameter, worth 9 points), and four, 4.8 in. concentric rings. From center: red (7 points), blue (5 points), black (3 points), and white (1 point). If arrow splits two colors, higher point-value scored. In drawing bow, tips of first three fingers of string hand (one that pulls bowstring) control arrow in style called Mediterranean Draw. In Mongolian (or Oriental) Draw, bowstring pulled back between thumb and bent index finger of string hand. To help hold string in place, thumb ring normally worn. Archer's arrows are held by a quiver, which is hung from back, worn in hip pocket, or fastened at belt or on bow, depending on type; ground or floor quivers rest on ground.

ARCHERY, CROSSBOW   Uses bolts instead of arrows. Bolts may be of any material and any length over 12 in., but must not cause unreasonable damage to target, and must be clearly marked for shooter identification.

ARCHIE   Bob Montana comic strip about high school students. Debuted 1941. Inspired by Henry Aldrich radio show and movies. "R" on title character Archie Andrews' sweater stands for Riverdale High, where Archie attends with pal Jughead. Vies for attention of coeds Betty and Veronica with conniving, slick- haired Reggie. They frequent Pop's Choklit Shoppe, soda fountain and hang-out, after school.

ARCHIMEDES (298–212 B.C.)   Great mathematician. Known for Archimedes' Principle, fundamental natural law of buoyancy: objects submerged or floating in liquid are buoyed upward by a force equal to the weight of the displaced liquid. Upon discovery, exclaimed "Eureka!" — a Greek word meaning "I have found it."

ARCHITECTURE   Art of building, design of space for human use. Called mother of arts. First acknowledged architectural style seen in 3,500 B.C., Mesopotamia.

ARCTIC CIRCLE   Describes southern boundary of the Arctic. Sixty-six degrees 30 minutes north latitude, 23½ degrees south of the north pole. Sun's rays never shine directly on the Arctic. This region loses more heat than it receives from the sun.

AREA CODES   U.S. major American cities' area codes:

1) New York (212)
2) Los Angeles (213)
3) Chicago (312)
4) Philadelphia (215)
5) San Francisco (415)
6) Houston (713)
7) Miami (305)
8) Boston (617)
9) Dallas (214)
10) Minneapolis (612)
11) Detroit (313)
12) Washington, DC (202)

ARGENTINA   South America's second-largest country. Named

from Latin word *argentum* meaning "silver." Spanish explorers hoping
to find silver there in 1500s called the region *Plata*, Spanish for
silver. Argentina exports silver but three-fourths of its wealth is from
its rich soil.

ARGON   Inert (non-reactive) gaseous element. Discovered in
1894. About 1% of the Earth's atmosphere is argon. Most light bulbs
are filled with argon because it cannot burn.

ARIZONA   State flower: Saguaro (Giant Cactus); State bird:
Cactus Wren; State tree: Paloverde; State motto: *Ditat Deus* (God
enrichens); State nickname: The Grand Canyon State; State song:
"Arizona" by Maurice Blumenthal (music) and Margaret Rowe Clifford (words). Origin of state's name: Spanish version of Pima Indian
word for "little spring place" or from Aztec arizuma meaning "silver-
bearing."

ARIZONA, THE   U.S. battleship. One of eight sunk in Japanese bombing at Pearl Harbor, December 7, 1941. Went down
with over 1,000 on board. Remained in commission. Presently a
monument to Americans who died in the attack.

ARLBERG EXPRESS, THE   Train departing Vienna at 8:10
nightly. Cities on train's route are: Vienna, Salzburg, Innsbruck,
Buchs, Zurich, Basle and Paris.

ARMADA   Navy in Spanish. Most famous example: Spanish
Armada which sailed in 1588 to invade England. Defeated by Lord
Howard of Effingham and his captains Sir Francis Drake, Jack Hawkins and James Frobisher. Surviving Spanish ships wrecked trying
to get home.

ARMSTRONG, NEIL ALDEN (1930–   )   American
astronaut. First person to walk on moon, 10:56:20 P.M., eastern
daylight time, July 20, 1969 during Apollo 11 mission. Stepped
onto lunar surface with left foot first. Described surface "fine and
powdery." Retired NASA, 1971. Professor of engineering, University of Cincinnati.

ARTESIAN WELLS   Named for Artios, France where first
dug. Wells in which water rises above water table. Can be dug
where sloping layer of water-rich sandstone is sandwiched between
denser rock.

AS THE WORLD TURNS   Soap opera, airing since 1956.
Suspended, along with all other regular TV schedules, immediately

following assassination of President John F. Kennedy, November 22, 1963. Suspension lasted until the funeral was over, November 25.

ASH WEDNESDAY First day of Lent, a forty-day period of fast and prayer. Congregation is blessed with ashes of burned palm from preceding year's Palm Sunday. Ashes remind of the need to prepare for a holy death.

ASHE, ARTHUR ROBERT (1943–   ) First black tennis player to win men's singles in U.S. Open (1968, beating Tom Okker of the Netherlands in final), Wimbledon (1975, beating Jimmy Connors in final), and to head U.S. ranking list for men's singles. Retired from active playing because of heart problems, became non-playing captain of U.S. Davis Cup team.

ASIMOV, ISAAC (1920–   ) Russian-born American science fiction writer and professor of biochemistry. His *Foundation Trilogy* (*Foundation, Foundation and Empire*, and *Second Foundation*, 1951–1953), considered one of greatest sci-fi works of all time. Fourth Foundation book, *Foundation's Edge* (1982). Also wrote short story "Nightfall" (1940); *I, Robot* (1950), many other fiction works.

ASPIRIN Acetylsalicylic acid. Probably the most widely-used drug in the world. Americans consume forty-two tons per day of this pain-killing fever reducer and anti-inflammation drug. First marketed in 1899 by Bayer A. G. of Germany.

ASSOCIATED PRESS Largest news gathering agency in the world. Nonprofit corporation. Owned by 4,000 member newspapers, radio and television stations. Formed, 1848, to collect and distribute foreign news to its members. Now has bureaus in over 50 countries.

ASTROLOGY The study of how heavenly bodies supposedly influence life and events on Earth. Astrologers cast horoscopes based on the positions of Earth, the planets, the zodiac, and the houses (12 divisions of Earth's surface) at the time of a person's birth (predictive charts). In 1975, 186 scientists, including 18 Nobelists, claimed that it had no scientific basis.

ASWAN HIGH DAM Controls floodwaters of Egypt's Nile River. Completed in 1970. Microscopic worms carrying schistosomiasis (disease causing intestinal and urinary infection) live in snails found along the Nile. Since dam halts flooding, worms are not washed away and they infect bathers' skin and clothing.

ATHENA   In Greek mythology, daugher of Zeus — full grown and in full armor, she sprang from his head. Earliest account (Homer's *Iliad*) portrays her as fierce battle goddess. In later poetry, portrayed as embodiment of wisdom, reason and purity. Athens was her special city; the owl (denoting wisdom) her special bird; the olive, which she created, was her tree.

ATHETOSIS   Condition characterized by succession of slow, writhing movements. Involuntary. Usually affects fingers and hands; sometimes toes, feet and other parts of the body. Generally results from damage to specific brain sites, particularly the basal ganglia. Seen in cerebral palsy.

ATLANTA   Georgia's capital and largest city. Founded in 1837 as Terminus, located at southern end of Western and Atlantic Railroad. Name changed to Atlanta in 1847 by railroad engineer J. Edgar Thompson, in honor of the railroad.

ATLANTA BRAVES. see MILWAUKEE BRAVES

ATLANTIC CITY   Seaside resort on coast of New Jersey. Situated on small island called Absecon Beach. Noted for its 6 mi. (10 km.) long boardwalk lined with hotels, theaters, shops. Home of Caesars Boardwalk Regency Hotel Casino and Convention Hall where the annual Miss America pageant takes place.

ATLANTIC OCEAN   World's second largest body of water (first is Pacific Ocean). Has no definite northern or southern boundaries. Runs into Arctic Ocean on the north and Antarctic Ocean on the south. Contains the point that is 0° longitude, 0° latitude.

ATLAS MOUNTAINS   Mountain range in northwestern Africa. Extends 1,500 mi. (2,140 km.). Named for Atlas, the Greek Titan. Highest peak Jebel Toubkal is located in Morocco at 13,665 ft. (4,165 m.).

ATLAS, CHARLES (1894–1972)   American body builder. Selected world's most perfectly developed man by Physical Culture magazine in 1922. Born Angelo Siciliano, Brooklyn, NY. Skinny and weak at 16, he began body building. Started mail-order marketing of his "dynamic tension" method of isotonic exercise in 1929. Ads show "97-pound weakling" getting sand kicked in his face and guarantee: "I can make you a new man."

ATMOSPHERE   The layer of air above the Earth. Although

it technically extends for about 1,000 mi., more than 99% of the air is within 120 mi. The atmosphere is about four-fifths nitrogen and one-fifth oxygen.

ATOLL Circular island made of coral surrounding a body of water called a lagoon. Sometimes formed on crater of volcano sunken below sea's surface. Found most often in Pacific Ocean.

ATOMIC BOMB Research began in 1942 with President Roosevelt's Manhattan Project, directed by J. Robert Oppenheimer. First bomb exploded, 1945, at Trinity Site, New Mexico, near Alamagordo Air Base. Soon after, the bomb was dropped on Hiroshima and Nagasaki, Japan. The following lists countries that have exploded atomic bombs, with the year of each country's first test: U.S. 1945; U.S.S.R. 1949; Great Britain 1952; France 1960; Peoples Republic of China 1964; India 1974.

ATTICA Maximum security prison near Buffalo, NY. The scene of a bloody prison riot that began September 9, 1971. Seventy-four prisoners and hostages died when the prison was retaken by over 1,000 state police and prison guards, September 13.

ATTILA THE HUN (A.D. 406?–453) King of the Huns, from about A.D. 433–453. Also called the "Scourge of God" because of his ruthless treatment of the people he attacked.

AUBERGE French country inn. *Auberges de France*, of *logis*, found off main roads and between towns. Usually serve food and have a dozen rooms or less. *Gites de France* are rural guesthouses — farms, cottages, furnished rooms — conforming to fixed standards of facilities and prices.

AUCKLAND ISLANDS Group of uninhabited islands off southern coast of New Zealand. Discovered 1806. Used as a depot for whaling and sealing activities in 1800s. Controlled by New Zealand.

AUERBACH, ARNOLD (RED) (1917–   ) Boston Celtics coach who led them to nine National Basketball Association championships between 1957 and 1966, including eight in a row. Retired to general manager after 1966 season. Famous for lighting a victory cigar on the bench when he felt game was won.

AUGUSTA, MAINE. see U.S. EXTREMITIES

AUGUSTUS (63 B.C.–A.D. 14) Roman emperor. Ruled during Rome's cultural development when the city underwent great construction. Many buildings left unfinished by Julius Caesar, his great uncle, were restored. Augustus once bragged of having "found Rome brick and left it marble."

AUSTEN, JANE (1775–1817)   English novelist. Often regarded as greatest woman novelist. Led sheltered family life as spinster daughter of country parson, yet turned it into innovative comedies of manners. *Pride and Prejudice* written when she was 21 but not published until 1813. Also wrote *Sense and Sensibility* (1811), *Emma* (1816) and *Northanger Abbey* (1818), all published years after written.

AUSTRALIA   Only country that is also a continent. East coast explored in 1770 by James Cook, who claimed it for Great Britain and named it New South Wales. Used as a penal colony beginning January 26, 1788, when Captain Arthur Phillip brought over first boatload of prisoners (by 1868, over 186,000 convicts had been sent). First white settlement established in 1788 near Botany Bay. Western region named New Holland by Abel Janszoon Tasman. In early 1800s it was discovered that Australia was one land mass, not two separate islands. Adopted its Latin name from the 1500s: Terra Australis Incognita, meaning unknown (*incognita*) southern (*australis*) land (*terra*). Became Commonwealth country in 1901. *Cities:* Five major cities, all located on country's coastlines, are Sydney (east coast), Melbourne (southeast coast), Adelaide (south coast), Brisbane (east coast), and Perth (west coast). *Flag:* Design has British Union Jack in upper left corner on a blue field. Five stars represent constellation of Southern Cross, and one larger star symbolizes the Commonwealth. *Rural:* Thirteen percent of inhabitants live in rural areas called "outback." Most farms are cattle and sheep stations. World's largest sheep population. *States:* New South Wales, Queensland, South Australia, Tasmania, Victoria, and Western Australia. *Surrounding waters:* Indian Ocean, Timor Sea, Arafura Sea, Coral Sea, South Pacific Ocean, and Tasman Sea.

AUSTRIA   Official name: Republik Osterreich. Was Holy Roman Empire's most powerful state, 1438–1806, when Hapsburgs were in control. Today, as neutral country, acts as center for exchange of ideas between Communist and non-Communist countries. *National anthem:* "Land der Berge, Land am Strome (Land of Mountains, Land at the River)." *National flower:* edelweiss. *Coat-of-arms:* eagle. *Cities:* Most populated cities are Vienna (1,640,106), Graz (250,300) and Linz (203,983). *Currency:* schilling, made up of 100 groschen. *Language*: roughly 98% speak German. Various dialects are spoken. Other common languages are Slovene, Magyar and Serbo-Croatian.

AUTO RACING—FIRST RACE Conflicting claims on first auto race. Some recognize 1878 201-mile race from Green Bay to Madison, WI, won by an Oshkosh Steamer. In 1894, race run between Paris and Rouen, France (78 mi.), won by steam-driven car with top speed of 11 m.p.h. Not all entrants made it to Rouen, and none was able to return immediately. In 1895, race run from Paris to Bordeaux and back (732 mi.), won by Frenchman Emil Levassor, average speed 15 m.p.h.

AUTO RACING—FLAGS Flags used in sport symbolize the following: Red : Race being stopped, competitors should come to immediate and complete stop. Green: Track clear, racing may resume. Yellow : Caution, no passing, danger ahead. Checkered : Winner has crossed finish line.

AUTO RACING—HAIRPINS Sharp turn in race course. May be as much as 180 degrees. Term also applies to slalom races in alpine skiing.

AUTO RACING—INTERCONTINENTAL First race from New York to Paris, 1908. Contestants were to drive New York to San Francisco, take steamer to Valdez, Alaska, drive across Alaska and Bering Strait to Siberia, then east to Paris. Route changed during race. Cars shipped by boat from U.S. to Japan. American entry— 1907 Thomas Flyer with driver Monty Roberts and mechanic George Schuster—won. Arrived in Paris 169 days after start, driving estimated 13,341 mi.

AUTOBAHNS Four-lane motorways in Germany, which have no specified speed limit. However, 80 m.p.h. (130 km.p.h.) is recommended.

AUTRY, GENE (1907–   ) Radio country singer turned movie star. Made his first film, *The Phantom Empire*, in 1935 and was voted number one Western star in 1937. Made numerous B-Westerns through 1953 with his horse Champion. His theme song was "Back in the Saddle Again." Had 1952 hit record, "Frosty, the Snowman." In 1960 "the Singing Cowboy" retired and became a successful businessman, investing in radio and TV stations and the California Angels baseball team. His recording of "Rudolf, the Red-Nosed Reindeer" still sells thousands of records annually.

AVENGERS, THE   British TV series, proved very popular in America. Starring Patrick Macnee as the very proper secret agent Jonathan Steed, and Diana Rigg playing the karate-chopping Mrs. Emma Peel. Series began in England in 1961 with Honor Blackman in role of Steed's assistant. American premiere, March 1966.

AVOCADO   Fruit of tree belonging to laurel family. Cultivated in U.S., South Africa and Mexico. Thrives in soil rich in humus (decomposed vegetable matter). Provides thiamine, riboflavin and vitamin A. Twenty to 30% oil. Highest caloric fruit: 167 calories per hundred grams.

AVON RIVER   Upper course of Swan River in Western Australia. Flows for 200 mi. (380 km.) Has northwest course. Joins Swan River at Northam.

AXIS SALLY (1900–   )   Radio announcer, World War II. Born Mildred Gillars. Germany's version of Tokyo Rose. Broadcast Nazi propaganda. Imitated Hitler's method of preaching to the masses about German superiority.

AZORES   Group of nine islands owned by Portugal. Located in Atlantic Ocean, west of Portugal, along route of cable and air lines that connect America and Europe.

B

B&B   Amber-colored liqueur made by blending Benedictine, believed to be world's oldest liqueur, with brandy to create drier Benedictine. Marketed since 1930. Abbreviation on label, D.O.M., for Latin *deo optimo maximo* ("to God, most good, most great").

B&O RAILROAD   Baltimore and Ohio Railroad. organized 1827. Oldest common carrier, or railroad that provides service to the public for a fee. Now part of Chesapeake and Ohio Railroad.

B-52 BOMBER   Strategic bomber. Designed to attack targets deep within enemy territory. Has eight jet engines; may reach speed of 660 m.p.h. (1,060 k.p.h.). Can fly roughly 10,000 mi. (16,000 km.) without refueling.

B.C.   Stands for "before Christ." Years counted backwards from 1 B.C., supposed day of Christ's birth. The lower the number, the more recently the event occurred. Year after 1 B.C. is A.D. 1, or 1 anno Domini, "in the year of the Lord."

BABAR   Little elephant in series of French children's books. Written and illustrated by Jean de Brunhoof (1899–1937). Widely translated; popular in U.S.

BACALL, LAUREN (1924–   )   Born Betty Pepske. Sultry actress who, at age 19, made screen debut opposite Humphrey Bogart in *To Have and Have Not* (1944); subsequently married him and had two children, Stephen Humphrey (1949) and Leslie Humphrey (1952). Other notable films include *The Big Sleep* (1946) and *How to Marry a Millionaire* (1953). Appeared on Broadway in 1970 in *Applause* and again in 1980 in *Woman of the Year.*

BACH, BARBARA (1949–   ) Actress and wife of former Beatle Ringo Starr. Wed in 1981. Reported that Starr proposed after they suffered an automobile accident. Appeared with Starr in 1981 movie *Caveman.* Starred opposite Roger Moore in James Bond film *The Spy Who Loved Me.*

BACH, RICHARD DAVID (1936–   ) American author and aviator. Wrote *Jonathan Livingston Seagull* (1970), best seller with popularity among children and adults. Illustrated with photos by Russell Munson. About seagull who devotes life to perfecting flying techniques and teaching others who don't want lives limited to daily search for food.

BACHARACH, BURT (1929–   ) Composer and singer responsible for many hit songs, often collaborating with lyricist Hal David. Hits include "What the World Needs Now," "Message to Michael" and "Raindrops Keep Falling on My Head." Wrote "The Look of Love" after seeing Ursula Andress.

BACKGAMMON Ancient board game developed in Orient. Played on rectangular board divided in half (inner and outer table) by "bar." Twelve triangles, called points, line each side of board and are alternately colored light and dark. Each player has 15 pieces, one set light, the other dark. Pieces known as "counters," "stones" or "men"; in modern game, "men" is commonly accepted term. Pieces move according to throw of dice.

BAD NEWS BEARS, THE Film comedy (1976) about beer-guzzling coach, portrayed by Walter Matthau, whose Little League team has change of luck when it acquires female star pitcher, played by Tatum O'Neal.

BAGHDAD Capital and largest city in Iraq. Situated on banks of Tigris River. Much of Iraq's income used for flood control in this city. Petroleum refining is major industry.

BAGNOLD, ENID (1890–1981) British novelist and playwright. Best known for *National Velvet* (1935), novel about young girl named Velvet who rides winning horse in Grand National, England's most prestigious steeplechase race. Twelve-year-old Elizabeth Taylor starred in 1944 film version, her first major role.

BAHAMAS Country made up of 700 islands. Located southeast of Florida's tip. Named from Spanish *baja mar* ("shallow water").

Islands' revenue generated from import duties, casino fees, land sales, post office, and public utilities. No income tax. Currency unit is Bahamian dollar, consisting of 100 cents.

BAILEY, F. LEE (1933–   ) Boston criminal lawyer. Gained notoriety defending Cleveland doctor Sam Sheppard, "Boston Strangler" Albert De Salvo and renegade heiress Patty Hearst. A flamboyant Perry Mason type, Bailey has had several TV series and has authored several books, including novels and autobiography *The Defense Never Rests* (1972).

BAILY'S BEADS Named for English astronomer. Spots of light that appear around moon just before and after total solar eclipse. Caused by sunlight shining between mountains of moon.

BAJA PENINSULA Located in northwestern Mexico; extends between Pacific Ocean and Gulf of California. Divided into two sections: the state of Baja California and the territory of Baja California Sur. Discovered by Spanish in 1533–1534.

BAKER'S ITCH Form of psoriasis often afflicting hands of bakers and cooks. Possibly caused by action of yeast. Baker's stigmas, corns on fingers, also caused by kneading dough.

BALBOA, VASCO NUNEZ DE (1475–1519) Spanish explorer and soldier. First European to see eastern shore of Pacific Ocean, September 25, 1513; named it the South Sea.

BALDWIN, JAMES (1924–   ) American novelist-essayist who became leading spokesman for American blacks in late 1950s and '60s. *Another Country* (1962), a novel about interracial relationships, and *Nobody Knows My Name* (1961), a nonfiction indictment of society that tolerates black suffering, among best-known works. Others: *Go Tell It on the Mountain* (1953) and *Notes of a Native Son* (1955).

BALI Island province in Lesser Sunda Islands, Indonesia. Situated 1 mi. from Java. Known for Ubud, center for European and North American artists. Tourism a major part of island's economy. Balinese known for fondness of music, poetry, dancing and festivals, as well as the arts and betting.

BALL, LUCILLE (1911–   ) Hollywood starlet turned TV comedienne. Married singer Desi Arnaz in 1940. Together they formed Desilu Productions in 1950 to produce the pilot of *I Love Lucy*, a phenomenally popular series that lasted until 1957. Lucy continued a weekly TV series until 1968. (see I LOVE LUCY)

BALLAD OF THE GREEN BERETS, THE Hit song performed by Sgt. Barry Sadler, 1966. Written by Sadler and author Robin Moore, song sold over two million copies within three months of its release.

BALLESTEROS, SEVERIANO (1957–   ) Spanish golfer. Youngest winner (23 years, 4 days) of Masters Tournament, 1980; Jack Nicklaus (1963) previous youngest. Shot 13-under-par 275 to win by four strokes over Gibby Gilbert and Jack Newton. Won again in 1983.

BALLISTICS Branch of engineering concerned with motion of projectiles in flight. Its experts study rockets, missiles and bombs. Forensic ballistics tell whether a particular bullet was fired from a particular gun.

BALTIC SEA Arm of Atlantic Ocean connected with North Sea. Located between cities of Riga, U.S.S.R., and Stockholm, Sweden. Total area: 160,000 sq. mi. (414,400 sq. km.). Storms make navigation treacherous.

BALTIMORE COLTS Beat New York Giants, 23-17, in 1958 National Football League championship game; first overtime game in NFL history. Colts, led by quarterback Johnny Unitas, drove downfield to tie game in regulation on Steve Myhra field goal; won at 8:15 in sudden death OT on touchdown by fullback Alan Ameche. Beat Giants again in 1959 championship game. Lost to New York Jets, 16-7, in Super Bowl III (1969); beat Dallas Cowboys, 16-13, in Super Bowl V (1971). Moved to Indianapolis, 1984.

BALTIMORE ORIOLES Along with St. Louis Cardinals and Toronto Blue Jays, one of three teams in baseball with "bird" nickname. When St. Louis Browns franchise moved to Municipal Stadium in 1954, Baltimore acquired this American League team. Browns had been in St. Louis since 1902, when franchise moved from Milwaukee. Won only one pennant (1944) in St. Louis. In Baltimore, won World Series in 1966, 1970, 1983.

BAMBI Walt Disney's animated feature released in 1942. About life of a deer in the wild forest with Thumper the rabbit, Flower the skunk, and his mate Faline, and their encounters with man and nature.

BANANA BOAT SONG, THE Harry Belafonte's hit song,

more commonly known as "Day-O," based on Jamaican work song; describes activities of Jamaican men unloading a boat. Launched "calypso craze" in late 1950s.

BANANAS Tropical fruit that grows in huge clusters on banana plants. Americans eat more bananas than any other fruit: a total of 11 billion a year.

BANFF NATIONAL PARK Oldest national park in Canada. Founded in 1887. Located in Alberta on eastern side of Rocky Mountains. Noted for glaciers, dense forests and hot mineral springs. Grizzly bears, elk and moose roam the park. Covers 2,500 sq. mi. (6,470 sq. km.).

BANG THE DRUM SLOWLY 1956 novel and 1973 film by Mark Harris. Poignant story of baseball catcher dying of Hodgkin's disease. In film Robert DeNiro plays catcher and Michael Moriarty is Henry "Author" Wiggin, pitcher and sometime writer who acts as narrator of this story and Harris' three other Wiggin novels: *The Southpaw, Ticket for a Seamstitch* and *It Looked like Forever.*

BANGER. See FOOD NAMES, ENGLAND

BANGLADESH Independent country in southern Asia, formerly part of East Bengal, a province of British-ruled India. In 1947 East Bengal joined with Sylhet district of Assam and became East Pakistan in new state of Pakistan. Differences with West Pakistan led East Pakistan to declare independence in 1971. Country became Bangladesh, meaning "the Bengal nation."

BANKS, ERNIE (1931–) Known as "Mr. Cub," played shortstop and first base for Chicago Cubs of National League, 1953–1971. Hit 512 lifetime homers; led league in home runs twice and runs batted in twice. 1958 and 1959 MVP despite team's losing record. Hit record five grand-slam home runs in season, 1955. Elected to Baseball Hall of Fame, 1977. Known for enthusiasm and saying, "Let's play two [games] today."

BANNERMAN, HELEN BRODIE COWAN (1863–1946) Scottish-born writer who lived in India for much of her life. Wrote and illustrated *The Story of Little Black Sambo* (1899), about adventures of son of Black Mumbo and Black Jumbo. On walk through jungle, Sambo loses his new clothes and encounters fierce tigers but finally returns home to eat 169 pancakes because he was very hungry. Following this success, Bannerman wrote several similar books, including *Little Black Mingo* (1901) and *Little Black Quibba* (1902).

BANNISTER, ROGER (1929–   ) British athlete who ran first four-minute mile (3:59.4), Oxford, England, 1954. Knighted, 1975. Current record (3:47.33) held by Sebastian Coe, England, 1981. *Sports Illustrated* Sportsman of the Year, 1954. Now neurologist in London.

BANTRY BAY Bay in southwestern Ireland near Cork. Approximately 25 mi. (40 km.) long. French tried to land here in 1689 and 1796 to help Irish insurrections but were unsuccessful.

BAPTISTA, FULGENCIO (1901–1973) Cuban politician. President, 1940–1944. Unconstitutionally reclaimed presidency after 1952 coup d'état. Overthrown by Fidel Castro, 1959; went into exile. Baptista regime known for restrictions of civil rights and strong ties to U.S. business interests.

BAR MITZVAH Ceremony marking a Jewish boy's passage into adult religious community. Usually takes place on Sabbath (Saturday) nearest the boy's 13th birthday. Bar Mitzvah is Hebrew, meaning "son of the commandment." Same ceremony for a girl is called Bat Mitzvah.

BARBADOS Easternmost island country of West Indies, an island group belonging to the North American continent. One of world's most densely populated countries, with 1,506 persons per sq. mi. (507 per sq. km.). Named by Portuguese sailors in reference to bearded fig trees.

BARBARY CORSAIRS Pirate ships. Roamed Mediterranean Sea, 1550–1816. Activities sanctioned by their governments in the North African region now Morocco, Algeria, Tunisia and Libya. A corsair is any pirate ship sanctioned by the country to which it belongs.

BARBER OF SEVILLE, THE Rossini's opera *Il Barbiere de Siviglia*, first produced in 1816. The story involves the love affair of Count Almaviva and Rosina with the help of their friend Figaro, the village barber.

BARBIE DOLL Grownup doll made by Mattel, Inc. Her boyfriend doll is called Ken. Other friends are Kelly, Skipper, Francie and P.J. Children collect dolls and dress them in contemporary doll fashion.

BARETTA TV series about an unconventional cop; premiered

September 1975. Tony Baretta, played by Robert Blake, is a master of disguise whose usual on-duty clothing consists of T-shirt and jeans. He lives in rundown old hotel with pet cockatoo, Fred.

BARNACLE   Saltwater shellfish. Fastens itself to underwater objects such as wharf piles, turtles, rocks and ship bottoms. Born with 12 legs and one eye. Grows to have 24 legs and 3 eyes. In third stage of life, loses its eyes.

BARNARD, DR. CHRISTIAAN (1922–1984)   South African surgeon. Performed first successful heart transplant, December 3, 1967. Patient died 18 days later from pneumonia. Transplants often rejected by body's immune system; drug therapy resists this rejection. Autobiography: *One Life* (1970).

BARNUM, PHINEAS TAYLOR (P. T.) (1810–1891) Born in Connecticut. At age 60 opened "The Greatest Show on Earth" in Brooklyn; in 1881 merged with James Anthony Bailey's carnival to create Barnum and Bailey's Circus. Attractions included giant elephant Jumbo and General Tom Thumb. Coined phrase "There's a sucker born every minute." On his deathbed, he inquired, "How were the receipts today at Madison Square Garden?"

BAROMETER   Mercury-filled glass tube that measures air pressure. Used to forecast weather and measure heights. Falling barometer suggests stormy weather; rising barometer calls for better weather.

BARRIE, SIR JAMES MATTHEW (1860–1937) Scottish playwright and novelist. Wrote *The Little Minister* (1897), *Quality Street* (1901) and *The Admirable Crichton* (1902). Best known for *Peter Pan, or The Boy Who Would Not Grow Up* (1904), first play written specifically for children, in which Peter Pan, who decides never to grow up, runs off to live with fairies in Never-Never Land, but returns to London to listen to bedtime stories told the Darling children, John, Michael and Wendy. Discovered by Wendy Darling, Peter tells her the origin of fairies: "When the first baby laughed for the first time, the laugh broke into a thousand pieces and they all went skipping about, and that was the beginning of fairies. And now, when every new baby is born, its first laugh becomes a fairy." But Peter warns: "Every time a child says, 'I don't believe in fairies,' there is a fairy somewhere that falls down dead." When he suggests the three Darling children fly with him to Never-Never Land, he says they can do so by thinking lovely thoughts and being sprinkled with fairy dust. Tinkerbelle is Peter Pan's fairy companion, so named because she mends the fairy pots and kettles. Peter Pan's adversary in Never-Never Land is Captain Hook, commander of the pirate ship Jolly Roger. Hook's hand was eaten by a crocodile who pursues him to finish the meal, but the crocodile has also swallowed an alarm clock, whose ticking warns Hook when the crocodile is near. Hook is haunted by fear that someday the clock will run down. After final duel with Peter Pan, Hook escapes by jumping from ship into crocodile's open mouth. Story of Peter Pan has been filmed twice, as a silent movie in 1925 and as an animated cartoon by Walt Disney in 1953. Mary Martin starred as Peter on Broadway and in a 1955 TV special.

BARTLETT, ENOCH (1878–1956) Bartlett pear named after him. Best-known and most widely planted pear. Originated in England around 1770. Max-red bartlett is a red-skinned mutation.

BASEBALL "America's National Pastime," also called "The Grand Old Game," "The Traditional Game" and "The Old Ball Game." Developed in U.S. in mid-1800s from English sports of cricket, an adult game, and rounders, a similar game for children. The two gradually melded together by youngsters who wanted to imitate their elders, incorporating many cricket rules into their game. Invention of Abner Doubleday in 1839, now considered legend. New Yorker Alexander Cartwright acknowledged as first true formalizer of baseball rules. Unlike football, basketball and other major sports, baseball has no clock or time limit, so game said never to be over until final out. This demonstrated many times in last-inning come-from-behind victories; has also become American metaphor for miraculous recoveries in business, health, politics, etc. New York Yankee Hall of Fame catcher and manager Yogi Berra famous for his own version: "It's not over 'til it's over."

BASEBALL GLOVE First used by first baseman Charles Waite of Boston, National Association, 1875. Waite's glove was flesh-colored, as not to be conspicuous, with large opening in back for ventilation. Baseball gloves now manufactured from cowhide.

BASEBALL HALL OF FAME Located in Cooperstown, NY, village in central part of state between Albany and Syracuse, due to legend that sport was invented here by Civil War Major Abner Doubleday in 1839. Opened June 12, 1939, as part of baseball's Centennial Celebration. Underwent $3 million renovation, 1980. Annual induction of new members and exhibition game between major league teams held every August. Five original members: Ty Cobb, Babe Ruth, Honus Wagner, Christy Mathewson, Walter Johnson (elected 1936, three years before formal dedication).

BASEBALL, NIGHT Cincinnati Redlegs beat Philadelphia Phillies 2-1 in the major leagues' first night game. Played May 24, 1935, at Crosley Field in Cincinnati. Attendance: 20,422. Chicago Cubs' Wrigley Field is only major league stadium without lights.

BASEBALL RULES *Balk:* Illegal motion by pitcher. If committed with one or more runners on base, each advances one base. If nobody on base, a ball is charged against pitcher. Called most frequently for illegally delivering a pitch or pickoff attempt.

Ball weight: Official Baseball Rule 1.09 states baseball must weigh not less than 5 nor more than 5 1/4 oz. International Joint Rules Committee on Softball and United States Slow Pitch Softball Association both require 12-in.-circumference ball that shall weigh "not less than 6 1/4 oz. nor more than 7 oz." Kapok-center softball is therefore heavier than official baseball.

Forfeit: Official Baseball Rules, section 2.0, states forfeited game as one declared ended by umpire-in-chief in favor of offended team by score of 9-0, for violation of rules. Umpire can declare forfeit for violation of any rule in book.

Ground rule double: Awarded to batter when batted ball lands in fair territory and then bounces out of playing area, or is interfered with by fan or nonplayer. If line drive hits bag at third base and bounces into grandstands, correct ruling would be to award batter second base and advance all base runners two bases, because third base considered inside fair territory.

Home plate: Five-sided slab of whitened rubber, 17 in. by 17 in. from front tip. Located at intersection of first-base line and third-base line. Plate is in fair territory. Batted ball hit off plate is in play.

Home run: Player must touch all three bases and home plate (90 ft. between each brings total run to 360 ft.). Batted ball that hits foul pole (one of poles at boundary of field used by umpire as vertical extension of foul line to determine if ball going over wall is fair or foul) and lands fair is considered home run. Foul pole and foul line considered fair territory.

Official game: Five complete innings, or 4 1/2 if home team ahead, make game official. If score tied when play halted after five innings, tie declared; game must be replayed from start, with all statistics counting. If stopped before five innings, no records count. Applies to games halted by umpires for any reason.

Pitcher's win: Starting pitcher must work five innings in order to be credited with a win. Official Baseball Rule 10.19(a): "Credit the starting pitcher with a game won only if he has pitched at least five complete innings and his team not only is in the lead when he is replaced, but remains in the lead for the remainder of the game."

Rubber: Rectangular slab of whitened rubber, 24 in. by 6 in. Set in ground so distance between it and rear point of home plate is 60 ft., 6 in. Inlaid on small hill called pitcher's mound, 18 ft. in diameter, 6 in. high at highest point, 6 in. in front of rubber.

Strike zones: Space over home plate between batter's armpits and top of knees when he assumes natural stance. Varies from batter to batter because of differences in height and stance of hitters.

Umpires: Major league regular season games have four umpires, one behind home plate and one at each base. In All-Star, playoff and World Series play, two additional umpires are used, one at each foul line. Minor leagues and other forms of baseball and softball normally use two or three umpires, one behind plate and others stationing themselves at various places in infield.

Warm-up pitches: When pitcher goes to mound for start of inning or when reliever comes into game, allowed not more than eight warm-up throws to catcher. If replacement is due to injury, umpire-in-chief can allow as many as necessary for new pitcher to warm up.

BASEBALL TERMS   *Battery:* Term for pitcher and catcher. Evolved from military term meaning two pieces of artillery acting as unit. Originally applied just to pitcher, considered key weapon of team's arsenal. Used to refer to both positions together since c.1868.

Catcher: Defensive position. Stationed behind home plate. Squats to receive ball thrown by pitcher and generally stands to return ball to pitcher. Squats again to receive next pitch, repeating this an average of 150 times per game.

Hit for cycle: Get a single, double, triple and home run in same game, regardless of order or number of times at bat. Through 1980, only 98 National Leaguers and 78 American Leaguers had done this. Bob Meusel (New York Yankees) and Babe Herman (Brooklyn Dodgers) did it three times each.

In the corn: Playing the outfield. Evolved from game being played in large, open country fields where outfielder might be playing on edge of or even in cornfields. Easy pop fly to outfielder called "can of corn."

Seventh-inning stretch: Fans' custom of standing during game's seventh inning, apparently started in order to relax after sitting on hard benches of grandstands and to observe lucky number seven. Reportedly originated in Cincinnati, 1869, or at Manhattan College, 1882.

Shag flies: Fielding practice in which players chase fly balls hit by another player or coach, who tosses ball lightly in the air and hits it as it falls. Also known as "hitting fungos." Light bat used known as "fungo bat."

Texas Leaguer: Short fly ball that falls between infielders and outfielders. Sportswriter in 1890 described hit that was specialty of Toledo player Art Sunday, veteran of Texas League, as "Texas League hit." Shortened through time to Texas Leaguer.

Triple Crown: Title given to league leader in home runs, batting average and runs batted in (RBIs). Batter's rarest feat. Only 12 titles given since 1900. Awarded twice to Ted Williams (1942, 1947) and Rogers Hornsby (1922, 1925). Given to Chuck Klein (National League) and Jimmy Foxx (American League) in same year (1933). Most recently awarded to Carl Yastrzemski, Boston Red Sox, 1967.

BASKETBALL   Originated at Training School of International YMCA College (now Springfield College), Springfield, MA, 1891, by instructor Dr. James A. Naismith to popularize use of indoor gymnasiums. Attached peach baskets to gym's balcony, giving sport its name. First game played January 20, 1892. Twelve of Naismith's original 13 rules still in effect.

BASKETBALL, FREE-THROW TWENTY-ONE   Basketball practice game for two. Player shoots free throws (foul shots) until he misses; then opponent gets chance to make rebound shot and, if he makes it, goes to foul line for free throws. One point per shot; played to 21 points.

BASKETBALL RULES   *Ball:* Diameter of 9 1/2–10 in.; newly approved women's ball slightly smaller.

Basket: Metal ring 18 in. in diameter, 6 in. from backboard and 10 ft. from floor. Traditionally painted orange, with net hanging below.

Free throw line: Parallel to end line and 15 ft. from the plane of face of backboard. Line is 2 in. wide and 12 ft. long (side to side).

Game length: In National Basketball Association, quarters are 12 min.

each (48 min. in regulation game); overtime periods, 5 min. each. In college, two 20-min. halves played; high schools generally play four 8-min. quarters.

Twenty-four-second clock: Offensive team gets 24 sec. to attempt shot at basket or loses ball. Used to speed up action of pro games and eliminate slowdown tactics. Bitterly opposed at first by some owners, now recognized as popularizing NBA. Introduced by Danny Biasone of Syracuse Nationals and used in NBA since 1954–1955 season.

BASKETBALL TERMS *Center:* Usually tallest on five-player team, plays "pivot" position, focal point of team's offense. Takes position near foul line (called "paint" because usually painted bright color). May be close to basket (low post) or near free throw line (high post). On defense, primary roles are shot blocker and rebounder.

Full-court press: Pressure defensive tactic. Team guards opponents more closely than usual to disrupt their play in intensive effort to get ball. Can be played in man-to-man or zone configurations.

Give and go: Play in which player passes to teammate, cuts around his defender toward basket for immediate return pass and shot. Maneuver also used in lacrosse, soccer and hockey.

BASKETBALL, PRIMITIVE Ancient Central and South American Indians played game in which object was to shoot solid rubber ball through stone ring mounted on wall. Winner awarded clothes of all spectators; loser put to death.

BASTILLE Paris prison. Built as fortress, 1370. Used by Louis XIII to impound political prisoners and criminals. Bombarded, July 14, 1789 (Bastille Day), marking start of French Revolution.

BAT Only flying mammal. Has fingers, toes, two eyes and teeth. Hangs upside down while resting. Some navigate by high-frequency echo location. Vampire bats approach victims on foot. Hoary bats travel south for winter. Blood is sole source of food; digestive apparatus specialized for this diet. Bite is relatively painless, yet rabies and other fatal diseases may be transmitted.

BAT MASTERSON Popular TV Western, premiered October 1958. Gene Barry portrayed the legendary lawman and gambler who roamed the Southwest, romancing the ladies and protecting the innocent.

BATHROOM More houses have flush toilets than fixed showers and baths. In U.S., 98% of occupied homes have toilets; in

Japan, 35%. Average person uses bathroom six times daily.

BATMAN AND ROBIN   Comic book (later film, newspaper comics, radio and TV) characters created by Bob Kane and writer Bill Finger in National Detective Comics, no. 27, May 1939. Batman (secret identity Bruce Wayne) and Robin (Dick Grayson) fight crime in Gotham City. Wayne, orphaned at 10 by brutal murder of parents, has no super powers, but keen mind and strong body. Original Batman, an avenging vigilante, later an honorary member of Gotham Police Force, chose name when he saw chilling silhouette of bat against full moon. Adopted Dick Grayson, young aerialist with traveling circus whose parents had been killed by extortionists, as his ward and trained him as Robin, "the Boy Wonder." ABC's TV series premiered in 1966 with Adam West (Batman) and Burt Ward (Robin) as "the Dynamic Duo"; added campy element to characters, with Robin making such exclamations as "Holy Barracuda!" and "Holy hole in the donut!" Together, they would POW!, WHAM! and BASH! such evildoers as The Riddler, The Penguin and The Joker. Batgirl was portrayed by Yvonne Craig.

BATON ROUGE   Louisiana state capital. Established in 1719 by French soldiers. Originally a military post to protect white travelers from Indians. Name means "red stick" in French and refers to a red-stained pole posted here to divide land of two Indian camps.

BATTERY   Device that converts chemical energy to electrical energy. Has two electrodes: one positive, called an anode; one negative, called a cathode. Electrical current flows from the anode.

BATTERY PARK   Southernmost tip of Manhattan, New York City, where Hudson and East rivers merge into New York Bay. Point where Italian navigator Giovanni da Verrazano first set foot after discovering New York Harbor, 1524. Statues and memorials in park commemorate area's history.

BATTLE CREEK, MICHIGAN   Home of cereal manufacturer magnate W. K. Kellogg (1860–1951), "King of the Corn Flakes." Made donations to the city and established his company's headquarters and Kellogg Foundation here.

BATTLE OF HASTINGS   William, Duke of Normandy, France, later known as William the Conqueror (1022–1087), invaded England, 1066. Defeated King Harold II. Assumed rule of England as King William I, 1066–1087. William claimed he had been promised the throne by his cousin Edward the Confessor, Harold's predecessor.

BATTLE OF LITTLE BIG HORN   Montana, June 25, 1876. Civil War General Custer (1839–1876), and 650 men attacked about 2,000 Cheyenne and Sioux Indian warriors, underestimating their number. Battle lasted possibly less than one hour. Custer and all his men killed. Only non-Indian survivor allegedly a horse named Comanche.

BATTLE OF MIDWAY   World War II. Naval battle fought near Midway Island in mid- Pacific. Commenced June 4, 1942, when planes from U.S. aircraft carriers *Enterprise, Hornet* and *Yorktown* attacked Japanese fleet. Japan lost four aircraft carriers and one heavy cruiser. U.S. lost a destroyer and *Yorktown* to submarines.

BATTLE OF MORNINGSIDE HEIGHTS   Student uprising at New York City's Columbia University, April 1968. Student dissidents besieged five buildings on Columbia's Morningside Heights campus, demanding more student-faculty say in running the university. Roughly 400 students arrested; charges later dropped.

BATTLE OF THE BULGE   World War II. Surprise counteroffensive in attempt to stop allied drive to German heartland. Launched by General von Rundstedt, December 16, 1944. Early success of this last great German offensive reversed by January 1945.

BATTLE OF THE SOMME   World War I. Began July 1, 1916. Marked introduction of the "tank." Over 1.1 million killed, 60,000 on first day alone.

BATTLE OF NEW ORLEANS   January 8, 1815. U.S. forces, under General Jackson, defeated British. Also called the Needless Battle because it was fought after the signing of the Treaty of Ghent, which officially ended the War of 1812.

BAUM, LYMAN FRANK (1856–1919)   American writer of children's stories. His classic *The Wonderful Wizard of Oz* (1900) tells story of Dorothy, little girl from Kansas hurled by cyclone to land of Oz, located "over the rainbow." Her house lands on Wicked Witch of the East, freeing little people called Munchkins from bondage. Trying to get back to Kansas, Dorothy is befriended by Scarecrow (looking for a brain), Cowardly Lion (looking for courage) and Tin Man (looking for a heart). They follow Yellow Brick

Road to Emerald City, capital of Oz and home of the Wizard, who first tests Dorothy's will and ultimately reveals secret way to get her home. In 1939 film version, Judy Garland played Dorothy, Ray Bolger played Scarecrow, Bert Lahr played Lion, Jack Haley played Tin Man and Frank Morgan played the Wizard.

BAXTER, TED   Character portrayed by Ted Knight on *The Mary Tyler Moore Show* (1970–1977). Baxter began his career at a 5,000-watt station in Fresno, CA, before becoming anchorman of six o'clock news for WJM-TV in Minneapolis. The swellheaded Baxter known to put his foot in his mouth both on and off the air.

BAY OF BISCAY   Extension of Atlantic Ocean. Lies on western coast of Spain and France. Named from Basques, people who live along rocky Spanish shore. Noted for heavy storms.

BAY OF PIGS   April 17, 1961, a force of anti-Castro Cuban exiles landed at the Bay of Pigs on the west coast of Cuba. The 2,506 Brigade, trained and funded by the CIA, invaded in the hopes that the Cuban masses would "rise up to sweep communism from the country." Three hundred of the invaders were killed, 1,200 captured. The plans, developed by the CIA during the Eisenhower administration, were carried out during President J. F. Kennedy's first year in office. Kennedy considered it the greatest mistake of his administration.

BAYONET   Steel dagger. Can be affixed to muzzle of rifle for close combat. Said to have been invented by Marechal de Puysegur of Bayonne, France, 1641. Used by his troops who fought for King Louis XIV.

BEACH BOYS, THE   Successful rock-and-roll band formed in 1961 by brothers Dennis, Brian and Carl Wilson, their cousin Mike Love and friend Al Jardine. Created "the California sound," with songs about surfing, driving and dating, and urging kids to "Be True to Your School." Early hits include "Surfin' Safari" (1962), "Surfin' U.S.A." (1963) and "I Get Around" (1964). Formed their own record label, Brother Records, in 1970. Ironically, Dennis Wilson drowned in a 1983 accident.

BEACON HILL   Fashionable residential section of Boston, located north of Boston Common. Served as Beacon Station for signaling ships in 1600s.

BEACON STREET   Large avenue located in Boston. Runs

along Boston Common. Lined with fashionable townhouses, the State House and the Boston Athenaeum, a private library.

BEAN, JUDGE ROY (1825?–1904)   Saloonkeeper and justice of the peace. Called himself the only "Law West of the Pecos," the Pecos being a river. Famous for his sometimes zany decisions, such as when he fined a dead body $40 for carrying concealed weapons.

BEARD, DITA (1918–   )   Lobbyist in Washington, DC, for ITT. Arranged for ITT to give $400,000 to Nixon administration's reelection fund in exchange for ITT's unhindered takeover of Hartford Fire Insurance Corp. Scandal exposed four months later by columnist Jack Anderson.

BEARD, JAMES (1903–   )   Rotund chef, gourmet and author. Wrote 18 books on food, including *Beard on Bread* and *James Beard's American Cookery*. Runs Greenwich Village cooking school in New York.

BEAT THE CLOCK   Radio game show moved to TV in March 1950 with Bud Collyer as host. Contestants attempt to perform stunts and beat amount of time shown on ticking 60-second clock.

BEATLES, THE   The most influential and popular rock-and-roll band from the 1960s. John Lennon, Paul McCartney and George Harrison began together in 1958 as The Quarrymen; with Ringo Starr from 1962, as The Beatles. Managed by Brian Epstein, who spotted group at a Liverpool nightclub, the Cavern, Beatles went on to make music history. First U.S. concert performed at Carnegie Hall. In 1964, first film, *A Hard Day's Night*, premiered. In age, Ringo is the oldest; George, the youngest. Hit songs include: "I Wanna Hold Your Hand"; "All You Need Is Love"; "Ob-La-Di, Ob-La-Da," a love song about Desmond and Molly Jones; "When I'm 64," a song that mentions grandchildren Vera, Chuck and Dave. Started own company, Apple Records, featuring "Granny Smith" apple on label. Cover of last album, *Abbey Road* (1969), shows Paul walking barefoot with his eyes closed. 1965 album *Rubber Soul* contains songs "Norwegian Wood," "It's Only Love" and the hit "Michelle."

BEAU GESTE   1939 feature about three brothers in Foreign Legion who battle their tyrannical officer (Brian Donlevy) and rescue a lady's honor. Gary Cooper plays title role.

BEAUTY AND THE BEAST Fairy tale in which beauty saves life of father by consenting to life with the beast, who, freed from evil spell by her love, becomes handsome prince and marries her. French filmmaker Jean Cocteau made surrealistic 1946 film version.

BEAVER Large, furry aquatic rodent. Paddle-like tail used to steer while swimming. Considered natural engineer, building intricate canals, dams and lodges in which it lives. Can hold breath underwater for 15 min. Despite water home, does not eat fish. Skin and fur used as currency in certain regions of North America, 17th century; also called hairy bank notes.

BECKET, THOMAS (1118?–1170) Archbishop of Canterbury. Ordered killed by King Henry II, December 29, 1170. Four of King's knights murdered Becket in his Canterbury Cathedral, until then considered a sanctuary.

BEDTIME FOR BONZO 1951 film starring Ronald Reagan as professor raising chimp to prove that environment determines a child's behavior. Bonzo played the chimp; Diana Lynn was Reagan's girl.

BEE'S KNEES Slang expression popular in 1920s, used to describe a superb person or thing, e.g., "He's the bee's knees." Also a cocktail made of 1 tsp. honey, one part lemon juice and two parts gin or applejack, depending on source.

BEER Beverage obtained by adding hops and water to yeast-fermented malted cereal. Amount of hops influences flavor; stout beers have bitter hop flavor.

Consumption

Country	Rank	Gallons consumed per person per year
West Germany	1	39.1
Czechslovakia	2	38.7
Denmark	3	35.3
U.S.	12	24.4

Foreign varieties: Austria - Puntigan, Norway - Frydenlunds, Ireland - Harp Lager Beer, Denmark - Tuborg, Carlsberg, Wiibroe, Italy - Peroni, Netherlands - Heineken

BEES Have six legs and four wings, like most insects. Gather nectar from flowers to produce honey. Average honeybee produces about one-tenth of a pound of honey in its life and may fly 1,300 mi. to do so. Only insect that produces food eaten by man. Honeybees have five eyes and can see ultraviolet light. In a honeybee hive there is only one active queen bee, whose sole duty is to lay eggs. It mates with drone bee, who is stingless. Drone cannot collect pollen or nectar. Honeybees comprise family Apidae. Commercial beekeeping is called apiculture. Colonies of bees are housed in apiaries.

BEETLES Of the nearly one million known species of insects, about three-quarters are beetles. There are more different kinds than any other living thing. The largest, the Goliath beetle, is 4 in. long.

BEGIN, MENACHEM (1913–   ) Israeli prime minister from 1977 to 1983, when he resigned. Imprisoned two years in Soviet labor camp, World War II. Later traveled to Palestine, where he led a guerilla organization against British rule. Received Nobel Peace Prize, 1979.

BELFAST Capital and largest city of Northern Ireland. Became capital when Northern Ireland and Ireland split into separate states in 1920. Textile factories produce delicate linen. *Titanic* was built here.

BELGIUM Small European country, roughly the size of Maryland. Strategic location made it Europe's most frequent ground for battles. Bordered by France, the Netherlands and West Germany, and is across the Channel from England. Divided into two official language groups in 1963: inhabitants of northern country, called Flemings, speak Flemish (56%); those living south of Brussels, called Walloons, speak French dialect called Walloon (32%). Eleven percent of country's people are classified as legally bilingual, speaking both Flemish and French; only 1% of Belgians speak German.

BELGRADE Capital and largest city of Yugoslavia. Lies where Danube and Sava rivers meet. Destroyed over 30 times by invading armies. Majority of inhabitants are Serbs.

BELL, ALEXANDER GRAHAM (1847–1922) American inventor. Created the telephone. First words spoken over the telephone: "Watson, come here, I want you."

BELLADONNA Or deadly nightshade. Bushy plant that produces potentially lethal drug, belladonna, its active principal the alkaloid atropine. Means "fair lady" in Italian, possibly because Italian ladies made cosmetics from the plant's juice. Belladonna also used by Leucota, Italian famous for poisoning beautiful women.

BELLI, MELVIN MOURON (1907–   ) Trial lawyer, famous since 1960s. Showy manner in court. Defended Jack Ruby, who had killed Lee Harvey Oswald, J. F. Kennedy's assassin. Also defended comedian Lenny Bruce, who was arrested on obscenity and drug possession charges throughout the early 1960s.

BELLOW, SAUL (1915–   ) American novelist and short-story writer. Novels deal with contemporary Jewish life in America. *Humboldt's Gift* won 1975 Pulitzer Prize for fiction, 1976 Nobel Prize. Other novels: *Herzog* (1964) and *Mr. Sammler's Planet* (1970).

BELMONT STAKES. See TRIPLE CROWN

BEN CASEY Popular TV medical drama series of 1960s, starring Vince Edwards as doctor in neurosurgical ward of County General Hospital. Casey's mentor, Dr. David Zorba, was played by Sam Jaffe, who spoke the show's opening words: "Man, woman, birth, death, infinity."

BEN HUR Lew Wallace's biblical adventure novel has been brought to the screen in two epic motion pictures. Ramon Novarro starred in the 1926 silent version; Charleton Heston played title role in 1959 remake. The latter version won a record number of 11 Oscars, including Best Picture and Best Actor.

BEN-GURION, DAVID (1886–1973) Statesman. First prime minister of State of Israel. Later resigned to become pioneer in remote part of Negev Desert. Ben-Gurion, meaning "son of lion," is his self-chosen name.

BENCHLEY, PETER BRADFORD (1940–   ) American novelist. *Jaws* (1974) opens with shark moving silently through water and attacking young woman taking midnight swim after making love. Her violent death begins terror at Amity Island resort. Shark hunted by local police chief, marine biologist and crusty fisherman Quint aboard his boat, *The Orca*, named for species of killer whale. Steven Spielberg directed 1975 film version. Benchley also wrote *The Deep* (1976) and *The Island* (1979).

BENELUX Economic union formed in 1948 by Belgium, the Netherlands and Luxembourg. Term made up of first letters in each country's name. Created a common foreign trade policy for all three countries.

BENNETT, TONY (1926–   ) Born Anthony Dominick Benedetto. Discovered singing in Greenwich Village night club by Bob Hope, who made him part of his variety troupe. Hit songs from the 1950s and '60s include "Rags to Riches," "I Wanna Be Around" and "(I Left My Heart in) San Francisco."

BENNY GOODMAN STORY, THE 1955 feature film based on life of famous swing bandleader and clarinet player. Steve Allen portray Goodman; many guest musicians appear as themselves, including Gene Krupa and Harry James.

BENNY, JACK (1894–1974) One of radio's most popular and enduring comedians. Began his career in 1929. Major, long-term sponsor: Jell-O. Appeared in movies and began TV career in 1950. Trademarks included: his ancient Maxwell automobile, violin playing, jokes about his age, and the line "Now, cut that out!" Comedy foils included Mary Livingston (actually his wife) and his valet Rochester, the black comedian Eddie Anderson. Don Wilson was his announcer.

BENZ, KARL (1844–1929) German. Most often credited with invention of gasoline automobile, in 1885, although cruder versions were built by others earlier. His car was a three-wheeled, rear-engine model. A steam-powered vehicle was built by Nicolas Cugnot of France in 1770.

BERGEN, EDGAR (1903–1983) Popular ventriloquist of radio and movies in 1930s and '40s. With puppets Charlie McCarthy and Mortimer Snerd, appeared in short subjects and features, including: *You Can't Cheat an Honest Man* (1939) and *I Remember Mama* (1948). Edgar and Charlie won an Honorary Wooden Oscar in 1937.

BERING STRAIT Narrow water passageway of 50 mi. (80 km.) between Bering Sea and Arctic Ocean, separating Soviet Union and U.S. (Alaska). Named for Vitus Bering, Danish navigator who proved in 1700s that water separated America from Asia.

BERKOWITZ, DAVID (1956–   ) Alias Son of Sam. Arrested August 10, 1977, for murder of six people and assault of seven others. Claimed he had been ordered by dog demons to commit the crimes. Later recanted demon story.

BERLE, MILTON (1908–   ) Known as "Mr. Television" during late 1940s and early '50s. His variety series was reason many people bought TV sets during this period; first telecast as *Texaco Star Theatre* in 1948. Berle continued to entertain on a weekly basis until 1959.

BERLIN BLOCKADE Isolation of West Berlin by East Germans, 1948. Blockade imposed when Western powers of Britain, France and U.S. refused to give over territory to Soviet control after World War II.

BERLIN WALL Built August 31, 1961, by East German police to stop exodus of East Germans into West Berlin. Escapes had begun in June 1961, when Russia threatened to sign its own pact with East Germany and end cooperation with West Germany. Occupied since World War II by U.S., U.K. and France. Berliners called wall Schandmauer (Wall of Shame). Measures 27 mi. (43 km.) long.

BERLIN, IRVING (1888–   ) Composer and lyricist of many popular songs and musical plays including *Annie Get Your Gun*. Among his songs are "God Bless America," "Oh, How I Hate to Get Up in the Morning," "Easter Parade" and "White Christmas."

BERMUDA British self-governing colony consisting of 360 small islands, of which only 20 are inhabited. Capital and chief port is Hamilton. Over 600,000 tourists visit per year.

BERMUDA BOWL. See BRIDGE, WORLD CHAMPIONSHIP

BERMUDA TRIANGLE Area of ocean between coasts of Florida, Bermuda and Puerto Rico. Since 1854, 50 ships and aircraft have vanished near or in it. Bodies of survivors seldom found. Some scientists attribute disappearances to storms or downward air currents. First reported disappearance: *U.S.S. Cyclops*, March 1918.

BERN Capital of Switzerland and Swiss canton (state) of Bern. Picturesque city with famous clock tower, the Zeitglockenturm, built in 1530. Bears are kept in a pit in eastern Bern and are city's symbol. Name derived from German word *Baren* ("bear").

BERNHARDT, SARAH (1844–1923) Born Rosalie Bernard, but known as Divine Sarah to critics and audiences who acclaimed this famous French stage actress.

BERNINI-BRISTOL HOTEL One of Rome's most luxurious hotels, located in city's busy square, Piazza Barberini. Renowned for shopping and sightseeing. Hotel's public rooms are decorated with marble and rich fabrics; private bedrooms and suites furnished in modern fashion.

BERNSTEIN, CARL (1944–   ) American journalist and author. With Bob Woodward, Washington *Post* reporter who uncovered Watergate scandal. Co-wrote Watergate books *All the President's Men* (1974) and *The Final Days* (1976) with Woodward.

BERNSTEIN, LEONARD (1918–   ) Composer who wrote scores for Broadway musicals, including: *On the Town* (1944), *Candide* (1956) and *West Side Story* (1957). Conductor of New York Philharmonic.

BERRY, CHUCK (1931–   ) Rock-and-roll singer/songwriter popular since mid-1950s. Hits include "Maybelline," "Rock and Roll Music," "Johnny B. Goode" and "Roll Over, Beethoven."

BETTY AND VERONICA. See ARCHIE

BIARRITZ Popular resort area in southwestern France. Offers mineral baths and sea bathing in Atlantic Ocean.

BIATHLON Winter Olympic event that combines cross-country skiing and target shooting. Competitors ski 10 or 20 km. and shoot at targets, incurring two-minute penalty for each miss. Introduced to Olympics at Squaw Valley, CA, 1960.

BIBLE, THE First words of its first book, Genesis, I: 1, are "In the beginning, God created the heavens and the earth."

BIBLIOPHILE A lover of books. From Greek *philo* ("lover") and *biblos* ("book"). Also original word for inner bark of papyrus plant from which forerunner of paper made. Word "Bible" also derived from *biblos*.

BIBLIOTHEK German word for "library." Derived from Greek *biblos* ("book") and *theke* ("case") Thus, a "bookcase." Compare: *bibliotheca* (Latin), *bibliothèque* (French), *biblioteca* (Spanish, Portuguese and Italian) and *biblioteka* (Russian).

BIG APPLE. See NEW YORK CITY NICKNAMES

BIG BANG Theory that universe began from a singular state of infinite density and has been expanding ever since. George Gamow coined term, 1946, to describe initial cataclysmic event.

BIG BEN Name of bell in clock tower of London's Houses of Parliament. First rang in 1859. Named for Sir Benjamin Hall, Commissioner of Works, whose nickname was "Big Ben." Clock connected to Big Ben is noted for its accuracy. Clock wound by hand until 1913; now wound by electric motor. Its four faces are lit by fluorescent lamps.

BIG BERTHA Long-range gun used in World War II. Manufactured by Krupp family firm, leading German producer of munitions, steel and machinery. Named for Bertha Krupp, daughter of Freidrich A. Krupp.

BIG DIPPER Part of larger constellation, Ursa Major, or the Great Bear. Like Little Dipper, forms outline of long-handled cup. Consists of seven stars; the two in front of cup point to North Star. Also known as the wagon or plow.

BIG SLEEP, THE 1946 film based on Raymond Chandler mystery novel. Humphrey Bogart stars as private detective Philip Marlowe, hired to rescue millionaire's daughter. Directed by Howard Hawks.

BIG SUR Considered scenic highway number one. Ninety-four-mile stretch in California from Carmel to Hearst Castle at San Simeon. Twisting roads offer breathtaking views of Pacific Ocean and Los Padres National Forest. Bordered on east by Santa Lucia Range.

BIG THREE OF IVY LEAGUE. See FOOTBALL, COLLEGE

BIG VALLEY, THE Popular TV Western of late 1960s. Barbara Stanwyck stars as Victoria Barkley, head of the clan, who battled lawless elements threatening her ranch. Richard Long, Peter Breck and Lee Majors co-star as her sons.

BIGGERS, EARL DERR (1884–1933) American mystery novelist. Created Charlie Chan, polite, sage Oriental detective for Honolulu police force. Lives with wife and 11 children in house on Punchbowl Hill, overlooking city. According to sons, who often try to help out their "Pop," he always gets his man. Played in films by Warner Oland, Sidney Toler, Roland Winters and others; on TV by J. Carrol Naish and Ross Martin. Among many screen Number One and Number Two sons were Victor Sen Young and Keye Luke.

BIKILA, ABEBE (1932–1973) Ethiopian distance runner who won marathon at 1960 Rome Olympics in Olympic record time—running barefoot. In 1964, in Tokyo, he repeated his victory, this time with shoes, bettering his time by more than three minutes.

Merkin & Frankel

BILL HALEY AND THE COMETS   Popular rock-and-roll group of mid-1950s. Hit songs include: "Shake, Rattle and Roll" (1955), "See You Later, Alligator" (1955), "Razzle-Dazzle" (1956), "R-O-C-K" (1956). Appeared in feature films *Rock Around the Clock* (1956) and *Don't Knock the Rock* (1956).

BILL, THE   Asking for the bill in four languages: *Ma jeg bede om regningen* (Danish); *L'addition, s'il vous plaît* (French); *Posso avere il conto, per favore* (Italian); *La cuenta, por favor* (Spanish).

BILLET-DOUX   Love letter. From French *billet doux* (literally, "sweet letter").

BILLIARDS   Game played on rectangular table with slate surface covered by tight green felt and surrounded by rubber cushions along edge. In U.S., "billiards" denotes game played on table without pockets; "pool" or "championship pocket billiards" denotes game played on table with six pockets, one at each corner and one in middle of each long side. In pocket billiards, balls are numbered 1 to 15; 1 through 8 are solid-colored, 9 through 15 are white with colored stripe. "Eight ball" is always black. Numbered balls arranged in triangular frame called rack, which sets balls in five rows and is then removed. Play begins with break shot: white unnumbered cue ball is shot at racked balls with long stick called cue, causing balls to carom off cushions. As long as player continues sinking designated numbered balls in designated pockets without sinking cue ball (scratching), his turn continues. Player may lean over table to make difficult shot, but one foot must always remain on floor.

BILLIARDS VARIATIONS   *Eight ball:* Player must sink all colored or striped balls, then eight ball. If wrong type of ball is sunk, player scratches (ends turn); if eight ball is sunk out of sequence, player loses.
Snooker: Played with white cue ball, 15 red balls and 6 balls of other colors. Object is to pocket red ball and colored ball alternately, each time returning colored ball to table until all red balls pocketed, then pocket all colored balls in numerical order. Player "snookered," ending turn, when he cannot make cue ball strike designated target ball before it strikes any other.

BILLINGSGATE MARKET   Fishmarket located in City of London, on River Thames. Approximately 400 tons of fish sold daily in 1875 yellow brick, arcaded building, topped with seated female figure held by several dolphins. Many fish weather vanes found here.

BILLY JOE MCALLISTER   Jumped off Tallahatchie Bridge in Bobbie Gentry's 1967 hit song "Ode to Billy Joe." Ballad won Grammy Award and inspired 1976 movie starring Robby Benson as Billy Joe. (see ODE TO BILLY JOE)

BILLY THE KID (1859–1881)   Outlaw, thought to have been born in New York City. Later moved to New Mexico. Chose name William H. Bonney; dubbed Billy the Kid. After mother's death, 1874, took to living in streets. Infamous for having killed one man for each of his first 21 years of life; actually killed seven or eight men. Captured, 1881, by Pat Garrett, former friend and newly elected sheriff. Later escaped by killing two guards. Finally tracked down and killed by Garrett, July 13, Fort Sumner, NM.

BIMONTHLY   Means every other month, or six times a year. Latin prefix *bi-* means "two." (Compare: bicycle, bifocals.) Biweekly means every other week. Sometimes confused with *semi-*, meaning "half" (semimonthly and biweekly would both describe publication that comes out every other week).

BINARY NUMBER SYSTEM   System using only two symbols: 0 and 1.

1 = 1	6 = 110	100 = 1100100
2 = 10	7 = 111	
3 = 11	8 = 1000	
4 = 100	9 = 1001	
5 = 101	10 = 1010	

BING CROSBY PRO-AM   Mid-January Professional Golfers Association event, one of oldest continuous stops on pro tour. Began 1937. Charity event hosted by late singer-actor until his death. Uniquely played on three courses in Pebble Beach, CA, on Monterey Peninsula: Pebble Beach, oceanside course in craggy hills over Carmel Bay; Cypress Point; and Spyglass Hill (replaced Monterey Peninsula CC, 1967). All par 72 with small greens. Tournament known for demanding courses and severe weather conditions.

BIRD, LAZLO AND GEORG   Inventors of ball-point pen, 1938. Patented by Lazlo in 1943. Originally marketed by Hungarian brothers as first pen to write underwater.

BIRDIE   Rock-and-roll singer Conrad Birdie in play (and movie)

Bye Bye Birdie, who gets drafted and causes problems for his songwriter manager (Dick Van Dyke, on stage and screen). Film premiered in 1963.

BIRDS

Swift:	world's fastest: 200 m.p.h.
Goose:	first domesticated bird.
Stork:	can stand on one leg due to self-locking joints.
Albatross:	largest web-footed marine-type. Greatest wingspan of any: called gooney bird.
Wild Turkey:	large game type; heaviest on-land variety on continent.
Penguin:	stout-bodied flightless; excellently adapted for swimming.
Three-wattled Bell:	Costa Rica; call heard for three miles.
Mound Builder:	flies immediately after hatching.
Hummingbird	world's smallest bird.

BIRDS, THE   1963 film, directed by Alfred Hitchcock, about a small town in California attacked by thousands of birds. Suzanne Pleshette plays schoolteacher whose eyes are pecked out.

BIRDSEYE, CLARENCE (1886–1956)   Refined frozen foods, 1924. During travels in Labrador, 1916, originated idea by preserving fresh vegetables in barrels of freezing water. Founded company to manufacture products; sold it four years later for more than $20 million. Became General Foods, Inc.

BIRTH OF A NATION, THE   1915 landmark film directed by D. W. Griffith. Epic story of two families during Civil War starred Lillian Gish, Mae Marsh and Henry B. Walthall.

BIRTHSTONES

Month	*Stone*	*Significance*
January	Garnet	Constancy
February	Amethyst	Sincerity
March	Aquamarine, Chalcedony	Courage
April	Diamond	Innocence
May	Emerald	Love, Success
June	Pearl, Alexandrite, Moonstone	Health

Month	Stone	Significance
July	Ruby	Contentment
August	Peridot, Sardonyx	Married happiness
September	Sapphire, Chrysolite	Clear thinking
October	Opal, Tourmaline	Hope
November	Topaz	Fidelity
December	Turquoise, Zircon	Prosperity

BISMARCK, THE   World War II German battleship. Eight guns, 52,600 tons; Germany's largest. Damaged one British battleship and sank another, the *Hood*, on first encounter. Combined British naval and air forces downed the *Bismarck* on May 27, 1941, one month after it had been launched. Also, hit song performed by Johnny Horton, written for 1960 film *Sink the Bismarck!*

BISMARCK, PRINCE OTTO EDWARD VON LEOPOLD (1815–1898)   First chancellor of German Empire, 1871–1890. Known as "the Iron Chancellor" for his "blood and iron" policies. Engaged in Franco-German War (1870–1871) and Austrian War (1866), which led to Unification of Germany. Forced to resign by Wilhelm II.

BIT   Internal coding system for most digital computers. Number 2 is used as base (radix) instead of 10. Binary digits represent one of two states: "on" or "off," "positive" or "negative." In binary number system, 0 and 1 are only numerals. Two is denoted ten, three denoted eleven, four, 100, etc.

BLACK FOREST   Mountainous region in West Germany. Called Schwarzwald in German. Mineral springs, fir and spruce trees fill the area. Inhabitants make toys, cuckoo clocks and musical instruments. Subject and site of several ancient German fairy tales.

BLACK HILLS   Low mountains in southwestern South Dakota and eastern Wyoming. Popular vacation spot. U.S. bought territory from Sioux Indians in 1876 after gold discovered.

BLACK HOLE OF CALCUTTA   Derogatory name for room in Calcutta where 146 Britons were imprisoned overnight. On June 20, 1756, the ruler of Bengal had stormed the British garrison, taking British as prisoners. By the next day, 123 had suffocated to death.

BLACK HOLES   Remnants of collapsed stars so dense that their gravity pulls light. A star the size of the sun would make a black hole 10 mi. in diameter. If measurable, one teaspoonful of black hole would weigh 15,000 tons. Existence of black holes has not been proven.

BLACK LABEL BEER   Product of Carling, Canadian brewer since 1840s, who acquired Cleveland auto factory, converted it into brewery, then pioneered idea of regional brewers making one nationally distributed beer. Also brews Red Cap Ale. Company now subsidiary of Heileman brewery. 1950s advertisement had waitress named Mabel being called to bring beer to her customers.

BLACK RUSSIAN   Cocktail made of 1 oz. vodka and ½ oz. Kahlúa or Tia Maria (coffee liqueurs). To mix White Russian, ½ oz. cream is added.

BLACK TUESDAY   October 29, 1929, day of the greatest crash of an American stock market in history. Followed by four-year period during which average stock price on New York Stock Exchange more than doubled. Panicked stockowners sold record 16,410,030 shares in one day.

BLACK VELVET   Drink made from champagne (or cider) and stout. Served chilled. Stout related to porter; very dark ale, malty, slightly bitter (best known is Guinness). Black Velvet also brand of Scotch.

BLACKJACK (TWENTY-ONE)   World's most popular card game. Played by dealer/banker and one or more players. Player's hand must add up to more than dealer's hand without going over 21, which means an immediate loss. Number cards count face value, court cards worth 10 points, ace counts 11 or 1 (at option of holder). Dealer must take card from deck if his hand shows 16 points or less. If over 17, dealer must stand pat.

BLACKOUT, THE   Faulty relay setting caused power failure, 5:16:11 P.M. EST, November 9, 1969. Relay switch near Niagara Falls accidently diverted Canadian electricity onto overloaded New York lines. Parts of nine northeastern states and two Canadian provinces blacked out up to 13½ hours. Affected an estimated 30 million people. Roughly 800,000 stranded in New York City subways. Popular belief that this event resulted in the conception of so-called "blackout babies."

BLANC, MEL (1908–   )   Voice actor, regular on many radio programs of 1940s (including *The Jack Benny Show*). Most famous as voice of many popular, animated cartoon characters, including: Bugs Bunny, Daffy Duck, Porky Pig, Foghorn Leghorn, Sylvester.

BLANDA, GEORGE (1927–   )   Quarterback and placekicker whose pro football career with Chicago Bears, Houston Oilers and Oakland Raiders spanned 26 years, 1949–1975. Retired at age 47 with NFL record of 2,002 points. In 1970, playing for Oakland at age 42, won five consecutive games with last-second heroics.

BLARNEY CASTLE   Located near Cork, Ireland. Home of Blarney Stone, which, according to legend, if kissed will bring one the gift of clever, expressive talk. Stone brought to tower in 1446. Today blarney means "skillful flattery" or "coaxing talk."

BLATTY, WILLIAM PETER (1928–   )   American novelist and screenwriter. Wrote *John Goldfarb, Please Come Home* (1963), *Twinkle, Twinkle "Killer" Kane* (1967), *The Legion* (1983) and *The Exorcist*, novel about 12-year-old Regan MacNeil, possessed by demons in her Georgetown home. Priests exorcise vile spirits from her body. 1973 William Friedkin film version starred Linda Blair.

BLINDMAN'S BLUFF   Game in which blindfolded player tries to catch and identify other players in room who try to avoid capture. When blindfolded player catches and correctly identifies his prisoner, that player becomes blind man. Also called blind cow, blind buck and blind fly.

BLITZKRIEG   German meaning "lightning war." Describes attack style of highly mechanized German army, World War II. Combined use of radio-equipped tanks, mechanized personnel carriers and dive bombers.

BLONDIE   Daily newspaper comic strip created by Chic Young in 1930. In the beginning, Blondie Boopadoop was a birdbrained flapper wooed by playboy Dagwood Bumstead. They married February 17, 1933, causing Dagwood's father to disinherit him. Blondie became devoted wife, and mother of Alexander (1934) and Cookie (1941), while inherently lazy Dagwood went to work for Julius Dithers, a tyrannical boss henpecked at home by his wife Cora.

BLONDIN, CHARLES (1824–1897)   French tightrope walker. Traversed Niagara Falls for first time, June 30, 1859, walking

1,100-ft. line suspended 160 ft. above falls. Later repeated feat, adding such variations as crossing on stilts and blindfolded.

BLOOD   Fluid of life. Carries food and oxygen to cells, removes waste and fights infection. Average adult has about 5 qts. of blood, which is about six times thicker than water. Type based on presence or absence of agglutinogens (factors A and B) in red blood cells. Most common types: A, B, AB and O. Type O has neither factor A nor B; person with type 0 is called "universal donor." Less common agglutinogen, Rh factor, with Rh positive and Rh negative blood types. Must know blood type to perform transfusions.

BLOOD CELLS   Red and white types, counted in test called blood count. Excess of white blood cells may suggest infection. Amount and color of red blood cells may indicate anemia.

BLOODY MARY   Several stories of origin of this mixture of vodka, tomato juice and spices. "Queen among drinks" said named after Mary, Queen of Scots, although Mary I of England was historically known as "Bloody Mary." Bartender Ferdinand L. Petiot made it at Harry's New York Bar in Paris, 1920. American entertainer Roy Barton named it "Bucket of Blood" after club in Chicago. Renamed "Red Snapper" after Petiot spiced it up with salt, pepper, lemon and Worcestershire sauce.

BLUE ANGEL, THE   This landmark film skyrocketed Marlene Dietrich to international stardom. Directed by Josef von Sternberg, it starred Emil Jannings as college professor enamored of nightclub performer Dietrich, who sings the haunting "Falling in Love Again."

BLUE GROTTO, THE   Wave-cut cave in Capri, an Italian island. Filled with sapphire-blue coloring when sun shines through waters. In Greek mythology, Capri was home of the Sirens, whose music enticed Ulysses and his sailors.

BLUE MOON   Under very rare circumstances, Earth's atmosphere is such that the moon appears to be blue. One such circumstance was the volcanic eruption of Krakatoa, 1833, which released large amounts of dust and water vapor into the atmosphere. Phrase "once in a blue moon" describes a rare occurrence.

BLUE WHALE   Up to 100 ft. (30 m.) long. Largest and heaviest known mammal, past and present. May weigh more than 100 short tons (91 metric tons). Sometimes called sulfur-bottom whale due to growth of sulfur-colored plants on its belly. Has most rapid rate of growth of any animal or plant.

BLUE, VIDA (1949–   )   Only pitcher in history to be started in major league baseball all-star games for both American and National Leagues. Started for Oakland A's, 1971 and 1975 (American League), and for San Francisco Giants, 1978 (National League). Finished career with Kansas City Royals, 1983; released midseason, later convicted of drug charges with three Royal teammates.

BLUES BROTHERS, THE   Dan Ackroyd (a.k.a. Ellwood Blues) and John Belushi (a.k.a. Jake Blues) created this tribute to 1950s rhythm-and-blues performers as a preshow warm-up act for TV series *Saturday Night Live*. They eventually used the act on the show and performed as opening act for comedian Steve Martin. Ackroyd and Belushi left *SNL* to make feature-length movie *The Blues Brothers*, released in 1980.

BOAT   According to U.S. Coast Guard and International Rules, the following must be displayed from sundown to sunrise: green light, starboard (right) side; red light, port (left) side. Lights must be visible for one mile. Bow (front) and stern (back) lights must be visible for two miles.

BOB & CAROL & TED & ALICE   1969 comedy feature film directed by Paul Mazursky. Story concerns efforts of sophisticated couple (Natalie Wood and Robert Culp) to introduce their best friends (Dyan Cannon and Elliott Gould) to the sexual revolution.

BOBSLED   Large racing sleds with two pairs of runners in tandem, long seat for two or four riders, and hand brake. Crew members push-start sled, then jump aboard. Front rider steers, rear rider brakes. Entire crew balances sled with precisely timed weight shifts. In Olympic competition (four-man since 1924, two-man since 1932) one country may enter two sleds in each category.

BOCCI   Italian game similar to lawn bowling. Played by two teams on boarded-in court 10 ft. by 60 ft. Jack ball rolled onto court, then each team tries to roll four balls closer to it than opponents do. One point awarded for every ball closer to jack ball than opponent's closest ball. Twelve points wins game.

BOCK'S CAR   American bomber. Dropped atomic bomb on Japanese port city of Nagasaki, August 9, 1945. Roughly 80,000 of city's 250,000 inhabitants killed.

BOEING 737   Short-to-medium-range twin-engine aircraft introduced in 1967. Fifty feet shorter than 707, but has same body width; hence, nickname "Fat Albert."

BOER   Dutch word for "husbandman" or "farmer." Also name for Dutch colonists in South Africa in late 17th and 18th centuries.

BOGART, HUMPHREY (1899–1957)   Tough-guy Hollywood actor. Won Oscar for *African Queen*, 1951. Last scene in Oscar-winning *Casablanca* (1942) shows Bogart (Rick) playing solitaire chess—a game that was Bogie's lifelong addiction. Taught by his father, Bogie played anytime, anywhere, in person, by phone or mail. Born of New York City blueblood stock, he had Princess of Wales as seventh cousin.

BOGOTA   Capital and largest city of Colombia. Situated in Andes Mountains. Three mountain peaks loom over city: one with large, white convent, one with statue of Christ and one with a cross.

BOHEMIA   Region in western Czechoslovakia that includes Prague, the country's capital. Origin of modern word *bohemian*, meaning a writer or artist living an unconventional life-style; became synonymous with gypsy because it was once believed that wandering tribes traveled through Bohemia. Connotes aimlessness and disregard for conformity.

BOILERMAKER   Shot of straight whiskey followed immediately with beer, called chaser or helper; sometimes whiskey is poured right into glass of beer. Term used since 1920s, often associated with American Southwest and with stevedores. "Boilermaker's delight" is term for moonshine or inferior whiskey. When tequila used, referred to as Submarino.

BOLEYN, ANNE (1507–1536)   Second wife of Henry VIII. The King broke from Roman Catholic Church, which would not annul his first marriage, in order to marry the 11-fingered Boleyn, 1533. Boleyn executed, May 19, 1536, on charges of adultery and incest. Henry said to have had her beheaded because she bore him no sons. Renowned for dignity and courage to the end. Last words were: "The executor is, I believe, very expert; and my neck is very slender."

BOLIVAR Standard coin of Venezuela. Made up of 100 centimos. Named for Simón Bolívar.

BOLIVAR, SIMON (1783–1830) South American liberator. Between 1819 and 1825, Bolívar gained independence from Spain for Colombia, Venezuela, Equador, Peru and Bolivia. Sometimes called the George Washington of South America and "El Liberatador" (The Liberator).

BOLOGNA City in northern Italy. Manufactures silks and velvets. Baloney first served here. Its university, founded in 1170 and one of world's oldest, is where Dante and Petrach studied.

BOMBAY Island city that lies off India's west coast in Arabian Sea. India's largest city. Overcrowding is serious problem; caused occasional riots due to food shortages in 1960s and '70s.

BOMBECK, ERMA (1927–   ) American syndicated columnist ("At Wit's End") and author. Books deal humorously with life of American housewife and mother. In *The Grass Is Always Greener Over the Septic Tank* (1977), views such typical suburban topics as Barbie dolls, school bus drivers, little leagues and shopping center parking lots.

BONANZA Popular TV Western, 1959–1973. The Cartwrights were Ben (Lorne Greene), the father; Adam (Pernell Roberts); Hoss (Dan Blocker); and Little Joe (Michael Landon). Maintained their ranch, the Ponderosa, in Nevada. Sheriff Roy Coffee (Ray Teal) patrolled the Virginia City vicinity where Ponderosa was located. Victor Sen Young played their cook, Hop Sing.

BONAPARTE, NAPOLEON (1769–1821) Born Napoleone Buonaparte on France's newly acquired island of Corsica; became French military commander and emperor. Although proud of his Italian heritage, he assumed French form of name in 1796 as French citizen; referred to himself privately as Napoleon Bonaparte even after naming himself Emperor Napoleon I in 1804.

BONAVENA, OSCAR (1943–1976) Argentinean heavyweight boxer. Lost fights to Muhammad Ali and Joe Frazier, but was never a major contender. Known as "Ringo" because of Beatlelike haircut. Lived in Nevada after retirement until his murder there in May 1976, nearby a brothel.

BOND STREET   Leads into Piccadilly in West End of London. Divided into Old and New Bond streets. Famous as center of London's fashionable shopping areas.

BOND, JAMES. See FLEMING, IAN

BOND, JULIAN (1940–   )   Black congressman from Georgia. Nominated for vice-president as symbolic gesture by liberal elements of Democratic party, 1968. Declined, citing constitutional provision that vice-presidents must be at least 35 years old. He was 28 at the time.

BONE CHINA   Type of porcelain developed in late 18th and early 19th centuries by English potters. Phosphate of lime or bone ash added to clay, a technique found to increase strength of material during and after firing.

BONES   Two hundred six bones in human body, although number decreases as some smaller bones fuse with age. Longest bone is femur, or thighbone. Smallest bones are in middle ear. Foot has 20 bones. Bone of upper arm is known as "funny bone" because its real name is humerus. The collarbone, or clavicle, is broken more often than any other bone.

BONN   West Germany's capital since 1949, when country was split into West Germany and East Germany. Birthplace of composer Ludwig van Beethoven. Noted for its university and villagelike atmosphere.

BONNEVILLE SALT FLATS, THE   Packed salt bed of ancient Lake Bonneville in Utah. Thirteen-mile strip on barren 100 sq. mi. plain, site of many attempts at world land speed record. Former official record (average of two-way run) set there October 23, 1970, by Gary Gabelich, who drove Dynamics Blue Flame an average 622.407 m.p.h. New official land speed record, 633.606, set by Richard Noble of Great Britain on October 4, 1983, in jet-powered Thrust II in Gerlach, NV.

BONNIE AND CLYDE   Clyde Barrow (1909–1934) and Bonnie Parker (1910–1934). American gangsters. Held up gas stations and small-town businesses, U.S. Southwest, early 1930s. Occasionally killed people who got in their way. Ambushed and gunned down, May 23, 1934, by Texas Rangers in Louisiana. Subject of 1967 hit feature film directed by Arthur Penn. Faye Dunaway and Warren Beatty starred. Country tune "Foggy Mountain Breakdown" was their getaway song.

BONSAI   Art of growing miniature trees in tray, or name of tree grown this way. Word means "tray-planted." Grower attempts to create small tree with characteristics of large tree in nature.

BONSPIEL. See CURLING

BOOKER T. AND THE M.G.'S   Popular soul musical group of 1960s. Booker T. Jones formed the group with Lewis Steinberg, Al Jackson and Steve Cropper in 1962. M.G. stands for Memphis Group, where band recorded. Hits include: "Green Onions" (1962), "Boot Leg" (1965), "Hig Hug Her" (1967) and "Time Is Tight" (1969).

BOONE, PAT (1934–   )   Pop singer of 1950s and early '60s who turned to acting in '60s. First hit, "Ain't That a Shame" (1955), followed by "I Almost Lost My Mind" (1956), "Don't Forbid Me" (1957), "April Love" (1957) and "Moody River" (1961), among others. Films include: *Journey to the Center of the Earth* (1959), *State Fair* (1962) and *Perils of Pauline* (1967).

BOOT HILL. See TOMBSTONE, ARIZONA

BORDEN, GAIL (1801–1874)   Invented process of evaporating water from milk to produce concentrated condensed milk. Patented, 1856. Comes canned, contains sugar. Largely replaced by sugarless evaporated milk.

BORDEN, LIZZIE ANDREW (1860–1927)   Sunday school teacher. Charged with murdering her father and stepmother with an ax, August 4, 1892. Acquitted after 13-day trial, June 20, 1893. Household maid, Bridget Sullivan, also home on day of murder, was never tried. Popular rhyme arose after this Fall River, MA, incident:

"Lizzie Borden took an ax
And gave her mother forty whacks;
When she saw what she had done,
She gave her father forty-one."

BORG, BJORN (1956–   )   Swedish tennis player who led his country to first Davis Cup victory, December 21, 1975. Beat Jan Kodes of Czechoslovakia in straight sets to win deciding match. First to win Wimbledon singles five straight times (1976–1980). Lost to John McEnroe in Wimbledon final that would have given him six straight titles.

BORGNINE, ERNEST (1915–   )   Character actor who gained fame with his Oscar-winning role as Marty (1955). Other films include: *The Vikings* (1958), *The Dirty Dozen* (1967) and *The Poseidon Adventure* (1972). Starred in TV series *McHale's Navy* (1962–1965). Has license plate: BORG-9.

BORN FREE   Elsa the lioness stole most scenes in this 1966 film from actors Virginia McKenna and Bill Travers, playing game wardens who kept her as a pet. Title song won Oscar for Best Song.

BORSCHT   Originated in Ukraine, where it is the national soup. Bouillon made tart by adding lemon juice, vinegar or kvass, a fermented liquid from rye or beets. Name from old Slavic word for "beet." Generally contains 15–20 ingredients, including beets, bacon, herbs, beef and potatoes.

BOSTON   Capital of Massachusetts and largest New England city. Its State House, built in 1713, has gold dome originally covered with copper by Paul Revere. Boston patriots were very active in American Revolution.

BOSTON BRUINS   National Hockey League's first team based in U.S. Entered league, 1924. Two more U.S. clubs (New York Americans and Pittsburgh Pirates, both defunct) joined league in 1925. Bruins were five-time winners of Stanley Cup championship: first in 1929; last in 1971–1972 season. Second U.S. team to win cup, after New York Rangers (1928).

BOSTON CELTICS   Winner of 15 National Basketball Association titles, more than any other team. Founded by owner Walter Brown, 1946, in Basketball Association of America. Became charter member NBA, 1949. Named after 1920s touring team, Original Celtics. Under coach Arnold "Red" Auerbach, won eight titles in a row, 1959–1966. Team colors: green and white. Irish shamrocks and leprechaun prominent in team's logo.

BOSTON COMMON   Located in downtown Boston and covers 45 acres. U.S.'s oldest public park. Designed by John Winthrop in 1634 as military training field and public pasture. Women found guilty of witchcraft were hanged here in late 1600s.

BOSTON STRANGLER, THE (1933–1973)   Albert H. DeSalvo, alias the Boston Strangler. Killed 13 Boston women between June 1962 and February 1964. Sentenced to life in prison. Stabbed to death by other inmates, 1973.

BOTTICELLI (1444 – 1510) Florentine Renaissance painter. Great colorist, master of rhythmic line. Mythological scenes as in *Birth of Venus* allude to triumph of love over brutal instinct. Also painted *Spring, Mars and Venus*.

BOUILLABAISSE Fish stew made of at least two and usually five different types of fish, seasoned with herbs and sometimes wine, and colored with saffron.

BOULLE, PIERRE (1912 –   ) French novelist. Best known for *The Bridge over the River Kwai* (1954), story of British POWs in Japanese prison camp in Burma during World War II, forced by egotistical commanding officer to build bridge to aid Japanese captors, and of efforts to destroy the bridge. Film version with Sir Alec Guinness named Best Picture of 1957. Boulle also wrote *Planet of the Apes* (1963).

BOUND FOR GLORY 1976 film based on autobiography of folksinger Woody Guthrie. David Carradine portrays Guthrie as young man in 1930s and his growth as a singer and composer through his involvement with the migrant labor movement in Oklahoma and California. (see GUTHRIE, WOODY)

BOUNTY, THE British naval ship. Mutiny occurred, April 28, 1789, when Captain Bligh was bringing breadfruit trees from Tahiti to Jamaica. Breadfruit used as substitute for flour that islanders could not get due to American Revolution. (see MUTINY ON THE BOUNTY; NORDHOFF, CHARLES BERNARD)

BOURGEOISIE French word meaning "middle class." Developed as business class in between aristocracy and peasants.

BOUTON, JIM (1939 –   ) Pitcher whose controversial diary, *Ball Four*, chronicled his 1969 season with Seattle Pilots and Houston Astros. Described behind-scenes baseball action in frank terms. Sequel, *Ball Five*, told story of his 1978 comeback attempt with Atlanta Braves. Nicknamed "Bulldog," had 62-63 lifetime mark, with 21-7 mark with New York Yankees in 1963.

BOW, CLARA (1905 – 1965) "The 'It' Girl," an actress whose personality personified Roaring Twenties. Films include: *Mantrap* (1926), *Wings* (1927), *The Wild Party* (1929).

BOWERY BOYS, THE Group of fun-loving hoodlums was the basis of a series of features from 1937. Originally "The Dead End Kids" in films like *Little Tough Guys* (1938), then known as "The

East Side Kids" until 1946. Group included Huntz Hall as Sach, Leo Gorcey as Slip, and Gabriel Dell as Gabe. Last film together was *In the Money* (1958).

BOWERY, THE   Home of New York City's bums. Once was Indian trail that led to Peter Stuyvesant's Bouwerie (farm). In early 19th century was fashionable amusement and theater center. Declined with people's movement north. Has been called "Street of Forgotten Men" for almost a century.

BOWIE, DAVID (1947–   )   Rock singer/songwriter turned actor. Born David Jones, changed name to avoid confusion with Monkees' lead singer. Named son Zowie Bowie. Hits include "Fame" and "Let's Dance." Films include *The Man Who Fell to Earth* and *The Hunger*.

BOWLING   Sport can be traced to ancient Egypt, 5200 B.C. Indoor lanes originated in U.S. mid-19th century. Today U.S. has more than 8,500 alleys and more than 155,000 lanes, with over 65 million bowlers. Largest bowling centers in the world have been in Japan: Tokyo World Lanes (now closed) had 252 lanes; Fukuyama Bowl in Osaka, current leader, has 144. Alleys found in nearly 50 countries. Tenpin (bigpin) bowling most common variation.

BOWLING, TENPIN   *Ball:* Bored with two to five holes, usually three. Most bowlers use three-finger grip, holding ball with thumb, middle and ring fingers in holes. In two-finger grip, thumb and middle finger used. Standard ball has maximum diameter of 8 ½ in., circumference of 7 in., and weighs 16 lbs.
Pins: Maplewood pins set in four rows: one pin (closest to bowler), two, three, four. Stand on spots marked within three-ft. triangle. Numbered one to ten, front to back, left to right. Number one pin called "headpin."
Perfect game: Takes 12 strikes to roll perfect 300 game. Ten frames, one strike per frame, plus two bonus balls for striking out in 10th frame.
Pocket: Right-handed bowler always aims for space between headpin and number three pin (right pin in second row). Left-handed bowler aims for space between headpin and number two pin (left pin in second row). Allows for best "mix" of pins when ball strikes. Headpin 60 ft. from foul line (point of ball's release).
Railroad splits: A seven/ten split (two corner pins in back row), most

difficult shot to make. Split occurs if two or more pins (not headpin) are standing after first ball has been bowled in frame, with one or more pins between them or in front of them already down.

Spares: When all 10 pins are knocked down with both balls rolled in one frame. Score of first ball from following frame added to score again. If bowler rolls spare on last ball of final (10th) frame, gets bonus ball. (Strike is knocking down all pins with first ball of frame.)

Turkey: Three strikes in a row. Term originated in late 1800s, when scoring was difficult and three consecutive strikes was a remarkable accomplishment. At Christmas and Thanksgiving, bowling alley operators would give free turkey to first player on team to achieve this.

BOWLING, VARIATIONS *Fivepin bowling:* Canadian fivepin bowling has 10 frames, three balls per frame. Ball, made of hard rubber, is 5 in. in diameter, has no finger holes. Pins, smaller than in tenpin bowling, have different point values according to position: five for headpin, three for two in second row, and two for the two in third row. Perfect score is 450.

Skittles: Popular English bowling game, played either singles or with teams up to five. Players take turns rolling ball or round disk, called a cheese, at nine wooden pins, called skittles, set up in diamond arrangement at end of alley 3 ft. by 21 ft. Each player gets three throws (a chalk) to knock down as many skittles as possible; if all knocked down before third throw, they are set up again.

BOXCARS. See CRAPS, NICKNAMES FOR THROWS

BOXER REBELLION Military uprising in China, 1898–1900, attempting to purge the country of foreigners and foreign influences. Militia units of Empress Dowager Tz'u-Hsi (Ch'ing Dynasty) were called "righteous harmony fists," known as "boxers" to foreign press.

BOXING Fistfighting. First recorded in England, 16th century. Pugilism, more refined 19th-century term; from Latin *pugil,* for fighter using protective hand cover. Also known as "the sweet science," term popularized by journalist A. J. Liebling's boxing book of that name. Phrase "sweet science of bruising" attributed to Englishman Pierce Egan in 1824 book *Boxiana.*

BOXING—GAMBLING Despite standardization and state licensing of boxing in U.S., Senate rackets committee and local investigations in late 1950s established links between boxing promoters and gamblers. Struggling fighters were frequently forced to "take a dive" or "go into the tank" in order to get future bouts scheduled. Betting on boxing dropped from $500 million annually in 1946 to $20 million annually in 1959, almost all on high-visibility championship fights.

BOXING, OLYMPIC Matches have three rounds, each three minutes long, with one-minute rest periods between rounds. Boxing became modern Olympic event in 1904 (St. Louis Olympics). Current Olympic weight classes: Light Flyweight, Flyweight, Bantamweight, Featherweight, Lightweight, Light Welterweight, Welterweight, Light Middleweight, Middleweight, Light Heavyweight, Heavyweight.

BOXING RULES Standardized under Queensberry Rules, introduced 1867, first fully used in London tournament, 1872. Named for John Sholto Douglas, 8th Marquis of Queensbury. Rules specified use of gloves, three-minute rounds with one-minute rest periods, and weight classes. First used in heavyweight championship bout in New Orleans, September 7, 1892; James J. Corbett knocked out John L. Sullivan in 21st round. Modern championship fights are usually 15 rounds, lasting maximum of 59 minutes (15 three-minute rounds plus 14 one-minute rest periods).

BOXING TERMS *Rabbit punch:* short, chopping punch to back of neck or base of skull, delivered with back of boxer's fist; illegal because of potential for causing severe injury. Likewise, "hitting below the belt" or "low blow" also illegal.
Throwing in the towel: to concede defeat; also called "sponge" (manager whose fighter is being badly beaten stops fight by throwing a towel or sponge into ring, two items readily at hand since they are used between rounds).

BOXING WEIGHT CLASSES Maximum Lbs. Allowed

Division	Amateur	Professional
Light flyweight	106	-
Flyweight	112	112
Bantamweight	119	118
Featherweight	125	126
Junior lightweight	-	130
Lightweight	132	135
Light welterweight	139	-

Junior welterweight	-	140
Welterweight	147	147
Light middleweight	156	-
Junior middleweight	-	154
Middleweight	165	160
Light heavyweight	178	175
Heavyweight	unl.	unl.

BOXING WINS Bout can be won by disqualification or by one of the following: knockout, in which boxer is knocked unconscious or knocked down and unable to resume within 10-second count administered by referee; technical knockout (TKO), in which boxer is unwilling or unable (in judgment of referee) to continue, although not counted out; decision, in which victory is awarded, based on scoring system involving number of points or rounds won if neither fighter has scored knockout or TKO. Scoring systems vary according to location of bout.

BOY SCOUTS Founded in Great Britain, 1907, by Sir Robert Baden-Powell. Incorporated in U.S., 1910. Has spread worldwide. Aimed at threefold development: mental, moral, physical. Every four years organization holds World Jamborees, huge camp gatherings that bring together Scouts and Guides (senior-level Scouts) from all over the world. First Jamboree held in England, 1920; first hosted by U.S., 1967, at Farragut State Park, ID.

BOYS TOWN Home and school for neglected and homeless boys. Founded 1917 by Father Edward J. Flanagan with $900 in borrowed money. Later moved to 320-acre Overlook Farm, which eventually housed over 900 boys. Farm renamed Boys Town in 1936 and incorporated as village of Boys Town, NE.

BOZO AND THE PINEAPPLE Derogatory name for 1976 Republican candidates for president and vice-president Gerald Ford and Robert Dole. Lost by 29 electoral votes to Jimmy Carter and Walter Mondale.

BRADBURY, RAY (1920–   ) American science-fiction writer. Known for combining fantasy with social criticism. Short stories in *The Martian Chronicles* (1950) concern Earth expeditions to Mars, 1999–2026. Martians give hostile reception to survivors of last large-scale war on Earth. *The Illustrated Man* (1951) is set in rural camping ground in 1930s. As young man looks at title character's tattoos, they come to life, telling stories they represent. Rod Steiger starred in 1969 film. *Fahrenheit 451* (1953) is a novel about a future world where books are banned and burned. Title refers to temperature at which paper burns. Oskar Werner and Julie Christie starred in 1966 film version.

BRADDOCK, BENJAMIN   Character portrayed by Dustin Hoffman in film *The Graduate* (1967). At graduation party, is advised to enter plastics business. Has affair with parents' friend, Mrs. Robinson.

BRADLEY, BILL (1943–   )   Basketball player and Rhodes Scholar. Elected to U.S. Senate from New Jersey, 1978, after retiring from New York Knickerbockers of National Basketball Association, 1977. College All-American at Princeton. Member of 1964 U.S. gold medal-winning Olympic team. Joined Knicks in 1967, after return from Oxford. Played on NBA champions 1970, 1973.

BRADY, PAT (1914–   )   Rodeo rider and fiddle player with Sons of the Pioneers. Appeared with this musical group in many Roy Rogers movies and became his sidekick on TV's *The Roy Rogers Show* (1951–1957). His jeep in series nicknamed Nellybelle.

BRAHE, TYCHO (1546–1601)   Danish astronomer. Reformed observation of planets by viewing them regularly; earlier astronomers had observed them only at specific points in their orbits. Lost part of nose in duel; wore gold-and-silver replacement.

BRAIN   Average adult variety weighs approximately 3 lbs., $\frac{1}{40}$ of body weight. Brain of three-month-old boy weighs just under 1 lb., or about $\frac{1}{10}$ of his weight. Regarded as organ of intellect for only last 300 years. Most ancient cultures believed heart was where thought took place. Greek scientist Aristotle held that brain served only to cool blood.

BRAIN CELLS   Called neurons. Specialized for carrying nerve impulses. Number from 10 to 100 billion; do not reproduce. Transmit information by release of chemical neurotransmitters such as acetylcholine, dopamine, norepinephrine and serotonin.

BRANDENBURG GATE   Built 1791. Situated in East Berlin. Section of Berlin Wall at gate separates East from West Berlin. Sign that reads "Warning! You are now leaving West Berlin" stands beside gate.

BRANDO, MARLON (1924–   )   Legendary movie star

whose "method acting" was influential in 1950s. Among his famous films: *A Streetcar Named Desire* (1951), *The Wild One* (1953), *Mutiny on the Bounty* (as Fletcher Christian, 1962) and *The Godfather* (1972).

BRANDOPHILE   Collector of cigars, specifically of cigar bands (paper marking rings that come around cigars). Also called cigrinophiler. "Brand" is from Old English, German, Danish word for "burn." Word "cigar" comes from Mayan word for smoking, which was observed by Columbus and brought back to Spain.

BRANDS HATCH   Motor circuit near Farningham in Kent, England, opened for Formula III racing in 1949. Now one of best-known and most frequently used British circuits, both for motor racing and for test driving. British Grand Prix hosted here in even-numbered years; hosted at Silverstone circuit in odd years.

BRANDT, WILLY (1913–   )   West German politician, writer and activist. Chancellor of West Germany, 1969–1974. Elected mayor of West Berlin 1957, 1958 and 1963, when he welcomed President J. F. Kennedy to country.

BRANDY   Pure alcoholic liquor distilled from wine or fermented fruit juice. Most famous form is cognac, made only in the Cognac district of France. Next in fame is magnac, made in the South of France. Both types are distilled from white wines made with white grapes. U.S. is world's leading importer.

BRASILIA. See RIO DE JANEIRO

BRAUN, EVA (1912–1945)   Saleswoman for Heinrich Hoffman, Hitler's photographer. Hitler's mistress beginning around 1930. Married, April 29, 1945, only to commit suicide together the next day.

BRAZIL   Largest and most populated South American country. Bordered by all other countries on continent except Chile and Ecuador. Only country passed through by both equator and Tropic of Capricorn. All but southernmost part lies within tropics. Recife is easternmost city and easternmost point in South America. São Paulo is its largest city (also largest on continent) and leading industrial center. Brasilia has been capital city since 1960, when government seat was moved from Rio de Janeiro. Currency: cruzieros, made up of 100 centavos. National anthem: "Hino Nacioal Brasiliero," which begins "On the peaceful banks of the Ypiranga / rang forth the cry." Music written in 1831 by Francisco Manoel da Silva.

Lyrics written by Voaquini Osorio Duque Estrada. Words replaced former lyrics, 1922.

BREAKFAST AT TIFFANY'S Popular 1961 feature film directed by Blake Edwards. Audrey Hepburn portrays Holly Golightly, a small-town girl who takes in the big city. Film contains Oscar-winning song "Moon River."

BREAKING AWAY 1979 hit film about four late-teenage friends in Indiana who don't know what to do with their lives. Nicknamed "the townies," they challenge local college students ("gownies") to a bicycle race. Stars Dennis Christopher.

BREARLY, HARRY (1871–1948) British metallurgist. Invented stainless steel, iron-based alloy, 1913. Chromium content (10–27%) renders it exceptionally resistant to rust, corrosion and oxidation, thus "stainless." Addition of nickel and other elements increases resistance to heat and cold.

BREASTS Human breast contains mammary (milk-producing) glands. One breast is larger in most women; 1–2% women have an extra nipple. Absence of one or both breasts, called amazia or amastia, is extremely rare. Breast development in men is called gynecomastia.

BRENNER PASS Pass between Austria and Italy at eastern end of Alps. Begins near Bolzano, Italy; descends to Innsbruck, Austria. Used by ancient Romans as link between Italy and Germanic lands.

BRESLIN, JIMMY (1930–   ) American journalist and novelist. Columnist for New York *Herald-Tribune*, New York *Daily News* and *New York* magazine. Ran for president of New York City Council, 1969, as mayoral candidate novelist Norman Mailer's running mate. Wrote *Can't Anybody Here Play This Game?* (1963) about New York Mets' first season. *The Gang That Couldn't Shoot Straight* (1969), his first novel, is about humorous Mafia-type family in Brooklyn. *Forty-Four Caliber* (1978), co-written with former *Trib* colleague and TV sports commentator Dick Schaap, is based on Son of Sam murders. Son of Sam (David Berkowitz) had written to Breslin during his killing spree.

BRETON Inhabitant of Brittany (Bretagne in French), a peninsula in northwestern France. Region noted for local traditions, fishing and beaches. Small group called Breton Liberation Front, attempting to achieve independence for area, has been responsible for bombings to gain attention.

BREZHNEV, LEONID ILYICH (1906–1982)   Russian politician. Succeeded Nikita Khrushchev (1894–1971) as first secretary of Soviet Communist party, 1964. Term in office marked by rise in soviet military power, invasions of Czechoslovakia (1968) and Afganistan (1980), and Moscow Summer Olympics (1980). Succeeded by Yuri Andropov.

BRIAN'S SONG   1971 TV movie about Brian Piccolo, Chicago Bears runner who died of cancer at age 26. Starred James Caan as Piccolo and Billy Dee Williams as teammate Gale Sayers. Screenplay focused on their friendship. Piccolo played with Bears 1966–1969.

BRICE, FANNY (1891–1951)   Comedienne popular in vaudeville and on Broadway and radio in 1920s and '30s. Appeared in films *The Great Ziegfeld* (1936) and *Everybody Sings* (1938), among others. Barbra Streisand portrayed her in two films: *Funny Girl* (1968) and *Funny Lady* (1975).

BRIDEY MURPHY (1798–1864)   Native of Belfast, Ireland. Danced a jig, according to tradition, at her wedding in 1816. Ruth Simmons is pseudonym of Pueblo, CO, housewife (1923–?) who reportedly regressed to former life as Bridey Murphy while in hypnotic trance, November 29, 1952.

BRIDGE OF SAN LUIS REY   Name of Pulitzer Prize–winning novel by Thornton Wilder, 1927. Story takes place in 1714 near Lima, Peru, where collapse of rope bridge kills five travelers.

BRIDGE OF SIGHS   Located in Venice, spanning canal between Doge's Palace and state prison. Named for prisoners who crossed it on way to trial. Those found guilty were sent back to execution by another bridge passageway. Bridge by same name stands between New York City Tombs prison and former Criminal Courts building.

BRIDGE ON THE RIVER KWAI, THE   Oscar-winning Best Picture of 1957, directed by David Lean. Story of British soldiers forced to build bridge while captives in Japanese prison camp. Won Oscar for Alec Guinness as British colonel. Jack Hawkins leads climactic attack on bridge.

BRIDGE   Origins in game of whist go back 400 years. First text on bridge was 1886 British leaflet giving rules for "Biritch, or Russian

Whist." Many rule books appeared between then and 1900. Widely popularized through newspaper columns by Ely Culbertson and Charles Goren. Has become all-time most popular card game in English-speaking world. Uses standard deck of 52 cards. Trump suit (changes for each game) is most powerful. Suits normally rank: spades (highest), hearts, diamonds, clubs (lowest).

BRIDGE, CONTRACT Version of game highest in popularity. Supplanted earlier form, auction bridge, in popularity after innovations made in 1925 by Harold S. Vanderbilt. Committee on Laws of Whist Club (of New York), chaired by Vanderbilt, authored Laws of Contract Bridge, effective April 1, 1943. Still used today. Game played by four in two partnerships. Highest bid on hand becomes "contract" for number of tricks highest-bidding partners predict they will take.

BRIDGE, WORLD CHAMPIONSHIP Bermuda Bowl is bridge's world team championship, played by countries. First played in Bermuda, 1950, won by U.S. Bridge Team Olympiad, takes place in Olympic years. Bermuda Bowl won most often by Italy's Blue Team: 1957–1959, 1961–1963, 1965–1967, 1969, 1973–1975. Team also won Bridge Olympiad in 1964, 1968 and 1972. Giorgio Belladonna, member of all these teams. U.S. has won second most times.

BRIGADOON Broadway musical by Frederick Lowe and Alan Jay Lerner, turned into 1954 Gene Kelly movie. Story of two Americans who come across little village in Scottish Highlands that comes to life for one day each 100 years. Film directed by Vincente Minnelli.

BRIGHAM YOUNG UNIVERSITY Coeducational school in Provo, UT, controlled by Church of Jesus Christ of Latter-Day Saints (Mormon). Founded by Mormon leader Brigham Young in 1875. Also has campus in Laie, Oahu, Hawaii.

BRIGHT EYES 1934 film starring Shirley Temple. Shirley is center of adoption case between her godfather, an airline pilot, and a crotchety old millionaire. Shirley sings "On the Good Ship Lollipop."

BRITAIN *Cars:* There are 263 cars and 3½ miles of paved road to every 1,000 people, making it the country with the highest ratio of cars per mile of road. After Norway, Britain has lowest death toll from auto accidents: 12 per 100,000, compared to 21 deaths per 100,000 in U.S.

Colonies: Two have succeeded in establishing independence. First was U.S., with signing of Declaration of Independence, 1776. Second was Rhodesia, 1965. In 1975 Rhodesian black majority took control and changed country's name to Zimbabwe.

Flag: British Union Flag is included in design of more flags than that of any other country; appears in flags of Fiji, New Zealand, Tuvalu, Canada (Royal Union Flag), Hong Kong, Australia and St. Helena. Flag's design is blue field with red cross bordered in white, and two diagonal red and white stripes in background.

Train stations: Largest in each division of Great Britain are Waterloo (England), Edinborough Railway Station (Scotland) and Cardiff Railway Station (Wales).

BRITISH ISLES In order of size: Great Britain, including countries England, Scotland and Wales; Ireland, including countries Ireland and North Ireland; Isle of Man; Hebrides; Orkney Islands; Shetland Islands; 5,500 smaller islands.

BRITISH MUSEUM, THE Founded in 1753. Best known for ancient Mediterranean civilizations and medieval European collections. Houses Elgin Marbles, sculptures from Parthenon in Athens, and Rosetta Stone, which permitted translation of ancient Egyptian writing.

BRITISH ROYAL FAMILY Name Saxe-Coburg-Gotha abandoned, 1917, at start of World War I because of German origin. Replaced by Windsor, name of royal residence, Windsor Castle. First monarch to bear new name was George V. Members of House of Windsor use rose petals in royal celebrations. Rose is England's national flower.

BRITISH, THE Nationality of enemy who "ran through the bushes where the rabbits couldn't go" in number one hit song "The Battle of New Orleans" (1959). Recorded by Johnny Horton, country singer who also had hits with "North to Alaska" and "Sink the Bismarck."

BROADWAY MELODY OF 1938 Film starring Robert Taylor as Broadway producer who hires unknown dancer (Eleanor Powell) with winning racehorse to star in his show. One of Judy Garland's earliest appearances; features her singing "You Made Me Love You" to a photo of Clark Gable.

BROKEN ARROW   TV Western series in which cowboys and Indians got together to fight injustice. Premiered September 1956 and starred John Lupton as army captain Tom Jeffords, and Michael Ansara as Apache chief Cochise.

BRONSON, CHARLES (1922–   )   Born Charles Buchinsky, this former coal miner began playing bit parts in 1951, working his way up to full-fledged leads in 1960s and finally to major stardom in *The Valachi Papers* (1972) and *Death Wish* (1974). Was member of *The Magnificent Seven* (1960) and *The Dirty Dozen* (1967).

BRONTE SISTERS   Anne (1820–1849), Charlotte (1816–1855) and Emily (1818–1848). English novelists and poets. Wrote under pseudonyms Currer, Ellis and Acton Bell. Anne best known for novel *Agnes Gray* (1847), published as set with Emily's novel *Wuthering Heights*. Charlotte, more prolific, wrote novels *Jane Eyre* (1847), *Shirley* (1849), *Villette* (1853) and *The Professor* (1857). *Wuthering Heights* (1847) is story of strange, uncouth and passionate character Heathcliff; written as journal of Mr. Lockwood, who is collecting material for history of mansion Wuthering Heights when besieged by ghost of heroine Catherine Earnshaw, who died in childbirth.

BRONZE   Oldest known alloy. Combination of copper and up to 25% tin. Extremely hard and durable. Resists corrosion. As copper content weathers, leaves distinctive green patina. Earliest known use 3000 B.C. in Mesopotamia.

BROOKLYN   One of New York City's five counties (boroughs). Founded by Dutch, 1636, who named it Breukelen ("Broken Land") after town in Holland. Leading U.S. seaport and manufacturing center. Located SW end of Long Island.

BROOKLYN DODGERS   Fans began referring to this National League baseball team as "Dem Bums" during lean times in 1930s. Popularized by New York *World-Telegram* sports cartoonist Willard Mullin, who used drawing of bum as team's symbol. After team moved to Los Angeles, 1958, Mullin's bum drawn with sports shirt, beret and dark glasses.

BROOMHILDA   Russell Myers' comic strip. Debuted 1970. Broomhilda is wacky witch; Gaylord, her disobedient pet buzzard. Her buddy is Irwin, a mindless troll.

BROTHERS, DR. JOYCE (1928–   )   TV psychologist who gained fame as winning contestant on television quiz show *The*

$64,000 *Question* in 1957. She was signed by NBC and has hosted a number of talk shows ever since.

BROWN, EDMUND GERALD, JR. (JERRY) (1938–   ) American politician. Former governor of California. Presidential hopeful, 1976. Romantically involved with pop-rock singer Linda Ronstadt, who accompanied him to Liberia and celebrated his birthday with him, 1979. Ronstadt denied all marriage rumors. Brown also had invited her to sing campaign fund-raising concerts for him. Educated as a Jesuit seminarian, one of his mottos was: "Inaction may be the highest form of action."

BROWN, HELEN GURLEY (1922–   ) American author and editor. Wrote *Sex and the Single Girl* (1962). Became editor-in-chief of *Cosmopolitan*, 1965. Turned general-interest magazine into one aimed at unmarried working women. Attracting new readers and advertisers, by 1981 ranked 16th in U.S. circulation with 2.75 million, 95% at newsstands due to provocative covers featuring "Cosmo girls."

BROWN, JIM (1936–   ) Top football running back of 1950s and early '60s. All-American at Syracuse University. Played for Cleveland Browns of National Football League, 1957–1965. First NFL back to gain 10,000 career yards, finishing with 12,312. Led league in rushing every year he played except 1962. Most Valuable Player, 1958, 1965. Retired at peak of career to become actor.

BROWN, JOHN (1800–1859) Radical abolitionist. Active member of "Underground Railroad". Raided federal arsenal in Harper's Ferry, VA, October 16, 1859, in effort to obtain arms for slave uprising. Caught, convicted of treason and hanged.

BROWN, LES (1912–   ) Orchestra leader who introduced Doris Day with hit tune "Sentimental Journey" (1944). Formed his "Band of Renown" in 1935, had many hits including his theme "Leap Frog." Has appeared with Bob Hope in live and TV performances since 1947.

BROWNING, ELIZABETH BARRETT (1806–1861) AND ROBERT (1812–1889) English poets. Married in 1846; traveled to Italy, where they lived and wrote until her death. Elizabeth, best known for *Sonnets from the Portuguese* (1850), love poems to her husband. Robert, known for dramatic monologues *Bells and Pomegranates* (1846), *Dramatis Personae* (1854) and *Dramatic Idyls* (1879–1880).

BRUCE, LENNY (1925-1966) American comedian. Satirized American life, often using four-letter words. Arrested several times. Died from narcotics overdose at 41. Autobiography *How to Talk Dirty and Influence People* (1965) sold well, as did *Essential Lenny Bruce* (1966), collection of nightclub routines.

BRUEGEL, PIETER (THE ELDER) (1525-1569) Flemish painter of peasant scenes, biblical allegories, innovative landscapes and crowd scenes. Painted *Months of the Year* series (1565), *Tower of Babel* (1563), *Peasant Dance* (1565). Member of family of outstanding painters.

BRUNDAGE, AVERY (1887-1975) American building contractor and president of U.S. Olympic Committee, 1929-1953. President of International Olympic Committee, 1952-1972. Outspoken advocate of amateurism in Olympic Games. Represented U.S. in decathlon in 1912 Olympics in Stockholm.

BRUSSELS Capital of Belgium. Main square includes Grand Place, with elaborate merchant and craft guilds built in 1600s. Other sights are town hall dating from 1400s, Manneke Pis fountain, royal palace and elegant residential neighborhoods.

BRYANT, ANITA (1940-   ) Singer and entertainer. Once Miss Oklahoma; runner-up for 1959 Miss America. Became Florida Citrus Commission's "public representative," the Sunshine-Tree Girl, 1968. Woman of the Year, 1970. Outspoken against homosexuality. Florida's governor, Reubin Askew, once remarked: "People connect orange juice, Florida and Anita Bryant so much that it becomes difficult to decide which to visit, which to listen to and which to squeeze." Bryant raised recognition of Florida orange juice from 50 to 80% of population.

BUCHAN, JOHN (1875-1940) Scottish writer and governor-general of Canada. Wrote many adventure stories in idyllic settings, like *Prester John* (1910), set in Africa. *The Thirty-Nine Steps* (1915), *Greenmantle* (1916) and *The Three Hostages* (1924) are spy novels featuring hero Richard Hannay. *The Thirty-Nine Steps* involves international plot against England and efforts of Hannay to expose it while fleeing police, who supect him of murder.

BUCK WHITE. See ALI, MUHAMMAD

BUCK, PEARL (1892-1973) American novelist. Raised in China by missionary parents. Won Pulitzer Prize for *The Good Earth* (1932), which tells of rise and fall of peasant farmer Wang Lung.

Other novels include *A House Divided* (1953) and *Dragon Seed* (1942). Won Nobel Prize in Literature, 1938.

BUCKINGHAM PALACE Home to British Monarch (currently Queen Elizabeth II) in West End, London. Includes four main wings surrounding courtyard; monarch resides in North Wing. Has 600 rooms and 40-acre garden. Built in 1703 by John Sheffield, Duke of Buckingham. Bought by King George III in 1761.

BUCKLEY, WILLIAM FRANK, JR. (1925–   ) American author, editor, columnist, TV commentator and orator. Leading conservative political spokesman. Founder and editor of *National Review*, "a journal of fact and opinion," monthly magazine started 1955. Also host of TV's *Firing Line*. Unsuccessful New York City mayoral candidate, 1965.

BUDAPEST Capital and largest city of Hungary. Home of 20% of country's population. Formed when cities of Buda, Pest and Obuda joined with Margaret Island in 1873. Lies on both banks of Danube River. Much destroyed in World War II, later rebuilt.

BUDDHA (563–483 B.C.) Born Siddhartha Gautama. Later called Buddha or "Enlightened One." Founder of Buddhist religion. Depicted in statues sitting cross-legged, meditating, with tranquil smile and closed eyes. Frequently commemorated in art and monuments.

BUDWEISER First brewed in St. Louis, MO, by Adolphus Busch and Carl Conrad in 1876, at small brewery opened in 1852; funded by Busch's father-in-law, Eberhard Anheuser. Today Anheuser-Busch brews Budweiser, Budweiser Lite, Michelob, Michelob Lite and Busch beers in 11 locations.

BUFFALO BILL (1846–1917) Born William Frederick Cody. Frontiersman and showman. Nickname derives from occupation as buffalo hunter. Formed Wild West Circus, featuring mock battles against Indians and sharpshooting displays. Toured U.S. and Europe.

BUFFETT, JIMMY (1946–   ) Singer/songwriter of 1970s. Gained fame with hit song "Margaritaville" (1977), in which Buffett spends time looking for his long-lost shaker of salt.

BUGABOOS Mountain range in Canadian Rockies, west of Calgary, Alberta. Commercial helicopter skiing started here in 1965. Later expanded to nearby ranges Cariboos and Monashees. Helicopter rides from lodge to summit provide unblemished powder skiing.

BUGLIOSI, VINCENT. See HELTER SKELTER

BULLET Bullet-shaped electronic train running on Japanese railroad system. Train called Shinkansen, known for reaching speeds of up to 130 m.p.h. (210 km.p.h). Seventy-five percent of railroad system operated by Japan National Railway, a government-owned system with private line connections. Trains travel throughout country and provide spectacular view of Mt. Fuji.

BULLFIGHTING Contest in which courage of matador is pitted against strength of bull, usually ending in bull's death. Portuguese, who fight on horseback, do not kill bull. Spanish term *corrida de toros* means "running of the bulls." World's largest bull ring, Plaza Mexico in Mexico City, seats 50,000. Seat prices vary depending on proximity to ring and whether in sunshine or shade (*sombra*). Most expensive seats, *barrera sombra*, front row in shade. Traditionally, bullfight starts at 5 P.M., but time varies according to locality and weather conditions. A band then strikes up *pasadoble* (two-step), and matadors stride into ring followed by their helpers (*cuadrillas*, composed of *banderilleros* and *picadors*). Matadors are usually 20 to 35 years old. Training begins at age 12; apprentice matadors traditionally work as bricklayers while undergoing extensive training with bulls. During bullfight, customary for three matadors to fight (and kill) two bulls apiece, although sometimes two matadors fight three bulls apiece. Each fight takes about 20 minutes. Forty-two major bullfighters have died in the ring since 1700.

BULLS AND BEARS Refers to opposing positions in stock market. "Bulls" expect stock prices to rise, while "Bears" anticipate falling prices. Nicknames probably derive from fact that bull raises its horns to fight, while bear sweeps its paws downward to attack.

BULOVA WATCH COMMERCIAL First commercial TV station, WNBT (later WNBC), aired first commercial ever for Bulova Watch Company on July 1, 1941. During a weather report, a watch bearing the name Bulova was shown ticking for 60 seconds.

BUNKER, CHANG AND ENG (1811–1873) Two Siamese brothers born joined at the chest, source of term "Siamese twins." Married two unattached sisters in 1843. Had 10 and 12 children, respectively. Died within hours of each other.

BUNNING, JIM (1931–   **)** Retired 27 consecutive New

York Mets to pitch perfect game on Father's Day, June 21, 1964, at Shea Stadium. Won 6–0. Also pitched no-hitter for Detroit Tigers, 1958. Had lifetime record of 224-184 in 17 seasons. Losing candidate for governor of Kentucky, 1983. Only eight other pitchers in major league history have pitched perfect games, including Don Larsen in 1956 World Series.

BUNYAN, JOHN (1618–1688) English author. While imprisoned 12 years for unlicensed preaching, wrote nine books, including *Grace Abounding to the Chief of Sinners* (1666). Later wrote allegory *Pilgrim's Progress* (Part I, 1678; Part II, 1684). Hero Christian leaves City of Destruction to find Zion, the City of God, reaching it after much travail. In Part II, Christian's wife and four sons and her friend Mercy all travel to Zion, following his example.

BURDICK, EUGENE (1918–1965) American novelist. With William J. Lederer, wrote *The Ugly American* (1958); with Harvey Wheeler, wrote *Fail-Safe* (1962), novel about accidental U.S. air attack on Russia. Sidney Lumet directed 1964 screen version, with Henry Fonda as U.S. president.

BURGER, HAMILTON. See GARDNER, ERLE STANLEY

BURMA ROAD Road 700 mi. (1,000 km.) long, built in 1937–1938, leading from Lashio, Burma, to Kunming, China. Allowed China to receive supplies during its war against Japan. Served as "back door" entrance into China, since Japan had blockaded the Chinese coast. United with Ledo Road, providing route from India to China, in 1945.

BURNETT, CAROL (1936–   ) Actress. Sued *National Enquirer*, March 1981, for its 1976 report that she had been drunk and had insulted diplomat Henry Kissinger at a Washington restaurant. Jury awarded Burnett $1.6 million, later reduced to $800,000.

BURNFORD, SHEILA (1918–   ) Scottish-born Canadian novelist. Wrote *The Incredible Journey* (1961) about old, white English bull terrier called Bodger; red-gold Labrador retriever called Luath, and slender, wheat-colored Siamese cat named Tao. Novel and Walt Disney film version are tearjerkers.

BURNS, GEORGE (1896–   ) Vaudeville comedian, teamed with his wife Gracie Allen successfully in radio, movies and TV. Renewed popularity as octogenarian. Played God in *Oh, God!* (1977) and *Oh, God! Book II* (1980). Won Oscar in 1975 for supporting role in *The Sunshine Boys*.

BURR, AARON (1756–1836) Third U.S. vice-president, 1801–1805. Fatally wounded political rival Alexander Hamilton in pistol duel, July 11, 1804. Fled; resumed vice-presidential duties until term ended.

BURROUGHS, EDGAR RICE (1875–1950) American novelist. Wrote 23 Tarzan books, beginning with *Tarzan of the Apes* (1914). In *Son of Tarzan*, Tarzan's son Jack flees from England to Africa and in presence of father's ape friend Akut is dubbed Korak, ape talk for "the killer." Korak's mother is former Jane Porter and his grandparents (Tarzan's parents) are Lord Greystoke (John Clayton) and Alice Rutherford Clayton. Tarzan's ape mother was named Kala. (see TARZAN)

BUS STOP Popular 1956 feature film about group of travelers stuck at snowbound bus station. Marilyn Monroe starred as Cherie, a sexy entertainer who catches the eye of cowboy Don Murray.

BUTCH CASSIDY AND THE SUNDANCE KID 1969 Western starring Paul Newman and Robert Redford as legendary outlaws on the run from authorities. Film introduced popular song "Raindrops Keep Falling on My Head." Katharine Ross portrayed Elfa Place, Butch and Sundance's friend.

BUTTER The fat removed from milk. Cream from 10 quarts of milk yields four cups or one pound of butter. Made by agitating cream until fat separates. Butter is 80% fat, has 3,200 calories per lb. and is rich in vitamin A.

BUTTERFIELD 8. See O'HARA, JOHN HENRY

BUTTERFIELD, ALEXANDER P. (1926–   ) White House aide. July 16, 1973, informed Senate committee investigating Watergate affair that Nixon had taped all of his Oval Office and Executive Office conversations since the spring of 1971. Tapes incriminated Nixon and top men around him.

BUTTERFLY Found throughout the world. Drinks nectar of flowers, carries pollen. Is caterpillar in earlier stage of life cycle. Does not grow in size with age. Roughly 90,000 kinds, including southern dog face, comma anglewing and great purple hairstreak.

BVD Bradley, Vorhees and Day, creators of long woolen underwear. Widespread use in trenches, World War I. BVD became synonymous with the article of clothing.

TRIVIAL CONQUEST

C

C-3PO Gold-plated, human-shaped robot (or droid) who, along with sidekick R2-D2, assisted their owner, Luke Skywalker, in *Star Wars* (1977) and its sequels, *The Empire Strikes Back* (1980) and *Return of the Jedi* (1983).

C.C.C.P. See SOVIET UNION

C.S.S.R. See CZECHOSLOVAKIA

CABARET 1972 musical film directed by Bob Fosse, based on hit Broadway play. Liza Minnelli stars as Sally Bowles, nightclub performer in Germany during rise of Nazism. Minnelli and Fosse won Oscars for their work. Joel Grey also starred.

CABBAGE Genus Brassica, family Cruciferae (mustard family). Red and green varieties. High in vitamin C, plus A, B_1, B_2, calcium and cellulose, which acts as a laxative. Eaten by early sailors to prevent scurvy. One of most common vegetables in U.S., Europe, and Asia. Yields more pounds per acre than any other vegetable. Broccoli, cauliflower, brussels sprouts, kale and kohlrabi are all vegetables developed from it. Sauerkraut is made from shredded cabbage.

CABER TOSSING Best-known of events featured in meets of Scottish athletes. Caber tree trunk of unspecified size should be "of length and weight beyond powers of best athlete to turn." Famed Braemer caber weighs more than 120 lbs., is 19 in. long. In perfect toss, caber revolves longitudinally, landing with base pointing away from competitor. "Twelve o'clock" toss lands caber pointing in exact direction competitor was facing at time of throw.

CABLE CAR   Vehicle pulled by cable. Invented in 1873 by Andrew S. Hallidie. First traveled on Clay Street in San Francisco. Tourist attraction and landmark of city. World's longest cable car line is 60 mi. (97 km.), located in Sweden.

CABOT LODGE, HENRY, JR. (1902–   )   Former Republican senator from Massachusetts and U.S. ambassador to United Nations. Vice-presidential nominee on Richard Nixon's losing ticket for presidency, 1960.

CADILLAC   Cadillac Automobile Company founded, 1900, by Henry Leland. Company named after French explorer Antoine de la Mothe Cadillac, founder of a colony at Detroit, 1701. Leland revolutionized car manufacturing by using interchangeable parts.

CAESAR, JULIUS (100–44 B.C.)   Roman general, statesman, orator and writer. Declared himself first Dictator of Roman Empire, 49 B.C. After defeating Pharnaces II, King of Pontus, in battle in 47 B.C., Caesar informed his senate: *"Veni, vidi, vici,"* meaning "I came, I saw, I conquered." Assassinated, as predicted, March 15, the Ides of March. Assassins included his friend Marcus Brutus, to whom Caesar supposedly said his last words: *"Et tu Brute?"* ("And you, Brutus?")

CAESAR, SID (1922–   )   Popular TV comedian. Starred on *Your Show of Shows* (1949–1954). In sketch comedies, his wife was played by Imogene Coca, Nanette Fabray and Gisele MacKenzie. In recent years he has played serious and comedic supporting roles.

CAINE MUTINY, THE   Herman Wouk's novel became 1954 film starring Humphrey Bogart as Captain Queeg, considered unfit by crew members Van Johnson and Robert Francis. Jose Ferrer was their defense attorney. (see WOUK, HERMAN)

CAIRO   Capital of Egypt. Largest and most populated African city. Part of Nile Valley and Nile Delta, one of Egypt's few areas with abundant water and fertile soil. Huge deserts lie to east and west.

CALCUTTA AIRPORT. See INDIA AIRPORTS
CALDWELL, ERSKINE BRESTON (1903–   )
American novelist. Author of *Tobacco Road* (1932) and *God's Little*

Acre (1933), both set in Georgia hills. First title about family of sharecropper Jeeter Lester; second concerns gold-digging mountaineer Ty Ty Walden. Photographer Margaret Bourke-White was Caldwell's first wife.

CALDWELL, JANET MIRIAM (TAYLOR) (1900 –   ) American novelist. Wrote best-selling romances, including *The Eagles Gather* (1940), *This Side of Innocence* (1946) and *Great Lion of God* (1970), biblical novel based on life of St. Paul of Tarsus, Jew who became apostle to Gentiles. Through extensive research, tried to convey religious and social implications for modern times.

CALEDONIA Ancient Roman name for northern Scotland; later referred to all of Scotland. In A.D. 83 Agricola, a Roman general, invaded Caledonia. The first Caledonians were called the Picts.

CALENDAR Calendar used throughout the world is the Gregorian, established by Pope Gregory II, 1582; has 365.25 days per year. Perpetual calendar uses series of 14 calendars; will give day of week for any date. First day of next century is a Monday.

CALENDAR—EARTH'S ORBIT Because Earth's orbit around sun is an ellipse, not a circle, distance between earth and sun changes. On January 1, sun is closest to earth, 91.4 million mi. away. On July 1, it is farthest, 94.5 million mi.

CALF ROPING. See RODEO

CALIFORNIA U.S. state with largest population. Noted for its large number of blondes and beautiful beaches. State was named after a treasure island in a popular Spanish tale. Bordered by three states: Oregon to the north, Nevada to the east, Arizona to the southeast.

CALIFORNIA, GULF OF Arm of Pacific Ocean between Baja Peninsula and Mexican mainland. Eastern shore has oyster beds; western shore has pearl and sponge fisheries. Once called Sea of Cortez, after Hernando Cortez, who first explored it in 1536.

CALIGULA (A.D. 12–41) Gaius Caesar. Roman emperor from 37 until his murder, 41. Nicknamed "Caligula", Latin for "Little Boot" because he wore military boots as a child. Atrocious ruler. Allegedly made his horse consul.

CALLAS, MARIA (1923–1977) Soprano opera singer. Born in New York City; raised in Athens, Greece. First public appearance, age 14, in opera *Cavalleria Rusticana* in Athens. First American performance in Chicago, singing lead soprano in Bellini's *Norma*. Dated Greek shipping magnate Aristotle Onassis after 1966 divorce from Italian industrialist Giovanni Batista Meneghini.

CALLEY, LIEUTENANT WILLIAM, JR. (1943–   ) American soldier. During U.S. involvement in Vietnam, led force into My Lai hamlet, South Vietnam, March 16, 1968. Massacred between 347 and 504 civilians. Only Calley was tried and found guilty. Court-martial proceedings began November 12, 1970, Fort Benning, GA. Calley convicted March 29, 1971, of murder of at least 22 unarmed civilians. Sentenced to life in prison; sentence later shortened after President Nixon reviewed the case. Served approximately five years in prison and under house arrest.

CALORIE   In physics: gram calorie is amount of heat required to raise temperature of 1 gm. of water 1° C; large calorie is quantity of heat equal to 1,000 gram calories. In physiology: unit equal to large calorie; expresses heat output of organism and fuel or energy value of food.

CAMBODIA   Southeast Asian country, target of secret bombing missions ordered by President Nixon and Henry Kissinger, March 1969. Missions directed at suspected Vietcong command and supply post inside neutral Cambodia during Vietnam war. Known for a time as "the Secret War."

CAMEL   Large desert-dwelling animal. Two kinds: Arabian or African with one hump and Bactrian with two humps. Humps are fat, not bone; camel's spine is really straight. These "ships of the desert" can go for long distances without food or water. Lawrence of Arabia used them in leading revolt against Turks, 1914–1918.

CAMELOT. See KENNEDY, JOHN F.

CAMERA SHUTTER SPEED   One of two controls to regulate exposure of film. Aperture size, or f-stop, controls size of aperture. Shutter speed determines amount of time aperture will remain open. Setting of 500 means shutter open for $\frac{1}{500}$ second; setting of "B" means flash bulb will be used.

CAMOUFLAGE   French word, added to American vocabulary in World War I, meaning to disguise appearance of troops, ships or guns with paint, nets, etc., in order to try to hide them. Also used as noun, meaning material for doing this.

CAMP DAVID   Presidential retreat. Founded by President F. D. Roosevelt, 1942. Named Shangri-La, after paradise in James Hilton's book *Lost Horizon*. Renamed by President Eisenhower after five-year-old grandson, David Eisenhower II.

CAMP DAVID ACCORDS   Two agreements for peace in Middle East, specifically between Egypt and Israel. Signed September 17, 1978, at Camp David, MD, by Egyptian President Anwar el-Sadat, Israeli Prime Minister Menachem Begin and U.S. President Jimmy Carter.

CAMPBELL, GLEN (1938–   )   Country/pop singer who recorded many hit songs, including "Gentle on My Mind" (1967), his TV theme song; "Wichita Lineman" (1968); "Galveston" (1969); "Rhinestone Cowboy" (1975). Has dagger tattooed on arm. Acted in movies, including *True Grit* (1969) and *Norwood* (1970).

CAMPTOWN RACETRACK   Five-mile-long racetrack made famous in Stephen Foster's song "Camptown Races," where a "bobtail nag" was running a race with a shooting star. Originally published in 1850 as "Gwine to Run All Night," has become a classic American folk song.

CANADA COASTLINE   Country with world's largest coastline: 151,488 mi. (243,797 km.). Bordering waters are Atlantic, Arctic and Pacific oceans, Hudson and James bays, and Hudson Strait.

CANADA, NATIONAL SYMBOLS   Maple leaf, which appears on country's flag, was made official emblem in 1860. Leaf has 11 points. Inspired song "Maple Leaf Forever," unofficial Canadian hymn written 1867 by Alexander Muir. Beaver is country's official animal.

CANADA PROVINCES   Provinces and their rank in area:
1. Quebec 594,860 sq. mi. (1,540,680 sq. km.)
2. Ontario 412,582 sq. mi. (1,068,582 sq. km.)
3. British Columbia 366,255 sq. mi. (948,596 sq. km.)
4. Alberta 255,285 sq. mi. (661,185 sq. km.)
5. Saskatchewan 251,700 sq. mi. (651,900 sq. km.)
6. Manitoba 251,000 sq. mi. (650,087 sq. km.)
7. Newfoundland 156,185 sq. mi (404,517 sq. km.)
8. New Brunswick 28,354 sq. mi (73,436 sq. km.)
9. Nova Scotia 21,425 sq. mi. (55,491 sq. km.)
10. Prince Edward Island 2,184 sq. mi. (5,657 sq. km.)

CANADA TERRITORIES Yukon and Northwest territories constitute more than one-third of Canada's land area, but less than .3% of its population. Only one U.S. state (Alaska) borders Yukon Territory; no U.S. states border Northwest Territory.

CANADA TIME ZONES Six time zones are Newfoundland, Atlantic, Eastern, Central, Mountain and Pacific.

CANARY ISLANDS, THE Group of 13 islands, seven of which are inhabited. Located in Atlantic Ocean and belong to Spain. Divided into two provinces: Santa Cruz de Tenerife and Las Palmas. Named Canaria from Latin word *canis* ("dog") because large fierce dogs were found here in ancient times.

CANASTA Partnership card game of rummy family. Originated in Uruguay in 1940s (means "basket" in Spanish). Reached U.S. in 1949 and became fad in early 1950s. Uses two standard decks and four jokers; jokers and all eight deuces are wild cards. Wild-Card Canasta (when all seven cards in hand are wild) is worth 2,000-point bonus; however, not considered legal in all types of canasta.

CANBERRA Capital of Australia, located in southeast corner of New South Wales. City plan developed by Walter Burley Griffen of Chicago, who won international competition to plan Australia's capital city in 1909.

CANDID MICROPHONE Popular radio program of 1940s; hosted by Alan Funt, who moved to TV in 1948, changed name to *Candid Camera* and continued to catch people off guard with practical jokes and unusual situations.

CANDLESTICK PARK San Francisco, CA, stadium. Opened April 12, 1960, two years after baseball Giants moved from New York (played two years in Seals Stadium). Seats 58,000 after expansion. Natural grass fields famous for windy conditions; diminutive Giants relief pitcher Stu Miller once blown off pitching mound during game. NFL's '49ers also play here.

CANNED FOOD French government offered prize to whoever could develop a simple method of preserving food to be used by Napoleon's army. Prize won by chef Nicholas Appert, 1795. Appert sealed food in bottles immersed in boiling water.

CANNIBAL. See ANTHROPOPHAGIST

CANTON BULLDOGS Early team in National Football

League. Played in NFL 1919–1926 (played in Cleveland, 1924). Won championship 1922, 1923.

CAPE CANAVERAL   Site of John F. Kennedy Space Center. Situated 10 mi. (16 km.) from Coco Beach, FL. Consists of Air Force Missile test center (established 1949), Army and Navy units, and Space Center (established 1958). Renamed Cape Kennedy in 1963 by President Johnson; name changed back in 1973 due to Floridians' preference.

CAPE COD   Hook-shaped peninsula on coast of Massachusetts. Cape Cod Bay lies inside hook. The Cape is 65 mi. (105 km.) long and 1–20 mi. (1.6–32 km.) wide. Named for codfish caught off its shores. Center of whaling industry in 1800s.

CAPE HATTERAS   High ridge jutting into Atlantic Ocean at tip of Hatteras Island, NC. Many lighthouses now warn ships of rocky area, after large number of shipwrecks here.

CAPILLARY   Blood vessel that connects artery and vein. Blood releases oxygen and food to artery and vein cells. Capillaries are one cell wide and less than a millimeter long.

CAPONE, ALPHONSE (1899–1947)   Chicago gangster and racketeer, 1920s and '30s. Nickname, "Scarface." Considered father of organized crime. Controlled Chicago underworld during prohibition era. Executed February 14, 1929, St. Valentine's Day Massacre in which his henchmen dressed as policemen and shot seven members of opposing Bugs Moran gang. Notoriously ruthless. Once remarked: "I've been accused of every death except the casualty list of the World War." Carried business card listing himself as secondhand furniture dealer. At peak, grossed $50 million annually. Had several bulletproof cars; favorite make, Cadillac. Convicted in 1931 of income tax evasion. Sentenced to 11 years. Died of syphilis. On one occasion said: "Public service is my motto."

CAPOTE, TRUMAN (1924–   )   American writer of novel *Breakfast at Tiffany's* (1958), short-story collection *Other Voices, Other Rooms* (1948) and "nonfiction novel" *In Cold Blood* (1965), true account of 1959 murder of four members of Clutter family in their Kansas farmhouse. Used fiction writing techniques to re-create characterization of victims and murderers Richard Hickock and Perry Smith, who were hanged April 14, 1965.

CAPP, AL (1909-1979)   Born Alfred Gerald Chaplin. American cartoonist. Began daily comic strip *Li'l Abner* in 1934. Popular burlesque inspired 1940 movie and 1957 Broadway musical comedy filmed in 1959. Strip set in Kentucky hills in place called Dogpatch. Among characters and features of strip: Li'l Abner, strapping son of Pansy Yokum (Mammy) and Lucifer Ornamental Yokum (Pappy), married to voluptuous Daisy Mae; Evil-Eye Fleegle, denizen of Brooklyn and master of the whammy; General Bullmoose, greedy, manipulative billionaire; Fearless Fosdick, Li'l Abner's detective hero, a parody of Chester Gould's Dick Tracy and a comic strip within a comic strip. First appeared in 1942. Sadie Hawkins Day, first Saturday after November 11, is day of race when girls of Dogpatch chase boys to catch a husband; invented for benefit of Sadie Hawkins, "the homeliest gal in all them hills." Kickapoo Joy Juice, powerful drink sold by Polecat Indian tribe in Dogpatch. Real soft drink of same name marketed briefly in 1950s.

CAPTAIN AHAB. See MELVILLE, HERMAN

CAPTAIN BLIGH   Cruel captain of *H.M.S. Bounty*, whose crew mutinied in three motion pictures. Captain portrayed by Charles Laughton in *Mutiny on the Bounty* (1935), by Trevor Howard in the 1962 remake and by Anthony Hopkins in *The Bounty* (1984). (See MUTINY ON THE BOUNTY; NORDHOFF, CHARLES BERNARD)

CAPTAIN BLOOD. See FLYNN, ERROL

CAPTAIN KANGAROO   Popular children's TV show, which began in 1955. Bob Keeshan starred as the Captain, keeper of the Treasure House, who explored many educational aspects to common situations with his helpers Mr. Green Jeans, Bunny Rabbit, Mr. Moose and Dancing Bear.

CAPTAIN MARVEL   Comic strip hero introduced 1940–1954; reincarnated in 1966 during superhero craze. When orphan Billy Batson says name of wizard Shazam, he magically transforms into Captain Marvel.

CAPTAIN MORGAN   Eighty-proof spiced Puerto Rican rum named for Welsh-born privateer Sir Henry Morgan. Born to wealthy parents, 1635. With sanction of Jamaican governor, Morgan directed his Spanish Main activities at ships of nations with which England was at war. Portrayed by Steve Reeves in 1960 film *Morgan the Pirate*.

CAPTAIN QUEEG   Mentally disturbed captain of fictional navy destroyer *Caine* in Herman Wouk's 1951 Pulitzer Prize novel *The Caine Mutiny*, from which came successful play *Caine Mutiny Court Martial* (1954) with Lloyd Nolan and film *Caine Mutiny* (1954) with Humphrey Bogart. Queeg gave away his anxiety by rolling two steel ball bearings in palm.

CAR ACCIDENTS   Thirty thousand Americans killed in car accidents every year. About one every nine minutes, as many as all other types of accidents combined. About one-half of automobile fatalities are alcohol-related, which may explain why more auto deaths occur on Saturday than any other day.

CAR BATTERIES   Secondary or storage cells that store electricity produced by generator when car engine is running. Stored electricity provides power to start car. Most car batteries are 12-volt.

CAR HORNS   First type was bulb horn, located on car's steering wheel or tiller and sounded by physically squeezing it. Later moved outside car next to driver; had long brass tube. Klaxon or "kah-loo-gah" type was electrically operated, its sound starting on B, below middle C, then rising to F sharp, above middle C, and back to B. Today, car horns are standard equipment; many varieties exist, but most often their sound is in key of F.

CARBON   Chemical element. Usually found in combination with other elements, as carbon dioxide. Present in all living things. Diamond and graphite, pure carbon. Changes directly from solid to gas; does not melt. Organic chemistry deals with carbon compounds.

CARCINOGEN   Substance or agent that produces or accelerates development of cancer. Known carcinogens: cigarette smoke, x-rays and sunlight. From Greek, meaning "that which generates cancer."

CARDINAL VIRTUES   According to Christian theology, Cardinal Virtues are faith, hope and charity. Plato's, however, were wisdom, courage, temperance and justice, sometimes called natural virtues. By 14th century combined into Seven Cardinal Virtues, able to battle Seven Deadly Sins: lust, pride, anger, envy, sloth, avarice and gluttony.

CARDS. See PLAYING CARDS

CARE   Acronym of Cooperative for American Relief to Everywhere. Nonprofit organization, originally founded in 1945 to provide clothing and food to vast areas of Europe destroyed in World War II. Now operates worldwide.

CAREERS   Parker Brothers board game. Players choose from eight occupations, formulating their plans for success. They get rewards, promotions and setbacks during game as they face challenges to their careers.

CARIBOU   Large member of deer family found in Alaska and Canada. Depended on by Eskimoes and northern Indians for food, clothing, shelter and tools. Caribou and reindeer are only animals that have antlers on the female as well as the male.

CARLOS I, JUAN (1938–   )   Became king of Spain, November 22, 1975. Designated successor by (and to) Franco (1892–1975) in 1969. Grandson of King Alfonso XIII. Relation of British royal family. Canceled plans to attend Prince Charles' wedding (1981) upon learning royal couple would depart from Gibraltar for honeymoon. Spain recently demanded return of Rock of Gibraltar, under British control since 1713. Under Carlos, Spain has become a democratic constitutional monarchy.

CARLOS, JOHN. See SMITH, TOMMIE, AND CARLOS, JOHN

CARLSBAD CAVERNS NATIONAL PARK   Situated in foothills of Guadalude Mountain in New Mexico. One of world's largest caverns. Has been explored to 1,100 ft. (535 mi.) below surface. Ends of some corridors have never been reached.

CARMICHAEL, HOAGY (1899–   )   Composer, pianist and singer turned actor. Wrote "Star Dust" as jazz instrumental in 1927; song became major hit four years later when lyrics were added by Mitchell Parish. Movie credits include: *To Have and Have Not* (1944) and *The Best Years of Our Lives* (1946).

CARMICHAEL, STOKELY (1941–   )   Black activist. Advocate and populizer of concept of "black power." Grew up in Harlem section of New York City. Led voter registration drives while in college. Briefly served as prime minister of Black Panthers, 1968.

CARNERIN, ANDRE JACQUES (1769–1823)   Made first parachute jump from balloon 2,230 ft. above Paris in 1797;

during jump, became first victim of airsickness. Albert Berry made first parachute jump from airplane in 1912 near St. Louis, MO.

CARROLL, DIAHANN (1935–   )   First black actress to star in TV situation comedy. As Julia Baker, a nurse, in *Julia* (1968–1971). Shows revolved around her work and home life with her son Corey.

CARROLL, LEWIS (1832–1898)   Pseudonym of Charles Lutwidge Dodgson. English mathematician and author of children's books. One of two best-known works is *Alice's Adventures in Wonderland* (1865), in which Alice follows white rabbit with pink eyes down hole under hedge after it says, "Oh dear! Oh dear! I shall be too late!" and takes a watch from its waistcoat pocket. In Wonderland, Alice drinks from bottle labeled "DRINK ME" and becomes smaller. She finds little glass box under table, containing very small cake on which words "EAT ME" are marked in currants; this makes her bigger. She meets Mock Turtle, who weeps constantly. Alice is one of three guests at March Hare's tea party. Others are March Hare, Mad Hatter and sleepy Dormouse. Mad Hatter, as drawn originally by John Tenniel, wore hat with sign "In this style 10/6." Tenniel drew hatter to resemble real-life furniture dealer Theophilius Carter, who always wore top hat (though not with price tag in band). Queen of Hearts orders Alice to play croquet. Every time queen loses or is crossed, shouts at offender: "Off with his head!" After Alice is attacked by pack of playing cards, she awakens and tells her sister, "Oh, I've had such a curious dream!" Sequel *Through the Looking-Glass* (1872), introduces Humpty Dumpty, scornful character who says words mean whatever he chooses them to mean, and twins Tweedledee and Tweedledum. In Tweedledee's poem "The Walrus and the Carpenter," twins entice some oysters to follow them; the two dine on oysters with vineger and pepper, bread and butter. Here chess pieces replace playing cards of first book.

CARSON CITY   Became Nevada's capital in 1861. Smallest state capital in U.S. Named after famous frontier scout Kit Carson.

CARSON, JOHNNY (1925–   )   TV personality, host of NBC's *Tonight Show* since October 1, 1962. Begins with humorous monologue ribbing public personalities and politicians about their lastest activities or styles. Once quipped: "Ronald Reagan doesn't dye his hair; he bleaches his face." Viewed by an average of 5,780,000 households nightly. As of 1983, highest-paid performer on air. Author of bestseller *Happiness Is a Dry Martini,* collection of one-liners published in 1965. Illustrated by Whitney Darrow, Jr. Fifth best-selling nonfiction book in 1965, with over 172,000 copies sold that year.

CARSON, RACHEL LOUISE (1907–1964) American naturalist and author. Wrote *The Sea Around Us* and *Silent Spring* (1962), indictment of fast-growing use of chemical insecticides and weed killers. Offers documented evidence of their destruction of environment. Shocked pesticide industry.

CARTER, DONALD JAMES (BOSCO) (1926–   ) Bowler of the Year six times (1953, 1954, 1957, 1958, 1960, 1962). Voted greatest bowler of all time in 1970 *Bowling* magazine poll. First president of Professional Bowlers Association.

CARTER, JAMES EARL (JIMMY) (1924–   ) Thirty-ninth U.S. president. Former governor of Georgia. Born October 1, at what was then called Wise Sanitorium in Plains, GA. First U.S. president delivered in hospital. During Carter administration, U.S.S.R. invaded Afghanistan, events in the Middle East caused gas prices to double, inflation rate spiraled and Iranian hostage crisis began, November 4, 1979. In February 1979 Carter pardoned Patricia Hearst for her involvement in Symbionese Liberation Army's 1974 bank robbery. Being frank about issues of aging, Carter disclosed to public the fact that he had hemorrhoid operations while in office. Interviewed in *Playboy* (November 1976), discussed views on pride and lust. *Time* magazine's Man of the Year, 1976.

CARTER, LILLIAN (1898–1983) Mother of President Jimmy Carter. Peace Corps volunteer at age 77. Of her children, she remarked: "When I look at my children, I say, Lillian, you should have stayed a virgin." Died at age 85 of cancer.

CARTER, WILLIAM (BILLY) (1924–   ) Brother of President Jimmy Carter. Honored in *Esquire,* 1970, as Most Dubious Man of the Year for his words to U.S. Senate subcommittee: "Billy Carter is not a buffoon, a boob or a wacko." Known for beer drinking; short-lived brand Billy Beer named for him.

CARVER, GEORGE WASHINGTON (1864–1943) Black American botanist and chemist. Best known for more than 300 products he developed from peanut plant, including peanut butter.

CASABLANCA Largest city in Morocco and major port in North Africa. Founded by Portuguese in 1515. Name means "white house" in Spanish. Site of President F. D. Roosevelt and Prime Minister Winston Churchill's World War II strategic planning in 1943.

CASABLANCA Best Picture of 1943, based on play *Everybody Comes to Rick's.* Gambling casino (Rick's Café American) explodes when old love walks in with husband, French freedom leader fleeing Nazis. Stars Humphrey Bogart as Rick Blaine and Ingrid Bergman as Ilsa Lund Laszlo. Peter Lorre is Ungarte; Claude Rains is Renaud; Dooley Wilson is Sam, who sings "As Time Goes By."

CASEY AT THE BAT. See THAYER, ERNEST

CASH, LAWRENCE (JOHNNY) (1932–   ) American country-and-western singer, songwriter and actor. Wrote and sang such hits as "I Walk the Line," "Ring of Fire" and "Folsum Prison Blues." Autobiography, *The Man in Black* (1975), recounts his musical successes, his problems with pills and his relationship with June Carter and God, which he says saved him. Wears only black when performing.

CASINOS, LAS VEGAS Casinos and hotels in Las Vegas, NV, line 3½-mile stretch of U.S. 91 called "the Strip." Bright lights attract gamblers to such games as blackjack, roulette and craps, Strip's biggest moneymaker. Popular casinos include Lucky Strike, Golden Nugget, Jackpot and Horseshoe.

CASPER, THE FRIENDLY GHOST Animated TV cartoon, debuted 1946. Later, beginning 1953, a comic book from Harvey Comics. Casper and girlfriend Wendy, the Good Little Witch, are cuddly, benevolent characters who sometimes battle evil Ghostly Trio and frolic about with Nightmare, the Ghost Horse.

CASPIAN SEA Salt lake below sea level. World's largest inland body of water. Surrounded by Russia on three sides and by Iran to the south. Covers 143,240 sq. mi. (371,000 sq. km.). Close to size of California.

CASTANEDA, CARLOS (1931–   ) American anthropologist and author. Wrote *The Teachings of Don Juan* (1968) and four follow-ups: *Tales of Power, Journey of Ixlan, A Separate Reality* and current *The Fire from Within.* All are based on experiences with hallucinogenic plants and bizarre philosophies encountered during four years as apprentice to Yaqui Indian medicine man and sorceror Don Juan in Sonora, Mexico.

CASTRATED ANIMALS   The males of many animals raised for meat are castrated (have their testicles removed) so they will gain weight faster or will become more manageable.

Animal	Male	Castrated Male
Cattle	Bull	Steer
Chicken	Rooster	Capon
Horse	Stallion	Gelding

CASTRO, FIDEL (1926–   )   Prime minister of Cuba, 1959 to present. July 26, 1953, made failed attack on Moncada Barracks, known as July 26 movement. Exiled to Mexico. Overthrew Batista dictatorship, 1959. Nationalized businesses. After U.S. Bay of Pigs invasion, allied with U.S.S.R.

CASTRO, RAUL (1931–   )   Cuban revolutionary. Younger brother of Fidel Castro, Cuba's present leader. Involved in failed revolt of 1953. Exiled with his brother; returned secretly, 1956. Instrumental in Castro's successful overthrow of government, 1959.

CAT BALLOU   1965 hit movie starring Jane Fonda as young schoolteacher out west in late 1890s, who teams up with cattle rustler (Michael Callan) and drunken uncle (Lee Marvin) to rob a train. Marvin won Oscar for Best Actor in dual role as reformed drunk, Kid Shelleen, and metal-nosed desperado.

CATCH-22   1970 film based on novel by Joseph Heller. War-weary Air Force officers try to get discharged using every gimmick possible. Alan Arkin, Martin Balsam and Richard Benjamin star. Bob Newhart plays Major Major.

CATCHER IN THE RYE. See SALINGER, J.D. (JEROME DAVID)

CATONSVILLE NINE   Nine Roman Catholics, led by Reverends Philip and Daniel Berrigan, who seized and burned 600 draft files, May 17, 1968, in Catonsville, MD. Seven besides Berrigans were: Thomas Lewis, Thomas Melville, Marjorie Melville, John Hogan, David Darst, George Mische and Mary Moylan.

CATS   Members of family Felidae. *Felis catus*, or domestic cats, date to ancient Egypt. Napoleon said to have fear of cats, or ailurophobia. Tabby named Mickey, of England, holds record for killing most mice: 22,000 in 23 years. Considered sacred by ancient Egyptians. Their killers were punished by death. Dead ones made into mummies; over 300,000 found. To express mourning, Egyptians shaved their eyebrows. Cats four rows of whiskers called vibrissae, or tactile hairs. Connected to nerves that transmit sensory information to brain. Domesticated variety have five claws on each forepaw and four on each hindpaw. Siamese cats come in two main varieties, seal point and blue point, although other colors such as chocolate, lilac and redpoint have been developed. Points are dark markings on face, ears, feet and tail.

CATTON, BRUCE (1899–1978)   American historian and journalist. Noted for work on Civil War, including Pulitzer Prize-winner *A Stillness at Appomattox* (1953). Also senior editor of *American Heritage*. *A Coming Fury* (1961) was first volume of his centennial history of Civil War.

CAVIAR   Delicacy made from salted or pickled eggs, or roe, of certain fish, especially sturgeon. Finest caviar is Beluga caviar from sturgeon found in Black and Caspian seas. Less expensive caviar is produced from other kinds of sturgeon or the lumpfish. Leading producers are Russia and Iran.

CAYMAN ISLANDS   British dependency northwest of Jamaica in Caribbean Sea. Comprise three islands: Grand Cayman, Little Cayman, Cayman Brac. Georgetown (in Grand Cayman) is capital and largest city.

CB LINGO   Slang used by truck drivers and others in talking on citizens band (CB) radios. Popularized by song "Convoy" by C. W. McCall, number one hit in 1976. Sampling of CB slang: meat wagon, blood box (ambulance); pregnant roller skate (Volkswagen); Smokey Bear (state police car); green stamps (money); ten-twenty (location).

CEDILLA   Hooklike mark put under letter *c* in some French words to show it is to be sounded like voiceless *s* (e. g., *garçon*).

CENTURY   From Latin *centuria*, meaning 100 years. Centuries described by ordinal numbers (1st, 10th, 20th, etc.) refer to 100-year period preceding. For example, the 21st century will span January 1, 2000, through December 31, 2099.

CEREBRAL PALSY   Or Little's disease. Type of paralysis that cripples more children than any other disease, afflicting about one out of every thousand babies born in U.S. Most often caused by disease or injury before, during or just after birth.

CEREBUS   Three-headed dog of Greek mythology that guards gates to Hades (Hell). Phrase "give a sop to Cerebus," meaning to give a bribe or quiet a troublesome person, comes from story of the Sibyl, who drugged dog with cake when taking Aeneas to the Underworld.

CERVANTES, MIGUEL DE (1547–1616)   Spanish novelist, dramatist and poet. Born near Madrid in central Spain; died April 23, 1616, same day as William Shakespeare. Author of *Novelas Ejemplares* ("Twelve Tales"), 1613. His masterpiece was *Don Quixote* (1605), novel about country gentleman/knight with chivalrous delusions. Famous for his joust with windmill. Travels with rolypoly squire Sancho Panza, who rides mule Dapple next to Quixote's scraggly old horse Rosinante. Quixote pays homage to woman named Aldonza Lorenzo, whom he dubs Dulcinea ("the sweet one") del Toboso. Name Dulcinea has become synonymous with "sweetheart." Novel opening "At a certain village in La Mancha" gives title to popular stage musical *Man of La Mancha*, which interweaves life of Cervantes with that of his fictional hero and includes song "The Impossible Dream." Book also includes line "All that glitters is not gold."

CEZANNE, PAUL (1839–1906)   French painter. Noted for vivid color, striving for depth in shadows and outlines. His work (still lifes, landscapes, and portraits) bridges gap between impressionism and modern painting.

CH'ING DYNASTY   Last imperial dynasty to rule China, 1644–1912. Led by members of the Manchu family, who had overthrown the preceding Ming Dynasty. Corruption of gentry bureaucrats and influence of Western thought led to decreased power and their ultimate abdication, 1912.

CHAMBERLAIN, NEVILLE (1869–1940)   England's prime minister, 1937–1940. Moving force behind Munich Agreement of September 29, 1938, which he said would ensure "peace in our time" and promised Britain would not go to war against Germany if that country surrendered Sudentenland in Czechoslovakia. Once said of Germany's Nazi leader: "Hitler has missed the bus." Succeeded in office by Winston Churchill, 1937.

CHAMBERLAIN, WILT (THE STILT) (1936–   )
Pro basketball player 1959–1973, the Philadelphia and San Francisco Warriors, Philadelphia 76ers and Los Angeles Lakers in National Basketball Association. Number two all-time career scorer, passed in 1984 by Kareem Abdul-Jabbar. Top career rebounder with 23,924. Scored NBA record 100 points in one game, vs. New York Knicks, March 2, 1962. Became interested in volleyball while in NBA and formed own team, Wilt's Big Dippers. Joined professional International Volleyball Association in 1975; its president since 1977.

CHAMPAGNE   Sparkling (bubbling) wine. True Champagne comes from Champagne region of France, northeast of Paris. Always served cold, 35–45°. Should be cooled gradually in refrigerator and put on ice shortly before being used. Young vintages call for colder serving temperature. Classified for sweetness: brut, driest; extra sec, dry; sec, somewhat sweet; demi sec, quite sweet; doux, sweetest. Container capacities for champagne and other sparkling wines: split (6.5 oz.), half-bottle (13 oz.), bottle (26 oz.), magnum (52 oz.) and jeroboam (104 oz.).

CHAMPS-ELYSEES   Main thoroughfare in Paris. Named in 1709 for Elysian Fields, tree-lined plain where avenue grew. At one end is Arc de Triomphe, where 12 boulevards intersect; at other end is Place de la Concorde, which leads to Tuileries Gardens and Paris' Impressionist museum, Jeu de Paume.

CHANDLER, RAYMOND (1888–1959)   American detective story writer. Created hard-boiled Los Angeles private investigator Philip Marlowe in *The Big Sleep* (1939) and many subsequent adventures. College-educated; quotes Browning, Eliot and Flaubert; relaxes with classical music and art and solves chess problems. Late in literary life, marries heiress Linda Loring (whom he meets in *The Long Goodbye*, 1954) but refuses to use any of her money. Played in films by Humphrey Bogart, Robert Mitchum, Eliott Gould, among others.

CHANEL, GABRIELLE (COCO) (1883–1971)   French fashion designer. Revolutionized women's fashion after World War I with straight, simple, uncorseted lines, the "Chanel Look." Created Chanel No. 5 perfume, 1922; named for fashion shows on fifth of each month (five was her lucky number). Introduced women to short hair, costume jewelry, collarless suit. Subject of Broadway musical *Coco*, 1969.

CHANEY, LON (1883–1933) Star character actor, known as "the Man of a Thousand Faces" for his many guises in silent films. Movies include: *The Hunchback of Notre Dame* (1923), *The Phantom of the Opera* (1925), *London After Midnight* (1927).

CHANG World's most common surname. Means "draw-bone," "open," "mountain" or "constantly." Of approximately 1,000 different Chinese surnames, only about 60 are common.

CHANNEL ISLANDS, THE British-owned islands, 10–30 mi. (16–48 km.) off coast of France, located in English Channel. Self-governing and not subject to parliamentary rule unless named in specific acts. Heavy French influence. Three main islands: Jersey, Guernsey and Alderney; occupied by Germans from 1940 to 1944. Because islands are located further from England than were sections of occupied France, they were of little value to the Germans.

CHAPIN, DWIGHT (1940–   ) Appointments secretary for Richard Nixon. Fired after 1974 conviction for lying about certain activities in Watergate affair. Sentence: 10 to 30 months.

CHAPLIN, CHARLIE (1889–1977) A legend in his own lifetime, comedian personified screen comedy in his guise of "The Little Tramp," with his baggy pants, derby hat, and cane in his left hand. His features and shorts are considered classics: *Easy Street* (1916), *The Kid* (1920), *The Gold Rush* (1924), *Modern Times* (1936) and many more. Was first actor to sign a million-dollar Hollywood contract. Married Oona O'Neill.

CHAPMAN, MARK DAVID (1955–   ) Killed John Lennon, former Beatle, December 8, 1980. Pleaded guilty by reason of insanity. Currently serving 20-year-to-life sentence. Immediately prior to killing, seen carrying copy of J. D. Salinger's *The Catcher in the Rye* (1951).

CHARADE 1964 film directed by Stanley Donen. Audrey Hepburn stars as woman returning to Paris home and finding husband murdered. Cary Grant helps her solve mystery of his death and of missing fortune hunted by the killers.

CHARLESTON, SOUTH CAROLINA South Carolina's second largest city. Important Atlantic seaport situated on peninsula between Ashley and Cooper rivers. Founded 1670. Named for King Charles II. Civil War began on Charleston waterfront in 1861.

TRIVIAL CONQUEST

Charlie Brown **102**

CHARLIE BROWN. See SCHULZ, CHARLES MONROE

CHARLIE CHAN. See BIGGERS, EARL DERR

CHARLIE'S ANGELS Popular TV detective show about three sexy police-trained sleuths, working for unseen boss named Charlie (voiced by John Forsythe). Original team starred Kate Jackson, Farrah Fawcett-Majors and Jaclyn Smith.

CHARRIERE, HENRI (1906–1973) Best-selling autobiographical novel *Papillon* (1970) describes Charrière's 1931 life imprisonment on Devil's Island for murder of Montmartre gangster. Describes his prison experiences and attempts to escape; escapes successfully in 1945, fleeing to Venezuela. Called Papillon (French for "butterfly") because of tattoo on his chest. Steve McQueen had title role in 1973 screen version, co-starring Dustin Hoffman.

CHARTERIS, LESLIE (1907–   ) American mystery writer. Born in Singapore as Leslie Charles Bowyer Yin, son of Englishwoman and Chinese doctor. Once wrote column for *Gourmet* magazine. Created suave fictional detective Simon Templar, beginning with *Meet the Tiger* (1928). Known as "the Saint" because his motives are pure. Calling card: small stick figure with halo. Hero of 46 books, several films, 1940s radio and 1960s TV series (with Roger Moore).

CHATTANOOGA CHOO-CHOO "The Chattanooga Choo-Choo" first left on Track Two at a quarter to four in 1941 movie *Sun Valley Serenade*. Harry Warren and Mack Gordon song became best-selling hit for Glenn Miller, who recorded it with his orchestra.

CHAUCER, GEOFFREY (1340?–1400) English poet. Most revered for *The Canterbury Tales* (begun 1396), 17,000 lines of heroic couplets telling tales of pilgrims on journey from Tabard Inn in London to Thomas à Becket's shrine at Canterbury. Thirty-one start 60-mile trip; pick up Canon's Yoeman on way, making 32. Although each requested to tell two tales on trip there and two on trip back, Chaucer finished only 20.

CHAVEZ, CESAR ESTRADA (1927–   ) Labor leader. Advocates rights of American migrant farm workers in U.S. Southwest. Organized National Farm Workers Association, 1962, which eventually became United Farm Workers of America (UFW),

Merkin & Frankel

1970, with Chavez as president. Led grape and lettuce pickers in strikes and boycotts.

CHECKERS Two-player board game. Called draughts (drafts) in England. Board has 64 squares, 8 by 8, of alternately light and dark colors (usually red and black). Each player starts with 12 black or red pieces (checkers) that move forward vertically unless capturing or "jumping" opponent's piece. Player with black pieces goes first. With infallible play on both sides, a draw is inevitable.

CHECKPOINT CHARLIE Checkpoint where foreigners cross between East and West Berlin.

CHEESE Over 400 varieties manufactured. Differ in moisture and fat content and microorganisms involved in ripening. Types include soft (high moisture), hard (low moisture), semihard (medium moisture) and blue-veined, the blue veins being mold. Processed varieties are blended with emulsifying salts.

CHEETAH Great cat of Africa and Asia. Fastest land animal, clocked at 65 m.p.h. in short bursts. Endangered species. Lives on plains and is up to 4 ft. tall.

CHERRY TREE Member of rose family; produces small white or pink flowers (blossoms) in spring. Some types grown for decoration. Japanese varieties renowned for their beauty.

CHERUBIM AND SERAPHIM According to medieval belief, seraphim are highest order of angels, having six wings and distinguished by ardency of their zeal and love. Subject of 1838 poem by Elizabeth Barrett Browning. Cherubim, angels of second order just below seraphim, are described as excelling in knowledge and depicted as chubby, rosy-faced children with wings.

CHESAPEAKE BAY Arm of Atlantic Ocean dividing Maryland in two. Contains ports of Baltimore, MD, and Portsmouth and Norfolk, VA. Ships can sail almost all of its 200 mi. (320 km.) between state's eastern and western shores. Annapolis, on western shore, is site of U.S. Naval Academy.

CHESS Originated in India or Persia in 6th century. Name taken from Persian word for "king." By 13th century, chess played throughout Europe. In recent years, Soviet players have dominated world competition. Called "the Royal Game" because of upper classes' favor. Played on checkerboard. Sixteen pieces move according to fixed restrictions as player tries to force opponent's principal piece (king) into checkmate, an inescapable position. Each player has two rooks (castles); two bishops; one queen; one king, usually with cross on top of crown, making it tallest boardpiece; and two knights (horses), which move "two up and one over" (in L-shape)—only pieces allowed to "jump" over others. Each set of pieces is either light or dark; light makes first move. White king starts on black square; black king on red square, at center of back row of pieces. Queen starts "on her own color."

CHESS TERMS *Castling:* Moving king two squares to left or right of original position, toward one of rooks (castles), then transferring that rook to square over which king has just passed. Permitted only once per game, and only if neither piece has moved from its original position and there are no pieces between them. *Stalemate:* Situation in which player cannot move any piece without placing his king in check. Results in draw.

CHESTERFIELD English royal family. Fourth Earl, Philip Chesterfield (1694–1773), wrote series of works on manners. His name given to type of sofa, topcoat and cigarette.

CHESTERTON, GILBERT KEITH (1874–1936) British artist, poet, journalist, critic, essayist, short-story writer and creator of Father Brown, one of most unusual whodunit detectives. Brown, quiet, gentle Roman Catholic priest, appears in 51 stories; views wrongdoers as souls needing salvation. Brown stories, uniformly good-humored and nonviolent, serve as springboard for Chesterton's religious philosophy.

CHEYENNE Wyoming's capital and second-largest city, situated in southeast corner of state. Founded in 1867 as terminal for western railroad. Known for lawlessness during 1860s. Became capital in 1890. Named for Indians living in area.

CHIANG CH'ING (1914–) Chinese actress and political figure. Became Mao Tse-tung's fourth wife, 1939. Leader of Cultural Revolution of 1960s. Joined Politburo, 1969. After Mao's death, arrested as member of Gang of Four.

CHICAGO Inhabited by American Indians more than 5,000 years ago. Name comes from Checagou, Indian name for river in area. Nicknamed "First City of the Plain" and "City in a Garden"; latter appears on Chicago's seal in Latin as *Urbs in Horto.* Also nicknamed "the Windy City" by New York City journalist Charles A.

Dana in 1893, in reference to amount of bragging Chicagoans did when they held World's Columbian Exposition to honor both Christopher Columbus and their city's accomplishments. This nickname often interpreted as reference to wind that blows across city from Lake Michigan.

CHICAGO CUBS   Baseball team that has gone pennantless longest since last National League win. Won pennant in 1945, but lost World Series to Detroit Tigers, four games to three. Last World Series win, 1908. Finished second (in Eastern Division), 1969, 1970, 1972.

CHICAGO FIRE   October 8, 1871, fire burned for over 24 hours, killing 300 people and razing homes of more than 90,000 residents. Popular belief is that it began when a cow kicked and knocked over a lighted lantern in the barn of a Mrs. O'Leary.

CHICAGO PIANO   Slang term for automatic machine gun in 1920s and '30s. Chicago was country's bootlegging and racketeering center; as a result, adjective "Chicago" came to mean tough and illegal-looking. "Chicago overcoat" was a coffin; "Chicago pineapple," a small bomb or grenade.

CHICAGO SEVEN   Originally eight, later seven men, accused of conspiracy to incite riot at 1968 Democratic National Convention in Chicago. Defendants were: two members of Youth International Party, or Yippies (Jerry Rubin, Abbie Hoffman); two members of National Mobilization Committee (Rennie Davis, David Dellinger); a Black Panther (Bobby Seale, later ejected from trial, making Chicago Seven); Lee Weiner and John R. Froines. Five-month trial (1969–1970) became battle between Judge Julius J. Hoffman and defense attorneys Kunstler and Weinglass. Convictions of conspiracy overturned, 1974. Hoffman did mete out punishments of contempt of court to defendants and their attorneys.

CHICKEN   More on earth than any other kind of fowl. More than 180 varieties. Largest, Jersey Black Giant, weighs up to 13 lb. First domesticated about 5,000 years ago. Roasters are 4 to 6 months old, usually male; broilers, fryers are 9 to 12 weeks old, male or female. Capons are males whose reproductive organs have been removed; most meaty. "Drawn" means internal organs removed; head, shanks and feet cut off. "Dressed" means killed, bled and plucked. "Parts" usually refers to breasts, thighs, wings and legs. Bruises sustained to any part of chicken's body during its lifetime may result in less tender meat.

CHICLE Chief ingredient of chewing gum. Milky white latex or sap from sapodilla tree grown in Mexico, Belize and Guatemala. Rubber latex added to bubble gum for necessary elasticity.

CHICO AND THE MAN TV comedy series about enterprising young Chicano and his partnership with cranky, sarcastic Ed Brown in Ed's Garage. Freddie Prinze played Chico; Jack Albertson was "the Man." Jose Feliciano wrote and sang show's theme.

CHILE Southernmost South American country. Indians named region Chilli, meaning "place where land ends."

CHIMPANZEE Ape of family pongidae. After human being, considered most intelligent primate. Can fashion and use tools, such as sponges made of leaves for soaking up drinking water. Used extensively in medical and psychological research, due to similarity to humans. Chimpanzee named Washoe was taught American sign language.

CHINA Population of three largest cities (including metropolitan area): Shanghai, 11,000,000; Peking, 9,029,000; Tiajin, 7,390,000. Four of many Chinese dialects are Mandarin, Wu, Tibetan and Vigus (Turkic). Mandarin Chinese is most spoken language in the world. Marriage laws established in Communist China in 1950 were first to allow individuals to choose their own mates; previously, parents arranged marriages. Bride wears red at wedding. Marriage is prohibited if one is impotent, has venereal disease, a mental disorder or leprosy. Buenos Aires, at 57° longitude, 35° South, is directly opposite 123° longitude, 35° North, which is in China.

CHINA AND JAPAN AT WAR Japanese plans to build empire in Western Pacific led to July 7, 1937, clash between Chinese and Japanese troops at Marco Polo Bridge near Peking. This incident resulted in full-scale war and Japanese occupation of most of China until 1944.

CHINA—LITERARY BAN Peking library lifted ban on Shakespeare, Dickens, Twain and others, January 7, 1978. Move toward westernization following death of Mao Tse-tung included easing of restrictions on freedom of expression, dress, travel and the economy's private sector and foreign policy.

CHINATOWN   1974 motion picture starring Jack Nicholson as J.J. Gittes, tough Los Angeles private eye of 1930s led into dangerous case by femme fatale Faye Dunaway. Director Roman Polanski makes cameo appearance as hood who knifes Gittes.

CHINATOWNS, U.S.   San Francisco's Chinatown is largest in U.S.; inhabited by 36,000 persons of Chinese ancestry, it is also largest Chinese community outside Asia. Other U.S. cities with large Chinatown areas include Chicago, Los Angeles and New York City.

CHINESE CHECKERS   Board is six-pointed star with holes or indentations to hold pieces (called marbles or pegs). Each point is different color, with 10 or 15 pieces of each color. Players (two to six) move pieces single steps or in jumps over other players' pieces into opposite point. Game won by first player to move all his pieces to opposite point. Derived from English checkers game Halma, Greek word for "jump."

CHINOOK   Warm, dry wind that blows down slopes of Rocky Mountains. Temperature increases 1° with every 180 ft. it descends (1°C for every 90 mi.). Early settlers believed it originated from region inhabitated by Chinook Indians. Pronounced "shih-nook."

CHIPMUNKS, THE   The sped-up voice of Ross Bagdasarian (a.k.a. David Seville) produced novelty record "The Chipmunk Song" in 1958, and he turned the success of this gimmick into an animated TV series called *The Alvin Show*. Alvin, Simon and Theodore were three singing chipmunks who lived with Dave Seville in original series, which began in 1961. Bagdasarian's son revived show with new cartoons in 1983.

CHIROPODY   Or podiatry. In medicine, care and treatment of human foot. From Greek *pod* ("foot"). Practice includes treatment of corns, calluses, skin, muscle, bone and joint disorders, as well as prescription of drugs, corrective shoes and preventive hygiene.

CHISHOLM, SHIRLEY (1924–   )   U.S. congresswoman representing New York City, 1969–1983. First black woman elected to this post. Unsuccessfully sought Democratic nomination for president, 1972. Published autobiography, *Unbought and Unbossed* in 1970.

CHITLINS   Southern slang for dish made from chitterlings, small intestines of pig. Plantation owners slaughtered pig and gave unused parts to slaves, who cooked this dish by boiling the cleaned intestines and flavoring with spices. Also prepared by frying batter-dipped intestines in deep fat. Akin to German *kutteln* (entrails, tripe), introduced to U.S. by Pennsylvania Dutch.

CHLOROPHYLL Pigment that makes plants green; also necessary for photosynthesis, process used by plants to convert carbon dioxide to sugar. Chlorophyll absorbs energy from sunlight.

CHRIST, JESUS. See JESUS

CHRISTIAN SCIENCE MONITOR International daily newspaper dealing with Christian Science as well as world news. Founded by Mary Baker Eddy in Boston, 1908. Publication's aim: "To injure no man, but to bless all mankind."

CHRISTIAN, FLETCHER Leader of Mutiny on the Bounty, 1790. Nine British mutineers, in addition to 6 men and 12 women from Tahiti, settled on Pitcairn Island. Men fought over women until only John Adams was left. Island still populated by his descendants.

CHRISTIE, AGATHA (1890-1976) English mystery novelist and playwright. Second to Shakespeare as most translated English author. Created detectives Miss Jane Marple and Hercule Poirot. Her highly publicized 11-day disappearance in 1926 resulted from amnesia induced by death of mother and breakup of her marriage. Known for saying: "Give me a decent bottle of poison and I'll construct the perfect crime." Among her most famous creations is *The Mousetrap* (1952), stage whodunit that opened in London on November 25, 1952, and still running; longest-running English-language play of all time. Five guests and detective gather during blizzard. When one is murdered, suspense heightens. Characters include Mollie and Giles Ralston, Christopher Wren, Mrs. Boyle, Major Metcalf, Miss Casewell, Mr. Paravicini and Detective-Sergeant Trotter. Hercule Poirot, internationally famous private detective, retired member of Belgian police force, appeared in 37 novels and short stories before dying in *Curtain* (written in 1940s, but not published until 1975). His death received front-page coverage in New York *Times*; Poirot first fictional character so honored. Among many other Poirot cases are *The Murder of Roger Ackroyd* (1926), considered Christie's most ingenious novel; *Death on the Nile* (1937) and *Murder on the Orient Express* (1934).

CHRISTIE, JULIE (1940–   ) Popular British actress in many notable roles since 1960s. Won Oscar for *Darling* (1965). Other films include *Doctor Zhivago* (1965), *Far from the Madding Crowd* (1967) and *Shampoo* (1975).

CHRISTINA, THE Sixteen-hundred-ton yacht that belonged to Aristotle Socrates Onassis, Greek shipping tycoon. After marriage to J. F. Kennedy's widow, Jacqueline Kennedy, Onassis held wedding party on board, October 1968.

CHROMOSOMES Bodies that carry genes in cells. Human cells have 46 chromosomes in 23 pairs, one-half from father, one-half from mother. People with Down's syndrome have extra chromosome.

CHRYSLER BUILDING Built in 1920. Took title of world's tallest building from Woolworth Building. Seventy-seven stories high, it reigned as tallest skyscraper until 1931, when Empire State Building rose to 102 stories. Situated in Manhattan, New York City.

CHUCKLES THE CLOWN Kiddie show host for WJM-TV in Minneapolis on *The Mary Tyler Moore Show*. Chuckles was never seen on camera; in show's most famous episode, "Chuckles Bites the Dust," was killed by an elephant.

CHUCKWAGON One wagon of a train in pre-railroad cattle drives. Used to prepare food for cowboys en route from range to market.

CHURCHILL, WINSTON (1874–1965) Statesman and British prime minister, 1940–1945, 1951–1955. Succeeded Neville Chamberlain (1869–1940). First prime minister to serve under Queen Elizabeth (crowned 1952). Knighted by Queen, 1953. Skillful orator; Great Britain's political and spiritual leader during World War II. In radio broadcast, October 1, 1939, as international tensions mounted in Europe, Churchill said: "I cannot forecast to you the action of Russia. It is a riddle wrapped in a mystery inside an enigma." Upon taking office, he stated: "I have never promised anything but blood, tears, toil and sweat." Son of Brooklyn-born Jenny Jerome and Lord Randolph Churchill, third son of seventh Duke of Marlborough, he was also seventh cousin, once removed, of U.S. President Franklin Delano Roosevelt. Married Clementine Hozier in September 1908. In 1963 made honorary citizen of U.S. by unprecedented special act of Congress. Died January 1965 and was given state funeral; first state funeral for commoner since 1898 and first commoner's funeral attended by reigning British sovereign (Queen Elizabeth II).

CIA/OFFICE OF STRATEGIC SERVICE   Central Intelligence Agency (CIA) replaced World War II intelligence agency OSS under National Security Act of 1947. Often controversial, CIA's undercover and occasionally illegal activities were investigated in 1970s, resulting in tighter organizational restrictions.

CIGAR   Consists of three parts: filler, binder and wrapper. Superior are handmade cigars from "long filler" and natural leaf wrapper; cheaper cigars are made from "short filler" or "scrap." Quality also reflects source of tobacco, with Cuban considered best. "Genuine Havanas," like Rafael Gonzales Vitola E, are handmade in Cuba entirely of Cuban tobacco. Cigars originally all made by hand; more and more machine-made since 1902. Nearly all U.S. domestic brands machine-made.

CINCINNATI KID, THE   1965 feature film directed by Norman Jewison, starring Steve McQueen as expert New Orleans gambler determined to take crown away from Lancy Howard (Edward G. Robinson), king of stud poker.

CIRCA   Latin, from *circum*, ("round about"). Means approximately; with dates, means about or around. In history, indicates exact date is not known. Abbreviation: c.

CIRCLE   Closed curve, all points of which are equidistant from center. Diameter divides circle in half. Circumference is length of distance around circle. Radius is distance from center to circumference, or half the diameter. Arc is curved line between any two points. No matter how a circular sphere is cut, the resulting flat area will be a circle.

CISCO KID, THE   This "Robin Hood of the Old West" was created, with horse Diablo and sidekick Pancho, by O. Henry and brought to screen in *In Old Arizona* (1929) starring Warner Baxter. Later featured in many 1940s B-Westerns with Cesar Romero and Gilbert Roland in title role. Duncan Reynaldo played role in oft-rerun TV version.

CISCO PIKE   First film for Kris Kristofferson, country singer turned actor/leading man in 1972. Kristofferson met wife Rita Coolidge while making *Pat Garrett and Billy the Kid* (1973). Other films include *Semi-Tough* (1977), *Convoy* (1978) and *Heaven's Gate* (1980).

CITATION   Horse that passed $1 million in career earnings by winning his last race, July 14, 1951, at Hollywood Park. Overall, won 32 of 45 races; "out of the money" only once. In 1948, as three-year-old, won 19 of 20 races (one second place), including Triple Crown (Kentucky Derby, Preakness, Belmont Stakes), and earned then record $709,470 in one year.

CITIZEN KANE   Classic 1941 motion picture starred in and produced and directed by Orson Welles. Based on life of William Randolph Hearst, story concerns rise from boyhood poverty to great wealth of newspaper publisher who aspires to politics but is ruined by personal scandal. Nominated for nine Academy Awards but won only Best Screenplay. Won 1972 poll among film critics as best film ever made. "Rosebud," mysterious last word spoken by Charles Foster Kane (Welles) at start of film, is name of his childhood sled.

CITY HALL   Name for city hall in four languages: hôtel de ville (French); quwai-sho (Japanese); das Rathaus (German); municipio (Italian).

CLAIBORNE, CRAIG (1920–   )   New York *Times* food editor and author/editor of many cookbooks, including *New York Times International Cookbook, Craig Claiborne's Kitchen Primer, The Gourmet Diet Book* and *A Feast Made with Laughter*, a memoir with recipes.

CLARK, RICHARD (DICK) (1929–   )   *American Bandstand* host. Accused of accepting gifts and cash, known as payola, in exchange for radio airplay; found innocent after testimony before U.S. Senate committee, April 29, 1960.

CLARKE, ARTHUR CHARLES (1917–   )   British science-fiction author, best known for collaborating with Stanley Kubrick to make movie 2001: *A Space Odyssey* based on his short story "Sentinel." Some of his ideas were used in developing first communications satellites and radar.

CLAVELL, JAMES DUMARESQ (1924–   )   English-born American novelist, screenwriter and director. Wrote *Shogun* (1975), novel set in 17th-century feudal Japan. Concerns shipwrecked English sea pilot John Blackthorne and Toranaga, most powerful warlord in Japan, who schemes to become Shogun (supreme military dictator). Made into top-rated TV mini-series with Richard Chamberlain. Clavell also wrote *King Rat* (1962), story of British and American prisoners in Japanese World War II prison camp in southeast Asia. Filmed in 1975 with George Segal in title role of unscrupulous opportunist. Also starred Tom Courtenay and James Fox. Directed by Bryan Forbes.

CLAY, CASSIUS. See ALI, MUHAMMAD

CLEMENTE, ROBERTO (1934-1972) Pittsburgh Pirates outfielder, 1955–1972. Won National League batting titles, 1961, 1964, 1965, 1968. National League MVP, 1966; World Series MVP, 1971. Lifetime hits equaled 3,000. Specially elected to Hall of Fame, 1973, after dying in December 31, 1972, plane crash en route from native Puerto Rico to deliver supplies to Nicaraguan earthquake victims.

CLEOPATRA 1963 film directed by Joseph L. Mankiewicz and costing $28 million. Cleopatra and her love affairs with Julius Caesar and Marc Anthony are lavishly portrayed by Elizabeth Taylor, Richard Burton and Rex Harrison.

CLEOPATRA (69–30 B.C.) Queen of Egypt, 51–49, 48–30. Last ruler of inbred, tyrannical Ptolemaic dynasty. Married and co-ruled with brother Ptolemy, then age 10. Later married another brother; had children by Julius Caesar and Mark Anthony. Killed herself by allowing poisonous snake, an asp, to bite her. Described as "the Serpent of the Nile" in Shakespeare's *Antony and Cleopatra*. Marriage between siblings was common among royal families of that time.

CLEVELAND BROWNS Named after original owner and coach Paul Brown. Founded in 1946 as member of All-American Conference. Joined NFL with two other AAC teams, 1950, won league title. Also won 1954 and 1955 titles under Brown, who was later coach and general manager of Cincinnati Bengals. Having no official emblem, Browns are only NFL team to have helmets without insignia (plain brown with white center stripe). Pittsburgh Steelers wore helmets without decoration until 1962, when steel industry logo was placed on one side.

CLOCK ACCURACY Atomic clock most accurate. Measures number of vibrations made by atoms of element cesium. Atom clocks will not gain or lose more than one second in 300 years. If 30 minutes lost per day, would take 24 days to read correct time.

CLOSE ENCOUNTERS OF THE THIRD KIND
1977 hit film about average guy (Richard Dreyfuss) who has contact

with UFO. Director Steven Spielberg re-released two years later a "special edition" with added footage.

CLUE   Parker Brothers detective board game, introduced in 1949. Players solve murder of Mr. Boddy by chasing six suspects through rooms of his mansion, trying to find out who did it, with what weapon, in which room. Six suspects: Col. Mustard, Mr. Green, Miss Scarlet, Professor Plum, Mrs. White, Mrs. Peacock. Six murder weapons: wrench, rope, revolver, lead pipe, knife, candlestick. Nine rooms: billiards room, library, study, hall, lounge, dining room, kitchen, ballroom, conservatory.

COAL MINER'S DAUGHTER   1980 film biography of country singer Loretta Lynn. Sissy Spacek won Oscar for Best Actress for portrayal of Lynn. Directed by Michael Apted.

COBB, TYRUS RAYMOND (TY) (1886–1961)   Baseball player, born in Narrows, GA; nicknamed "the Georgia Peach." Center fielder for Detroit Tigers, 1905–1926; Philadelphia A's, 1927–1928. All-time hit leader with 4,191. Won 12 batting titles in 13 years, 1907–1919. Highest lifetime batting average (.367). Original member of Baseball Hall of Fame; named on 222 of 226 ballots cast in 1936 election.

COCA-COLA   Invented in 1866 by John Pemberton, Atlanta drugstore owner. "7X" is serum ingredient whose identity is known only by two or three people: only seven have ever known it. Contained cocaine until 1903. Since that date, cocaine has not been involved in manufacture of Coca-Cola in any capacity. Main ingredients: carbonated water, sugar, caramel color.

COCCYX   Last bone of vertebral column in man and tailless apes. Pronounced "kock-sicks." Named from Greek *kokkyx*, meaning "cuckoo," because of resemblance to a cuckoo's beak.

COCK ROBIN   In first verse of nursery rhyme, Sparrow admits killing him with bow and arrow: "The fly saw him die, the fish caught his blood, / the beetle'll make the shroud, the dove'll be chief mourner; / All the birds of the air fell a-sighing and a-sobbin',/ When they heard the bell toll for poor Cock Robin." (see ANDERSEN, HANS CHRISTIAN)

COCKFIGHTING   Sport of matching fighting roosters (gamecocks). Winner acknowledged either by time limit or when one is is killed or so badly hurt that it is withdrawn by its handler. When beaten, rooster's comb (crown or crest on top of head) slumps over; hence term "crestfallen." Gambling and cruelty associated with this sport render it illegal in virtually all places.

CODFISH Among most important of food fishes. Largest cod-producing regions are Grand Banks off Newfoundland and George's Banks off Cape Cod, MA. Biggest Cape Cod turkey, as cod are sometimes known, ever caught weighed 211 lbs.

CODING SYSTEMS Methods of communication in which only persons with key can understand message. Letter *B*, for example, is represented 1) in Morse code by dash followed by three dots, 2) in International Radio Code by word Bravo, 3) in International Alphabet Flag Code by notched red flag.

COFFEE Probably most popular nonalcoholic drink in the world. U.S. is largest coffee-drinking country, consuming about 500 million cups a day. Brazil produces about one-half of world's coffee. Instant variety first introduced in 1939 by Nestlé Corporation. Brand name: Nescafé. Powdered form. Nestlé's Taster's Choice, freeze-dried, first introduced in 1966. Superior blend.

COGNAC French town in department of Charente, on Charente River, where brandy cognac is distilled from Charente and Charente-Maritime white wines. Grand Marnier liqueur also made here. Considered best brandy in world. U.S. is world's leading importer of cognac. (see BRANDY; VSOP)

COIN COLLECTING Or numismatism. Started as major hobby in 1850s; now most popular hobby in U.S., with about 10 million collectors. Numismatists generally interested in origin, history, rarity and value of coins. Collected by variety, date, types or design. Highest price paid for single coin: $725,000 for 1787 uncirculated Garrett gold Brasher doubloon.

COLD Human viral disease. Takes two to five days to develop after infection; lasts four to six days. Average person has two to four colds per year, but in isolated areas such as North Pole people have fewer or none.

COLERIDGE, SAMUEL TAYLOR (1772–1834) British poet. Wrote 1798 poem *The Rime of the Ancient Mariner*. Narrator is seaman who must do supernatural penance for shooting albatross, bird of good omen. Part of penance is regular repetition of tale.

COLLODI, CARLO (1826–1890) Pen name of Italian author Carlo Lorenzini. Wrote children's story *Pinocchio: The Story of a Puppet* (1881). Given piece of wood that laughs and cries by carpenter friend, Geppetto creates talented but headstrong puppet Pinocchio, who later turns into real boy and becomes his son. Walt Disney 1940 cartoon version introduced Jiminy Cricket as Pinocchio's conscience, along with pets Cleo the goldfish and Figaro the kitten.

COLOGNE West German city and airport on Rhine River. Produces toilet water called eau de cologne, made here for over 200 years.

COLOMBIA Northernmost country on South American continent. Only country on continent to face both Caribbean Sea and Pacific Ocean. Bogotá is capital and largest city. Country named for Christopher Columbus; however, Spanish explorer Alonso de Ojeda arrived here first in 1499, three years before Columbus.

COLOR Black: not so much a color as a description of object's incapacity to reflect light; absorbs most colors without a trace. Black and white cancel each another out because they are equal in strength. Objects that absorb light appear black. Yellow: when combined with black, is highly visible because it is most light-reflective of all colors (other than white).

COLOR BLINDNESS Also, daltonism. Inability to distinguish colors. More common in men than in women. Dichromatic vision, or confusion of red and green, is most common form. Achromatic vision, or blindness to all colors, is extremely rare. Both are incurable.

COLORADO Highest peaks of entire Rocky Mountain chain, which extends from Alaska to New Mexico, are those of Colorado Rockies. Thus Colorado has highest overall elevation of all U.S. states. Highest Rocky and Colorado peak is Mt. Elbert, 14,433 ft. (4,399 m.), located in Sawatch Mountains.

COLORADO RIVER Flows across 1,360 mi. (2,189 km.) of U.S. and 90 mi. (145 km.) of Mexico. Rises in Rocky Mountains of Colorado and empties into Gulf of California. For millions of years ground away at rock bed, eventually creating Grand Canyon.

COLOSSEUM Largest and most famous Roman amphitheater. Built by Emperor Vespasian in A.D. 80. More than one-third of outer arcade still stands. Elliptical arena was pit surrounded by high wall to protect spectators from wild animals sported in arena. Today hundreds of stray cats make it their home.

COLT, SAMUEL (1814–1862) Developed first successful revolver; patented this repeating pistol in 1836. Colt .45 six-shooter used in Wild West produced by his company.

COLUMBIA SPACE SHUTTLE First reusable manned spacecraft. Maiden 54-hour flight on April 12, 1981, with U.S. astronauts John Young and Bob Crippen. Thirty-two thousand heat-reflecting silica tiles protect craft during reentry to Earth's atmosphere. Survived second flight without tile loss. Four flights to date.

COLUMBO Popular TV detective, Lt. Philip Columbo, portrayed by Peter Falk on series, 1971–1977. Driving beat-up car and wearing rumpled trench coat, Columbo solved many murder mysteries for Los Angeles police.

COLUMBUS, CHRISTOPHER (1451–1506) Italian explorer, born in Genoa. Received support from Queen Isabella I of Spain in attempt to reach Asia by going west. Denied common assumption that earth was flat. Departed from Spain; hence later known as "Iberia's Pilot," after Spanish peninsula Iberia. After about two and a half months of sailing, *Nina, Pinta* and flagship *Santa Maria* arrived at what is now known as America. Columbus also discovered many West Indian islands, including Jamaica. Since 1581, his remains have rested in cathedral in Santo Domingo, Dominican Republic.

COLUMBUS, OHIO State capital. State leaders wanted to call capital Ohio City, but General Joseph Foos, legislator from Franklin County, proposed "Columbus" to honor explorer Christopher Columbus.

COMANECI, NADIA (1961–   ) Romanian gymnast who received seven perfect scores (first perfect 10s in Olympics) en route to three gold medals in 1976 Montreal Olympics: all-around exercise, balance beam, uneven parallel bars. Fourteen years old, 4 ft., 11 in., and 86 lb., Nadia was highlight of all gymnastic exhibitions at games.

COMFORT, ALEX (1920–   ) English fiction writer with Ph.D. in biochemistry. Director of research in gerontology at University Center, London, and author of best-selling sex guides *The*

Joy of Sex: A Cordon Bleu Guide to Lovemaking (1972) and *More Joy* (1974). Takes cookbook approach to sex and includes Indian, Chinese and Japanese erotic art and explicit drawings of modern couple making love.

COMMA   From German *komma*. Punctuation mark used most often in English. Sets off nonrestrictive or parenthetical sentence elements, quotations and items in series, or indicates slight pause.

COMO, PERRY (1912–   **)**   Popular singer of 1940s and '50s, known as "Mr. C" (short for Como and class). Hits include: "A—You're Adorable" and "Hot Diggity."

COMPASS POINTS   There are 360 degrees in a circle. Therefore, on a compass, North and East are at right angles, or 90° apart. North and Northeast are then half that, or 45° apart. So if North is 0°, Northeast is 45°.

Thirty-two different points:

North	South
North by East	South by West
North Northeast	South Southwest
Northeast by North	Southwest by South
Northeast	Southwest
Northeast by East	Southwest by West
East Northeast	West Southwest
East by North	West by South
East	West
East by South	West by North
East Southeast	West Northwest
Southwest by East	Northwest by West
Southeast	Northwest
Southeast by South	Northwest by North
South Southeast	North Northwest
South by East	North by West

COMPLETE SCARSDALE MEDICAL DIET, THE   Two-week crash diet book by Dr. Herman Tarnower. Best seller, 1978. Named after town north of New York City where he worked. Was murdered, March 1980, by Jean Harris, his mistress for 14 years.

COMPUTER LANGUAGE   Combination of letters, words and symbols. Language used depends on job to be done. For business data, COBOL (Common Business-Oriented Language). For scientific tasks, ALGOL (algorithmic language). Others include: FOR-TRAN, BASIC and Pascal.

CONCORDE Supersonic transport (SST) airliner (travels faster than speed of sound). Built jointly by Aerospatiale of France and British Aircraft Corporation. First test run, 1969. Service between Paris and Washington began in 1976. Flight from Paris to New York takes less than four hours. Flown by England (British Airways) and France (Air France). Plane's high noise created controversy in U.S.

CONDON, RICHARD (1915–   ) American novelist. Best known for *The Manchurian Candidate* (1959), in which Raymond Shaw, captured during Korean War and brainwashed, enters trance at mention of game of solitaire and was ready to accept instructions when queen of diamonds appeared; made into 1962 film with Laurence Harvey as Shaw. Also wrote *An Infinity of Mirrors* (1964), *Winter Kills* (1974) and *The Entwining* (1980).

CONFEDERACY. See U.S. CIVIL WAR

CONGREVE, WILLIAM (1670–1729) English dramatist. In tragedy *The Mourning Bride* (1697) wrote: "Heaven has no rage like love to hatred turned, / Nor hell a fury like a woman scorned." Also known for Restoration comedies *The Double Dealer* (1693), *Love for Love* (1695) and *The Way of the World* (1700).

CONKERS Popular British children's game played with chestnuts. Two players each have a "conker" (a chestnut or sometimes a hazelnut) threaded on knotted string. Players take alternate hits at opponent's conker. Game won when one nut is destroyed.

CONNALLY, NELLIE Wife of Texas governor John B. Connally, Jr. Rode in car in which J. F. Kennedy was assassinated and Governor Connally seriously wounded. Approximately 30 seconds before Kennedy was shot, she said: "Mr. President, they can't make you believe now that there are not some in Dallas who love you and appreciate you."

CONNERY, SEAN (1930–   ) Scottish actor, born Thomas Connery. Has tattoo on right arm that reads: "Scotland Forever." Gained fame as James Bond in films such as *Dr. No* (1962), *Diamonds Are Forever* (1971) and *Never Say Never Again* (1983).

CONNOLLY, MAUREEN CATHERINE (1935–1969) American tennis player. Dubbed "Little Mo" upon winning first U.S. Open title, 1951, because of youth (age 16) and height

(5 ft., 5 in.). First woman to win tennis Grand Slam, 1953. Won U.S. Open and Wimbledon singles three times each. Serious riding injury before 1954 U.S. Open ended career. Died 15 years later at age 34.

CONNORS, CHUCK (1921–   )   Major league first baseman with Dodgers and Cubs. Left baseball for acting career: starred in *The Rifleman, Arrest and Trial* and *Thrillseekers* on TV; movies include *Geronimo* (1962) and *Soylent Green* (1972).

CONRAD, JOSEPH (1857–1924)   Polish-born English novelist. Original name: Teodor Josef Konrad Korzeniowski. Worked at sea on merchant ships, attaining rank of captain. Best known during lifetime as writer of sea stories. Among his works are *Lord Jim* (1900) and *The Secret Agent* (1907). In *The Nigger of the Narcissus* (1897), negro sailor James Wait, dying on board ship *Narcissus*, brings out best and worst in crew. Sailor Donkin almost stirs them to mutiny. In *Heart of Darkness* (1902), whose title refers both to jungle and to heart of primitive man, narrator Marlow tells story of his search for white trader Kurtz in Belgian Congo. This novelette inspired Francis Ford Coppola film *Apocalypse Now*, with setting changed to Vietnam during war. Martin Sheen played Marlow character; Marlon Brando was Kurtz.

CONSTITUTION, THE   U.S. supreme law of the land. Establishes framework of government and defines basic rights of all citizens. Sections known as articles and amendments. First 10 amendments make up Bill of Rights. Signed, 1787; ratified, 1788. Begins: "We, the people..."

CONTACT LENSES   Invented in 1887. First covered whole eye. Smaller lenses introduced in 1950s; soft lenses, in 1971; lenses that can be worn for weeks, in 1981. Most are tinted, usually blue, to make them easier to handle.

CONTINENTAL DIVIDE, THE   U.S. boundary separating areas that drain into Atlantic Ocean (east-flowing streams) from those that drain into Pacific Ocean (west-flowing streams). Created by Rocky Mountain range. Enters Mexico from New Mexico; enters Canada from Montana.

CONTINENTAL SHELF   Part of continent that slopes about 600 ft. (180 m.) under water. Covered with continental deposit that rivers have brought down from land.

CONTINENTS

Continent	Area in sq. mi	Area in sq. km	Number of Countries
Asia	17,128,500	44,362,800	38
Africa	11,707,000	30,321,100	51
North America	9,363,000	24,250,200	17
South America	6,875,000	17,806,250	15
Antarctica	5,500,000	14,245,000	-
Europe	4,057,000	10,507,600	33
Australia	2,966,100	7,682,200	1

CONTOUR LINES   On topographic maps: lines that indicate points of equal elevation. Close-spaced contour lines describe steep slopes; wide-spaced contour lines indicate more gradual slopes.

CONVOLUTIONS OF BROCA   Important speech area located on left frontal lobe of brain. Often, stroke victims will have damage in this region and will lose ability to speak while still able to understand speech. Named for Paul Broca, who discovered them in 1861.

COOK COUNTY   County seat: Chicago. County has approximately 5.5 million residents, ranking second in population behind Los Angeles County. Chicago's metropolitan area includes six Illinois counties.

COOL HAND LUKE   1967 film starring Paul Newman as young man sentenced to chain gang for cutting heads off parking meters. Bet that he could eat 50 eggs in an hour. George Kennedy won Oscar for Best Supporting Actor.

COOLIDGE, CALVIN (1872–1933)   Thirtieth U.S. president. Born July 4, 1872. Sworn in by his father, a notary public, in dining room of their Vermont farm after Warren Harding's death, 1923. Known for silence and strict traditional New England ideals.

COOPER   Person who makes or repairs casks or barrels. Not many around today, but was common occupation at time when commodities were shipped or stored in barrels.

COOPER, ALICE (1945–   )   Vincent Furnier, son of preacher, became hugely popular as Alice Cooper with rock band of early 1970s. Stage show notorious for bizarre theatrics (live boa constrictor and chopping up of baby dolls). Career highlights include hit single "School's Out" (1972), 1975 TV special and album *Welcome to My Nightmare.*

COOPER, D. B.   Name given by hijacker of Northwest Boeing 727, November 1971, who demanded that $200,000 and four parachutes be given to him upon landing in Seattle. After giving orders for the plane to take off again, Cooper parachuted out over northwest American wilderness. He remains unfound.

COOPER, JAMES FENIMORE (1789-1851)   First major American novelist. Wrote series of five novels on frontier life, known collectively as *The Leatherstocking Tales.* Series features white hunter raised among Delaware Indians, known variously as Natty Bumpo, the Deerslayer, Pathfinder and Hawkeye, and includes (in alphabetical order): *The Deerslayer* (1841), *The Last of the Mohicans* (1826), *The Pathfinder* (1840), *The Pioneers* (1823), *The Prairie* (1827).

COPENHAGEN   Denmark's capital and largest city, located on country's largest island, Sjaelland. More than half of Denmark's shipping passes through Copenhagen harbor, where incoming boats are greeted by statue of "The Little Mermaid" from Hans Christian Andersen's fairy tale. City is home of Tivoli Gardens Amusement Park, where visitors enjoy rides, concerts and ballet. Many streets here are closed to motor vehicles and have special bicycle paths.

COPERNICUS, NICHOLAS (1473-1543)   Polish astronomer who founded present-day astronomy. Rejected Ptolemy's theory that earth was center of universe, advancing idea that earth and planets revolve around sun. Opposition from Roman Catholic Church delayed publication of his masterpiece, *Concerning the Revolutions of the Celestial Spheres,* for 13 years.

COQ AU VIN   French recipe for chicken (*coq*) casserole in wine (*vin*) sauce. Dry red wine used for color as well as flavor; abroad, darker brown color of dish achieved by adding chicken's blood to gravy as last-minute thickener. *Coq* also French term for shipboard galley chef.

CORBETT, JAMES J. (1866-1933)   Heavyweight boxing champion, 1892-1897. Former bank clerk who brought image of respectability to boxing; hence nickname, "Gentleman Jim." Knocked out John L. Sullivan in 21st round, September 1892, to become first heavyweight champion under Queensberry rules requiring gloves and three-minute rounds.

CORDOBES, EL (1937–   ) Born Manuel Benitez Perez. Spanish bullfighter. Passed *alternativa* (event in which apprentice matadors graduate from facing older bulls) in 1963. Became millionaire in two years as result of success and flamboyant style in bullring, earning more than $3 million annually at height of career. Appeared in 111 corridas (bullfights) in 1965. Displays of courage enamored him even to detractors of this sport.

CORDON BLEU SCHOOL OF COOKING Founded in Paris, 1895. Noted for excellent training, using 18th-century implements such as whisk and hand sieve. Owned by Mrs. Brassard. Offers two-hour cooking demonstrations and four-week sessions.

CORDUROY From French *cord du roi* ("cord of the king"). Type of fabric with lengthwise ridges called wales, usually made from cotton.

CORFU One of Ionian islands, belonging to and off western coast of Greece. Second largest in island group. Also called Kerkira. Area: 227 sq. mi. (588 sq. km.). Invaded by Italians and Germans during World War II, but returned to Greek control.

CORN Nearly half world's supply of corn produced in U.S. In terms of weight and acres covered, is largest crop here. Roughly $13 billion worth harvested annually. Three-fifths of crop used as feed for livestock.

CORNWALLIS, MARQUIS CHARLES (1738–1805) British general. Surrendered at Yorktown, VA, October 19, 1781, to U.S. General George Washington, ending Revolutionary War. Treaty of Paris, marking official end to war, not signed until September 3, 1783.

CORPORAL KLINGER Maxwell Klinger, aide to doctors of 4077th Mobile Army Surgical Hospital, portrayed by Jamie Farr on TV series *M*A*S*H* (1972–1982) and *After M*A*S*H* (1983). During hitch in Korean war, Klinger frequently dressed in women's clothes in attempt to get discharged as mentally unfit.

CORRIGAN, DOUGLAS (WRONG-WAY) (1907–   ) Airplane pilot and mechanic who set speed record in flight from California to New York, July 1938. On return trip, became disoriented in fog and ended up, 24 hours later, landing in Ireland. His plane had no radio and his compass was faulty.

CORSICA French-owned island in Mediterranean Sea, located between southeastern France and northwestern Italy. Birthplace of Napoleon, who reclaimed it for France from British in 1796. Occupied by Italians and Germans during World War II; freed by Allied forces in 1943.

CORVAIR   1960 Chevrolet, one of first compact cars. Aircooled, six-cylinder engine in rear. Described as "unsafe at any speed" by Ralph Nader in 1965 book bearing same name. Nader argued that automobile industry placed profit and style ahead of safety.

CORVETTE STINGRAY   Corvette Blue Flame, first American sports car, introduced by General Motors in 1953. New Stingray design introduced in 1963. Immediately popular, with demand exceeding supply. Had plunging hood, folding headlights, independent rear suspension and no real grille.

COSBY, BILL (1938–   )   Comedian and one of first black performers to star in weekly network TV series (*I Spy*, 1965); also, first to win Emmy. Had own TV series, *The Bill Cosby Show* (1969). Comic creations Weird Harold and Fat Albert became basis for longrunning Saturday morning cartoon show, *Fat Albert and the Cosby Kids* (1972), featuring such other characters as Mush Mouth and Russell (Bill's brother). Feature films: *Hickey and Boggs* (1972), *Devil and Max Devlin* (1981) and *Bill Cosby—Himself* (1983).

COSELL, HOWARD (1920–   )   American broadcaster who hit big on network TV but still "tells it like it is" on daily radio sports show. Known as "Howard the Mouth," speaks with Brooklyn accent and rhetorical flourish. Covers Monday night football, boxing, some Olympics and some baseball for ABC-TV and radio. Former laywer; graduated Phi Beta Kappa from New York University Law School.

COSMOLOGY   Brand of astronomy that deals with structure and history of universe. Two different theories in cosmology: Big Bang theory holds that universe was formed in explosion 10 or 20 billion years ago; Steady State theory holds that universe has never changed.

COSTA DEL SOL   Resort area on coast of Spain. Beaches and golf courses attract visitors to towns such as Málaga, Torremolinos and Los Monteros.

COSTA RICA   Bordered by: Nicaragua to north; Pacific Ocean to south and west; Caribbean Sea and Panama to east.

COTTON BOWL. See FOOTBALL, COLLEGE— BOWL GAMES

COUNTRIES—ALPHABETIZED First three: Afghanistan, Albania, Algeria. Last three: Zaire, Zambia, Zimbabwe.

COUNTRIES—LARGEST AREA World's five largest in area: 1) Soviet Union, 8,649,490 sq. mi. (22,402,179 sq. km.); 2) Canada, 3,851,787 sq. mi. (9,976,139 sq. km.); 3) China, 3,691,000 sq. mi. (9,559,690 sq. km.); 4) United States, 3,623,420 sq. mi. (9,384,658 sq. km.); 5) Brazil, 3,284,426 sq. mi. (8,506,663 sq. km.).

COURT MARTIAL OF BILLY MITCHELL, THE 1955 film directed by Otto Preminger. Gary Cooper stars as Billy Mitchell, war hero fighting for truth. Based on actual events.

COUSTEAU, JACQUES (1910–   ) Famed French marine explorer. Aboard boat *Calypso*, headed four-year expedition using specially designed equipment and succeeded in exploring ocean floor at unprecedented depth of 4½ mi.

COUSY, BOB (1928–   ) Basketball player, Boston Celtics, 1950–1963. One of game's great passers. Point guard of Celtics NBA champions, 1957, 1959–1963. MVP, 1957. In college, led Holy Cross to NCAA championship, 1947. Coached Cincinnati and Kansas City in NBA, 1969–1974. Basketball Hall of Fame, 1970.

COW Female adult of bovine group. Milk stored in baggy organ called udder, which has four nipples (teats) for milking. Machine milking uses suction to extract milk. Males are called bulls. Cows and bulls, like dogs, have sweat glands on their nose.

COW THAT JUMPED OVER THE MOON In nursery rhyme "High Diddle Diddle, the Cat and the Fiddle": when cow jumped over the moon, "the little dog laughed, to see such a craft, and the dish ran away with the spoon."

COW'S STOMACH Divided into four components: the rumen and reticulum, where food is stored and partially digested by microorganisms; the omasum, where water is absorbed; and the abomasum, or true stomach, where most digestion occurs. Cow can bring food back from rumen to be rechewed in form of cud.

COWARD, SIR NOEL PEIRCE (1899–1973) English

playwright, actor, composer and director. Among his plays: *Private Lives* (1930) and *Blithe Spirit* (1941). In poem "Mad Dogs and Englishmen," wrote: "Mad dogs and Englishmen go out in the midday sun; / The Japanese don't care to, the Chinese wouldn't dare to; / Hindus and Argentines sleep firmly from 12 to 1; / But Englishmen detest a siesta." Title gave name to British rock touring band of early 1970s, featuring vocalist Joe Cocker and American keyboardist Leon Russell.

COWPUNCHER   Or cowboy, cowpoke, cowhand, wrangler, vaquero, buckaroo, gaucho: man who tended cattle in Western frontier days. Outfit was working uniform, from wide-brimmed hat that kept sun out of eyes to leather chaps that protected legs from thorns and branches.

CRABBE, CLARENCE (BUSTER) (1908–1983)   Four-hundred-meter freestyle swimming gold medalist, 1932 Los Angeles Olympics. Took bronze in 1928 games for same event. Turned actor and made one Tarzan movie (*Tarzan and the Fearless*, 1933). Played Tarzan, Flash Gordon and Buck Rogers in movie serials and Captain Gallant on TV. Co-starred with fellow Olympian and Tarzan, Johnny Weissmuller, in 1950 Jungle Jim film *Captive Girl*.

CRANE, STEPHEN TOWNLEY (1871–1900)   American novelist, poet and short-story writer known for vividly realistic style. Died of tuberculosis at 28. Wrote *Maggie: A Girl of the Streets* (1893) and *The Red Badge of Courage* (1895), Civil War novel about bravery of Henry Fleming, New York farmhand fighting at battle of Chancellorsville. Also wrote *The Open Boat and Other Tales* (1898).

CRAPS   Game played with dice. Most popular and biggest-betting private and banking dice game in Las Vegas, U.S. and world. Spontaneity of action, variety of plays and high level of participation among its attractions. Casino game with best odds: besides card game baccarat, only one in which player gets same wagering position as house.

CRAPS—NICKNAMES FOR THROWS   "Snake-eyes" (2); "cock-eyes" (3); "Little Dick" (4); "Little Joe" or "Little Joe from Kokomo" (5); "Johnny Hicks" (6); "Ada (or Eighter) from Decatur" (8); "ninety days" (9); "Big Dick" (10); "boxcars" (12, by two 6s).

CRAPS—PLAY   On first throw ("come out" throw), shooter who throws 7 or 11 has thrown "natural" and dice "pass" (player wins immediately); shooter who throws 2, 3 or 12 has thrown "craps" and dice "crap out" (player loses immediately); shooter who throws 4, 5, 6, 8, 9 or 10 has thrown "point" and to win must "make the point" by throwing same number again before throwing 7—no other numbers matter. If shooter throws 7 before throwing his number again, dice "miss out" (lose). Since there are more ways to make two dice add up to 7 than any other number (six ways: 1 and 6, 2 and 5, 3 and 4, 4 and 3, 5 and 2, 6 and 1), the probability of rolling 7 is higher. Odds of making specific number on single roll are determined by comparing number of ways to roll that number with number of ways to roll anything else. Odds of rolling 7: 6 out of 30, or 5 to 1.

CRATCHIT, BOB. See DICKENS, CHARLES

CRAWFORD, CHRISTINA (1939–   ) Adopted daughter of film star Joan Crawford. Author of *Mommie Dearest*, originally called *The Hype*. Story of life with mother, which she claims included beatings, psychological manipulations and embarrassment. Movie (1982) starred Faye Dunaway as mother.

CRAWFORD, JOAN (1908–1977) Film actress. Appeared in over 80 movies. Won Academy Award for performance in *Mildred Pierce* (1945). Served as director of Pepsi-Cola Company after death of husband, chairman of board, in 1959.

CRAZY HORSE (1844–1877) American Indian. Chief of Oglala Sioux during Sioux Wars of 1875. With main ally, Chief Sitting Bull of Cheyenne tribe, defeated General George Custer at Battle of Little Big Horn, also known as "Custer's Last Stand."

CRAZY HORSE SALOON Parisian cabaret. Famous for distinguished, "intellectual" striptease show begun by Alain Bernardin in 1950s. Phone number: 723.32.32.

CREAM Rock-and-roll group formed in 1966 by drummer Ginger Baker, bassist Jack Bruce and guitarist Eric Clapton. Hit singles include "Sunshine of Your Love" (1968) and "White Room" (1968). Disbanded 1968.

CREWEL Embroidery worked in colored wool on plain cloth background. Similar to needlepoint, in which entire surface, including background, is embroidered. Large sewing-type needles used. Developed in England and America in 17th century. Traditionally uses floral and scroll patterns. Name derived from crewel wool, two-ply worsted yarn.

CRIBBAGE   Card game played with standard deck. Score kept on wooden cribbage board with four rows of 30 holes for each player. Each player has two pegs and moves them along to mark score. "Pegging out" means winning by moving pegs through all score holes and off board. In meld scoring after each hand, face cards count 10 points; all others count face value (ace counts 1). Game to 121 points. Perfect hand (29 points) would be four 5s and jack of same suit as card turned up on playing table. Two points awarded for each pair (four 5s make up six pair for 12 points); 2 points awarded for each combination adding up to 15 (jack combines with each 5 for 15, thus another 8 points); four 5s themselves can be made into four combinations adding up to 15, for another 8 points; 1 additional point since player has jack as same suit as turned-up card.

CRICKET   English outdoor sport, roughly equivalent to American baseball. Played by two teams of 11 each, using stumps (supports of wickets, 28 in. high), bails (top pieces of wicket, 4⅜ in. long) and bats (flat-edged, shaped like paddle). Batter defends wicket with bat, knocking away bowler's pitches and trying to score by knocking over three stumps and two bails of wicket.

CRIMEAN PENINSULA, THE   Projects from southern Russia into Black Sea and Sea of Azov. Covered with cedar, magnolia forests, olive trees and vineyards. Capital is Simferopol. Part of Ukrainian Soviet Socialist Republic.

CRIMEAN WAR (1853–1856)   Fought in Turkey between Turks, British, French and Sardinians against Russians. Site of "Charge of the Light Brigade" and battlefield nursing services of Florence Nightingale.

CROCKETT, DAVID (DAVY) (1786–1836)   Frontiersman and congressman from Tennessee. Known for trademark coonskin cap, which became fad among teenagers in mid-1950s. Died in Battle of Alamo in Texas, March 6, 1836.

CROCODILE   Large, carnivorous reptile. Differs from alligator in that it has pointed, not rounded snout and is more aggressive. African crocodile kills more people than other African animals. Eyes and nostrils are uppermost on head; favors floating in shallow water.

CRONKITE, WALTER (1916–   )   Newscaster on CBS for over 25 years. Hosted *The Twentieth Century* documentary series,

1957–1967. Replaced Douglas Edwards as anchorman on *CBS Evening News*, 1962. Announced President Kennedy's assassination, November 22, 1963. Concluded last newscast by saying: "Old anchormen, you see, don't fade away. They just keep coming back for more. And that's the way it is, Friday, March 6, 1981."

CROQUET, ASSOCIATION Older, more complicated version of lawn croquet, played in U.S. by two or four players. Court has one central peg and six hoops. Object is to hit balls with mallet through prescribed course of hoops and finally against center peg. Game won by side that finishes course first or scores most points (one per hoop, in both directions, plus one for peg, or 13 per ball) in agreed time. Hoops made of rounded iron painted white. Crown of first hoop is blue; crown of last is red.

CROQUET, LAWN Outdoor lawn game for two to eight players. Ball propelled by mallet (long handle attached to two-headed striking area) through hoops stuck in ground (wickets). Play starts and ends in front of south (or home) stake, located at end of court.

CROSBY, BING (1904–1977) Real name Harry Lillis Crosby. Popular singer turned actor of 1930s, '40s and '50s. Made seven "Road" pictures with Bob Hope, which led them to Singapore (1940), Zanzibar (1941) and Morocco (1942). Won Oscar as Father O'Malley in *Going My Way* (1944). Other films include *Holiday Inn* (1942), *The Country Girl* (1954) and *High Society* (1956). 1942 recording of "White Christmas" sold over 30 million copies, a world record. Died on golf course in Spain, October 14, 1977.

CROSSBOW Or alabast. Missile weapon widely used in Middle Ages. Consists of short bow fixed transversely on stock. Designed for firing while lying behind crosshatches of castle's parapet.

CROSSBOW ARCHERY. See ARCHERY, CROSSBOW

CRUSADES Holy wars, 1095–1270, during which European Christians fought Muslim Turks in attempt to regain Holy Land from Arabs.

CRUSOE, ROBINSON. See DEFOE, DANIEL

CRUZEIRO. See SOUTH AMERICA CURRENCY

CUBA Largest island in West Indies; belongs to Antilles island group. Country consists of one large island and over 1,600 smaller islands. Isle of Pine is only inhabited small island. Called by coun- trymen "Pearl of the Antilles" because of its physical beauty. Orig- inally Spanish colony; gained independence in 1898. Ruled by U.S. military government until 1902. Fidel Castro overthrew leader Ful- gencio Batista in 1959 and formed present Cuban Communist party.

CUBE In geometry: solid of six equal square sides, all edges equal in length. Volume equals length of an edge multiplied by itself three times, or cubed.

CUBE ROOT Number that when multiplied by itself three times yields original number. E.g., cube root of 64 is 4 (4x4x4 = 64); cube root of 27 is 3 (3x3x3 = 27).

CUBIT Unit of length based on distance from elbow to tip of middle finger. Used by many ancient civilizations, unit of course varied because of differences in arm's length. Modern English cubit is 18 in.

CUGAT, XAVIER (1900–　　) Latin bandleader, popular since 1940s. Often photographed carrying Mexican Chihuahua un- der arm. Introduced Dinah Shore and Desi Arnaz, as well as his wives Abbe Lane and Charo, to American public. Film appearances include *You Were Never Lovelier* (1942) and *Neptune's Daughter* (1944).

CURFEW From Middle French *cov refeu*. In Middle Ages, town's bell was rung every night at same time, requiring people to cover (put out) fires, extinguish lamps and go to bed. Bell called "curfew bell." Line "curfew must not ring tonight" from 1882 poem of that name by Ross Hartwick Thorpe (1850–1939).

CURIE, MARIE (1867–1934) Chemist and physicist. First female lecturer at Sorbonne. Won two Nobel prizes, 1903 and 1911; only woman to do so. Discovered radioactivity and isolated radium. Death from leukemia thought to have been caused by exposure to radioactivity.

CURLING Game resembling shuffleboard, played on 138-ft. strip of ice between two teams of four players each. Players, called lead, no. 2, no. 3 and captain or "skip," slide round "stones" using handle that screws into center hole and aim at marked target area ("house") at opposite end of ice. One point scored for each stone inside house and closer to center ("tee") than any opponent's stone. Curling tournament called "bonspiel." Popular sport in Canada.

CURTIS, TONY (1925–　　) Born Bernard Schwartz in

Bronx, NY. Took stage name from Anthony Curtis, character he played in screen debut, *Criss Cross* (1948). Other films include: *Some Like It Hot* (1959), *The Great Race* (1965) and *The Boston Strangler* (1968). Once married to actress Janet Leigh. Their daughter is actress Jamie Lee Curtis.

CUSP In astrology: imaginary line separating one zodiac sign from adjoining sign. Used in nativity calculations. Uncertainty as to planet's location; ambiguity as to planet's influence.

CWT. See WEIGHT MEASUREMENTS

CY YOUNG AWARD Created in 1956 by Commissioner Ford C. Frick, who was disturbed that pitchers were not getting enough recognition in MVP balloting. Named for baseball's all-time winningest pitcher, Cy Young (511, with more than 200 in each league). Since 1967, winner named in each league. Steve Carlton of Philadelphia Phillies only four-time winner through 1983.

CYCLAMATES Artificial sweetener used in soft drinks. Thirty times as sweet as sucrose; lacks bitterness some taste in saccharin. Banned in 1969, when high uses of synthetic sweetener shown to cause bladder tumors in laboratory animals.

CYCLING Sport of racing or touring with bicycles. Conducted on steeply banked oval tracks or on public roads, often without restriction of normal traffic. Federal Highway Act of 1973 legitimized bicycles on U.S. roads. Cyclists learn to obey traffic rules and drive defensively. When riding in group, lead cyclist who sees car approaching shouts, "Oil!" or, more commonly, "Car up!" Rear cyclist who sees car approaching from behind group yells, "Car back!"

CYCLOPS In Greek mythology: member of Cyclopes, race of one-eyed giants. Some forged Zeus' thunderbolts. Most famous was Polyphemus, who threatened Odysseus (called Ulysses in Roman mythology) in Homer's epic poem *The Odyssey*. Name means "circular eye."

CYPRUS—FLAG Has white background with map of country in copper-yellow (symbolizing metallic element copper) above two green crossed olive branches (symbolizing peace). Only country with map on flag.

CZECHOSLOVAKIA Official name: Cskoslovenska Socialisticka Republika (Czechoslovakia Socialist Republic). Abbreviation: C.S.S.R. Divided into two sections: Czech Socialist Republic (Bohemia and Moravia) and Slovak Socialist Republic (Slovakia). Each has own prime minister, cabinet and elected legislature. Invaded by troops from Soviet Union, Bulgaria, East Germany, Hungary and Poland, August 1968, ending brief period of liberal reform.

D

DAILY PLANET, THE. See SUPERMAN

DAIQUIRI   Cocktail named after Cuban nickel mining town near Santiago. Mining engineer Jennings S. Cox credited with naming drink in 1900, although first printed reference comes in F. Scott Fitzgerald novel *This Side of Paradise*, 1920. Mixed by combining 1 oz. white rum, 1 oz. lime juice and 1 tsp. sugar. Served cold or frozen.

DAISY   The Bumstead pup. Has appeared in comic strip *Blondie* almost since its inception in 1931. Invariably drawn by cartoonist Chic Young with a perplexed expression, Daisy can generally be found next to Dagwood's favorite chair.

DALAI LAMA PALACE   Located in Lhasa, Tibet's capital. Spectacular castlelike structure where Dalai Lama lives. Dalai Lama regarded by Buddhists as ruler of country and as spiritual leader; had great influence in Tibet until Chinese Communists invaded in 1950.

DALEY, RICHARD (1902–1976)   Mayor of Chicago, 1955–1976. Used police to squelch anti-Vietnam war protest at 1968 Democratic National Convention. Though convention came just months after severe racial riots erupted throughout city, Daley assured delegates: "As long as I am mayor of this city, there's going to be law and order in Chicago."

DALI, SALVADOR (1904–   ) Spanish painter, influenced by psychoanalyst Sigmund Freud and futurism. By 1929 had become leader in new style, surrealism. Precise style enhanced nightmare effect of his painting. Best known for *Persistence of Memory* (1931), featuring seemingly dripping watches, and *Crucifixion* (also called *Christ of St. John of the Cross*, 1951), one of series of religious paintings. Known for the outrageous in painting (e.g., *Soft Self-Portrait with Grilled Bacon*) and appearance (e.g., outlandish waxed mustache).

DALLAS Texas' second-largest city, called "Big D" by its residents. Purportedly named for George M. Dallas, U.S. vice-president, 1845–1849, under President Polk. Of its inhabitants, 98% were born in U.S.

DAM SQUARE. See AMSTERDAM

DAMASCUS Capital of Syria, famous for skilled craftsmen. Lies on Barada River. Pleasant climate occasionally interrupted by khamsin, desert wind.

DAMN YANKEES 1958 musical comedy based on hit Broadway play. Red-haired devil (portrayed by Ray Walston) and his temptress Lola (Gwen Verdon) transform middle-aged baseball fan into young star player who leads Washington Senators to pennant.

DANA, BILL (1924–   ) Gained fame through characterization of José Jimenez on *The Steve Allen Show*. Introduced himself with line "My name José Jimenez." TV series *The Bill Dana Show* (1963–1965) placed José in job of bellhop in big-city hotel.

DANA, RICHARD HENRY, JR. (1815–1882) American novelist and lawyer. His classic sea story *Two Years Before the Mast* (1840), based on diary he kept as sailor on voyage around Cape Horn (Africa), concerns captain's brutality and crew's lack of means of redress.

DANDELION From French *dent de lion* ("lion's tooth"), has toothlike notches on leaves. Common lawn weed. Leaves can be used in salad and flowers made into wine.

DANIEL BOONE TV Western series of 1960s. Fess Parker portrayed Daniel Boone, American folk hero who encountered many friendly and hostile Indians in Tennessee–Kentucky territory.

DANIEL, MARGARET TRUMAN (1924–   ) Daughter of Harry Truman (U.S. president, 1945–1953) and wife of New York *Times* editor Clifton Daniel. Author of novel *Murder in the White House* (1980) and follow-up novel *Murder on Capitol Hill* (1981).

DANNY & THE JUNIORS   Rock singers from Philadelphia, popular in late 1950s. Danny Rap, Joe Terranova, Frank Mattei and Dave White formed group in mid-1950s and had hits including "At the Hop" (1957) and "Rock and Roll Is Here to Stay" (1958).

DANSKE, HOLGER   National folk hero of Denmark. Important character in medieval French romance, known as valiant warrior and rebel. Story chronicled in *Chansons de Geste.*

DANUBE RIVER   Second largest river in Europe. Flows 1,777 mi. (2,860 km.) from southwest Germany through Austria, Czechoslovakia, Hungary, Yugoslavia, Romania and Bulgaria, emptying into Black Sea on Russian-Romanian border. Flows through capital cities of Austria (Vienna), Hungary (Budapest) and Yugoslavia (Belgrade).

DARLING   Film drama (1965) starring Laurence Harvey, Dirk Bogarde and Julie Christie. Christie won Oscar for portrayal of model with questionable background who marries Italian prince.

DARROW, CLARENCE. See SCOPES TRIAL

DARTMOUTH COLLEGE   Privately endowed coeducational liberal arts college in Hanover, NH. Founded in 1769 under charter granted to Eleazar Wheelock by King George III. Member of Ivy League.

DARTS   Each player starts with prescribed number of points (usually 301 or 501) and subtracts points scored on each three-throw turn, trying to get to zero. Player must hit a double (outer ring of board) to begin subtracting his scoring darts, another double at end of game in order to win (called doubling in and out). Perfect throw of three darts earns 180 points, highest score possible on one turn; scored by throwing all three darts into inner (triple) ring of 21-point sector, yielding three 60-point darts for 180 total. Bull's-eye is divided into two concentric circles on dartboard. Inner circle ("bull") worth 50 points; outer worth 25. Inner diameter ½ in.; outer, 1⅛ in. Officially, center of inner bull should be 5 ft., 8 in. off ground and 8 ft. from toe line, where thrower stands. Standard dartboard is made of cork, bristle or elm. Eighteen inches in diameter, it has 20 numbered segments marked off by wires. Segment

20 (counting 20 points) at 12 o'clock, then numbered (in clockwise direction) 1, 18, 4, 13, 6, 10, 15, 2, 17, 3 (at 6 o'clock), 19, 7, 16, 8, 11, 14, 9, 12 and 5.

DARWIN, CHARLES ROBERT (1809-1882) British naturalist and biologist. Studied plant and animal specimens during travels aboard *H.M.S. Beagle*. Argued that present species evolved from a few common ancestors. Theory of natural selection explains why some species more successful than others. Married cousin, Emma Wedgewood, 1839.

DASH Most cookbooks define both "dash" and "a few grains" as "less than ⅛ tsp." and "tsp." as 60 drops. A dash, therefore, is 6 drops, or just less than ⅛ tsp.

DATES Fruit of date palm, Middle East and North Africa palm tree. Date palms grow to 100 ft. and produce up to 600 lb. a year. Also grow in California, Arizona and Texas.

DAVE CLARK FIVE, THE British rock-and-roll group popular in mid-1960s. The Five included Dave Clark, Mike Smith, Rick Huxley, Lenny Davidson and Dennis Payton. Among hits: "Glad All Over" (1964), "Bits and Pieces" (1964), "Catch Us If You Can" (1965).

DA VINCI, LEONARDO (1452–1519) Florentine painter, sculptor, architect and engineer. Painted *Mona Lisa* (c. 1503 – 1505), also known as *La Gioconda*, smiling-faced portrait of wife of Florentine banker Zanobi del Giocondo. Oil on panel, approximately 30 in. by 21 in. Most looked-at painting in Louvre museum, Paris. Stolen from Louvre, August 21, 1911, by patriotic Italian determined to return it to his native land; recovered, 1913. Da Vinci also painted *The Last Supper*, which hangs in Monastery of Santa Maria delle Grazie in Milan, Italy; traditional arrangement of apostles and Christ changes from line of 13 to several small groups.

DAVIS CUP, THE Officially, International Lawn Tennis Challenge Trophy. Gift of Dwight F. Davis, leading American player, in 1900. Held every year except war years, 1901 and 1910. Shreeve, Crump & Low (Boston silversmiths) created 13-in.-high bowl from 217 troy oz. sterling silver.

DAVIS, ADELE (DAISIE) (1904–1974) American nutritionist, author, natural foods crusader and expert on vitamins. Among her books: *Let's Cook It Right* (1962), which includes more than 400 healthy recipes; *Let's Have Healthy Children* (1959); *Let's Get Well* (1965).

DAVIS, ANGELA (1944–) Communist and radical. Lost assistant professorship at University of California–Los Angeles in 1975, after school received threats following her appointment. In same year acquitted of murder and kidnapping charges stemming from shootout at Marin County Courthouse.

DAVIS, MILES (1926–) Jazz trumpet player, popular since 1950s. In 1960s pioneered fusion of jazz and rock with albums *Miles in the Sky, Bitches Brew* and *Live at the Fillmore.*

DAVIS, NANCY. See REAGAN, RONALD

DAVIS, SAMMY, JR. (1925–) Singer, actor and entertainer since 1930s. Began career as Silent Sam, the Dancing Midget. Guest-starred on many TV series; played lead in 1965 Broadway hit *Golden Boy.* Starred in many movies, including *Porgy and Bess* (1959), *Ocean's Eleven* (1960), *Robin and the Seven Hoods* (1964) and *Salt and Pepper* (1968). Wrote autobiography, *Yes I Can.*

DAVY JONES' LOCKER In sailors' folklore: where bodies of drowned sailors come to rest. Name may derive from Jonah, biblical figure swallowed by whale.

DAY AT THE RACES, A 1937 film starring three Marx Brothers. Groucho was Hugo Z. Hackenbush, horse doctor who treats patients at bankrupt sanitarium and tries to keep it going by winning at the track.

DAY OF THE JACKAL, THE 1973 film based on novel by Frederick Forsyth. Edward Fox stars as the Jackal, international contract killer and master of disguise hired to kill Charles de Gaulle. (see FORSYTH, FREDERICK)

DAY, DENNIS (1917–) Irish tenor and featured regular on *The Jack Benny Show* on radio and TV. Prefaced questions with "Gee, Mr. Benny." Hit records of Irish tunes included "My Wild Irish Rose."

DAYAN, MOSHE (1915–1981) Israeli statesman. Helped plan Israeli campaigns in 1963 and 1973 wars. Negotiated and signed Camp David Accords leading to peace with Egypt. Lost left eye in invasion of Syria, 1941, World War II; wears eye patch.

DAYS OF THE WEEK

Day	Named for
Sunday (first day of week)	Sun
Monday	Moon
Tuesday	Tyr, Norse god of sky and war
Wednesday	Odin, chief Norse god
Thursday	Thor, Norse god of thunder
Friday	Freya, Norse goddess of love and beauty
Saturday	Saturn, Roman god of agriculture

DAYS OF WINE AND ROSES Film drama (1962) about alcoholic couple, portrayed by Jack Lemmon and Lee Remick. Won Oscar for Henry Mancini's theme song. Directed by Blake Edwards.

D DAY. See NORMANDY INVASION

DDT Dichloro-diphenyl-trichloro-ethane, first synthetic insecticide (1939). Affects nervous system. Passed on to human beings who eat animals or plants that have been contaminated. Banned for most purposes, 1972. Used in World War II to fight typhus.

DE GAULLE, CHARLES (1890-1970) French general, World War II, and president of Fifth Republic, 1959–1969. Presidency saw increasing French influence in international affairs despite his question: "How can you govern a nation that has 350 kinds of cheese?"

DE HAVILLAND, OLIVIA (1916–   ) Actress starring in costume dramas including *A Midsummer Night's Dream* (1935), *Adventures of Robin Hood* (1938) and as Melanie in *Gone with the Wind* (1939). Won Oscars for *To Each His Own* (1946) and *The Heiress* (1949). Sister of actress Joan Fontaine.

DE MILLE, CECIL B. (1881–1959) Hollywood pioneer, producer and director famous for epic productions. Films since 1913 include *The Squaw Man* (1913), *King of Kings* (1927), *Reap the Wild Wind* (1942) and *The Greatest Show on Earth* (1952). Said, "Give me a couple of pages of the Bible, and I'll give you a picture." The result: *The Ten Commandments* (1923) and its 1956 remake.

DE SADE, MARQUIS COUNT DONATIEN ALPHONSE FRANÇOIS (1740–1814) Deranged French philosopher and writer. From 1777 until his death, resided in prison or in lunatic asylum at Charenton for major role in Marseilles sex scandal. There wrote novels and plays detailing philosophy responsible for word "sadism" (sexual perversion in which gratification is obtained by infliction of physical or mental pain on others; delight in cruelty). Wrote *120 Days of Sodom* (1785) and *Justine* (1790).

DEAD SEA Situated in Israel and Jordan. World's saltiest body of water; has nine times more salt than any ocean. Contains no fish and very little plant life. Believed by some to be a curing sea. First mentioned as "Salt Sea" in Bible (Genesis 14:3).

DEAD SEA SCROLLS Ancient Hebrew biblical texts, dated between 67 B.C. and A.D. 237. Found by two shepherd boys, 1947, in area of Khirbet Qumram near Jericho on western shore of Dead Sea.

DEAN, JAMES (1931–1955) Young actor of 1950s who died in car crash while driving Porsche Spyder. Acclaimed for *East of Eden* (1955), *Rebel Without a Cause* (1955) and *Giant* (1956).

DEAN, JAY HANNA (DIZZY) (1911–1974) and DEAN, PAUL (DAFFY) (1913–   ) Pitching brothers of St. Louis Cardinals. Pitched 1934 "Gas House Gang" to World Series win over Detroit Tigers, winning two games each. Dizzy was 150-83, 1930–1937; Daffy was 50-43, 1934–1939. Both retired because of injuries. Dizzy became sports announcer known for honest sentiments and awful grammar, as in "They woulda had 'im at second, but he slud" and "Base runners have to return to their respectable bases."

DEAN, JOHN WESLEY, III (1938–   ) American politician. White House counsel to President Nixon. First to testify at length about White House involvement in Watergate break-in. Said of Watergate scandal, "There is a cancer within, close to the presidency, that is growing." For his own involvement, served four-month prison term. Recounts his story in *Blind Ambition* (1967).

DEARBORN, MICHIGAN Home of Ford Motor Company's main plant, built in 1919 by Henry Ford. Ford industries employ more than one of every four workers in Dearborn. Henry Ford Museum and Greenfield Village attract about two million tourists a year. Birthplace of Henry Ford.

DEATH IN VENICE Luchino Visconti directed 1971 film based on Thomas Mann's novel about aging writer, recuperating from illness, who confronts image of perfect beauty in golden-haired boy staying at same hotel. Dirk Bogarde played dying artist.

DEATH OF A SALESMAN. See MILLER, ARTHUR

DEATH ON THE NILE. See CHRISTIE, AGATHA

DEATH VALLEY   Located in eastern central California, north of Mojave Desert. Named in 1849 for desolate desert environment. Length: 130 mi. (209 km.). Width: 6–14 mi. (10–23 km.). Western hemisphere's lowest elevation is near Badwater in Death Valley, 282 ft. (86 m.) below sea level. U.S.'s highest recorded temperature, 134°F (75°C), reported here in 1913. Small portion of Death Valley lies in Nevada.

DEATH VALLEY DAYS   TV Western anthology series. Premiered 1972; sponsored by Borax Bleach. Show featured stories about Western pioneers and was hosted by Stanley Andres, Ronald Reagan, Robert Taylor and Dale Robertson throughout 20-year run.

DEBAKEY, DR. MICHAEL (1908–   ) Surgeon at Baylor College of Medicine in Texas. Credited with first human artificial heart transplant, 1969. Transplant unsuccessful.

DECATHLON. See TRACK AND FIELD

DECLARATION OF INDEPENDENCE. See JEF-FERSON, THOMAS

DEEP THROAT   Secret informant. Guided Washington *Post* reporters Bob Woodward and Carl Bernstein in their investigation of Watergate break-in, cover-up and scandal. Guessing who Deep Throat was is still a popular pastime.

DEERSLAYER, THE. See COOPER, JAMES FENI-MORE

DEFENDERS, THE   TV courtroom drama series about father-and-son law firm of Preston & Preston, played by E. G. Marshall and Robert Reed. Premiered September 1961.

DEFIANT ONES, THE   Academy Award–winning story of two escaped convicts (Tony Curtis and Sidney Poitier) chained together while fleeing police. Their mutual hate, because of racial differences, disappears as they struggle to remain free. Stanley Kramer directed this 1958 film.

DEFOE, DANIEL (1660–1731)   English journalist and novelist. Called father of modern journalism and of the English novel.

Wrote journal of European affairs, 1704–1713. His *Life and Strange Surprising Adventures of Robinson Crusoe* (1719), widely considered first English novel, was based on true story of Alexander Selkirk. Crusoe shipwrecked on island for 28 years, 2 months, 19 days; rescues man from cannibals and names him Friday, because that was day it happened. Friday eventually helps Crusoe capture passing ship, and they return to England.

DEGAS, EDGAR (1834–1917) French Impressionist noted for paintings of ballerinas in split-second poses of arrested movement. Studied infinite variety of particular movements that make up dancers' continuous motion. Unlike other Impressionists, a superb master of the line. Helped organize first Impressionist exhibition, 1874. Failing eyesight in later years caused him to abandon precise style for softer, more colorful pastels. Among famous works: *Absinthe* (1876) and *Prima Ballerina* (1876).

DEIGHTON, LEN (1929–   ) British writer of spy novels *The Ipcress File* (1962), *Horse Under Water* (1963), *Billion-Dollar Brain* (1966), *Spy Story* (1974) and *Funeral in Berlin* (1964), in which British agent gets involved with smuggling Russian scientist out of East Berlin with connivance of Russian security officer.

DEJA VU French, meaning "already seen." Altered state of consciousness in which one's environment seems familiar and the future predictable, though both are unknown. May be caused by activity in brain's temporal lobes.

DEKAGRAM. See METRIC PREFIXES

DELAWARE U.S. state located midway between New York City and Washington, D.C. Most of state is flat, with elevations rising only about 60 ft. (18 m.). Highest elevations are within Piedmont province of Appalachians; rise to about 442 ft. (134 m.).

DELAWARE RIVER Forms boundary between New York/Pennsylvania, Pennsylvania/New Jersey and New Jersey/Delaware.

DELILAH Bribed by Philistines to entice Samson into telling her the secret of his strength. Eventually he revealed that his power was in his hair, left uncut because of his Nazarite's vow. She had his seven locks of hair shaved while he slept, weakening him so Philistines could take him prisoner. Story told in Book of Judges.

DELIVERANCE 1972 film directed by John Boorman and

starring Burt Reynolds, Jon Voight, Ned Beatty and Ronny Cox as four men on camping trip through mountain wilderness that turns into terrifying nightmare. Film features musical hit "Dueling Banjos."

DELTIOLOGIST Picture postcard collector. From Greek *deltio* (small writing tablet). Deltiologists of America formed 1960; publish magazine *Deltiology*. J. R. Burdick was U.S. pioneer of postcard collecting.

DEMOCRATIC NATIONAL CONVENTION, 1968 Held in Chicago. Widespread rioting and violence broke out when anti-Vietnam war protesters converged on city. Democratic party already torn apart by war sentiment into "hawks" and "doves."

DEMPSEY, WILLIAM HARRISON (JACK) (1895–1983) Boxer born in Manassa, CO; hence nickname "Manassa Mauler," coined by writer Damon Runyon. Won heavyweight title, July 4, 1919. Lost crown to Gene Tunney, 1926. Rematch in 1927 thwarted by loss to Tunney in 10-round decision: the controversial "long count" fight. After retirement, devoted time to business interests (including Times Square restaurant in New York City) and sports promotion.

DENIM JEANS First worn by adventurers of California Gold Rush, 1849. Made, according to legend, from canvas of covered wagons. Designed to hold up under demanding conditions of Old West.

DENMARK Scandinavian country, in northern Europe, surrounded almost entirely by water. Consists mainly of Jutland Peninsula, which shares 42-mi. (68-km.) border with West Germany to south. Also made up of 482 islands. Flag: red field with two white stripes that intersect slightly left of center. Believed to have come to King Valdemar II from sky during battle in 1219 as victory symbol. Has remained unchanged longer than any other country's flag.

DENNIS THE MENACE Root beer–loving comic strip character created by Hank Ketchum, 1951. Appears in newspapers as daily single-panel and Sunday color strip. His dog's name is Ruff. CBS-TV version, in 1960s, starred Jay North as Dennis.

DENSITY Mass or amount of matter in a unit volume. Equals mass divided by volume. Density of irregularly shaped objects is determined by measuring volume of liquid they displace when submerged.

DENVER, JOHN (1943–) Country/pop singer and songwriter popular in 1970s. Hits include: "Take Me Home, Country Road" (1970), in which he called West Virginia his mountain mama; "Annie's Song" and "Rocky Mountain High" (both 1974); "Thank God I'm a Country Boy" (1975). Born Henry John Deutchendorf, Roswell, NM.

DEOXYRIBONUCLEIC ACID Or DNA. Chief material in chromosomes. Carries genetic information that is passed on, via cell division, from one generation to next. Model of DNA's molecular structure devised by biologists James Watson and Francis Crick.

DES MOINES Capital and largest city in Iowa. Originally inhabited by Indians. U.S. Army built post to protect Indians but viewed them as "untaught children" and took control of area. Indians gave up rights to territory in 1845.

DESERT FOX, THE 1951 war movie starring James Mason as Field Marshal Erwin Rommel. Henry Hathaway directed World War II saga of battle in African desert and Rommel's defeat.

DESIDERATA. See EHRMANN, MAX

D'ESTAING, VALERY GISCARD (1926–) President of France, 1974–1981, and founder of French Independent Party, 1962. Defeated in 1981 by François Mitterrand, a socialist.

DETROIT Largest city in Michigan. Detroit River lies to south, separating U.S. from Canada. City situated directly north of Windsor, Ontario. Hardest-hit city during 1960s civil rights riots. In summer of 1967 five-day riot left 42 dead and over $40 million in property damaged. President Johnson sent army troops to assist police and National Guard in restoring order. Rioting also occurred in black neighborhoods of Watts (Los Angeles), Washington, D.C., and Newark, NJ.

DETROIT RED WINGS National Hockey League team. Winner of seven NHL titles, third-highest among teams in league. Players Ted Lindsay and Gordie Howe teamed with Sid Abel on Wings' "Production Line," 1946–1952. Alex Delvecchio took Abel's place when he retired in 1953.

DEVIL'S ISLAND. See FRENCH GUIANA

DEVLIN, JOSEPHINE BERNADETTE (1948–)

Politician and activist. Elected at age 21 to British House of Commons, April 17, 1969. Youngest woman to occupy seat here. Independent Unity candidate from Belfast; led Ireland's civil rights movement, seeking to prevent discrimination against Catholics.

DEW POINT Temperature at which water vapor in air condenses to liquid water. Dew point depends on humidity of air.

DEWEY DECIMAL SYSTEM Book classification system using numbers 000 to 999 to cover general fields of knowledge and decimals within them to fit specialized areas. Invented 1874 by Melvil Dewey (1851–1931) while acting librarian at Amherst College. Now being replaced by Library of Congress classification system in many libraries.

DIAL M FOR MURDER. See KNOTT, FREDERICK

DIAL SOAP Product of Armour-Dial Inc., Phoenix, AZ. One of country's most successful soap advertising campaigns shows woman showering (from neck up) with caption: "Aren't you glad you use Dial Soap! (Don't you wish everybody did?)."

DIAMOND Crystals of element carbon. Hardest known substance and best heat conductor. Although gem diamonds are colorless (or pale yellow, blue or pink), diamond dust used as abrasive is black. Gem diamonds are judged by four Cs: color, clarity, carat and cut. Simplest gems in chemical composition. Largest ever found: Cullinan, found in South Africa in 1905 and weighing 3,106 carats (about 1¼ lbs.). Largest cut diamond: Star of Africa (530.2 carats), cut from Cullinan in 1908. Roughly two tons of diamonds are mined annually.

DICE Plural of *die*, English word derived from Middle English *de*. Saying "The die is cast," attributed to Julius Caesar at Rubicon River, means irrevocable decision has been made. Dice are small cubes usually made from ivory (called "ivories" by gamblers), bone, wood or plastic. Six sides numberd by one to six dots, placed so sum of dots on opposite sides equals seven. Found in Egyptian tombs and ruins of Babylon; dice playing popular in ancient Greece and Rome. Loaded (fixed) dice found in 1748 at Pompeii, Roman city buried by Mt. Vesuvius, A.D. 79. Total number of dots on two dice: $1+2+3+4+5+6=21$, times $2 = 42$.

DICK AND JANE. See ARBUTHNOT, MAY HILL

DICK VAN DYKE SHOW, THE Popular TV situation

comedy, 1961– 1966. Dick Van Dyke starred as Rob Petrie, head writer of *The Alan Brady Show*. Fellow writers were Buddy Sorvell (Morey Amsterdam) and Sally Rogers (Rose Marie). At home was wife Laura (Mary Tyler Moore) and son Ritchie (Larry Mathews). Carl Reiner portrayed Alan Brady. Rob and Laura resided at 148 Bonnie Meadow Road in New Rochelle, NY.

DICK, ALBERT BLAKE (1856–1934) Inventor. Created mimeograph machine, 1884. Original model had electric pen that perforated type of wax paper to render paper copies. Name comes from Greek words *mime* (to copy) and *graphos* (writing).

DICKENS, CHARLES JOHN HUFFON (1812– 1870) English novelist. Used pseudonym Boz. Among his many popular novels is *Oliver Twist* (1838), depicting world of crime, poverty and the workhouse of 19th-century London. Oliver, a foundling, is raised in workhouse, where he commits unspeakable crime of asking for more gruel for supper—twice. Later becomes pupil of Fagin, head of school for pickpockets; is backward learner, unlike Fagin's prize pupil, the Artful Dodger. *A Christmas Carol* (1843) tells of conversion of Ebenezer Scrooge, "grasping old cheapskate" of whom Dickens wrote: "Darkness was cheap, and Scrooge liked it." Scrooge visited by four ghosts on Christmas Eve—dead partner Jacob Marley and spirits of Christmas Past, Present and Future— who offer him last chance to escape eternal damnation. As evidence of Scrooge's conversion, novel ends "and it was always said of him that he knew how to keep Christmas well, if any man alive possessed the knowledge. May that be truly said of us, and all of us!" And so, as Tiny Tim (lame son of Scrooge's underpaid clerk, Bob Cratchit) observes: "God Bless Us, Every One!" Dickens called this work a "ghostly little book to raise the ghost of an idea" and said he laughed and cried over it as no other story he wrote. *David Copperfield* (1850) is the story of a boy, David, who serves as go-between for coachman Barkis and Clara Peggoty, his nurse. He tells Peggoty "Barkis is willin'," and eventually the two are married. *A Tale of Two Cities* (1859) is set in London and Paris during French Revolution. Novel opens: "It was the best of times, it was the worst of times." *The Mystery of Edwin Drood* (1870) leaves Drood's disappearance unsolved because novel was never finished.

DICKEY, JAMES LAFAYETTE (1923–   ) Ameri-can poet and novelist. Wrote *Into the Stone* (1960) and *Deliverance*

(1969), latter about four Atlanta businessmen on weekend canoe trip who wind up defeated by strength of river. 1972 film version, starring Burt Reynolds and Jon Voight, had Dickey in bit part as Southern sheriff.

DIEM, NGO DINH (1901–1963)   First president of Republic of South Vietnam. Strong anti-Communist and anti-Buddhist Roman Catholic. Backed by U.S. Became increasingly unpopular with his people. Assassinated by own generals in 1963 military coup d'état.

DIEN BIEN PHU   Site of French fortress in Indochina. Fortress lost in battle whose significance for French imperialism in Indochina was equivalent of Napoleon's defeat at Waterloo.

DILLINGER, JOHN (1902–1934)   American outlaw. Famous for bank robberies and prison escapes. FBI public enemy number one, 1933. Ambushed and killed in front of Biograph Theater, Chicago, by FBI agents after betrayal by mysterious "Lady in Red." Has been suggested that another man was killed and that Dillinger escaped.

DiMAGGIO, JOE (1914–   )   Baseball Hall of Famer. New York Yankees center fielder, 1936–1951. Known as "Yankee Clipper" and "Joltin' Joe." Fifty-six-game hitting streak (1941) considered one of baseball's greatest achievements. Was married to Marilyn Monroe. Known today for Mr. Coffee commercials.

DIMENSIONS   There are three in mathematics: height, width and length. Solid figure has all three dimensions; plane figure has two; line has one; point has none. Some mathematicians believe time is fourth dimension.

DINAR   Currency used in Iraq, Jordan, Kuwait, Southern Yemen, Algeria, Tunisia, Yugoslavia. Used in Middle East from 8th to 19th centuries. Brought to Yugoslavia with Turkish invasions.

DING DONG SCHOOL   Educational TV series for pre-schoolers, 1952–1956. Dr. Frances Horwich, known as Miss Frances to viewers, was schoolmarm. Show telecast from Chicago.

DIONNE QUINTUPLETS   Emilie, Marie, Annette, Cecile and Yvonne, born to Oliva and Elzire Dionne in Corbeil, Canada, May 28, 1934. First quintuplets to survive beyond birth. Emilie died, 1954; Marie, 1970.

DIPHALLIC TERATA   From Greek *di* (twice), *phallos* (penis) and *teras* (monster): having partial or complete doubling of penis or clitoris. Usually called diphallus in reference to person or condition.

DIPLOMACY Board game of political strategy and maneuvering; appropriately, favorite game of former Secretary of State Henry Kissinger. Patented by Games Research Inc., 1954. Each player takes role of different country in Europe at turn of century. By waging battles, forming and breaking alliances, and negotiating, players try to capture majority of military bases situated around board. More neighbors a country has, more vulnerable it is. Turkey, with two neighbors, would seem easiest to defend; England, France and Italy each have three.

DIRKS, RUDOLPH (1877–1968) Created cartoon characters Katzenjammer Kids, December 12, 1897, for *The American Humorist*, Sunday supplement of New York *Journal*. Twins Hans and Fritz, also called "the Katzies," rebel against all authority, most often "die Mama," "der Captain" (former shipwrecked sailor acting as their surrogate father) and "der Inspector" (representing school authorities).

DIRTY DOZEN, THE 1967 war movie starring Lee Marvin as tough army major assigned to train 12 convicts for suicidal behind-the-lines mission during World War II. Ernest Borgnine, Jim Brown, Telly Savalas and George Kennedy co-star; Charles Bronson is only member of team to survive.

DIRTY HARRY San Francisco police inspector Harry Callahan wields .44 Magnum and is not afraid to use it. Appears in four films starring Clint Eastwood: *Dirty Harry* (1971), *Magnum Force* (1973), *The Enforcer* (1976) and *Sudden Impact* (1983).

DISEASES Leading causes of death in North America: 1) heart disease, 2) cancer, 3) stroke, 4) motor vehicle accidents, 5) other accidents, 6) chronic lung disease, 7) pneumonia 8) diabetes mellitus, 9) chronic liver disease and cirrhosis, 10) atherosclerosis.

DISMAS AND GESTAS Two robbers crucified next to Jesus Christ. Gestas blamed Christ for their crucifixion. Dismas reprimanded Gestas, earning Christ's forgiveness. St. Dismas is patron saint of people in prison.

DISNEYLAND Three-hundred-acre amusement park at 1313 Harbor Boulevard in Anaheim, CA. Opened 1955; based on characters by entertainment mastermind Walter Elias Disney (1901–1966).

DISPLACED PERSON Or "D.P.": a refugee. "D.P." came into vogue during Vietnam war with advent of Refugee and Immigration Act, 1961.

DISTRICT OF COLUMBIA   Capital of United States. Occupies 67 sq. mi. (110 sq. km.). Formerly in Maryland. Coextensive with city of Washington. Citizens first given right to vote in presidential elections in 1964.

DIXIE   Name associated with American South and title of minstrel song. Origin uncertain. One theory suggests that Citizen's Bank of New Orleans in 1850s issued $10 bills with *dix* ("ten" in French) written on back. Bills were called "dixies" and New Orleans was called "land of dixies."

DIXVILLE NOTCH   New Hampshire town. Population, 37; 27 registered voters. Earliest voters in presidential primaries, casting ballots minutes after midnight on primary day. Tradition began in 1960.

DOBIE GILLIS, THE MANY LOVES OF   TV comedy series starring Dwayne Hickman as Dobie, typical American teenager. Each episode opened with Dobie, next to statue of "the Thinker," pondering his fate. Maynard G. Krebs (Bob Denver) was Dobie's sidekick; Chatsworth Osborne, Jr. (Stephen Franken) was his enemy.

DODGE, MARY MAPES (1831–1905)   American editor and writer of children's books. Edited children's magazine *St. Nicholas* and wrote *Hans Brinker, or The Silver Skates* (1865), novel about poor Brinker family in little Dutch village on Zuider Zee. Hans and sister Gretel enter skating contest; Gretel wins prize of silver skates.

DOG BREEDS   American Kennel Club registered breeds in 1982: 1) poodle, 88,050; 2)cocker spaniel, 87,218; 3) Doberman pinscher, 73,180; 4) Labrador retriever, 62,465; 5) German shepherd, 60,445; 6) golden retriever, 51,045; 7) miniature schnauzer, 36,502; 8) beagle, 35,548; 9) dachshund, 32,835; 10) Shetland sheepdog, 30,512.

DOGS   Bodies function similarly to human bodies; however, dog's body temperature is about 2°F warmer, their hearts beat 40 times a minute faster, and they have cooling sweat glands only on noses and feet, which is why they pant when hot. Smallest dog is Chihuahua, averaging 4 lbs. (1.8 kg.), 5 in. (13 cm.) high at shoulder; named after state in New Mexico. Tallest is Irish wolfhound, up to 34 in. (86 cm.) high. Heaviest is St. Bernard. up to 200 lbs. (90 kg.). Only non-pink-tongued dog is chow chow, which has black tongue. Mexican hairless may have sparse hair on top of head and tip of tail; another hairless breed is the xoloitzcuintli from Mexico.

DOGPATCH. See CAPP, AL

DOLDRUMS Or intertropic convergence zone. Calm region of Atlantic and Pacific oceans near equator, so named because of difficulty sailing there (doldrum means inactivity or stagnation).

DOLLAR BILL Portrait of George Washington depicted on front. On back are two sides of nation's Great Seal. Bill has four eyes in total: Washington's (two), American eagle's (one) and "Eye of Providence," which hovers over pyramid made of 13 stones representing original colonies.

DOLOMITES Part of Alps, located in northeastern Italy and in Austrian Tyrol. Name from Déodat de Dolomieu, who discovered magnesium-calcium rock called dolomite. Highest peak: Marmolada, 10,965 ft. (3,342 m.).

DOLPHIN Small, toothed whale. Mammal unlike fish in that it feeds young with mother's milk and is warm-blooded, thus maintaining steady body temperature. Considered most intelligent animal after man. Travels in groups. Communicates by sounds called phonations.

DOMINIQUE 1963 number one hit single by "the Singing Nun" (Soeur Sourire). Her life story was made into feature film *The Singing Nun* (1966), starring Debbie Reynolds.

DOMINOES Table game brought from China to Europe in 14th century. Made up of 24 (standard Western set) rectangular tiles of wood, ivory, stone, plastic or bone, commonly called "bones" or "pieces." Face of each tile divided by central line, with halves either blank or marked with indented dots called "pips."

DONALD DUCK Walt Disney character. First appeared in 1934; by 1940s had developed into character loved by many. Fan clubs include German Organization for Non-Commercial Supporters of Donaldism.

DONOVAN (1946–   ) Popular singer-songwriter of late 1960s. Among hit records: "Catch the Wind" (1965), "Sunshine Superman" (1966), "Mellow Yellow" (1967) and "Hurdy Gurdy Man" (1968).

DON QUIXOTE. See CERVANTES, MIGUEL DE

DOORS, THE Popular rock-and-roll group of 1960s. Formed

in 1965 by Jim Morrison and Ray Manzarek, with Robby Krieger and John Densmore. Hits include "Light My Fire" (1967), "People Are Strange" (1968) and "Touch Me" (1969). Lead singer Morrison died of heart attack, July 3, 1971.

DOROTHY   Kansas farmgirl, portrayed by Judy Garland in movie *The Wizard of Oz* (1939), who is whisked off via tornado to Land of Oz. Pair of ruby slippers and phrase "There's no place like home" returns her to aunt and uncle.

DOS PASSOS, JOHN (1896–1970)   American novelist. Wrote trilogy *U.S.A.*, composed of *The 42nd Parallel* (1930), *1919* (1932) and *The Big Money* (1936). Featured kaleidoscopic technique combining narration, stream of consciousness, biographies and quotations. Left-wing stance of early novels later tempered into conservative tone.

DOSTOEVSKI, FEODOR (1821–1881)   Russian novelist. Wrote *Brothers Karamazov* (1879–1880), detailing Dimitri's arrest and trial for murder of his father. Other brothers: Ivan, Alyosha and Smerdyakov. Novel reflects social life and intellectual attitudes of 19th-century Russia. Other novels: *Crime and Punishment* (1866) and *The Possessed* (1871).

DOUBLE AXEL   In figure skating: maneuver performed by jumping off forward outside edge of one skate, spinning fully around in air two and a half times and landing on rear outside edge of other skate. Notable for prolonged height attained. Axel: two times around. Triple axel (first performed in competition by Vern Taylor of Canada in 1978 world championships): three times around.

DOUBLE EAGLE II   First balloon to successfully cross Atlantic, August 11–16, 1978. Since 1958, 13 previous attempts had failed. Flight time: 5 days, 17 hours, 6 minutes. Distance: 3,120 mi. (5,023 km.).

DOUBLE-JOINTED   Having joints that allow more movement than normally occurs. Term first cited in 1831. Anatomical reason for such movement unclear; possible cause is added elasticity of ligaments, which secure bones together at joints.

007. See FLEMING, IAN

DOUGLAS, KIRK (1916–   ) Ruggedly handsome American actor who has often eschewed typical leading-man parts for meatier character roles, as in *Champion* (1949), *Lust for Life* (1956), in which he played painter Vincent Van Gogh, *The Vikings* (1958) and *Lonely Are the Brave* (1962).

DOVE   Bird closely related to pigeon. In Bible, Noah sent doves from Ark to find land. They also symbolize peace; hence those opposed to war are often called doves.

DOVER   Capital of Delaware. Major industries include canning and latex products. State's third-largest city, behind Wilmington and Newark.

DOYLE, SIR ARTHUR CONAN (1859–1930)   British physician and author. Abandoned medicine after immediate success of first story featuring detective Sherlock Holmes, "A Study in Scarlet," which appeared originally in *Beeton's Christmas Annual* for 1887 and was published in book form in 1888. There is little doubt that Holmes was named for author-physician Oliver Wendell Holmes, about whom Conan Doyle wrote: "Never have I so known and loved a man I have never seen." The fictitious detective had a giant intellect as well as uncanny deductive powers. Among his distinguished works on various erudite subjects was *Upon the Distinction between the Ashes of Various Tobaccos* ("Precisely 140, Watson"). He lived at 221B Baker Street, where 17 steps led to his second-floor flat and where Dr. Watson was his occasional roommate; previously lived on Montague Street near British Museum. Habits included smoking vile shag tobacco (kept in toe of Persian slipper in cluttered flat) and cigars (kept in coal scuttle). Early in career had "affection" for cocaine, up to three doses a day by 1887; mentioned little in later adventures, may have given it up. Fond of scratching away absentmindedly at violin while in contemplation; also a virtuoso, could calm Watson's nerves with melodious air. Had solved first case as 20-year-old Oxford student and upon graduating had become world's first consulting detective; continued at it for 23 years. Retired when only woman he loved, opera singer Irene Adler, died in 1903. Kept bees on southern slopes of Sussex Downs, accompanied by Mrs. Hudson.

Other characters in 60 Holmes stories include Dr. John Watson, who, upon returning to London after stint in India, met Holmes by answering his advertisement for roommate. Watson became trusted friend and assistant, and chronicler/narrator of Holmes' adventures. Mycroft Holmes, older than Sherlock by seven years (and larger and stouter), was much respected by him for his powers of observation and deduction; nevertheless, Sherlock decried his laziness and lack of ambition. Mycroft was founder and member of Diogenes Club, Pall Mall, which (according to Sherlock) contained the most unsociable and unclubbable men in town." No conversation was allowed at club, where Mycroft could be found from 4:45 to 7:40 most every evening. Arch-enemy Professor James Moriarty posed as mild-mannered math professor but was "Napoleon of Crime" to Holmes and his match intellectually. When they battled physically on edge of Reichenbach Falls in Switzerland, Moriarty plunged to his supposed death (*The Final Problem*). Mrs. Martha Hudson, Holmes' landlady and housekeeper, lived in flat below his. In *The Naval Treaty*, Holmes observed: "Her cuisine is a little limited, but she has as good an idea of breakfast as a Scotswoman."

In the movies, Sherlock Holmes has been basis for films since 1903. Basil Rathbone portrayed the detective in *Hound of the Baskervilles* (1939), with Nigel Bruce as Watson. This team made 13 more films throughout the 1940s, including *The Scarlet Claw* (1944) and *Terror by Night* (1946).

DR. DOOLITTLE   Amiable and extraordinary country doctor created by English-born American writer Hugh Lofting (1886–1947) in 1920. Doolittle's parrot taught him to talk to animals, including strange ones he kept at his home in Puddleby-on-the-Marsh: pet duck named Dab Dab and two-headed llama he called a Pushmi-Pullyu. Stories began as letters written to children during World War I and were illustrated by Lofting himself. Made into movie musical with Rex Harrison, 1967.

DR. KILDARE   Popular TV medical drama of 1960s, starring Richard Chamberlain as Dr. James Kildare. Raymond Massey was Dr. Leonard Gillespie, Kildare's mentor at Blair General Hospital.

DR. NO   1961 film that launched James Bond series. Sean Connery starred as Bond, investigating murders in Jamaica and discovering secret base responsible for sabotaging American rockets.

DR PEPPER   Fruit-flavored drink originated in 1885 at corner store in Waco, Texas. Once the number three soft drink. Advertising campaign shifted in 1982 from seeking national standing to maintaining its stronghold in South and Southwest.

DR. SEUSS. See GEISEL, THEODORE SEUSS

DR. STRANGELOVE   1964 black comedy film directed by Stanley Kubrick. Psychotic Air Force general launches A-bomb attack on Russia while U.S. President Merkin Muffley (played by

Peter Sellers in one of three roles) tries to work with Soviet premier to save the world. Ultimately, bombs are dropped, with actor Slim Pickens riding one out of plane to tune of "We'll Meet Again."

DR. ZHIVAGO 1965 epic motion picture based on Boris Pasternak novel. Omar Sharif and Julie Christie played couple caught in Russian Revolution. "Lara's Theme" helped musical score win Oscar.

DR. ZORBA Chief of surgery at County General Hospital and mentor to young Dr. Ben Casey. Portrayed by Sam Jaffee on popular TV series *Ben Casey* (1961–1966). First name: David.

DRACHMA Official monetary unit of Greece: copper-nickel coin equaling of 100 lepta. Formerly composed of silver. In ancient Greece, equaled six obols.

DRACULA Transylvanian count who became a vampire. Created by Bram Stoker in 1897 novel and portrayed on screen many times since 1923, most notably by Bela Lugosi in *Dracula* (1931) and Christopher Lee in Hammer Studio's *Horror of Dracula* (1958).

DRAFT CARD August 31, 1965, congressional bill provided jail terms and fines for willful destruction of draft cards. Measure aimed at protests against U.S. involvement in Vietnam war.

DRAG RACING In straight-line racing (sprints), track or strip is ¼ mi. (440 yds.) long, with breaking distance of additional ½ mi. Width must be at least 50 ft.

DRAGNET TV crime drama series based on actual cases from Los Angeles Police Department, though "all names were changed to protect the innocent." Jack Webb created and starred in show as Sgt. Joe Friday, whose line "Just the facts, ma'am" became national catchphrase.

DRAGONFLIES Insects that are beneficial to man because they feed on flies and mosquitoes. One of fastest insects, flies 50–60 mph. Some extinct dragonflies had 2½-ft. wingspreads.

DRAMAMINE Antihistaminic drug that prevents motion sickness and controls nausea and vomiting. Reduces activity of central nervous system. May cause drowsiness.

DRAMATIS PERSONAE From Latin; literally, "people of drama." Cast of play, novel, poem or film.

DRAW A BOW. See ARCHERY

DRUGS Chemical substances that cure or prevent disease or alter mental or physical abilities. Drug addiction, sometimes called narcomania, is serious health problem. Most often abused drug is alcohol. Alcoholism is sometimes called dipsomania.

DRUMS   Percussion instrument consisting of hollow cylinder with membrane stretched tightly over one or both ends; tapped or thumped rhythmically by drumstick. Popular instrument in marching bands and jazz and rock groups. Many comedians end jokes with drummer performing "rim shots."

DRURY LANE   London street forming eastern border of Covent Garden, fashionable shopping and dining area. Also, name of theater in London on Catherine Street.

DUBLIN   Capital and largest city of Republic of Ireland. Established by Vikings in mid-800s. Main shopping street, O'Connell, is one of Europe's widest. Situated at mouth of Liffey River, city is busy port and manufacturing area.

DUBROVNIK. See YUGOSLAVIA

DUCK-BILLED PLATYPUS   Or spiny anteater. Native to Australia, considered mammal because it has hair and nurses its young. Only egg-laying mammal. Has bill like duck's, no teeth and webbed feet; lives near streams.

DUCKING THE BOOM   Bending low on deck to avoid being hit by boom, horizontal pole to which bottom of sail is attached. Boom swivels around mast to keep sail at proper angle to wind. If boat or wind direction shifts, boom can swing fast.

DUKE OF EARL   Hit song by Gene Chandler (1962), in which nothing can stop the Duke of Earl. Other Chandler hits include "Just Be True" (1964) and "Nothing Can Stop Me" (1965).

DULLES INTERNATIONAL AIRPORT   Washington, DC, airport dedicated in 1962 to John Foster Dulles (1888–1959), secretary of state under President Eisenhower. Dulles was most traveled American secretary of state in his time, flying nearly 500,000 mi. (800,000 km.) and making over 60 trips abroad.

DUM DUM INTERNATIONAL AIRPORT. See INDIA, AIRPORTS

DUMAS, ALEXANDRE (1802–1870)   French novelist. Published almost 300 books, working with group of nameless collaborators. Accused of stealing plots and rewriting history. Among best-known works is *The Count of Monte Cristo* (1844), in which Edmond Dantes, falsely inprisoned for political reasons, escapes, finds treasure on island of Monte Cristo and returns as nobleman to gain revenge. In *The Three Musketeers* (1844), Athos, Porthos and Aramis, joined by penniless d'Artagnan, were heroic members of Louis XIII's bodyguard in 17th-century France. With motto "All for one, one for all," they battled evil Cardinal Richelieu. Novel based on historic figures; had two sequels.

DUMBO 1941 animated feature by Walt Disney. Circus elephant, Mrs. Jumbo, receives visit from stork, and her child is nicknamed Dumbo because of his especially big ears. With help of his only friend (a mouse) and some crows, Dumbo learns to fly.

DUNCAN TAVERN HISTORIC SHRINE Kentucky tourist attraction consisting of Duncan Tavern and Anne Duncan House. Tavern built in 1788 of limestone and furnished with period pieces; watering hole to Daniel Boone. Anne Duncan, the tavern keeper's widow, built house next door in 1800.

DUNGRI Section of Bombay, India, where denim fabric originated. Dungarees, or blue jeans, are made from this sturdy, coarse material.

DUNKIRK Port Dunkerque (Dunkirk), France, scene of German blockade of Allied forces in World War II. On June 4, 1940, 850 British vessels rescued approximately 200,000 British and French trapped here and were escorted safely across English Channel under cover of Royal Air Force.

DUODECIMAL SYSTEM Numerical system based on 12 rather than 10 (as in decimal system). Inch and foot units of measurement form duodecimal system because there are 12 inches to the foot.

DU PONT Largest chemical company in the world, founded in 1802 by Eleuthère Irénée du Pont de Nemours. First made gunpowder and explosives. Dacron and Orlon fibers and Teflon are Du Pont products.

DURAN, ROBERTO (1951–) Defeated Sugar Ray Leonard on June 20, 1980, in "Brawl in Montreal": welterweight championship fight in Montreal's Olympic Stadium, site of Leonard's 1976 Olympic gold medal triumph. Duran won close, unanimous 15-round decision in fight called one of hardest-hitting of all time. Leonard won rematch with 8th-round TKO in New Orleans, November 25, 1980.

DURANTE, JIMMY (1893–1980) Comedian famous for his long nose, or "schnozzola." Theme song: "Inka Dinka Doo." Ended performances with: "Goodnight, Mrs. Calabash, wherever you are." Films include *Little Miss Broadway* (1938), *The Great Rupert* (1950) and *Jumbo* (1962).

DURBAN South Africa's chief eastern seaport and most popular resort area, founded in 1834. Noted for trade and industry. Bay Beach and Indian Market's jewelry, fruit and herb stalls are major tourist attractions.

DUROCHER, LEO (1906–) Baseball player and manager of New York Giants, who uttered famous remark: "Nice guys finish last" (also title of 1975 autobiography). Remark intended to explain why scrappy player Eddie Stanky was doing well and the Giants, with better players, were in last place. "They're nice guys," Durocher said, "but they think they're giving you 100% on the ballfield, and they're not."

DUSTMAN British slang for garbage collector. Besides usual meaning, "dust" in England refers to household refuse; hence also "dust bin" for garbage can and "dust cart" for garbage truck.

DUVALIER, FRANCOIS (1907–1971) Oppressive dictator of Haiti, 1957–1971. Liked to be called "Papa Doc." Succeeded by son Jean Claude Duvalier, 1971.

DYER, WAYNE (1940–) Author of *Your Erroneous Zones: Bold but Simple Techniques for Eliminating Unhealthy Behavior Patterns* (1976), an indictment of the "psychological establishment." Claims mental health is only common sense. "Erroneous zones" are areas of self-defeating behavior. Book advocates living for the moment.

DYLAN, BOB (1941–) Born Robert Zimmerman in 1941. Influential folk/rock singer and songwriter with folk hits "Blowin' in the Wind," "A Hard Rain's A-Gonna Fall," etc., in early 1960s. Made electric debut in 1965 at Newport Folk Festival backed by rock band. Later hits include "Like a Rolling Stone" (1965) and "Lay, Lady, Lay" (1969).

DYNAMITE Nitroglycerin-based explosive, trinitrotoluene (TNT), invented in 1867 by Alfred Nobel, who also founded Nobel Prize. Patented, 1875; also called blasting gelatin. U.S. annual industrial use: roughly 2½ million lbs. (1,130,000 kg.).

E

E Most written letter in English, used once in every eight letters. Derived from Egyptian hieroglyph and Phoenician and Hebrew sign "he." Most used because it has replaced vowels *a*, *i*, *o* and *u* of Old English words; for example, modern *when* comes from Old English *hwanne*. Most common initial letter in English is *t*.

E PLURIBUS UNUM The Great Seal of the U. S., adopted June 20, 1789. Depicts American bald eagle in whose beak is a ribbon with the words *E Pluribus Unum*, Latin meaning "from the many, one."

E = MC² Formula relating mass and energy. Developed by Albert Einstein. Reveals that a very small amount of mass, if completely transformed into energy, can produce an extremely large amount of energy. E stands for energy, m for mass, and c for the speed of light, squared.

EAGLETON, THOMAS (1929–   ) McGovern's running mate against President Richard Nixon, 1972. Reporters uncovered Eagleton had been hospitalized for depression. McGovern, who originally backed Eagleton "1000 percent," was forced to drop him.

EARDRUM, THE Tympanic membrane. Important organ for hearing. Stretched across end of auditory canal, much like a drumhead. Sound waves travel through air, strike eardrum, cause it to vibrate. Vibrations are transmitted to inner ear where they are converted to nerve signals and sent to brain.

EARHART, AMELIA (1897–1937) Pioneer in aviation. First woman to fly across the Atlantic Ocean (1928), first woman to cross it solo (1932), and first woman to earn the Distinguished Flying Cross. Disappeared somewhere near Howland Island in the Pacific Ocean while attempting to fly around the world, 1937.

EARN YOUR VACATION TV quiz show of summer, 1954. Host Johnny Carson would select members of studio audience to participate in question-and-answer game, in which prize would be their dream vacation.

EARP, WYATT. See O.K. CORRAL

EARTH Four-and-one-half billion years old. Land area, about 30% of total surface area; water area about 70%. Roughly 70% of earth underwater. Deepest part of ocean: Challenger Deep, Pacific, 36,198 ft. (11,033 m.) below surface. Average ocean depth, 12,450 ft. (3,795 m.). Traveling at a speed of 66,600 mi. (107,200 km.) per hour, one orbit around the sun, a sidereal year, takes 365 days, six hours, nine minutes and 9.54 seconds. Covers a distance of 595 million mi. (958 million km.). Weighs 6.6 sextillion or 6,600 billion billion short tons (6.0 sextillion metric tons).

EARTH'S WATER Earth contains more than 300 million cubic mi. of water. 97% percent is in the oceans and another 2% is frozen in glaciers and icecaps. About 1% is drinkable fresh water in lakes, rivers, underground and in the air.

EARTHBALL Informal game played with inflated ball several feet in diameter (largest ball used in sports). No player limits, time limits, referees, or formal rules. Ball placed in middle of large field. Opposing teams start on opposite goal lines, rush ball and try to get it across opponent's goal line. Game is good-humored, spontaneous, and limited in time only by players' energy.

EARTHQUAKES Ground movements caused by sliding of rock within the Earth's crust. Focus of an earthquake is area of movement within crust. Epicenter is point on surface directly above focus. About 6000 earthquakes a year are detected worldwide, but only 15 are very destructive.

EARTHWORM Found throughout the world. Some, several feet long. Although legless and eyeless, some have five hearts. All are both male and female, but never mate themselves.

EAST BERLIN Capital of East Germany, Communist ruled.

Separated from West Berlin by Berlin Wall. An unmarked grass-covered mound is all that remains of the bunker in which Adolf Hitler died.

EAST GERMANY   Five largest cities in East Germany:

Name	Approximate population
East Berlin	1,128,983
Leipzig	563,980
Dresden	514,508
Karl-Marx-Stadt	313,850
Magdeburg	283,109

EAST IS EAST   According to Rudyard Kipling's 1889 poem "The Ballad of East and West,": "Oh, east is east, and west is west, and never the twain shall meet; Till Earth and sky stand presently at God's great Judgment Seat."

EASTER   Celebrated by Christians to commemorate resurrection of Christ. Since marked on religious calendar, does not fall on same date annually. Celebrated on first Sunday after first full moon after vernal equinox.

EASTER ISLAND   Chilean island in eastern Pacific Ocean. Famous for giant prehistoric monuments called Mauis, carved from volcanic stone. Discovered by Dutch navigator Jacob Roggeveen on Easter Sunday, 1772.

EASY RIDER   Influential, low-budget feature film, 1969, directed by Dennis Hopper. Hopper and Peter Fonda (wearing a stars-and-stripes-decorated helmet) set out on their motorcycles to "find America." Jack Nicholson became a star after his Oscar-nominated supporting role in this film.

EATING BREAD AND HONEY   Second verse, "Sing a Song of Sixpence": "The king was in the countinghouse, Counting out his money; The Queen was in the parlor Eating bread and honey."

EATING HABITS   Carnivore: eats animal flesh, e.g. dolphin. Herbivore: eats plants, e.g. horse. Insectivore: eats insects, e.g. aardvark. Omnivore: eats plants and animals, e.g. human being.

EBONY   Leading national magazine aimed at black readers, selling 1.4 million copies monthly, ranking 44th among U.S. general interest magazines. Its closest competitor, *Jet*, sells 760,000 weekly. Company also publishes *Ebony Jr.*, a children's magazine.

ECUADOR   Small South American country. Lies between Colombia and Peru. Andes Mountains occupy much of country. The equator (*ecuador* in spanish) crosses the country giving it its name.

EDAM, NETHERLANDS   Town in Netherlands, where well-known red-crusted Edam cheese is produced. Gouda and Leydan cheeses are also made here.

EDERLE, GERTRUDE (1906–   )   American swimmer. First woman to swim English Channel (France to England), 1926. Broke existing men's record with time of 14 hrs., 34 min., from Cape Gris-Nez to Deal, England on August 6, 1926. Had won two bronze medals in sprints in 1924 Olympics. Florence Chadwick of U.S. first woman to swim Channel from England to France, 1951. England's Matthew Webb first to make crossing (England to France), 1875.

EDISON, THOMAS ALVA (1847–1931)   Improved or invented more than 1000 devices including the electric light, typewriter, motion picture camera (first American to register for a patent), stock ticker and telephone. Patented phonograph in 1877. The first words he recorded were, "Mary had a little lamb." Called Prince of Light. Quoted as having said: "Everything comes to him who hustles while he waits." Described as "1% inspiration and 99% perspiration." In 1876 moved to Menlo Park, NJ, and established laboratory of the same name. It was here that he invented electric light, earning title, The Wizard of Menlo Park.

EDSEL   Car introduced by Ford's Lincoln-Mercury Division in 1957 after massive market research and public relations. Named for Edsel Ford, only son of Henry Ford and father of then Ford Company president Henry Ford II. Car, with its distinctive horse-collar grille, was a failure, lasting three model years 1958–1960. 110,000 total produced.

EDWARD VIII (1894–1972)   Duke of Windsor. Son of King George V and Queen Mary. Became King of England, January 1936. Fell in love with twice-divorced American woman Wallis Warfield Simpson, beginning what was to become the "world's greatest romance." British government opposed to accepting Simpson as Queen. After a 325-day reign, Edward abdicated the throne, finding it impossible "to carry the heavy burden of responsibility and to discharge my duties as king as I would wish to do without the help and support of the woman I love." They later married. Edward went into self-imposed exile.

EGGS Produced by nearly all anir .als. Purpose, to produce young. Chicken egg composition: 65.5% water, 12% protein, 11.5% minerals, and 11% fat. Yolk contains most calories, fat, iron and half of the protein and riboflavin. Scrambled, 20% less riboflavin than hard-boiled. The average hen lays 200 or more per year. White leghorn variety lays 300 per year. Chicken eggs must be kept at 100°F for 21 days to hatch. Annual consumption of eggs per person per year, steadily declining from 334 in 1960 to 263 in 1982. Annual egg production per hen increasing from 174 in 1950 to 235 in 1976.

EGYPT Over a million tourists visit each year to see pyramids, Great Sphinx in Giza, and ancient tombs in Valley of the Kings. Travelers are required to donate $3 to save monuments in ancient region of Nubia.

EHRMANN, MAX (1872–1945) Indiana-born poet and writer of science fiction and fantasy stories. Actually wrote "Desiderata" (1927), poem allegedly discovered in Old St. Paul's Church, Baltimore, MD, dated 1692—according to inscription on poster widely circulated since 1960s. Adlai Stevenson gave copies bearing Ehrmann's credit to contributors to his presidential campaign, 1956. Opening line is, "Go placidly amid the noise and haste, and Remember what peace there may be in silences."

EICHMANN, ADOLF (1906–1962) Lieutenant colonel in German S.S., World War II. Supervised deportation of Jews and other minorities from Germany and German-occupied countries to concentration camps where millions were killed. After war, escaped to Argentina. Lived on Garibaldi Street in Buenos Aires. Seized there by Israeli agents and taken back to Israel, 1960. Tried for war crimes and hanged, 1962.

EIFFEL TOWER Built in Paris, by French engineer Alexandre Gustave Eiffel (1832–1923) for Paris World's Fair in 1889. Stands 984 ft. (300 m.) from base. Elevators and stairways of 1792 steps lead to top. Used for military observation in World War I, experiments and television transmission since. Cost over million U.S. dollars to build.

EINSTEIN, ALBERT (1879–1955) German-born American physicist. At age 26, advanced Theory of Relativity. Stated that nothing can move faster than speed of light. Theory laid basis for the release of atomic energy. Informed President Roosevelt, 1939, of possibility of building an atomic bomb. In describing his quantum theory said, "God does not play dice." Declined Israel's 1952 offer to become president, claiming he was unsuitable for the job and knew nothing about human relations.

EISENHOWER, GENERAL DWIGHT DAVID (IKE) (1890–1969)   Thirty-fourth U.S. president. Directed Allies, invasion of Normandy, June 6, 1944. First president on color television, 1955; also held first televised news conference, January 19, 1955, at the State Department. The president had been given tips on how to act on camera by actor Robert Montgomery. News conference was edited for later broadcast. During World War II, unspoken qualification for officers on his staff was playing bridge.

EL DORADO   Rumored City of Gold. Spanish explorer Francisco Coronado led expedition through American Southwest into present-day Kansas in search of it, 1540. No gold was found.

EL GORDO   Literally "The Fat One." Spain's national, government-run lottery. Gives most prize money in world—equivalent of U.S. $334 million awarded in 1983, split 46 ways, was $7.3 million, with 10,419 prizes in all. Tickets (in 1983) cost equivalent of U.S. $158, which is often divided into shares.

EL GRECO (c.1548–1614)   Greek-born (on Crete) painter, sculptor and architect, who lived in Spain most of his life. Emigrated to Italy as young man; in Venice, influenced by Titian and Tintoretto. Lived in Toledo, Spain, after 1577, becoming Spanish citizen and introducing Renaissance elements into Spanish painting. Painted *The Burial of Count Orgaz* (1586), and *Martyrdom of St. Maurice and Theban Legion* (1584).

EL SALVADOR   Smallest Central American country. Area 8,124 sq. mi. (21,041 sq. km.). Bordered by Guatemala on northwest, Honduras to northeast, Pacific Ocean to south. About one-half country's annual income is earned by 3% of population. Western hemisphere's most densely populated country, with approximately 645 persons per sq. mi. (249 per sq. km.). Total population is about 5,323,000.

ELDER, LEE (1934–   )   First black player in prestigious Masters golf tournament. Players must win major tournament to qualify for following year's event; Elder won 1974 Monsanto Open to qualify for 1975 Masters. First qualified for PGA tour in 1967 after years on all-black United Golf Association circuit.

ELECTROCARDIOGRAM Or ECG. A technique doctors use to record electrical activity in the heart. Electrodes which can detect currents in the heart are placed on a patient's skin and a graph of electrical activity is produced. This graph can be used to detect or monitor certain heart malfunctions.

ELEMENTS, FOUR GREAT Elements are substances which all matter can be broken down. Over 100 known elements, although ancient Greeks believed there were only four: earth, wind, fire and water.

ELEPHANT Largest land animal and second-longest-living land mammal after man, living 60 or more years. The largest known stood 13 ft. 2 in. at the shoulder and weighed 12 tons. Only the giraffe is taller. Elephants can run 25 mph. (40 kph.) and raise their trunks when threatened. Can be trained to ride bicycles and stand on their heads, but cannot jump. The two species, African and Indian, can be distinguished by large ears of the African. Are the only mammals with four knees. Also, only Indian variety are trained. Do not drink through their trunks.

ELEPHANT AND CASTLE Busy traffic center in London. Named after former pub. Redesigned in 1957–64 as two round-abouts with a shopping precinct. Also the name of a subway stop on London's Underground system.

11 DOWNING STREET London residence of Britain's financial minister, Chancellor of the Exchequer, who prepares annual budget and is Cabinet member. Term "exchequer" comes from Old French *eschequier* ("chessboard") and it refers to medieval custom of calculating revenues on checkered table.

ELIOT, GEORGE (MARY ANN EVANS) (1819–1880) English novelist. Adopted male pseudonym (1857) for contemporary acceptance in 19th-century England. Among her famous works: *Adam Bede* (1859); *The Mill on the Floss* (1860); *Silas Marner* (1861); and *Middlemarch* (1871).

ELIOT, THOMAS STERNS (T. S.) (1888–1965) American-born English poet, critic and dramatist. Became British subject 1927. Known for *Murder in the Cathedral*, a drama in verse set in England's Canterbury Cathedral, dealing with assassination of St. Thomas à Becket, and *The Waste Land*, a lengthy poem.

ELIZABETH I (1533-1603)   Queen of England, 1558-1603. Daughter of Henry VIII, who declared her illegitimate after he beheaded her mother, Anne Boleyn. After his death, her place in line of succession to throne was restored. Never married, thus became known as the Virgin Queen. Also referred to as Good Queen Bess.

ELIZABETH II, QUEEN ALEXANDRA MARY (1926-   )   Queen of England, 1952-present. Also known as Defender of the Faith. Eldest daughter of King George VI. Married distant cousin Prince Philip Mountbatten, November 20, 1947, in Westminster Abbey. June 2, 1952, four months after her father's death, crowned Queen. Mother of: Charles Philip Arthur George, 1948, Prince of Wales and current heir to throne; Anne Elizabeth Alice Louise, 1950; Andrew Albert Christian Edward, 1960; and Edward Anthony Richard Louis, 1964. Queen's royal tour, 1953-1954, included visit to New Zealand, December, 1953, first visit by a reigning British king or queen. From there she delivered her Christmas address; first time it was not made from Great Britain. In the January 5, 1953 issue of *Time* magazine, Queen was distinguished as their "Man of the Year." In her case, however, cover read: "Woman of the Year."

ELLINGTON, DUKE (1899-1974)   Popular orchestra leader, piano player, and composer of the 1930s, '40s and '50s. Compositions include: "Mood Indigo" (1931), "Sophisticated Lady" (1933), and "It Don't Mean a Thing" (1932). Later hits "Take the A Train" and "Satin Doll" became his theme songs.

ELLSBERG, DANIEL (1931-   )   One time U.S. military strategist and Vietnam War hawk. Grew disillusioned and, as a result, provided New York *Times* with Pentagon Papers, classified studies of U.S. involvement in Indochina from World War II through late 1960s. Indicted, 1971. Charges dropped, 1973.

ELMER GANTRY   Acclaimed 1960 film about an opportunist (Burt Lancaster) who teams up with traveling evangelist show headed up by girl (Jean Simmons), while newspaperman (Arthur Kennedy) and a prostitute (Shirley Jones) try to expose them. Lancaster won Best Actor Oscar and Jones took Best Supporting Actress Award for performances.

ELMER J. FUDD   Famed "wabbit" hunter and archenemy of

Bugs Bunny. Voiced from 1939 through 1957 by actor Arthur Q. Bryan.

ELYSEE PALACE   Official residence of France's presidents since 1873. Built in 1718 by Claude Mollet for Count d'Everux. Became King's residence in 1764. Napoleon resigned here in 1815.

EMMANUEL III, VICTOR (1869–1947)   Last royal king of Italy, 1900–1946. In an attempt to avoid civil war, called upon Mussolini to form a cabinet. Mussolini was later to become fascist premier. King died in exile.

EMBRACEABLE EWES   Cheerleaders for Los Angeles Rams of National Football League. Popularity of Dallas Cowboy cheerleaders in 1970s inspired many other NFL teams to recruit their own squads to increase fan interest. Others include Buffalo Jills and San Diego Chargettes.

EMERALD   Hexagonal (six-sided) dark green stone. Said by the Roman Pliny to have "out-greened nature." May's birthstone. Thought to signify love and success. Variety of mineral beryl.

EMPIRE STATE BUILDING, THE   Located in New York City. 1,250 ft. (381 m.) high with 102 stories. Completed in 1931 at cost of U.S. $40,948,900. World's fourth tallest skyscraper. Made of 10 million bricks. Erected on site of old Waldorf-Astoria Hotel. Once New York City's tallest skyscraper. At 9:49 A.M. on July 28, 1945, a twin-engined B-25 bomber lost in dense fog crashed into the building. 78th and 79th floors destroyed. Thirteen killed including the three crew members.

EMPIRE STRIKES BACK, THE   1980 film sequel to *Star Wars* (1977). Continues battle by Rebels against the Empire and introduces new characters: Lando Calrissian portrayed by Billy Dee Williams; and Yoda, a troll-like mentor to Luke Skywalker, who teaches Luke the ways of the Jedi.

ENAMEL   Hard, white tissue covering the crown of teeth. Enables them to withstand pressure, heat and cold. Wears with age revealing yellowish dentin underneath. Hardest substance in the body.

ENCEPHALITIS   Inflammation of brain. Pressure caused by swelling results in headache. May also cause convulsions, coma or death. Result of viral infection; symptoms may take years to appear.

ENDLESS SUMMER, THE   Feature-length 1966 film documentary about two surfers looking for the "perfect wave." Glorious footage of surfing spots worldwide captures beauty and exhilaration of the sport. Directed, written and photographed by Bruce Brown.

ENGLISH World's second-most-spoken language, with about 358 million speakers. Mandarin Chinese with 650 million is first, Russian third, and Spanish fourth. English evolved from languages of Angles and Saxons, original inhabitants of British Isles, with additions from conquerors Romans (Latin) and Normans (Norman French).

ENGLISH CHANNEL, THE Arm of North Sea separating France and England. Length: 350 mi. (563 km.). Width 21–100 mi. (34–160 km.). Narrowest point is between Dover, England, and Calais, France, called the Strait of Dover. These are usual points used for the English Channel swim. Other English points used— South Foreland, Shakespeare Beach and Deal; other French point used—Cape Gris-Nez and Sangatte. French call channel La Manche, meaning "the sleeve." England and France believed to be connected before Channel formed.

ENOLA GAY U.S. B-29 bomber. Dropped atomic bomb "Little Boy" on Hiroshima, Japan, 9:15 A.M., August 6, 1945. Pilot, Colonel Paul Warfield Tibbets (named Enola Gay for his mother); bombadier, Major Thomas Ferebee. Approximately 78,000 killed instantly, 70,000 wounded, and 10,000 unaccounted for. The uranium fission bomb roughly equivalent to 20,000 tons TNT. Ferebee's immediate log entry, "My God." Second bomb dropped on port city of Nagasaki, August 9, 1945. Japan formally surrendered to U.S., August 14. The bombings occurred eleven days after Truman, Churchill and Chiang Kai-Shek issued an ultimatum to Japan to surrender unconditionally. No mention of newly created bomb was made. Japan refused.

ENTEBBE RAID Palestinian terrorists hijacked French airplane to Entebbe, Uganda, 1976. Over 100 passengers held hostage for one week. Israeli commandoes led surprise raid, July 4, to rescue hostages, freeing 103. One commando, three hostages, seven hijackers and 20 Ugandan soldiers killed in crossfire.

ENTERPRISE First atomic-powered aircraft carrier. Launched September 24, 1961, Newport News, VA. Fueled by eight nuclear reactors. Capable of cruising five years without refueling.

EQUATOR Purely imaginary band circling the earth, 90° at every point from north and south poles. In the beginning, the Greeks recognized the earth's shape as spherical. We now know that the earth is an irregular sphere bulging at the equator and flattening out at the north and south poles. Hottest days: March 21 and September 23 (vernal and autumnal equinoxes), when sun is 90° above horizon. Passes through following countries: Brazil, Colombia and Equador (South America); Congo, Gabon, Kenya, Somalia, Uganda and Zaire (Africa); and Indonesia.

EQUINOXES Occur twice annually when the sun is directly above the equator, making both day and night twelve hours long. Vernal equinox occurs in March; autumnal equinox occurs in September.

ERDMAN, PAUL E. (1932–   ) Canadian-born American novelist. Writes about high finance. Wrote *The Billion-Dollar Sure Thing* (1973), *The Silver Bears* (1974), and *The Crash of '79* (1976), in which Saudi Arabians hire retired banker to improve world banking's treatment of Saudis. In process, he observes events that lead to war in Middle East and crash of Western economies.

ERLICHMAN, JOHN DANIEL (1925–   ) Domestic affairs assistant to President Richard Nixon, 1969–74. Played major role in Watergate scandal. Resigned; convicted of conspiracy, obstruction of justice and perjury (1975), imprisoned (1976), and released (1978). *The Company* (1976), thinly disguised novel of Watergate affair, features President Richard Monckton, a hate-filled, self-deluded moralizer.

ERVIN, SAM (1896–   ) North Carolina Democratic Senator. Chairman of Senate Select Committee that investigated Nixon's relation to corruption of his administration and Watergate affair, 1973.

ESKIMO ROLL Stunt roll used in canoeing or kayaking. Paddler leans to one side of boat, causing it to capsize, then rights it with hip movement, coming up on opposite side to complete continuous circular motion. Record is 1000 times in 65 min., 39.3 sec., set by Bruce Parry in Australia, 1977.

ESPERANTO Most successful attempt at inventing artificial universal language. Based mainly on Romance languages, has all its nouns end in o. Invented by Dr. Esperanto, pseudonym of Polish eye doctor and linguist Ludwik Lazanz Zamenhof (1859–1917) in *Fundamento de Esperanto* (1905). Language's name derived from Latin-type word for optimist.

ETHIOPIA   Country in northeastern Africa. Name means "sun-burned faces" in Greek. Formerly called Abyssinia, referred to as such in Old Testament. Early inhabitants arrived about 1500 B.C. Coffee is major export crop.

EUCALYPTUS   Large tree native to Australia. There are several species. Noted for their fragrance and because koala bears will eat only eucalyptus leaves in the wild.

EUCHRE   Game played with 32-card "piquet pack," eliminating all below the seven. In trump suit, the jack (called right bower) is highest. Other jack of the same color as trump (red or black) becomes second-highest trump (left bower).

EUCLID (c. 300 B.C.)   Greek mathematician. Laid foundations for modern geometry. One of his fundamental assumptions: given a straight line and a point not on it, only one straight line through that point is parallel to given line.

EUPHRATES RIVER   One of western Asia's longest rivers. Rises in mountains of Turkey and flows 2,235 mi. (3,597 km.) into the Persian Gulf. Irrigates Iraq's farms.

EUREKA   California state motto adopted in 1849. From Greek word *heureka* meaning "I have found it." Refers to California's successful gold rush.

EUROPE, COUNTRIES BEGINNING WITH "A"

Countries starting with an "A":	*Countries ending with an "A":*
Albania	Bulgaria
Andorra	Czechoslovakia
Austria	Malta
Albania	Romania
Andorra	Russia
Austria	Yugoslavia

EUROPE, EXTREMITIES

Outermost points in Continental Europe:
Southernmost point— Cape Tarifa, Spain
Northernmost point—North Cape, Norway
Easternmost point—Eural Mountains,. Soviet Union
Westernmost point—Cape Roca, Portugal

EUROPE, LARGEST COUNTRIES

1.	Soviet Union	2,151,000 sq. mi.	(5,592,600 sq. km.)
2.	France	210,038 sq. mi.	(543,998 sq. km.)
3.	Spain	194,881 sq. mi.	(504,742 sq. km.)
4.	Sweden	173,665 sq. mi.	(449,792 sq. km.)

EUROPEAN ECONOMIC COMMUNITY   Also called Common Market. Established 1958 to integrate economies of western Europe. Founding members: Belgium, France, Luxembourg, The Netherlands and West Germany. In 1973, Great Britain, Ireland, and Denmark were admitted as members. Greece was last country admitted, 1979.

EUROPEAN FOLK DANCING   Fandango (Spain) and Laendler (Austria)—dances based on gestures of courtship. Sword Dance (Scotland)—celebrates battle victories. Tarantella (Italy)—originated as technique for curing tarantula bite.

EUSTON STATION   One of 16 British Rail stations in London. Lines are Northern Line and Victorian Line. Situated on Eversholt Street off Euston Road.

EVEN-NUMBERED PAGES   Usually on left-hand side of a book. Modern printing allows printing on both sides of page, odd-numbered pages follow page one on right side, even-numbered pages on back, or left side.

EVERGLADES NATIONAL PARK   Located on southwestern tip of Florida. Contains Gumbo Limbo trail, and Anhinga trail, a boardwalk leading into jungle where tropical plants and swamp animals are found.

EWBANK, WEEB (1907–   )   Coached New York Jets in American and National Football Leagues, 1963–1973, including 16-7 win over Baltimore Colts in Super Bowl III, January 1969. Also coached Colts to 1958 and 1959 NFL championships. Only man to coach champions in both leagues. Member Pro Football Hall of Fame.

EXEMPLI GRATIA (E.G.)   Latin, meaning "for example." Literally, "for the sake of example." Properly abbreviated (e.g.) only when used to introduce example. Sometimes usage confused with i.e., *id est*, or "that is."

EXORCIST, THE   Hit 1973 horror film about a 12-year-old girl, Regan MacNeil (portrayed by Linda Blair), who is possessed by the Devil. Max von Sydow played the title role.

EXPLORER I   First American satellite in orbit. Launched February 1, 1958, nearly four months after the U.S.S.R. launched its first satellite, Sputnik II. Explorer I collected scientific data.

EXPO 70. See OSAKA, JAPAN

EXXON   America's leading corporation in sales. Followed by Mobil and General Motors. Before AT&T broke up in 1983, it claimed highest percentage of profits, assets and market value.

EYE—IRIS   Round, colored disk behind the cornea. Color derives from melanin; brown eyes have more melanin than blue. Black opening in center called the pupil. Dilator and sphincter muscles regulate pupil size, controlling how much light enters the eye.

EYE OF THE NEEDLE, THE   1981 film based on Ken Follett best seller. Donald Sutherland stars as "Die Nagel," a German agent during World War II stranded on a British island where he meets a lonely woman (portrayed by Kate Nelligan).

F

F TROOP Television comedy series premiered September 1965, about the incompetent personnel of Fort Courage during the late 1800s. Ken Berry starred as Capt. Wilton Parmenter, Forrest Tucker as Sgt. Morgan O'Rourke, and Larry Storch, Corporal Randolf Agarn.

F.A. CUP. See WEMBLEY STADIUM

FABARES, SHELLY (1944–   ) Television actress who started as a teenager in the '50s. Played Mary Stone on The Donna Reed Show (1958-1966); had hit record, "Johnny Angel," in 1962; was a regular on other series, *The Little People* (1972), *The Practice* (1976), *Forever Fernwood* (1977), and since 1978, *One Day at a Time.*

FAHRENHEIT, GABRIEL DANIEL (1686–1736) German physicist who developed Fahrenheit temperature scale. First to make a thermometer with mercury instead of alcohol; enabled more accurate measure.

FAIL-SAFE 1964 thriller directed by Sidney Lumet. Henry Fonda stars as the president who faces the crisis of a plane accidently ordered to bomb Moscow. (see BURDICK, EUGENE)

FAISAL. See KING FAISAL

FALCONRY Sport employing the training of falcons, hawks and other predatory birds in pursuit of game. Dates from Assyria, 7th century, and flourished during the Middle Ages. Still practiced in Europe, U.S, and other parts of the world.

FALLOPIAN TUBES Two tubes in the female reproductive

system which lie near ovaries. Approximately once every 28 days, ovulation occurs: ovary releases an egg which is carried by fallopian tube to the uterus. If unfertilized, egg dies and is discharged during menstruation. Tubes removed in a hysterectomy.

FALLOW   Or summer fallow. Land kept free of vegetation for one crop season to allow storage of moisture for the next year's crop. A practice of dry farming, the production of crops without irrigation.

FANDANGO. See EUROPE, FOLK DANCING

FANEUIL HALL   Built in Boston by Peter Faneuil in 1742 as a public market and meeting place. Scene of colonial protests before American Revolution. Today it has a library, historical paintings and a military museum.

FANGIO, JUAN MANUEL (1911–   )   Italian-born Argentine race car driver. Won five World Grand Prix Championships (1951, 1954, 1955, 1956, 1957) for four different manufacturers (Alfa Romeo, Mercedes Benz, Maserati, Ferrari). Won 24 Grand Prix races before retiring after 1958 French Grand Prix. Oldest driver to win World Championships (46 years, 55 days old when he last won, August 18, 1957).

FANTASTICKS, THE   Long-running off-Broadway musical about a set of parents hoping their children will fall in love and marry. Opened in New York in 1960. Songs by Tom Jones and Harvey Schmidt, including "Try to Remember."

FARINE, JEAN MARIE (1685–1766)   Or Johann (Giovanni) Maria Farina. Italian-born, settled in Cologne, Germany, 1709. Invented *eau de cologne*, "cologne water." Original perfume still manufactured under Farina name. Contains oils of lemon, orange, bergamot, neroli and rosemary and is diluted with rose water.

FARMER, FANNIE MERRITT (1857–1915)   Director of Boston Cooking School, known as "Mother of Level Measurements" for creating cookbook (1896), which provided carefully worked-out measurements and easy-to-follow directions. Called for "cupful, teaspoonful, tablespoonful," etc., for first time. Later wrote cooking page for *Woman's Home Companion*.

FARRIER   Or horseshoer, formerly a practitioner of veterinary skills. At one time the term was interchangeable with veternarian. Horse's hooves, which grow at rate of ⅓ in. (8 mm.) per month, must be replaced every six weeks to enable a balanced stride.

FARROW, MIA (1945–   ) Actress; daughter of Maureen O'Sullivan. Gained fame as a regular of the TV series *Peyton Place* (1964). Married Frank Sinatra at the Sands Hotel, Las Vegas, in 1966. Films include: *Rosemary's Baby* (1968), *See No Evil* (1971), *The Great Gatsby* (1973) and *Broadway Danny Rose* (1984).

FATHER OF THE BRIDE 1950 film starring Spencer Tracy as a father who becomes aggravated after a series of blows which start when his daughter, portrayed by Elizabeth Taylor, announces her engagement. Directed by Vincente Minnelli.

FATHER TIME Classic personification of time. Old man pictured with scythe (long-handled tool used for cutting grass or grain) and hourglass. Comes from folklore, with cultural, literary, biblical and historical allusions.

FATHOM A unit of length equal to six feet used to measure rope or cable and depth of water. From Old English word for "outstretched arms," and from sailors' practice of measuring rope from fingertip to fingertip on extended arms.

FAULKNER, WILLIAM HARRISON (1897– 1962) American novelist from old Mississippi family. Created "Yoknapatawpha County," (MI) in *The Sound and the Fury* (1929), about surviving members of aristocratic Southern family. Won Nobel Prize in literature, 1949, and Pulitzer Prizes for fiction in 1955 (for *A Fable*) and 1963 (for *The Reivers*). Among other works: *Sanctuary* (1931), *Light in August* (1932), and *Requiem for a Nun* (1951).

FEAR OF THE LORD "The fear of the Lord is the beginning of wisdom," Psalm 111, verse 10, the Bible.

FEAR STRIKES OUT 1957 film biography of baseball player Jimmy Piersall, his rise to fame, and his problems with mental illness. Anthony Perkins starred.

FEATHERS Distinguish birds from all other animals. Two kinds: contour, long and smooth, used for flight; and down, short and fluffy, used for warmth. Probably evolved from scales of birds' reptile ancestors.

FEBRUARY Second month of year. Has 28 days except on leap years when it has 29. Shortest month; may have only three moon phases. From latin *februa*, "feast of purification," February 15.

FEDERATION CUP International tennis team competition

for women. Inaugurated in 1963 as equivalent of men's Davis Cup, commemorating 50th anniversary of International Lawn Tennis Federation. Unlike Davis Cup, all matches are held at one site. National teams compete in two singles and one doubles match, with winners advancing. U.S. and Australia have dominated.

FEEDBACK   Noun form of verb phrase *feed back* (two words). Term used originally in electronics, describing feeding back of part of output to input. Now also used in psychology (response) and computer technology. Shortest English word containing all of first six letters of alphabet.

FERDINAND, FRANCIS (1863–1914)   Archduke of Austro-Hungary and heir to the crown of the Austro-Hungarian Empire. Assassinated June 28, 1914, in Sarajevo, capital of Bosnia, now in Yugoslavia, by Gavrilo Princip, a student. The event triggered World War I.

FERRIES, ENGLAND-BELGIUM   The following are ferry routes between English and Belgian ports: Dover–Ostende; Dover–Zeebrugge; Felixstower–Zeebrugge; Folkeston–Ostende; Harwich–Ostende.

FEZ   Morocco's religious center. Home of Karaouiyine University, one of world's oldest schools, established 859. Also name of tall rimless cap made in Fez. Originally the caps were dyed red from berries found only in Morocco.

FIA   *Fédération Internationale de l'Automobile*, governs sport of auto racing. *Fédération* established after World War II, to set rules, encourage technical advancement, and institute safety controls for drivers.

FIDDLER ON THE ROOF   Hit Broadway musical and film based on short stories by Sholem Aleichem. Zero Mostel created starring role of Tevye; Topol played it in film. Popular song, "If I Were a Rich Man."

FIDDLER'S GREEN   According to sailor's folklore, the place where good sailors go. Also called sailor's heaven. Derives from legends about Davy Jones, The Spirit of the Ocean, in which those sailors drowned or buried at sea allegedly go to Davy Jones' locker.

FIELDING, HENRY (1707–1794)   English author. Best known for bawdy novel *The History of Tom Jones, a Foundling* (1749), in which Tom is in love with Sophia Western but considers himself unworthy. After series of adventures, he marries her, becoming a devoted husband and good citizen.

FIELDS, W.C. (1879–1946)   Juggler turned silent-screen comedian. Gained popularity and fame with screen characterization as boozy eccentric in the 1930s. In films since *Pool Sharks* (1915), Fields is best remembered for sound films: *Alice in Wonderland* (1933) as *Humpty Dumpty; David Copperfield* (1934); *My Little Chickadee* (1940), teamed with Mae West; and *The Bank Dick* (1940). Kept his library in his bathroom. Wrote much of his own dialogue—asked, "What contemptible scoundrel stole the cork from my lunch?" and, "I think I'll go out and milk the elk," and "A woman drove me to drink, and I never had the courtesy to thank her," and "Who put the pineapple juice in my pineapple juice?" Portrayed by Rod Steiger in 1976 film *W. C. Fields and Me.*

FIFTH AVENUE   Manhattan thoroughfare lined with old mansions, air-conditioned apartments, exclusive clubs, luxury hotels, churches, museums, art galleries, antique shops, high-price cafés. Portion of it faces Central Park. Was address of Carnegie, Vanderbilt, Woolworth and other business giants. Called "Millionaire's Row."

FIGHT NIGHT. See FRIDAY NIGHT FIGHTS

FIGHT OF THE CENTURY. See FRAZIER, JOE

FILLMORE WEST   Rock club opened by Bill Graham in San Francisco. Became center for San Francisco 60s rock music. At the same time, Fillmore East was opened in New York City.

FILLY. See HORSE RACING TERMS

FILM SOUND TRACK   The first movie to have sound track was Warner Bros., *Don Juan* (1926), a silent movie with synchronized music and sound effects. First words heard in film, "You ain't heard nothin' yet, folks," spoken by Al Jolson, created sensation in *The Jazz Singer* (1927).

FINGER LAKES   Group of narrow lakes in western New York. Notable lakes include Seneca, Cayuga, Keuka, Canandiagua, Owasco and Skaneateles.

FINGERPRINTS   Dactylograms, from Greek word for "finger picture." Patterns formed by ridges on human fingertips, with every person's being unique, even in identical twins. Four classes of patterns: loop, arch, whorl, and accidental. First used in crime detection at beginning of 20th century.

FINIAN'S RAINBOW   1947 Broadway musical which featured song, "How Are Things in Glocca Morra?" Book by E.Y. Harburg and Fred Saidy; music and lyrics by Burton Lane and E.Y. Harburg. Became feature film in 1968, directed by Francis Ford Coppola and starring Fred Astaire, Petula Clark and Tommy Steele.

FINLAND   Country in northern Europe. Northernmost region located inside Arctic Circle. Called "Land of the Midnight Sun"; sun shines 24 hours a day for long periods in the summer. Bordered by Sweden to the west, Norway to the north and Russia to the east.

FIREWORKS   Or pyrotechnics. Important part of many celebrations throughout the world. Date from 12th-century China. Most are made of gunpowder tightly packed into paper tubes.

FIRPO, LUIS ANGEL (1895–1960)   Argentinian heavyweight nicknamed "Wild Bull of the Pampas," fought Jack Dempsey in front of 88,000 at Polo Grounds, New York, September 14, 1923. Knocked Dempsey down seven times in first round, then sent him through ropes. Friends pushed Dempsey back into ring, and he knocked Firpo out. Fight lasted less than four minutes. In career, the six ft. three in., 220-lb. fighter had 30 wins, and only three losses.

FIRST FAMILY, THE   Comedy record album spoofing the John F. Kennedy administration. Vaughn Meader starred and gained fame for his impersonation of the president. Naomi Brossart portrayed his wife, Jackie. Was number one on the charts in December 1962. Sequel album released in 1963 was not as popular.

FIRTH OF FORTH   Large mouth of Scotland's river, Forth, along country's east coast. Connects with North Sea. One of world's longest suspension bridges spans the firth at Queensferry.

FISA. See ROWING FISCHER

FISCHER, ROBERT JAMES (BOBBY) (1943–   )
First American to win World Chess Championship (title first established 1866; Paul Morphy of New Orleans [1837-1884], considered top player of his time, but never won official crown). Beat Russian Boris Spassky to win title in Reykjavík, Iceland, on September 1, 1972, at age 29. Held title until 1975, when he refused to defend

championship under rules of International Chess Federation and was stripped of title. Official Elo system rates him greatest Grandmaster of all time. Has 187 IQ; became youngest Grandmaster ever at age 15; was U.S. chess champion, 1963–1967 and 1971–1972.

FISHER, EDDIE (1928–   ) Nightclub singer and actor in films: *Bundle of Joy* (1956), and *Butterfield* 8 (1960). Most famous for his marriages to Debbie Reynolds, Elizabeth Taylor and Connie Stevens.

FISHERMAN'S RING Gold ring on which pope's seal is carved. Shows apostle Peter, leader of Christ's "fishers of men," fishing from boat. Name of reigning pope set around goal seal.

FISHING The popular sport of catching fish, usually with a lure or baited hook attached to a line extending from a fishing pole. "Plug": a lure made mostly of wood, plastic or cork, with one or more hooks emerging. May be floating (or surface) plug, or sinking plug. "Leader": the length of line used to connect main line with hook or lure; it is made of heavier gauge than rest of line to protect against sharp teeth of some fish.

FISHING LICENSES State leaders in paid fishing licenses granted in 1982: 1) California, 2,480,158; 2) Texas, 1,909,503; 3) Minnesota, 1,677,611 (note: Minnesota, with its smaller population, has higher per capita average).

FISSION The splitting of an atomic particle, which results in release of energy. Atomic bombs are based on fission of heavy atoms, such as plutonium and uranium. The union of atoms, called fusion, also results in energy release.

FITZGERALD, FRANCIS SCOTT KEY (1896–1940) American novelist and short-story writer who epitomized the jazz age. Also known as leading writer of what Gertrude Stein called "Lost Generation" of young, aimless Americans after World War I. Suffered from tuberculosis, depression and alcoholism throughout adult life, once saying, "I have drunk too much and that is certainly slowing me up. On the other hand, without drink I do not know if I could have survived this time." Became Hollywood screenwriter in 1930s. Died of heart attack. Works include *This Side of Paradise* (1920), his first novel and an instant success: Midwesterner Amory Blaine attends Princeton, has unrequited love for Isabelle Borge, serves in France in World War I, and returns to go into advertising, world-weary, cynical, and regretful before age 30, prototype of "Lost Generation" hero. In *The Great Gatsby* (1925), boot-legger Jay Gatsby earns fortune during Prohibition, has mansion at West Egg on Long Island, and is motivated by desire to win Daisy Buchanan from her husband. In *Tender is the Night* (1934), story set in post–World War I Europe, Nicole (wealthy mental patient modeled after Fitzgerald's wife, Zelda), falls in love with young psychiatrist, Dick Diver. They marry, but as her mental health improves, his deteriorates. Novel was public failure; Fitzgerald did many post-publication rewrites. *The Last Tycoon* (1941), about movie moguls in 1920s and '30s, was left unfinished at time of Fitzgerald's death, but is considered among his best works. *Last Tycoon* character, Monroe Stahr, allegedly based on producer Irving Thalberg.

FITZGERALD, ZELDA (1900–1948) Née Zelda Sayre. Beautiful southerner, met novelist F. Scott Fitzgerald while he was in army and married him in 1920 (same year as publication of Fitzgerald's successful first novel, *This Side of Paradise*). Incurable mental illness. Biography, Nancy Milford's *Zelda*.

555 Fictional telephone exchange commonly heard on TV when script calls for phone number.

FLAK JACKET Flak is anti-aircraft fire. Slang word derived from German *Flieger Abwehr Kanonen*, meaning "flier defense cannons." Because early war planes were not armored, fliers wore jackets to protect themselves.

FLAMINGO HOTEL Opened by mobster, Benjamin "Bugsy" Siegel, in Las Vegas, 1946. Named after Siegel's mistress, Virginia Hill. Constructed by the Syndicate for $6 million to be country's first classy, legal gambling establishment.

FLEA Tiny wingless insects that suck blood of birds and mammals. Dangerous vermin because they can carry germs causing bubonic plague and typhus. Able to jump more than 100 times farther than their length.

FLEET STREET Main artery of British press. Home to such papers as *Daily Telegraph* and *Daily Express*. At turn of 18th century, coffeehouses in area were frequented by journalists such as Joseph Addison and Sir Richard Steele.

FLEMING, IAN LANCASTER (1908–1964) English adventure writer. Also wrote children's story, *Chitty-Chitty-Bang-Bang* (1964). Most famous characters were in spy novels:

James Bond, Secret Agent 007 on Her Majesty's Secret Service, licensed to kill in line of duty (as indicated by double-0 number earned in first Bond novel, *Casino Royale* (1953). Bond, son of Swiss mother, Scottish father, schooled at Eton but expelled after trouble with a maid. Later graduated from University of Geneva. Secret Service cover: that of an employee of Universal Import and Export Co. Bond novels set in exotic locales; *You Only Live Twice*, for example, takes place in Japan, where Fleming toured in 1959 and 1962. In the novel, Bond loses his double-0 classification. Ernst Stavro Blofeld is Bond's archenemy, head of SPECTRE (Special Executive for Counterintelligence, Terrorism, Revenge, and Extortion). Blofeld kills Bond's wife of one day, Tracy di Vicenzo, but Bond has his revenge, killing Blofeld in *You Only Live Twice.*

Goldfinger: First name, Auric, derived from Latin word for "gold." In novel, *Goldfinger* (1959), Bond thwarts Goldfinger's plan to rob Fort Knox.

Oddjob: Indestructible Korean bodyguard of Goldfinger. In 1964 movie version Harold Sakata plays Oddjob, whose favorite weapon is steel-rimmed hat. Shirley Bassey performed the title song, "Goldfinger," penned by John Barry.

Pussy Galore: In *Goldfinger*, Bond is helped by Pussy, a flying school instructor and aid of villain, Auric Goldfinger. Honor Blackman portrayed her in 1964 film.

Felix Leiter: Bond's contact in Central Intelligence Agency. Fleming took name from millionaire friend, John Leiter.

M: Admiral Sir Miles Messervy, head of British Secret Service, man whom Bond says, "holds a great deal of my affection and all of my loyalty and obedience."

Miss Moneypenny: M's secretary, played in James Bond movies by Lois Maxwell.

Bond's trademarks include beautiful women, a Ronson lighter, foreign sports cars, martinis ("shaken, not stirred"), champagne, cognac and gambling. James Bond has been portrayed on the screen by Sean Connery (*Dr. No, Goldfinger, Never Say Never Again* and others), David Niven (*Casino Royale*), George Lazenby (*On Her Majesty's Secret Service*), and Roger Moore (*Live and Let Die, Octopussy* and others).

FLEMING, PEGGY (1948–   ) Gold medalist in women's singles figure skating in 1968 Winter Olympics (only U.S. win) in Grenoble, France. Previously world champion, 1966–1968. Went on to professional ice show career and later broadcasting.

FLINTSTONES, THE   Long-running animated cartoon TV series, a parody on modern suburban life, set in the Stone Age. Fred and Wilma Flintstone lived on 39 Stone Canyon Way in the town of Bedrock, next to their neighbors and best friends, Barney and Betty Rubble. The Flintstones had a baby girl named Pebbles and pet dinosaur named Dino. Premiered 1960.

FLORENCE   Italian city, called *Firenze* in Italy, and *Fiorenza* during Renaissance. Name means "city of the flower." Birthplace of Renaissance. Controlled by wealthy Medici family for over 300 years, beginning in 15th century. Leonardo da Vinci, Michelangelo, Dante, Machiavelli, Galileo were masters who lived or worked there. Michelangelo's statue, *David*, considered symbol of city's spirit. City houses nearly half of Michelangelo's statues, including Florentine *Pieta* in Cathedral of Florence, and tombs for two Medici princes in Medici Chapel. Uffisi Museum, housed in Renaissance Palace, designed by Vasari, contains paintings by Botticelli, Masaccio and Piero della Francesca. Pitti Palace houses paintings by Rafael, Titian and Andrea Del Sarto.

FLORIDA   Called "The Sunshine State." Southernmost contiguous U.S. state. Produces three-quarters of nation's oranges and grapefruits. Major industry is tourism; visitors spend average of $20 billion per year. Miami has country's greatest concentration of luxury hotels. More sunken treasure found on Florida's shore than on that of any other U.S. state.

FLU   Or influenza. Infectious disease spread by breathing exhaled air of one who is infected. Higher incidence in winter due to people being indoors, and thus in closer proximity. Often occurs in epidemics, as with the Asian Flu (1957–1958), which originated in China.

FLUID OUNCE. See LIQUID MEASURE

FLUSH TOILET   Invention usually credited to Englishman, Thomas Crapper. Product was advertised "By Appointment to Her Majesty the Queen." Biography titled, *Flushed With Pride*.

FLYING PURPLE PEOPLE EATER, THE   Hit 1958 song by actor-singer-songwriter, Sheb Wooley. Flying creature of song's title had one eye and one horn on its head. Wooley co-starred as Pete Nolan on TV's *Rawhide*.

FLYING SCOTSMAN Name of fast, diesel-powered passenger trains from London to Edinburgh. Trip is 393 mi. (629 km.), and is made in under six hours. Originated as a nickname, became official name for train in 1923.

FLYNN, ERROL (1909–1959) Former boxer from Tasmania turned actor. Propelled to fame with starring role in *Captain Blood* (1935). Portrayed virile, handsome hero in numerous swashbucklers, including *The Adventures of Robin Hood* (1938), *The Sea Hawk* (1940) and *The Adventures of Don Juan* (1948). His 1959 autobiography was entitled *My Wicked, Wicked Ways*. Also wrote novel, *Showdown*.

FLYNT, LARRY (1942–   ) Publisher of *Hustler*, third leading adult magazine after *Playboy* and *Penthouse*. Constantly in censorship battles since magazine started in 1974. Paralyzed from knees down after being shot in 1979 assassination attempt.

FODOR'S GUIDES. See FODOR, EUGENE

FODOR, EUGENE (1905–   ) Hungarian-born American travel correspondent and editor. Editor-publisher *Fodor's Modern Guides* (1949–1964); president, 1964–present. Company's tourist guides have won *Grand Prix de Literature de Tourisme* and the Award of the National Association of Travel Organizations. Publishes guides to virtually every tourist-oriented country in world including the U.S.

FOLLOW THE SUN 1951 film biography of professional golfer, Ben Hogan. Glenn Ford stars as Hogan from amateur status, his shattering auto accident, and his triumphant comeback.

FOOD NAMES, ENGLAND Differences for terms used for foods in England and the U.S.:

England	U.S.
Jelly	Jell-O
Prawns	Shrimp
Sultanas	Raisins
Banger	Sausage
Aubergines	Eggplants

FOOT Twenty-six bones, forming three arches. Cartilage helps make arches shock absorbent. Has as many muscles as the hand. Part of the body most subject to insect bites. Corns, bunions, and calluses may result from ill-fitting shoes. Safest time to purchase shoes is late afternoon.

FOOT REFLEXOLOGY "Big toe" (first in line of toes), is head's pressure point in terms of foot reflexology. Big toe also contains pressure joints for pineal and pituitary glands. Holistic medicine claims massage of big toe cures headache.

FOOTBALL, COLLEGE *Big Three:* Harvard, Yale and Princeton formed informal Big Three long before Ivy League was formally created (1956). Those three teams, particularly Yale, dominated football in pre-forward-pass era, earning nickname. Today they still rank one-two-three in total college football victories. National championships: Yale, eight; Princeton, seven; and Harvard, six.

Draft: National Football League originated annual draft of college players in 1936 to prevent richer teams from buying all talented players. Teams granted draft choices in reverse order of position in final standing of most recent season, but may trade them.

First Game: First intercollegiate football game, November 6, 1869, at New Brunswick, NJ, played by Princeton and Rutgers under modified soccer rules. Used 25 players per side. Rutgers won, 6-4.

Southern Conference: University of Arkansas Razorbacks, Fayetteville, AK; University of Texas Longhorns, Austin, TX; Southern Methodist University Mustangs, Dallas, TX; Baylor University Bears; Waco, TX; Rice Institute Owls, Houston, TX; University of Houston Cougars, Houston, TX; Texas A & M U. Aggies — College Station, TX; Texas Christian University Horned Frogs, Fort Worth, TX; Texas Tech Red Raiders, Lubbock, TX

FOOTBALL, COLLEGE BOWL GAMES   Games with year founded:

Bluebonnet Bowl	:	Houston, TX, 1959 (now Astro-Bluebonnet Bowl)
Cotton Bowl	:	Dallas, TX, 1937
Fiesta Bowl	:	Phoenix, AZ, 1971
Gator Bowl	:	Jacksonville, FL, 1946
Hula Bowl	:	All-star game, Honolulu, HI
Liberty Bowl	:	Memphis, TN (founded 1959, Philadelphia)
Orange Bowl	:	Miami, FL, 1933
Peach Bowl	:	Atlanta, GA, 1968
Pecan Bowl	:	Defunct
Rose Bowl	:	Pasadena, CA, 1902 (Michigan defeated Stanford, 49–0. Played in Durham, NC in

1942 due to post-Pearl Harbor West Coast scare.)

Sugar Bowl	:	New Orleans, LA, 1935
Sun Bowl	:	El Paso, TX, 1936
Tangerine Bowl	:	Orlando, FL, 1968 (now Florida Citrus Bowl)

FOOTBALL, COLLEGE TEAM NICKNAMES *Bulldogs*: University of Georgia. Member Southeastern Conference. Team colors, red and black. Games played in Sanford Stadium on campus in Athens, GA, capacity 82,122.

Cyclones: Iowa State University. Member of Big Eight Conference. Team colors, cardinal and gold. Play games at Iowa State stadium, Ames, IA, capacity 50,000.

Horned Frogs: Texas Christian University. Nickname from species indigenous to Fort Worth region. Member Southwest Conference. Team colors, purple and white. Play at TCU-Amon Carter Stadium, Fort Worth, TX, capacity 46,000.

Tigers: Nickname most common to college football teams in U.S. Among them: Auburn University, Clemson University, Grambling State University, Jackson State University, Memphis State University, University of Missouri, Pacific University, Princeton University, Tennessee State University, Texas Southern University, Louisiana State University. Among Division I (large) schools, second most common nickname is Wildcats.

Volunteers: University of Tennessee athletic teams. Member Southeastern Conference. Team colors, orange and white. Games played in Neyland Stadium, Knoxville, TN, capacity 91,000.

FOOTBALL, CANADIAN Teams have 12 on a side, 12th being a fifth back on offense and a defensive back or linebacker on defense. Field is longer (110 yds.) and wider than in U.S., with 25 yd. deep end zones. Teams get three downs to make ten yds. for a first down. One point (a *rouge*) scored if receiving team cannot return a kick out of its end zone.

FOOTBALL, RULES American football has most rules of any sport: 48 printed pages for formal rules and 71 pages for rules plus official comments and interpretations. High school, college, and professional rules differ slightly. *Ball*: Oval inflated bladder, pointed at ends. Length is 11 to 11¼ in. and weight is 14 to 15 oz. Cover consists of four panels of pebble-grained leather with no corrugations other than four seams joining panels together. Raised stitching for grip on one seam. NFL requires home team to have 24 balls available for testing by referee one hour before game time. In case of bad weather, a playable ball is substituted upon request of offensive captain. Wilson is official supplier of NFL footballs.

Clipping: Blocking an opponent (other than ball carrier) from behind, especially by hitting or throwing the body across the back of the opponent's legs. Carries a 15 yd. penalty from point of infraction.

Goal post: In NFL, goal posts centered at back of end zone. Crossbar 10 ft. off ground. Length is 18½ ft. with 20-ft. bars extending upward at both ends. In college football, crossbar 23-ft., 4 in. long.

Kickoffs: At beginning of each half and after every touchdown or field goal is scored, U.S. professional football teams kick off to opponents from own 35 yd. line. Prior to 1974 season, pros kicked off from 40 yd. line; college teams still kick from there. After safety, team caught in end zone gets free kick (can be placekicked or punted, but opponent cannot attempt to block it) from its own 20 yd. line.

Offside: Penalty called when any part of player's body is beyond line of scrimmage (or restraining line on kickoff) when ball is put into play. Incurs 5 yd. penalty.

Safety: Occurs if ball becomes dead in possession of offensive team in its own end zone, or if it goes out of bounds in end zone while in offensive team's possession. Two points scored for defensive team, which then receives free kick from offensive team's 20 yd. line.

Touchback: Occurs when offensive player downs ball in his team's defensive end zone, with impetus to down it coming from opposing team, or when punt or kickoff goes through end zone without being touched by receiving team. No score. Offensive team retains possession on its own 20 yd. line.

Wild card playoff team: Team that qualifies for postseason play because it has best record of all teams in conference that do not automatically qualify by winning their division. First used in National Football League for 1970 playoffs because realigned league had three divisions in each conference. 1980–1981 Oakland Raiders first wild card team to win Super Bowl. National Basketball Association has also used wild card concept.

FOOTBALL, TOUCH   Six to eleven players on a team. Field should be 70–100 yds. long. Tagging ball carrier halts advancement. Emphasis on passing. Rules are localized to fit game in progress.

FOOTBALL, TERMS   *Bomb*: Long forward pass, especially

one resulting in touchdown. Longest possible, 99 yds., done four times in NFL history: Frank Filchack to Andy Farkas for Washington vs. Pittsburgh, October 15, 1939; Sonny Jurgenson to Gerry Allen for Washington vs. Chicago, October 15, 1958; George Izo to Bobby Mitchell for Washington vs. Cleveland, September 15, 1963; Karl Sweetan to Pat Studstill for Detroit vs. Baltimore, October 16, 1966.

Chain gang: Members of football officiating team (all of whom wear vertically striped shirts) with responsibility of holding and moving markers (sticks) signifying first down. Sticks joined by 10 yd. piece of chain which is brought on field for close measurements.

Slotback: In "Slot T" offensive formation, back who lines up in "slot" between tackle and end.

Tailback: In "I," single wing, or "pro set" offensive formations, back who lines up furthest from center. Generally team's speediest runner.

FORD, EDWARD CHARLES (WHITEY) (1928–   ) Pitcher for N.Y. Yankees, 1950–1967. Started three games against San Francisco Giants in 1962 World Series. Won game one, no decision in game four, lost game six. Nicknamed "Chairman of the Board." Had 236-106 lifetime mark and record 10 World Series wins. Elected to Baseball Hall of Fame in 1974.

FORD, GERALD RUDOLPH JR. (1913–   ) Thirty-eighth U.S. president. Originally named Leslie King after his father. Renamed, age two, by his stepfather after his mother remarried. Football star, University of Michigan. Elected to Congress, 1949. Succeeded vice-president Spiro Agnew, October 10, 1973. (Agnew had resigned in fear of possible imprisonment upon charges that he had received illegal kickbacks as both governor of Maryland as well as vice-president.) Ford also assumed the presidency without having been elected. He was sworn in, April 9, 1974, after Nixon's resignation in the wake of the Watergate scandal. Soon after taking office, Ford said, referring to Watergate, "Our long national nightmare is over." On September 5, 1975, 26-year-old Lynnette "Squeaky" Fromme, a follower of Charles Manson, tried to shoot the President. Fromme claimed she only "wanted to get some attention for a new trial for Charlie and the girls" who were serving time for Beverly Hills Manson murders. Seventeen days later, September 22, 45-year-old Sara Jane Moore, a fringe radical and one-time FBI informant, fired one shot at the President in San Francisco. He was not wounded. Ford was the first president to appear on the weekly NBC news show, *Meet the Press.*

FORESTER, CECIL SCOTT (1899–1966)   Prolific English author. Won wide following with series of 11 historical novels depicting naval career of Horatio Hornblower. British officer during Napoleonic Wars. Also wrote *The African Queen* (1935), in which the owner of old steam launch of that name reluctantly rescues a missionary from Germans during World War I. Humphrey Bogart won Oscar opposite Katharine Hepburn in 1951 film version.

FORK   Introduced in 1100 by the wife of Doge Domenice Silvie of Venice. Two-pronged table utensil, unpopular until Renaissance. By 1600s forks had four prongs, as they do today.

FORMICARY   A nest of ants. Word from Latin *formica,* meaning "ant."

FORSYTH, FREDERICK (1938–   )   British journalist and novelist. Wrote *The Day of the Jackal* (1971), about plot to murder French president, Charles De Gaulle; *The Odessa File* (1972), bestseller about German journalist tracking former Nazi officers living under new identities. "Odessa," acronym for organization established to shield ex-Nazis; and *The Dogs of War* (1974). Title refers to group of white mercenaries who liquidate half-mad dictator of obscure West African republic and replace him with puppet president who will grant mining rights to mining magnate who hired them.

FORT KNOX   U.S. Army Center. Located just south of Louisville, KY. Named Camp Knox in 1918 for first secretary of war, Major General Henry Knox. Renamed Fort Knox in 1933. Contains U.S. Treasury Department's gold depository worth $6 billion.

FORTUNE COOKIE, THE   1966 feature film about a TV cameraman (Jack Lemmon), hurt while covering a football game. Advised by shyster lawyer brother-in-law (Walter Matthau) to stay in bed in order to get a big insurance settlement. Matthau won Oscar for Best Supporting Actor.

45 R.P.M. RECORDS   Like 78s and 33⅓s, 45 r.p.m.'s have only one groove on each side (r.p.m. is abbreviation for revolutions per minute).

FOSBURY, DICK (1947–   )   With unorthodox style (called Fosbury Flop) won high jump at 1968 Mexico City Olympics with record jump of 7 ft. 4¼ in. Fosbury turned his back on bar just as he reached it and flipped over backwards, landing on nape of neck. Most jumpers use traditional scissors or roll styles jumps.

FOSSE, BOB (1927–   )   Broadway and Hollywood dancer of the 1950s, turned choreographer and film director. Films as director include: *Sweet Charity* (1968), *Cabaret* (1972), *Lenny* (1974), *All That Jazz* (1979), and *Star 80* (1983).

FOSSIL FUELS   Any energy source derived from organic matter in the earth's crust. Coal, oil and natural gas the most important types. All are formed from remains of sea plants and animals that lived millions of years ago.

FOUR HORSEMEN OF THE APOCALYPSE, THE   1921 film directed by Rex Ingram. Rudolf Valentino stars as artist who enlists as soldier during World War I. Alice Terry plays his love.

FOUR SCORE AND SEVEN YEARS   Old English phrase. Opening line of Lincoln's 1864 Gettysburg Address dedicated to soldiers who died on Gettysburg Field during the Civil War. As a "score" equals 20 years, four score and seven equals 87 years.

FOUR SEASONS, THE   Formed in 1956 as "The Four Lovers." First hit single was "Sherry" (1962). Frankie Valli, lead singer, stayed with group until 1967, recording with them such hits as "Big Girls Don't Cry," "Walk Like a Man" and "Rag Doll."

FOUR-H CLUB   Youth organization teaching skills and values. Head, heart, hands, and health, four H's. Members participate in farming, community service, and personal improvement.

FOUR-MINUTE MILE   xxxx minute mile barrier May 6, 1954 at Oxford University, England, during meet between British AAA and Oxford. His time was 3:59.4. Australian John Landy lowered record to 3:57.9 in June of that year, then Bannister beat Landy in Vancouver in August with a time of 3:58.8 Current record is 3:47.33 run by England's Sebastian Coe in 1981.

FOURTH ESTATE, THE   Term for the press. Often credited to British statesman Edmund Burke, but actually first used in 1826 by Thomas Macaulay: "The gallery in which the reporters sit has become a fourth estate of the realm" meaning press was as powerful as first three estates of Parliament: Lords Spiritual, Lords Temporal and Commons.

FOWLES, JOHN (1926–   ) English novelist. Author of *The Magus* (1966), *The Ebony Tower* (1974), *Daniel Martin* (1977) and *The French Lieutenant's Woman* (1969), set in England in the 1860s and 1870s. Lovers' triangle involes Ernestina, her fiance, Charles, and Sarah, the title character. Film version starred Meryl Streep as Sarah and Jeremy Irons as Charles. *The Collector* (1963) is about butterfly collector who holds young woman hostage in hope she will learn to love him. 1965 film starred Terence Stamp and Samantha Eggar.

FOXES Small animals related to dogs and wolves. Female foxes are known as vixens, their young are pups, kits, and cubs, and their bushy tails are called brushes. Fox fur can be among the most valuable furs.

FRANC Belgium, Switzerland, Luxembourg and several other countries use the franc as their national currency. Only France and Monaco use the French franc as their basic monetary unit.

FRANCE *Cheese:* French consume more cheese per capita than any other people. France ranks third in cheese production, behind the U.S. and Russia, making 1,113,000 short tons (1,010,000 metric tons) per year. Popular French cheeses include Camembert, Port du Salut, Roquefort and Brie.
Flag: Called "the tricolor." Has three vertical stripes: blue, white, and red. First used by King Louis XVI in 1789.
National Anthem: "La Marseillaise," adopted in 1795. Royalist Claude Joseph Rouget de Lisle wrote words and music in 1792 as "A War Song for the Army of the Rhine."

FRANCIS, ANNE (1932–   ) Leading lady of films in 1950s. Appeared in *The Blackboard Jungle* (1955), *Forbidden Planet* (1956), *Don't Go Near the Water* (1957), among others. Starred in TV detective series *Honey West* in 1965.

FRANCIS, CONNIE (1938–   ) Popular singer of late 1950s/early 1960s. A 1923 tune, "Who's Sorry Now?" became her first hit record in 1958, followed by other oldies: "Among My Souvenirs" (1960) and "Together" (1961). Appeared in films, including *Where the Boys Are* (1960). Other hit songs include: "My Happiness" (1959) and "Everybody's Somebody's Fool" (1960).

FRANCIS, THE TALKING MULE Donald O'Connor starred in six films featuring Francis (whose off-screen voice was provided by Chill Wills). Movie titles include: *Francis Goes to the Races* (1951), *Francis Covers the Big Town* (1953), and *Francis Joins the WACs* (1954). Inspired TV series *Mr. Ed* (1961–1965).

FRANCO, FRANCISCO (1892–1975) Spanish general and head of state, 1936–1975. Led nationalists in successful *coup d'état*, toppling democratic republic in Spanish Civil War (1936–1939). Final victory, April 1, 1939.

FRANK, ANNE (1929–1944) German-Jewish girl whose family hid from Nazis in Amsterdam, Holland, warehouse located at 263 Princengracht. Her *Diary of Anne Frank*, covering years of hiding, found after she was caught and exterminated. Published 1947, became Broadway play and 1959 movie starring Millie Perkins as Anne, and Shelley Winters in an Oscar-winning supporting role.

FRANKFORT Capital of Kentucky. Divided by Kentucky River. Its "Corner of Celebrities" is a three-block area of old homes once belonging to famous Kentucky statesmen, judges and military-men.

FRANKLIN, BENJAMIN (1706–1790) American states-man, inventor, writer and printer. Published *Pennsylvania Gazette* and *Poor Richard's Almanac* (1732–1757), collection of agricultural and astronomical data to which he added practical wisdom and moral maxims. Venture successful enough to allow him to retire from business in 1748 at age 42 and pursue other interests. "Early to bed, early to rise, makes a man healthy, wealthy and wise," one of Poor Richard's maxims (1735). James Thurber, in *Fables for Our Time* (1940), wrote "Early to rise and early to bed makes a man healthy and wealthy and dead." Franklin is credited with the invention of the Franklin stove and bifocal lenses. While flying a kite in a thunder-storm, he noted that a bolt of lightening traveled down kite wire causing key attached at end to spark. Laid basis for development of lightning rod.

FRAZIER, JOE (1944–   ) Heavyweight boxer who re-tained world championship in March 8, 1971 "Fight of the Century" against Muhammad Ali at New York's Madison Square Garden (Ali's first professional loss). Frazier won one-round bout on points. Crowd of 20,455 paid $1,352,500 to see bout live. Grossed more than $20 million with closed-circuit TV income. Frazier and Ali were paid

$2.5 million each in unprecedented meeting of two undefeated heavyweight champions. After George Foreman beat Frazier (1973) and Ali beat Foreman (1974), Ali won rematch with Frazier in 14th-round knockout in October 1, 1975, "Thrilla in Manila." Frazier became nightclub performer and manager of son Marvis, heavyweight contender.

FRECKLES Groups of pigment cells called melanocytes in the skin. When exposed to sun they darken, resulting in the familiar spots. Most common in children, people with red hair, and tend to run in families.

FREED, ALAN (1922–1965) Disc jockey who popularized the term "Rock and Roll" and who brought the sound to white teenagers by playing "race" records (black rhythm and blues music) in the early 1950s. Became America's top D.J. by 1959. A scandal involving him with payola forced him out of radio in the early 1960s.

FRENCH FOREIGN LEGION Often romanticized group of fighters. Founded 1831. Originally stationed in Africa to protect France's "possessions" there. Later moved to present location on the Italian island of Corsica.

FRENCH GUIANA Overseas department of France on northeast coast of South America. Noted for its cruel prisons. Convicts sent from France for 150 years. Political prisoners kept on offshore island called Devil's Island. Others sent to Kourou and Saint Laurent prison camps. In 1945 convicts were sent back to France.

FRENCH PRESIDENCY Seven-year term. President's authority aided and checked by Parliament. System established 1958 as compromise between parliamentary and presidential systems. General Charles De Gaulle, first to serve under new system.

FREQUENCY MODULATION (FM) Frequency of one wave, the carrier, varied in response to frequency of another wave, the modulator. Advantage over amplitude modulation (AM): more resistant to noise and interference, which cause static. Only FM is used for TV audio.

FREUD, SIGMUND (1856–1939) Austrian neurologist and founder of psychoanalysis, field originally called "talking cure," based on free association to discover unconscious motivations. Sexuality and oedipal trauma are central to Freud's interpretation of neurosis.

Freud alleged American women aroused him to have erotic dreams. Published *The Ego and the Id*, 1923.

FRIDAY NIGHT FIGHTS   Gillette Cavalcade of Sports televised boxing from Madison Square Garden, New York City, every Friday night, 1944–1964. TV exposure eventually decreased arena attendance for all but championship fights. Caused fade in popularity of small boxing clubs, which were sport's minor-league system.

FRIED CHICKEN   Leads the list of preferred main dishes at sit-down restaurants in U.S. Others, in order of popularity, are: roast beef, spaghetti, turkey, baked ham, fried shrimp, beef stew, meat loaf, fish, macaroni and cheese, pot roast and Swiss steak.

FRIEDAN, BETTY (1921–   )   Feminist writer. *Feminine Mystique* (1963), her first book, known as "*Uncle Tom's Cabin* of women's movement," credited with reviving women's movement in U.S.A. Founder and past president of National Organization for Women, 1966–1970. Mother of Daniel, Jonathan and Emily. Divorced husband Carl Friedan in 1969 after 22 years of marriage.

FRISBEE   Toy and sport which grew from post–World War II recreation of Yale students who scaled pie plates from Frisbie Baking Co. Idea sold to Wham-O company, who manufactured plastic saucer first as "Pluto Platter," then as "Wham-O Flying Saucer," finally as "Frisbee." Competitive play began 1957, supervised by International Frisbee Disc Association. Players compete on teams and individually in events including throwing for distance and MTA, (Maximum Time Aloft). Current recognized records: 444 ft. for distance, 15.2 sec. for MTA, both set 1978. Two events combine in third event: throwing Frisbee, then running and catching it; current record for distance in that event is 271.2 ft. set in 1979.

FRITZ THE CAT   Robert Crumb's underground comic book star turned controversial feature film by Ralph Bakshi. The first animated cartoon to receive an X rating. Film parodied the hippie life-style of 1960s.

FROGS AND TOADS   Tailless amphibians. Major differences: skin—toad's dry, frog's wet; teeth—toads without, frogs with. Largest frog almost 12 in., can jump up to 6 ft. Frogs locomote more rapidly than toads.

FROM HERE TO ETERNITY   1953 Best Picture Oscar winner about the lives and loves of a group of soldiers stationed at

Pearl Harbor just before World War II. Burt Lancaster starred as tough sergeant who makes love to Deborah Kerr on beach. Frank Sinatra won Oscar for Best Supporting Actor as Maggio in his first nonsinging role, rescuing his career. Montgomery Clift played Prewitt, a private having an affair with bad-girl Donna Reed, who won Oscar for Best Supporting Actress.

FROM RUSSIA WITH LOVE   1964 James Bond movie, the second of series to be filmed. Sean Connery as 007, sent to steal a secret Russian device.

FROMMER, ARTHUR   Author of travel guide books that help travelers follow a budget. Recommended budgets have increased over the years. For example, two of his books are: *Europe on $5 a Day* (1968); and *Europe on $20 a Day* (1981–1982).

FRONTS (WEATHER)   Term describing zone where a warm and a cold air mass meet. Area along which most changes in weather occur. Cold fronts cause sudden changes in weather, warm fronts, more gradual. Cold fronts travel twice as fast.

FROST, ROBERT LEE (1874–1963)   American poet. Four-time Pulitzer Prize winner (1924, 1931, 1937 and 1943). Known for verse about New England. First work not published until age 40. "…promises to keep and miles to go before I sleep" from "Stopping by the Woods on a Snowy Evening" (1923). Wrote "good fences make good neighbors," in "Mending Wall" (1914); and "The Road Not Taken" (1916), in which he wrote, "Two Roads diverged in a wood, and I—took the one less traveled by,/And that has made all the difference." At John F. Kennedy's presidential inauguration, January 1961, Frost read his poem, "The Gift Outright."

FULLER, R. BUCKMINSTER (1895–1983)   American architect and engineer. Best known for designing Geodesic Dome, spherical buildings which have no internal support and whose strength increase with size. Discussed in Sidney Rosen's 1969 book, *Wizard of the Dome: R. Buckminster Fuller, Designer of the Future.*

FULTON, ROBERT (1765–1815)   American inventor, artist and engineer. Designed and built Clermont, first commercially successful steamboat. Made its first journey from New York City to Albany, 1807.

FUNAMBULIST   Tightrope walker. From Latin *funis*, meaning "rope," plus *ambulare*, "to walk." Literally, "rope walker" or "rope dancer". Also called schoenobatist. Among most famous: Charles Blondin, who walked across Niagara Falls; Steve McPeak, who carried fiancée across canyon of Nevada's Boulder Dam, getting married in middle (afterward arrested for being public nuisance); and The Flying Wallendas, circus family act.

FUNNY GIRL   Broadway hit musical which made star of Barbra Streisand. Became her first feature film in 1968. Streisand won Oscar for her portrayal of comedienne Fanny Brice. (see BRICE, FANNY). Sequel *Funny Lady* (1975) continued the story.

G

GABLE AND LOMBARD   1976 film based on true romance and marriage of Clark Gable (portrayed by James Brolin) and Carole Lombard (Jill Clayburgh).

GABLE, CLARK (1901–1960)   Leading man of movies for over 30 years and known as "the King of Hollywood." His most famous films include *Mutiny on the Bounty* (1935) and *Gone with the Wind* (1939). Won Oscar for *It Happened One Night* (1934). Last film: *The Misfits* (1960). Entered the air force one week after his wife, Carol Lombard, was killed in an airplane crash, January 16, 1942. Hermann Goering, commander of Nazi Germany's air force, offered $5,000 for Gable's capture.

GABOR, ZSA ZSA (1921–   )   Actress. Former Miss Hungary of 1936 (title taken away because she was underage). Sisters Eva and Magda also performers. Starred in films, including *Moulin Rouge* (1953) and *Queen of Outer Space* (1959). Has said, "I've never hated a man enough to give him his diamonds back."

GAGARIN,   YURI   ALEKSEYEVICH   (1934–1968)   Soviet cosmonaut. On April 12, 1961, became first man to orbit Earth, aboard Vostok 1. Landed safely one hour and 48 minutes later. Died in plane crash. Neil Armstrong and Edwin Aldrin left one of Gagarin's medals on the moon as tribute.

GAINSBOROUGH, THOMAS (1727–1788)   English painter. Though best known for elegant, lively portraits like *The Blue Boy*, his favorite subject was English landscapes.

GALAHAD. See KING ARTHUR

GALAPAGOS ISLANDS, THE   Located in Pacific Ocean. Island group belonging to Ecuador. Made of volcanic peaks. Inhabited by rare animals and birds such as cormorants (birds which cannot fly), penguins, a type of mockingbird found only there, iguanas and 500 lb. (230 kg.) turtles. *Galápagos* means turtle in Spanish.

GALILEI, GALILEO (1564–1642)   Seventeenth-century Italian astronomer and physicist. Made contributions to theory of gravity and discovered Jupiter's moons and Saturn's rings. In 1632 he was tried by the Inquisition for heretical theories set forth in his books *The Starry Messenger* and *A Dialogue on the Two Principal Systems of the World*.

GALLANT HOURS, THE   1960 film which recounts the fighting on Guadalcanal in 1942. James Cagney portrays Admiral William F. Halsey, World War II naval hero who planned the defense of the island.

GALLOPING GOURMET, THE   A daily TV series starring Australian chef Graham Kerr, which ran from 1969–1973. In front of a live audience, Kerr demonstrated how to prepare gourmet meals, and introduced guest stars and humor to the cooking show format.

GANDHI, INDIRA PRIYADARSHINI (1917–   )   Prime Minister of India, 1966–1977; first woman to hold the post. Only daughter of Jawaharlal Nehru, first prime minister of independent India. Jawaharlal succeeded by Bahadur Shastri, who held the post two years until his death. Indira's husband, Feroze Gandhi, bears no relation to the leader of India's independence, Mohandas Gandhi.

GANDHI, MOHANDAS KARAMCHAND (1869–1948)   Hindu nationalist leader. Known as "Mahatma," meaning "great soul", and "The Little Brown Saint." Led Indian National Congress in nonviolent achievement of Indian independence from Britain, 1947. Began as a student of law in England, 1888. Practiced as an advocate for fellow Indians in South Africa. Entered Indian political scene, 1919, protesting British sedition laws. Assassinated, January 30, 1948, and cremated the next day on the banks of Hindu's most sacred river, the Ganges. His policy of civil disobedience has influenced 20th-century political activists.

GANGES RIVER   Hindu's sacred river located in India, flowing into Bay of Bengal. Thought to have sprung from head of Lord S'va, one of the three major deities. Thousands of Hindus make pilgrimages to its banks to bathe, drink its water and meditate. Some come to die in it, believing they will be brought to paradise. Cities such as Calcutta, Banaras and Patna are situated on river.

GANJA. See JAMAICA

GARBO, GRETA (1905–   ) Born Greta Gustafson. Actress in Sweden, came to America and became screen legend in Hollywood movies in the 1920s and '30s. Classic films include *Flesh and the Devil* (1927), *Anna Christie* (1930), *Queen Christina* (1933), *Camille* (1936) and *Ninotchka* (1939).

GARCIA   Most common Spanish family name. Spanish form of Gerald. Translates to mean "spear," "firm," "youth" or "prince." It is the 58th most common surname in U.S.

GARDNER, ERLE STANLEY (1889–1970)   American author of detective fiction. Wrote 85 mysteries featuring defense attorney Perry Mason, beginning with *The Case of the Velvet Claws* (1933), which was rejected by several publishers before William Morrow and Co. decided to publish it and make Mason into series (all titles of which begin with "The Case of the . . . "). In *The Case of the Terrified Typist* (1956), Mason loses case (only time in published series), although there is a twist ending after court adjourns. Gardner, himself a lawyer until becoming successful at writing, also created Bertha Cool-Donald Lam series under pseudonym A. A. Fair. Other characters in Mason series (which went to TV from 1957–1967, with Raymond Burr in Emmy-winning portrayal of Mason):

   Hamilton Burger, district attorney, Mason's courtroom adversary in most Mason novels, never winning (did not prosecute in *Terrified Typist*). Played in TV series by William Tallman.

   Paul Drake, Mason's private investigator, doing the legwork. Played in TV series by William Hopper, son of Hollywood gossip columnist Hedda Hopper. Drake suffers from habitual indigestion.

   Della Street, Mason's secretary. He proposed to her five times, but she always turned him down because she wanted to keep working, and knew Mason would never permit his wife to work. Steadfastly loyal, she was also arrested five times while performing her job. Note: In film version of *The Case of the Velvet Claws* (1936), they get married, but it never happened in a Mason book.

GARLAND, JUDY (1922–1969) Born Frances Gumm. Legendary actress and singer. Among her famous films: *The Wizard of Oz* (1939), for which she won a special Academy Award for "outstanding performance by a screen juvenile"; *Meet Me in St. Louis* (1944); *Summer Stock* (1950); and *A Star Is Born* (1954). Emotionally unstable. Daughter Liza Minnelli said of her, "When she was sad, she was sadder than anyone." Died of drug overdose.

GARLIC Honored by the Lovers of the Stinky Rose, member of the lily family, native southern Europe. Fifteenth-century Europe, revered as contraceptive device worn around neck on string while making love.

GARNET The most common color is red to very dark red. Used both as gemstones as well as abrasives. For many years, was cut and sold as a ruby with the dealer sincerely believing he had a ruby. The words *cape ruby* and *ceylon ruby* are still applied to the garnet.

GARRISON, JAMES (1921–   ) Louisiana district attorney. Claimed to have uncovered 1963 Kennedy assassination conspiracy. Remarked, February 23, 1966, "My staff and I solved the assassination weeks ago." Arrested several suspects, whom he alleged were homosexuals. All were acquitted.

GARRY MOORE SHOW, THE Popular television variety show from 1958–1964. Moore, a crew-cut bow-tied entertainer on radio and TV since 1939, made a star out of regular performer Carol Burnett; Durwood Kirby was Moore's sidekick and announcer.

GARSON, GREER (1908–   ) Popular actress of the 1940s and '50s. Won Oscar for *Mrs. Miniver* (1942). Her half-hour acceptance speech prompted the Academy to limit the thank-yous at subsequent ceremonies. Other films include *Madame Curie* (1943), *Julie Misbehaves* (1948), *Julius Caesar* (1953) and *Sunrise at Campobello* (1960), in which she played Eleanor Roosevelt.

GAS HOUSE GANG, THE Name given by sportswriter Frank Graham to 1934 St. Louis Cardinals baseball team. Famous for wild, unpredictable behavior on and off field. Members included Pepper Martin, Joe "Ducky" Medwick, Leo Durocher, Dizzy and Daffy Dean, Rip Collins and player-manager Frankie Frisch. Cardinals are one of three Major League teams with bird nicknames (Toronto Blue Jays and Baltimore Orioles are others).

GASOHOL   Fuel, 10% methyl alcohol, 90% unleaded gasoline. Increased use after gas shortages of late 1970s and early 1980s. Greatest use as automobile and truck fuel. Roughly same performance and mileage as gasoline.

GASOLINE ALLEY. See INDIANAPOLIS MOTOR SPEEDWAY

GATEWAY ARCH   Arch (630 ft./192 m.) in St. Louis, Missouri. Honors city's role in settlement of the West. Stands beside Mississippi River. Visitors ride on trains inside the arch up to an observation deck on top.

GATWICK AIRPORT. See LONDON AIRPORTS

GAUCHOS   Cowboys of South America, usually of mixed Spanish and Indian blood. Noted for skill on horseback and dramatic costume (wide-brimmed hat, baggy trousers, silver belt). Caught and sold wild cattle years ago; now largely replaced by peons (day laborers).

GAUGUIN, (EUGENE HENRI) PAUL (1848–1903)   French painter and woodcut artist. First a sailor, then a stockbroker, later a painter, and friend of Dutch artist Vincent van Gogh. Quit brokerage in 1883 at 35. Worked on Panama Canal digging for 15 days in 1887. Settled in Tahiti, 1891, and painted natives in post-Impressionist style.

GAYLE, CRYSTAL (1953–   )   Loretta Lynn's younger sister; became a country/pop singer in the late 1970s with hits including "Don't It Make My Brown Eyes Blue," "I'd Do It All Over Again" and "I'll Get Over You."

GEHRIG, HENRY LOUIS (LOU) (1903–1941)   Baseball player for New York Yankees. Known as "The Iron Horse" and "Pride of the Yankees." Played 2,130 games consecutively between June 2, 1925 and May 2, 1939. Replaced Wally Pip at first base during second game of streak; had pinch hit the day before. Replaced 14 years later by Ellsworth ("Babe") Dahlgren. Lou Gehrig Day at Yankee Stadium instated July 4, 1939, at which time he said, "Today I consider myself the luckiest man on the face of the earth." Gehrig knew at the time he was dying of rare disease that has since borne his name. First major-leaguer to have number (4) retired.

GEISEL, THEODORE SEUSS (1904–   )   American writer and illustrator. Wrote under name Theo Le Sieg but best known as Dr. Seuss. *And To Think That I Saw It on Mulberry Street*

(1937), rejected by many publishers, was his first children's book and an instant success. Began revolution in children's books featuring absurd and floppy animals that invented new words. Former ad writer, has no children. "You have 'em, I'll amuse 'em," he said. Won Pulitzer Prize, 1984. Among many characters: Yertl the Turtle; Horton, the egg-hatching elephant; the Grinch Who Stole Christmas; and the Cat in the Hat.

GELLER, URI (1948–   )   Israeli psychic. Best known for bending spoons, nails and keys supposedly with psychokinesis, or mind over matter. Also claims to fix stopped watches through television.

GEMINI   Constellation. Also called The Twins. Named after Castor and Pollux, twin gods of Greek mythology. Also known as the Dioscuri, meaning "sons of Zeus." Patron gods of athletes, protectors of seamen and controllers of wind and waves.

GENE KRUPA STORY, THE   1960 filmed biography starring Sal Mineo as the famous drummer. Story portrays his rise in the jazz music world, his battle with drugs and his comeback.

GENERAL ASSEMBLY   Main deliberating body of the United Nations. Makes recommendations regarding international actions. Has no enforcement powers. Founding 51 members first met in London, 1945, soon after end of World War II.

GENERAL ELECTRIC COLLEGE BOWL, THE   Popular TV quiz show which pit scholars from two competing colleges against each other in answering difficult questions. Winners received $3,000 scholarship grant. Alan Ludden hosted the show on CBS from 1959–1963; Robert Earle continued the hosting chores on NBC from 1963–1970.

GENERAL TOM THUMB (1838–1883)   Charles S. Stratton, a 25-in. midget renamed and exhibited by P. T. Barnum in the mid-1800s. Married Lavinia Warren, a 32-in. woman, in 1863.

GENESIS. See BIBLE, THE

GENTLEMEN PREFER BLONDES   1953 film starring Marilyn Monroe and Jane Russell as two showgirls en route to Paris seeking rich husbands. Directed by Howard Hawks from the 1949 musical play by Joseph Fields and Anita Loos; includes the song "Diamonds Are a Girl's Best Friend."

GEORGE III (1738–1820)   King of England, 1760–1820.

Ruled during American Revolutionary War, French Revolution and Industrial Revolution. In 1801, Britain changed its name to the United Kingdom.

GEORGIA   Of all U.S. states east of Mississippi River, Georgia is largest. Covers 58,876 sq. mi. (152,488 sq. km.). Nicknamed "The Empire State of the South," due to size and prosperous industries. Contains 159 counties including Bacon, Macon and Fulton, the largest.

GEORGIE PORGIE   In nursery rhyme, "Georgie Porgie, pudding and pie, / Kissed the girls and made them cry, / When the boys came out to play, / Georgie Porgie ran away."

GEORGY GIRL   1966 film starring Lynn Redgrave in the title role as ugly duckling who marries a wealthy older man (James Mason) for the sake of the illegitimate baby of her roommate (Charlotte Rampling). Title song became pop hit by The Seekers.

GERMAN   Considered sister language of English because both are members of West Germanic group of Germanic subfamily of Indo-European language family. English also related to Yiddish, Afrikaans, Dutch, Flemish, Plattdeutsch and Frisian.

GERMAN MEASLES   Also rubella or three-day measles. Highly contagious disease. Symptoms appear two to three weeks following exposure. If contracted during first trimester of pregnancy, may cause birth defects such as blindness, deafness, mental retardation and heart damage.

GERMANY   Divided country in central Europe consisting of West Germany (called Bundesrepublik Deutschland, BRD) and East Germany (called Deutsche Demokratische Republik, DDR) West German flag is black, red and gold. It represents German Confederation and Weimar Republic, and was adopted in 1950 East German flag was the same as West Germany's from 1955–1959, when the Communists added their coat of arms.

GERONIMO (1829–1909)   Last warrior chief of Chirahua band of Apache Indians. Led tribe in series of attacks against U.S. and Mexican settlements, 1876–1886. Surrendered to General George Crook. Converted to Christianity. Given name, Goyathhay, meaning "yawning one." Nicknamed "Geronimo" by Mexicans.

GERSHWIN, GEORGE (1889–1937)   Musical composer born in New York. First Broadway show *La La Lucille* (1923) Composed the suite *Rhapsody in Blue* in 1924. *Of Thee I Sing* (1931), first musical to receive Pulitzer Prize for Drama; wrote first American folk-opera, *Porgy and Bess* (1935).

GERULAITIS, VITAS (1954 –) American tennis player, born in Brooklyn. Son of Lithuanian immigrants. Joined pro circuit, 1974. Won Australian Open, 1977. Nicknamed "Broadway Vitas," for love of New York nightlife, expensive cars.

GESTAPO Short for the German *Geheime Staatspolizei*, founded, 1933, Nazi Germany. Notorious for brutality to opponents of Nazi Party. Became regular State Police Force, 1936.

GESTATION PERIODS

Bear:	6–8 months
Horse:	11 months
Cat:	63 days
Lion:	108 days
Cattle:	9 months
Human:	9 months
Dog:	58–63 days
Rat:	22 days
Elephant:	21 months
Whale:	10–17 months

GET SMART TV comedy series starring Don Adams as Maxwell Smart, Agent 86 of the U.S. intelligence agency C.O.N.T.R.O.L. Premiered September 1965. Smart, assisted by Agent 99 (Barbara Feldon) and taking his orders from the chief (Edward Platt), would battle agents of K.A.O.S., an international organization of evil. Smart was inept but lucky and had a hidden telephone in his right shoe. His main verbal defense against his enemies was "Would you believe. . .?" and he'd apologize to his boss Thaddeus, "Sorry about that, Chief!"

GETAWAY, THE 1972 film, directed by Sam Peckinpah, about a husband and wife who plan and execute bank robbery, then attempt a complicated getaway from police and former accomplices. Steve McQueen and Ali MacGraw star, and get away.

GETTY, JEAN PAUL (1892–1976) American business executive. Amassed an estimated one billion dollars by the time of his death. Entered his father's business, age 22. A millionaire by age 24. Received roughly $15 million after his father's death, 1930. Bought oil stock at depression-low prices. Owner Getty Oil Corporation. Founded Getty Museum, Malibu, CA. Once remarked: "A billion dollars isn't what it used to be."

GIANT PANDA   Black and white, bearlike animal. Classification debated. Found in bamboo forests of China and Tibet. Endangered. Food supply unstable. Weighs up to 300 lbs. (140 kg.). Symbol of World Wildlife Fund.

GIBBON, EDWARD (1737–1794)   English historian. Wrote *The Decline and Fall of the Roman Empire*, 18th-century study of 13 centuries of Roman power. Concludes history is "little more than the crimes, follies and misfortunes of mankind."

GIBRALTAR   Located on a narrow peninsula on Spain's southern coast. Britain's only European colony. Official state flag is that of Great Britain, the Union Jack or British Union Flag. Also flies an unofficial civil flag picturing the colony's coat of arms. Separated from northern Africa by the Strait of Gibraltar, a narrow body of water (8–23 mi./13–37 km.) connecting the Atlantic Ocean and the Mediterranean Sea. At each side of the strait's eastern end is a huge rock, collectively called The Pillars of Hercules, consisting of the Rock of Gibraltar (Europe) and the Jebel Musa (Africa). This rocky peninsula is home to the Barbary apes, the only wild monkeys remaining in Europe. Gibraltar also contains the famous Trafalgar Graveyard.

GIBRAN, KAHLIL (1883–1931)   Novelist, poet, and author. Wrote 1923 prose poem *The Prophet*. Born in Lebanon, moved to Boston at 12. *The Prophet's* 28 sections deal with love, freedom, friendship, prayer and death. Considered his masterpiece, has been translated into 20 languages.

GILDA   1946 film starring Rita Hayworth and Glenn Ford. South American casino owner (George MacCready) hires Ford as his assistant; the owner's wife (Hayworth) falls in love with Ford. Introduces the song "Put the Blame on Mame."

GILLETTE, KING CAMP (1855–1932)   American inventor and manufacturer. At 21, was traveling salesman. Longed to invent a disposable item. Invented the safety razor, 1895. Idea came in a vision as he was examining his own razor.

GILMORE, GARY MARK (1941–1977)   Convicted murderer. Executed in Utah, January 17, 1977, by firing squad. Execution marked end to 10-year suspension of capital punishment in the U.S.

GIN Distilled rye, corn or other grain flavored with essential oils. Juniper berries give it its characteristic flavor. Sloe gin is a liqueur made from a type of plum.

GIN RUMMY Card game for two players (more can play by dividing into two teams and holding separate but simultaneous games between pairs of players). Each player gets 10 cards to start, then alternately gets to pick additional cards from top of unused portion of deck or turned-up discard pile, trying to arrange hand into runs (or melds) of three or more. When scoring, face cards worth 10 points, others worth face value.

GINZA. See TOKYO

GIRAFFE Genus *Giraffa*, species *camelopardalis*. Tallest animal. Up to 18 ft. (5 m.) in height; 6 ft. (1.8 m.) tall at birth. Can gallop up to 30 m.p.h. (48 km.p.h.). Has tongue 17 in. (43 c.m.) long. Has highest blood pressure of any mammal, to ensure blood flow to head. Almost never utters a sound.

GI'S Nickname for American army military troops. Name derives from "General Issue" the term stamped on their clothing, equipment and supplies. Popular figures as liberators of Nazi-occupied Europe, 1944–1945. Their unrestrained manner led some Europeans to describe them as "overpaid, oversexed and over here."

GISH SISTERS Two acting sisters, discovered by pioneer moviemaker D. W. Griffith. Lillian Gish (1896–   ) appeared in *Birth of a Nation* (1914) and *Intolerance* (1916). Dorothy Gish (1898–1968) starred in *Hearts of the World* (1918) and *Orphans of the Storm* (1922).

GLACIATION The process of glacier formation. Periods of glaciation are called Ice Ages, which last about 50,000 years with about 40,000 years in between. The last occurred about 20,000 years ago. Cirques, drumlins and eskers are geological features formed during glaciation.

GLADIOLUS Also sword lily. Flowering plant of iris family. Over 200 species, grows from bulbs called corms. Tall-stemmed; leaves resemble swords. Word from Latin *gladius*, meaning "sword," from which we get gladiolus, gladiator and gladiate.

GLASGOW Largest city in Scotland. One of world's major shipbuilding centers. Its docks and shipyards heavily bombed by Germans in World War II. Its two airports are Prestwick International

Airport and Glasgow Airport.

GLASS   Made chiefly from sand, soda and lime. First manufactured around 3000 B.C. Nature makes glass when: 1) lightning strikes sand; and 2) when heat from volcanic eruptions fuses rocks and sand into glass called obsidian.

GLAUCOMA   Eye disease from Latin meaning "cataract." Occurs when aqueous fluid cannot drain into blood vessels outside the eye. Pressure builds; may damage optic nerve, causing blindness.

GLEASON, JACKIE (1916–　　) "The Great One," a comedy star who came to TV from nightclubs, radio and Broadway. Recreated his radio role as the original Chester Riley for *The Life of Riley* (1949) on TV. *The Jackie Gleason Show* began in 1952, and he developed his repertoire of comic characters: Reggie Van Gleason; The Poor Soul; Ralph Kramden; and Joe the Bartender, who sang "My Gal Sal" at the show's opening. The June Taylor Dancers appeared each week in elaborate musical numbers.

GLENFIDDICH   Single malt Scotch is a product of Single, named distillery. Contains no grain spirits. Name means "Valley of the Deer." Unveiled Christmas Day in 1887. Delicate with a slightly sweet flavor, known as among world's best.

GLENN, JOHN HERSCHEL (1921–　　) American astronaut and U.S. senator from Ohio. First American to orbit the earth. His spacecraft *Friendship* 7 orbited the earth three times in less than five hours on February 20, 1962. Unsuccessful U.S. presidential bid in 1984.

GLIDER   Motorless monoplane with long, slender wings to make best use of air currents for soaring. Two methods for launching: bungey launching, men pulling plane with rubber rope from top of steep hill; or car-towing, car pulling glider by rope on flat land until airborne, then pilot releases rope.

GLUTEUS MAXIMUS   Round muscle at back of hip. Largest of body's muscles. Along with gluteus medius and quadriceps femoris, provides support that enables standing. Also involved in walking and running.

GO-KART   Tiny-wheeled motorized vehicle. Usually has bodyless tubular frame and small-capacity, single-cylinder engine mounted toward rear. Single seat for driver. Go-Kart Company formed 1957. Activities include pure racing, dragging, hill climbing. American

Stan Mott drove one around world, which took 3½ years.

GOAT Sheeplike mammal, genus Capra of the cow family Bovidae. Sometimes referred to as "the Poor Man's Cow." Essentially a mountain dweller. Used for milk, meat and goatskin. Mohair from fleece of Angora goat. Regarded by Cornell University study to be best suited for space travel with man.

GOAT ISLAND Divides Niagara Falls into American Falls and Horseshoe Falls. Located in Niagara River in western New York. Length is .75 mi. (1.2 km.).

GOBEL, GEORGE (1919–   ) Nightclub comedian-turned-TV-star in the 1950s. Affectionately known as "Lonesome George" because of his persona, a bewildered, innocent, born loser whose catch phrase, "Well, I'll be a dirty bird" became a popular byword.

GODEY, JOHN (1912–   ) American author. Wrote *The Taking of Pelham One, Two, Three* (1973), made into a 1974 film directed by Joseph Sargent, starring Walter Matthau, Robert Shaw and Martin Balsam. Story involves four criminals who take New York City subway train and passengers hostage for $1 million ransom.

GODDARD, ROBERT H. (1882–1945) American inventor and physicist. Considered the Father of Modern Rocketry. Patented over 200 rocketry inventions, some of which were useful many years later in America's space program.

GODFATHER, THE Oscar-winning Best Picture of 1972. Story of a syndicate chieftain, his daily life and his operations in the crime world. Based on Mario Puzo novel, film intentionally omitted the word "mafia" from the screenplay. Marlon Brando won Oscar for his portrayal of Don Corleone; Robert Duvall was nominated in his role of the family lawyer. Co-starring Al Pacino as heir Michael Corleone and Diane Keaton as his second wife. James Caan was Sonny Corleone. Directed by Francis Ford Coppola. Sequel, *The Godfather Part II* (1974), also won Best Picture Oscar. (see PUZO, MARIO)

GODZILLA Monster created by Japanese special effects genius Eiji Tsuburaya. Actually played by actor in rubber suit in *Godzilla, King of the Monsters* (1954), starring Raymond Burr. The monster, which had a mate (Gojilla), and a son (Minya), supposed to be Tyrannosaurus Rex aroused from hibernation by American nuclear tests in Pacific. Was 164 ft. (30 stories) tall, with incendiary radioactive breath. Helped create monster craze and made covers of *Time* and *Newsweek*.

GOEBBELS, JOSEPH (1897–1945) Minister of Propaganda and Enlightenment, Nazi Germany. A failed writer and poet, Goebbels quickly rose to power when he joined Hitler's Nazi Party. Committed suicide, with Hitler, May 1945, during Fall of Berlin.

GOERING, HERMANN WILHELM (1893–1946) German Nazi politician. Hitler's second in command, World War II. President, German legislative, 1928. Driving force behind Germany's prewar rearmament. Led development of Lüftwaffe, the air force, and its method of attack, blitzkrieg, meaning "lightning war." Sentenced to hanging for war crimes. Committed suicide with poison a few hours prior to scheduled execution.

GOING MY WAY 1944 Oscar-winning Best Picture about a young priest who is assigned to a church in a rough neighborhood. Bing Crosby starred and won Best Actor Oscar as Father O'Malley. Songs included "Swinging on a Star" and "Going My Way." Sequel, *The Bells of St. Mary's* (1945).

GOLD Pure gold is weak. Strengthened when alloyed with copper, silver, nickel and zinc. This also changes the color. Karat (K) denotes proportion of pure gold. 24K, pure gold; 18K, 75% pure; 14K, 58.3% pure. Yellow variety is 90% gold, 10% copper. Chemical symbol, Au.

GOLD RUSH Discovery by James Wilson Marshall at Sutter's Mill, January 24, 1848, marked start of California Gold Rush. By 1849, thousands of hopefuls known as "forty-niners" flocked west in search of fortune. Led to rapid expansion of the West. In 1896, gold found in Klondike Region of Yukon territory by George Carmacks, his Indian wife, Kate, and her relatives Shookum Jim and Tagish Charlie. Klondike gold rush produced $200 million in gold by 1928.

GOLD, FRANKINCENSE AND MYRRH. See MAGI, THE

GOLDEN GATE STRAIT Located in northwestern California. Five mi. (8 km.) long and 1–2 mi. (1.6–3.2 km.) wide. Connecting San Francisco Bay and Pacific Ocean. Spanned by Golden Gate Bridge connecting Oakland to San Francisco. Named by John Charles Frémont in 1846.

GOLDEN HIND, THE   Sixteenth-century ship. Used by Sir Francis Drake to sail around the world, 1577–1580. Originally named "Pelican"; renamed "Golden Hind" after the emblem of one of the voyage's financial backers.

GOLDFINGER. See FLEMING, IAN

GOLDFISH   Variety of carp originating in China and Japan. Bred from dull wild types to produce brilliant colors, unusual shapes and fins. Can be red, gold, orange, bronze, gray, black or white; become brown like their ancestors when returned to the wild. Also fade in color when kept in running or poorly lit water.

GOLDILOCKS AND THE THREE BEARS   Fairy tale. Definitive version attributed to Robert Southey, first published in 1837 in book of essays titled *The Doctor*. Southey said he learned story from his uncle William Dove, but it has many antecedents in folklore. Originally called "The Story of the Three Bears." Spoiled Goldilocks eats porridge of three bears, finding one bowl too cold, one too hot, one "just right."

GOLDWATER, BARRY (1909–   )   American politician. Republican senator from Arizona, 1952 to present. Archconservative. From a family of politically active Democrats. Ran for president against Lyndon Johnson, 1964. Advocated total worldwide victory over Communism and decreased Federal power. Used chemical symbols of gold and water as campaign emblem (AuH_2O). At the Republican Convention in San Francisco he said, "Extremism in defense of liberty is no vice, [and] moderation in pursuit of justice is no virtue." Despite backing by influential businesses and newspapers including the *Los Angeles Times*, Goldwater lost by one of the largest vote margins in U.S. history. Later favored military intervention in Vietnam and opposed détente with U.S.S.R.

GOLF   *Apron:* Closely cut grass surrounding green. Cut shorter than fairway but not as short as putting green itself.
Ball: Made of rubber with liquid core, has a surface with 336 slight depressions ("dimples") that reduce drag, improve accuracy and distance of flight. Maximum weight allowed is 1.62 oz. Minimum diameter: 1.68 in. for U.S., 1.62 in. for United Kingdom, Canada and international competitions.
Big three: Americans Jack Nicklaus and Arnold Palmer along with Gary Player of South Africa. Dominated professional golf through-

out the 1960s and early '70s. From 1960 to 1967, one of these three won the Masters title each year.

Grand Slam: Includes U.S. Open (begun 1900), Masters (begun 1934), the Professional Golfer's Association (PGA) Championship (begun 1920) and British Open (begun 1920). Only Masters (Augusta, GA, National) has permanent site. No golfer has ever won all four in one year.

Highest course: Tuctu Golf Club, Morococha, Peru, 14,335 ft. above sea level at lowest point. Golf has also been played on moon and in Tibet at altitudes over 16,000 ft.

Hole: Also called a cup. Diameter is 4¼ in., depth is 4 in. Flagstick or pin centered in cup displays the number of the green. Can be removed while player is putting.

Lowest course: Furnace Creek, Death Valley, CA, average 220 ft. below sea level.

Nineteenth hole: Golfers' terminology for clubhouse. After playing round of 18 holes of golf, players gather for drinks and talk at "19th Hole," the clubhouse bar.

Ryder Cup: Biennial tournament between teams of U.S. and British professional golfers. Started 1927, not held between 1937–1947. British have won only three times; last time 1973.

Scotch foursome: Golf match in which four players compete on two teams with each side playing only one ball. Partners take turns hitting the ball.

Slow play: According to rules administered by United States Golf Association (USGA), and Royal and Ancient Golf Club of St. Andrew's (Scotland), play must be "without undue delay," both during play on hole and between holing out and starting play from following tee. Penalties: in match play, loss of hole; in stroke play, two strokes with disqualification for repeated violation. If infraction occurs between holes, penalty strokes charged to upcoming hole.

Tee: Small wooden or plastic peg with concave top on which golf ball is placed prior to being driven. Golfers originally used small mound of dirt. George Grant of Boston was issued a patent on December 12, 1899, for tee with wooden stem and flexible tubular head. First marketable, all-wooden tee was Reddy Tee, invented 1920 by dental surgeon William Lowell.

United States Golf Association: Originated in 1894 after a meeting of golf clubs' officers, predominantly from the East Coast. Organized to standardize the sport, adopt uniform rules and regulate member status. Ruling organization of U.S. golf.

GOLF CLUBS Player may use maximum of 14 during a round. May replace damaged clubs, or add clubs, if starting with less than 14. Rule applies to partners sharing set of clubs. Three types of clubs: woods, numbered 1–7, used for long shots; irons, numbered 1–10, used for shorter shots approaching green; and putter, used for putting ball into cup.

Driver: No. 1 wood. Normally used for driving ball from tee. Wood club has head relatively broad from front to back. Usually made of persimmon wood, sometimes plastic.

Mashie-Niblick: Clubs originally had names instead of numbers. Mashie-niblick is 7-iron; halfway between a mashie (5-iron) and niblick (9-iron). Other names that have survived are driver, driving iron (1-iron), and wedge (10-iron).

GOLF ON THE MOON Astronaut Alan Shepard of Apollo 14 crew left three balls on moon, February 6, 1971. Using six-iron head attached to geology tool, swung one-handed at balls he dropped from space suit. Missed first; hit second about 200 yd., third about 400 yd. Normal six-iron shot travels about 140 yd., but moon has one-sixth of earth's gravity. Shepard awarded Metropolitan Golf Writers' Mulligan Award, a mulligan being a golfer who hits a shot again if he dislikes first shot.

GOLF, ORIGINS. See ST. ANDREWS

GOLF, PAR Standard score that an expert playing errorless golf under ordinary weather conditions would be expected to make on given hole. Based on distance from tee to hole. Yardage guidelines of the U.S. Golf Association:

Par	Men	Women
3	up to 250 yd.	up to 210 yd.
4	251–470 yd.	211–400 yd.
5	471 and over	401–575 yd.
6	—	576 and over

Birdie: one under par
Bogey: one over par
Double Bogey: two over par
Double Eagle: three under par
Eagle: two under par

GONDOLA. See VENICE

GONE WITH THE WIND. See MITCHELL, MARGARET

GONZALES, RICHARD ALONZO (PANCHO) (1928–   ) Los Angeles-born tennis player. Early star of pro tennis tour. Nickname, "Pancho," given to him at 17 by high school tennis player Charles Pate, who also gave him old racket, tennis balls and fundamental instructions (only coaching or lesson Gonzales had on way to U.S. Open titles, 1948–1949, and stellar pro career).

GOODBYE GIRL, THE 1977 film written by Neil Simon. Marsha Mason stars as title character who can't keep a man until an unwanted Richard Dreyfuss moves in. Dreyfuss won Best Actor Oscar for performance.

GOODBYE, NORMA JEAN 1976 feature film about early life of Marilyn Monroe. Misty Rowe plays Norma Jean Baker on her rocky road to stardom.

GOODING, GLADYS First of stadium organists. Played for Brooklyn Dodgers at Ebbets Field, 1940–1956, at Madison Square Garden for N.Y. Rangers of National Hockey League and N.Y. Knicks of National Basketball Association. Baseball and hockey use organists most often. Nancy Faust of Chicago White Sox awarded gold record by Mercury Records for reviving sales of "Kiss Him Goodbye (Na Na Hey Hey)," song she plays when opposing pitcher leaves game.

GOODMAN, BENNY (1909–   ) Jazz bandleader and clarinetist, known as "King of Swing." First musician to play jazz at Carnegie Hall (1938). Life portrayed by Steve Allen in feature film *The Benny Goodman Story* (1955).

GOODYEAR, CHARLES (1800–1860) American inventor. Discovered vulcanized rubber by lucky accident. In 1834, he dropped a piece of rubber on a stove and discovered that it became more stable. Before vulcanization, natural rubber was not useful because it was not durable in extreme heat or cold.

GOOLAGONG-CAWLEY, EVONNE (1951–   ) Tennis player. One of few Aborigines (native Australian) to achieve worldwide prominence. Won 1971 Wimbledon singles championship at age 19, and again in 1980. Married Roger Cawley, 1975. Lost U.S. Open finals four times in a row (1973–1976).

TRIVIAL CONQUEST

GOONS, THE British radio comedians consisting of Harry Secombe, Peter Sellers, Michael Bentine and Spike Milligan. Broadcast on BBC radio in the 1950s, the series pioneered the mixture of burlesque, farce, satire and fantasy, and inspired many of today's comedy TV series.

GORDON TRACY. See GOULD, CHESTER

GORDON, CHARLES (1833–1885) British soldier. Began as second lieutenant in Royal Engineering, 1852. Distinguished fighter in Crimean War, 1853–1856. In 1863, made commander of 3,500 Chinese peasants. Earned nickname "Chinese Gordon" for his victorious command. Died defending Khartoum against Sudanese rebels.

GORDY, BERRY, JR. (1929–) Former boxer turned founder of Motown Records. A songwriter since 1957; hits include "Lonely Teardrops" (1957) and "You Got What It Takes" (1959). Created Motown in Detroit during 1963 and groomed such talent as Stevie Wonder, Diana Ross and the Supremes, and Smokey Robinson. Produced movie *Lady Sings the Blues* (1972).

GORE, LESLEY (1946–) Singer/songwriter who achieved success at 17 with hit single "It's My Party" (1963). Other hits include: "Judy's Turn to Cry" (1964), "That's the Way Boys Are" (1964), "Sunshine, Lollipops and Rainbows" (1965) and "California Nights" (1967).

GOREN, CHARLES (1901–) American expert on card game of bridge. Born 1901, Philadelphia. Invented point-count bidding system, which has become standard. Wrote first bridge book, *Winning Bridge Made Easy*, 1936. Won world championships, 1950 and 1957, and 26 U.S. titles. Gave up law practice to concentrate on bridge.

GORGEOUS GEORGE. See WRESTLING, PROFESSIONAL

GORILLA Anthropoid (manlike) ape, only in Africa. Most powerful and largest of primates, averaging 5 ft. (1½ m.) in height and 600 lbs. (270 kg.). Typically shy. Male will pound chest with clenched fists if nervous or to frighten intruders. Considered less intelligent than chimpanzee and orangutan.

GORKY PARK Also known as Park of Culture and Rest. Located in Moscow, U.S.S.R. Named after writer Maksim Gorky.

Founded in 1928, it consists of a number of old gardens belonging to public or private buildings. Filled with cafés and open bandstands.

GOSPELS, THE   First four books of New Testament. Basically biographies of Jesus attributed to disciples Matthew, a tax collector; Mark; Luke, a physician; and John, a fisherman.

GOSSAMER ALBATROSS   Human-powered aircraft piloted and powered by California biologist Bryan Allen. In June 1979, became first human-powered aircraft to cross the English Channel, winning a $220,000 prize offered by a British industrialist. The 75 lb. plane made the 22½ mi. flight in less than 3 hours.

GOTHAM. See NEW YORK CITY NICKNAMES

GOULD, CHESTER (1900–   )   American cartoonist. Created Dick Tracy detective comic strip, 1931. First realistic police strip, although Tracy did use electronic gadgets like two-way wrist radio (later wrist TV). Tracy, scrupulously honest cop with square jaw and eagle-beak nose, inspired half-dozen movie serials, 1937–1947, first of which included character of brother Gordon, brainwashed to do evil deeds to Dick. Tracy also inspired 1940s radio series, 1950s TV series, 1960s animated cartoon series and Al Capp's L'il Abner parody, Fearless Fosdick.

GOYA, FRANCISCO JOSE DE (1746–1828)   Spanish artist. Gained early fame for portraits and genre work depicting human folly, then for painting war heroes. Late paintings were macabre treatments of nightmares. Paintings include, *Los Caprichos* (1796) and *May 3, 1808* (1814–1815). Etchings include *Disasters of War* series (1810–1813).

GRABLE, BETTY (1916–1973)   Movie actress who was the top box-office draw during World War II. Became GIs' favorite pinup girl and nicknamed "The Legs." Films include *Moon Over Miami* (1941), *Coney Island* (1943) and *Pin-Up Girl* (1944).

GRADUATE, THE   Hit 1967 film starring Dustin Hoffman in his first major role. Story of a young college grad who has an affair with one of his parent's friends and marries her daughter. Anne Bancroft starred as Mrs. Robinson. Director Mike Nichols won Oscar for direction. Song "The Sounds of Silence" opens the film, and other songs by Simon and Garfunkel used throughout, including "Mrs. Robinson."

GRADY, JAMES (1949–   )   American author. Wrote *Six*

Days of the Condor (1974), about sole survivor of a mass murder at a branch office of American CIA. Man tries to avoid police, FBI and CIA pursuers to find out who in his agency sold out. Robert Redford and Faye Dunaway starred in Sydney Pollack's *Three Days of the Condor* (1975), which compressed action into a long weekend. Also wrote *Shadow of the Condor* (1976) and *Catch the Wind* (1980).

GRAFFITI Singular, graffito. English adoption of Italian word for scribbling or scratching, has come to mean anonymous self-expression. Wall writing found in Pompeii preserved by eruption of Mt. Vesuvius in A.D. 79. Among best known graffito is "Kilroy was here," dating from World War II.

GRAHAM CRACKER Popular snack food. Originallly eaten by followers of Sylvester Graham (1794–1851), Presbyterian minister and advocate of dietary reform. Argued that consumption of meats and fats resulted in sexual excesses. Promoted vegetable diet as cure for alcoholism. Stressed substitution of whole wheat or graham flour for white flour.

GRAHAM, BILLY (1918–   ) Born William Franklin. American evangelist. Uses TV to spread his message. Became known after his 1949 conversion of several prominent Hollywood celebrities to Christianity. To justify his wealth he once said, "There is nothing in the Bible that says I must wear rags."

GRAHAM, SHEILA Hollywood gossip columnist and author of several nonfiction books, notably *Beloved Infidel* (1958, co-written with Gerold Frank) and others about her relationship with novelist F. Scott Fitzgerald in last years before his death in 1940. Filmed in 1959 with Deborah Kerr as Graham and Gregory Peck as Fitzgerald.

GRANATELLI, ANDY (1923–   ) Former auto racer, later owner of Indianapolis 500 cars. Wears badge No. 500 at race. Introduced turbine engines to Indianapolis in 1967, with driver Parnelli Jones at wheel, using Pratt and Whitney engine. Car was in lead when gear problem stopped it with four laps left. Granatelli also chairman and spokesman for STP oil and gasoline additives, called "the racer's edge."

GRAND CANYON, THE Giant gorge 217 mi. (347 km.) long and 1 mi. (1.6 km.) or more deep in northwestern Arizona. Deepest land gorge in world. Extends from mouth of Little Colorado, south of Marble Canyon, west to Grand Wash Cliffs. Explorers can take Bright Angel Trail down to Colorado River. Canyon's sides formed millions of years ago when Colorado River cut through the rock.

GRAND CENTRAL STATION   Located at 42nd Street and Park Avenue, New York City. Built from 1903–1913. World's largest train station. Concourse leading from waiting room is 385 ft. (115.5 m.) long, 125 ft. (37.5 m.) wide.

GRAND COULEE DAM   Largest concrete dam in U.S. and greatest single source of water power. Dams Columbia River in state of Washington. Built with roughly 12 million cu. yd. (9 million cu. m.) of concrete. Has three power plants.

GRAND HOTEL   1932 film, which won Best Picture Oscar, about a day in the life of guests in Berlin Hotel. Starring Greta Garbo, a lonely ballerina; John Barrymore, a jewel thief; Joan Crawford, an ambitious stenographer and Wallace Beery, a hardened businessman.

GRAND MARNIER   Orange-flavored French liqueur made from Cognac. First made 1880. Comes in two varieties: cordon rouge and cordon jaune. 80 proof.

GRANGE, HAROLD (RED) (1903–   )   Football player known as "the Galloping Ghost." All-American halfback at University of Illinois, 1923–1925, scored first four times he touched ball (vs. Michigan, 1924). Played for Canton Bulldogs, New York Yankees, and Chicago Bears in pro career. Made several films while playing; became radio and TV sportscaster after retirement.

GRANT'S TOMB   The $600,000 memorial in New York City, finished in 1897, holds the bodies of Ulysses S. Grant (1822–1885) and his wife (1826–1902). Grant was 18th U.S. president, 1869–1877.

GRAPEFRUIT   Or *citris grandis*, large citrus fruit. U.S. produces 60% of world's total, 75% of which is grown in Florida. Majority of crop is canned, frozen or made into juice. So called because it grows in clusters like grapes.

GRAPES   Smooth, juicy berries that grow in clusters on vines. Used to make wine, brandy, champagne and sherry, eaten as table fruit; dried as raisins, and used for juice and jelly. The U.S. Department of Agriculture meat inspection stamp uses a purple dye derived from grapes.

GRAPES OF WRATH, THE   Epic 1940 film based on John

Steinbeck novel. Story of the Okie migration to California during the depression won Jane Darwell an Oscar for Best Supporting Actress. John Ford directed and won Academy Award. Theme song, "The Red River Valley." (see STEINBECK, JOHN)

GREASE One of the longest-running musicals on Broadway, became a hit movie in 1978. John Travolta and Olivia Newton-John star as high school lovers. Songs include "Beauty School Dropout" and "We Go Together."

GREAT BARRIER REEF World's largest coral formation. Located off northeast coast of Australia. In recent decades, crown-of-thorns starfish have been eating the reef's living coral, thus destroying the chance for new reef to grow.

GREAT BRITAIN Europe's largest island (mainland 94,251 sq. mi./244,108 sq. km.). Consists of England, Northern Ireland, Scotland and Wales. Official name: The United Kingdom of Great Britain and Northern Ireland.

GREAT DICTATOR, THE 1940 film by Charlie Chaplin, which satirizes Adolph Hitler. Chaplin plays dual role of Jewish ghetto barber and dictator Adenoid Hynkel of Tomania. Jack Oakie co-stars as Napaloni, a takeoff of Mussolini.

GREAT ESCAPE, THE Popular 1963 war movie about a group of POWs planning a mammoth breakout from a German prison camp during World War II in three tunnels named Tom, Dick and Harry. Steve McQueen starred as "the Cooler King"; Charles Bronson played "the Tunnel King." Only three escape in the end.

GREAT IMPOSTER, THE 1961 feature film starring Tony Curtis as Ferdinand Waldo Demara, a high school dropout who successfully posed as a college professor, a penologist and a Royal Canadian Navy surgeon.

GREAT LAKES *Lake Michigan:* N cen U.S. (22,400 sq. mi./58,016 sq. km.)
Lake Huron: E cen N. America (23,010 sq. mi./59,560 sq. km.)
Lake Superior: U.S. and Canada, northernmost and westernmost (31,820, sq. mi./82,414 sq. km.)
Lake Erie: E cen N. America, U.S./Canada boundary (9,940 sq. mi./25,745 sq. km.)
Lake Ontario: U.S. and Canada, easternmost, all Great Lakes empty into it (7,540 sq. mi./19,529 sq. km.)

World's largest group of freshwater lakes. Only Lake Michigan lies entirely within the U.S.; all others border Ontario, Canada's second largest province. The lakes border eight U.S. states: Wisconsin, Michigan, Illinois, Indiana, Ohio, Pennsylvania, New York and Minnesota. Major cities located on the lakes: Chicago (largest), Milwaukee and Gary (all on Lake Michigan); Buffalo, Cleveland and Toledo (on Lake Erie); and Duluth, Superior and Thunder Bay (on Lake Superior).

GREAT RACE, THE   1965 comedy film directed by Blake Edwards. Tony Curtis plays hero; Natalie Wood, heroine. Jack Lemmon, as villainous Professor Fate, drives his Hannibal Twin 9 in an auto race that spans three continents.

GREAT SALT LAKE   Remnant of prehistoric Lake Bonneville which once covered one-fourth of the state of Utah. Largest lake in the state. Fed by the Bear, Weber and Jordan rivers. Continual shrinking adds to the salt concentration. Sinking impossible due to salt content.

GREAT TRAIN ROBBERY   Allegedly first train robbery, 1855. Ronald Biggs, posing as rich businessman, stole trainload of gold bullion destined for Crimea. The gold was intended to pay English troops at war there.

GREAT WALL OF CHINA, THE   Built entirely by hand, taking hundreds of years. It averages 25 ft. high, 15–20 ft. wide, and stretches 1,684 mi., about the distance from New York to Ohama. Is only structure built by man that can be seen from space.

GREAT WHITE HOPE, THE. See SACKLER, HOWARD

GREAT WHITE WAY   Nickname for section of Broadway adjacent to Times Square that comprises theater district in New York City. Named for the glow of the rows of white lights on theater marquees.

GREATEST STORY EVER TOLD, THE   1965 film based on life of Jesus Christ. Directed by George Stevens with an all-star cast led by Max von Sydow as Christ.

GREECE   Site of first European civilization, which began more than 2,000 years ago. Ancient Greeks called themselves Hellenes and their land Hellas. Official name of Greece today is *Elliniki Dimokratia*, meaning Hellenic Republic.

TRIVIAL CONQUEST

Islands: More than 200 of the country's islands are in a group called Cyclades, located in Aegean Sea. Kythnos, siphnos and Mikonos are included in this group.

GREEK ALPHABET

Alpha	Nu
Beta	Xi
Gamma	Omicron
Delta	Pi
Epsilon	Rho
Zeta	Sigma
Eta	Tau
Theta	Upsilon
Iota	Phi
Kappa	Chi
Lambda	Psi
Mu	Omega

GREEK PREFIXES

Greek	*English*
aero-	air
cardio-	heart
cyto-	cell
encephalo-	brain
eu-	good
geo-	earth
masto-	breast
ornitho-	bird
pseudo-	false
sclero-	hard
xeno-	foreign

GREEN BAY PACKERS National Football League team owned by citizens of Green Bay, WI, smallest city (87,899) to have major-league franchise in any sport. Team organized 1919 by Curly Lambeau. Indian Packing Corp. supplied money for equipment, hence team name. Joined NFL 1921, dominated in 1960s (five titles) under coach Vince Lombardi. Winners of first two Super Bowls.

GREEN MONSTER Green, 37-foot-high left-field wall at Fenway Park, Boston, home of Boston Red Sox. Extends from left field corner (315 ft. from home plate) to left-center field (379 ft. from plate). Inviting target for right-handed hitters, "monster" for pitchers. 23-foot-high net installed above wall to prevent home-run balls from sailing into adjacent street.

GREENE, GRAHAM (1904–) English novelist, short-story writer and playwright. Many works set in exotic locales. Most famous for *The Third Man* (1950), story of writer searching post–World War II Vienna for dead friend Harry Lime. Also wrote *The Power and the Glory* (1940), *The Quiet American* (1955), *Our Man in Havana* (1958) and *The Comedians* (1966).

GREENLAND World's largest island. Province of Denmark. Official languages are Danish and Greenlandic. Most inhabitants have Eskimo and Danish ancestors. Named Greenland by Vikings to attract tourists though even in summer only coastal areas are green.

GREENWICH, ENGLAND London borough located on 0° longitude (the Prime Meridian). Astronomers designated line passing through Royal Greenwich Observatory as earth's Prime Meridian, 1884. Greenwich mean time (GMT) standard time for world.

GRENADINE SYRUP Red, acidic juice of pomegranate, basis of red sweet syrup of little or no alcoholic content called grenadine. Used as sweetener or coloring agent, provides ruddy glow in a Tequila Sunrise.

GREY, JOEL (1932–) Broadway actor who won an Oscar for his portrayal as emcee of Kit Kat Club in *Cabaret* (1972). Other movie credits include *Buffalo Bill and the Indians* (1976) and *The Seven Percent Solution* (1976).

GREY, ZANE (1872–1939) American novelist and short-story writer. Wrote at least 54 formulaic novels about America's Wild West, including *The Last of the Plainsmen* (1908) and *Riders of the Purple Sage* (1912). Abandoned career in dentistry when books became best-sellers. Also wrote nonfiction books on camping and game fishing.

GREYHOUND AND WHIPPET RACING Introduced to U.S. in 1907 by Owen Patrick Smith, inventor of mechanical rabbit, which dogs chase. Races usually ¼ mi., run counterclockwise. Famous races include St. Petersburg Derby, Flagler International and English Derby. Greyhounds and whippets, smaller breed of greyhound, are both used for parimutuel racing.

GRISSOM, VIRGIL (1926–1967) First U.S. astronaut to

change orbit in flight, and to make more than one flight. First flight aboard spacecraft Mercury landed in the Atlantic. Craft accidentally filled with water. Killed, 1967, in test preparations of Apollo flight designed to land astronauts on moon.

GROSS   Twelve dozen or 144. Adopted from French *grosse* meaning "big." Also called a small gross, as opposed to a great gross, which is 12 gross, or 1,728.

GROUNDHOG DAY   February 2. The day when groundhog emerges to look for its shadow. Legend has it that shadow forecasts six more weeks of winter. From European belief that a sunny, thus shadow-producing, Candlemas Day (February 2) predicts six more winter weeks.

GUCCIONE, BOB (1930–   )   Born in Brooklyn, NY. Former artist and greeting card designer. Started *Penthouse* in 1965 as competitor to *Playboy*. Has also published *Forum, Viva, Photo World* and *Omni*. Produced and directed film *Caligula* (1979).

GUESS WHO'S COMING TO DINNER   Hit 1967 feature film starring Spencer Tracy and Katharine Hepburn as parents shocked when their daughter (played by Katharine Houghton) brings her fiancé to dinner and discover he is black (portrayed by Sidney Poitier). Hepburn won Oscar for Best Actress. Tracy's last film.

GUESS WHO, THE   American rock group. Performed "American Woman" at the White House under the Nixon administration. The administration set a record in entertaining at a rate of 45,000 guests per year.

GUEVARA DE LA SERNA, ERNESTO (1928–1967)   Revolutionary. Known by nickname, "Che." Prominent figure in Cuban revolution that brought Fidel Castro to power, 1959. Born in Argentina. Traveled widely in Latin America. Suddenly disappeared at height of his power. Resurfaced, leading a guerrilla attempt to overthrow Bolivian government. Killed, October 9, 1967, by Bolivian army, which put his body on display.

GUGGENHEIM MUSEUM   Founded by Solomon R. Guggenheim in 1937 to promote art and education. Located in New York City on Museum Row on Fifth Avenue. Building designed by Frank Lloyd Wright.

GUINNESS, ALEC (1914–   )   British actor of stage and screen. Played eight roles in *Kind Hearts and Coronets* (1949). Other roles include *The Man in the White Suit* (1951), *The Ladykillers* (1955) and *Dr. Zhivago* (1965). Won Oscar for Best Actor playing Colonel Nicholson in *The Bridge on the River Kwai* (1957). Recently seen as Obi Wan-Kenobi in *Star Wars* (1977) and its sequels.

GULF OF BOTHNIA   Long gulf between Sweden and Finland, extending from northern side of Baltic Sea. Aland Islands (Finland) form barrier across its mouth.

GULF OF MEXICO   World's largest gulf. Bordered by five U.S. states: Texas, Alabama, Florida, Louisiana and Mississippi.

GULF OF PANAMA   Last leg of Panama Canal when entering from the Atlantic. Flows into Pacific Ocean. Canal connects Atlantic and Pacific Oceans. Average passage time, eight hours.

GULF STREAM, THE   Large ocean current originating in Gulf of Mexico. Warm water current flows an average of 4 m.p.h., influences climate of eastern North America and northwestern Europe.

GULLIVER, LEMUEL. See SWIFT, JONATHAN

GUM DEPARTMENT STORE. See RED SQUARE

GUNGA DIN. See KIPLING, RUDYARD

GUNS OF NAVARONE, THE   1961 film based on novel by Alistair MacLean. Six men are sent to do an impossible mission: destroy two huge guns on a German-held island which cannot be attacked from air or sea. Gregory Peck stars. David Niven plays demolitions expert.

GUNSMOKE   The longest-running Western TV series began its run September 1955. John Wayne turned down lead role for fear of being stereotyped as a cowboy. James Arness accepted and starred as Marshal Matt Dillon of Dodge City, KS, and other supporting characters included Doc Adams, played by Milburn Stone; Chester Goode, played by Dennis Weaver; and Kitty Russell, owner of Longbranch Saloon, played by Amanda Blake. Burt Reynolds played Blacksmith Quint Asper 1962–1965. Was top-rated TV series 1957–1961.

GUNTHER, TOODY   Partner of Officer Francis Muldoon in patrol car number 54 in TV series *Car 54, Where Are You?* (1961–1963). Toody portrayed by Joe E. Ross; Muldoon by Fred Gwynne.

GUSTAV V (1858–1950)   King of Sweden, 1907–1950.

Reigned during period of neutrality and socialistic development. Fostered cooperation among Scandinavian countries.

GUTENBERG BIBLE, THE Properly called Mazarin Bible, from 1760 discovery in library of Cardinal Mazarin in Paris. First typeset book. Printed by Johann Gutenberg (1400–1468), German printer who invented movable type. Has 42 lines to page. Only 21 copies remain in existence, with one bringing $2 million at an April 1978 auction. Another located at Huntington Library, San Marino (near Los Angeles), CA.

GUTHRIE, JANET (1938–   ) First woman to drive in Indianapolis 500 auto race. Qualified in 1977, her second attempt. Finished 29th after car broke down. Improved placing to 9th in 1978. Drove for championship car builder Rolla-Vollstedt. Until 1972, women not even allowed into pit and refueling areas at Indianapolis.

GUTHRIE, WOODROW (WOODY) (1912–1967) Folk singer, composer of over 1,000 ballads. Composed "This Land is Your Land" and "Union Maid." Influenced by Great Depression. Died of Huntington's chorea, hereditary disease of basal ganglia and cerebral cortex, characterized by choreiform (dancelike) movements, psychosis and intellectual deterioration. Autobiography entitled *Bound for Glory*, also a 1976 film starring David Carradine as Guthrie.

GWINNETT, BUTTON. See JEFFERSON, THOMAS

GYMNASTICS, SCORING Perfect score in gymnastics is 10. Each exercise is scored 10 to zero, with deductions of whole, ½ and ¹⁄₁₀ points. Gymnasts penalized for general faults (lack of assurance or elegance) and for faults specific to apparatus.

GYPSY ROSE LEE (1913–1970) Burlesque queen, onstage from age six. Sister of actress June Havoc. Appeared in films, including, *Belle of the Yukon* (1944) and *Screaming Mimi* (1957). Life story made into Broadway musical *Gypsy*.

H

H-BOMB Or hydrogen bomb. One of most powerful. Energy derives from fusion (joining together) of hydrogen atoms. Produces lethal radioactive fallout. Hydrogen fusion occurs in the sun and stars, producing heat.

HABEAS CORPUS Legal term from Latin meaning "you have the body." Refers to a variety of writs whose object is to bring a party before the court. Protects against illegal detainment or imprisonment.

HACKETT, SIR JOHN WINTHROP (1910–   ) Author. Wrote 1978 best-seller with other top-ranking NATO staff and military advisers describing political and military scenarios leading up to war between NATO and Warsaw Pact forces, scheduled to take place August 1985. Western forces suffer serious early losses but stall Pact countries in later years. Also wrote essay collection, *Sweet Uses of Adversity: An Experience* (1974).

HADRIAN'S WALL Barrier built by Roman Emperor Hadrian, A.D. 120s, where no natural boundary existed. Separated England and Scotland and ran for 73 mi. (117 km.). Ruins remain.

HAGGARD, MERLE (1937–   ) Country music singer and composer. Nicknamed "The Okie from Muskogee," after his popular song. Has written many songs, which have become country standards, including, "Sing Me a Sad Song," "Hungry Eyes" and "Today I Started Loving You Again."

HAGMAN, LARRY (1930–   ) Television actor best

known for his portrayal of J. R. Ewing, the principal character of the series *Dallas*. Son of actress Mary Martin, Hagman gained fame as Tony Nelson, the "master," on *I Dream of Jeannie*. (see J. R.)

HAIFA   Israel's chief and largest port and on the eastern Mediterranean. Located on the Bay of Acre. Third largest Israeli city. Has oil refinery, factories, seamanship and technical schools.

HAIG, ALEXANDER (1924–   )   American politician. Reagan's Secretary of State, 1981–1982. After Reagan was shot, March 30, 1981, declared, "I'm in control now." Resigned from the post, 1982. Formerly supreme commander of NATO forces, 1974–1979. Named army vice-chief of staff, 1973. Left to become Nixon adminstration's chief of staff.

HAIL   Hard, round balls of ice. Onionlike structure. Falls from clouds during thunderstorms, especially in spring and summer. Extremely rare in tropics, polar regions, and over oceans.

HAIL TO THE CHIEF   Music by James Sanderson, words from Sir Walter Scott's play *Lady of the Lake*. Since 1828, played at public appearances of U.S. president.

HAILEY, ARTHUR (1920–   )   English-born American novelist of fast-paced soap operas with glamorous backgrounds. *Hotel* (1965), best-seller set in New Orleans luxury hotel St. Gregory. Deals with hotel management, an attempted rape, a racial incident and a robbery. *Airport* (1968), epic about a disaster at Lincoln International Airport. In it, a snowstorm downs a 707, blocking runway 29, and a man with a bomb is aboard the plane. Helen Hayes won Best Supporting Actress, 1970 film version. *Overload* (1965), novel about public utility industry. Hero Nim Goldman is executive of Golden State Power and Light Co. in California.

HAIPHONG HARBOR   North Vietnam. Mined by the U.S., 1972, in a last-ditch effort to halt a major invasion of South Vietnam.

HAIR   Broadway musical about the hippie movement of the late 1960s opened in 1968. Hits from the show include "Good Morning, Starshine" and "Aquarius." In the song "Hair," wearing a toga made of long beautiful hair will cause a gaga at the go-go. Feature film made in 1979.

HAITI   Western portion of island Hispaniola located in West Indies. Physician and voodoo authority Dr. Francois Duvalier (1907–1971) elected president in 1957 and president for life in 1964. He kept a secret police force called the *ton ton macoutes*, meaning "bo-geymen."

HALDEMAN, HARRY ROBBINS (H.R.) (1926–   ) Nixon's Chief of Staff, 1969–1973. Called the "Iron Chancellor" and "Nixon's S.O.B." His involvement in the Watergate break-in and cover-up caused him to resign and serve 18 months in prison. Succeeded by Alexander Haig.

HALEY, ALEX PALMER (1921–   ) American black author whose *Roots* (1976), tracing his family heritage from Africa, won a special citation 1977 Pulitzer Prize and became successful TV mini-series. Helped black Muslim and civil rights leader Malcolm X (1925–1965) write *The Autobiography of Malcolm X* (1965), finishing it after Malcolm X's assassination (February 21, 1965). Frequent contributor to *Playboy*, conducted *Playboy* interviews with jazz musician Miles Davis, Martin Luther King, Jr., Malcolm X and American Nazi Party leader George Lincoln Rockwell.

HALLEY'S COMET Spectular comet that can be seen from earth every 75 to 79 years, averaging about 76. Expected to return in 1986. Named for English astronomer who correctly predicted its arrival in 1682.

HALSEY, ADMIRAL WILLIAM F. (1882–1959) World War II commander in the Pacific. Defeated Japanese repeatedly, egging his men on with motto, "Hit hard, hit fast, hit often." His manner and success earned him the nickname "Bull."

HAMILTON, GEORGE, IV (1937–   ) Country singer popular since mid-1950s. Hit songs include, "A Rose and a Baby Ruth," "West Texas Highway," "Break My Mind" and "Abiline," number-one hit about the "prettiest town" he has ever seen.

HAMLIN, VINCENT T. (1900–   ) American cartoonist. Created *Alley Oop* (1933), caveman in the Kingdom of Moo. Mounted on faithful pet dinosaur Dinny, brings order to prehistoric kingdom, which is perpetually going to pot under inept leadership of King Guzzle.

HAMMETT, (SAMUEL) DASHIELL (1894–1961) American writer who created the first "hard-boiled" private eye, Sam Spade. Met Lillian Hellman in early 1930s and began love affair that lasted until his death 30 years later. He taught her how to write (see HELLMAN, LILLIAN). Hammett wrote five novels.

Red Harvest (1920) and *The Dain Curse* (1929) featured the Nameless Continental Operative. *The Maltese Falcon* (1930), only novel featuring San Francisco detective Sam Spade (also appeared in three short stories collected in *Adventures of Sam Spade and Other Stories*, 1944). Spade calls Frisco "my burg," knows city inside and out. Searches for statue of black bird, stolen in Orient, and for killer of his partner, Miles Archer. Bird, said to be worth a fortune, turns out to be fake. Novel filmed three times in ten years, twice as *The Maltese Falcon* (1931 and 1941) and once as *Satan Met a Lady* (1936). Last version starred Humphrey Bogart as Spade, considered an American classic. *The Glass Key* (1931) featured detective Ned Beaumont, Hammett's favorite character. *The Thin Man* (1934) featured husband and wife detectives Nick and Nora Charles and their dog, Asta.

HANCOCK, JOHN (1737–1793)   American Revolutionary statesman. Wealthy. Made generous contributions to the Revolution. Affixed most flamboyant signature to Declaration of Independence, July 4, 1776. Remarked: "There, I guess King George can read that." Little known about actual signing; only signers present.

HANDWRITING ANALYSIS   Or graphology. Examination of handwriting as a reflection of personality, tension and physical and emotional state. Holds that upward slant marks enthusiasm; downward slant, discouragement; pointed letters, competition and aggression. Used by psychologists as diagnostic aid.

HANGING GARDENS OF BABYLON   Presumably built for one of his wives by King Nebuchadnezzar II, ruler of Babylon (605–562 B.C.). No trace of gardens remain. Babylonian priest described it as laid out on brick terraces 400 ft. (120 m.) square, 75 ft. (23 m.) above ground. Only living wonder of the Seven Wonders of the Ancient World.

HANNIBAL (247–183 B.C.)   North African leader and military strategist. When Rome declared war on Carthage, 218 B.C., Hannibal led troops, horses and elephants over the Pyrenees and Alps to battle. When Rome demanded his surrender, he committed suicide.

HAPPY BIRTHDAY TO YOU   Traditional birthday song written in 1893 by Patty and Mildred Hill for Patty's kindergarten school. Other children's songs written by duo include "Good Morning Song" and "Rainy Day Good Morning."

HARDY BOYS, THE. See STRATEMEYER, ED-WARD L.

HARDY, ANDY   The typical American teenager of the late 1930s and early 1940s as portrayed by Mickey Rooney in a series of films produced by MGM. Andy lived in the middle American town of Carvel with his mother (Fay Holden) and his father, a judge (Lewis Stone).

HARDY, OLIVER (1892–1957)   The overweight half of Laurel & Hardy, known for his tie twiddle, long-suffering looks into the camera, and the line, "This is another fine mess you've gotten us into!" Features include *Sons of the Desert* (1933), *Way Out West* (1937) and *Blockheads* (1938). Won Oscar for short *The Music Box* (1932).

HARDY, THOMAS (1840–1928)   English novelist and poet. Wrote melancholy novels about men fighting fate and environment. Among his works: *Far from the Madding Crowd* (1874), *The Return of the Native* (1878), *Tess of the D'Urbervilles* (1891) and *Mayor of Casterbridge* (1886), about mayor of town in Wessex County, England, shortly before 1830. Twenty years earlier, in drunken frenzy, mayor had sold his wife and daughter to a sailor, and they return.

HARLEM GLOBETROTTERS   All-black basketball team whose combination of skill, vaudeville and worldwide travel is credited with making the sport international. Since founded by Abe Saperstein, nearly 100 million people in 90 countries have seen them play in last 50 years, winning more than 98 percent of their 12,000 games. "Sweet Georgia Brown" is theme song.

HARLOW, JEAN (1911–1937)   American actress. First female film star to make cover of *Life* (May 1937) as "the Sex Symbol." Died one month later.

HARNESS RACING   Racing in which horse (called a Standardbred) pulls driver in a sulky, a light rig with bicycle-type tires. Shafts and harness attach the sulky to the horse; its freewheeling action and balance make weight of driver relatively unimportant. Two categories are pacing and trotting. In pacing, horse moves both legs on one side of the body forward simultaneously. A free-legged pacer is one that races without hoppies, the leg harness that guides horse's stride. Sometimes called "sidewheelers" because of rolling gate. A trotter moves left front leg and right rear leg simultaneously, then right front and left rear. Pacing's Triple Crown consists of Little Brown Jug, Cane Futurity and Messenger Stakes. Little Brown Jug is its principal leg, a one-mile race which has run since 1946 (Delaware, OH), and is named for world-champion pacer of 19th century. Trotting's Triple Crown consists of Kentucky Futurity, Hambletonian and Yonkers Trot.

HAROLD AND MAUDE   Bud Cort stars as a 20-year-old obsessed by death, who strikes up a relationship with 79-year-old swinger Ruth Gordon. Cat Stevens' music provides entertaining listening in this black comedy, ignored upon initial release but now a cult classic.

HARRIS, JOEL CHANDLER (1848–1908) American writer who adapted black folk legends in *Uncle Remus—His Songs and Sayings* (1880), humorous tales told in dialect. Uncle Remus is happy-go-lucky, elderly black servant who tells stories to little white boy about Br'er Fox and Br'er Rabbit, natural enemies of the briar patch. Basis for Walt Disney film *Song of the South* (1946), which combined live action and animation.

HARRIS, RICHARD (1932–   ) Irish actor, starring in many films including *Mutiny on the Bounty* (1962), *Major Dundee* (1965), *Camelot* (1967), *Cromwell* (1970) and *A Man Called Horse* (1969). Had hit record, "MacArthur Park," in 1968.

HARRIS, TOM (1913–   ) Psychotherapist and author. Wrote *I'm OK, You're OK* (1967), preaching Transactional Analysis as manual for survival of humankind. Tells people how to overcome worry that they are wrong and others right by believing in and constantly being aware of their own values.

HARRISON, GEORGE (1943–   ) Played lead guitar and wrote songs for The Beatles from 1958–1970. When The Beatles broke up, he released a three-record set, *All Things Must Pass* (1971), which included the number-one single "My Sweet Lord," a song which caused a lawsuit on the grounds it sounded too much like the Chiffons' 1963 hit, "He's So Fine." (see BEATLES, THE)

HARRY AND TONTO   1974 feature film directed by Paul Mazursky. Art Carney won an Oscar for Best Actor in this story of a 72-year-old-man who makes a cross-country trip with his best friend, a cat named Tonto.

HARRY'S NEW YORK BAR   Famous bar in Paris. Opened

in 1911 by Tod Sloans, taken over by Harry MacElhone in 1913. Watering hole for F. Scott Fitzgerald and Ernest Hemingway. Bloody Marys invented here in 1920.

HART, JOHNNY (1931–   )   Creator, caveman B.C. comic strip. Began 1958. B.C., strip's hero, is "average caveman." Emphasizes timelessness of human nature. Turned down by five syndicates before *Herald-Tribune* syndicate bought it.

HARTFORD   Capital of Connecticut. Home of roughly 50 insurance companies' headquarters, hence, known as "Insurance Capital of the World." In 1835, Hartford Fire Insurance Company was able to pay its claims after a serious fire in New York City, giving Hartford its reputation for dependable insurance companies.

HARVARD LAMPOON, THE   Harvard University's century-old humor magazine. Takes name from French refrain *lampons*— "let's drink"—in 17th century French satirical drinking songs. Term applies to any pointed mockery of individual or institution. Alumni of Harvard magazine founded National Lampoon humor monthly.

HARVARD UNIVERSITY   The country's first university. Founded, 1636, in Massachusetts, just 16 years after the first landing of the Pilgrims. Followed by the College of William and Mary in 1693, and by Yale University, 1701.

HARVEST MOON   Name of the full moon that occurs closest to the autumnal equinox (about September 23), usually in October. Called Harvest Moon because it is so bright that farmers can harvest at night by its light.

HARVEY WALLBANGER   Cocktail made of 1 oz. vodka, 6 oz. orange juice and 1/2 oz. Galliano, an Italian liqueur created in the 1800s and named after Italian Major Giuseppe Galliano. The liqueur is made from herbs and flowers, is golden, spicy, aromatic and floats on top of the wallbanger.

HARWICH-OSTENDE FERRY. See FERRIES, ENGLAND-BELGIUM

HATFIELD-MCCOY FEUD   Savage fighting between two 19th-century southern clans. Began 1882 when Johnse Hatfield attempted to elope with Rosanna McCoy. In the ensuing quarrel, three McCoys and a Hatfield were killed. Led to nine years of battles along the border of Kentucky and West Virginia. Feud ended with the marriage of a Hatfield to a McCoy, March 21, 1891.

HAUPTMANN, BRUNO RICHARD (1900– 1936) Convicted criminal. Tried for kidnapping and murder of Charles Lindbergh, Jr. Proceedings began January 1, 1935. Considered the "Trial of the Century." Guilt never absolutely determined. Executed.

HAVERSIAN CANALS Microscopic channels in bone that blood vessels pass through.

HAWAII Only U.S. state not on mainland of North America. Made completely of islands in South Pacific Ocean, hence has no borders. *Science Digest* calls Hawaii the most healthful state. First part of the U.S. to be attacked in World War II, when Japanese bombed naval base at Pearl Harbor on December 7, 1942.

Rainfall: Receives greatest amount of rain in the world, average 460 in. (1,168 cm.) per year.

Pineapple: State's second largest crop behind sugarcane. Produces one-fifth of the world's pineapples on its 47,000 acres of plantations. Island of Lanai ("The Pineapple Island") is owned by the Dole Company, and all its cultivated land is on one plantation.

Volcanoes: Of the state's eight major islands, only Hawaii has active volcanoes: Mauna Loa (last eruption 1978) and Kilauea (last eruption 1983). World's largest dormant volcano, Halaekala Crater, is on island of Maui.

Last state to join Union, 1949.

HAWN, GOLDIE (1945–   ) TV actress turned movie star. Regular on TV series *Laugh-In*. Won Oscar for Best Supporting Actress in *Cactus Flower* (1969). Appeared with Peter Sellers in *There's A Girl In My Soup* (1970) and Warren Beatty in *Shampoo* (1975).

HAWTHORNE, NATHANIEL (1804–1864) American novelist and short-story writer. Wrote *Twice-Told Tales* 1837 and 1842), *The House of the Seven Gables* (1851), *The Blithedale Romance* (1852) and *The Marble Faun* (1860). In novel *The Scarlet Letter* (1850), set in 17th-century Puritan Massachusetts, heroine Hester Prynne must wear scarlet letter *A* for adultery.

HAYDEN, STERLING (1916–   ) American film actor. Quit school at 16 to go to sea. Returned at age 24, went to Hollywood. Published 700-page epic sea novel, *Voyage* (1976), in which voyage from New York to San Francisco around Cape Horn serves as microcosm of class struggle in U.S. during 1896 presidential election.

HAYDEN, TOM (1940–   ) Founder of Students for a Democratic Society (SDS), 1961. Member of the "Chicago Seven." Second husband of actress Jane Fonda. Ran unsuccessfully for U.S. senate in California, 1976. With Fonda, runs Campaign for Economic Democracy.

HAYES, GABBY (1885–1969) Character actor who personified the Western sidekick with his scratchy beard and toothless smile. He was paired with the biggest Western stars, including John Wayne, Gene Autry, Roy Rogers and Hopalong Cassidy. Had his own TV series in the 1950s.

HAYES, HELEN (1900–   ) Acclaimed actress, considered the First Lady of the American Stage. On Broadway since her late teens. Won Oscar for *The Sin of Madelon Claudet* (1931), her first talkie. Other movie roles include *A Farewell to Arms* (1932), *Anastasia* (1956) and *Airport* (1969).

HAZEL TV situation comedy series adapted from *Saturday Evening Post* cartoons of Ted Key about a maid who runs the family she works for. Shirley Booth played Hazel, Don DeFore was George Baxter, her boss, whom she called "Mr. B."

HEAD, EDITH (1898–1981) Dress designer who became famous Hollywood costume designer. First credit on *She Done Him Wrong* (1933), designing for Mae West. Has won the most Oscars for costume design for films, including *Samson and Delilah* (1951) and *A Place in the Sun* (1952).

HEADLESS HORSEMAN, THE. See IRVING, WASHINGTON

HEALTHY, WEALTHY AND WISE. See FRANKLIN, BENJAMIN

HEARING In normal population, no significant difference in acuity of right versus left ear. Left ear favored for phone use in right-handed individuals. Hearing impairments generally afflict one ear more than the other. Hearing ability often slightly reduced after consuming a large meal.

HEARST CASTLE Luxurious mansion, San Simeon, CA. Built and owned by publishing tycoon William Randolph Hearst (1863–1951). Filled with valuable antiques, paintings, tapestries and furniture. Turned over to State of California, 1958.

HEARST, PATRICIA (1955–   ) Daughter of William

Randolph Hearst, newspaper magnate. Kidnapped, February 4, 1974, by Symbionese Liberation Army. Captors demanded and received $2 million in food for the poor from her father. Patricia was with fiancé Steven Weed the night of her abduction. Soon after, she joined the army in terrorist activities going by the name "Tania." She surfaced, two months later, as a party to a Liberation Army bank robbery. For this she was tried and convicted, serving nearly two years in prison. Upon capture, she gave her occupation as "Urban Terrorist." In February 1979, President Carter granted her clemency.

HEART   Four-chambered, hollow muscle. Beating caused by contraction and relaxation of the heart muscle. Provides body with vital oxygenated blood. Beats more slowly from infancy to adulthood, from 120 to approximately 70 beats per minute.

HEART DISEASE   More people in industrial nations die from it than from any other cause. Over one million Americans a year are felled by heart and vascular disease, nearly half of all deaths. Leading causes of heart disease are cigarette smoking, high fat diet, lack of exercise and stress.

HEARTBREAK HOTEL   Located on "Lonely Street" with a "desk clerk draped in black." Heartbreak Hotel, a haven for forgotten lovers, was immortalized by Elvis Presley in a 1957 hit song which became one of his biggest-selling records.

HEATHROW   World's busiest airport. Handles approximately 24 million passengers per year. Situated 15 mi. (24 km.) west of London's center. All three of its terminals are linked to Heathrow Central Station, where Piccadilly Line can be taken to downtown London.

HEAVEN   God's name for firmament. Genesis 1:14: "Let there be light in the firmament of the heaven." Proper definition: home of God and his angels; but Bible also uses it for air and upper heights. Modern word from Old English *heofon*.

HEAVEN CAN WAIT   Film co-directed by and starring Warren Beatty (1978). Football player (Beatty) taken to heaven ahead of schedule must find another body to return to life. A remake of *Here Comes Mr. Jordan* (1941).

HEDONISM   Philosophy that pleasure is highest good and should be aim of action. In psychology, theory that person's actions always have pleasure as purpose. Ancient hedonism of two schools: from Aristippus, that pleasure achieved by gratification of sensual desires; and from Epicurus, that pleasure achieved through rational control of desires.

HEFNER, HUGH (1926–   ) American editor and publisher. Founded *Playboy*, 1953. Serves as its editor and publisher. Served in same capacity for Playboy Club quarterly *VIP* (1963–1975), circulation 750,000; now listed as publisher. Founded *Oui* (1972) as racier version of *Playboy*; first relinquished editorship in late 1970s. Sold publication to Laurant Publishing, 1981. Has steered Playboy Enterprises into film production and cable television. (see PLAYBOY)

HEIDEN, ERIC (1958–   ) American speed skater. Won five gold medals at 1980 Lake Placid Winter Olympics (500 m.; 1,000 m.; 1,500 m.; 5,000 m.; and 10,000 m.—all possible events). Set new Olympic record in each event. Sister Beth also an Olympic medalist at Lake Placid.

HEIMLICH MANEUVER First-aid procedure started in 1974 to dislodge objects blocking air passages causing one to choke. Standing behind victim, wrap arms around waist, place fist against abdomen and press with sharp upward thrust. Maneuver has caused drastic reductions in number of deaths from choking.

HEINLEIN, ROBERT ANSON (1907–   ) American science-fiction writer. Noted for "historical" style of his novels, set in future, and for conservative ideology. Winner of four Hugo Awards for best sci-fi novel of the year. Best known for *Stranger in a Strange Land* (1961), which introduced word *grok* into modern lexicon. Popular college campus book in the 1960s. Also wrote *Farmer in the Sky* (1950); *Orphans of the Sky* (1963).

HEISMAN TROPHY, THE Awarded each year to most outstanding college football player. Presented by New York's Downtown Athletic Club annually since 1935. Named for John Heisman, 1892–1927, college coach and later club's athletic director. University of Chicago halfback Jay Berwanger first winner. Archie Griffin of Ohio State only player to win twice (1974, 1975).

HELENA Capital of Montana. Town grew when gold was discovered in Last Chance Gulch, 1864. Today gulch is Helena's main street. During an 80-day period in 1935, city was shaken by earthquakes causing $3.5 million in damages.

HELIOLOGY   The study of the sun. The root word plays a great role in history. Heliopolis, an ancient city in Egypt, was the center of sun worship. And Helios was the Sun God in Greek mythology. Every morning he leaves his palace, crosses the sky in a golden chariot and then returns among the river oceans.

HELIUM   A lightweight gas and an inert (nonreactive) element. Only hydrogen is more abundant than helium in the universe, although helium is not common on earth. Most is found in natural-gas fields. Is lighter than air, making helium-filled balloons rise.

HELLER, JOSEPH (1923–   )   American novelist and playwright. Wrote novels *Something Happened* (1974) and *Good as Gold* (1979), and play, *We Bombed in New Haven* (1968). Also wrote *Catch-22* (1961), his first novel, originally titled *Catch-18*, but publisher changed name because of popularity of Leon Uris' *Mila-18* (see URIS, LEON). Novel about absurdities of war, an immediate best-seller, considered masterpiece of black humor. Main character Yossarian, member of American World War II bomber squadron in Italy, tries to get out of war by claiming insanity, but if he's rational enough to want out, he's not insane—that's "catch-22," ever since, a phrase synonymous with a no-win situation. Lt. Milo Minderbinder, a psychiatrist, and the confused Major Major, are other characters.

HELLMAN, LILLIAN (1905–   )   American dramatist and author of autobiographical books including *Pentimento* (1973), part of which was the basis for Jane Fonda–Vanessa Redgrave film, *Julia*. Had 30-year love affair with detective writer Dashiell Hammett (see HAMMET, DASHIELL). Among her plays: *Watch on the Rhine* (1934), *The Little Foxes* (1959) and *The Children's Hour* (1934), the penetrating drama of young female teachers at a boarding school who are beset by malicious rumors of their lesbianism. Basis for films *These Three* (1963) and *The Children's Hour* (1962) starring Audrey Hepburn and Shirley MacLaine.

HELSINKI   Finland's capital and largest city. Located on country's southern coast on Gulf of Finland. Its latitude is close to that of Oslo (Norway's capital) and Stockholm (Sweden's capital), yet it is farthest north of the three cities. Known as "White City of the North."

HELTER SKELTER   Prosecuting attorney Vincent Bugliosi's 1975 account of crimes and trial of Charles Manson and four co-

conspirators (called "The Manson Family") for ritualistic murders of actress Sharon Tate and six others. Book co-written with Curt Gentry. Title comes from Beatles' song "Helter Skelter" on *The White Album*, which Manson said included secret message that motivated killing spree.

HEMINGWAY, ERNEST (1899–1961)   American novelist and short-story writer. Known for intensely masculine writing and adventurous personal life that was background for his work. Won Pulitzer Prize (1953) and Nobel Prize (1954). Nicknamed "Papa." Originally reporter in Kansas City and Toronto. Quit to write short stories but later served as foreign correspondent, covering Spanish Civil War for North American Newspaper Alliance (NANA) and World War II for *PM* and other magazines. Well-publicized bon vivant and sportsman, his escapades (which included once catching 468-pound marlin without harnessing himself to boat) often covered in popular magazines such as *Life* and *Esquire*, pictured with rugged outdoor grin, hairy chest and giant fish or game just bagged. Also had spectacular death, shooting himself with shotgun. Among his works: Nick Adams, the protagonist and narrator of many Hemingway short stories, introduced in boyhood in story collection, *In Our Time* (1924), later appears in *The Killers* (1927) and many others. Prototype for many later Hemingway heroes. Bears some resemblance to the author himself. *The Torrents of Spring* (1926) was his first novel. Sold poorly. Considered a parody of Sherwood Anderson's *Dark Laughter*. Wrote it so he could get out of contract with Liveright, Anderson's publisher, and switch to Scribner's. *The Sun Also Rises* (1926), novel which about "lost generation" of expatriated Americans in Europe after World War I, established Hemingway's reputation. Set in Spain with Pamplona bull run as backdrop. Story told by Jake Barnes, American rendered impotent by war wound. *A Farewell to Arms* (1929) concerns World War I romance of Frederic Henry, an American serving in Italian ambulance corps, and English nurse Catharine Barkley. Superb descriptions of World War I destruction. *Death in the Afternoon* (1932) is nonfiction work about all that's "important and interesting" about bullfighting. Drawing on his experience in journalism, book is considered one of the definitive works on the subject. He later wrote about bullfighting for *Sports Illustrated* (was paid $15 per word) and had used it as backdrop in novel *The Sun Also Rises*. *Green Hills of Africa* (1935) is nonfiction account of Africa hunting expedition. Participants on hunt treated like characters in novel. Also contains literary criticism. *For Whom the Bell Tolls* (1940) describes idealistic American college professor Robert Jordan's experiences in Spain during Civil War, 1936–1939. Title comes from passage in English poet John Donne's "Devotions": ". . . never send to know for whom the bell tolls; It tolls for thee." *Across the River and Into the Trees* (1950) is novel about aging World War II hero who returns to scene of his wounding. Unanimously rated as inferior Hemingway work. *The Old Man and the Sea* (1952) is short novel about Santiago, an old Cuban fisherman who hooks and boats a giant marlin but loses it to sharks. Won Pulitzer Prize for fiction, 1953. Led to winning Nobel Prize for Literature, 1954. *Islands in the Stream* was published posthumously in 1970 and is not well regarded. Divided into three parts: "Bimini," "Cuba" and "At Sea," all recounting episodes in life of Thomas Hudson before, during, and after World War II. Made into feature film (1977) starring George C. Scott, David Hemmings, Claire Bloom, Susan Tyrell, Gilbert Roland, and Richard Evans. Considered one of Scott's better performances.

HEMISPHERES   Northern and Southern Hemispheres divided by the Equator. Northern Hemisphere contains Europe, the Soviet Union, North America and almost all of Asia, thereby encompassing majority of world's countries. Southern Hemisphere contains Antarctica, part of South America, tip of Africa and Australia. Three largest countries entirely within Southern Hemisphere: Australia (2,966,200 sq. mi./7,686,848 sq. km.), Argentina (1,065,189 sq. mi./2,776,889 sq. km.), and Peru (496,222 sq. mi./1,285,216 sq. km.).

HEMOPHILIA   Hereditary disease. Blood lacks substances necessary for normal clotting. Caused by defective gene on X chromosome. Afflicts mostly males. Females more likely to be carriers. Also known as the Royal Disease; or "Disease of Kings," due to frequency among males of inbred royal families.

HENDRIX, JIMI (1942–1970)   An innovative and influential rock guitarist of the late 1960s. Formed his first band in 1965, Jimmy James and the Blue Flames. In 1966, The Jimi Hendrix Experience was created and albums included *Are You Experienced?* (1967) and *Electric Ladyland* (1968).

HENIE, SONJA (1912–1969)   Norwegian skater who notched record 10 world figure-skating championships, 1927–1936.

Won Olympic gold medals in women's singles skating, 1928, 1932, 1936. Retired from amateur skating at age 23 (1937) to skate professionally and make movies. First full-length skating film, *One in a Million* (1936), increased public awareness of sport; by 1939 was third biggest movie box-office draw behind Shirley Temple and Clark Gable, making her top-earning sports figure of her time. Among other music-and-ice films for Twentieth Century–Fox: *Thin Ice* (1937), *Everything Happens at Night* (1939), *Sun Valley Serenade* (1941).

HENRY FORD MUSEUM. See DEARBORN, MICHIGAN

HENRY VIII (1491–1547) King of England, 1509–1547, during reign of Tudor family. Second son of Henry VII and Elizabeth of York. Broke with Roman Catholic Church; established Church of England, 1534. Had six wives.

HENRY, PATRICK (1736–1799) Virginia statesman, governor and orator. Influential during American Revolutionary War period. Famous for saying to Virginia's Provincial Convention, 1775, "Give me liberty or give me death" as he pressed them to arm the state's militia against England.

HEPATITIS Inflammation of the liver. Often accompanied by jaundice, a yellowing of the skin, whitening of the eye and mucous membranes. Viral and toxic types. Word from Greek hepar meaning "liver."

HEPBURN, KATHARINE (1907–   ) Popular actress since the 1930s. Has the most Oscar nominations and wins of any actress; winner of four, for *Morning Glory* (1933), *Guess Who's Coming to Dinner* (1967), *The Lion in Winter* (1968) and *On Golden Pond* (1982).

HERCULES Greek mythological hero. To cleanse himself of guilt over his killing of his wife Megara and three sons in fit of rage induced by goddess Hera, submits himself as slave to cousin Eurystheus, who devises series of twelve dangerous, nearly impossible tasks for Hercules to perform. These "Labors of Hercules" are: 1) killing lion of Nemea; 2) killing nine-headed Hydra; 3) bringing back alive stag with gold horns; 4) capturing great boar; 5) cleaning Augean stables in one day; 6) driving away Stymphalus birds; 7) capturing bull that Poseidon had given Minos; 8) stealing man-eating mares of King Diomedes of Trace; 9) bringing back girdle of Hippolyta, Queen of Amazons; 10) bringing back cattle of Geryon, monster with three bodies; 11) bringing back Gold Apples of Hesperides; and 12) bringing three-headed dog Cerebus up from Hades.

HERLIHY, JAMES LEO (1927–) American novelist
and playwright. Novels include *All Fall Down* (1960), and *Midnight
Cowboy* (1965), about friendship of Joe Buck and Rico "Ratso" Rizzo
in sleazy Times Square tenement. Made into 1968 film with Jon
Voight and Dustin Hoffman. Herlihy's plays include *Blue Denim* (1957)
and *Crazy October* (1958).

HERMITAGE MUSEUM Located in Leningrad, Soviet
Union. Owns more than 6,000 works of art. Famous for ancient
Greek and Roman sculpture, Islamic art, and Baroque, Renaissance
and French Impressionist paintings.

HERRIOT, JAMES (1916–) British veterinarian and
author. Pseudonym, James Alfred Wight. Best-sellers *All Creatures
Great and Small* (1972), *All Things Bright and Beautiful* (1974) and *All
Things Wise and Wonderful* (1977) about life of a country vet.

HERSHEY, PENNSYLVANIA Town founded by Milton
S. Hershey in 1903. Famous for Hershey Foods Corporation, which
produces chocolate.

HERTZ Car rental agency. Became one of top companies in the
business with the slogan, "Hertz puts you in the driver's seat." Avis
succumbed to the passenger seat with its ad, "Number two and trying
harder."

HESS, RUDOLPH (1894–) German Third Reich min-
ister and Hitler's representative. Transcribed Hitler's book *Mein Kampf*.
As of 1939, second in succession to Hitler after Goering. Parachuted
into Scotland, 1941, to discuss terms for peace with Great Britain.
Captured and tried for war crimes by International Tribunal at Nu-
remburg, 1946. Sentenced to life in Spandau, Berlin's internationally
appointed prison. Since 1966, he has been its only prisoner.

HESSE, HERMANN (1877–1962) German author. Wrote
1927 novel *Steppenwolf*. Hero Harry Haller's inability to fit in causes
him to regard himself as a "steppenwolf," lone wolf of the steppes.
American rock band led by German born John Kay adopted name
in late 1960s. Their hits included motorcycle anthem "Born to Be
Wild", "Magic Carpet Ride", "The Pusher and Monster".

HEYERDAHL, THOR (1914–) Norwegian ethnolo-
gist and author of *Kon-Tiki* and *Aku-Aku*. Sailed balsa-wood raft *Kon
Tiki* from Peru to Polynesia in 1947; proved that Polynesia islands

could have been settled by South American Indians. Sailed *Ra I* and *II*, boat made of reeds, Morocco to Barbados 1969–1970. Observed oil pollution.

HIAWATHA   Henry Wadsworth Longfellow's epic poem *Song of Hiawatha* (1855) based on North American Indian legend about mythical warrior sent to clear forests and fishing grounds and teach peace. Lives "on the shores of Gitchee Gumee, by the shining Big-Sea-Water." (see LONGFELLOW, HENRY WADSWORTH)

HIBERNATION   Period of dormancy some animals undergo in the cold winter months, during which the body temperature, heart rate and metabolic rate decrease drastically. Estivation is identical to hibernation but occurs in summer or during long droughts.

HIBERNIA   Old name for Ireland believed to originate from Latin "Juverna," the name Julius Caesar and fellow Romans gave to the country. Greek geographer Ptolemy referred to the name when he described the region in detail.

HICKOK, WILD BILL (1837–1876)   James Butler Hickok. Frontier marshal and famous gunfighter. Also known for dealing a good hand (all aces and eights) at poker. Shot in the back and killed by Jack McCall, Deadwood, SD, while playing poker.

HIGGINS, PROFESSOR HENRY. See SHAW, GEORGE BERNARD

HIGH ASWAN DAM. See ASWAN HIGH DAM

HIGH NOON   Oscar-winning Western starring Gary Cooper as Will Kane, a sheriff who has no support from the town in his duel with an outlaw gang. Cooper won Best Actor Oscar for his role.

HIGHWAY PATROL   TV crime drama series based on actual experiences of highway patrol officers across U.S. Broderick Crawford played Dan Matthews, chief of Highway Patrol; William Boyett was his assistant, Sgt. Williams. Premiered in 1956.

HILLARY, SIR EDMUND PERCIVAL (1919–   ) New Zealand explorer and mountaineer. Formerly a beekeeper. With Nepalese Sherpa guide Tenzing Norkay became first to reach summit of Mount Everest, Nepal, world's highest peak. Upon reaching summit, May 29, 1953, he photographed Norkay. Hillary later knighted by Queen Elizabeth II for the feat. Currently active in Nepalese school-building program.

HILTON, JAMES (1900–1954)   English novelist. Created mythical utopia of Shangri-La in 1933 novel *Lost Horizon*. Land of eternal youth and peace, supposedly in Tibet. Term has come to mean any ideal refuge. Also created kindly Latin teacher Mr. Chipping, or "Chips," as his pupils lovingly called him, in *Goodbye, Mr. Chips* (1934).

HIMMLER, HEINRICH (1900–1945)   German Nazi politician. Managed Gestapo, Hitler's secret police force. Established concentration camps. Devised means for mass-murdering Jews and political prisoners. Committed suicide, 1945, after being captured by Allied troops. Swallowed a vial of poison he had concealed in his mouth.

HINDENBURG   German dirigible. Used for transatlantic passenger trips. Caught fire and exploded, May 6, 1937, over Lakehurst, NJ. Killed 36. Cause of fire, unknown. Ended public confidence in this form of air travel.

HINES, DUNCAN (1880–1959)   American gourmet. Beginning with *Adventures in Good Eating* (1935), listing of 160 superior restaurants, built rating "Recommended by Duncan Hines" to one valued and exhibited by more than 10,000 eating places. Wrote many other restaurant and hotel guides.

HIPPOCRATES (460?–377? B.C.)   Greek physician. Laid down principles of medical science in Greece, 4th century B.C. Often called the Father of Medicine. Hippocratic oath is still given to many graduating medical students. Oath begins: " I swear by Apollo, the Physician. . ." Apollo was patron god of physicians of ancient Greece and Rome.

HIPPODROME   In ancient Greece and Rome, course for horse and chariot races. Surrounded by tiers of seats built up in oval. *Ben-Hur* famous chariot race scene took place in one.

HIPPOPOTAMUS   Second heaviest land animal, weighing up to four tons. Although Hippopotamus means "river horse," it is actually the pig's largest relative. Are native to Africa and spend most of their time in water.

HIROSHIMA. See ENOLA GAY

HIRSCH, ELROY (1923–   )   Pro football end for Chicago Rockets and Los Angeles Rams, 1946–1957. Nicknamed "Crazy Legs" for his great speed and ability to make quick cuts. Caught

387 passes in 12-year pro career after starring at University of Wisconsin (1943-1945), where he is now athletic director.

HIRSUTE   Means hairy. Often used in reference to pubescent, with stiff, rough hairs.

HISPANIOLA   West Indian island on which Haiti and Dominican Republic, two independent republics, are situated. Discovered in 1492 by Columbus, who named the island La Isla Espanola.

HISS, ALGER (1904–   )   Former U.S. State Department official. Accused by Whittaker Chambers, allegedly his conspirator, of spying for Soviet Union, 1949. Proved his conviction with the "pumpkin papers," microfilm containing confidential dispatches from Hiss to Chambers. Sentence, two years prison, 1950.

HITCHCOCK, ALFRED (1899-1980)   British director of suspense films, moving to Hollywood in 1940s. Began making silent films in Europe; gained worldwide attention with *The Man Who Knew Too Much* (1934). Among his U.S. productions: *Spellbound* (1945), *Rear Window* (1954) and *Psycho* (1960). Made cameo appearances in almost all his films. Hosted two TV series, *Alfred Hitchcock Presents* (1955-1962) and *The Alfred Hitchcock Hour* (1962-1965).

HITLER, ADOLF (1889-1945)   German chancellor and Führer. Roman Catholic. Espoused philosophy of Nietzsche and music of Wagner to support belief in mystically unified Germany and Aryan supremacy. At age 16, application to Academy of Fine Arts in Vienna was rejected. Lived there several years working as commercial artist before moving to Munich, 1913. Early phase of Nazi Party, sought to gain publicity for Party's campaign to overthrow current government. Night of November 8, 1923, he and well-known retired general announced national revolution in Munich beer garden called Burgerbrau Keller. Became known as the Beer Hall Putsch. After losing Germany's 1923 presidential election to Paul von Hindenburg, convinced Hindenburg to appoint him chancellor, January 1923. After Hindenburg's death, 1934, assumed presidency without an election. By 1936, he had made Germany a totalitarian state. After signing Franco-German Armistice, gaining control over most of France, June 22, 1940, he danced a jig at Compeigne, France. Document signed in same railroad car, at same spot in forest where Germans surrendered, World War I. Planned to build empire, the Third Reich, to last 1,000 years. Capital would be Berlin, to be renamed Germanis. Many of his statements reflected belief that ultimate supremacy of his people and of himself would justify all measures to achieve it. Once said, "The victor will never be asked if he told the truth." *Time* magazine's "Man of the Year," 1938. Favorite movie, *King Kong*, 1933 classic about a giant gorilla tearing up elevated railway tracks and scaling Empire State Building. Wrote *Mein Kampf* (1924), translated as *My Struggle*. Autobiographical work dedicated to Rudolf Hess and written in Lansberg Prison.

HO CHI MINH CITY   Largest city in Vietnam, formerly called Saigon. Renamed in 1975 by Provisional Revolutionary Government following Communist North Vietnam's defeat of South Vietnam. Named for Ho Chi Minh, late president of North Vietnam.

HOCKEY   *Goal:* Extends vertically 4 ft. above surface of ice with goal posts 6 ft. apart, measured from inside of posts. Goalie protects 24 sq. ft. area from pucks traveling sometimes more than 120 m.p.h. *Puck:* Round disk, 1 in. thick, 3 in. diameter. Made of vulcanized rubber. Weighs between 5½ and 6 oz. In National Hockey League, home team must have supply frozen before game.
Substitution: Allowed during course of play, called substitution "on the fly." Players may be changed at any time in front of team benches, provided those leaving ice are out of flow of play before change. Must be accomplished with precision to avoid losing any advantage in play. With 16-man roster and 6-man teams, National Hockey League coaches try to rotate fresh skaters into play frequently. Lacrosse has similiar substitution rule.

HOCKEY, OLYMPIC   Instituted in 1920 Summer Olympics, switched to Winter Olympics, 1924. Of 15 Olympic hockey competitions, 1924–1984, Canada has won six (1920, 1924, 1928, 1932, 1948, 1952). Soviet Union, by winning 1984 gold medal, has pulled even (1956, 1964 ,1968, 1972, 1976, 1984). United States won gold in 1960 and 1980.

HOCKEY, WORLD CHAMPIONSHIP   1949, Canada (Sudbury Wolves) beat Denmark, 47–0. Jim Russell led Canadians with eight goals. Canada scored 13 goals in first period, 16 in second, 18 in third. Championship took place on February 12, 1949, in Stockholm, Sweden. Eventual tournament winner, however, was Czechoslovakia.

HODGES, GIL (1924–1972)   First baseman with Brooklyn and Los Angeles Dodgers, N.Y. Mets, 1943–1963. Manager,

Washington Senators, 1963–1967. Manager, N.Y. Mets, 1968–1971. Won National League pennant and World Series (over Baltimore, four games to one) with 1969 "Miracle Mets," 1962 expansion team with no previous winning record.

HOFFA, JAMES RIDDLE (1913–?)   Labor leader. Former president of the International Brotherhood of Teamsters, a reportedly corrupt truckers union linked to organized crime. Disappeared from Michigan restaurant July 30, 1975. Circumstances suggested abduction or murder.

HOFFMAN, ABBIE (1936–)   Counterculture leader, 1960s. Member of the "Chicago Seven," charged with disrupting the 1968 Democratic Convention in Detroit. At his trial, claimed he was an orphan of America. Later convicted of selling cocaine, jumped bail and surrendered six years later in 1980.

HOGAN, BEN (1912–)   Only golfer whose life story was made into a movie, *Follow the Sun*, 1951. Glenn Ford played Hogan, champion player critically injured at peak of career in 1949 highway accident. Told he'd never walk again, Hogan limped to victory in 1950 U.S. Open Playoff. Also won 1951 and 1953 U.S. Opens, 1951 and 1953 Masters, and 1953 British Open, among many others.

HOLIDAY, (ELEANORA) BILLIE (1915–1959)   American jazz singer in late 1930s and '40s. Struggled with heroin addiction during later years. Her autobiography, co-written with William Duffy, called *Lady Sings the Blues* (1956). Diana Ross portrayed "Lady Day" in 1972 film version, winning Oscar nomination. Famous for "Willow Weep for Me" and many others.

HOLLANDER, XAVIERA   Indonesian-born Dutch woman; New York City madam-turned-author. Gained prominence with autobiographical book *The Happy Hooker* (1972). Later wrote other books on sex and sex advice column in *Penthouse* magazine, publisher Bob Guccione's rival to *Playboy*.

HOLLYWOOD OR BUST   1956 film starring the comedy team of Dean Martin and Jerry Lewis. Movie-nut and crooner drive to Hollywood in search of fame and fortune. Directed by Frank Tashlin.

HOLLYWOOD SQUARES   Popular TV game show, putting celebrities in a tic-tac-toe board; contestants win square if they determine the celebrity answer to trivia question is correct or bluff.

Peter Marshall was host; Paul Lynde had the most appearances as regular panelist.

HOLLYWOOD TEN   Alvah Bessie, Herbert B. Lieberman, Lester Cole, Edward Dmytryk, Ring Lardner, Jr., John Howard Lawson, Albert Maltz, Sam Ornitz, Adrian Scott and Dalton Trumbo—ten film directors, producers and writers required to testify to the House Committee on Un-American Activities, October 1947. Committee was investigating the presence of Communism in Hollywood. The accused cited Fifth Amendment right not to incriminate themselves. Found guilty, imprisoned and blacklisted.

HOLMES, LARRY (1949–)   Heavyweight boxing champion since 1978. Beat Muhammad Ali in his last comeback, Las Vegas, October 2, 1980, 11-round technical knockout. At one time Holmes was Ali's sparring partner.

HOLOGRAM   A three-dimensional picture produced with a laser. Means "complete picture" in Greek. Can be either a transparency (slide) or a flat picture (print). Requires laser for 3-D effect to be seen. Holographic movies have been developed but not perfected.

HOLY BIBLE, REVISED STANDARD EDITION, THE   Published 1952. Translated from original languages and first set forth 1611 (King James version), subsequently revised 1881–1985 and 1901. Revised again, 1946–1952. Best-seller, 1952–1954, combining beauty of 1611 King James version with revisions based on original sources and histories.

HOLY KAABA   Small, flat-roofed stone building in Mecca which Moslems face when praying. South wall contains sacred Black Stone, believed to be sent from heaven by God.

HOLY TOLEDO   Exclamation of surprise. Refers to Toledo, Spain, which became an outstanding Christian cultural center following its liberation from the Moors in 1085. Toledo's famous 13th-century Gothic Cathedral is one of the largest in Europe.

HOMER   Blind Greek epic poet. Existence long disputed but attributed as writer of two epic poems, The *Iliad* and *The Odyssey*. *Iliad* focuses on Greek hero Achilles in last days of Trojan Wars. *Odyssey* recounts adventures of hero Odysseus on his lengthy return home from Troy.

HOMESTEAD GRAYS   Baseball team in Negro National

League, based in Pittsburgh. Negro leagues formed 1920, lasted until early 1950s, when baseball became integrated at major and minor league levels, after Jackie Robinson broke in with Brooklyn Dodgers, 1947. Among famous Grays were future Baseball Hall of Famers Josh Gibson (the Babe Ruth of the Negro Leagues), outfielder Richard "Cool Papa" Bell and first baseman Buck Leonard (called "the Lou Gehrig of the Negro Leagues").

HOMO SAPIENS   1) Scientific classification of human beings. 2) Includes extinct human species. 3) All existing persons belong to subspecies *Homo Sapiens*. 4) From Latin *homo* meaning "human being," and *sapiens*, meaning "wise."

HOMOSEXUALITY   In 1895 author Oscar Wilde (1854–1900) accused by Marquess of Queensberry of being a sodomite because of his affair with Lord Douglas, the Marquess' son. Douglas' poem "Two Loves" ("I am the love that dare not speak its name") was quoted at the trial. Wilde convicted and sentenced, two years' hard labor.

HONEYCOMB   Hit 1957 song by singer-songwriter Jimmie Rodgers. Tune became number one the week Russian satellite *Sputnik* went into orbit. Rodgers followed song with other hits, including "Kisses Sweeter than Wine" and "Secretly."

HONEYMOONERS, THE   Popular TV comedy series (1956) starring Jackie Gleason as bus driver Ralph Kramden. His wife, Alice, was portrayed by Audrey Meadows; his best friend, Ed Norton, a sewer worker, was played by Art Carney, and Norton's wife, Trixie, was portrayed by Joyce Randolph. Ralph's reaction when Alice disapproved of any of his great ideas was to threaten to belt her with the line: "One of these days... Pow!—right in the kisser!"

HONG KONG   British dependency on southern coast of China. Consists of two cities, Victoria and Kowloon, separated by a harbor called Hong Kong. Name means "fragrant bay." British gained 99-year lease for Hong Kong in 1898. China disputes British right to the area.

HONOLULU   Capital, largest city and chief port of Hawaii. Home to large concentration of Buddhists; city has over 30 Buddhist Temples. Location of Iolani Palace, former State Capitol building and country's only royal palace, now being restored as a museum.

HOOVER DAM   One of world's highest concrete dams. Located in Black Canyon of Colorado River, connecting Nevada with Arizona. Contains 4,400,000 cu. yds.(3,360,000 cu. m.) of concrete, enough to pave a two-lane highway from New York to San Francisco. Supplies electric power to Arizona, Nevada, California. Completed in 1936.

HOPALONG CASSIDY Black-garbed cowboy hero created by novelist Clarence E. Mulford. Portrayed in movies and TV by William Boyd since 1935. "Hoppy" and his white horse, Topper, appeared in over 50 features, including *Bar 20 Justice* (1938), *Twilight on the Trail* (1941), and *False Paradise* (1948).

HOPE, BOB (1903–   ) Popular comedian for over 40 years. Boxer, under the name Packy East, turned vaudeville performer and radio entertainer. First film, *The Big Broadcast of 1938*. Teamed with Bing Crosby in many "Road" pictures which led to *Singapore* (1940), *Zanzibar* (1941), and *Morocco* (1942). Host of many Oscar ceremonies; won special Academy Awards in 1940, 1944, and 1952. Theme song, "Thanks for the Memory."

HOPSCOTCH Lines form diagram with several compartments. Player hops from one to another in prescribed order, having to kick or pick up puck tossed before turn starts. Many variations. "Scotch" means "line on ground," so name of game correctly suggests game in which player hops over lines.

HORLICK, WILLIAM (1846–1936) American industrialist remembered for developing malted milk, 1887, a mixture of malt extract and powdered milk. President, Horlick's Malted Milk Co., 1906–1921.

HORNUNG, PAUL, AND KARRAS, ALEX National Football League Commissioner Pete Rozelle suspended stars Hornung (halfback, Green Bay Packers) and Karras (defensive tackle, Detroit Lions), 1963, for gambling. Reinstated, 1964 season. Five other Lions and the team were fined but not suspended.

HOROLOGY Science of time measurement. Horologists design and build clocks. Sundials, called shadow clocks, were probably first clocks, used as early as 2000 B.C. Modern clock invented 1300s. Atomic clocks most accurate, lose a few seconds in 100,000 years.

HORSE RACING Called "Sport of Kings" since 12th century when Henry I of England began racing military horses to amuse fellow aristocrats. Fastest horses traditionally owned by royal and rich. Although Oriental cultures and Greeks raced horses well before dawn of Christian era, England could be termed cradle of modern thoroughbred horse racing. Every thoroughbred racer today traces ancestry back to one of three English sires: Matchem, Herod or Eclipse, descendants of horses brought to England from Turkey (Byerly Turk), Syria (Darley Arabian) or northern Africa (Godolphin Barb). Today, after 31 years as top U.S. spectator sport, horse racing (including harness racing) has slipped to second place behind baseball. Attendance in 1983: baseball, 78,051,343 (including Major and Minor Leagues, college games, World Series, and play-offs); horse racing, 75,784,430 (including thoroughbred and harness tracks).

HORSE RACING, BETS   *Across the board:* Bet on one horse to finish first (win), second (place), or third (show) in the same race. With normal $2.00 wagering, an "across the board" bet would cost $6.00. If the horse wins, bettor collects on all three bets; if horse places, place and show bets collected; if horse shows, only show bet collected. If horse finishes fourth or lower, it is "out of the money."

Daily double: Wager in which bettor must pick winners of two consecutive races to win bet. Usually first and second races, although some tracks have experimented with a second daily double in the last two races in order to encourage spectators to remain at track longer. First daily double run at Connaught Park, Ottawa, Canada, 1930.

Parimutuel betting: Literally, "betting among ourselves." Devised by French shopkeeper Pierre Oller in 1872. Tickets on race entrants, purchased in any quantity. Betting receipts (minus handling commission, called take-out) distributed to winners in proportion to number of winning tickets they hold. Also used in dog racing and jai alai.

Tote board: Also called totalizator. Used in parimutuel betting. Calculates odds for race based on amount of money wagered on each horse. Electric totalizator first used in England, 1929. Arlington Park in Chicago had first in U.S. In general use today.

HORSE RACING TERMS   *Backstretch:* Straightaway on opposite side of infield from finish line. Farthest from spectator area and usually closest to stable area; also referred to as "the backstretch" in racing lexicon. Straightaway leading to finish line called "homestretch."

Extra weight: Handicap carried by faster horses to even things out in handicap race. Added by placing lead bars in saddlebags under jockey. Track racing secretary assigns weights based on past performances and level of competition. In true handicap, difference between highest and lowest assigned weights can be as much as 15 pounds.

Filly and mare: Female racehorse called filly if thoroughbred age four or less (flat racing); if standardbred, age three or less (harness racing). Once past that age, called a mare. Males called colts if four or less (thoroughbred; three, standardbred); once past that age, called horses.

Furlong: One-eighth of a mile (220 yds.). Distance races are measured in.

Hand: Measure of a racehorse's height. Equal to 4 in. (10 cm.).

Horseshoe: Flat, U-shaped shoe for horse consisting of narrow strip of metal (usually steel or aluminum) shaped to fit outline of hoof. Nailed to bottom of hoof through eight holes. Also called plate.

Maiden: Racehorse, male or female, that has never won. Some "break their maiden" in first race, while others may retire as "maidens." Maiden races pit entire field of maidens against one another, with at least one shedding that label.

Mudder: Horse that runs well on muddy or sloppy track, rain or shine. Track conditions hold key to "mudder's" success: if raining for short time, track may still be rated "fast" or "good" despite rain; if raining long enough, track can remain "sloppy" long after rain stops. Theories on why some horses do well on sloppy track range from uniquely shaped hoof to simple disposition: some horses enjoy running in mud, while others dislike poor footing and constant shower of mud in their eyes.

Near side: The left side of the horse. Right side called "off" side. Horse normally mounted and dismounted on near side.

Photo finish: Mechanically taken photograph of horse or horses at moment they reach "the wire" (finish line of race), enabling placing judges to determine exact order of finish. Introduced at Hialeah Park, FL. Most famous "photo" in racing history was dead heat (two or more horses finishing at same time) at Aqueduct, NY, 1944 Carter Handicap, when Brownie, Bossuet and Wait a Bit finished together.

Silks: Jockey's racing uniform. Introduced in 1762 at Newmarket, England, for convenience in distinguishing horses while running. Different combinations of bright colors adopted by stable to identify its horses; thus, jockeys wear colors of specific stables in each particular race.

Stirrups: In horse racing, called "the irons." Pair of rings hanging from saddle used to support jockey's feet. Jockey riding particular horse said to be "in the irons," "up" or "on board."

HORSESHOE see HORSE RACING TERMS

HORSESHOE PITCHING   Sport in which competitors pitch specially manufactured horseshoes at stakes located at both ends of court 40 ft. apart. Played by two or four "pitchers" who toss shoes from 6 ft. sq. "pitcher's box" toward stake in center of opposite pitcher's box. Points scored when horseshoe comes within 6 in. of stake. Ringer: shoe that encircles stake so that straightedge could touch its two prongs without touching stake; scores three points.

HOSPITAL   Translated in four languages: French, Hotel-Dieu; German, Hoypital; Hawaiian, Haukapila; Zulu, Isibhedlela.

HOSTAGES   Fifty-two Americans taken hostage in Iran, 1979. Held captive 444 days. Released just minutes after Ronald Reagan's inauguration as president, January 20, 1981.

HOSTESS DING DONG   Chocolate cake product made by Continental Baking, maker of Ho-Ho's, Hostess Cup Cakes, Twinkies, Snoballs and Wonder Bread. Ding Dongs are round, covered with chocolate and have vanilla cream inside.

HOT LIPS HOULIHAN   Nickname of Margaret Houlihan, head nurse of the 4077th Mobile Army Surgical Hospital, featured on the TV series *M*A*S*H*. Portrayed by Loretta Swit, "Hot Lips" had an affair with Dr. Frank Burns (Larry Linville), but during the run of the series, married, then divorced Lt. Col. Donald Penobscott. Role originated in film version by Sally Kellerman. (see M*A*S*H).

HOT LINE   Teletype link between Moscow and Washington, D.C. Instituted June 1963, following nuclear threat presented by the Cuban Missile Crisis. Developed as an attempt to control nuclear crisis.

HOTEL DE VILLE See CITY HALL

HOTEL-DIEU See HOSPITAL

HOUSE OF COMMONS   Along with House of Lords, makes up English Parliament. Reigning monarch forbidden entry to Commons; maintains theoretical veto power, not exercised since 1708. Other royal family members may observe the proceedings.

HOUSE OF THE RISING SUN, THE   Hit 1964 song by rock group The Animals. In song, house in New Orleans has "ruined many a poor boy." The Animals had many other hits, including "We Gotta Get Out of This Place" (1965) and "San Franciscan Nights" (1967).

HOUSE OF TUDOR   English royal family. Descended from the Lancasters. Ruled the throne of England for 118 years.
Henry VII (1485–1509)
Henry VIII (1509–1547) — son of Henry VII
Edward VI (1547–1553) — son of Henry VIII
Mary I (1553–1558) — daughter of Henry VIII
Elizabeth I (1558–1603) — daughter of Henry VIII

HOUSEFLIES   Among most dangerous pests known due to carrying of germs, which they leave on any object they touch. Over 100,000 types of flies. Scientific name is *Diptera*, meaning "two wings" in Greek. Allegedly, state of Alaska is free of these pests.

HOUSES, NORTH AMERICAN   Most common house colors: 1) white, 2) brown, 3) dark red.

HOUSTON   Largest city in Texas. Fifty miles (80 km.) from Gulf of Mexico. One of world's major seaports. Leading trade center in Southwest. Further south than Jacksonville, FL, or New Orleans, LA.

HOUSTON ASTRODOME   First enclosed baseball and football stadium. At highest point, dome reaches 208 ft. (63 m.). Venue for athletic events and annual Houston Livestock Show and Rodeo. Once called "the Eighth Wonder of the World."

HOUSTON, SAM (1793–1863)   Texas soldier and politician. Commander of the Army when Texas declared independence from Mexico, 1836. Twice president of New Found Republic, he became its senator when it was annexed in 1845.

HOW TO MURDER YOUR WIFE   1965 comedy film starring Jack Lemmon as bachelor cartoonist who wakes up after drinking party to find he is married. Virna Lisi plays his wife, who suspects she may not be around long.

HOWDY DOODY   Popular children's TV series, 1947–1960. Buffalo Bob Smith was the host and friend of Howdy Doody, a red-haired, freckle-faced boy puppet whose sister Heidi and twin brother,

Double, made frequent appearances. Their mutual enemy, Phineas T. Bluster, caused trouble in Doodyville. Live audience of kids sat in Peanut Gallery.

HOWE, GORDIE (1928–   ) Played with Detroit Red Wings of National Hockey League, 1946–1971. Retired after 1971 season. Holds NHL records for most years, games played, All-Star games played (22), points, goals and assists. Came out of retirement, 1973, to play for Houston Aeros and New England Whalers of World Hockey League. Teammate of sons Mark and Marty. Whalers joined NHL for 1979–1980 season, enabling Howe to add to records and pass 800-goal mark (NHL) 1,000-goal mark (overall). Retired second time after 1979–1980 season at 52, after career spanning parts of five decades.

HUCK FINN. See TWAIN, MARK

HUD 1963 feature film about hard-driving, woman-chasing young man (portrayed by Paul Newman) who is idol of his nephew and scorn of his father. Patricia Neal won Oscar for Best Actress as housekeeper who repulsed Newman's advances. Directed by Martin Ritt.

HUDSON, HENRY British explorer. Discovered Hudson River, 1609. Sailed as far north as Albany. First European to sail Harbor of New York. Leif Ericson, a Dutchman, may have sailed past it, A.D. 1000. In 1611, while exploring Hudson Bay in eastern Canada, mutiny broke out on board. Hudson, his son and seven loyal crew members cast out into a small boat and were never heard from again.

HUDSON BAY Landlocked sea in northeast Canada. Area is approximately 475,750 sq. mi. (1,230,250 sq. km.), including James Bay extension. Connected to Atlantic Ocean by Hudson Strait and to Arctic Ocean by Foxe Channel. Close proximity to Magnetic Pole causes compasses to be pulled from their true direction.

HUDSON RIVER Largest river lying entirely within state of New York. Length is 306 mi. (492 km.). One of most important rivers in U.S. Named for Henry Hudson, one of its earliest explorers. Spanned by George Washington Bridge. Holland Tunnel built underneath, 1927, connecting Manhattan Island with New Jersey. Mouth of river determined site of New York City, now its harbor. Hudson rises in Lake Tear-of- the-Clouds in Adirondack Mountains.

HUEY, DEWEY AND LOUIE Tormenting nephews of

TRIVIAL CONQUEST

comic strip and cartoon character Donald Duck. Their October 17, 1937, debut in *Donald Duck* daily comic strip (signed by Walt Disney, actually drawn by Al Taliaferro) boosted strip's popularity. Donald's Uncle Scrooge is their great-uncle.

HUGHES,   HOWARD   ROBARD   (1905–1967) Industrialist, billionaire, aviator and eventual recluse. Besides *Hell's Angels* (1930) and *Scarface* (1932); produced *The Outlaw* (1943) with Jane Russell; allegedly designed unique supportive brassiere for her. Designed largest plane of 1940s, nicknamed "Spruce Goose," actually a wooden flying boat whose first and last flight was in 1947; flew 1 mi. (1.6 km.) at altitude of 70 ft. (21 m.).

HUGHES, THOMAS (1822–1896)   English author and social reformer. Best-known as author of schoolboy novel *Tom Brown's School Days* (1857) and its college-day sequel, *Tom Brown at Oxford* (1861). *School Days* set at English public school Rugby, which is also name of model community Hughes tried unsuccessfully to start in Tennessee (1879).

HUGO AND NEBULA AWARDS   Given annually for excellence in science-fiction writing. Hugo initiated at 1953 World Science-Fiction Convention; named in honor of Hugo Gernsbach, founder of *Amazing Stories*, first sci-fi magazine. Nebula, first awarded 1966, presented by Science-Fiction Writers of America.

HUGO, VICTOR (1802–1864)   French novelist, poet, dramatist and political figure. Wrote *Notre Dame de Paris* (*The Hunchback of Notre Dame*), 1831, about hunchback bell ringer Quasimodo, and *Les Misérables*, about ex-convict Jean Valjean. Exiled 1855–1870 because he opposed Napoleon III. Returned in triumph, 1870; elected to French national assembly and senate in later years.

HULA HOOP   Introduced by Wham-O Co. in March 1958; sold between 80 and 120 million in six months at $1.98 each. Company produced more than 100,000 units per day at 50 cents apiece but ultimately made only $10,000 because craze died out. Idea for circular, hollow plastic hoop maneuvered by gyrating hips originated in Australia. Wham-O revived it in 1967 with ball bearings inside to produce a whirring noise and again in 1982 with scented peppermint powder inside.

HUMAN BODY   Has over 600 muscles (40% of body's weight) and 206 bones (25% of body's weight). About two billion cells die and are replaced each day. By age 70, average person's heart will have pumped at least 46 million gallons (174 million liters) of blood.

HUMPHREY, HUBERT HORATIO (1911–1978) U.S. senator from Minnesota. Lost 1968 presidential campaign to Republican Richard M. Nixon. As prominent New Deal Democrat, ran for vice-president with incumbent President Lyndon B. Johnson in 1964 and won.

HUNDRED YEARS' WAR Fought between England and France, 1337–1453. Began when Edward III of England claimed title to French throne. Longest war to date.

HUNGARY In October 1956 Hungary rebelled against domination by U.S.S.R. Six days after rebels seized power, eight soviet tanks were used to squash rebellion in country's capital city, Budapest.

HUNGARY'S BORDERS Countries that border Hungary: Czechoslovakia to north; Russia to northeast; Romania to east; Yugoslavia to south; Austria to west.

HUNT BROTHERS Nelson Bunker Hunt and W. Herbert Hunt. Monopolized significant portion of silver market, 1979–1980, buying futures contracts on margin. Silver price in January 1979 was $6.50 per oz.; in January 1980, $50.35 per oz. Regulatory changes, 1980, sent price of silver down. Closed March 28 at $10.80 per oz. Brothers took out $1.1 billion in loans to recover from their losses.

HUNT, EVERETTE HOWARD, JR. (1918–   ) Agent for American Central Intelligence Agency for 21 years, also writing 42 spy novels and short stories under pseudonyms David St. John, Robert Dietrich and others. After retiring from CIA (1970), recruited Cubans to break into office of Pentagon Papers informant Daniel Ellsberg's psychiatrist and Democratic Party headquarters at Watergate Hotel in Washington, 1972. Served 33 months in prison. Wrote autobiography *Undercover: Memoirs of an American Secret Agent* (1974).

HURLING Irish game combining elements of hockey and Gaelic football. Played on field (80 x 140 yd.) by two teams of 15 players. Tapered, curved, broad-bladed sticks ("hurleys") cast ball to another teammate or toward the goal. Ball ("slitter") is 10 in. in circumference, cork-centered, made of rubber and covered with horsehide.

HUSH HUSH...SWEET CHARLOTTE 1965 horror film starring Bette Davis as Charlotte, blamed for ax murder of her fiancé over 30 years before. Olivia de Havilland, Joseph Cotten and Agnes

Moorehead play her tormentors. Patti Page sings title tune.

HUSTLER, THE 1961 film starring Paul Newman as pool hustler Fast Eddie Felson, who meets his match in Minnesota Fats (portrayed by Jackie Gleason). Features Piper Laurie as lame girl who befriends Felson. Directed by Robert Rossen.

HUTTON, BARBARA (1912–1979) Unlucky heiress of seven failed marriages. Known as "the poor little rich girl." Heir to Woolworth fortune built by grandfather F. W. Woolworth, who began empire in 1878 with five-and-dime store.

HUXLEY, ALDOUS (1894–1963) English writer. Wrote futuristic satire *Brave New World*, set in 632 A.F. (After Ford); phrase refers to Ford (sometimes called Freud), legendary father of standardization, who has been deified. In Shakespeare's *Tempest*, Miranda says, "Oh brave new world that has such people in it." Huxley also wrote *Point Counter Point* (1928) and *The Art of Seeing* (1942), the latter about improving his vision. He was virtually blind since 17.

HYDROGEN Lightest element, $\frac{1}{14}$ as heavy as air. Tasteless, odorless and colorless gas, liquid at $-253°C$ $(-423°F)$. Name means "water former" in Greek. Burns to yield water (H_2O). Most abundant element in universe.

HYDROPONICS Technique whereby plants are grown in fluid solutions instead of soil. Mostly used for careful study of plant growth requirements; also used commercially to grow crops in barren areas and to grow out-of-season crops indoors.

HYPOXEMIA From New Latin *hypo-* ("less than normal"), *ox* ("oxygen") and *-emia* ("blood"). Deficient oxygenation of the blood. May cause death.

HYSTERECTOMY Surgical removal of uterus. Usually involves removal of ovaries, as preventive measure against ovarian cancer. Upsets hormonal balance; menopausal symptoms such as hot flashes and fatigue may result. Usually performed to treat bleeding that accompanies benign or malignant disease.

HYSTERIA Psychological disorder involving surfacing of unconscious conflicts surface as physical illness. Originally thought due to disturbance of uterus because women were more prone to this disorder. Word from Greek meaning "belonging to the womb." Hysterectomy, removal of the uterus.

I

I AM CURIOUS (YELLOW)   Swedish film released in U.S. in 1969. Became notorious for explicit sex scenes which caused it to be banned in 15 states.

I CHING   Or *Yi Ching* (Chinese for "Book of Changes"). Ancient Chinese book developed from teachings of Confucius. The *I Ching* is used to make predictions based on throwing of six coins or bones.

I LOVE LUCY   Popular TV series starring Lucille Ball and Desi Arnaz, 1951–1959. Desi played Ricky Ricardo, bandleader whose dizzy wife, Lucy, was trying to break into show business. Was number one rated show in America, 1952–1955.

I WAS A TEENAGE WEREWOLF   Horror-monster film (1957). Michael Landon, best known for role on TV's *Bonanza*, starred.

I'M OK, YOU'RE OK. See HARRIS, TOM

I'VE GOT A SECRET   Popular TV quiz show, 1952–1967. Panelists tried to guess contestant's secret. Hosts were Garry Moore (1952–1964) and Steve Allen (1964–1967). Panelists included: former Miss America Bess Myerson, Betsy Palmer, Bill Cullen and Henry Morgan.

I.N.R.I.   Latin, meaning "Jesus of Nazareth, King of the Jews." Inscribed on Christ's cross by Roman soldiers after Crucifixion.

I.O.U.   Slang abbreviation for "I owe (unto) you." Promissory note; personal voucher containing as little as a date, statement "I owe you," the amount of debt and signature of debtor.

I.Q.   Intelligence quotient: number used by psychologists to describe a person's intelligence. It is a quotient because it is a person's mental age, determined by tests, divided by actual age and multiplied by 100. Average I.Q.: 100. Below 25 person considered an idiot; below 70 considered mental retardation; above 140 is genius. One-half of population has I.Q. of 100. Binet-Simon scale is an I.Q. test.

IAN   Scottish equal of John, most common boy's name. Found in almost every language. Other Scottish forms: Iain, Jock, Johny. In French, Jean; in Russian, Ivan.

IBERIAN PENINSULA   Ancient name for peninsula occupied by Spain and Portugal. Spain occupies 194,855 sq. mi. (504,750 sq. km.) and Portugal occupies 35,553 sq. mi. (92,082 sq. km.). Original Iberians among oldest European peoples. Inhabitants of northern Spain, called Basques, still use some Iberian words in their language. Lusitania Express train runs on peninsula between Madrid and Lisbon, the capitals of Spain and Portugal, respectively.

IBIZA   Spanish resort island. Haunt of artists who visited and stayed. First discovered by Phoenicians. Settled by Carthaginians in 654 B.C. Arabs later occupied island and left Moorish-style architecture.

IBM   Formerly International Business Machines; has 274,108 employees, about the population of Birmingham, AL. First president, T. J. Watson, adopted "Think" as company slogan.

ICARUS   In Greek legend, he and his father Daedalus escaped from Labyrinth at Knossos by using wings made of wax and feathers. Icarus' wings melted when he flew too close to sun against his father's warning, and he fell into Icarian Sea. Daedalus landed safely at Naples.

ICE CREAM   Dates to biblical times, but variety of flavors didn't start until Howard Johnson's introduced 28 in 1928. In North America, vanilla is still the most popular, followed by chocolate and strawberry. Neapolitan variety is a combination of vanilla, chocolate and strawberry, layered. Neapolitan may also be used to describe any dish made in three contrasting layers. Adjective neapolitan means "of or in the manner of Naples."

ICEBERG   Mass of ice that breaks off from glacier. Pure fresh water. One-eighth to one-tenth of mass visible above water. Hazard to oceangoing vessels. Passenger liner *Titanic* struck iceberg, April 1912; maiden voyage. All 1,500 aboard died.

IDLEWILD. See JOHN F. KENNEDY INTERNA-TIONAL AIRPORT

ILIAD, THE. See HOMER

ILLINOIS Five bordering states: Wisconsin to the north; Indiana to the east; Kentucky to the southeast; Missouri to the southwest; and Iowa to the west.

ILLYA KURYAKIN Russian spy who worked for United Network Command for Law and Enforcement on TV series *The Man From U.N.C.L.E.* Portrayed by David McCallum, Illya was partnered with Napoleon Solo (played by Robert Vaughn); Mr. Waverly (Leo G. Carroll) was their boss.

IMF Impossible Missions Force was subject of popular adventure series *Mission Impossible* (1966–1973). Jim Phelps (Peter Graves) led his four special agents on dangerous missions involving foreign countries and organized crime.

IMPOTENCE Inability to copulate. Term used to describe condition in males. From Latin *impotens* ("lack of self-control"). Grounds for divorce in Alaska, Massachusetts, Rhode Island, Utah and 20 other states. Cannot divorce for impotence in California or New York.

IN THE HEAT OF THE NIGHT 1967 film starring Sidney Poitier as Philadelphia detective investigating a murder in Mississippi and earning respect of racist local police chief. Rod Steiger plays chief; won Best Actor Oscar for his portrayal.

INDEX FINGER. See TOUCH

INDIA Four major international airports: Dum Dum International Airport, Calcutta; Sahar International Airport, Bombay; Palam International Airport, Delhi; Meenambakam International Airport, Madras. Language: Inhabitants speak approximately 180 languages, including 16 major tongues. About 700 dialects also spoken. Hindi is official language; English is associate official. *Bharat* is Hindi word for India; country's official name. Grows tea more than any other nation, about 1,246,000,000 lb. (565,180,000 kg.) per year. Some famous Indian teas are Darjeeling, Assam, Dooars, Cachar and Sylnet, all named after districts where grown.

INDIA, STATES OF

Andhra Pradesh	Haryana
Assam Himachal	Pradesh
Bihar	Jammu and Kashmir
Gujarat	Kanataka (includes city of Mysore)
Kerala	Manipur
Madhya Pradesh	Meghalaya
Maharashtra	Nagaland
Punjab	Orissa
Rajasthan	Tamil Nadu (capital city is Madras)
Tripura	Sikkim
West Bengal	Uttar Pradesh

INDIAN LOVE CALL   Song from Rudolf Friml operetta *Rose Marie*, with line "When I'm calling you-ooo-ooo-ooo-ooo-ooo-ooo!" made famous in Jeanette MacDonald, Nelson Eddy film of 1936.

INDIANA   Called Hoosier State. Name may have come from Indiana pioneers' traditional greeting to visitors: "Who's here?" Or from "husher," slang word for fighting man who could "hush" others with his fists.

INDIANAPOLIS 500 AUTO RACE   Five-hundred-mile race for open-wheel racing cars, commonly called Indy cars, after this race and Indianapolis Motor Speedway where it takes place. Run annually since 1911 on Memorial Day, recently on Sunday of Memorial Day weekend. Consists of 200 laps of 2½-mile course. Begins with command "Gentlemen, start your engines," modified in 1977 when Janet Guthrie became first woman driver in race. Ends with winner drinking from traditional bottle of milk in ride down "Victory Lane." Has largest attendance for single-day U.S. sports event (about 300,000). Current average speed record: 163.621 m.p.h., by Rick Mears, 1984. This race an important factor in developing passenger car features like high-compression engines, hydraulic shock absorbers and advances in brakes, tires and lubricants.

INDIANAPOLIS MOTOR SPEEDWAY   Site of Indy 500 race, opened 1909 by Carl G. Fischer and other automakers as test track. Called "the Brickyard" because original track surface composed of three million red bricks; paved over, 1963. Term "Gasoline Alley" originally referred to pit area here; now generic term for pit and service area.

INDUS RIVER   Greatest river in Pakistan. Gave name to country of India. Rises in Tibet, empties into Arabian Sea. Called "King River" in ancient poetry of India.

INFLUENZA   Also called flu or grippe, is a viral disease. Symptoms, including headache, fever and bodyaches, usually last about a week. A worldwide flu epidemic killed about 20 million people in 1918–1919.

INFORMATION, LONG-DISTANCE   Telephone directories have been printed since 1878. First "Information Service" number established 1910. Long-distance information number is area code followed by 555-1212. About 600 million long-distance information requests annually. Charge of 50 cents for each interstate information request instituted May 25, 1984.

INHERIT THE WIND   1960 film dramatizing the world-famous Scopes "Monkey Trial," as lawyers battle the theory of evolution in courtroom. Spencer Tracy and Fredric March starred in film based on Broadway play.

INSECT   Any small, six-legged animal. More than 800,000 known varieties. Estimated 1 to 10 million kinds yet to be discovered. Largest, oldest and most varied class of animal. On earth at least 400 million years. Contitutes more than two-thirds of species known to man. Extremely adaptable. Rapid reproduction.

INSULIN   Hormone produced by pancreas. Discovered 1922 by Sir Frederick Grant Banting and Charles Best. Revolutionized treatment of diabetes. Diabetics either lack insulin production or do not utilize it efficiently.

INTERMEZZO   Love story featuring Swedish actress Ingrid Bergman in her American film debut (1938). Leslie Howard, Edna Best and Cecil Kellaway co-starred in this film about a famed, married musician's affair with his protégée.

INTERNATIONAL COURT OF JUSTICE   Highest judicial agency of United Nations. Settles international legal disputes. Decisions based on international law and cannot be appealed. Headquartered in Peace Palace at The Hague, Netherlands.

INTERNATIONAL DATE LINE   One hundred and eighty degrees longitude in Pacific Ocean. Established 1884 to standardize beginning of each day. Travelers crossing International Date Line eastward gain a day.

TRIVIAL CONQUEST

INTERNATIONAL FLAT EARTH SOCIETY

Founded 1800 to "establish as fact that this earth is flat and plane and that it does not spin and whirl at 1,000 miles an hour." The 100 members believe North Pole is center of earth.

INTERNATIONAL MORSE CODE

A .–	N –.			
B –...	O –––			
C –.–.	P .––.	1 .––––		
D –..	Q ––.–	2 ..–––		
E .	R .–.	3 ...––		
F ..–.	S ...	4 ....–		
G ––.	T –	5		
H	U ..–	6 –....		
I ..	V ...–	7 ––...		
J .–––	W .––	8 –––..		
K –.–	X –..–	9 ––––.		
L .–..	Y –.––	0 –––––		
M ––	Z ––..			

INTERNATIONAL RADIO CODE Also called Alpha Code.

A-Alpha	J-Juliet	S-Sierra
B-Bravo	K-Kilo	T-Tango
C-Charlie	L-Lima	U-Uniform
D-Delta	M-Mike	V-Victor
E-Echo	N-November	W-Whiskey
F-Foxtrot	O-Oscar	X-X ray
G-Golf	P-Papa	Y-Yankee
H-Hotel	Q-Quebec	Z-Zulu
I-India	R-Romeo	

INTERNATIONAL RED CROSS Humanitarian organization. Founded by Jean Henri Dunant, 1863, to provide basic services to civilians and prisoners of war during war or following disaster. Only organization to receive Nobel Peace Prize, World War I. American Red Cross founded 1881 by Clara Barton. Barton cared for wounded in Civil War. Known as "Angel of the Battlefield."

INTERPOL Acronym of International Criminal Police Organization, international network of police forces. Founded in Vienna,

1923. Membership: 126 nations. Each nation maintains an information clearinghouse on domestic criminals and their activities; detains criminals wanted in other countries.

INTOURIST   Soviet Union's travel agency, run by the state. Has contact with about 80 travel agents in U.S. Arranges hotels, sightseeing tours and transportation for foreign visitors to Soviet Union. Headquartered in Moscow; established 1929.

IRAQ   Arab country at head of Persian Gulf. Longest portions of Tigris and Euphrates rivers run through it. Called Mesopotamia, meaning "between the rivers" to ancient Greeks. Most inhabitants live in region between rivers. Grows more dates than any other country.

IRISH FAMINE   One of world's major famines. Caused by destruction of potato crop by fungus, 1843–1849. Many migrated to U.S. after 1846. By 1840, potato was Ireland's most important food crop.

IRMA LA DOUCE   Billy Wilder's 1963 comedy about policeman (Jack Lemmon) who loses job when he arrests all the prostitutes in Paris, but falls in love with one streetwalker (Shirley MacLaine) and becomes a pimp.

IRON   Metallic element. Chemical symbol, Fe, from *ferrum*, Latin for "iron." One of most abundant elements on earth, necessary for all living things. Steel, an alloy of iron and carbon, is most widely used metal.

IRON AGE   From roughly 1,500 B.C. until A.D. 1740, when steel came into widespread use. Process of iron smelting developed early in Bronze Age, about 3,000 B.C.

IRVING, CLIFFORD (1930–   )   American novelist who obtained $765,000 from McGraw-Hill publishers in 1971 for "autobiography" of reclusive billionaire Howard Hughes (1905–1976). Irving said book based on more than 100 meetings with Hughes, but Hughes denied knowing him. Irving and his wife later pleaded guilty to conspiracy, larceny and forgery charges, returned remainder of McGraw-Hill money and went to jail for 17 months.

IRVING, WASHINGTON (1783–1859)   American essayist and storyteller. Wrote *A History of New York from the Beginning of the World to the End of the Dutch Dynasty*, as Diederich Knickerbocker, a crusty Dutchman. Spent many years working in U.S. embassy in

Spain. Later wrote *The Legends of the Alhambra* (1832, enlarged 1852), group of tales and sketches on Spanish subjects. Returned to Spain as U.S. ambassador, 1842–1846. Lived in Tarrytown, NY, estate Sunnyside; and best-known for Hudson River tales like: "Rip Van Winkle" (1820), published in *Sketch Book of Geoffrey Crayon, Gent.*— henpecked Rip wanders into Catskill Mountains before Revolutionary War, helps group of dwarfs drink a keg and falls asleep for 20 years, returning to find wife dead, daughter married, and George Washington President; and "The Legend of Sleepy Hollow" (1820), also published in Crayon's Sketch Book—schoolmaster Ichabod Crane encounters headless horseman who haunts pre-Revolutionary Hudson Valley (although it's really Brom Bones, his rival for affections of Katarina Van Tassel), and Crane is scared out of town.

IS PARIS BURNING? Multimillion-dollar film account of liberation of Paris. Filmed in 1966 and starring an international cast including Jean-Paul Belmondo, Charles Boyer, Leslie Caron, Kirk Douglas, Glenn Ford, Gert Frobe, Orson Welles and many others. Written by Francis Ford Coppola and Gore Vidal.

ISCARIOT, JUDAS One of the 12 disciples of Jesus Christ. According to the Gospel, the redheaded apostle betrayed Jesus to the authorities. Hanged himself soon after Jesus was crucified. Word *Judas* used as noun means "traitor."

ISLANDS IN THE STREAM 1977 film of Ernest Hemingway novel about sculptor and three sons. George C. Scott stars in Franklin J. Schaffner's film. (see HEMINGWAY, ERNEST)

ISLANDS, WORLD'S LARGEST World's three largest: Greenland, 840,000 sq. mi. (2,184,000 sq. km.); New Guinea, 306,000 sq. mi. (795,600 sq. km.); Borneo, 280,100 sq. mi. (728,260 sq. km.).

ISRAEL Founded on May 14, 1948, in what was Palestine on eastern shore of Mediterranean Sea as homeland for Jews. Bordering countries (Egypt, Iraq, Lebanon, Syria and Jordan) invaded following day over territorial disputes. Though Israel won, disputes continue. Flag has two blue stripes on white background; between stripes is blue Star of David, an ancient Jewish symbol.

ISTANBUL Largest city in Turkey. Only city in world located on two continents, Asia and Europe. Called Constantinople from 330–1453; was capital of the Byzantine Empire. Became capital of Ottoman Empire in 1453 and was renamed Istanbul.

ISTHMUS OF CORINTH   Narrow, windswept strip of land, connects central Greece to Peloponnesus. Width: 4–8 mi. (6.4–13 km.). In 1893, Corinthian Canal cut through it, shortening journey from Adriatic Sea to Piraeus by more than 202 mi. (320 km.).

IT'S A MAD, MAD, MAD, MAD WORLD   1963 film comedy featuring cameo appearances by more than 50 stars. Stanley Kramer directed this story of group of people racing to find buried treasure. Spencer Tracy starred as police captain who keeps an eye on their activities. Filmed in Cinerama.

ITALY   Flag: Green, white and red. Adopted, 1870. First used by Italians supporting Napoleon Bonaparte of France during war against Austria, 1796. Napoleon designed flag to look like French flag, replaced blue with green, his favorite color. Islands: Capri, home to the famous cave, the Blue Grotto; Elba, where Napoleon was exiled in 1814; Ischia, a summer resort which has suffered from earthquakes and volcanic eruptions. All three of these islands are situated off the country's western coast. Transportation: *aeroporto* (airport), *automacchina* (automobile), *stazione autobus* (bus station), *stazione ferroviaria* (train station), *strada pubblica* (highway). Having signed alliance treaty known as Rome-Berlin Axis with Germany in 1936, Italy under fascist dictator Mussolini entered World War II in June 1940. After overthrow of Mussolini, June 1943, and Allied Invasion of Italy, September 1943, Italy surrendered and next month declared war against former ally Germany.

IVANOV   Most common Russian family name. Derived from John. Variations include Evanoff, Evanow and Vana.

IVORY   Hard, white substance from teeth, tusks or horns of some animals. Elephant tusks produce best ivory, but walrus tusks, whale and hippopotamus teeth are also used.

IWO JIMA   Middle island of three Volcano Islands in northwest Pacific Ocean. Mt. Suribachi (volcano) is situated at southern end of island. Soil made of gray volcanic ash. Over 6,000 men died capturing this island of 8 sq. mi. from Japanese in World War II. Six marines who raised U.S. flag are depicted in Marine Corps War Memorial, Arlington, VA.

J

J&B. See JUSTERINI & BROOKS

J. R. J. R. Ewing, portrayed by Larry Hagman on series Dallas (1978–   ), is responsible for one of top-rated individual TV shows in history. The 1979 season ended with J.R. being shot, and "Who Shot J.R.?" became national catch-phrase. The 1980 season opener revealed that Kristin Shepard, J. R.'s sister-in-law, (acted by Mary Catherine Crosby) had pulled the trigger. (See HAGMAN, LARRY)

JACK Traditional nursery rhyme name for any lad; Jill is corresponding female name, as in "Jack and Jill went up the hill to fetch a pail of water." Other examples are *Jack and the Beanstalk, Jack the Giant Killer, Little Jack Horner*. Also name of son of Mother Goose, legendary character who created fairy tales and rhymes, originating in French literature, 1697. According to rhyme: "She had a son Jack, a plain-looking lad; / He was not very good, nor yet very bad." In rhyme, Jack buys goose that lays golden egg, and Mother Goose turns him into the Harlequin and his sweetheart into Columbine. In tale *Jack and the Beanstalk*, trades mom's cow to butcher for handful of beans which she throws out window. Overnight, they grow into tall beanstalk to clouds, where bloodthirsty giant guards golden-egg-laying goose.

JACK DANIEL'S Sour-mash whiskey produced in oldest U.S. distillery located in Lynchburg, TN. Springwater from limestone cave used in distillation. Sour mash is residue of fermentation of malted barley, corn and rye. Daniel acquired distillery from Dan Call after U.S. Civil War.

JACK RABBIT   Large North American hare. Lives on plains. Called jack rabbit because its long ears resemble donkey's ears. Brownish fur of white-tailed jack rabbit turns white in winter.

JACK SPRAT   In nursery rhyme, "Jack Sprat could eat no fat. / His wife could eat no lean, / And so between them both, you see, / They licked the platter clean."

JACK THE RIPPER   Name given to London murderer. Killed seven prostitutes, 1888. Murderer's identity never discovered. Some believe he was Duke of Clarence, Queen Victoria's grandson. Name comes from letters received by police presumably written by killer.

JACKSON, REGINALD MARTINEZ (REGGIE) (1946–)   Slugging outfielder for Oakland Athletics, Baltimore Orioles, New York Yankees, California Angels. Earned nickname "Mr. October" for World Series and playoff hitting. In final game of 1977 World Series hit three homers to lead Yankees over Los Angeles Dodgers. Hit home runs on consecutive at-bats in fourth, fifth and eighth innings, all on first pitch.

JACKSON, THOMAS (1824–1863)   Confederate general. Nickname "Stonewall" derives from Battle of Bull Run, where his outnumbered troops stood their ground like a "stone wall." Killed on nighttime scouting mission when his own troops, mistaking him for the enemy, shot him.

JAGGER, JOSEPH. See JAGGERS, WILLIAM

JAGGER, MICK (1943–)   Lead singer and founder of The Rolling Stones. Attended London School of Economics before forming group. Starred in motion pictures: *Ned Kelly* (1970) and *Performance* (1970). (See ROLLING STONES, THE)

JAGGERS, WILLIAM   Scottish engineer. Found flaw in roulette wheel, Monte Carlo, making it favor certain numbers. Won 2.4 million francs in four days, 1886. Casino eventually stopped by rotating parts of wheels, making them wear evenly.

JAGUAR   Largest and most powerful cat in Western Hemisphere. Considered god of strength and courage by ancient Maya Indians. Import and export of jaguars or their pelts prohibited in U.S. Found only in Mexico and Central and South America.

JAI ALAI   Pronounced "hi-li," known as *pelota* in Spain. Ball (pelota), harder and heavier than golf ball, made from virgin de-para rubber from Brazil, covered with hand-woven layer of linen thread and two layers of goatskin. Ball hurled with *cesta* (basket), hand-held scoop; clocked at more than 150 m.p.h., fastest ball movement in any sport. Miami first city in U.S. to have fronton, arena in which spectators bet on games using parimutuel system.

JAKARTA Capital and largest city of Republic of Indonesia. Located on northwest coast of Java. Named Djakarta, meaning "glorious fortress." Official spelling is Jakarta. Characterized by its *kalis*, canals that supply water for drinking, bathing and washing clothes.

JAMAICA Independent island country in West Indies. Part of North American continent. Belongs to Commonwealth of Nations; previously British colony. Originally called Xaymaca, meaning "island of springs." Jamaican slang words include *susu* (local gossip), *ganja* (marijuana), *foo foo* (foolish), *wash-mouth* (breakfast) and *blue-swee* (cunning, elusive).

JAMES I (1566–1625) King of Great Britian, 1603–1625. James VI of Scotland since age one. Strong advocate of expanding the empire. Unpopular monarch. Contemplating origin of man's consumption of oysters, James once said: "He was a very valiant man that first adventured on eating oysters."

JAPAN Asian island country between Sea of Japan and Pacific Ocean. Its islands form a 1,300 mi. (2,090 km.) archipelago along Asia's northeastern coast. Four main islands are Honshu (88,000 sq. mi./227,920 sq. km.), Hokkaido (30,077 sq. mi./77,899 sq. km.), Kyushu (16,240 sq. mi./42,062 sq. km.), and Shikoku (7,246 sq. mi./18,767 sq. km.). Countrymen call their nation Nippon, meaning "source of the sun." Japan suffers from approximately 1,500 minor tremors per year and a severe quake every few years; more earthquakes than any other country, due to location on unstable part of Earth's crust. Major exports to U.S. include automobiles, motorcycles, TVs, frog's legs, steel and textiles. Language is branch of Ural-Ataic family prevalent in Asia. Spoken in many dialects. Written with Chinese characters and its own additions, making it the most complex written language of any developed nation. *N* is the only final consonant sound. Japanese *N* has peculiar sound made with mouth open and tongue not touching roof of mouth. Pronounced only at end of word when it precedes (sound of) *s, z, h, y* or *w*. National anthem is "Kimi ga yo (Reign of our Emperor)." Music written by Hyashi Hirokami, 1880.

JARRY PARK   Home of Montreal Expos of National League, 1969–1976. First site outside U.S. to host official major league baseball game, April 14, 1969. Capacity 28,000. Expos moved to site of 1976 Olympic Games (baseball capacity, 58,000) for start of 1977 season. Jarry Park (or Parc Jarry in French) measured 340 ft. down foul lines and 420 ft. to center field.

JASON   In Greek mythology, led sailors on ship *Argo* (the Argonauts) on quest for Golden Fleece of winged ram sacrificed to Zeus and hung on tree in Colchis (located in modern Black Sea coastal area of Russian Georgia), guarded by dragon. Jason reclaims his kingdom from uncle by giving him Golden Fleece.

JAWBONE   Consists of right and left maxillae, or upper jawbones, and horseshoe-shaped mandible, or lower jawbone. Word "mandible" comes from Latin *mandere* ("to chew"). Only bone in body whose ends are mirror images of each other. Extremely strong.

JAWS   The number one hit film of 1975, based on best-selling novel by Peter Benchley. Steven Spielberg directed this story of three men who set out to kill great white shark, terrorizing residents of Amity Island. Roy Scheider was town sheriff; repeated role in *Jaws II* (1978). (See BENCHLEY, PETER)

JAZZ SINGER, THE   Story of young man who makes it as singer rather than cantor. Three film versions starred Al Jolson (1927), Danny Thomas (1953) and Neil Diamond (1980). 1927 version famed for being first feature-length talking motion picture with sound on film.

JEEP   Military slang for "G.P., General Purpose car." Four-wheel drive vehicles became popular recreational cars after World War II, when term originated.

JEEVES   Character created by P. G. Wodehouse; Bertie Wooster's impeccable butler. Quintessential gentleman's gentleman, Jeeves constantly rescues his master, an amiable, extravagant nitwit.

JEFFERSON CITY   Capital of Missouri, named in honor of Thomas Jefferson. Located on banks of Missouri River, midway between Kansas City and St. Louis. Home of Lincoln University.

JEFFERSON, THOMAS (1743–1826)   Statesman, scholar

and architect. Virginia delegate to Continental Congress, 1775–1776. Chosen June 1776, to write Declaration of Independence. Completed 18 days later. He later became known as "the father of the Declaration of Independence" which was ratified July 2, 1776, and adopted July 4, 1776, Independence Day. Fifty-six signed the Declaration, including John Hancock, the largest signature, and Button Gwinnett, in the upper left-hand corner. Jefferson became third U.S. president, 1801–1809. As U.S. government had been officially moved from New York City to Washington, DC in 1790, Jefferson was first president to take oath of office there.

JEREZ City in southwestern Spain, at one time a Roman colony. Noted for its sherry, named for the town. Also known for raising horses.

JERUSALEM Capital of Israel, holy city of Jews, Christians and Muslims. West Jerusalem is modern section of city, inhabited mainly by Jews. East Jerusalem contains Old City, inhabited mainly by Arabs. Three Sabbaths are observed: Friday (Muslim), Saturday (Jewish) and Sunday (Christian).

JESSEL, GEORGE (1898–1981) Vaudeville entertainer turned actor and Hollywood producer. As actor, films include *Lucky Boy* (1929), *Stage Door Canteen* (1943) and *The Busy Body* (1957). Nicknamed "the Toastmaster General of the United States."

JESUS CHRIST (4–8?B.C.–A.D.29?) Source of Christian religion and Savior in Christian faith. Son of Mary. Jesus and his disciples are often symbolized by the fish. Their practice of gathering followers often compared with fisherman catching fish. Fish was also early symbol of Christian baptism. Ring worn by Pope is called "the Fisherman's Ring." In Book of John, 8:7, Pharisees wanted him to stone a woman accused of adultery, or refuse, which would have forced Jesus to break the law. He avoided trap by saying, "He who is without sin among you, let him cast the first stone." Book of John, 11:35, is shortest in Bible. Jesus had just found that his friend Lazarus, brother of Martha and Mary, had died. After weeping, he brings Lazarus back from the dead.

JESUS CHRIST SUPERSTAR Tim Rice and Andrew Lloyd Webber rock opera, turned Broadway show and feature film, depicts last week in Jesus Christ's life. 1973 film by Norman Jewison starred Ted Neeley as Christ.

JEW'S HARP Musical instrument, dating from 1500s, consisting of frame of metal pressed between teeth and plucked with finger, causing twanging sound.

JEWELL, DEREK (1927–) Jazz critic of London *Sunday Times*, and author of *Duke: a Portrait*, a 1977 biography of jazz pianist-composer Duke Ellington (1899–1974). Jewell followed Ellington's music for 30 years and on English tours interviewed the bandleader-composer of "Mood Indigo" and "Satin Doll."

JEZEBEL Bette Davis won second Oscar for Best Actress in role of Southern vixen who creates scandal and loses fiancé by wearing daring red gown to society ball. Released in 1938, film also starred George Brent, Henry Fonda and Fay Bainter.

JINGLE BELLS Popular Christmas song about racing through snow in sleigh pulled by bell-ringing horse named Bobtail.

JINGLES JONES Sidekick to Wild Bill Hickok in 1957 TV series. Jingles, riding his horse Joker, would forever call out, "Hey, Wild Bill, wait for me!" Andy Devine portrayed Jingles, partner of Guy Madison as Wild Bill on this popular Western show.

JOAN OF ARC (1412–1431) French national heroine. Born Jean la Pucelle. Led troops that liberated city of Orléans, 1429. For this, nicknamed, "Maid of Orleans." At age 17, had visions from God telling her to lead French from British occupation. Captured by British, 1430, who tried her as witch and heretic. Burned at stake, 1431. In 1456, Pope pronounced her innocent. Made a saint, 1920.

JOCKEY. See HORSE RACING TERMS

JOHANNESBURG City in South Africa. Founded by prospectors in 1886. Deep gold mines, some below sea level, are found beneath city. Gold has made it South Africa's most important industrial and commercial city.

JOHANSSON Most common Swedish family name. Also common in Norway and Denmark. Means "son of John." Variations include Johannsen, Johanson and Johansen.

JOHANSSON, INGEMAR (1922–) Only Swedish heavyweight champion. Knocked out Floyd Patterson in third round of championship bout, June 26, 1959, at Yankee Stadium. Last white boxer to hold heavyweight title. First foreigner to hold title since Primo Carnera in 1933. Patterson regained title with fifth round KO of Johansson, June 20, 1960, and knocked him out again in sixth round, March 13, 1961.

JOHN F. KENNEDY INTERNATIONAL AIRPORT

Located in New York City on 5,000-acre landfill near Jamaica Bay. Formerly called Idlewild. Renamed in memory of President J. F. Kennedy following his assassination, November 22, 1963. Painters began changing signs December 20, 1963.

JOHN THE BAPTIST (c.7 B.C.–A.D. 28)   Distant relative of Jesus. Preached on banks of Jordan River in ancient Judea. Predicted coming of messiah. Name derives from ceremonies of repentance and baptism he performed on followers, including Jesus.

JOHN, ELTON (1947–   )   Born 1947 as Reginald Dwight. Took stage name from Long John Baldry and saxophonist Elton Dean. First performer since The Beatles to have four albums in top ten simultaneously, in 1971: *Elton John; Tumbleweed Connection; 11–17–70*, a live album; and *Friends*, a movie soundtrack. Other hit albums include *Goodbye Yellow Brick Road* and *Captain Fantastic and the Brown Dirt Cowboy*. Many hit singles, including "Daniel," "Bennie and the Jets" and "I'm Still Standing." In 1979 was first rock star to perform in Soviet Union.

JOHNNY APPLESEED   Name given to John Chapman (1775–1847), born near Boston, who believed his mission in life was to plant apple seeds in wilderness. Did this for last 48 years of life, especially in Ohio and Indiana.

JOHNNY HICKS. See CRAPS, NICKNAMES FOR THROWS

JOHNSON, ANDREW (1808–1875)   Seventeenth U.S. president. Assumed office after Lincoln's assassination, April 15, 1865. Southern Democrat. Often faced hostile Republican-controlled Congress. Impeached and tried by U.S. Senate for issues relating to post–Civil War restoration of the union. Only president ever impeached; found not guilty. His administration saw freeing of slaves and purchase of Alaska.

JOHNSON, LUCI BAINES (1947–   )   Daughter of President Lyndon Baines Johnson. Married August 6, 1966, to Patrick Nugent, 23, business student from Waukegan, IL. Ceremony unrivaled in size or splendor by wedding of any other presidential daughter in American history.

JOHNSON, LYNDA BYRD (1944–   )   Daughter of President Lyndon Baines Johnson. Married Marine Captain Charles

Robb, December 9, 1967, at White House. This marriage made Johnson second president to give away two daughters while in office.

JOHNSON, LYNDON BAINES (1908–1973) Thirty-sixth U.S. president, 1963–1969. Graduate of Southwest State Teachers College, 1930. Assumed presidency after J. F. Kennedy's assassination, November 22, 1963. In one of most abrupt presidential transitions, Johnson phoned three Dallas lawyers to find out presidential oath of office. Those contacted were Waddy Bullion, Irv Goldberg and U.S. District Court Judge Sarah Hughes who finally administered the oath. Sworn in aboard presidential jet *Air Force One* two hours after Kennedy pronounced dead. First words as President were: "Let's get this goddamn thing airborne." First Congressional address, November 27, began: "All I have I would have given gladly not to be standing here today." First State of the Union address, January 8, 1964, outlined his "War on Poverty" program. Congress approved $948 million to increase medical insurance, food stamp and educational programs. In May 1964 he said: "... we have the opportunity to move not only toward the rich society and the powerful society, but upward to the Great Society." "Great Society" became catchname for his domestic program. Frustrated with lack of progress at home and with Vietnam war abroad, he announced on March 31, 1968, that he would not seek reelection. Criticized for picking up pet beagle by ears.

JOLLY ROGER Pirate flag. Depicts white skull with two crossed bones beneath on a black field. Pirate ships not considered vessels of any country. Piracy is armed robbery on high seas or assaults by ships against land. Still occurs in areas of South Pacific.

JOLSON STORY, THE Actor Larry Parks starred in many B-pictures, famous for performance as Al Jolson in *The Jolson Story* (1946). Made sequel, *Jolson Sings Again*, in 1950. Songs included "Swanee," "Mammy" and "April Showers," dubbed by Jolson.

JONES, JAMES (1921–1977) American novelist whose first novel, *From Here to Eternity* (1951), won a National Book Award. First of pre– and post–World War II trilogy (others were *Some Came Running*, 1957, and *The Thin Red Line*, 1962). In *From Here to Eternity*, about Army life in Hawaii before Pearl Harbor, Private Prewitt preserves his integrity by refusing to box, expressing his conscience in lonely wail of his bugling. Film version (1953) won three Oscars, including Best Picture.

JONES, REV. JAMES WARREN (JIM) (1931–1978)   Leader of People's Temple cult who ordered more than 900 members of his Guyana commune to commit suicide by drinking cyanide-laced Kool-Aid, then killed himself with bullet to head. James Reston, Jr., conducted extensive investigation of Jones to write *Our Father Who Art in Hell* (1981), about Jones and the scheming that led hundreds to complicity in their own deaths.

JONES, ROBERT TYRE (BOBBY) (1902–1971)   Made amateur's version of Grand Slam of Golf in 1930 by winning U.S. and British Opens and Amateurs. Only player ever to accomplish these wins in one year. Professional Grand Slam—Masters, U.S. Open, British Open and PGA Championship—has never been won by one player in same year. Established Masters Tournament at Augusta National Club. Nicknamed "Emperor Jones." Won U.S. Amateur five times, U.S. Open four times.

JONG, ERICA MANN (1942–   **)**   American novelist and poet noted for bawdy, seemingly autobiographical novels. *Fruits and Vegetables* (1973) and *Loveroot* (1975) are books of poems. Among novels *Fanny* (1980), complete title, *Fanny: Being the True History of the Adventures of Fanny Hackabout-Jones.* Feminist response to John Cleland's *Fanny Hill*, about 18th-century English woman of pleasure. *Fear of Flying* (1973), first novel. Its heroine Isadora Wing is young, Barnard-educated and in Vienna with her second husband, a psychiatrist. Restless, she goes on two-week erotic binge.

JOPLIN, SCOTT (1868–1917)   Piano player and composer known as "King of Ragtime." Wrote over 50 ragtime songs, considered classics, including "The Maple Leaf Rag" (1899) and "The Entertainer" (1902). Latter used as theme in movie *The Sting* (1973); its use in film caused revival of his music during 1970s.

JORGENSON, GEORGE W., JR. (1926–   **)**   Bronx youth. Served two years in army. Became a biologically correct female, December 1952, after "five major operations, a minor operation and almost 2,000 hormone injections" in Copenhagen hospital. Took name Christine Jorgenson. This sex change was elective surgery.

JOSEPH   Received "coat of many colors" from his father Jacob, but hated by brothers who viewed gift as sign of Joseph's favored status. They sold Joseph into slavery and returned bloodstained coat to Jacob, saying wild animal had killed him. Brought to Egypt, he eventually rose to high office and later convinced his family, in time of famine, to move there.

JOSEPHINE (1763–1814)   French empress. Wife of Vicomte Alexandre de Beauharnais. Mother of Eugene (1781–1824), prince of Eichstatt, and Hortense (1783–1824), wife of Louis Bonaparte and mother of Napoleon III. Vicomte was guillotined in French Revolution. Josephine became first wife of Napoleon I, 1796; he later divorced her, convinced she could not have children. In 1813 she wrote to Napoleon, then exiled on Elba Island, asking to be allowed to join him. Died before receiving his response.

JOUSTING   Ancient sporting event in which armored knights on horseback charged each other with lances at command "Charge, sir knight!" Peaked in popularity during 12th century. Mock battling replaced actual battle as method of proving courage and gaining glory. Tournaments gave nobles opportunity to display prowess in arms and courtesy toward enemies.

JOYCE, JAMES (1882–1941)   Irish novelist and short-story writer. Dublin, setting for most famous works, *Dubliners* (1914), *Portrait of the Artist as a Young Man* (1916) and *Ulysses* (1922). Banned in U.S. until 1933 for obscenity charges. Wore patch over eye.

JUAN DE FUCA STRAIT   Narrow body of water separating Vancouver Island, Canada and state of Washington, U.S. Ships pass through strait into Pacific from Seattle, Vancouver and Victoria. Named for Greek navigator in service for Spain; his claim to its discovery was proven false, but name was kept.

JUDGE ROY BEAN   Legendary self-appointed judge of Old West has been portrayed on screen by many throughout the years, including Walter Brennan (who won an Oscar for his portrayal) in *The Westerner* (1940), Edgar Buchanan in 1956 TV series *Judge Roy Bean* and Paul Newman in feature film *The Life and Times of Judge Roy Bean* (1972).

JUDGMENT AT NUREMBERG   1961 film dramatizing German war crimes trials. Spencer Tracy starred as U.S. judge presiding over trials. Maximilian Schell won Best Actor Oscar as German defense lawyer.

JUDO   Japanese sport that makes use of principles of jujitsu, weaponless system of self-defense. Created 1882 by Dr. Jigoro Kano, Japanese jujitsu expert, who modified or dropped many holds too dangerous to use in sport.

JUKEBOX   Coin-operated phonograph. First was John Gabel automatic entertainer, introduced 1906. Contained 20 10-in. records. First electric jukebox introduced 1927.

JULIET. See SHAKESPEARE, WILLIAM

JULIUS DITHERS. See BLONDIE

JUNEAU   State capital of Alaska. Largest area of any U.S. city, covering 3,108 sq. mi. (8,050 sq. km.). Northernmost U.S. state capital. Lies at base of steep mountains. Named after prospector Joe Juneau in 1880.

JUPITER   Fifth planet from sun and largest in solar system, 1,300 times the size of Earth. A 150 lb. person would weigh 396 lbs. on Jupiter. Named for Roman god known as Jove, center of Jovian system. Its clouds are marked by the Great Red Spot, a severe atmospheric disturbance. Roughly 25,000 mi. (40,000 km.) long and 20,000 mi. (32,000 km.) wide. Resembles a hurricane.

JUSTERINI & BROOKS   Bottlers of J&B, a blended Scotch whisky. Company founded 1749 as wine merchant. Began distilling and bottling blended whisky (British spelling) mid-19th century. Blending malt whiskies and grain spirits gives liquor smoother taste. J&B Scotch distilled and bottled "in the Highlands."

K

K-K-K-KATY, THE STAMMERING SONG Geoffrey O'Hara's famous "stammering song" popular ever since it was written in 1918 and recorded that year by vaudevillian Billy Murray. Jack Oakie performed song in feature film *Tin Pan Alley* (1941).

K2. See MOUNTAINS, WORLD'S HIGHEST

KABUL Afghanistan's capital and largest city. Situated on Kabul River. Became capital in 1776. Ancient coins have led historians to estimate that city first existed between 500 and 300 B.C.

KAHLUA Liqueur, 53 proof, product of Mexico. Cane spirit base flavored with coffee. Served straight, on ice, added to coffee or ice cream, with milk or cream, or vodka.

KAMIKAZE Name used by Japanese suicide pilots during World War II. In Japanese, means literally "The Divine Wind," from *kami*, "God or Goddess" in Shinto religion, plus *kaze*, "wind."

KAMPALA Capital and largest city of Uganda. Exports cotton, coffee and sugarcane. Replaced Entebbe as capital when Uganda became independent in 1962.

KANGAROO Or wallaby, name for a number of Australian marsupials. Usually have one offspring a year which develops within marsupium, a pouch in belly. Self-defense using forearms comes naturally to Australia's national animal. Elder male (called old man) dominates other males (called boomers) by biting, kicking, and boxing, in order to control herd, including females (flyers) and babies (joeys).

KANSAS CITY   Cities in Kansas and Missouri which are separated by Kansas River. Both named for Kansa Indians who once populated area. Former names: Wyandot, KA (renamed in 1886); and The Town of Kansas, MO (renamed in 1889).

KANSAS CITY MONARCHS   Baseball team in Negro American League. Negro Leagues, formed 1920, played to early 1950s, when baseball became integrated at all levels following Jackie Robinson breaking color line with Brooklyn Dodgers, 1947. Robinson had played for Monarchs, as did future Hall of Fame pitcher Satchel Paige, pitcher Hilton Smith, and second baseman Newt Allen. Outfielder Richard "Cool Papa" Bell played for KC and Homestead Grays.

KARAMAZOV BROTHERS. See DOSTOEVSKI, FEODOR

KARATE   Literally "empty-hand" fighting. Has variety of forms. When *kyu* (student) becomes *dan* (graduate), entitled to wear black belt with karate robe; dan or black-belt grades go from first to tenth dan. Dans from eighth-grade up, called *Sheehan* (honorable professor) by their juniors, can wear solid red belt, or continue to wear black belts.

KARRAS, ALEX. See HORNUNG, PAUL, AND KARRAS, ALEX

KARTOFFEL. See POTATO

KATMANDU   Capital and largest city of Nepal. Lies on Baghmati River. Founded, A.D. 723. Home of many beautiful Hindu and Buddhist temples. Independent kingdom until 1768, when it became Nepal's capital.

KEATON, BUSTER (1895–1966)   Born Joseph Francis Keaton. Appeared in family vaudeville act as youngster. Became silent-screen comedian known as "The Great Stone Face." Classic films include *Sherlock Junior* (1924), *Seven Chances* (1925), and *The General* (1926).

KEATS, JOHN (1795–1821)   English poet. In Book I of long allegory *Endymion* (1818) wrote: "A thing of beauty is a joy forever: Its loveliness increases; it will never pass into nothingness; but still will keep a bower quiet for us, and a sleep full of sweet dreams, and health, and quiet breathing." In "Ode on a Grecian Urn" (1819), about perfection and timelessness of art, wrote, "Beauty is truth, truth beauty—that is all Ye know on earth, and all Ye need to know."

KEENE, CAROLYN   Pseudonym of Harriet Stratemeyer Adams, daughter of Edward Stratemeyer (who wrote *Hardy Boys* series under name of F.W. Dixon). Keene wrote more than 100 books under a half-dozen pen names. Also wrote *The Bobbsey Twins*.

KELLER, HELEN (1880–1968)   Author, lecturer, humanitarian. Illness at 19 months old left her blind and deaf. Taught by Anne Sullivan to speak, read Braille and write with a special typewriter. Graduated from Radcliffe College, *cum laude*, 1904.

KELLY, GRACE (1929–1982)   American actress and leading lady of the 1950s, retired from films to marry Prince Rainier III of Monaco. Films include *Rear Window* (1954) and *High Society* (1956). Won Oscar for Best Actress in *The Country Girl* (1954). Became a member of Board of Directors to 20th Century-Fox. First actress to appear on a postage stamp. Bore three children, Caroline (1957–   ) and Albert (1958–   ) and Stephanie (1965–   ).

KELVIN SCALE   The international standard for scientific temperature measurement. Developed by Lord Kelvin. Uses gas thermometer. Absolute zero equals -273.15°C (-459.67°F). Scale does not use word *degree* or degree symbol.

KEMELMAN, HARRY (1908–   )   American mystery writer. Famed for detective series featuring Rabbi David Small, starting with *Friday the Rabbi Slept Late* (1964). Others: *Saturday the Rabbi Went Hungry* (1966), *Sunday the Rabbi Stayed Home* (1969), *Monday the Rabbi Took Off* (1972), *Tuesday the Rabbi Saw Red* (1973), *Wednesday the Rabbi Got Wet* (1976), *Thursday the Rabbi Walked Out* (1978).

KENNEDY SPACE CENTER   Cape Canaveral, FL. Contains Launch Complex 39, spaceport designed for huge Saturn Rocket. Vehicle Assembly Building, 525 ft. (160 m.) high, used for rocket assembly. Tours available by TWA.

KENNEDY, EDWARD MOORE (TED) (1932–   )   American politician. Democratic senator from Massachusetts. After losing 1980 presidential nomination to Jimmy Carter, delivered moving speech that concluded, "For all those whose cares have been our concern, the work goes on, the cause endures, the hope still lives, and the dream shall never die." Campaign reawakened public awareness of his July 1969 automobile accident on Chappaquiddick Island, MA. After driving off an unmarked and railless bridge, his passenger Mary Jo Kopechne drowned and he suffered a concussion. Kennedy wandered around for eight hours, apparently in shock, before reporting the incident to the police. Pleaded guilty to leaving the scene of an accident. Attended Kopechne's funeral wearing a neck brace.

KENNEDY, JACQUELINE. See ONASSIS, JACQUELINE KENNEDY

KENNEDY, JOHN FITZGERALD (1917–1963) Thirty-fifth U.S. president (1961–1963). First president born after turn of the century. At age 43 the youngest president elected. (Theodore Roosevelt, who assumed office after McKinley's assassination, was 42). Education began at London School of Economics: Then transferred to Princeton where, after an attack of jaundice, he was forced to leave. Graduated from Harvard, where he was voted "most likely to succeed." In 1943, Kennedy was commander of the motor torpedo boat PT-109, sunk by the Japanese during operations in the southwest Pacific. Kennedy and his crew swam three miles to a deserted island where they were rescued. Later received Navy and Marine Corps Medal and the Purple Heart. Kennedy was the first veteran of the Navy to become president. In 1946, he was elected to Congess as a representative of Massachusetts, the same year as first-term Congressman Richard Nixon. At the July 13, 1960 Democratic National Convention in Los Angeles, in one of the closest races in history, defeated Democratic contenders Lyndon Johnson, Stuart Symington and Adlai Stevenson on the first ballot. Kennedy's youthful optimism reflected in campaign song "High Hopes." He went on to win a narrow victory over Republican candidate Nixon, becoming the first Roman Catholic president. Though his Catholicism was an obstacle for many voters, the fact that Vice-President Lyndon Johnson was a southern Protestant aided Kennedy in his election. Kennedy's theme for his presidency was called the "New Frontier." Goals were improvements in civil rights, education, health care and reduced unemployment through worker retraining. As part of official European tour, Kennedy visited West Berlin, June 23, 1963. In speech expressing solidarity with the people of West Berlin, the President frequently proclaimed *"Ich bin ein Berliner,"* German meaning "I am a Berliner." He also spent three days in Duganstown, Ireland, where Kennedy family originated. He was first president to hold live televised news conferences on a regular basis. Having exceptional command of TV medium, some called the broadcasts the best matinee in town. On Friday, November 22, 1963, Kennedy was shot and killed by accused assassin Lee Harvey Oswald while visiting in Dallas. The President's last words were, "My God, I'm hit." He is buried in Arlington National Cemetery in Virginia, where eternal flame burns near his grave. Because of his youth, optimism and vision of social progress, the Kennedy administration was sometimes compared with Broadway show *Camelot*, which depicted a strong, well-loved young king in ancient England. Only U.S. president to win Pulitzer Prize, *Profiles in Courage*, 1956.

KENNEDY, JOSEPH P. (1888–1969)   Financier and public official. Father of John F., Robert F. and Edward. Bank president, 1914. First Chairman, Security and Exchange Commission, 1943. Resigned to become ambassador, British Court of Saint James, 1937. Quit post to protest U.S. aid to Allies, World War II.

KENNEDY, ROSE FITZGERALD (1890–   ) Matriarch of American political family. Noted for inner strength displayed in face of personal tragedies: loss of eldest son in World War II, assassination of sons President John F. and Senator Robert F., air crash death of one daughter, and mental retardation of another. In *Times to Remember* (1974), she writes about her ancestors, her husband (Joseph), her nine children, and her thoughts while raising them.

KENNEDY,   ROBERT   FRANCIS   (1925–1968) American lawyer and politician. Campaign manager and Attorney General under brother President J. F. Kennedy from 1961 until his resignation, 1964. Stressed civil rights and eradication of organized crime. Elected U.S. senator from New York, 1965. March 24, 1965, became first person to scale Mount Kennedy in the Yukon territory. (The mountain had been renamed in 1964 by Canadian government in honor of the recently assassinated J.F. Kennedy.) The senator planted a black-bordered flag at summit and left several PT-109 clasps that J.F.K. had used during his 1960 presidential campaign. Ran for president, 1968. Assassinated by Sirhan Sirhan in Los Angeles, CA, June 5, 1968, the day after he had won California Democratic primary. He had won five of six primaries he entered. Survived by widow Ethel.

KENNEDY–NIXON DEBATE   First televised presidential

debates, beginning September 26, 1960. Four total. Moderated by journalist Howard K. Smith. Audiences of 60–75 million watched each one.

KENSINGTON GARDENS Located in London's Hyde Park. Covers 275 (originally 20) acres of park's total 615 acres. In the 18th century, Round Pond, octagonal basin surrounded by trees and flowers, was constructed. Other features of gardens include Broad Walk, Edwardian Sunken Garden and statue of Peter Pan.

KENT STATE University in Ohio. In May 1970, National Guardsmen shot four students and wounded nine others demonstrating against U.S. involvement in Cambodia. Public outcry prompted Congress to demand U.S. troop withdrawal. Nixon complied, June 1970.

KENTUCKY State nickname: "The Bluegrass State." State Motto: "United We Stand, Divided We Fall." State Song: "My Old Kentucky Home," words and music by Stephen Collins Foster.

KENTUCKY DERBY, FIRST RACE All but one of 15 jockeys in the first race, 1875, were black, including Oliver Lewis, rider of winner Aristides. In first 28 runnings, black jockeys rode 15 winners. Most famous black jockey, Isaac Murphy, won Derby three times. By 1912, racial prejudice had moved black jockeys out of Derby picture. (see TRIPLE CROWN)

KEROUAC, JACK (1922–1969) Born Jean-Louis Lebrid de Kerouac. American novelist and poet. Originated and defined term "Beat Generation" in his 1957 novel *On the Road*. Main Character, Dean Moriarty and his friends make endless trips across U.S. Long on description, short on plot, "The Bible of the Beat Generation" has lyrical, syncopated rhythm in writing characteristic of beatnik poetry. Also wrote *The Subterraneans* (1958) and *The Dharma Bums* (1958).

KESEY, KEN (1935–   ) American author. Wrote *One Flew Over the Cuckoo's Nest*, based on experiences as orderly in Oregon mental hospital. Also wrote, *Sometimes a Great Notion*. Leader of 1960s LSD experimenters Merry Pranksters, subject of Tom Wolfe's book *Electric Kool-Aid Acid Test*.

KEW GARDENS Also known as Royal Botanical Gardens. Contains one of the world's largest collections of trees and hothouse plants. Found in Richmond, outside of London.

KEY LARGO　1948 film directed by John Huston, about a gang of hoods who take over hotel in Florida Keys, intimidating the proprietor, Humphrey Bogart. Claire Trevor won Best Supporting Actress Oscar as gangster Edward G. Robinson's moll.

KEY, FRANCIS SCOTT (1779–1843)　Attorney and poet. Wrote words to "Star Spangled Banner," 1814, which became the National Anthem. Describes the British shelling of Fort McHenry, MD, during the War of 1812. Words set to tune of popular drinking song.

KEYES, DANIEL (1927–　　)　American writer. His *Flowers for Algernon* (1966), written first as short story, later expanded to novel. Written in diary form, story of mentally retarded man who becomes highly intelligent through surgery, then returns to former state. Filmed in 1968 as *Charly*, with Cliff Robertson in Oscar-winning role.

KEYSTONE KOPS　Group of slapstick comedians created by Mack Sennett at Keystone Studios. Ford Sterling led police force in wild chases in numerous shorts from 1912 through 1920.

KHARTOUM　Capital of Sudan. Lies at junction of Blue Nile and White Nile. Founded by Egyptian Muhammad Ali in the 1820s.

KHAYYAM, OMAR (1048?–1122)　Persian astronomer-poet. Well-known during lifetime for contributions to astonomy, mathematics and law. His *Rubiayat* (written 12th century), discovered, translated and arranged in quatrains by English poet Edward Fitzgerald (1859). Among its famous verses: "Here with a loaf of bread beneath the bough / A flask of wine, a book of verse—and thou / Beside me singing in the Wilderness / And Wilderness is Paradise enow."

KHOMEINI, AYATOLLAH RUHOLLAH (1900–　　)　Religious and political leader of Iran. Ordered imprisonment of American hostages in U.S. Teheran embassy, 1975–1976. *Time* magazine's 1979 Man of the Year, did most to change the news for worse.

KHRUSHCHEV, NIKITA SERGEYEVICH (1894–1971)　Soviet premier, 1958–1964. Succeeded Joseph Stalin as first Secretary of Soviet Communist Party, 1950. Economic, agrarian and industrial policies met with opposition. September 29, 1960, he upset the 15th session of United Nations General Assembly when he yelled, interrupting speaker Harold MacMillan (England's prime minister), and took off shoe and whacked it on desk, in rhythm, for emphasis. Khrushchev wanted the Secretary-General replaced with a three-man committee, or troika. In June 1961, 16 months prior to the Cuban missile crisis, Khrushchev gave President Kennedy, among other gifts, a puppy named Pushinka. Dog's mother, Strelka, had traveled into space. In 1964, after several bad harvests at home and failure of the Cuban missile crisis, he was forced out of office by a group led by Leonid Brezhnev, his successor. Khrushchev is survived by his widow, Nina. Once quoted as having said, "We will in my lifetime rule the world by invitation."

KIBITZER Spectator in bridge or other card game, especially one who offers advice. From Yiddish *kiebitz* meaning "meddlesome onlooker." Has come to mean, in general, a meddler.

KICK THE CAN Form of hide-and-seek using tin can as base. When "it" person spots another player, both must race to can and kick it as far as possible. The one who doesn't kick the can must retrieve can, and becomes "it."

KID, THE Film directed by Charlie Chaplin (1921). Jackie Coogan played title role of street-wise orphan taken in by the Tramp. Chaplin's first feature, combination of slapstick and sentiment.

KILLANIN, LORD MICHAEL MORRIS (1914–   ) Irishman who succeeded American Avery Brundage as president of International Olympic Committee after 1972 Munich Olympics. Allowed Canada's right to bar Taiwanese from 1976 Montreal Olympics, immediately indicating he would not wield dictatorial power as Brundage had.

KILLEBREW, HARMON (1936–   ) Major league baseball player 1954–1975. Played with the Minnesota Twins, 1961–1974. Known as "the Killer." Lifetime home runs numbered 573. Led American League in homers six times. Won RBI title three times. American League MVP 1969. Twins retired his number (three), 1975. Elected Hall of Fame, 1984.

KILLY, JEAN-CLAUDE (1943–   ) French skier who won all three alpine skiing events at 1968 Olympics, Grenoble, France, men's downhill (1:59.85), giant slalom (3:29.28) and slalom (1:39.73). Controversy developed over charges that Killy displayed brand name of sponsors on his skis. Skiers henceforth required to tape over brand names to prevent commercialism.

KILMER, ALFRED JOYCE (1886–1918) American poet. Wrote for New York *Times Magazine* and *Book Review*. Last lines of his poem "Trees" (1914): "Poems are made by fools like me, but only God can make a tree." Killed in France during World War I.

KILO. See METRIC PREFIXES

KILROY WAS HERE Phrase used worldwide during World War II. American Transit Company staged contest to locate the "real" Kilroy. Turned out to be James J. Kilroy, an inspector during the war for Bethlehem Steel, who used phrase to certify equipment.

KIMBERLEY One of world's most important diamond centers. Until 1908 mines at Kimberley and Pretoria produced most of world's diamond market. Founded by prospectors, 1871.

KIMBLE, RICHARD Starring character, portrayed by David Janssen, of the TV series *The Fugitive* (1963–1967). Wrongly convicted of murdering his wife, he was pursued by Lt. Philip Gerard (played by Barry Morse) while trying to find one-armed man who actually committed crime.

KING ARTHUR Legendary king of England, part myth, part historical. Earliest references in 6th century Welsh literature. Sir Thomas Malory's *Le Morte d'Artur* (c. 1469) is first major prose collection of Arthurian legend. Later versions including Tennyson's *Idylls of the King* (1859–1872), Mark Twain's *A Connecticut Yankee in King Arthur's Court* (1889) and T. H. White's *The Once and Future King* (1958), which inspired the Lerner and Loewe musical *Camelot* (1960). All draw heavily on Malory. Characters are the same, but interpretations change. Among key elements:

Camelot: Capital city of Arthur's England, "Rosy-red city, half as old as time." His court, where the Knights of the Round Table convened. Historians place real-life basis for legend at one of four sites, usually at Cadbury in Somerset.

Excalibur: Arthur's magic sword. In some versions, Arthur pulls it from stone anvil in which it's embedded, proving he is rightful King of England.

Galahad: Purest and noblest of Knights of the Round Table. In *Le Morte d'Artur*, he is illegitimate son of Sir Lancelot and Princess Elaine. Later goes on quest for Holy Grail. Name has become synonymous with chivalry.

Guinevere: Arthur's queen and, in *Idylls of the King* and other versions, lover of bravest knight, Sir Lancelot. Arthur loves them both and tries to overlook their affair, but treacherous Mordred (Arthur's bastard son) exposes them, leading to their exile, a war, and death of Arthur.

Merlin: Magician and seer of Arthur's court. His mistress is Vivien, Lady of the Lake, who made Excalibur. She ultimately imprisons Merlin in enchanted tower so she can conjure up Arthur whenever England needs him.

KING FAISAL (1909-1975)   Saudi Arabian king. Important figure in Mid-East politics. Shot and killed by nephew who had history of mental illness. Assassination occurred at reception in honor of birthday of Prophet of Islam, Mohammed.

KING KONG   1933 fantasy film about giant ape, brought from Skull Island to New York. Fay Wray played his love interest. Jessica Lange portrayed the role in the 1976 remake.

KING LEAR. See SHAKESPEARE, WILLIAM

KING MIDAS   In Greek mythology, King of Phrygia. Asked gods to make everything he touched turn to gold. When his food turned to gold, prayed they take favor back.

KING RAT   1965 film based on James Clavell novel. George Segal starred as title character, an American corporal at odds with British marshal for wealth he has gained by trading with enemy while captives of Japanese World War II prison camp.

KING, BILLIE JEAN MOFFITT (1943–   )   American tennis player. Won record 20 Wimbledon titles, 1961–1979: 6 women's singles, 10 women's doubles, 4 mixed doubles. Won 4 U.S. Open singles titles and ranked number one in world 4 times, 1965–1973. First woman chosen *Sports Illustrated* Sportsman-of-the-Year, 1972 (co-winner with UCLA basketball coach John Wooden). Trounced Bobby Riggs in famed "Battle of the Sexes," September 20, 1973, in Houston Astrodome winning $100,000.

KING, MARTIN LUTHER JR. (1929–1968)   American clergyman and civil rights leader. Trained as Baptist minister. King rose to lead nationwide civil rights movement, in 1950s and '60s. In 1955, he led year-long struggle to integrate Montgomery, AL public transit system. An admirer of Mahatma Gandhi, used Gandhi's doctrines of civil disobedience and nonviolence to win change in Montgomery and throughout Southeast. In the process, he with 114 others, was arrested, fingerprinted, photographed (mug shot number 7089) and later freed on $300 bond. In 1957, he founded

Southern Christian Leadership Conference (SCLC) to coordinate civil rights movements across the country. On August 28, 1963, 250,000 people assembled in Washington, DC, to stage civil rights rally. There, King delivered his famous "I Have a Dream" speech. Won Nobel Peace Prize, 1964. In speech describing his vision of racially equal society, he said, "I have been to the mountaintop." He was assassinated by James Earl Ray on April 4, 1968, in Memphis, where he was leading strike of local sanitation workers. His epitaph reads "Free at last, free at last. Thank God Almighty, I am free at last."

KINGDOM OF NATURE   Since at least 1642, natural world has been categorized into three great divisions of natural objects; the animal, vegetable and mineral kingdoms. Classification first cited in M. R. Besler's *Gazophylacium Rerum Naturalium.*

KINGFISH   One of most popular and long-running radio programs of all time was "Amos 'n Andy," created by and starring Freeman Gosden and Charles Correll. Show centered on the lives of Amos Jones, Harlem cab driver; Andy Brown, his pal; "Kingfish," head of their lodge; and Sapphire, his wife. Became TV series in 1951.

KINSEY, ALFRED (1894–1956)   American zoologist. Surveyed sexual behavior and values of Americans. Interviewed 18,000 people for his controversial 1948 book *Sexual Behavior in the Human Male.*

KIPLING, RUDYARD (1865–1936)   English poet, novelist and short-story writer. Won first Nobel Prize in Literature awarded to English writer, 1907. Born in India of British parents. Established career with stories about India, where he returned and spent many years of his life. Known for many years as "Bard of the Empire," in later years called racist and imperialist. Refused laureateship and Order of Merit. Among his poems: "White Man's Burden," "If," "Gunga Din" (1892), about Indian soldier, ends with line, "You're a better man than I am, Gunga Din!" *Jungle Book* (1894 and 1895), two volumes of stories in which central figure is human Mowgli raised by Mother Wolf. Also wrote *Captains Courageous* (1897), *Kim* (1901), and *Just So Stories* (1902).

KISSINGER, HENRY ALFRED (1923–)   American politician and scholar; Harvard professor. German-born. Adviser on national security to Presidents Eisenhower, Kennedy and Johnson. National Security Adviser to President Nixon, later Secretary of State for Nixon and Ford. At the forefront of Nixon's policy of "detente" with U.S.S.R. Declared "Peace is at hand" less than one month before bombing of North Vietnam escalated. Led U.S. delegation in talks resulting in cease-fire in Vietnam. Awarded 1973 Nobel Peace Prize along with North Vietnamese negotiator Le Duc Tho. In final days before Nixon's resignation Kissinger and president were known to pray together. Kissinger is noted for having said: "Power is the ultimate aphrodisiac." Wrote *The White House Years* (1980), first of two-volume memoirs, covering 1969 to early 1973.

KITCHEN DEBATE Debate between Richard Nixon, President Eisenhower's emissary abroad, and Soviet Premier Nikita Khrushchev, 1958. The meeting took place at a display of kitchen appliances at American National Exhibition, which Nixon had gone to Moscow to open.

KIWI. See NEW ZEALAND

KLONDIKE GOLD RUSH. See GOLD RUSH

KNITTING Formation of fabric by intermeshing loops of yarn. Two basic stitches are knit and purl. Popcorn stitch, also called bumps or bobble stitch, creates raised design in knitting. To "yarn over" is to wrap yarn around needle, one per stitch, unless otherwise directed. "Casting on" is forming first row of loops on knitting needle, laying foundation for work.

KNOCK-KNEE From latin *Genu valgum*, meaning "bow-legged." Inward curvature of legs causing knees to knock while walking. Also called baker's leg, baker-feet and baker-knees due to high incidence among bakers.

KNOSSOS Ancient city on island of Crete, Greece. Archeological excavation by Sir Robert Evans (1851–1941) revealed that it was sophisticated Minoan Bronze Age culture. Neolithic artifacts were found.

KNOTS Interlacing ropes to form loop or knob to secure ropes together or to an object. Classified as bends (joining two ropes together) or hitches (fastening rope to object or own standing part). Distinctions not absolute. Fisherman's Bend used to secure rope to anchor, spar or ring; bucket hitch for tying to buckets, bait pots, etc.

KNOTT, FREDERICK (1918–   ) Wrote *Dial M for Mur-*

der (1952 play, 1954 film). Hitchcock film featured Ray Milland and Grace Kelly. Solution to murder revolves around key to apartment left under carpet of fifth step of outside stairway. Knott also wrote *Wait Until Dark* (1966), another thriller play later turned into film (with Audrey Hepburn).

KNUTE ROCKNE—ALL AMERICAN   1940 film biography of Notre Dame's famous football coach portrayed by Pat O'Brien. Ronald Reagan portrays George Gipp, "the Gipper."

KODAK   Manufacturer of photographic equipment. Founded, 1908, by George Eastman. Photography revolutionized, 1885, by Eastman's introduction of roll film, made possible by use of paper in place of glass. Foremost consumer of silver; silver nitrate and chloride used in photographic processes.

KOJACK   Popular TV police series starring Telly Savalas as Lt. Theo Kojack of New York Police Department. Sucking lollipops was his trademark. Kevin Dobson portrayed Lt. Bobby Crocker, Kojack's plainclothes partner.

KOPECHNE, MARY JO (1940–1969)   Former staff worker for Robert F. Kennedy. Drowned July 18, 1969, when car she and Senator Edward Kennedy were riding in fell off bridge on Chappaquiddick Island, MA. Kennedy pleaded guilty to leaving scene of accident.

KORBUT, OLGA (1955–   )   Russian gymnast. Olympic gold medalist in floor exercise and balance beam at age 17 in 1972 Munich Olympics, noteworthy for her emotional performance. Older, and slightly injured, managed only a silver medal in balance beam in 1976 Montreal Olympics.

KOREAN WAR   North Korea's surprise attack on South Korea marked beginning of war, June 25, 1950. Unification of Korea had not been agreed upon since its occupation, at end of World War II, by the U.S.S.R. in North and U.S. in South. Armistice signed, July 27, 1953.

KOUFAX, SANDY (1935–   )   Left-handed (southpaw) pitcher for Brooklyn and Los Angeles Dodgers, 1955–1966. Named MVP in 1963 World Series; won twice in Dodgers' four-game sweep of New York Yankees. Retired due to arthritic elbow, 1966. Member Hall of Fame. Pitched four no-hitters, one perfect game. Won three Cy Young Awards (top pitcher) and 1963 MVP in National League.

KREMLIN   Fortress in Moscow. Originally built and designed by Italian architects in 1400. Much of it burned down when Napoleon invaded city in 1812. Rebuilt in classical style of 1800s. Lavish interior with red castellated walls. Guilded domes and pyramidal gate towers constitute exterior. Burial place of 47 czars. Contains historical jewels, paintings and crowns worn by czars. Closed by communists in early 1900s, made government center. Parts reopened to public as national museum, 1955.

KRUGER NATIONAL PARK   South Africa's most popular tourist attraction. Famous game reserve in Middleveld section of country's region called The Plateau. Wild animals roam the park freely.

KRYPTON   Fictional planet and birthplace of Superman. Scientist father Jor-El launched his and wife Lara's infant son Kal-El in rocket to Earth seconds before planet exploded. Green rocks from Krypton (kryptonite) can harm Superman on Earth.

KUBRICK, STANLEY (1928–   )   Photographer for *Look* magazine turned film writer-director-producer. Films include *Paths of Glory* (1958), *Lolita* (1962), and *Dr. Strangelove* (1963). The technically sophisticated *2001: A Space Odyssey* (1968) was the most courageous film of 1960s. It was followed by *A Clockwork Orange* (1971) which received X rating for explicit sex and violence.

KUHLMAN, KATHRYN (1907–1976)   American faith healer and author. Established organization devoted to missionary work, drug rehabilitation and education of blind children. Died of complications following open-heart surgery. *I Believe in Miracles* (1962) gives as evidence for her faith 21 factual and dramatic stories of people who have been cured of diseases ranging from lung cancer to creeping paralysis.

KUNSTLER, WILLIAM. See CHICAGO SEVEN

KUWAIT   Desert country with no rivers or lakes, bordering Iraq, Saudi Arabia and the Persian Gulf. Smaller than New Jersey yet it houses one-tenth of the world's petroleum reserve. More than one-half of its population are foreigners.

KYBER PASS, THE   Steep, rocky route between Afghanistan and Pakistan. Of great strategic and historic importance as gateway to India from the West. Central point in Britain's attempt to control Afghan border in the 19th century.

KYOTO   Located on Honshu Island, Japan. Capital from 794 to 1868. Name means "capital city" in Japanese. Tokyo replaced Kyoto as capital in 1868. Both cities are spelled with same letters.

KYSER, KAY (1897–   )   Bandleader of 1930s and '40s, hosted radio quiz show *Kollege of Musical Knowledge*. Appeared in a few films, including *That's Right, You're Wrong* (1939), *My Favorite Spy* (1942) and *Swing Fever* (1944).

L

LA DOLCE VITA Italian expression: Living life of luxury, softlife in Rome. Gained worldwide popularity when it became title of Frederico Fellini's 1960 movie with Marcello Mastroianni and Anita Ekberg.

LA PAZ Largest city in Bolivia. Acts as country's capital, although Sucre is official capital. La Paz is world's highest capital city, at 12,795 ft. (3,900 m.) above sea level. Location of El Alto Airport, world's highest commercial landing field.

LACRIMAL FLUID Or tears. Salty fluid that lubricates eyes and fights infection. People blink about 25 times a minute, spreading tears over eyes. Strong emotion can cause tear glands to release tears.

LACROSSE Outdoor field game between two teams of 10 players using netted sticks to throw ball into goal. From North American Indian game baggataway; when French missionaries saw game, thought sticks resembled bishop's crosier (in French, *la crosse*). Unofficial national Canadian sport since 1844. Also played in U.S., Australia, England and Ireland. Its ball, made of India rubber, is colored white or orange. Weighs 4½ to 5 oz., with circumference of 7¾ to 8 in.

LADBROKES OF LONDON National chain of "betting shops" in England. Largest bookmaking firm (legal) in world. Annual turnover nearly U.S. $1 billion. Accepts bets on anything from soccer and horse races to space race and sex of royal babies. England, where betting shops legalized 1960, called "gambler's paradise."

LADY CHATTERLY. See LAWRENCE, DAVID HERBERT

LADY GODIVA Legendary wife of 11-century English Earl of Mercia. Made her husband cancel some taxes on commoners by riding naked through streets of Coventry. In later addition to legend, only townsperson to look was tailor Peeping Tom, who was struck blind.

LAETRILE Controversial drug for treatment of cancer. Derived from pit of apricot. Argued that cancer cells contain enzymes that break down laetrile, causing the release of cyanide. Believed that cyanide then kills cancer cells. Illegal to transport laetrile over state borders.

LAGOS Nigeria's capital and largest city. Major slave market until 1851, when it became a British protectorate. Annexed by Britain in 1861, made capital in 1914. Primary outlet for country's animal hides and skins.

LAGUARDIA, FIORELLO (1882–1947) American lawyer and politician. Republican congressman and mayor of New York City, 1934–1945. Known for socially progressive policies. Nickname, "The Little Flower," derives from first name, Fiorello.

LAIKA First dog sent into space, November 1957, by Soviet Union, in preparation for manned space mission. Spent one week in orbit then died in space.

LAKE COMO Located in northern Italy at foot of Alps. Shores lined with summer homes, fertile vineyards. Como is chief town on lake and popular tourist spot.

LAKE ERIE Bordered by New York, Pennsylvania, Ohio and Michigan. Principal cities on the lake are Detroit, MI; Toledo, Sandusky and Cleveland, OH; Erie, PA and Buffalo, NY.

LAKE LUCERNE Located in central Switzerland. Scene of many adventures of Swiss patriot William Tell. Covers 44 sq. mi. (114 sq. km.). Surrounded by Swiss Alps.

LAKE MARACAIBO South America's largest lake. Located in northwestern Venezuela. Covers 6,300 sq. mi. (16,316 sq. km.). Oil wells are found in lake and on its shores.

LAKE ONTARIO Smallest and easternmost of five Great Lakes. Located between Ontario, Canada, and New York state.

Covers 7,540 sq. mi. (19,529 sq. km.). Can be navigated year round. Toronto is largest city on its shores.

LAKE SAM RAYBURN. See SAM RAYBURN RESERVOIR

LAKE SUPERIOR   One of five Great Lakes. World's largest freshwater lake; largest lake in North or South America. Covers 31,700 sq. mi. (82,103 sq. km.). Lies between Canada and U.S. About 200 rivers empty into it.

LAKE TITICACA   World's highest navigable lake, 12,507 ft. (3,812 m.) above sea level. Surrounded by Andes Mountains. Forms part of Bolivia and Peru border in South America. Called "the lake of the clouds."

LAKE VICTORIA   Large freshwater lake in Africa. Second largest freshwater lake in world, after Lake Superior, U.S. Headwater source of White Nile River. Borders on Kenya, Tanzania and Uganda. Equator crosses lake.

LAKE, VERONICA (1919–1973)   Starring actress known as "the peek-a-boo girl" because of her "peek-a-boo bang" (long blonde hair obscuring one eye). Films include *Sullivan's Travels* (1941), *This Gun For Hire* (1942), *Duffy's Tavern* (1945) and *The Blue Dahlia* (1946).

LAKER, SIR FREDERICK A. (1922–   )   Founder, Laker Airways Ltd., 1966. Established the Skytrain (1977), a cut-rate, no reservation air-shuttle between London and Los Angeles. He was knighted by Queen Elizabeth II, 1979. Since its start, his business has folded twice. "Fly me, I'm Freddie," line he used in TV commercials, also title of life story.

LAKES, WORLD'S LARGEST   Three largest:
1. Caspian Sea—Asia-Europe 143,240 sq. mi./371,000 sq. km.
2. Lake Superior—North America 31,700 sq. mi./ 82,103 sq. km.
3. Lake Victoria—Africa 26,720 sq. mi./ 69,200 sq. km.

LAMOTTA, JAKE (1921–   )   Middleweight boxing champion, 1949–1951. "Raging Bull" was his nickname and also title of his 1970 autobiography. Robert DeNiro won Oscar for his portrayal of LaMotta in 1980 film *Raging Bull*.

LAMOUR, DOROTHY (1914–   )   Actress nicknamed "The Sarong Girl" because of her many appearances in films in which a sarong was her costume, including *The Jungle Princess* (1936), *The Hurricane* (1937), *Her Jungle Love* (1938) and *Aloma of the South Seas* (1947). Teamed with Bob Hope and Bing Crosby in their many "Road" pictures.

LANDERS, ANN (1918–   ) AND VAN BUREN, ABIGAIL (1918–   ) Esther Pauline (Landers) and Pauline Esther (Van Buren) Friedman, identical twin sisters. "Eppie" started writing "Your Problems," 1955, and "Popo" started her "Dear Abby" column about a year later. Both offer advice.

LANDIS, KENESAW MOUNTAIN (1866–1944) U.S. district court judge who became first commissioner of baseball, 1920, in wake of 1919 Black Sox scandal, banned eight Chicago White Sox for their part in purported fix of World Series. Ruled baseball with iron hand until his death. Elected Hall of Fame, 1944.

LANDON, ALFRED MOSSMAN (1887–   ) American politician. Governor of Kansas, 1932–1938. During first term, balanced state budget, which brought him national attention. Republican presidential candidate, 1936. Defeated by Franklin Delano Roosevelt.

LANE, DICK (NIGHT TRAIN) (1928–   ) National Football League defensive back with L.A. Rams, Chicago Cardinals and Detroit Lions, 1952–1965. Green Bay coach Vince Lombardi once called him best cornerback he had ever seen. Nicknamed after blues song "Night Train" by saxophonist Jimmy Forrest.

LANE, MARK (1927–   ) New York City attorney, with comedian Dick Gregory (1932–   ), collaborated on *Code Name Zorro*, 1978 book about April 4, 1968, assassination of Rev. Dr. Martin Luther King, Jr., civil rights leader shot on outside balcony of Lorraine Hotel, Memphis, TN. Claimed convicted assassin James Earl Ray was part of larger conspiracy. Lane, who wrote *Rush to Judgment*, critical of Warren Commission report on Kennedy assassination, was formerly Democratic New York State assemblyman from New York, arrested in 1961 Freedom Ride. Was write-in candidate for vice-president in Gregory's 1968 presidential campaign, getting 200,000 votes.

LANGUAGES Most commonly spoken in North America: 1. *English:* Official language of the Bahamas, Barbados, Canada, Dominica, Grenada, Jamaica, St. Lucia, St. Vincent and the Gren-

adines, Trinidad and Tobago and the United States.
2. *Spanish*: Official language of Costa Rica, Cuba, the Dominican Republic, El Salvador, Guatemala, Honduras, Mexico, Nicaragua and Panama.
3. *French*: Official language of Canada, Haiti.
4. *Italian*: Fourth most often spoken language in North America.

LANOLIN   Wax made from a coating on sheep wool. Mixes well with water, easily absorbed into skin. Used in salves, ointments and cosmetics, as well as leather processing.

LAPIS LAZULI   Latin for "blue stone." Brilliant blue mineral used as gem or ornament. Egyptians and Romans used it in jewelry. Finest variety comes from Afghanistan.

LARGE YACHT RACING   Racing of majestic J-type boats (up to 135 ft. long) and 12-meter boats in America's Cup-style racing (up to 65 ft. long); most expensive competitive sport. Ownership confined to multimillionaires or syndicates. Word *yacht* from Dutch, meaning "to hunt" or "to chase."

LARSEN, DON (1929–   )   Pitched perfect game in 1956 World Series leading New York Yankees to win over Brooklyn Dodgers, 2–0. Struck out pinch hitter Dale Mitchell to end game. Catcher Yogi Berra jumped into pitcher's arms. Sal "The Barber" Maglie was losing pitcher. Yankees won series.

LARYNX   Section of air passage of the throat. Box-shaped; upper portion contains vocal cords, thus commonly known as voice box. Shape and stretch of vocal cords determines pitch.

LAS VEGAS   Nevada's largest city. Famous for night clubs and casinos. Attracts 10 million visitors annually. Founded in 1905. Gambling legalized in 1931. Also famed for large number of wedding chapels—more per capita than any other U.S. state.

LASERS   Stands for "light amplification by stimulated emission of radiation." Device which provides narrow, strong, uniform light beam. Developed 1950s–1960s, used today in industry, communications, medicine and navigation.

LASSIE   Collie. First appeared in *Lassie Come Home*, a novel by Eric Knight. In the 1943 movie, Pal starred. Pal, Jr., starred in the television series. Became first animal elected to Animal Hall of Fame,

1969. All Lassies have been male. Had own TV series from 1954–1971, his masters included Jeff Miller (Tommy Rettig), Timmy Martin (John Provost) and Forest Ranger Corey (Robert Bary).

LAST PICTURE SHOW, THE   1971 film directed by Peter Bogdanovich. Jeff Bridges, Ellen Burstyn and Cybill Shepard star in this study of life in a small Texas town during the 1950s. Ben Johnson and Cloris Leachman won Best Supporting Oscars.

LAST SUPPER, THE   Christ's last meal before his arrest. Announced to the 12 disciples that one would betray him. At the supper were Jesus, the fishermen Andrew, Peter, James and John, Matthew (tax collector), Simon (zealot), Judas of Iscariot (betrayed Jesus to the authorities), Bartholemew, Philip, James the Less, Jude and Thomas.

LAST TANGO IN PARIS   Critically acclaimed 1972 feature directed by Bernardo Bertolucci. Marlon Brando plays a widower in Paris who has an affair with a young woman (Maria Schneider). Banned in Alabama and Louisiana as obscene. Film received an X rating in February 1973.

LAUGH-IN. See ROWAN AND MARTIN'S LAUGH-IN

LAWFORD, PETER (1923–   )   Actor. Son of Sir Sidney and Lady Lawford. Married Patricia Kennedy, John F. Kennedy's sister, 1955. Divorced, 1966. Appeared in *The Thin Man* TV series and film *The Longest Day* (1962).

LAWRENCE OF ARABIA. see LAWRENCE, THOMAS EDWARD

LAWRENCE, DAVID HERBERT (D. H.) (1885–1930)   English writer. Regarded sex, primitive subconscious and nature as cures for man's difficulties in industrial society. His novels include *Sons and Lovers* (1913), story centering on attachment between Paul Morel and his mother, an attachment that prevents his loving another woman. First part of book autobiographical. Also wrote *Women in Love* (1921), sequel to *The Rainbow* (1915). Describes later life of Ursula Brangwen and her sculptor sister Gudrun, and their relationships with the men in their lives. Characters and relationships probably based on Lawrence and his wife and their friends John

Middleton Murry and his wife Katherine Mansfield. *Lady Chatterly's Lover* (1928) concerns Lady Constance Chatterly, her paralyzed husband, and Mellors the gamekeeper, the unspoiled man she runs off with. Banned as obscene in U.S. until 1959 and England until 1960.

LAWRENCE, STEVE (1935–) Nightclub and television singer appearing frequently with his wife, Eydie Gorme. Both starred in their own TV variety shows in 1958.

LAWRENCE, THOMAS EDWARD (T. E.) (1888– 1935) English archeologist, soldier and author known as Lawrence of Arabia. Aided Arabs in revolt against Turks during World War I. His autobiography, *Seven Pillars of Wisdom* (1926) later abridged into *The Revolt in the Desert* (1927).

LBJ RANCH Cattle ranch near Stonewall, TX, birthplace of President Lyndon B. Johnson. Became informal White House, where Johnson entertained friends and political associates. Sections of ranch, family cemetery, L. B. J.'s birthplace and boyhood home are all part of LBJ National Historic Site.

LE CARRE, JOHN (DAVID JOHN MOORE CROMWELL) (1931–) English author of espionage fiction. Was World War II British intelligence and Foreign Service officer assigned to Bonn, setting of fifth novel, *A Small Town in Germany* (1968). Heroes Alan Turner, Alec Leamas of *The Spy Who Came in from the Cold* (1963, his breakthrough book) and, frequently, George Smiley, embody Le Carre's unglamorous spy antihero. Smiley, plump, myopic, middle-aged, thoroughly anonymous man with a precise mind, appears as minor character in some novels, as main character in *Call for the Dead* (1960), *A Murder of Quality* (1962), *Tinker, Tailor, Soldier Spy* (1974). Latter became PBS TV series with Alec Guinness as Smiley.

LE FIGARO. See PARIS NEWSPAPERS

LE MANS 24-HOUR TEST OF ENDURANCE Sports car race held annually since 1923 on Le Mans circuit in Sarthe district of France. Original course 10.726 mi., now 8.34 mi. because of growth of nearby town.

LEAD Chemical element. Pure lead, soft. Often mixed with other metals to increase strength, called lead alloys. Used in production of lead-acid storage batteries, used in automobiles and other vehicles. Chemical symbol, Pb, from Latin word *plumbum* meaning "lead."

LEAD POISONING Called "Plumbism," from the Latin word for lead. Also called "Painter's Colic," as lead was a common ingredient in paint and could cause a serious illness. Children are especially vulnerable. Can cause stomach pain, weakness, paralysis, convulsions and death.

LEADER OF THE PACK Hit 1964 song by girl singing-group The Shangri-las. In song, Betty meets her love, the leader of the pack, at the candy store. Song inspired answer record, "Leader of the Laundromat" from The Detergents.

LEADVILLE, COLORADO Called "cloud city" because it is U.S.'s highest incorporated city. Lies 10,200 ft. (3,060 m.) above sea level. Named for its lead ore. World's largest molybdenum mine is nearby.

LEAGUE Unit of length. Land league: 3 statute mi. (4.83 km.). Marine league: 3 nautical mi. (5.56 km. or 3,041 fathoms). Also in poetical and rhetorical expressions of distance; e.g. Byron, 1818, "I never yet saw the picture...which came a league within my conception."

LEANING TOWER OF PISA Built in Pisa, Italy, 1173–1372. Originally the campanile, or bell tower, in the set of three buildings that included a cathedral and baptistry. Ground beneath the tower causing it to lean. It is now about 17 ft. (5.2 m.) out of line. Measurements taken since 1911 show its lean increasing by 1.25 mm. per year. Predicted to fall over between years 2010 and 2020. Considered one of the seven wonders of the modern world. Winding staircase of 296 steps leads to top.

LEAP YEAR Has 366 days, a day more than a standard year. Every year that can be divided evenly by four, such as 1976, is a leap year. Exceptions, century years: only those that can be divided by 400 are leap years. For example, 2000 will be a leap year, 1900 was not. On non-leap years, July 2 is the midpoint of the year.

LEAR, EDWARD (1812–1888) London landscape painter, also wrote and illustrated nonsense verse to amuse his friends' children, publishing four books of these rhymes and becoming known as "Poet Laureate of the Limerick." In "The Owl and the Pussycat," (1871), they elope by sailing off in a pea green boat, looking for place to be married.

LEARY, TIMOTHY FRANCIS (1920–   ) Clinical psychologist. Lecturer, Harvard University. Discovered and experimented with LSD. Leader of the Psychedelic Movement, late 1960s. Known to young drug culture as Uncle Tim. Famous for having said, "Turn on to the Scene. Tune into What's Happening. Drop Out." In 1963, Harvard refused to renew his contract. Arrested, 1970, drug-related charges. Imprisoned, 10-year sentence. Escaped to Algeria, six months later.

LEAVE IT TO BEAVER Popular TV comedy series 1957–1963. Jerry Mathers starred as Theodore "Beaver" Cleaver, and the show revolved around his world and Wally, his brother (Tony Dow), Ward, his father (Hugh Beaumont), June, his mother (Barbara Billingsley), Miss Landers, his teacher (Sue Randall) and Gus, the fire chief (Burt Mustin). Wally's friend Eddie Haskell (Ken Osmond) was a troublemaker (although in real life Osmond became a policeman).

LEBANON Independent nation since 1943. Borders with Syria, Israel and the Mediterranean Sea. Beirut, the capital, often referred to as "gateway between Asia and Europe." Trade is major source of income. Coldest month averages 40°F (5°C). Unlike all other Arab countries, Lebanon has no desert.

LEIF ERICKSON PARK Recreational area in Duluth, MN. Contains statue of Norwegian explorer Leif Erickson and a half-size model of the boat in which he voyaged to America (A.D. 997). Boasts impressive rose garden.

LEIGH, VIVIEN (1913–1967) British actress in American films; won Oscars as best actress in *Gone With the Wind* (1939) and *A Streetcar Named Desire* (1951). Other films include *Dark Journey* (1937), *A Yank at Oxford* (1938) and *Lady Hamilton* (1941).

LEMA, ANTHONY (CHAMPAGNE TONY) (1934–1966) American golfer who served champagne to the press after winning 1964 British Open at St. Andrews, Scotland. Tradition thereafter, every time he won—thus, nickname. He and his wife Betty died in the crash of his private plane en route from Akron, OH, to Lansing, IL, following 1966 PGA championship tournament.

LEMAY, GENERAL CURTIS E. (1906–   ) Ran on American Independent Party ticket with George Wallace, 1968. Received roughly 10 million popular votes and 46 electoral votes, carrying five states.

LEMMON, JACK (1925–   ) Actor proficient in comedic

and dramatic roles. Starred in such films as *Some Like It Hot* (1959)—appearing in drag with co-star Tony Curtis—and *The Days of Wine and Roses* (1962), portraying an alcoholic couple with Lee Remick. Won Oscars for *Mr. Roberts* (1955), as Ensign Pulver, and *Save the Tiger* (1973).

LENIN, VLADIMIR ILYICH (1870–1924)   Russian founder of Bolshevism. Exiled, returned to Russia immediately after revolution, gaining control of revolutionary movement and overthrowing provisional government to become first U.S.S.R. premier (1918–1924). While in Swiss exile, founded revolutionary journal *Iskra* (*Spark*, 1900), and later, St. Petersburg underground paper *Pravda* (1912), which became official Communist Party newspaper. (see PRAVDA)

LENINGRAD   Russia's second largest city, after Moscow. Founded in 1703 by Czar Peter I (The Great) as St. Petersburg. In 1914 at the start of World War I, Russians changed name with German ending "burg" to Petrograd meaning "Peter's City" in Russian. Upon Lenin's death in 1924, city was renamed Leningrad.

LENNON, JOHN (1940–80)   Formed The Beatles with Paul McCartney and George Harrison in 1960. At the height of their popularity, in 1966 said, "We're more popular than Jesus," and sparked controversy. Remained popular singer/songwriter after Beatles disbanded, with hits including "Imagine" (1971) and "(Just Like) Starting Over" (1980). (see BEATLES, THE)

LENS (EYE)   Or crystalline lens. Indirectly controlled by ciliary muscle. Enables accommodation to objects at various distances. Focuses light rays onto retina. Continues growth throughout life.

LEONOV, ALEKSEI (1934–   )   Soviet cosmonaut. First man to float in space. Spacecraft: *Voskhod Z*, launched March 18, 1965. Also a painter and caricaturist; called the "artist-cosmonaut."

LEOPARD, BLACK   Or panther. One of largest members of cat family. Entire body is spotted; spots on back and sides form circular pattern called rosettes. Generally nocturnal. Is a mutant.

LEPIDOPTERIST   One who collects or studies *Lepidoptera*, order of insects comprised of butterflies and moths; i.e., those insects with four membrous wings covered with scales. Varieties of colorful butterflies most revered collecters' items. John Fowles novel (later film) *The Collector* about mad lepidopterist. (See FOWLES, JOHN).

LEPROSY   Also Hansen's disease. Chronic infection of skin and superficial nerves. Results in skin lesions, skin thickening and progressive loss of sensation in hands, feet and elsewhere. Especially in tropical areas. Incidence twice as high in men. Common in medieval Europe. Leper is one who is infected.

LESBOS   Island located off northwest coast of Turkey in Aegean Sea. Along with Lemmos and Hagios, it forms Lesbos department, Aegean Island division, Greece. Inhabitants called Lesbosians. Known for its 7th-century B.C. lyric poets, such as Alcaeus and Sappho.

LET'S MAKE A DEAL   Popular TV game show 1963–1976. Studio audience dressed in strange costumes in order to attract attention of host Monty Hall and be selected as contestants.

LEUKEMIA   Medical term for proliferation of abnormal blood-forming cells. Symptoms: weakness, anemia, hemorrhages and enlarged spleen, liver or lymph nodes. 20% of patients survive 5 or more years after the appearance of symptoms; only 6% live 10 or more years.

LEVIN, IRA (1929–   )   American novelist and playwright. Plays include *No Time for Sergeants* (1956) and *Deathtrap* (1978). Novels include *Rosemary's Baby* (1967), *The Stepford Wives* (1972) and *The Boys from Brazil* (1976), in which a secret corps of ex-Nazis living in Brazil hopes to establish a Fourth Reich with 94 blue-eyed clones of Third Reich Führer Adolf Hitler.

LEWIS, CHIVE STAPLES (C.S.) (1898–1963)   Author. Created fantasy world Narnia in *The Lion, the Witch and the Wardrobe* (1940) and six subsequent books. Intended as children's Christian allegories, won widespread adult readership much as Tolkien's Hobbit trilogy.

LEWIS, JERRY (1926–   )   Wild comedian turned actor-director. Teamed with singer Dean Martin from 1946—appeared on first Ed Sullivan show for $200. Went on to make films *My Friend Irma* (1949), and *Jumping Jacks* (1952). In 1955 he hosted the Academy Awards. Went solo in 1958 and wrote and directed many starring vehicles: *The Bellboy* (1960), *The Nutty Professor* (1963) and *Cracking Up*.

LEWIS, SINCLAIR (1885–1951)   American novelist. Best-known works portrayed American small-town provincialism: *Main Street* (1920), *Arrowsmith* (1925), *Elmer Gantry* (1927) and *Dodsworth*

(1929). Main character of *Babbit* (1927), well-to-do realtor in town of Zenith, typifies American go-getter. In 1930, Lewis became first American to win Nobel Prize in Literature.

LHASA, TIBET   Capital of Tibet called the "roof of the world" because of its extraordinarily high mountains and plateaus. Town with highest elevation in world.

LI'L ABNER. See CAPP, AL

LIBERACE (1919–)   Flamboyant pianist who starred in his own TV series in 1952. Outlandish wardrobe, curly hair and ornate candelabra atop his Steinway were trademarks. Loved by fans, ridiculed by critics, Liberace countered them with line, "I cried all the way to the bank." His brother George, a violinist, led the orchestra.

LIBERIA   West African nation. Became a republic, 1847. Founded by American Colonization Society as place to send freed American slaves. Capital, Monrovia, named after James Monroe, fifth U.S. president.

LIBERTY BELL   Cast in England, 1752. Named by American abolitionists, 1839. Inscription reads: "Proclaim Liberty throughout all the land and unto all the inhabitants thereof." Bought by Pennsylvania for $300. Cracked on first being rung; recast 1753. Rung every anniversary of adoption of Declaration of Independence until 1835, when it cracked at funeral of Supreme Court Chief Justice John Marshall. Housed in Independence Hall, Philadelphia, PA.

LIBRA   Latin for "scales." Source of abbreviation lb. for pound weight and £ for British monetary pound.

LIBRARY OF CONGRESS   Established 1800 by Thomas Jefferson. This Washington, DC, library is world's largest. Created to serve Congress, now also serves as public reference library. Receives copies of all American copyrighted works, now includes more than 70 million items. Largest collection of incunabula (books printed before 1501). Bookshelves measure approximately 327 mi.

LIBROCUBICULARIST   Someone who reads in bed. From Latin *libro* meaning "book" and *cubiculum* meaning "bedroom or cubicle." Suffix *-ist* means "one who does."

LIDDY, G. GORDON BATTLE (1930–)   Leader of Watergate burglars. Offered to allow himself to be executed for failure of the bugging of Democratic national headquarters. As the least cooperative of the Watergate defendants, served the longest term of 52 months.

LIDO, THE Famous cosmopolitan resort island 15 minutes from Venice across Venetian Lagoon. Faces Adriatic Sea. Main setting for Thomas Mann's novella, *Death in Venice.*

LIE, TRYGVE HALVDAN (1896–1968) First secretary-general of UN, 1946–1952. Resigned under pressure from Soviet Union because of his support of UN's intervention in Korean War. Norweigian born.

LIFE MAGAZINE General interest photographic essay magazine. Founded by *Time* founder Henry R. Luce, November 23, 1936, 10-cent cover price. Last weekly issue, December 29, 1972, "Goodbye" in lower right-hand corner. Returned as two dollar monthly, 1978. Actress Elizabeth Taylor appeared on record 11 *Life* covers, first time July 14, 1947 (runner-up is actress Marilyn Monroe with 9). From 1936 to 1972, 290 *Life* covers—about one in every six—featured movie stars. Also interested in politics and controversy, *Life* paid Abraham Zapruder approximately $50,000 in 1963 for his 8-mm. film of John F. Kennedy assassination in Dallas. Never released in its full form by *Life* (single frames were printed). Returned it to Zapruder family in 1975. Only two authorized copies (made for Secret Service and FBI) now in National Archives, Washington.

LIFEBOAT 1944 film directed by Alfred Hitchcock about eight survivors in a lifeboat at sea after a Nazi U-Boat destroys their freighter. Hitchcock makes his cameo appearance in a newspaper ad.

LIFESAVERS Top-selling hard roll candy in U.S. Shaped like shipboard life preserver. Peppermint first of several flavors made by Beech-Nut, also makers of chewing gum, Breath Savers and formerly of baby foods. Since 1968 merger, company owned by Squibb, manufacturer of Bubble Yum, the top-selling bubble gum. Beech-Nut heir Edward Noble started American Broadcasting Company (ABC).

LIFFEY RIVER. See DUBLIN

LIGER The offspring of a lion and tiger. Usually a man-induced mating, while animals are in captivity. Also called tiglon or tigon.

LIGHT-YEAR Astronomy, unit of measurement. Distance light travels in one year at speed of 186,282 mi. (299,792 km.) per second. One light year is equal to 5.88 trillion mi. (9.46 trillion km.).

LIGHTNING Electrical spark in sky whose bolt can be 100 mi. long, 15 million volts and travel 100 million ft. per second. Empire State Building hit by lightning 50 or more times a year. People who are hit often become deaf. Causes more deaths in U.S. than hurricanes or tornadoes. Safest to be in automobile or steel-framed building equipped with lightning rods.

LILIES OF THE FIELD 1963 film about ex-G.I. who helps group of German refugee nuns build chapel in Arizona desert and learn to speak English. Sidney Poitier won Oscar for Best Actor.

LIME-JUICER Nickname for English sailor or ship. Stems from 1854 regulation that all passengers on long ocean voyages take lime juice every 10 days to prevent scurvy, disease caused by Vitamin C deficiency.

LIMELITERS, THE Folk-singing trio formed in 1959 by Glenn Yarborough, Louis Gottlieb and Alex Hassilev. Made many TV appearances singing their hits "The Hammer Song," "Molly Malone" and "Gari, Gari."

LIMERICK Humorous five-line poem with three long (first, second and fifth) and two short (third and fourth) lines. Long lines rhyme with each other, as do short lines. Rhyming words are sometimes misspelled to heighten humor.

LINCOLN Nebraska's second-largest city and capital since 1867. Originally called Lancaster, renamed after President Lincoln. Home to two campuses of University of Nebraska—Nebraska-Wesleyan University and Union College.

LINCOLN PARK ZOO Located in Chicago's sprawling Lincoln Park. Established in 1874, same year as the Philadelphia zoo. Ranks in age behind Central Park Zoo in New York City (1864) and Buffalo, NY, Zoo (1870).

LINCOLN, ABRAHAM (1809–1865) Sixteenth U.S. president (1861–1865). Born in log cabin in Illinois, the first president from state outside the original 13. A caricature done just after Civil War, playing on his unsophisticated background, featured him, as the "Illinois Railsplitter"—along with Andrew Johnson, the "Tennessee Tailor"—at work trying to repair the Union. At 6'4" Lincoln was tallest president. He is also remembered as having a wart on his face. Less than one week after end of Civil War, on April 14, 1865, the President was assassinated at Ford's Theatre in Washington, DC, while watching a production of Tom Taylor's play *Our American Cousin*. The assassin, celebrity-actor John Wilkes Booth, shot Lincoln in back of head. Booth then leaped out of Lincoln's box onto stage, tripped and broke his leg, and exited saying *"sic semper tyrannis"*, Latin meaning "thus ever to tyrants." Booth escaped to Virginia, but died during a gun battle with federal troops, April 25. His three co-conspirators were quickly tried and hanged for their part in the crime. The nation mourned as Lincoln's body was transported from DC to Springfield, IL. It is alleged that his ghost still roams the White House. His assassination occurred on Good Friday, the day Christ died on the cross.

LINCOLN, ELMO. See TARZAN

LINDBERGH, CHARLES AUGUSTUS (1902–1974)   American aviator. Piloted first nonstop transatlantic flight. Aircraft, *The Spirit of St. Louis*. Originated, Roosevelt Field, Long Island. Landed, 33½ hours later, Le Bourget, Paris, May 21, 1927. Flying solo, earned nickname "The Lone Eagle." Became an instant celebrity. Returned to U.S. aboard U.S. Navy cruiser sent by President Coolidge. In 1929, married Anne Morrow, daughter of U.S. ambassador to Mexico. Three years later, their 20-month-old son, Charles Lindbergh, Jr., was kidnapped and murdered. In April 1941, joined America First Committee, which included prominent business leaders opposed to American involvement in World War II. Lindbergh attracted thousands to the movement, attacked by President F. D. Roosevelt as a defeatist. This led to Lindbergh's resignation from the air force. Throughout 1940s Americans danced to the lindy hop (or jitterbug) named for the famed aviator.

LINDBERGH, CHARLES JR. (1930–1932)   First of six children of famous aviator Charles Lindbergh. Kidnapped, March 1, 1932, age 20 months. Held for ransom, then murdered. His death considered the "crime of the century." Bruno Richard Hauptmann convicted and executed, 1936. In 1932, Congress passed the Lindbergh Act making kidnapping a federal offense.

LINDSAY, JOHN (1921–   )   Mayor of New York, 1965. Ran on Republican and Liberal tickets. Despite municipal strikes, New York City remained peaceful compared to the race riots that erupted in other urban areas. Abraham Beame, a Democrat, won the mayoral election in 1973.

LINKLETTER, ART (1912–   ) Canadian-American broadcaster. Hosted several radio and TV shows, including *House Party* and *People Are Funny*, in 1950s and '60s. Author of several books including *Kids Say the Darndest Things* (1957), collection of best lines emerging from his *House Party* interviews with more than 15,000 children.

LIPPIZANER STALLIONS White horses, originally bred in Spain from crossing of Arabian and Berber stallions and Andulusian mares. Imperial Court of Vienna established stud farm in Lippiza, village near Trieste, 1580. Renowned for beauty and grace, "dancing white horses" of Vienna's Spanish Riding School have performed all over Europe and North America. School preserves classical art of riding in purest form.

LIQUID MEASURE U.S. and British units of liquid measure are not identical. U.S. gallon is about four-fifths of a British imperial gallon. However, U.S. fluid ounce is one-sixteenth of a U.S. pint, making it larger than the British fluid ounce, which is one-twentieth of imperial pint. One pint equals four noggins, which equal four gills.

LIQUID MEASURE VOLUME EQUIVALENTS

3 teaspoons =	1 tablespoon
2 tablespoons =	1 fluid ounce
1 cup =	8 ounces, or 1/2 pint
2 cups =	16 ounces, 1 pint or 1 pound
2 pints =	1 quart or 2 pounds
4 quarts =	1 gallon or 8 pounds
8 quarts =	1 peck
4 pecks =	1 bushel

LISBON Portugal's largest and capital city. One-fifth of Portugal's population lives in area. Lies on Tagus River. Colonized in ancient times by Greeks, Carthaginians and Romans. Moors conquered city in 700s. Retaken by Christian Portugese in 1147. Though Lisbon is located on European mainland, and Glasgow and Dublin are on the British Isles off European mainland, Lisbon is farther west than these other cities.

LISTON, SONNY (1932–1971) Won world heavyweight

boxing championship by knocking out Floyd Patterson in first round, September 1962. KO'd Patterson second time, July 1963, also in first round. Lost title to Cassius Clay (Muhammad Ali) in seventh round, February 1964. In rematch, Clay's phantom punch floored Liston in round one, May 1965. "The Big Bear," 38, who learned how to box while in jail, died in his Las Vegas home, January 5, 1971, of a suspected drug overdose.

LITMUS PAPER Contains dye made from lichens, type of plant; detects acid or base. Blue litmus paper will turn red in acid and be unchanged in base; red litmus paper stays red in acid and turns blue in base.

LITTLE AMERICA Established by Commander Richard E. Byrd's expedition in Antarctica's Ross Ice Shelf, 1928. Series of bases set up there. Byrd kept airplanes there and in 1929 became first person along with Floyd Bennett to fly over North Pole. World War II forced expedition to leave bases.

LITTLE ANTHONY AND THE IMPERIALS Singing group of the 1950s and '60s formed by Anthony Gourdine. Hits include "Tears on My Pillow" (1958), "Shimmy, Shimmy Ko-Ko Bop" (1960) and "Goin' Out of My Head" (1964).

LITTLE BLACK SAMBO. See BANNERMAN, HELEN BRODIE COWAN

LITTLE BOYS In nursery rhyme, made of "snakes [some versions say snips] and snails and puppy-dogs' tails." Little girls made of "sugar and spice and everything nice."

LITTLE BOY BLUE Character in nursery rhyme: "Little boy blue, come blow your horn, / The sheep's in the meadow, the cow's in the corn; / But where is the boy who looks after the sheep? / He's under the haycock, fast asleep. / Will you wake him? No, not I, / For if I do, he'll be sure to cry."

LITTLE BROWN JUG. See HARNESS RACING

LITTLE DIPPER, THE Northern Hemisphere group of stars. Arrangement suggests a ladle, hence the name. Forms part of constellation Ursa Minor (Little Bear). Contains Polaris, the North Star, used by navigators to find due north.

LITTLE EVA Eva Boyd at 17 was babysitting for songwriters Carole King and Gerry Goffin, who asked her to record a song they just wrote, "The Loco-Motion" (1962). The resulting record became a number one hit, and Little Eva followed it with others, including "Keep Your Hands Off My Baby" and "Let's Turkey Trot."

LITTLE JOHNNY GREEN   In nursery rhyme, "Ding, dong, bell, / Pussy's in the well. / Who put her in? / Little Johnny Green." Anonymous poem sometimes known as "Plato's Song."

LITTLE MISS MUFFET   Ate curds and whey when sitting on tuffet. Curds, coagulated milk used to make cheese; whey, liquid left after cheese is made. In Mother Goose rhyme, spider sat down beside her and frightened her away.

LITTLE ORPHAN ANNIE   Comic strip created by Harold Gray. Debuted August 5, 1924, in New York *News*. Annie and all other characters drawn with blank eyes. First fended for herself and dog Sandy, then adopted by millionaire "Daddy" Warbucks. Basis for radio serial, two movies, and Broadway musical. Gray died in 1968, but strip continues, trying to infuse updated themes.

LITTLE ROCK   Capital and largest city of Arkansas. Called "La Petite Roche" (The Little Rock) by French explorer Bernard de la Harpe, who recommended to the French government that it be made a trading post. Though his idea wasn't passed, when the Arkansas Territory was established the town thrived.

LIVER   One of most important organs in the body, and largest gland. The liver of an adult weights three or four lbs. It stores sugar, some vitamins, minerals and protein, and is vital for digestion of fats.

LIVERPOOL   Industrial city, major port in northwest England. Approximately 180 mi. (288 km.) from London. Residents called Liverpudlians. Pier Head is center of city life.

LIVINGSTONE, DR. DAVID (1813–1873)   Scottish physician, missionary and explorer. Crossed African continent twice, 1853–1856. Found waterfall of Mosioatunya on Zambezi River. Renamed it Victoria Falls, after Queen Victoria of England. In 1869 Henry Morton Stanley (1841–1904), newspaper reporter for the New York *Herald*, was sent to find him, as he had not been heard from in several years. After meeting at Ujiji on Lake Tanganyika, November 10, 1871, Stanley inquired, "Dr. Livingstone, I presume?" Together they attempted to find source of Nile.

LLAMA   Domesticated guanaco, relative of camel, native to

South American Andes Mountains. Raised for fur, meat and as pack animals. When annoyed, will spit in face of offender.

LLOYD'S LUTINE BELL   Salvaged from 1857 shipwreck. Tolls to inform whether a ship is overdue or lost. One toll means good news, two tolls, bad.

LLOYD'S REGISTER OF SHIPPING. see LLOYD'S OF LONDON

LLOYD'S OF LONDON   Association of underwriters. Handles all traditional forms of insurance, except life insurance. Originally handled only shipping insurance. Began in coffee house of Edward Lloyd, late 17th century. Publishes annual register listing all ships, English and foreign, and Lloyd's Register of Yachts, covering all methods of yacht construction.

LOBSTERS   Best to steam or boil in salt water, which boils hotter than fresh water, allowing crustacean to cook quicker and retain more protein. To cook, cover live lobsters with cold sea or salt water, bring to boil and cook for five minutes; reduce heat, and simmer for 15 minutes, or less if lobsters have recently shed and have softer shell.

LOCH NESS MONSTER   Nicknamed Nessie. Large animal believed to live in Lake Loch Ness, Scotland. Sonar investigations verify presence of large moving bodies in the lake. Described as having long neck, flippers and two humps.

LOFTLEIDER AIRLINES   Founded in Reykjavik, 1947. Name of Iceland's national airline until 1979. Name means "sky trails." Now called Icelandair. Flies to 11 countries. U.S. offices located in New York, Chicago and Washington, D.C.

LOLITA   1963 film directed by Stanley Kubrick from Vladimir Nabokov novel. Teenaged Lolita (portrayed by Sue Lyon) with heart-shaped sunglasses becomes involved with middle-aged college professor (James Mason). Shelly Winters co-stars as her mother and Peter Sellers as another love.

LOMBARD, CAROLE (1908–1942)   Actress and comedienne, starred in many hit films of the late 1930s, including *Twentieth Century* (1934), *My Man Godfrey* (1936), and *Nothing Sacred* (1937). Married Clark Gable in 1939. Last film, *To Be or Not to Be* (1942), released after her death in a plane crash in mountains near Las Vegas.

LOMBARDI, VINCENT THOMAS (VINCE) (1913–1970) Football player and later Hall of Fame coach for Green Bay Packers, 1959-1967. Member of Fordham University's "Seven Blocks of Granite" line. Led Packers to five National Football League titles (1961-1962, 1965-1967) and wins in first two Super Bowls. Retired 1968, but came back to coach Washington Redskins, 1969. Quote "Winning isn't everything, it's the only thing" attributed to him in 1960s, but actually said earlier by actor John Wayne in 1953 film *Trouble Along the Way.*

LOMBARDO, GUY (1902–1980) With his Royal Canadians, kept audiences dancing for more than 50 years with what was known as "the sweetest music this side of heaven." The Canadian bandleader's hits include "Boo Hoo" and "Enjoy Yourself," as well as his perennially popular theme song, "Auld Lang Syne."

LONDON *Airports:* Heathrow handles approximately 24 million passengers each year, while Gatwick handles approximately 5 million.
Fog: Known for its pea-soupers. At the turn of the century, the city had heavy fog due to air pollution. Air was cleaned before World War II.
Hotels: Posh hotels include Claridges (Brook Street), Dorchester (Park Lane), Ritz (Piccadilly), Savoy (Strand), and Inn on the Park (Park Lane).

LONDON BRIDGE Built 1823–1831 in London, England. Dismantled in 1967 because it was settling into River Thames. Reconstructed in Lake Havasu City, Arizona.

LONDON, JOHN GRIFFIN (JACK) (1876–1916) American novelist, short-story writer and essayist. Highest paid writer of his time. Best remembered for novels *The Call of the Wild* (1903), story of Buck, dog who goes from U.S. to Klondike as a sled dog, becomes leader of a wolf pack, and *The Sea-Wolf* (1904), novel about Wolf Larsen, ruthless captain of tramp steamer *Ghost*, rival of passenger Humphrey Van Weyden for poet Maude Brewster's affections.

LONE RANGER, THE Western hero on radio since 1933, and on TV from 1949 through 1957. Theme song: "The William Tell Overture." A silver bullet symbolized justice and law. Would start each chase, "Hi-ho, Silver." Indian Tonto called him "Kemo

Sabe," which means "faithful friend." Portrayed on TV and movies by Clayton Moore.

LONG GOODBYE, THE   1973 film directed by Robert Altman. Elliott Gould starred as detective Phillip Marlow trying to solve two murders. Based on the novel by Raymond Chandler.

LONG ISLAND   Located in southeastern New York. Includes New York City boroughs Queens and Brooklyn. State's largest island. Discovered by Henry Hudson in 1609. Location of popular summer resort areas.

LONG, HUEY PIERCE (1893–1935)   Governor and U.S. senator from Louisiana. Also known as the Kingfisher. Shot to death in the state capital by Dr. Karl Austin Leiss, 1935.

LONGCHAMPS   Hippodrome de Longchamps, in Bois de Boulogne, Paris, is racetrack operated by the *Societe d'Encouragement pour l'Amelioration des Races de Chevaux en France* (Society for the Encouragement and Betterment of Horse Racing in France). Site of one of world's foremost races, *L'Arc de Triomphe*, run on turf (grass).

LONGEVITY   Man is the longest living mammal. The most reliable longevity record is 113 years 124 days for Pierre Joubert (1701–1814), a Canadian shoemaker, although unauthenticated accounts of people living much longer have been reported. The highest life expectancy average is 71.85 years for males and 76.54 years for females in Sweden. Whales, elephants, hippoes and horses are the only other mammals that consistently live past 50.

LONGFELLOW, HENRY WADSWORTH (1807–1882)   American poet. Famous for *The Wreck of the Hesperus*, *The Village Blacksmith*, and *Excelsior* (1842), *Evangeline* (1847), *The Courtship of Miles Standish* (1858), *Paul Revere's Ride* (1860) and *The Song of Hiawatha* (1855). The latter tells a North American Indian legend about a mythical warrior sent to clear forests and fishing grounds and to teach peace. Lives "on the shores of Gitchee Gumee, by the shining Big-Sea-Water." Hiawatha's mother was Nokomis and his wife was Minnehaha.

LONGITUDE   Imaginary lines drawn on the earth from pole to pole. Unlike latitude lines, longitude lines are all of equal length. There are 360 degrees, corresponding to the 360 degrees of a circle. A degree of longitude is an angular measurement whose length varies from about 51 nautical mi. at the equator to zero mi. at the poles.

LOOMIS, BERNARDOTTE (BERT)   Alleged inventor of basketball dribbling, although not acknowledged by National Basketball Hall of Fame. Dr. James Naismith's original rules (1891) did not include dribbling. Loomis, captain of New Britain, CT YMCA team, is supposed to have introduced it in 1896 in a game attended by Naismith, who declared it legal. Nominated but never elected to Hall of Fame, Loomis died in 1959.

LOOP, THE   Chicago's central business district. Includes area five blocks wide, seven blocks long. Called the Loop because it's surrounded by a loop of elevated train tracks.

LORD HAW HAW (1906–1946)   American, born William Joyce. Propagated Nazi propaganda in English over German radio, World War II. After the war, captured in Germany and convicted of treason. Sentenced to death by hanging, by the British.

LOS ANGELES   Ranks third in population in U.S., behind New York City (first) and Chicago (second). California city on Pacific coast, yet farther east than Reno, NV, because country's coast indents at southern region of state.

LOST IN SPACE   Science fiction TV series about a family of astronauts marooned in outer space. Guy Williams starred as Prof. John Robinson; June Lockhart played his wife, Maureen. Most of the episodes concerned the exploits of their son, Will (Billy Mumy), cowardly Dr. Smith (Jonathan Harris) and their robot, who would caution "Warning, aliens approaching."

LOT'S WIFE   Became pillar of salt when she looked back at destruction of cities Sodom and Gomorrah. Lot and wife permitted to flee cities, but angels sent by God had warned them not to look back.

LOU GRANT   WJM-TV news producer, portrayed by Edward Asner, on *The Mary Tyler Moore Show* (1970–1977). A management change at the station ended Grant's job there, and he moved to California to take on the job of city editor for the Los Angeles *Tribune* on his own series, *Lou Grant* (1977–1982).

LOUIS   Christian name meaning "famous warrior." Chosen for 10 French kings. The first, Louis the Pious, was King of France and Holy Roman Emperor; succeeded his father, Charlemagne, in 814.

TRIVIAL CONQUEST

Louis XIV, the "Sun King," built Versailles Palace, 1685. Louis XVI married Marie Antoinette, 1770, and was deposed and executed during French Revolution, 1793.

LOUIS, JOE (1914–1981) Born Joseph Louis Barrow. World heavyweight boxing champion longer than any other boxer—more than 11 years, 1937–1949. Fought record 25 title defenses. Beat James J. Braddock in Chicago, June 22, 1937, to gain title. Successfully defended it against German Max Schmeling, who had given him his only early defeat. "Brown Bomber" retired in 1949, then lost to Rocky Marciano and Ezzard Charles in 1950 comeback attempt. Lifetime record 68-3.

LOUISIANA Some annual events: International Rice Festival; Louisiana Shrimp Festival and Fair; Gumbo Festival; Festival of Flowers.

LOUISIANA PURCHASE May 2, 1803, U.S. purchased about 827,987 sq. mi. (2,144 sq. km.) from France. Cost $15 million. Largest single purchase of land in U.S. history. All or parts of 15 states eventually formed out of the territory.

LOVE BUG, THE 1969 comedy film from Walt Disney. Dean Jones starred as an unemployed race driver who has a change of luck when he purchases a white Volkswagon with a mind of its own. Buddy Hackett co-starred and nicknamed the car "Herbie."

LOVE ME TENDER 1956 film that featured Elvis Presley's screen debut. Story of a family, during the Civil War time, divided by rivalry among brothers for the same girl. Elvis sings "Love Me Tender," "Poor Boy" and "We're Gonna Move." (see PRESLEY, ELVIS)

LOVE MEANS NEVER HAVING TO SAY YOU'RE SORRY. See SEGAL, ERICH

LOVE OF MONEY, THE "The love of money is the root of all evil." Biblical quotation from Book of Timothy, I: VI, 10.

LOVE STORY. See SEGAL, ERICH

LOVELY RITA Song by John Lennon and Paul McCartney performed on the Beatles album *Sgt. Pepper's Lonely Hearts' Club Band* (1967). Lovely Rita is a meter maid. (see BEATLES, THE)

LOVIN' SPOONFUL, THE Rock-and-roll group featuring John Sebastian on guitar, Steve Boone on bass, Zal Yanovsky on lead guitar and Joe Butler on drums. Hits include "Do You Believe in Magic," "Summer in the City" and "Rain on the Roof." Appeared in Woody Allen's film *What's Up, Tiger Lily?* (1967), and Paul Simon's *One-Trick Pony* (1980).

LSD   Abbreviation for German spelling of lysergic acid diethylamide. Hallucinogenic drug first synthesized by Swiss chemist Albert Hofmann, 1938. Dr. Hofmann discovered LSD's psychedelic properties by accident five years later. Average dose is one-three hundred thousandth of an ounce.

LUDLUM, ROBERT (1927–   )   American author. Often wrote espionage fiction in which unsuspecting amateur is sucked into plot. In *The Scarlatti Inheritance* (1971), U.S. agent Matthew Canfield foils pro-Hitler financier. His 10 other novels include *The Ostermann Weekend* (1972), *The Rhinemann Exchange* (1974), and *The Acquitaine Progression* (1984).

LUGE   Also called a toboggan, a one or two-man sled used for racing. Olympic sport since 1964. Rider(s) lie on back of sled with head just high enough to see twisting course ahead. Steered by shifting body weight and by pushing in on one sled runner while lifting up on the other.

LUGOSI, BELA (1882–1952)   Hungarian actor who became typecast in many cheap horror films. His definitive performance in *Dracula* (1930) stuck with him throughout his career. Other films include *White Zombie* (1932), *The Black Cat* (1934), *Return of the Vampire* (1943) and *Bride of the Monster* (1936). He was buried wearing the black cape he wore in *Dracula*.

LUKE SKYWALKER   Lead character of the *Star Wars* series of movies by George Lucas. Together with his robots, C-3PO and R2-D2, his sister Princess Leia and friend Han Solo, he battled the evil Empire—led by his father, Darth Vader.

LUSITANIA   British oceanliner. Hit by torpedoes from German U-2 submarine, May 7, 1915. Sank off coast of Ireland, killing 1,198 passengers, 124 of them Americans. Despite the outrage, the U.S. did not enter World War I until 1917.

LUSITANIA EXPRESS. See IBERIAN PENINSULA

LUXEMBOURG   Official name Grand Duchy of Luxembourg. One of the oldest and smallest independent countries in Europe.

TRIVIAL CONQUEST

Formed in 900s. Became independent in 1867. One of the world's most industrialized nations. Grand Duchy is a constitutional monarchy headed by a Grand Duke or Duchess.

LUXEMBOURG GARDEN   One of several famous gardens in Paris, France. Others include the Tuileries, the Bois de Boulogne, the Jardin des Plantes and the Bois de Vincennes. Paris is often described as a woman with flowers in her hair because of its beautiful gardens and parks.

M

M*A*S*H Successful 1970 comedy film about 4077th Mobile Army Surgical Hospital, starring Elliot Gould as Hawkeye and Sally Kellerman as Hot Lips. Became phenomenally popular TV series in 1972, starring Alan Alda as Hawkeye and McLean Stevenson as Lt. Col. Henry Blake. Movie and TV theme song was "Suicide Is Painless."

MA AND PA KETTLE Crusty but lovable hayseeds played by Marjorie Main and Percy Kilbride first appeared in 1947 Fred MacMurray comedy, *The Egg and I*. They proved so popular that Universal bought characters and made nine films about Kettles between 1949 and 1957.

MA BARKER Leader of family of criminals—portrayed on screen by Blanche Yurka in *Queen of the Mob* (1940), Claire Trevor on TV's *Untouchables* and Shelley Winters in *Bloody Mama* (1970).

MAC AND MC Gaelic word for son, occuring as prefix in many Irish and Scottish names of Celtic origin. Equivalent of English suffix *-son*, Hebrew *ben*.

MACARTHUR, GENERAL DOUGLAS (1880–1964) General, World War II and Korea. Recalled from retirement to command U.S. forces in Far East, World War II. Left Corregidor Island, Philippines, 1942, to wage more promising war against Japan, with words: "I came through, though, and I shall return." He did, October 24, 1944, when Allies were in stronger position to protect Philippines. Awarded Medal of Honor for his defense of the Islands. Commanded postwar occupation forces in Japan. Appointed supreme UN commander of forces in Korea, July 14, 1950, following North Korea's invasion of South Korea. When China entered war on North Korean side, called for air strikes on China. President Truman opposed his aggressive tactics. After MacArthur publicly expressed disagreement with president, he was relieved of command April 11, 1951. Ended 52 years of military service. Famous for having said: "Old soldiers never die, they just fade away." His trademarks were aviator-style glasses, heavily gold-braided hat and corncob pipe.

MACBETH. See SHAKESPEARE, WILLIAM

MACDONALD, JOHN DANN (1916–   ) American mystery writer. Most novels set in Florida, including Travis McGee series. Detective-thief McGee lives in Ft. Lauderdale on boat, *The Busted Flush*, which he won in poker game. Makes living recovering stolen property. Often works with neighbor Meyer, successful economist. McGee first appeared in 1964, with *The Deep Blue Goodbye*. All McGee novels have color in title.

MACHIAVELLI, NICCOLO (1469–1527) Florentine philosopher whose *The Prince* (1513) outlined his theories of government and pragmatic rule. Instructs rulers to retain power by exploiting weaknesses, saying, "the ends justify the means." Sometimes considered father of modern political science.

MACHINE GUN Charles E. Barnes invented first machine gun, 1856. Called an "improved automatic cannon." Hand-cranked. First rapid-fire machine gun, invented 1862 by Richard Jordon Gatling. It fired 250 shots per minute. Machine guns widely used by American criminals and bank robbers. George "Machine Gun" Kelly, Kate "Ma" Barker and Bonnie and Clyde all used 0.45-caliber Thompson submachine gun, invented by John Thompson, 1920.

MACHU PICCHU Site of an ancient city 50 mi. (80 km.) northwest of Cusco, Peru. Inhabited by Incas, South American Indians whose civilization created large empire. Hiram Bingham discovered Machu Picchu's ruins while on mountain, 1911.

MACK THE KNIFE Song that won singer Bobby Darin two Grammy Awards (Best New Artist, Record of the Year, 1959), comes from 1928 German musical, *The Threepenny Opera*. Song is about gangster MacHeath, who carries jackknife.

MACLAINE, SHIRLEY (1934–   ) Dancer turned

screen actress. Sister of Warren Beatty. Films include, *The Trouble With Harry* (1955), *The Apartment* (1959) and *Sweet Charity* (1968). Starred in TV series *Shirley's World* in 1971. Won Best Actress Oscar in *Terms of Endearment*, (1983).

MACLEAN, ALISTAIR STUART (1922–   ) Scottish author of adventure novels *Ice Station Zebra* (1963), *Where Eagles Dare* (1967) and *The Guns of Navarone* (1957), latter about World War II Allied commandos trying to destroy two heavily guarded German guns defending passage in Aegean Sea.

MACMILLAN, MAURICE HAROLD (1894–   ) British prime minister, 1957–1963. Spoke before UN General Assembly, September 29, 1960, urging U.S.S.R. to resume disarmament talks. Interrupted twice by Soviet Premier Khrushchev's yelling and shoe-pounding. Khrushchev walked out after speech.

MACY'S DEPARTMENT STORE   Located at Broadway and 34th Street in New York City. Largest department store in world, occupying 50.5 acres of floor space. Sells over 400,000 items and employs approximately 12,000 people. Rowland Hussey Macy established his first store (on Sixth Avenue, New York City), 1858.

MAD HATTER. See CARROLL, LEWIS

MAD MAGAZINE   American satirical humor magazine. Cover price $.10 when started, 1952, now "$1.25 (Cheap)." Publisher, William M. Gaines. Symbol/hero/mascot, cartoon character Alfred E. Neuman, whose motto is "What, me worry?" Drawn by Norman Mingo, made cover debut, 1956. Name is from minor character on Henry Morgan radio show.

MADAGASCAR   African country made of one large and many small islands. Located in Indian Ocean, 250 mi. (402 km.) southeast of mainland Africa. Large island, also called Madagascar, is world's fourth largest island. World's greatest vanilla producer.

MADAMA BUTTERFLY   Puccini's tragic opera first produced 1904. Story of Japanese maiden who falls in love with American navy lieutenant. Abandoned by her lover, she commits suicide using her father's hari-kari sword.

MADAME TUSSAUD'S WAXWORKS MUSEUM   London, England. Famous for historical models and Chamber of Horrors. Founded by Marie Grosmolte Tussaud, 1834. Originally located on Baker Street, later moved. Tussaud was Swiss wax sculptor whose figures of prominent people are still on display at museum. Suspected of sympathizing with king of France, forced to model heads of French revolutionary leaders and victims of guillotine.

MADDOX, LESTER GARFIELD (1915–   ) Governor of Georgia, 1967–1971. Lieutenant governor, 1971–1975, under Jimmy Carter. Before entering politics ran grocery store, furniture business and diner, from which he evicted three blacks rather than serve them in 1964.

MADEIRA ISLANDS Located off northwest coast of Africa in Atlantic Ocean. Belong to Portugal. Noted for their exotic flowers and trees. Rain only falls in winter months, so water must be rationed and distributed from mountains to farms and villages by stone aqueducts called *levadas*. Wine is chief industry.

MADRID Spain's capital and largest city. Its center is plaza called the Puerta del Sol, meaning "gate of the sun." Became capital because location is at almost exact geographical center of Spain.

MAE WEST Inflatable life jacket worn over the chest. First used in World War I, then again in World War II. When inflated, it suggests voluptuous figure of American film actress, Mae West, for whom it was named.

MAGALLANES Province in southern Chile. City of Punta Arenas is southernmost city in world next to small village of Ushuaia in Argentina. Punta Arenas contains 60% of Magallanes' population. Province formed 1849. Was penal colony for Spanish, 1843.

MAGEE, SAM Title character of "The Cremation of Sam Magee," poem by Robert W. Service (1874–1958), English-born Canadian writer of Klondike ballads such as "The Shooting of Dan McGrew." Magee cremated on the "Marge [edge] of Lake Labarge" after dying from cold on Dawson Trail to Klondike gold mines. Being thrown into fire thawed him back to life. First published in *Songs of a Sourdough* (1907).

MAGI, THE In Matt. 2:2, three wise men bring baby Jesus gold, frankincense and myrrh; latter two are aromatic gum resins gathered from incisions into bark of trees indigenous to Africa and Arabia. Both used for making perfume and incense. Frankincense especially valuable as one of four spices used in preparation of incense used in Jewish temple worship.

MAGICIAN Or prestidigitator or conjuror. Entertainer who appears to control events by supernatural means. In primitive societies, served as doctors and spiritual leaders.

MAGNA CARTA   Basis of English system of rights and liberties. Signed by King John in field of Runnymede, Northhampton, 1215. The King, under threat of civil war, was forced to sign "Great Charter," which in effect, limited his own power.

MAGNET   Device, often made of metal, that can attract iron and steel and some other types of metal. In bar-shaped magnets, more magnetism is concentrated at poles than at middle. North pole of a bar-shaped magnet always points north if suspended; it is attracted to Earth's magnetic south pole (located at geographic North Pole). Circular magnets' polarity is oriented outward from plane of circle. Magnetism results when electric charges move, as in aligned atoms of metal magnet or in electric current through electromagnet.

MAGPIE   Bird of crow family. Black- and yellow-billed types; both have black and white feathers. Travels in groups. Mimics calls of other birds; will also eat their young. Considered ominous if one lives near your home.

MAGYAR   Official language of Hungary. Uralic-Altaic language related to Estonian and Finnish. Various dialects spoken in certain areas. Also called Hungarian.

MAH-JONGG   Tile game of Chinese origin that became popular in America in the 1920s. Name means "the sparrows." Each of four (or three) players collects sets of tiles, trying to make two, three or four of a kind. Scores settled after each hand, with winner accumulating most points at end of play. Players designated by name of wind: east, south, west, north. Standard game uses 144 tiles; American version, easier to learn and score, uses 152 tiles. Players build four-sided, two-decked wall with tiles to begin game.

MAILER, NORMAN (1923–   )   Pulitzer Prize–winning American novelist and journalist (*Armies of the Night*, 1968). Ran for mayor of New York City, 1969, on platform calling for statehood of city and legalized gambling at Coney Island. Columnist Jimmy Breslin was his running mate. Among his books: *The Naked and the Dead* (1948), his first novel, about U.S. attack on Japanese-held Pacific Island in World War II; *Marilyn* (1973), a biography of sex goddess–actress Marilyn Monroe. Covers her life, suicide and film career. Illustrated with more than 110 photographs from exhibit "Marilyn Monroe—The Legend and the Truth"; *The Executioner's Song*

(1979), which recounts story of Gary Gilmore, executed by firing squad in Utah, January 17, 1977, for murdering gas station attendant. Gilmore gained notoriety for insisting state proceed with execution (first in U.S. in more than a decade). Gilmore's last words: "Let's do it."

MAINE   Forms northeastern corner of U.S. Its peninsula, West Quoddy Head, is easternmost piece of U.S. land. Largest state in New England. Only state to border just one other state (New Hampshire). Ninety percent of land is covered by forests. Nicknamed "the Pine Tree State."

MAKE ROOM FOR DADDY   Danny Thomas' popular TV series debuted in 1953 and continued through 1964. Danny was Danny Williams, loud but softhearted dad. Jean Hagen played his first wife through 1956; Marjorie Lord joined family in 1957. Stories usually involved kids: Rusty Hamer, Sherry Jackson, Angela Cartwright. Danny's Uncle Tonoose (played by Hans Conreid) was regularly featured.

MALAY SEA   Body of water surrounding the Malay Archipelago, a group of islands in Indian and Pacific Oceans.

MALCOLM X (1925–1965)   Born Malcolm Little. Advocate of black nationalism. Converted to Black Muslim movement. Became Orthodox Muslim, 1964, and founded rival Organization for Afro-American Unity. Assassinated, February 1965, by those thought to be connected with Black Muslims.

MALDIVE ISLANDS   Asia's smallest independent country. Group of 2,000 coral islands in Indian Ocean. Major industry is fishing. Boats are usually made of coconut. Most of trade is with Sri Lanka.

MALENKOV, GEORGI MAXIMILIANOVICH (1902–   )   Top lieutenant for Joseph Stalin. Served as first party secretary in first few weeks following Stalin's death, 1953. Lost position to Khrushchev following a power struggle. Expelled from party, 1961.

MALTA   Island country in Mediterranean Sea. Formerly a British colony, an independent commonwealth nation since 1964. Became a Republic in 1974. Consists of islands Malta, Comino, Cominotto, Filfla, Gozo. Most inhabitants speak Maltese, a West Arabic dialect with some Italian words. Both Maltese and English are official languages.

MALTESE CROSS   Cross of eight points or cross of Malta, a devoutly Roman Catholic nation. Also a perennial flower of the pink family, *Lynchnis chalcedonica*, native to Siberia. Named so because petals are notched like arms of Maltese cross.

MALTESE FALCON, THE   1941 detective film starring Humphrey Bogart as Dashiell Hammett's fictional hero Sam Spade. Mary Astor as his client, Sydney Greenstreet as "the Fat Man," Casper Gutman, Peter Lorre as Joel Cairo, all searching for a gem-filled statue of falcon.

MAMMOTH CAVE NATIONAL PARK   Located in central Kentucky covering 51,354.4 acres. Surrounds world's largest single cave, containing eight waterfalls, three rivers, two lakes. Blindfish, blind beetles, crayfish and crickets inhabit cave.

MAN FRIDAY. See DEFOE, DANIEL

MAN IN THE GRAY FLANNEL SUIT, THE   1956 film starring Gregory Peck in title role of public relations man. A study of his life at work and at home, and of the effect of news he is father of boy conceived in Italy during the war.

MAN O'WAR   Associated Press chose "Big Red" greatest race horse of all time. Won 20 out of 21 races at two and three years of age, 1919 and 1920. Only loss (second place) to appropriately named "Upset" in Saratoga's Sanford Stakes, 1919, winning $249,465.

MAN OF LA MANCHA   Broadway musical (1965) that introduced song "The Impossible Dream." Based on Cervantes' *Don Quixote*. Richard Kiley starred in play; music by Mitch Leigh and Joe Darion.

MAN WHO CAME TO DINNER, THE   Play by Moss Hart and George S. Kaufman (1939). Friendly burlesque on Alexander Woolcott, critic and radio personality, fictionalized as Sheridan Whiteside. Immobilized by accident at home of Midwest family, he insults virtually everyone in town.

MAN WHO KNEW TOO MUCH, THE   1956 film by Alfred Hitchcock. American doctor and wife witness murder of secret agent who tells them of assassination plot. Oscar-winning song "Que Serà, Serà" is key to film's climax.

MAN WITH THE GOLDEN ARM, THE   1955 film directed by Otto Preminger, starring Frank Sinatra as drug addict trying to kick habit. Eleanor Parker plays his crippled wife in this film based on Nelson Algren's novel.

MANATEE   Or sea cow, a large awkward sea animal. It is believed sailors too long at sea mistook unattractive manatee for a beautiful woman, and this was source of mermaid legend.

MANCHESTER, WILLIAM (1922–   ) American biographer. Wrote *Portrait of a President* (1962); *The Arms of Kruppd* (1968), and *Death of a President* (1967). Jacqueline Kennedy, widow of slain president John F. Kennedy, commissioned Manchester to write story of assassination. After several disputes about portions of book, changed her mind, and sued unsuccessfully to halt publication. Also wrote *American Caesar: Douglas MacArthur, 1880–1964* (1978), which examines life and controversial career of U.S. forces World War II Pacific commander, later director of postwar occupation of Japan and UN commander-in-chief in Korean War until President Truman relieved him for insubordination.

MANDRILL   Large, fierce, gregarious baboon native to West Africa. Males of this monkey are very colorful, with red noses, blue cheeks, bright red and blue rumps.

MANHATTAN   Cocktail prepared with 1½ oz. rye or blended whiskey, ¾ oz. sweet vermouth, one dash aromatic bitters. Usually decorated with cocktail cherry or twist of lemon. For Dry Manhattan, dry vermouth is used.

MANHATTAN CLAM CHOWDER   Red-colored chowder actually developed in Rhode Island in 1930s by adding tomatoes to clams and clam sauce. Debate has raged since over practice; met with scorn from fanciers of white, creamy New England clam chowder, developed in Massachusetts and Maine.

MANHATTAN ISLAND   Borough of New York City. Named after Manhattan Indians who lived there until 1626 when they sold it to Dutchman, Peter Minuit, for $24 worth of axes, kettles and cloth.

MANIFEST DESTINY   Term describing U.S. mid-19th century expansionist policy. Coined by John O'Sullivan to justify annexation of Texas, 1845. Term used to vindicate U.S. expansion across entire continent.

MANNEKE PIS FOUNTAIN. See BRUSSELS

MANSFIELD, JAYNE (VERA JAYNE PALMER) (1934–1967)   Blonde bombshell of such films as *Will Success Spoil Rock Hunter?* (1957), in which she also appeared on Broadway; *The Wayward Bus* (1957); *Kiss Them for Me* (1957), and many B-movies. Twentieth Century-Fox promoted her as rival for Marilyn Monroe. Also appeared as nightclub singer and as model on cover of more than 500 magazines. Died in auto crash near New Orleans. Allegedly had same bust size as Marie Antoinette, Queen of France.

MANSON, CHARLES (1934–   )   Convicted murderer and incarcerated, Vacaville state prison. Assisted by his "family," a group of mostly women, under his control. Charged with August 10, 1969, murder of Leno and Rosemary LaBianca. Murdered Sharon Tate (Mrs. Roman Polanski) and her four guests the preceding night. Formed musical group, Family Jams, from California jail cell, 1970. Recorded album entitled *Lie.*

MANTLE, MICKEY (1931–   )   New York Yankee center fielder, 1951–1968. Played most games of any Yankee (2,401). Hit 536 career home runs. Struck out 1,710 times in entire career. Switch hitter (bats from both sides of plate) and stellar defensive player until slowed by leg injuries. His uniform number (seven) retired by Yankees, 1969. Elected to Hall of Fame, 1974.

MAORI WARS   Fought between British colonizers and native Maori tribes, New Zealand, 1840–1847. Maori defeated by forces commanded by Sir George Grey.

MAORIS   Original inhabitants of New Zealand. Belong to Polynesian race. Nine percent of New Zealand's population. Generally tall, with broad faces, dark eyes and dark hair. Speak English but at large gatherings called *hui* speak Maori, the native language.

MAPLE LEAF. See CANADA, NATIONAL SYMBOLS

MARATHON   Modern Olympic marathon distance, 26 mi., 385 yd. Distance standardized in 1908, when race from Windsor to London, England, measured 26 mi. and runners were required to cover additional 385 yds. in order to finish opposite King Edward VII's Royal Box at stadium.

MARBLES   Ancient children's toy and game played worldwide. Small spheres (usually ⅓ in. to 2 in. in diameter). At one time most frequently made from marble chips; nuts, beans, stone, clay, glass and hollow steel also used. "Alleys" are marbles derived from alabaster—translucent, whitish and perhaps banded; "aggies" come from agate. In game, cheap marbles to be "shot" at called gibs, mibs, immies, hoodles, ducks and marrididdles (marbles homemade from clay); "shooters," or better grade marbles, are alleys, aggies, cinas, glassies, steelies, etc. New York's Institute for the Investigation of Rolling Spheroids reputedly studies history and playing intricacies of game.

MARCH HARE. See CARROLL, LEWIS

MARCIANO, ROCKY (1923–1969) Born Rocco Francis Marchegiano in Brockton, MA. Undefeated world heavyweight boxing champion (only one in sports history) 1952–1956. In 49 pro fights, won 43 by knockout, 6 by decision. Nicknamed "Brockton Blockbuster" or "Brockton Bomber." Beat Jersey Joe Walcott to win title. Retired April 27, 1956. Died in 1969 plane crash one day before 46th birthday.

MARGARITA Cocktail inspired by Mexican method of drinking tequila. Made from juice of one-half lime or lemon, 1½ oz. tequila, and ½ oz. Triple Sec. Served in glass rimmed with salt. Developed in Los Angeles, was springboard for rise of tequila consumption in U.S.

MARIANA TRENCH Located in Pacific Ocean near Guam. World's deepest trench at 36,198 ft. (11,033 m.) deep. A trench is a narrow and long depression in ocean floor.

MARINER SPACECRAFT Ten unmanned space probes launched by U.S. to gather information on planets. Mariner II passed over Venus, 1962, found temperature to be 800°F. Other Mariner probes went to Mars and Mercury.

MARIS, ROGER (1934–   ) Hit 61 home runs in 1961 to break Babe Ruth's season record of 60 set in 1927. Maris' record set in 162-game season; Ruth's in 154-game, so Commissioner Ford Frick ruled Maris' mark must have asterisk in record book. Hit number 61 off Tracy Stallard, Boston Red Sox, in Yankee Stadium on last day of regular season. Teammate Mickey Mantle hit 54 homers that year. Yanks won American League pennant and World Series under manager Ralph Houk.

MARKSMAN Expert shot in hunting, war and sport shooting

(i.e., rifle and pistol shooting, trap and skeet shooting). Someone who can "hit the mark" (target).

MARMADUKE   Comic strip Great Dane created by cartoonist Brad Anderson (1954). Dog's size frequently causes problems for his owners, the Winslow family.

MARNIE   1964 film directed by Alfred Hitchcock. Tippi Hedren plays Marnie, a compulsive thief, who becomes upset whenever she sees color red.

MARS   Fourth planet from sun. Reddish appearance led to its being named after Roman god of war, Mars. Also known as the red planet. Color derives from mineral limonite.

MARSEILLES   Greatest seaport in France and on Mediterranean. Second largest French city. Built in a half-circle around natural harbor called "Old Harbor." Founded 600 B.C. by Greeks. Site of many battles during French Revolution. Name given to French national hymn, "La Marseillaise."

MARSHALL PLAN   Strategy of economic assistance offered to war-damaged countries by the Truman administration following World War II. Named for Secretary of State George C. Marshall, who discussed it in his Harvard graduation address, June 5, 1947. Ultimately paid out $12.5 billion by time Korean War started.

MARSHALL, THURGOOD (1908–   )   Civil rights lawyer. First black U.S. Supreme Court justice. Appointed, 1967, by Lyndon B. Johnson. Won 29 of 32 cases he argued before Supreme Court. Represented the NAACP in landmark decision Brown vs. Board of Education.

MARTHA'S VINEYARD   Popular summer resort island 4 mi. (6 km.) off southeastern coast of Massachusetts. 6,000 year-round residents, 40,000 summer tourists. Explorer Bartholomew Gosnold named island for his daughter and for grapevines he found there, 1602.

MARTIN, DEAN (1917–   )   Singer and Hollywood leading man, teamed with Jerry Lewis until 1956, then enjoyed solo success in 1960s. Movies include, *Kiss Me Stupid* (1964) and *Airport* (1969). Starred as secret agent Matt Helm in four films, beginning with *The Silencers* (1966).

MARTIN, STEVE (1945–   )   American comedian, actor, writer. Has appeared on TV, in films *The Jerk*, *The Muppet Movie*,

Pennies from Heaven and *The Lonely Guy*. Wrote *Cruel Shoes* (1979), collection of humorous short pieces including "The Serious Dogs," "The Gift of the Magi Indian Giver" and "Poodles... Great Eating."

MARTINI Origin not definite, earliest known recipe 1862. Became progressively drier over years, with standard recipe changing from equal parts gin and dry vermouth to 15 parts gin and just a splash of vermouth. Ultimate is "naked martini," or gin on the rocks. Olive or onion is preferred garnish. Most popular U.S. cocktail. John Doxat's book *Stirred—Not Shaken*, named after fictional British spy James Bond's martini preference.

MARTINIQUE Island in West Indies. An overseas department of France since 1946. Three deputies from Martinique attend French National Assembly. Island also has its own local government.

MARTY 1955 Oscar-winning Best Picture that propelled its star, Ernest Borgnine, to fame. Based on Paddy Chayefsky's TV play about a 35-year-old butcher (Rod Steiger) from the Bronx who fumbles his way into romance with schoolteacher (Betsy Blair).

MARVEL COMICS Comic book publishing house founded by Stan Lee in 1961. With artist Jack Kirby, Lee created Fantastic Four in November 1961. The Hulk premiered May 1962. Marvel continued to expand one superhero at a time. Spiderman followed Hulk, and Thor premiered in "Journey into Mystery," August 1962.

MARX BROTHERS, THE Comedian brothers, successful in vaudeville, on Broadway and later in movies. The act originally included Groucho, Harpo, Chico, Zeppo and Gummo, the first three gaining greatest fame in films, including, *Duck Soup* (1933), *A Night at the Opera* (1935) and *Go West* (1940).

MARX, JULIUS (GROUCHO) (1890–1977) One of Marx Brothers, along with Harpo, Chico, Zeppo and Gummo, appeared in many Broadway shows in 1920s. Moved with brothers (minus Gummo) to the screen in 1929 with *The Cocoanuts*. Taking Harpo's pulse in *A Day at the Races* (1937), he quipped, "Either he's dead or my watch was stopped." Appeared without his brothers in *Copacabana* (1947), *Mr. Music* (1950), *Skidoo* (1968) and other films. Hosted TV quiz show, *You Bet Your Life* (1952–1961) in which announcer George Fenneman would introduce him, "Here he is, the one, the only—Groucho!" Once observed, "You're only as young as the woman you feel." Wrote autobiography *Groucho and Me* (1959) and sequel, *Memoirs of a Mangy Lover* (1963). (See MARX BROTHERS, THE)

MARX, KARL HEINRICH (1818–1883) German political philosopher and socialist. Developed social theories collectively known as communism. Advocated that workers unite and take control over means of production, factories and capital funds. Regarded religion as "opiate of the masses," that diverts people from identifying source of their oppression and from organizing to overcome it. Prolific author. Works include *The Communist Manifesto* (1848), written with Friedrich Engels (1820–1895), and the three-volumed *Das Kapital* (1867–1894). Buried at Highgate Cemetery, London. Inscribed on his tomb are words, "Workers of All Lands Unitez...".

MARY CELESTE November 1872, Captain B. S. Briggs, his wife, daughter and crew of seven set off for Genoa from Boston. *Mary Celeste* found four weeks later with everything in its place except the 10 people and lifeboat. Mystery never satisfactorily explained.

MARY HARTMAN Middle-aged housewife who resided at 343 Bratner Avenue in Fernwood, OH, as portrayed by Louise Lasser on TV series *Mary Hartman, Mary Hartman* (1976). Produced by Norman Lear, series was spoof of soap operas.

MARY POPPINS 1964 film from Walt Disney. Based on book by P. L. Travers. Julie Andrews won Oscar for Best Actress for her performance as magical nanny of two neglected children. Dick Van Dyke co-starred as chimney sweep Bert, who introduced kids to word *supercalifragilisticexpialidocious*.

MARY TYLER MOORE SHOW, THE Popular comedy series (1970–1977) about Mary Richards (Mary Tyler Moore), single woman who moves to Minneapolis and gets job as assistant producer of news show on local station WJM-TV (Channel 12). Her co-workers included Lou Grant (Edward Asner), Murray Slaughter, head news writer (Gavin MacLeod) and Sue Ann Nivens (Betty White) who hosted "The Happy Homemaker." On last episode, everyone was fired except Ted Baxter (Ted Knight), inept anchorman.

MARY, QUEEN OF SCOTS (1542–1587) Became Queen of Scotland six days after birth. Married Lord Darnley, 1565, who was murdered two years later. Soon thereafter she was imprisoned by Scotch nobles. Fled to England. Eventually executed for treason.

MARZIPAN Candy. Paste of almonds and sugar. Often molded into fruit shapes and colored as the fruit would be. Origins centuries ago in Orient, where almond sweetmeats were served at feasts.

MASON-DIXON LINE   Boundary line between Maryland and Pennsylvania surveyed 1763–1767 by Charles Mason and Jeremiah Dixon. Before Civil War, states south of line were considered slave states and those north of line were nonslave states. Surveyors were called to settle boundary dispute between Pennsylvania and Maryland. Runs at 39°, 43′, 26.3″ north latitude.

MASTERS, THE   Winner of prestigious Grand Slam of Golf event given green blazer of host club Augusta (GA) National. April tournament established there, 1934 by former amateur champion Bobby Jones. Players invited to compete, usually on basis of major tournament in year before. All past wearers of "green jacket" also qualify for all future Masters' tournaments.

MATA HARI (1876–1917)   Dutch dancer-entertainer. Born Margaretha Geertruida Zelle. Well known in Europe where she billed herself as a Javanese temple dancer. Allegedly joined World War I spy network after her act's popularity declined. Executed by French authorities who accused her of being German spy.

MATCHES   Invented early 1800s. First book matches invented by Joshua Pusey, Philadelphia patent lawyer, 1892. Packages of 50, striking surface on inside. Modern books typically contain 20 matches and have safety striking surface on outside.

MATHEMATICAL SYMBOLS

$\therefore$	= therefore
$\because$	= because
∞	= infinity
\\	= absolute value
$>$	= greater than
$<$	= less than
$\approx$	= approximately equal to
$\sqrt{}$	= square root
$\parallel$	= parallel to
$\perp$	= perpendicular to

MATHIAS, BOB (1930–   )   Only two-time Olympic decathlon winner, 1948 and 1952. American athlete won grueling event at 17, again at 21, setting world record then. Pioneer in use of fiberglass pole in pole vault, one of decathlon's 10 events.

MATILDA   A knapsack which "waltzes" or bounces as it is carried by poor, walking Australian worker or "swagman" in song "Waltzing Matilda," written 1903 by A. B. Paterson and Marie Cowan.

In song, "a jolly swagman" asks Matilda to come a-waltzing. Has unofficially become Australia's national song.

MAU MAU UPRISING   Kenya, 1952–1956. Revolutionary campaign against country's British government. Led by Mau Mau (origin unknown), militant nationalists. Though beaten in 1956, their influence led to Kenyan independence, 1963.

MAUDE   TV comedy series 1972–1978. Beatrice Arthur starred as Maude Findlay, an upper-middle-class wife living with her husband, Walter, her divorced daughter Carol and Carol's son Phillip, in suburb of New York.

MAUGHAM, WILLIAM SOMERSET (1874–1965)   English writer. First known as playwright, then for short stories and novels, many set in tropics. Among them, *Of Human Bondage* (1915), novel about doctor's infatuation with vulgar waitress (filmed three times: 1934, with Leslie Howard and Bette Davis in her first major role, 1946, with Paul Henreid and Eleanor Parker and 1964, with Laurence Harvey and Kim Novak). *The Moon and Sixpence* (1919), fictionalized biography of French painter Paul Gauguin, who left stock-brokering to become painter in Tahiti. (Maugham calls character Charles Strickland). *The Razor's Edge* (1949), in which worldly young man leaves inheritance for holy life in Hinduism.

MAURITANIA   Large African country. Borders Atlantic Ocean on the east, Sahara Desert on the west. Ninety-nine percent of population are Muslims. Economy is agriculturally based.

MAVERICK   TV western series with a sense of humor, from 1961. It spoofed Western genre and other TV series. James Garner starred as Bret Maverick, who with his brother Bart (Jack Kelly) would roam the west playing poker and aiding those in distress.

MAXIM'S   Expensive, fashionable restaurant located in Paris at 3 rue Royale. Recently bought by designer Pierre Cardin. Art Nouveau decor. Established at turn of century.

MAYAGUEZ   U.S. merchant vessel. Seized by Cambodian patrol boats, May 12, 1975. Thirty-nine-man crew and vessel rescued, May 14, after U.S. bombed mainland and invaded Cambodian island where crew was thought to be. Fifteen U.S. marines killed, 50 wounded.

MAYBERRY   The North Carolina town which was setting for *The Andy Griffith Show* (1960–1968) and *Mayberry R.F.D.* (1968–

1971). Leading citizens of Mayberry included sheriff, Andy Taylor, and his deputy, Barney Fife; gas station attendant Gomer Pyle and Floyd Lawson, the barber.

MAYFLIES Members of insect family *Ephemerida*, which means "living for a day" in Greek. Actually, live longer than a day, although some are adults for one day. Many trout flies are designed to imitate mayflies.

MAYFLOWER Ship that carried first pilgrims to America. Departed Plymouth, England, 1620, with 102 Puritans on board. Pilot, Christopher Jones, part owner of vessel. Arrived off Plymouth, MA, December 26, 1620. One birth and one death occurred during 65-day voyage.

MAYO CLINIC One of largest medical centers in world. Located, Rochester, MN. Founded by William Worrall Mayo and his sons, 1889. Registers estimated 225,000 patients each year. Approximately 500 staff physicians assisted by 650 doctors undergoing training.

MAYS, WILLIE (1931–) "The Say Hey Kid." Began major baseball career with Giants in New York, 1951, moved with them to San Francisco. Finished career with New York Mets, 1973, with 660 career homers. Hit famous 600th home run with San Francisco on September 22, 1969. First black captain of major league team, New York Giants, 1954. Elected to Baseball Hall of Fame in 1979.

MCCARTHY, CHARLIE Ventrilioquist Edgar Bergen's dummy. Awarded college degree "Master of Innuendo and Snappy Comeback" by Northwestern University, August 28, 1938.

MCCARTHY, EUGENE JOSEPH (1916–) American politician. Bid for 1968 Democratic presidential nomination crystalized popular opposition to Vietnam War. Served five terms in House of Representatives. Elected to U.S. Senate, 1958, 1965. Never received Democratic presidential nomination.

MCCARTHY, MARY THERESE (1912–) American novelist and writer about politics, art, travel. Best known for novels *The Company She Keeps* (1942), *The Group* (1963), story of eight members of Vassar College's all-woman Class of '33, from post commencement wedding of Kay Strong to her funeral seven years later.

MCCARTNEY, PAUL (1942–   ) Former Beatle, successful on his own since 1970. After two solo albums (*McCartney*, 1970; *Ram*, 1971), formed group Wings, with albums including *Wild Life* (1971); *Band on the Run* (1973), with a jacket that featured McCartney with film actors James Coburn and Christopher Lee; *At the Speed of Sound* (1976). Married Linda Eastman, American photographer, at Marleybone Registry office, London, March 12, 1969. (see BEATLES, THE).

MCCULLOUGH, COLLEEN (1937–   ) Australian author. Wrote 1977 novel *The Thorn Birds* about three generations of Cleary family, who go from poverty in New Zealand to wealth in Australia, sending members to London stage and Vatican. Praised for portrayal of Australia.

MCDONALDS Fast-food restaurant chain. Ray Kroc (1902–1984), founder. First restaurant, Chicago, 1955. Hamburgers were sold for $.15 throughout early 1960s. Today, burgers average $.65 apiece. Introduced hot apple pie and Big Mac, 1968. In 1975, began using marketing slogan and trademark for the Big Mac: "two all-beef patties, special sauce, lettuce, cheese, pickles, onions and a sesame seed bun." Presently 7,500 outlets throughout U.S. and 31 countries. Outsells closest competitor, Burger King, by more than three to one.

MCENROE, JOHN (1959–   ) American tennis player. Known for brilliant all-around game and ornery on-court behavior. Nicknamed "Super Brat." Won U.S. Open, 1979, 1980, 1981. Won Wimbledon 1981, halting Björn Borg's consecutive singles titles at five, then fined $2,000 and suspended 21 days for "bad language and verbal abuse" and "conduct bringing game of tennis into disrepute."

MCGOVERN, GEORGE STANLEY (1922–   ) American politician. Democratic candidate for president, 1972. Took 17 of 537 electoral votes, winning in Massachusetts and Washington, DC. Lost to reelected President Richard Nixon. Nixon carried 60.7% of the popular vote; McGovern, 38% One of the largest landslides in U.S. history.

MCGUIRE, BARRY (1937–   ) Singer-songwriter whose only hit record, "Eve of Destruction" (1965), was rock's first protest song. Previously with the New Christy Minstrels, and was lead singer of their hit "Green, Green" (1963).

MCKINLEY, MOUNT. See MOUNTAINS, U.S.

MCKINLEY, WILLIAM (1843–1901) Twenty-fifth U.S. president, 1897–1901. During his administration, Spanish-American War occurred; Arizona, New Mexico, Oklahoma became states. Assassinated, September 6, 1901, shortly after winning reelection. Shot by Leon Czolgsz, anarchist, Buffalo, NY. Died September 14.

MCLEAN, DON (1945–   ) Folksinger-songwriter whose 1972 number-one hit single "American Pie" (1971) was inspired by the death of Buddy Holly. Other songs included "Vincent" (1971), a tribute to Vincent van Gogh and "Castles in the Air"(1970).

MCLUHAN, HERBERT (MARSHALL) (1911– 1980) Canadian communications expert, author, educator. Observer of technical change in communication theories. *The Gutenberg Galaxy: The Making of Typographic Man* (1963) was his first major work, followed by *Understanding Media* (1964) and *The Medium Is the Message* (1967). Argues that because each medium encourages some styles of communication and rejects others, the "medium is the message," regardless of what it says. Describes world as "a global village" in which all information can be shared instantaneously via electronic communication.

MCNAMARA, ROBERT STRANGE (1916–   ) Secretary of Defense under Presidents Kennedy and Johnson, 1961– 1968. Former head of Ford Motor Company. President of World Bank, 1968.

MCQUEEN, STEVE (1930–1980) Popular actor of 1960s and '70s. Portrayed bounty hunter Josh Randall on TV series *Wanted: Dead or Alive* (1958). Starring roles in many films including *The Great Escape* (1963) and *Bullitt* (1968), in which he drove white Mustang in classic car chase through San Francisco. Last film, *The Hunter* (1980), released shortly before his death.

MCWHIRTER, NORRIS DEWAR (1925–   ) AND ALAN ROSS (1925– 1975) Authors and editors of *Guinness Book of World Records, Dunlap Illustrated Encyclopedia of Facts* and others. Twin brothers initiated Guinness book in fall 1954 at urging of managing director of Guinness Stout brewery, who believed Britain needed source book to settle pub arguments. First version, called *Guinness Book of Superlatives*, became instant success. Sales of annual new editions average 3 million. Ross was murdered in 1975 Irish

Republican Army terrorist attack after offering $100,000 reward for information leading to arrest of bombers.

MEAD, MARGARET (1901–1978)   American anthropologist. Most famous studies were those of Pacific Islands. *Coming of Age in Samoa* compares adolescence in Samoa to Western society.

MEASUREMENT   The International Bureau of Weights and Measures standardizes units of measurement. Only the kilogram still defined by physical standard. A platinum-iridium kilogram standard kept at Bureau; duplicates kept in 37 countries. Meter is defined by light wavelengths.

MECCA   City located in western Saudi Arabia. Birthplace of prophet Muhammed, founder of Islam, religion of Muslims. Holiest city of Islam, restricted to Muslims only. Site of Great Mosque, Muslims' center of worship.

MEDITERRANEAN SEA, THE   Latin name meaning "in the middle of land." Surrounded by Europe at north, Asia at east, Africa at south. Separates cities of Barcelona, Marseilles, Rome, Naples, Athens (northern shore) from Algiers, Tripoli, Bengasi, Alexandria, Tel Aviv (eastern shore). Covers 969,100 sq. mi. (2,510 sq. km.). World's largest sea. Famous trade route and tourist attraction. Called *Mare Nostrum* "Our Sea" by Romans.

MEDULLA OBLONGATA   Nervous tissue of brain. Extends from front of cerebellum to spinal cord. Most vital part of central nervous system. Center of autonomic control over breathing, blood pressure. Destruction is fatal.

MEERSCHAUM   Tobacco pipe made from meerschaum (sepiolite), soft, absorbent mineral that looks like white clay. Often carved into ornate forms. Vienna is center of meerschaum carving. Pipes are waxed; turn rich brown with use.

MELVILLE, HERMAN (1819–1891)   American novelist whose books reflected his experience as seaman. Had early success, then became obscure until 1920s revival. Most famous works: *Billy Budd*, matching innocent young foretopman Billy against evil master-at-arms Claggart. Billy, victim of circumstances, is hanged. Also *Moby Dick* (1851) about Captain Ahab, stern skipper of *Pequod*, wears ivory leg to replace one bitten off by cunning and ferocious white whale Moby Dick, that Ahab stalks obsessively. Whale symbolizes evil, unpredictable forces of universe. Book begins with "Call me

Ishmael," referring to narrator of tale, which Melville intersperses with text about whaling. Silent Indian Queequeg, Stubb, Starbuck are other members of *Pequod* crew.

MEN IN SPACE

Astronaut	Date	Country
1) Yuri Gagarin	April 12, 1961	U.S.S.R.
2) Alan B. Shepard, Jr.	May 5, 1961	U.S.
3) Virgil (Gus) Grissom	July 21, 1961	U.S.
4) Gherman Titov	August 6–7, 1961	U.S.S.R.
5) John H. Glenn, Jr.	February 20, 1962	U.S.

MENDEL, GREGOR (1822–1884)   Austrian botanist. Considered founder of modern genetics, study of biological inheritance. In 1866, reported work with pea plants discovering principles of dominant and recessive traits.

MENDELSSOHN-BARTHOLDY, JAKOB LUDWIG FELIX (1809–1847)   Classical German composer, pianist and conductor. Began writing at 12. His most famous compositions include "Wedding March" (1843), "Fingal's Cave Overture" (1832) and "Spring Song" (1845).

MENSA   Organization of those whose IQ is in top 2% of population, or genius. Founded 1961; approximately 50,000 members. Conducts research on persons of exceptional intelligence. Grants college scholarships.

MERCATOR PROJECTION   On a flat map, type of cylindrical projection. Lines of longitude do not converge at poles. Distances between parallels become greater approaching poles; makes areas in high latitudes appear larger than they are. Ideal for navigation charts.

MERCHANT OF VENICE, THE. See SHAKE-SPEARE, WILLIAM

MERCURY   Closest planet to sun. Most rapid orbit and shortest year; 88 earth-days. Travels at speed of 30 mi. (48 km.) per second. Named after fleet-footed Roman messenger god, Mercury.

MERCURY   Chemical element, symbol, Hg. Shiny metallic liquid. Heavy: weighs 13.6 times as much as equal volume of water.

Extremely toxic. 15th–mid-20th century, used to cure syphilis. From Greek *hydrargyrum* meaning "liquid silver" or "quick silver."

MEREDITH, JAMES HOWARD (1933–   ) First black to attend University of Mississippi at Oxford, 1962. Escorted to campus by Federal marshals. Attempts to register barred by state, local officials. Shot and wounded by sniper while campaigning for black vote registration, 1966.

MERRICK, JOSEPH (JOHN) (1862–1890) Born with severe deformity. Gained notoriety in Victorian England. Nickname, "the elephant man." Suffered neurofibromatosis, now commonly known as "elephant man's disease." Affects 100,000 Americans annually.

MERRIE MELODIES Series of cartoons released by Warner Bros., which introduced such stars as Bugs Bunny, Pepe LePew, Tweety and the Roadrunner. Every cartoon ended with line, "That's all, folks!"

MERSEY RIVER One of world's most important trade waterways. Rises in Pennine Hills of England; enters Irish Sea at Liverpool. Length is 70 mi. (110 km.). Railway tunnel under river connects Liverpool with Birkenhead.

METALIOUS, GRACE (1924–1964) Born Grace de Repentigny. American novelist. Wrote *Peyton Place* (1956), on bestseller list for two years. Recounts scandals of small New England town through her heroine, 16-year-old Allison MacKenzie. In *Return to Peyton Place* (1960), MacKenzie publishes successful novel *Samuel's Castle* about her hometown, causing furor that results in stepfather losing job as school principal. Basis for 1957 movie and first night-time TV soap opera; Mia Farrow as Allison.

METEOROLOGY Study of atmosphere and weather. Meteorologists make predictions and prepare maps for forecasters. Work closely with computers. Research meteorologists investigate ways to control weather.

METHUSELAH In Genesis 5:27, son of Enoch. Oldest man in Bible, 969 years old. Name synonymous with old age.

METRIC PREFIXES

Pico	-	trillionth
Nano	-	billionth
Micro	-	millionth

Milli	-	thousandth
Centi	-	hundredth
Deci	-	tenth
Deca or Deka	-	ten
Hecto	-	hundred
Kilo	-	thousand
Mega	-	million
Giga	-	billion

METRIC TON Unit of mass equal to 1,000,000 g., 1,000 kg. or 2,264.6 lb. avoirdupois. Approximately equivalent to 1.1 U.S. tons. The word *ton* as unit of measure derives from the Old French tonne cask, large wine container dating from 16th century.

MEXICO Bordered by four U.S. states: Texas, New Mexico, Arizona and California.

MEXICO CITY Capital of Mexico and largest city in Mexico, Latin America and Western Hemisphere. Second-largest city in world (after Shanghai). Fourth-most-populated city in world: city, approximately 8,988,230; metropolitan area, 13,993,866. Oldest American capital city. Villages established on its site by 1500 B.C. Capital of Aztec Indian Empire, 1325.

MGM GRAND HOTEL Luxury hotel, Las Vegas, NV. Fire, November 21, 1980, killed 84 people. Over 3,500 guests rescued by helicopter from roof. Fire alarms and sprinklers never worked. Presumed cause, electrical short.

MGM LION Leo, the MGM lion, has roared at start of every film released by Metro-Goldwyn-Mayer since company was formed in 1925.

MIAMI Fifty-eight percent of city's inhabitants born in U.S. Cubans make up ⅓ of population. Strong Latin culture. Once known as "Little Havana." Distance from Cuba 200 mi. (320 km.). Miami Beach, famous resort and suburb of Miami, lies across Biscayne Bay; accommodates more than 200,000 visitors at a time, more than two million annually.

MIAMI DOLPHINS Coached by Don Shula, 1972–1973, Miami team of American Football Conference remained unbeaten by sweeping 14 regular-season games and three play-off games, including 14–7 win over Washington in Super Bowl VII in Los Angeles. Among stars were quarterbacks Bob Griese, Earl Morrall, running backs Larry Csonka, Jim Kiick and Mercury Morris, receiver Paul Warfield, kicker Garo Ypremian.

MICHAEL ANTHONY Character portrayed by Marvin Miller on popular TV series *The Millionaire* (1955–1960). Anthony would deliver one-million-dollar cashier's check to an unsuspecting individual, money from account of eccentric multibillionaire John Beresford Tipton.

MICHELANGELO (1475–1564) Most prolific and admired artist of Italian Renaissance. Born Michelangelo di Lodovico Buonarroti Simoni. Painter, sculptor and architect known for monumental projects and noble renderings in all forms. Among his best-known works *The Pietà* (c. 1500), statue of Mary holding Jesus after he is taken down from the cross, stands in St. Peter's, Rome; *David* (1504). Returning home to Florence in 1501, Michelangelo was commissioned by city to work on giant block of marble no other sculptor had been able to use. Carved *David*, 18 ft. statue located in Galleria dell Accademia, Florence; Sistine Chapel (1508–1512), Pope Julius II commissioned Michelangelo to paint ceilings and walls of Pope's private chapel (built 1473). On ceiling used principal themes of Bible: creation (with God's right hand reaching out to Adam with spark of life); man's temptation and fall; Noah and the flood. Medici Tombs (1520–1534), designed and decorated chapel for Medici family, rulers of Florence, patrons of artists. Sculpted tomb of Lorenzo di Medici "the Magnificent"(1449–1492) and other family members.

MICHENER, JAMES ALBERT (1907–   ) American novelist. Work features exotic locales and historical figures. Recently known for *Hawaii* (1965), *Centennial* (1974), *Chesapeake* (1978) and *Poland* (1983). Also wrote *Tales of the South Pacific* (1947), winner, 1948 Pulitzer Prize for Fiction. Vignettes about American servicemen and women on New Caledonia and Solomon Islands during World War II. Rodgers and Hammerstein turned it into musical *South Pacific. The Bridges at Toko-Ri* (1953), Korean War story about pilot on dangerous mission while wife awaits his return. William Holden, Grace Kelly and Mickey Rooney starred in 1954 film version. *Iberia: Spanish Travels and Reflections* (1968), travelogue of 10 Spanish cities, observing art, history, customs, politics and mystique. Photos by Robert Vavra. *Sports in America* (1976) was his far-ranging personal look at participatory and spectator sports and its relation to public, role of media and government control, with extensive section on big-time college athletes; Pulitzer Prize—winner.

MICHIGAN Auto-making center of United States. Longest shoreline 3,288 mi. (5,292 km.) of any inland state. Touches four Great Lakes, Michigan, Superior, Huron, Erie. Lake Michigan separates the state from Milwaukee, WI and Chicago, IL.

MICKEY MOUSE Trademark of Walt Disney Productions. Starred in first synchronized sound cartoon, *Steamboat Willie* (1928). Many short subjects co-star girlfriend Minnie and dog Pluto. Appeared in *Fantasia* (1940) as the Sorcerer's apprentice. Received special Academy Award in 1932, becoming first nonhuman to win Oscar. Walt Disney performed as Mickey's voice from 1928–1947.

MICKEY MOUSE CLUB, THE Popular children's TV series produced by Walt Disney. Host Jimmie Dodd and "Big Mooseketeer" Roy Williams would lead Mouseketeers (Annette Funicello, Cubby O'Brien, Karen Pendleton, Doreen Tracey, Bobby Burgess, Cheryl Holdridge, others) in story and song.

MIDEAST WAR Joint attack on Israel by Syria and Egypt, October 6, 1973. Egypt driven back quickly, signed a cease-fire, November 11. War with Syria continued until May 31, 1974. Because Arab countries chose to attack on Israel's highest holy day, Yom Kippur, the war also known as Yom Kippur War.

MIDLER, BETTE (1945–   ) Singer who first performed at Continental Baths, a gay bathhouse in New York City. Turned actress. First album, *The Divine Miss M* (1972). Starred in films, including *The Rose* (1979) and *Jinxed* (1982).

MIDNIGHT COWBOY First X-rated motion picture to win Best Picture Oscar. Directed by John Schlesinger, 1969; film about young Texan (Jon Voight) who comes to New York City looking for easy money, and is befriended by street-wise punk (Dustin Hoffman). Theme song, "Everybody's Talkin'," sung by Harry Nilsson.

MIKADO, THE Gilbert and Sullivan's operetta about son of Japanese emperor who disguises himself as wandering minstrel to forget his lost love, first filmed in 1939.

MILE HIGH STADIUM Home of NFL's Denver Broncos and Denver Gold (U.S. Football League). Capacity 75,103. So named because Denver's elevation is 5,280 ft. above sea level ("the Mile High City").

MILES   Statute mile: 5,280 ft. (1.609 km.), or 1,760 yd. Square mile: Measure of area equal to content of square with a side whose length is one mile. Nautical mile: Unit of length equal to 1.5616 statute mi. (6,080.27 ft/1,853 km.).

MILK   America's most popular beverage, nearly complete food nutritionally, since it is almost perfectly balanced. Dairy products, America's most widely used products, account for 13% of food annually consumed.

MILKY WAY   Spiral galaxy. Contains solar system. Consists of stars, gas and dust, giving it milky appearance. All stars visible to naked eye are part of it. Approximately 500 million galaxies within reach of largest telescopes.

MILLER, ARTHUR (1915–   )   American dramatist whose plays deal with social issues such as anti-Semitism, fascism and political persecution. Among them: *Death of a Salesman* (1949), Pulitzer Prize–winning play, written in six weeks, centering on last two days in life of 63-year-old salesman Willy Loman, his relationship with his family. Lee J. Cobb created role, played by Frederick March in 1952 film version. Dustin Hoffman starred in 1984 Broadway revival. *The Crucible* (1953), based on witch trials and hangings in Salem, MA, in 1692. Some mischievous girls make spurious accusations, and by play's end otherwise good, pious people are condemning others to gallows. Parable for McCarthy-era witch hunts. *After the Fall* (1964), autobiographical drama in which heroine Maggie is modeled on Miller's second wife, actress Marilyn Monroe, who died in 1962. Miller wrote screenplay for her final film, *The Misfits* (with Clark Gable, 1961).

MILLER, GLENN (1904–1944)   Bandleader, composer and trombone player, whose "new sound" was immensely popular during World War II. Hits include "In the Mood" and "Chattanooga Choo Choo." Theme song, "Moonlight Serenade." James Stewart starred in film biography, *The Glenn Miller Story* (1953), featuring singing trumpet-player Louis Armstrong.

MILLER, HENRY (1891–1980)   American novelist. His books were banned in U.S. and Britain until 1960s because of alleged obscenity. *Tropic of Cancer* (1934) and *Tropic of Capricorn* (1939) not published in U.S. until 1961. *The Rosy Crucifixion*, an autobiographical trilogy consists of *Sexus* (1949), *Plexus* (1953) and *Nexus* (1959). Became eloquent spokesman against censorship.

MILLER, JASON (1939–) Playwright. Wrote *That Championship Season*, 1973 Pulitzer Prize and Tony Award winner. Debuted 1972. About reunion of four middle-aged men, ex-members of state championship basketball team honoring their coach.

MILLER, MITCH (1911–) Record producer turned TV host and star of *Sing Along With Mitch* (1961–1966). Old favorites and current popular songs were sung by Mitch's Sing-Along Gang or featured guest vocalists.

MILLER, ROGER (1936–) Country singer, composer of over 300 songs, many of which have been million-sellers. Hits include "Dang Me," "Chug-A-Lug," and "King of the Road" in which "rooms to let" cost $.50 cents. Winner of 11 Grammy Awards.

MILLER, WILLIAM EDWARD (1914–1983) American politician. Congressman from New York, 1951–1964. Chairman, Republican National Committee, 1961–1964. Ran for vice-president, 1964, on Barry Goldwater's conservative Republican ticket. Lost by 15,951,244 votes to Democratic incumbent Lyndon B. Johnson. Quit politics after this defeat.

MILLETT, KATE (KATHERINE MURRAY) (1934–) American sculptor, teacher, feminist author. *Sexual Politics* (1970) grew out of her Ph.D. dissertation at Columbia University. *Flying* (1974), an autobiographical work in which she describes her marriage, love affairs and relationship with her disapproving mother.

MILLS, WILBUR (1909–) Democratic congressman from Arkansas, 1939–1977. His 1976 affair with striptease dancer Fanne Fox, nicknamed the "Argentine Firecracker," and his alcoholism became public. He did not seek reelection.

MILNE, ALAN ALEXANDER (A. A.) (1882–1956) English dramatist, novelist, humorist, best remembered for his children's books. Originally written for his son Christopher Robin, *Winnie-the-Pooh* (1926) and *The House at Pooh Corner* (1928) have toy bear Pooh as their hero. Other characters include Eeyore the Donkey, Tigger the Tiger, Kanga and Roo—a kangaroo and her child—and Piglet. Christopher Robin is only human character. Other Milne children's books include *When We Were Very Young* (1924) and *Now We Are Six* (1927), both collections of verse.

MILTON, JOHN (1608–1674) English poet and essayist. Becoming progressively blind during life, wrote through secretaries.

Epic poem *Paradise Lost* (1667) about Adam and Eve's expulsion from Garden of Eden. Sequel *Paradise Regained* (1671) deals with Christ's struggle against Satan in the wilderness. Also wrote sonnets and political pamphlets.

MILWAUKEE BRAVES   Baseball team. Moved to Atlanta following 1965 season. Franchise had moved to Milwaukee after playing in Boston 1876–1952. While in Milwaukee, won National League pennants in 1957, 1958 and World Series 1958. Among great Milwaukee Braves: Hall of Famers Hank Aaron, outfield; Eddie Matthews, third base; Warren Spahn, pitcher.

MILWAUKEE COUNTY STADIUM   Home of Milwaukee Brewers of American Baseball League since 1970, when Seattle Pilots franchise arrived. Home of Milwaukee Braves, 1953–1965. Green Bay Packers of National Football League play some games there. Capacity 53,192 (baseball), 55,958 (football). Drawing on city's brewing tradition, also site of "world's largest beer barrel"— actually, little house shaped like beer barrel; after Milwaukee homer, Brewers' team mascot Bernie Brewer slides down "barrel" into simulated mug of beer, unleashing helium balloons.

MINNEAPOLIS   Largest city in Minnesota, nicknamed "City of Lakes." Word from Indian *minne* meaning "water" and Greek *polis* meaning "city." Due to northern latitude, has average temperature of 14°F (−10°C) in January. Farther north than Toronto, Canada and Milwaukee, WI.

MINNESOTA   State with lake area covering more than 4,000 sq. mi. (10,400 sq. km.). Called "Land of 10,000 Lakes" but actually has 20,000.

MINNESOTA FATS (1913–   )   Pool hustler born Rudolf Wanderone, Jr., portrayed by Jackie Gleason in 1961 movie *The Hustler*, co-starring Paul Newman. Real-life Fats hosted TV shows *Minnesota Fats Hustles the Pros* and *Celebrity Billiards*. Member Pool Hall of Fame; still plays some exhibitions and TV specials.

MINNESOTA VIKINGS   National Football League team that lost a record four Super Bowls: 1970 to Kansas City Chiefs, 23-7; 1974 to Miami Dolphins, 24-7; 1975 to Pittsburgh Steelers, 16-6; 1977 to Oakland Raiders, 32-14. Dallas Cowboys have lost three. Miami Dolphins and Washington Redskins have each lost two. Pittsburgh Steelers (1975, 1976, 1979, 1980) have won the most.

MINOAN CIVILIZATION   Ancient Cretan Bronze Age culture, approximately 2500–1400 B.C. Named after legendary King Minos, who is said to have built labyrinthian palace at Knossos, where the Minotaur lived. Civilization destroyed by fire and earthquakes.

MINOW, NEWTON (1926–) Chairman of F.C.C. (Federal Communications Commission) appointed by President Kennedy in 1961. Won high visibility with speech at Broadcasters Convention, May 9, 1961, in which he declared TV programming to be a "vast wasteland."

MINT JULEP Cocktail traditionally served at Kentucky Derby. Winning owner toasts horse with silver Julep Cup, later inscribed with winner's name and added to Churchill Downs' collection. Made with one tsp. sugar, shaved ice, Kentucky bourbon; decorated with fresh mint.

MIRACLE METS. See NEW YORK METS

MIRACLE ON 34TH STREET Director George Seaton adapted Valentine Davies' story for 1947 movie about department store Santa Claus in Macy's New York City store. Natalie Wood played doubting little girl. Seaton and Edmund Gwenn, for his portrayal of Kris Kringle, won Oscars. Kris Kringle is Pennsylvania Dutch name for Santa Claus.

MIRACLE WORKER, THE 1962 film based on true story of teacher Anne Sullivan's dedicated efforts to help young Helen Keller emerge from sightless and soundless world. Anne Bancroft won Best Actress Oscar as Sullivan; Patty Duke was Best Supporting Actress as Keller.

MIRRORS: SUPERSTITIONS Breaking of mirror thought to bring seven years of bad luck. First mirrors: lakes and pools. Used to view one's fate. If face seemed distorted, taken as portent of evil.

MISFITS, THE Dramatic 1961 film written by Arthur Miller, about young divorcée with three cowboys on savage hunt for wild mustangs. The last film for its stars Clark Gable and Marilyn Monroe.

MISS AMERICA Pageant held each year in Atlantic City, NJ. Contest first held in 1921; 16-year-old Margaret Gorman was first winner. In 1948, Miss Montana and her gaited palomino horse almost tumbled into orchestra pit; animal acts have been barred ever since. Bert Parks gained fame as host of contest since 1965. Ron Ely replaced Parks in 1979.

MISS JEAN BRODIE Fictional Scottish spinster school-teacher whose students were "la crême de la crême" was portrayed on screen by Maggie Smith, in *The Prime of Miss Jean Brodie* (1969), which won her Oscar for Best Actress.

MISS MONEYPENNY. See FLEMING, IAN

MISS PIGGY Jim Jenson's Muppet superstar Miss Piggy graced cover of August 1980 *Life* magazine after her role in 1979 *Muppet Movie*. Stories about her also appeared that year in *Harper's Bazaar*, *Redbook*, *Saturday Evening Post*, *McCall's*, *Seventeen* and *People*. After starring in sequel, *The Great Muppet Caper* (1981), she wrote *Ms. Piggy's Guide to Life*, collaborating with humorist Henry Beard, a founder of *National Lampoon* (1970) and co-author (with late *Lampoon* editor Doug Kenney) of *Harvard Lampoon's* 1969 J. R. R. Tolkien parody *Bored of the Rings*.

MISSION: IMPOSSIBLE TV adventure series, 1966–1973. A select group of agents for the IMF (Imposssible Missions Force) would take on top-secret assignments to save the Free World. Each mission would be described on audio tape—which, after being played, would self-destruct in five seconds.

MISSISSIPPI State flower: magnolia; State bird: mickingbird; State tree: magnolia; State song: "Go Mis-sis-sip-pi!" by Houston Davis.

MISSISSIPPI RIVER Fourth longest river in Western Hemisphere: 2,300 mi. (3703 km.). Mississippi Valley claimed for France, 1682, by explorer Robert Cavelier. United States bought most of area in Louisiana Purchase, 1803. U.S.'s longest and North America's chief river. Flows 2,384 mi. (3,799 km.) from Lake Itasca, MI to Gulf of Mexico. Called "The Father of Waters," because many of its tributaries turn into major rivers: Illinois River, Missouri River, Ohio River, Arkansas River. Major cities along river's banks include St. Louis, New Orleans, Memphis, Kansas City, Pittsburgh, Cincinnati, Louisville, Nashville. Also on its banks are the Twin Cities (Minneapolis and St. Paul), which the river divides.

MISSOURI U.S. battleship. Largest ever built. Main batteries of nine 16-inch guns, capable of firing 23 miles; 45,000 tons displacement. Scene of Japan's formal surrender ending World War II, September 2, 1945, Tokyo Bay.

MISSPELLS Commonly misspelled. Made up of *spells* and prefix *mis*, meaning "wrong." Spelled with three *s*'s. Same construction for words like *missay* and *misspeak*.

MISTRAL Train which at one time traveled from Nice to Paris. Service discontinued, 1981. TRV (Train Grand Vitesse) now makes trip. One must travel from Nice to Marseilles and change trains to continue to Paris. Entire trip takes approximately 8½ hours.

MITCH RYDER AND THE DETROIT WHEELS Popular rock group in the late 1960s. Hit songs include "Jenny Take a Ride" (1966) and "Sock It to Me Baby" (1967). Biggest hit was a medley of "Devil with a Blue Dress On" and "Good Golly Miss Molly" in 1966.

MITCHELL, MARGARET (1900–1949) American novelist whose only book, *Gone with the Wind* (1936), sold more than eight million copies and won Pulitzer Prize (1937) by time of her death. First edition weighed three pounds, had 1,037 pages and sold for $3. Turned into sweeping movie success which won nine Oscars and opened at Loew's Grand Theatre in Atlanta, GA, on December 15, 1939. Film starred Clark Gable, Vivien Leigh, Leslie Howard, Olivia de Havilland, Thomas Mitchell, Hattie McDaniel—who became first black to win an Oscar—and Butterfly McQueen as Prissy, the ever-nervous maid. Soap opera-type movie running nearly four hours, based on novel depicting Civil War and Reconstruction from Southern viewpoint. Opens with 19-year-old Tarleton twins Brent and Stuart predicting inevitability of war to heroine Scarlett O'Hara, but she is interested only in herself and upcoming picnic at Twelve Oaks, mansion of Ashley Wilkes, whom she wants to marry. After Wilkes spurns her for Melanie Hamilton, she marries Melanie's brother Charles for spite. He and second husband, Frank Kennedy, both die and after living in Atlanta (which she hates because it's full of "pushy people"), she returns to mansion Tara, whose land is her true love, and marries dashing but shady entrepreneur Rhett Butler. They have child, Bonnie Blue, who dies when thrown from her pony (Rhett shoots it). In last chapter of book and last scene of movie, he leaves Scarlett with famous line, "Frankly, Scarlett, I don't give a damn." Scarlett intends to go back to beloved Tara—all she had left—and says her closing line, "Tomorrow is another day."

MITCHELL, BILLY (1879–1936) Combat air commander, World War I. Promoted to brigadier general, 1918, leading largest armada of the time (1,500 planes). In 1925 he accused War and Navy Departments of negligence. After court-martial and suspension of rank, he resigned.

MITCHELL, MARTHA (1918—1976) Wife of Attorney General John Mitchell. Known for candor with the press. Advocated discipline for Vietnam war protestors and suppression of the press if it continued to reveal government secrets. After Watergate scandal broke, she openly criticized many members of the administration.

MIX, TOM (1881–1940) Real-life cowboy who became a star of silent western films. With Tony the Wonder Horse, he starred in many movies from 1910 on, including *Prairie Trails* (1920), *Riders of the Purple Sage* (1925), *Destry Rides Again* (1932) and *The Miracle Rider* (1935).

MOBY DICK. See MELVILLE, HERMAN

MOCHA Either a choice variety of coffee or flavoring made from coffee and chocolate.

MOCK TURTLE Pathetic character Alice meets in Wonderland. Never stops crying in Lewis Carroll's *Alice's Adventures in Wonderland* (1865), and sequel, *Through the Looking Glass and What Alice Found There* (1872). Author (real name Charles Dodgson) modeled Alice after Alice Liddell, daughter of colleague at Oxford.

MODEL T FORD Introduced, 1909; one of most successful cars ever. By 1920, nearly a million, nicknamed "Tin Lizzie" or "Flivver," were sold a year. Henry Ford said, "Any customer can have a car of any color he wants, provided it's black."

MODERN TIMES 1936 film by Charlie Chaplin which spoofs the perils of machine age. His last "silent film"—soundtrack had only sound effects, and music (including his song "Smile"). Paulette Goddard played his true love.

MOHAMMED (570–632 A.D.) "The Prophet." His preachings formed basis of the religion Islam, main religion of Africa, Middle East and parts of Asia. Followers of Islam are known as Muslims for the Arab word meaning "one who submits to God."

MOLASSES Sweet syrup which is by-product of sugar refining. Added to white sugar to make brown sugar. Good source of iron. Rum is made from it.

MONA LISA, THE. See DA VINCI, LEONARDO

MONACO   Tiny principality covering 0.6 sq. mi. (1.6 sq. km.), bordering Mediterranean Sea. Coastline only 3.5 mi. (5.6 km.) long, shortest of any country. Noted as shelter from income taxes. Revenue comes from indirect taxes, such as excise, transfer, stamp and estate taxes. Contrary to opinion, famed Monte Carlo casinos earn only 3% of government revenues. Capital is Monaco-ville, where prince's palace, oceanographic museum and 19th-century Romanesque Byzantine cathedral are all located. Country has highest population density: 45,195 per sq. mi. (17,450 per sq. km.). Ruled by Grimaldi family since late 13th century. Current monarch, Prince Ranier III, married former movie actress Grace Kelly.

MONGOOSE   Small animal of Africa and Asia famous for its snake-killing ability. Introduced into some Caribbean islands to control rats, but became over-populated pests. Law banning their importation into U.S. passed 1902. Plural is *mongooses*, not *mongeese*, because word has nothing to do with fowl. English spelling derived from Hindi word *mangus*. Kipling's Rikki-Tikki-Tavi in *The Jungle Book* is mongoose kept as pet.

MONITOR AND MERRIMAC   Iron-plated warships. Also called "ironclads." Fought famous yet stalemated battle, March 8, 1862, during American Civil War. Battle was first encounter between armored ships; first in which ships relied solely on steam power for maneuvering.

MONKEY WRENCH   Type of pipe wrench with adjustable jaws. First wrenches with movable jaws probably date from about 1700 in France. First wrench patent granted to Solyman Merrick in 1835. First truly practical pipe wrench with adjustable jaws was the Stillson wrench, for which Daniel Stillson of Massachusetts was granted patent No. 184,993 in 1876.

MONOPOLY   Board game based on business and real estate. Names of "properties" taken from Atlantic City, NJ, where inventor Charles Darrow vacationed. Patented, 1833. Has sold more than 80 million copies since Parker Brothers purchased rights, 1935. Sold in 24 countries, translated into 15 languages. Banned in U.S.S.R.

MONOPOLY BANKROLL   Before game begins, each player receives $1,500 from bank: two $500 bills, two $100 bills, two $50 bills, six $20 bills, five $10 bills, five $5 bills and five $1 bills. During game, each player receives an additional $200 from banker every time his or her token passes GO! square.

MONOPOLY BOARD   Has total of 40 spaces: 28 properties, including 22 avenues, 4 railroads and 2 utilities; 3 Chance spaces; 3 Community Chest spaces; 1 Income Tax space; 1 Luxury Tax space; 1 Jail space; 1 Go to Jail space; 1 Free Parking Space and GO. Railroads are Reading, Pennsylvania, B&O and Short Line, each costing $200; utilities are Electric Company and Water Works, each costing $150. The avenue properties are separated into eight color groups: purple—Mediterranean ($60), Baltic ($60); light blue—Oriental ($100), Vermont ($100), Connecticut ($120); maroon—St. Charles Place ($140), States ($140), Virginia ($160); orange—St. James Place ($180), Tennessee ($180), New York ($200); red—Kentucky ($220), Indiana ($220), Illinois ($240); yellow—Atlantic ($260), Ventnor ($260), Marvin Gardens ($280); green—Pacific ($300), North Carolina ($300), Pennsylvania ($320); dark blue—Park Place ($350) and Boardwalk ($400). When a player lands on another's property, rent must be paid to the owner. Rent varies according to property value; lowest is $2 for Mediterranean ($250 with hotel), highest is $50 for Boardwalk ($2,000 with hotel). Chance and Community Chest spaces prompt player to draw top card from pile (16 of each type). Cards may be in player's favor (winning second prize in beauty contest—collect $10), or to their disadvantage (paying poor tax of $15).

MONOPOLY LANDING PROBABILITIES   In order of probability,

Colors most often landed on:
1. Orange
2. Red
3. Yellow
4. Green
5. Maroon
6. Lt. Blue
7. Dk. Blue
8. Purple

Spaces most often landed on:
1. Jail (sent to)
2. Illinois Avenue
3. GO
4. B&O Railroad
5. Free Parking

MONOPOLY TOKENS   Eight tokens are shoe, top hat, thimble, flat iron, dog, wheelbarrow, race car and battleship. Each player moves his token according to throw of dice or instructions from card or board.

MONOSODIUM GLUTAMATE (MSG)   Flavor enhancer; accentuates taste without contributing its own flavor. Origins in Far East: seaweeds used for centuries to improve flavor of soups. Overconsumption may cause illness sometimes known as Chinese Restaurant Syndrome, characterized by facial pressure, chest pain and tingling sensations throughout body.

MONROE, MARILYN (1926–1962)   Actress, singer and sex symbol. Born Norma Jean Mortenson. Daughter of schizophrenic mother. Raised by dozens of foster parents. Married James Doughtery, aircraft worker, to escape being ward of state. Later married and divorced both ballplayer Joe DiMaggio (1954) and playwright Arthur Miller (1956). Admirer of Frank Sinatra's music; Sinatra once presented her with white poodle named Mafia. Attended President Kennedy's 45th birthday celebration, May 19, 1962, at Madison Square Garden, where she sang "Happy Birthday." Her figure was used by Walt Disney as model for Tinkerbell. Found dead, June 21, 1962, of overdose of sleeping pills.

MONROVIA   Capital and educational center of Liberia. Named for James Monroe, fifth president of U.S. Founded in 1922 by American Colonization Society.

MONSOON   Seasonal wind. Result of difference in temperature of air over Asia and Indian Ocean. Southwesterly monsoon, April–October, brings heavy rains. Australia, Africa and North America also have monsoons.

MONT BLANC TUNNEL   First all-year, all-weather road connection through the Alps between France and Italy. Built under Mont Blanc Massif, 1965.

MONTANA   U.S. state bordered by Canadian provinces of British Columbia, Alberta and Saskatchewan (all to the north) and U.S. states of Idaho (to the west and southwest), Wyoming (to the south), South Dakota (to the southeast) and North Dakota (to the east).

MONTEVIDEO   Largest city and capital of Uruguay, South America's smallest republic. Active port located on country's southern coast. Fifty percent of country's population live in Montevideo.

MONTHS, NAME ORIGINS

Month	Origin
January	After Janus, god of doors, gates, beginnings
February	Month of *februa* or "purification feast."
March	After war god, Mars.

April	Possibly from *aperine*, "to open," for spring month opening the year.
May	After goddess Maiia.
June	After Juno, goddess of marriage, childbirth and adult life.
July	After Julius Caesar.
August	After Emperor Augustus.
September	From Latin *septem* meaning seven; seventh month.
October	From Latin *octo* meaning "eighth."
November	From Latin *novem* meaning "nine."
December	From Latin *decem* meaning "ten."

MONTREAL   Largest city in Canada and largest French-speaking city after Paris. Located on Island of Montreal, triangular island in St. Lawrence River at eastern end of St. Lawrence seaway. Built around Mount Royal. One of world's largest inland seaports.

MONTREAL CANADIENS   Through 1984, "Les Habitants," as they are known by their fans, had won 21 Stanley Cup championships (National Hockey League trophy). Won five in a row, 1956-60, four in a row, 1976-79. Last win, 1979. Closest to the "Habs" are Toronto Maple Leafs (11) and Detroit Red Wings (7).

MONTY PYTHON   Ensemble name for group of British nonsense comedians who were very popular on TV in 1970s. Members Graham Chapman, John Cleese, Terry Gilliam, Terry Jones, Eric Idle and Michael Palin; also made theatrical films including *Monty Python and the Holy Grail* (1975) and *The Life of Brian* (1979), biblical parody banned in Scotland.

MOON   Completes one trip around the earth in 27⅓ days, about one month. The period from full moon to full moon lasts about 29½ days. The moon revolves once around its axis also in about one month. Its gravity is ⅙ that of earth: a 180-pound man weighs 30 lb. Moon is slowly moving further from Earth, at rate calculated to be about one-half inch per year.

MOON WALK   Goal set by President J. F. Kennedy in 1963 was achieved when *Apollo 11* landed on moon, 4:17 EST, July 20, 1969. First men to step onto moon's surface were Neil Armstrong and Edwin Aldrin, Jr. The New York *Times* headline the following day read: "Men Walk on the Moon."

MOON'S A BALLOON, THE. See NIVEN, DAVID

MOON, REVEREND SUN MYUNG (1920–)
Founded Unification Church, 1950s in Korea. Religion claims over three million followers in 40 countries. Introduced to U.S., 1971. Based on Christian doctrine, Moon's religious revelations and anticommunism.

MOORE, ARCHIE (1916–   )   Boxer known as "The Mongoose" or, more frequently, "Old Man River," because he fought until nearly age 50. Held world light-heavyweight championship, 1952–1960. At age 44 in 1960, when stripped of title for nondefense, was oldest to hold world boxing title. Lost to Rocky Marciano (1955) and Floyd Patterson (1956) in bids for heavyweight title. Had record 140 career knockouts.

MOORE, CLEMENT CLARKE (1779–1883)   American poet and educator. Best known for poem "A Visit from St. Nicholas," written for his children in 1822, first published anonymously in Troy, NY *Sentinel* (1823), reprinted in *Poems* (1844). In poem, which begins," 'Twas the night before Christmas," he names Santa's reindeer, and describes visions of sugar plums dancing in dreams of children asleep on Christmas Eve. Moore also founded, in 1819, and taught at General Theological Seminary.

MOORE, ROBIN (ROBERT LOWELL) (1925–)
American novelist. Wrote *The French Connection* (1969), which became 1971 Oscar-winning film and *The Green Berets* (1965), book of short-stories based on operations of U.S. Special Forces in South Vietnam where he served as correspondent and underwent Special Forces training, earning coveted green hat of title and of group's nickname.

MORAL MAJORITY   Controversial religious and political organization. Founded, 1979, by Virginia evangelist Reverend Jerry Falwell. Opposes pornography, abortion, homosexuality and the E.R.A.; supports school prayer.

MORE, SIR THOMAS (1478–1535)   English statesman and author. His *Utopia* (1516) described imaginary Pacific island ruled by philosophers who formulated ideal state built on reason. "Utopia" has come to mean any ideal place. More beheaded for treason after refusing to accept Act of Supremacy making Henry VIII head of Church of England. Roman Catholic saint whose life is basis of play and film *A Man for All Seasons*.

MORMONS   Mormon Church, also called Church of Jesus Christ of Latter-Day Saints. Founder, Joseph Smith. Believe religious benefits bestowed on living proxies can have beneficial effect on dead. Settled Salt Lake City, Utah, 1847.

MOROCCO   Located in North Africa. Ruled by Hassan II. Inhabitants' favorite foods are lamb, chicken, fruits and vegetables. Mechoui (whole roasted lamb) and pastilla (salted pie containing lamb, eggs, pigeon, chicken, vegetables, spices) are popular dishes. Coca-Cola is most popular soft drink.

MORPHINE   Narcotic painkiller. Addictive. Used as sedative, to relieve breathing difficulties, to treat diarrhea, occasionally as anesthetic. Also used to control labor pains in pregnant women. Named after Greek god of dreams, Morpheus.

MORRIS THE CAT   The "finicky" cat in "9-Lives" cat food TV commercials, also appeared in Burt Reynolds movie *Shamus* (1973). The original Morris died at height of success at age 17.

MORSE, SAMUEL F. B. (1791–1872)   American inventor and artist. Built first telegraph in U.S., 1844. Line ran from U.S. Supreme Court, Washington, DC, to Baltimore, MD. First message was biblical phrase, "What hath God wrought." Inventor of Morse Code.

MORTALITY AND LIFE EXPECTANCY   In U.S.:

Mortality Age	Probability/1000	Life Expectancy
Newborn	13.8	73.3 years
10	0.2	74.6
20	1.3	75.0
30	1.3	75.7
40	2.4	76.4
50	6.2	77.6
60	14.9	79.7
70	31.1	83.1
80	75.1	88.1

MORTON, JELLY ROLL (1885–1941)   Jazz pioneer Ferdinand Morton, nicknamed "Jelly Roll," was one of first musicians to forge ragtime, blues and popular music into what is now American jazz. Pianist, composer and bandleader, Morton's biggest hits include "Wolverine Blues" and "King Porter Stomp."

MOSCONI, WILLIAM JOSEPH (WILLIE) (1913–)
World pocket billiards champion, 1941–1948 and 1950–1957.
Technical assistant for movie *The Hustler*, (1961). Holds record for
longest billiards run: 526 straight balls. Still plays exhibitions and
special TV events.

MOSCOW   Capital of U.S.S.R. and location of Europe's tallest
building—Television Center, Moscow, 1,179 ft. (353.7 m.), tops
other European structures including Eiffel Tower, Paris, 984 ft.
(295.2 m.); M. V. Lomonosov State University, Moscow, 787 ft.
(236 m.); Palace of Culture and Science, Warsaw, 741 ft. (222.3 m.).

MOSES   Before leading Jews from Egypt and receiving Ten Commandments, Moses had been forced to flee Egypt after murdering
a man. Stopping by a well in Midian, defends seven sisters from
sheperds preventing them from drawing water. In thanks, their father
takes Moses in and he lives as shepherd in Midian for 40 years,
until God calls him from Burning Bush and sends him back to Egypt.

**MOSES, GRANDMA (ANNA MARY ROBERTSON
MOSES) (1860–1961)**   American primitive painter, untrained
in art, who began painting in her seventies. A farm wife, she painted
simple, colorful, carefree scenes of New England farm life.

MOSLEMS   Those who practice Islam religion, founded by Muhammad in A.D. 600s. *Muslim* means "one who submits (to God)"
in Arabic. Holy book, the Koran, requires followers to obey Five
Pillars of Islam. Also forbids them to eat pork, drink liquor or
gamble. Muslim mourners must wear white.

MOSQUITO   Two-winged fly. May carry germs which cause
malaria, yellow fever and encephalitis. Only females bite—to provide nourishment for developing eggs. Bite stabs victim with six
needlelike prongs. Like all insects, they have no teeth. Females may
live three times longer than males.

MOTHER TERESA (1910—   )   Founder of Missionaries
of Charity in Calcutta, 1948. Awarded Nobel Peace Prize, 1979.
She has since opened facilities for the poor in blighted areas of New
York City and Newark, NJ.

MOTHER'S DAY   American version, which occurs on second
Sunday of May, was originally idea of Julia Ward Howe, author of
"The Battle Hymn of the Republic." She named July 4 Independence
Day and urged that the day be used for promoting peace.

MOUNT ETNA   Rises 11,122 ft. (3,390 m.) on eastern coast and most populated region of Sicily. First recorded eruption in 700 B.C. Eighty have since occured.

MOUNT EVEREST   World's highest mountain. Rises 29,028 ft. (8.9 km.) above sea level. Part of Himalayan range in Tibet and Nepal. Named for British surveyor-general of India, Sir George Everest. Called "Goddess Mother of the Earth" by locals.

MOUNT FUJI   Highest, 12,388 ft. (3,776 m.) and most sacred mountain in Japan. Rises in an almost perfect cone from lake-covered plain. Favorite theme for Japanese art and poetry. World's most painted, photographed and climbed mountain.

MOUNT HOOD   Inactive volcano. Part of Cascade mountain range in northern Oregon. Rises 11,235 ft. (3,424 m.), Oregon's highest elevation.

MOUNT KENNEDY   Located in southwestern Yukon, Canada, in Saint Elias mountain range. Height: 13,905 ft. (4,172 m.).

MOUNT KILIMANJARO   Extinct volcano in eastern Africa. Two peaks: Kibo, Africa's highest point at 19,340 ft. (5,859 m.), always snow-covered, about 200 ft. (61 m.) deep; and Mawenzi, often called "the mountain of the cold devils" at 17,564 ft. (5,320 m.), which has no glaciers. Coffee is grown on volcano's lower slopes. Highest mountain in continent is not part of a mountain range.

MOUNT OLYMPUS   Greece's highest mountain. Ancient Greeks believed 12 major gods had palaces here. When Greeks discovered mountain was not center of world, and decided gods should be living farther from their worshipers, they began to believe in a heavenly Mount Olympus.

MOUNT RUSHMORE   Located in Black Hills of South Dakota. Granite cliff with carvings commemorating presidents George Washington, Thomas Jefferson, Theodore Roosevelt (only one wearing spectacles) and Abraham Lincoln. Designed by Gutzun Borglum and completed by his son Lincoln, 1941.

MOUNT ST. HELENS   Volcano in Seattle, WA. Erupted several times in 1980 causing millions of dollars damage. More than 60 people reported missing or dead. Explosions blasted away more than 1000 ft. (300 m.) from peak. Chosen "Ashhole of the Year," by *Esquire* magazine in 1980.

MOUNT VERNON Estate of George Washington. Covers 500 acres in Fairfax County, VA. Includes mansion, 15 smaller buildings and tombs of George and Martha Washington. Named after Washington's half brother's British navy commander, Admiral Edward Vernon.

MOUNT VESUVIUS Volcano 4,190 ft. (1,277 m.) overlooking Bay of Naples, Italy. Europe's only active volcano (on mainland). Inactive for several centuries, until August 24, A.D. 79, when erupted and killed 10% of the population of Pompeii, Herculaneum and Stabine.

MOUNTAIN CLIMBING Also called mountaineering. Three principal types: trail climbing; rock climbing, which for the ascent of steep slopes requires use of nylon ropes and pitons (steel spikes driven into rock with piton hammer); and ice climbing, which takes place above timberline.

MOUNTAINS, CONTINENTS' HIGHEST The highest mountains in each continent: Asia, Mt. Everest at 29,028 ft. (8,848 m.); South America, Mt. Aconcagua at 22,831 ft. (6,959 m); North America, Mt. McKinley at 20,320 ft. (6,194 m.); Africa, Mt. Kilimanjaro at 19,340 ft. (5,895 m.); Europe, Mt. Elbrus at 18,481 ft. (5,633 m); Antarctica, Mt. Vinson Massif at 16,864 ft. (5,140 m); Australia, Mt. Kosciusko at 7,310 ft. (2,228 m.);

MOUNTAINS, NORTH AMERICA Three highest mountains in North America:
Mt. McKinley in Alaska, U.S. at 20,320 ft. (6,194 m.); Mt. Logan in Yukon, Canada at 19,524 ft. (5,951 m.); Citlaltepetl (Orizaba) in Pueblo Veracruz, Mexico at 18,855 ft. (5,747 m.).

MOUNTAINS, U.S. Three highest mountains in 48 contiguous states:
Mt. Whitney, CA at 14,494 ft. (4,348 m.); Mt. Elbert, CO at 14,433 ft. (4,329 m.); Mt. Rainier, WA at 14,410 ft. (4,329 m.). Three highest mountains in all 50 states:
Mt. McKinley, AK at 20,320 ft. (6,096 m.); Mt. Whitney, CA at 14,494 ft. (4,348 m.); Mount Elberg, CO at 14,433 ft. (4,329 m.).

MOUNTAINS, WORLD'S HIGHEST Mt. Everest, Tibet/Nepal at 29,028 ft. (8,708 m.); K2, (or Mt. Godwin-Austen),

Kashmir at 28,250 ft. (8,475 m.); Kanchenjunga, India at Nepal 28,208 ft. (8,462 m.).

MOUNTIE   Name for officer of Royal Canadian Mounted Police, Canada's national law enforcement agency. Official uniform consists of broad-brim hat, scarlet jacket and dark blue pants with yellow stripe.

MOUSE THAT ROARED, THE   Peter Sellers and Jean Seberg starred in this 1959 British farce, in which government of Grand Fenwick declares war on U.S. knowing it will lose and, it hopes, be entitled to American financial aid after its surrender.

MOUSETRAP, THE   Play, based on Agatha Christie's short story "Three Blind Mice," failed on Broadway, but is longest-running production in history of British stage. Opened in England, 1952, and still performing.

MOVIE THEATERS   Soviet Union has 154,100, United States 11,110, Rumania 6,084, Italy 5,920, France 5,844.

MOZART, WOLFGANG AMADEUS (1756–1791)   Austrian composer. Wrote "Twinkle, Twinkle Little Star" at age five. Went on concert tour with violinist father at seven. Operas include *The Marriage of Figaro* (1786), *Don Giovanni* (1787) and *The Magic Flute* (1791).

MR. BELVEDERE   Clifton Webb portrayed self-centered genius in three comedy films: *Sitting Pretty* (1948), *Mr. Belvedere Goes to College* (1949) and *Mr. Belvedere Rings the Bell* (1951).

MR. CHIPS. See HILTON, JAMES

MR. MAGOO   Nearsighted old man who starred in many cartoons from 1950 on. Won Oscar for *When Magoo Flew*, Best Short of 1954. Jim Backus was his voice.

MR. PEEPERS   TV comedy series, broadcast live (1952–1955). Wally Cox starred as Mr. Robinson Peepers, shy science teacher, and Tony Randall played his friend, history teacher Harvey Weskit.

MR. ROBERTS   1955 film starring Henry Fonda in title role as cargo ship officer yearning for combat. James Cagney played his eccentric captain; William Powell portrayed the philosophical doctor. Jack Lemmon won Best Supporting Actor Oscar as Ensign Pulver.

MR. SPOCK   Pointy-eared, green-blooded science officer on starship *Enterprise*, portrayed in science-fiction TV series *Star Trek*

(1966–1969) by Leonard Nimoy. Half-human, half-Vulcan, and completely logical, Spock was second-in-command to Captain James T. Kirk (William Shatner). Subject of *Star Trek III: The Search for Spock*. (see STAR TREK)

MRS. MINIVER   1942 Oscar winner for Best Picture, about British family in war-torn England trying to lead normal life during siege of German Blitz. Greer Garson won Best Actress award performing the title role.

MRS. ROBINSON   Hit song by Simon and Garfunkel from 1967 film *The Graduate*. Mrs. Robinson in film, played by Anne Bancroft, seduces lead character, portrayed by Dustin Hoffman. Song discusses Jesus' love for Mrs. Robinson. (see SIMON AND GARFUNKEL)

MULE   Offspring of male donkey and female horse. Cross between female donkey and male horse is a hinny, more difficult to breed. No records of fertile male hinnies or mules; females rarely come into heat. Horses have 64 chromosones; donkeys, 62; hinnies and mules, 63.

MUMBLETY-PEG   Also called Bites, Stagknife, Knifey, Stick Knife, others. Contest to complete series of feats with pocketknife. Knife tossed in air from series of starting positions (e.g., palm of hand, back of hand, atop clenched fist), trying to make knife stick in ground. Was originally victor's privilege to drive peg into ground with as many blows of knife handle as loser needed additional throws to complete game. Vanquished, as penance, had to pull peg out of ground with teeth; hence, "mumble-the-peg," or "mumblety-peg."

MUNICH   West Germany's third-largest city. Capital of Bavaria. Called München in German, meaning "place of the monks." In A.D. 700s, Abbey of Tegernsee located here, giving town its name. Known for producing stained glass for churches. Most important export is beer. Called "Monaco of Bavaria" by Italians. Where Hitler founded Nazi party, 1918.

MUNSON, THURMAN (1947–1979)   New York Yankee catcher and captain. Died August 2, 1979, in plane crash at Akron-Canton Airport near his Ohio home while practicing flying a twin-engine plane he had just purchased. Two others in plane escaped death.

MUNSTERS, THE   Unusual family portrayed in popular 1964

TV comedy series. Herman Munster, who looked like the Frankenstein monster, his wife Lily and father "Grandpa," who both had
vampire tendencies and little Eddie, an aspiring werewolf, lived at
1313 Mockingbird Lane with their niece Marilyn, the only normal
one in the bunch.

MUPPETS, THE   A unique combination of puppets and mar-
ionettes created by Jim Henson. Though around for 20 years on
various variety shows, Henson's creations gained fame on children's
series *Sesame Street* (premiered 1969). Their own *The Muppet Show*
made stars of Kermit the Frog, show's host, and Miss Piggy, who
is in love with him. Have appeared in theatrical feature films: *The
Muppet Movie* (1979), *The Great Muppet Caper* (1981) and *The Muppets
Take Manhattan* (1984).

MURPHY, AUDIE (1924 – 1971)   America's most decorated
soldier in World War II, returned home to write, then star in film
of his autobiography, *To Hell and Back* (1955).

MUSCOVITE   1. Native or resident of city of Moscow or ancient principality of Moscow. 2. Mineral consisting of common or
potassium mica that is usually colorless or pale brown. 3. Color that
is dark greenish gray.

MUSEUMS   World's largest museum is American Museum of
Natural History, covering 23 acres of floor space. Located in New
York City. Second largest is Louvre in Paris, France. Third largest
is British Museum in London, England.

MUSHROOMS   Reproductive organs of certain fungi. Fungus
itself is moldlike and lives in soil or decaying wood. Most mushrooms
have a crown, a top and a stalk; also, gills that release spores.

MUSIAL, STAN (1920 –   )   Outfielder-first baseman for
St. Louis Cardinals, 1941 – 1963. Cardinals retired his number (6)
after career in which he won seven National League batting titles
and three MVP awards and scored 3,630 lifetime hits. Played in 24
All Star games. Nicknamed "Stan the Man." Played on 1942, 1944,
1946 World Series winners. Elected to Hall of Fame, 1969.

MUSIC MAN, THE   1962 film based on Meredith Wilson
Broadway musical. Fast-talking traveling salesman comes to River
City, IA, c. 1912, to organize a boys' band. Robert Preston and
Shirley Jones star.

MUSKIE, EDMUND SIXTUS (1914 –   )   Politician.

Maine's first Democratic senator, 1959–1980. Ran for vice-president on Hubert Humphrey's ticket, 1968. Lost to Nixon-Agnew. Remembered for weeping in public during 1972 New Hampshire Democratic presidential primary campaign after newspaperman William Loeb insulted his wife. Incident cost Muskie credibility, though he won primary by narrow margin. Withdrew from race, July 1972.

MUSLIMS. See MOSLEMS

MUSSOLINI, BENITO (1883–1945) Italian premier, 1922–1945. Founder of facism. Came to power after abduction and murder of former prime minister Giacomo Matteotti, 1924. Mussolini assumed full responsibility for the crime. Called for return to days of Roman Empire. Conquered only Ethopia, 1935. Joined forces with Germany, World War II. Army, unreliable and ill-disciplined. Respected the *iettatore*, or people with the "evil eye." Superstitious of number 13; would never start anything important on a Friday. Put his right hand on specific part of his body to ward off evil. In 1945, allied forces invaded Italy. Mussolini and his mistress, Clara Petacci, captured and shot by Italian underground. Hung from their heels outside Milan gas station.

MUTINY ON THE BOUNTY Classic adventure of 18th-century sea voyage and mutiny against tyrannical Captain Bligh, was made into a movie three times: 1935 version starred Charles Laughton as Bligh and Clark Gable as Fletcher Christian. 1962 remake had Trevor Howard portraying Captain Bligh, with Marlon Brando as Christian. 1984 version starred Anthony Hopkins and Mel Gibson. (see NORDHOFF, CHARLES BERNARD)

MUTT AND JEFF Bud Fisher's comic strip introduced November 15, 1907, as A. Mutt. Jeff appeared March 27, 1908, to be his married friend's buddy. First six-day-a-week strip; by 1920s had become one of America's most widely read comics, although its popularity has declined in recent decades. "A real Mutt-and-Jeff combination" describes two people with opposite characteristics: Mutt (first name Augustus) is the tall one; little Jeff invents the get-rich-quick schemer.

MY DARLING CLEMENTINE "Oh, My Darling Clementine," popular American folk song about days of California gold rush, was written, 1884, by Percy Montrose. In song, Clementine, a miner's daughter, died when she "hit her foot against a splinter," fell into the river and drowned.

MY FAIR LADY   1964 Best Picture, based on the Lerner and Lowe Broadway musical. British elocution teacher takes a London street peddler, mercilessly trains her and passes her off as aristocrat, to win a wager. Audrey Hepburn and Rex Harrison starred. Julie Andrews gained fame as flower-vender Eliza Doolittle on Broadway.

MY FAVORITE MARTIAN   TV comedy series about ship-wrecked Martian Uncle Martin (Ray Walston) and his earthly adventures with his "nephew," earthling reporter Tim O'Hara (Bill Bixby).

MY LITTLE CHICKADEE   1940 comedy film which featured the only team-up between Mae West and W. C. Fields. Out West, Mae is looking for rich husband but falls for bad man.

MY LITTLE MARGIE   TV comedy series, 1952–1955. Margie Albright (Gale Storm) lives with her father Vern (Charles Farrell) and gets mixed up in crazy schemes with their kindly old neighbor, Mrs. Odetts (Gertrude Hoffman).

MY THREE SONS   TV comedy series, 1960–1972. Fred MacMurray starred as Steve Douglas, widower raising his three boys with only the help of his father-in-law, "Bub" O'Casey (William Frawley), and later Uncle Charley (William Demerest). The boys were Mike (Tim Considine), Robbie (Don Grady), Chip (Stanley Livingston) and—after Considine left the cast—Ernie (Barry Livingston). Dog was Tramp.

MYRTLE BEACH   City in southeast South Carolina. One of Atlantic coast's most popular resorts. Beach has miles of soft white sand. About 350,000 vacationers visit each summer. Named for its many myrtle trees.

N

NABOKOV, VLADIMIR (1899–1977) Russian-American novelist and short-story writer. Satirical novel *Lolita* (1955), about middle-aged Professor Hubert Humbert's obsession with 12-year-old title character, made him internationally famous. Wrote *Ada* (1969) and *Pale Fire* (1962).

NADER, RALPH (1934–   ) American lawyer and consumer advocate. Gained national attention for book *Unsafe at Any Speed: The Designed-In Dangers of the American Automobile* (1965), documenting safety defects in American cars, particularly Chevrolet Corvair. Prompted government studies of auto safety and subsequent legislation. Nader himself does not drive. Founded Center for Study of Responsive Law, 1969. Because of his popularity with young people, Dannon Yogurt Co. started using fictitious consumer advocate called Ron Raider in its advertising, 1974–1975; Nader sued Dannon and won $15,000 settlement.

NAGY, DON. See CARTER, DONALD JAMES

NAGY, STEVE JOSEPH (1913–1966) Bowler of the Year, 1952–1955. Set all-time doubles record, 1952, with Johnny Klares. Bowled four 299 games, six 300 games. Steve Nagy Sportsmanship Award now given to "nice guy" bowler of year.

NAILS Hardened skin cells. Grow from skin beneath, called matrix. Crescent or moon-shaped region at base of each nail called lunula, from latin *luna* (moon). Whiteness of lunulas due to smaller cells, which carry less blood. All nails grow at same rate. Diet, abuse and general health affect rate of growth.

NAIROBI   Capital and largest city of Kenya. Popular tourist center. Busiest airport and biggest safari center in East Africa. Home of Nairobi National Park, large wildlife refuge.

NAKED CAME THE STRANGER   Allegedly written by Penelope Ashe, "demure Long Island housewife," this 1969 sex spoof sold more than 90,000 hardbacks and two million paperbacks. Actually written by 25 writers and editors of *Newsday* (Long Island daily newspaper) over one weekend, to demonstrate that trash novel could be written, produced and sold fast. Each chapter written by different person.

NAMATH, JOE WILLIE (1943–   )   Quarterback who led New York Jets to 1970 Super Bowl III upset of Baltimore Colts, 16-7; quoted as saying, "We'll win—I guarantee it." All-American at Alabama under coach Paul "Bear" Bryant. His January 2, 1965, signing for $427,000 gave credibility to American Football League, eventually forcing merger with NFL. Nicknamed "Broadway Joe" for his flamboyant New York life-style.

NAME THAT TUNE   Popular game show in which contestants competed with each other to identify titles of songs played by studio orchestra. Hosts have included Red Benson (1953), Bill Cullen (1954) and George De Witt (1955–1959). Astronaut John Glenn appeared on show and won $25,000.

NANCY DREW   Teenage detective of Carolyn Keene series. Aimed at readers 8 to 13. Debuted in *Secret of the Old Clock*, 1930. Has since appeared in more than 52 novels, selling over 60 million copies.

NANOMINUTE. See METRIC PREFIXES

NAPALM   Jellied gasoline used in bombs and flamethrowers. This mixture of gasoline and naphthenic and palmitic acids sticks to anything when it ignites and kills by burning or suffocating. Used in World War II and Korean and Vietnam wars.

NAPOLEON (1769–1821)   Or Napoleon Bonaparte. Emperor of France, 1804–1815. Born August 15, 1769, in Ajaccio, Corsica; known there as Corsica's most famous son. Also nicknamed "the Corsican General," "the Little Corporal," "the Little Wolf," "the Nightmare of Europe," "Boney," "Tiddy-Doll" and "Corporal Violet" (for swearing he'd return from exile when the violets were in bloom). In 1804 he coerced French senate into naming him emperor. During coronation, as Pope prepared to crown him, grabbed crown and placed it on own head. A military genius, extended empire to cover most of Western and Central Europe at its peak. Loved by his soldiers, once said, "Soldiers win the battles and generals get the credit." Exiled to Elba, small Mediterranean island, April 1815. Organized army to confront Prussian, English and Dutch forces at Waterloo, near Brussels, where he met final defeat. Returned to Paris and abdicated. Exiled permanently to St. Helena, October 1815, where he died, May 5, 1821.

NARCISSUS Beautiful youth of Greek mythology who loved own reflection in pool. Upon dying, turned into flower that now bears his name. Narcissism: neurotic obsession with self.

NARWHAL Whale of Artic. Male has spiral ivory tusk, 8 ft. (2.4 m.) long, extending from left side of head. This feature likens it to unicorn, single-horned animal described in Greek and Roman myths. Young narwhals use tusk in play-fighting; use among adults is unknown.

NASH, OGDEN (1902–1971) Writer of light verse, known for sophisticated whimsy and satire that set tone for *The New Yorker* magazine. Wrote line "Candy is dandy, but liquor is quicker" in "Reflections on Ice-Breaking." Appeared in 1945 collection *Many Years Ago*.

NASSER, GAMAL ABDEL (1918–1970) Egyptian politician and revolutionary nationalist. First president of Republic of Egypt, from 1956 until death in 1970. Led 1952 coup d'état that forced King Farouk from throne.

NASTASE, ILIE (1946–   ) Romanian-born tennis player. Nicknamed "Nasty" because of temperament; also title of 1978 autobiography. Won U.S. Indoor championship, 1970; U.S. Open, 1972; French Open, 1973. Wimbledon runner-up, 1972, 1976. Led Romania to finals of Davis Cup Challenge Round, 1969, 1971, 1972, losing to U.S. each time. Honored as Romanian Master of Sport, 1969.

NATATORIUM Swimming pool, particularly indoor pool; also, building in which swimming pool housed. From Latin *natare* (to swim).

NATCHEZ TRAIL Commercial and military trade route between Nashville, TN, and Natchez, MS. Pioneers traveling down Mississippi River to New Orleans often returned north via this route. Cuts through city of Tupelo, MS.

NATION, CARRY AMELIA MOORE (1846–1911) Temperance activist. Known for violent crusade to stop sale of liquor in U.S. Efforts partially responsible for Prohibition, enacted 1919. First husband, a drunkard, died soon after their marriage. Nation stood 6 ft. tall.

NATIONAL AUDUBON SOCIETY, THE First organization concerned with national conservation in North America; founded, 1905. Aims to educate population as to need and value of protecting plants, soil, water and wildlife. Named after John James Audubon, famous bird painter.

NATIONAL GEOGRAPHIC SOCIETY, THE Largest educational and scientific organization. Founded in 1888, this non-profit organization has eight million members in 185 countries. Publishes *National Geographic* magazine.

NATIONAL VELVET. See BAGNOLD, ENID

NATO. See NORTH ATLANTIC TREATY ORGANIZATION

NATURALS. See CRAPS—PLAY

NAVAL ORANGE Seedless fruit grown for table use in U.S. Actually double fruit because navel is underdeveloped second fruit. Grown by grafting trunks of seedless varieties onto root stocks of other citrus fruits.

NAVRATILOVA, MARTINA (1956–) Defected to U.S. 1975. First Czech tennis player to win women's singles at Wimbledon. Titles won in 1978, 1979, 1982, 1983. Also won 1982 French Open and 1983 U.S. Open. Top woman money-winner in tennis, 1982 ($1.475 million).

NAZCA Of or relating to ancient culture dating back to 2000 B.C. in southern Peru. Known for hard coil pottery and vivid painting, irrigation in area now desert, and weaving. Famous for line drawings of huge triangles, animals, straight lines and spiral forms, made 3,000–4,000 years ago in desert plains between Nazca and Palpa. Great speculation exists as to how designs were created and whether forms are calendars or stellar images.

NBA. See BASKETBALL

NEARSIGHTEDNESS Or myopia. Occurs when eyeball is

too long and images are focused in front of retina. Farsightedness, or hyperopia, occurs when eyeball is too short and images are focused behind retina.

NEGRO Spanish for "black," from Latin *niger*. Applied to race of people living in Africa and sold into slavery in America.

NEHRU, JAWAHARLAL (1889–1964) Indian nationalist. First prime minister of Independent India, 1947–1964. Associated with Gandhi's Congress Party, 1919. Arrested and jailed for political activity, 1921. Helped found Swaraj Party, 1923. Credited with coining expression "Third World," describing underdeveloped countries. In late 1960s Nehru jacket became fashion epidemic, consisting of high-collared jacket worn over turtleneck, often with pendant.

NEIMAN-MARCUS Exclusive department store founded by Herbert Marcus, Sr., his sister Carrie Marcus Neiman and her husband A. L. Neiman, 1908, in Dallas, TX. Twenty-one branches in U.S.: three each in Dallas and Chicago; two in Houston; one each in Ft. Worth, Newport Beach (CA), San Diego, Beverly Hills, Washington, DC, San Francisco, Bal Harbour (FL), Ft. Lauderdale, Atlanta, St. Louis, Boston, Los Angeles and White Plains (NY).

NELSON, GEORGE (BABYFACE) (1908–1934) American outlaw. Born Lester Gillis. Member of Dillinger gang of machine-gun bank robbers. Became public enemy number one after Dillinger killed, 1934. First convicted of larceny at age 13. Nicknamed "Babyface" after first bank robbery. Killed in shootout with FBI agents, November 28, 1934.

NELSON, HORATIO (1758–1805) British admiral and naval hero. Commander of 27 that defeated Napoleon's French fleet, along with entire Spanish fleet, October 21, 1805, in Battle of Trafalgar off coast of Spain's Cape Trafalgar. Battle establishing British naval superiority began when Nelson, from ship *Victory*, hoisted code signal to fleet: "England expects that every man will do his duty." Nelson, earning nickname "the Hero of Trafalgar," died in battle. (See TRAFALGAR SQUARE)

NERO WOLFE. See STOUT, REX

NETWORK 1976 feature film satirizing network TV. Starred Faye Dunaway and acclaimed British actor Peter Finch, who won Oscar posthumously as Best Actor.

NEUMAN, ALFRED E. See **MAD MAGAZINE**

NEUTRON BOMB   Or radio enhancement weapon. Atomic bomb, developed in late 1970s, that releases deadly nuclear radiation. Designed to kill people without damaging surroundings.

NEVADA   U.S. state with smallest population. Called "the Silver State" because of vast amount of silver once found here. Contains many ghost towns. Major industry is mining. Less rain falls here than in any other U.S. state (average of only 7.4 in./18.8 cm.). State flower: sagebrush. State bird: mountain bluebird. State tree: single-leaf piñon. State song: "Home Means Nevada."

NEVER-NEVER LAND. See **BARRIE, SIR JAMES MATTHEW**

NEW JERSEY   Nicknamed "the Garden State" for its many orchards and gardens; words "Garden State" displayed on NJ license plates. Also nicknamed "the Cockpit of the Revolution" for battles fought here during American Revolution.

NEW ORLEANS   Some of this city's major tourist attractions include: Mardi Gras, Preservation Hall, St. Louis Cathedral, exhibition of original streetcar named "Desire" and French Quarter.

NEW YORK CITY   Most populated city in U.S., with approximately 7,017,030 people. Blacks make up approximately 25% of population, numbering roughly 1,784,000 (more than in any other city in the world). City comprises five areas called boroughs: Manhattan (city's center and smallest borough), Brooklyn, Queens (largest), Bronx and Staten Island. Nicknames: "Gotham," derived from legendary English village whose inhabitants are known for their foolishness (coined by Washington Irving, who regarded New Yorkers of his day as know-it-alls); "the Big Apple," originally jazz term for Harlem (center of jazz in 1930s) and name given to city in 1971 by president of New York's Convention and Visitors Bureau. Sources of water supply: Delaware Aqueduct (50%), Catskill Aqueduct (40%) and Croton Aqueduct (10%).

NEW YORK CITY, U.S. CAPITAL   Nation's capital, 1785–1790. Scene of President Washington's inauguration, 1789. Capital moved to Washington, DC, 1790, to settle political battle between northern and southern states over war debts.

NEW YORK INSTITUTE FOR THE INVESTIGATION OF ROLLING SPHEROIDS. See **MARBLES**

NEW YORK JETS   Changed name from New York Titans in 1963 when new coach and general manager Weeb Ewbank took over team. Moved from Polo Grounds to new Shea Stadium, 1964, and began drawing sellout crowds with new quarterback Joe Namath. Won Super Bowl III over Baltimore Colts, 16-7.

NEW YORK METS   Set record on September 15, 1962, by losing 117 games; finished season 40-120, in last place. Seven years later, nicknamed "Miracle Mets" because with no previous winning record won National League East pennant, swept Atlanta Braves in NL championship series and beat Baltimore Orioles (4-1) in World Series.

NEW YORK TITANS. See NEW YORK JETS

NEW YORK TIMES, THE   New York City daily newspaper, first published in 1851; bought by Adolf S. Ochs in 1896. Coined motto "All the News That's Fit to Print." Most respected newspaper in country. Has second-largest Sunday circulation after *Daily News*, which has circulation of 2,004,835 and daily circulation of 1,513,941 vs. *Times'* 1,563,531 and 963,443.

NEW YORK YANKEES   Major league baseball team that has played most World Series games: 186 (through 1983), with 109-77 record. Has been in 33 World Series, with 22 wins. Nicknamed "Bronx Bombers" for tradition of sluggers like Babe Ruth, Joe DiMaggio, Mickey Mantle, Roger Maris and Reggie Jackson. Known as "New York Highlanders" until 1913; name changed after move from Hilltop Park on Broadway to Polo Grounds so local newspapers could have shorter name to fit into one-column headlines. In 1966 finished last for first time in 54 years. Famed 1927 line-up, "Murderer's Row," won 110 games and lost only 44. Featured three future Hall of Famers: Babe Ruth (RF), Lou Gehrig (1B) and Earle Combs (CF). Other members included: Tony Lazzeri (2B), Mark Koenig (SS), Joe Dugan (3B), Bob Meusel (LF) and Pat Collins (C).

NEW YORK, NEW YORK   1977 feature film, directed by Martin Scorsese, that introduced title song sung by Liza Minnelli. Minnelli played 1940s band vocalist who was romanced by saxophone player (Robert De Niro).

NEW ZEALAND   Island country in southwest Pacific Ocean. Part of large island group called Polynesia. Two main islands are North Island and South Island; several dozen smaller islands include Stewart and Chatham. Was once part of British Empire and is now independent member of Commonwealth of Nations, although Great Britain's Queen Elizabeth is recognized as its monarch. British influences remain in form of pubs, cricket and similar speaking accent. Inhabitants known as "Kiwis," after native bird with tiny wings useless for flight and no tail; only bird with nostrils at tip of beak.

NEWHART, BOB (1923–   ) Accountant turned nightclub comedian and actor. First comedy album, *The Button-Down Mind of Bob Newhart* (1960), reached number one on charts and led to Emmy-winning TV variety series in 1961. Movies include *Hot Millions* (1968) and *Cold Turkey* (1970). Two successful situation comedy series since 1972.

NEWS Word erroneously believed formed from first letters of north, east, west and south. Actually came into English with Norman Conquest (1066), from *nouvelles* (plural of French word for "new"), and was originally spelled "newes." Root is Greek *neos*.

NEWTON, SIR ISAAC (1642–1727) English physicist, inventor and natural philosopher. Most important figure in scientific revolution of 17th century. In *Philosophiae naturalis principia mathematica*, 1687, explained universal gravitation and laws of motion. Developed first effective telescope and the calculus, and made profound discoveries about nature of color and light. Had dog named Diamond.

NFL. See FOOTBALL

NICHOLAS II (1868–1918) Last czar of Russia, 1894–1917. Deposed March 1917 in February Revolution. Descendant of Romanov family from Lithuania or Germany. (First Romanov czar, Michael, 1613.) Nicholas II presumably shot in 1918, with his family.

NICKLAUS, JACK (1940–   ) American golfer, born 1940. Nicknamed "Golden Bear"; also, less complimentary "Blobbo" and "Ohio Fats" when he was heftier in younger days coming out of Ohio State. Became most dominant player of his generation. Won British Open three times, Masters five times, U.S. Open four times, Professional Golfers' Association Championship five times. Recorded no tournament wins in 1979, but next year, at 40, won U.S. Open in June with record 272 and followed it in August with another PGA tournament win. Partially red-green color blind; cannot distinguish these colors from more than 100 yards away, leading to difficulty in reading leader boards (scoreboards) on which strokes under par are shown in red and strokes even with or over par are shown in green.

NICTITATING MEMBRANE Thin membrane capable of being drawn across eyeball. When utilized by one person toward another, is taken in social language to be a wink.

NIETZSCHE, FRIEDRICH (1844–1900) German philosopher. Despite his stated opposition to anti-Semitism and empire building, his "Overman" or "Superman" model was used by Hitler and Mussolini to justify their racist authoritarian theories.

NIGERIA Most populated African country, with about 89,118,000 people. Ranks 9th in world population. Density is 249 per sq. mi. (96 per sq. km.). Country is 70% rural and 30% urban. Official language is English, taught in schools but not most common language spoken. Each of 250 ethic groups (largest are Hausa, Yoruba and Igbo) speaks own distinct language.

NIGHT GALLERY, THE Supernatural TV series, 1970–1973, hosted by Rod Serling. Anthology show like Serling's *Twilight Zone* whose stories usually involved occult.

NIGHT STALKER, THE 1971 made-for-TV movie about reporter who discovers modern-day Dracula murdering people in Las Vegas. Darren McGavin starred in this popular film, which spawned sequel in 1972 and weekly series in 1974.

NIGHT TO REMEMBER, A Fateful maiden voyage of fabulous *Titanic* was subject of this 1958 British-made drama. Starred Kenneth More, David McCallum and Honor Blackman; adapted faithfully from Walter Lord's best-selling book of same name.

NIGHTINGALE, FLORENCE (1820–1910) English nurse and philanthropist. Cited as founder of modern nursing. Wounded British soldiers in Crimean War knew her as "the Lady with the Lamp." First woman to receive British Order of Merit.

NIHILISM Philosophy originating in Russia, mid-1800s. First mentioned in Ivan Turgenev's book *Fathers and Sons*. Began as rejection of authority and influenced revolutionary movement. In Western Europe came to mean disbelief in objective values and truths. From Latin *nihil* (nothing).

NILE RIVER World's longest river, flowing north for distance of 4,145 mi. (6,632 km.). Gathers water from nine countries: Burundi, Rwanda, Tanzania, Kenya, Uganda, Zaire, Sudan, Ethiopia and Egypt.

NINE   Considered lucky by more people around the world than any other number. This is probably because when digits of any two-digit multiple of nine are added, nine is sum. Four, seven and twelve are also often considered lucky.

NIVEN, DAVID (1910–1983)   Scottish-born American actor known for playing British roles. Leading man since 1935, won 1958 Best Actor Oscar for *Separate Tables*, and played Phileas Fogg in *Around the World in Eighty Days* (1956). Summed up his lighthearted approach to life in memoirs *The Moon's a Balloon* (1971) and sequel *Bring on the Empty Horses* (1975). Was on stage when streaker invaded 1974 Academy Awards presentation.

NIXON, PATRICIA (THELMA CATHARINE RYAN) (1912–   )   Wife of former president Richard Nixon. Named among most admired women in Gallup polls, 1968–1971. Lester David's 1978 biography *The Lonely Lady of San Clemente* describes her as stoic and strong, despising politics and shut out by husband.

NIXON, RICHARD MILHOUS (1913–   )   Lawyer and 37th U.S. President (1969–1974). Elected to Congress, 1946, same year as J. F. Kennedy. Lost by slim margin to Kennedy, 1960 presidential race. On Republican ticket, lost 1962 California gubernatorial election to Edmund G. Brown. After defeat, he complained of unfair treatment by press: "You won't have Nixon to kick around any more. This is my last press conference." After 1968 presidential victory, Nixon and Secretary of State Henry Kissinger established detente with Soviet Union. Became first U.S. president to visit Moscow. In 1969, began Strategic Arms Limitation Talks (SALT) with Russia. With success of *Apollo 11* mission, fulfilled Kennedy's hope of landing man on moon by end of decade. Nixon's name is engraved on plaque alongside those of astronauts. In preparation for 1972 presidential campaign, Committee to Re-Elect the President (CREEP) was organized. Watergate hearing disclosed that CREEP channeled millions of dollars into slush funds to be used for Nixon's reelection. In aftermath of CREEP's activities, Federal Election Commission passed laws regulating maximum contributions to presidential campaigns. November 7, 1972, Nixon won reelection over Democratic candidate George McGovern in one of country's biggest landslides, taking every state except Massachusetts. He won 520 of 537 electoral votes, and 60.7% of popular vote. Nixon referred to backers as "the silent majority." Later revealed that since 1968, the President had been abusing the concept of national security by engaging in surveillance of political opponents and antiwar spokesmen. This surfaced June 17, 1972, at arrest of five men apparently burglarizing office of Democratic National Committee headquarters in Watergate Hotel, Washington, DC. Public suspicion aroused, his middle name gave rise to quip that "behind every mill house (Milhous) there's a water gate." October 30, 1973, Nixon fired Archibald Cox when Cox disobeyed his order to end attempts to obtain White House records during Watergate investigation. This led to immediate dismissal of Attorney General Ruckelhaus and resignation of Attorney General Richardson. Nixon insisted: "The White House has no involvement whatever in this particular incident." The investigation proved otherwise. August 9, 1974, aboard jet flying 30,000 ft. (9,000 m.) over Missouri River, Nixon offered his resignation to Secretary of State Kissinger. At the same time, Gerald Ford was being sworn in as country's 38th president. Nixon maintained, "I am not a crook." Author of *Six Crises* (1962), written after 1960 defeat to J. F. Kennedy, released prior to 1962 California gubernatorial campaign. The crises: Alger Hiss case, the Checkers speech, Eisenhower's heart attack, Communist mobs during visit to Caracas, Venezuela, encounters with Krushchev (the Kitchen Debate) and 1960 campaign. Also wrote *RN* (1978), autobiography, published by Grossett and Dunlap, containing 1,020 pages; opening sentence: "I was born in a house my father built." Self-proclaimed number one football fan in U.S. Sent trick play to Washington Redskins' coach George Allen before Super Bowl VII (1973). Redskins lost to Miami, 14-7. The scar on left side of Nixon's head, hidden by hair, was acquired when, after falling from carriage at age three, wheels of carriage rolled over his head. Nixon married in 1950, and had two daughters, Patricia (1946) and Julia (1948).

NOAH'S ARK Old Testament tale of righteous man God spared from flood that covered earth for 40 days and nights. Eight people— Noah, his wife, three sons Shem, Ham and Japeth and their wives— rode on ark Noah built. Also carried male and female animals. According to Genesis VIII:6–12, Noah sent out raven from ark and it did not return; then sent dove which returned after finding no place to land. Seven days later, Noah sent dove again, which returned with olive branch indicating water had subsided. Dove with olive branch, symbol of peace. His ark, made of gopher wood, landed atop Ararat Mountains, Turkey.

NOB HILL   Hill in downtown San Francisco. Originally fashionable residential section. Site of city's luxury hotels, the Fairmont and the Mark Hopkins. Located just west of Chinatown.

NOBEL PRIZE   Established 1901 by will of Swedish philanthropist Alfred Nobel. Encourages and awards those who work for betterment of humanity. Various categories awarded annually by Norwegian Nobel Committee. 1976, U.S. became first country to win all prizes: for literature, Saul Bellow; for chemistry, William Numm Lipscomb, Jr.; for physics, Burton Richter and Samuel C. C. Ting; for physiology or medicine, D. Carleton Gajdusek and Baruch S. Blumberg and for economics, Milton Friedman. 1940–1942, prizes suspended due to World War II. Notable political leaders who later received the peace prize: Henry Kissinger and Vietnamese negotiator Le Duc Tho, 1973, for talks resulting in a cease-fire in Vietnam; and Israeli Prime Minister Menachem Begin and Egyptian President Anwar Sadat, 1978, for negotiating a peace treaty and normalizing relations between the two countries.

NOGGINS. See LIQUID MEASURE

NORDHOFF, CHARLES BERNARD (1887–1947) AND HALL, JAMES NORMAN (1887–1951)   American novelists and travel writers. Most famous for trilogy of novels about *The Bounty*, ship captained by William Bligh. Lloyd Byron's poem "The Island" first popularized *Bounty* story, but is based on real incident, 1787 mutiny of crew of British war vessel. Nordhoff and Hall's trilogy consisted of *Mutiny on the Bounty* (1932), *Men Against the Sea* (1933) and *Pitcairn's Island* (1934). Last tells how Bligh and 17 followers, leaving Tahiti, row 1,200 miles to tiny island where they live for 20 years. Leader of mutiny was Fletcher Christian.

NORMANDY   Region in France situated along English Channel. Named for Norse tribes who conquered area in 800s. France won region from England, 1449. Joan of Arc fought during this time.

NORMANDY INVASION   Allied invasion of Normandy,

June 6, 1944. Landed on beaches of Omaha, Juno and Gold. Called "Operation Overlord," password for maneuver was "Mickey Mouse." General Dwight D. Eisenhower (1890–1969) directed landing of 125,000 British, Canadian, and American soldiers and over 5,000 ships and boats. Largest fleet ever assembled. Over next 100 days, 2.2 million men landed, driving Germans out of France. Marked beginning of end of World War II.

NORTH ATLANTIC TREATY ORGANIZATION (NATO) Mutual defense group. Organized to support North Atlantic Treaty of 1949. Members include Belgium, Canada, Denmark, France, West Germany, Greece, Iceland, Italy, Luxembourg, the Netherlands, Norway, Portugal, Turkey, the U.K. and the U.S.

NORTH BY NORTHWEST Suspenseful 1959 film directed by Alfred Hitchcock. Cary Grant is advertising man mistaken for spy. After Grant is attacked by biplane crop duster, danger builds to exciting climax on face of Mount Rushmore. James Mason is agent out to get him.

NORTH CAROLINA Called the Tar Heel State since Civil War. Supposedly North Carolinians (originally with Confederacy) threatened to put tar on heels of Confederates retreating from North Carolina soil so soldiers would "stick better in next fight."

NORTH DAKOTA Agricultural products such as wheat, beef cattle, barley, potatoes and corn, comprise 70% of income from goods produced in this state. North Dakotans work in agriculture more any than other state's people, making it U.S.'s most rural state. Fifty-six percent of population live on farms or in farming areas.

NORTH POLE North geographic pole: center of Arctic. Where lines of longitude meet. Receives more sunlight than South Pole. Instantaneous north pole: Where Earth's imaginary axis meets surface. North magnetic pole: Point toward which north-seeking compass needles point. Between March 20 and September 21, North Pole tilts toward sun.

NORTH SEA Arm of Atlantic Ocean between Great Britain and mainland Europe. Norway juts into the sea. Important economically to Europe because of petroleum and natural gas deposits beneath sea floor.

NORTHERN IRELAND Part of United Kingdom. Consists of six former counties: Antrim, Armagh, Down, Fermanagh, Londonderry and Tyrone; and two former county boroughs; Belfast and Londonderry. Agricultural roots but more income now generated by industry.

NORTHWEST PASSAGE   Route from Europe to Asia through northern extremities of North America. Explorers have searched for it since 1534. Sir Martin Frobisher discovered Frobisher Bay, 1576 and thought it was the passage. Baffin Bay was named after William Baffin, 1616, who went 300 mi. (485 km.) beyond earlier expeditions. Sir John Franklin died leading expedition, 1845. No ship traversed passage until 20th century.

NORWAY   Located on northwestern edge of Europe. One third lies above Arctic Circle. Called Land of the Midnight Sun because sun shines 24 hours each day in summer. Jostedal Glacier 300 mi. (780 km.) is largest ice field in Europe outside Iceland. Country is northernmost in Scandinavia.

NOSE PRINTS   Like human fingerprints, no dog's nose print is identical. Dog breeders use nose prints for positive identification. Healthy dogs should have moist noses. Dogs recognize objects by smell.

NOTAPHILE   Collector of bank notes, certificates on which banks promise to pay bearer on demand. Often referred to as circulating notes or currency. Person who saves or hordes money could be considered one, although term refers to legitimate hobby of collecting rare paper money.

NOTRE DAME, FOUR HORSEMEN OF   Notre Dame University football backfield, 1922–1925. Named by sportswriter Grantland Rice after Four Horseman of Apocalypse. Notre Dame version: (QB) Harry Stuhldreher; (HB) Don Miller; (HB) Jim Crowley; (FB) Elmer Layden. Their 1924 blocking line, known as "Seven Mules": (E) Ed Huntsinger; (E) Charles Collins; (T) Joe Back; (T) Edgar (Rip) Miller; (G) Noble Kizer; (G) John Weibel and (C) Adam Walsh.

NUCLEAR REACTOR   Facility for controlled nuclear fission. First built, 1942, Chicago. Over 500 built in U.S. Produce enormous amounts of heat which can lead to meltdown or disintegration of core of reactor. Its nuclear power plant is about 30% efficient.

NUMBERS

Name of Numeral	*Number of Zeros*
Thousand	3
Million	6
Billion	9
Trillion	12
Quadrillion	15
Quintillion	18
Sextillion	21
Septillion	24
Octillion	27
Nonillion	30

NUREYEV, RUDOLF (1938–)   Dancer who defected from Leningrad Kirov Ballet, 1961. Has acted in movies, including *Valentino* (1977) and *Exposed* (1983).

NURMI, PAAVO (1897–1973)   Finnish distance runner known as "Flying Finn," "Peerless Paavo," "Phantom Finn" (other Finnish runners Hans Kolehmainen and Ville Ritola also known as Flying Finns). Won nine Olympic gold medals: 10,000–m. run and 10,000–m. cross-country, individual and team, 1920; 1,500– and 5,000–m. runs, 10,000–m. cross-country relay, 1924; 10,000–m. run, 1928. Also won three Olympic silver medals, and broke 20 world records during career.

O'CONNELL STREET, DUBLIN. See DUBLIN

O'HARA, JOHN HENRY (1905–1970) American novelist and short-story writer. Collection *Pal Joey* (1940) became successful Cole Porter musical and film. Novel *Butterfield 8* (1935) about juvenile delinquent Gloria Wandrous. Title comes from phone exchange known as Butterfield 8 (BU-8). Elizabeth Taylor won Best Actress Oscar in 1960 film version.

O'HARA, MARY (1885–1980) Author. Wrote 1941 story *My Friend Flicka* about boy and horse. First of three horse novels written after moving to Wyoming ranch. Also composer, wrote *Wyoming Suite for Piano* (1946).

O'NEAL, TATUM (1963–   ) Actress, daughter of actor Ryan O'Neal, won Oscar at age 10 for Best Supporting Actress in *Paper Moon* (1973), her first film. Has since appeared in *Nickelodeon* (1976), *Bad News Bears* (1976), *International Velvet* (1978), and *Little Darlings* (1980).

O'NEILL, EUGENE (1888–1953) American playwright. Only U.S. playwright to win Nobel Prize (1936) for literature. Autobiographical *Long Day's Journey into Night* written 1939-41, first published and performed posthumously, 1956. Also wrote *The Emperor Jones*, *Desire Under the Elms*, and *The Iceman Cometh*.

O.K. CORRAL Tombstone, AZ. Scene of confrontation between Earp and Clanton clans, October 26, 1881. Doc Holliday, Wyatt, Virgil and Morgan Earp engaged in a gunfight touched off by a local dispute between ranchers. Morgan Earp, three Clantons (including Billie) and the McLowery brothers were killed. The Earp brothers were James C. (1841–1926), Virgil W. (1843–1906), Wyatt B. S. (1848–1929), Morgan (1851–1881), Warren B. (1855–1900). They also had a half brother, Newton Jasper Earp (1837-1928), and a full sister, Adelia. (see Tombstone, Arizona)

OAHU One of Hawaii's 132 islands. Home to about 80% of state's population. Pearl Harbor, one of the Pacific's largest natural harbors, is on island's southern coast. Home to the state's capital, Honolulu.

OAKLEY, ANNIE (1860–1926) Phoebe Anne Oakley Mozee. American markswoman. Known to Indian Sitting Bull as Little Sure Shot. Joined Buffalo Bill's Wild West Show. Once shot off the end of a cigarette held in the mouth of Berlin's Crown Prince William, later Emperor William II.

OBERAMMERGAU Bavarian village near Munich, West Germany. Every 10 years, residents perform *The Passion Play*, which portrays the suffering and death of Jesus. Tradition began with a vow made in 1633 by villagers when a plague devastated town. Play lasts eight hours, and has 1,200 performers.

OBRIGADO. See THANK YOU

OCCIDENT, THE Countries of the Western Hemisphere. From Latin word *occidere*, meaning "to fall" or "to set" (where the sun sets). Its opposite, the Orient, meaning the countries of the Eastern Hemisphere, comes from Latin *oriens*, meaning "the rising of the sun."

OCEAN'S ELEVEN 1960 caper film starring Frank Sinatra and his "Rat Pack": Dean Martin, Sammy Davis, Jr., Peter Lawford and Joey Bishop. Danny Ocean (Sinatra) rounds up his ex-paratrooper buddies to pull a Las Vegas robbery.

OCEANS World's oceans in size order are Pacific (64,186,300 sq. mi., 166,884,380 sq. km.), Atlantic (33,420,000 sq. mi., 86,892,000 sq. km.), Indian (28,350,500 sq. mi., 73,711,300 sq. km.), Arctic (5,105,700 sq. mi., 13,274,820 sq. km.). Experts disagree about the official status of the fifth ocean, the Antarctic. Oceans cover 71% of the earth's surface. Ocean water is 3½ dissolved minerals, accounting for its salty taste. Eighty-one percent of Southern Hemisphere is covered by ocean waters; Northern Hemisphere, 61%.

OCTOBER REVOLUTION ISLAND Central island of the Severnaya Zemlya group. Located in Arctic Ocean. Belongs to Soviet Union.

OCTOPUS Sea-dwelling relative of the clam and snail. Has eight tentacles, five hearts, and travels by jet propulsion. Largest is 28 ft. from tentacle tip to tip.

ODD COUPLE, THE 1965 hit Broadway play by Neil Simon. Became a movie in 1968 with Jack Lemmon as Felix Ungar, the neat and tidy photographer, and Walter Matthau as Oscar Madison, the gruff, sloppy sportswriter, both divorced and sharing an apartment out of need for companionship. Tony Randall portrayed Felix, and Jack Klugman was Oscar on the popular comedy TV series (1970–1975).

ODE TO BILLY JOE Hit 1967 song by Bobby Gentry in which the third of June was another sleepy, dusty delta day. Song was basis for 1976 feature film starring Robby Benson.

OFFICIAL PREPPY HANDBOOK, THE Guide to the tradition, mannerisms, etiquette, dress codes and correct social behavior of being "really top drawer" (upper crust). Going to prep school not prerequisite: "You don't even have to be a registered Republican." Lisa Birnbach edited; written by her, Jonathan Roberts (who originated concept), and others.

OH, SADAHARU Baseball player called "Babe Ruth of Japan." Retired November 5, 1980, at age 40 after 21 years at first base for Yomiuri Giants of Tokyo. Hit 868 career homers (major league leader Hank Aaron hit 755 and Ruth hit 714). Led league in home runs 15 times.

OIL! See CYCLING

OIL DRUMS Large metal containers used for shipping oil across great distances. Used as musical instrument by East Indian steel bands, who create unique sound by beating rims with sticks.

OKLAHOMA U.S. state located directly north of Texas. Name formed from two Choctaw Indian words: *okla*, meaning "people," and *homma*, meaning "red." Four percent of its 3,177,000 residents are Indians, higher percentage of Indian population than any other U.S. state.

OKTOBERFEST   Annual fair in Munich, Germany, held for two weeks from late September into October. Fairgrounds located on Theresiewiese. Huge beer halls seat thousands, who raise glasses and chant *Prosit!* meaning "Cheers!" or "To your health!" First Sunday of fest marked with parade in which Bavarian brass bands play, and folklore groups march.

OLD BAILEY, THE   London's Central Criminal Court located on Old Bailey Street. Once a feudal castle that formed part of a bailey (area between inner and outer city walls in medieval London). Held treason trial for King Charles I and moral trial of author/ playwright Oscar Wilde.

OLD FAITHFUL. See YELLOWSTONE NATIONAL PARK

OLD IRONSIDES   Nickname for navy vessel U.S.S. *Constitution*. Commissioned 1797. Made with wood; weighs 1,576 tons. Famed for battles in War of 1812. Saved from the scrapyard by Oliver Wendell Holmes' poem "Old Ironsides." Presently in Boston Harbor.

OLD KING COLE   In children's rhyme, "Old King Cole/Was a merry old soul,/And a merry old soul was he. / He called for his pipe,/And he called for his bowl,/And he called for his fiddlers three."

OLD MAID   Card game played with standard deck. One of the queens is removed to leave deck with odd queen—the Old Maid.

OLD SHELL GAME   Widely acknowledged as world's oldest swindle. Earliest known version called "Cups and Balls" (c. second century A.D.). Later called "Thimbles and Peas." Walnut shells instead of thimbles began being used approximately 1915. Since known as "Three Shell Game" (or "Shell Game," "Pea and Shell Game"). Standard stratagem: let mark win a few times, then use sleight of hand to remove pea from chosen shell.

OLD WOMAN IN THE SHOE   In nursery rhyme, she had so many children she didn't know what to do, so "she gave them broth without any bread, then whipped them all soundly and put them to bed."

OLD YELLER   1957 film produced by Walt Disney. Tommy Kirk starred as Western farmboy who adopts a yellow hunting dog, but must shoot it because of rabies. Based on novel by Fred Gipson.

OLIVE OYL   Popeye's girlfriend. Lives with parents Cole Oyl (her father) and Nana Oyl (her mother), and her brother Castor Oyl. Appears in comic strips, animated cartoons and was played by Shelley Duvall in the 1980 feature film. (see POPEYE)

OLYMPIC AIRWAYS   National airline of Greece. Formerly called TAE. Bought from government in 1957 by Aristotle Onassis, who changed its name. Resold to government in 1975. Transatlantic flights began in 1966. Currently flies to 5 continents using 38 commercial aircrafts.

OLYMPIC GAMES   Ancient Greek games reinstituted as international competition under leadership of Frenchman Baron Pierre de Coubertin at Athens, Greece, 1896. Summer Games held every four years since, except during World Wars. Winter Games began 1924 in Chamonix, France.

OLYMPIC GAMES, SUMMER

Year	Site	Unofficial Winner
1896	Athens	United States

Planned at 1894 Paris meeting of Athletic Sports Union. Nine nations participated. First gold medal awarded in hop, step and jump (now called triple jump) to James B. Connolly of South Boston, MA, with distance of 45 ft.

1900	Paris	United States

Held on grounds of Racing Club de France in Bois de Boulogne.

1904	St. Louis	United States

Because of costs involved in sending teams to U.S., few European countries competed. Additional Games held 1906 in Athens, also won by U.S., not officially recognized by International Olympic Committee.

1908	London	United States
1912	Stockholm	United States
1916	Berlin	

Canceled because of World War I.

1920	Antwerp	United States
1924	Paris	United States

1928	Amsterdam	United States

1932	Los Angeles	United States

1936	Berlin	Germany

U.S. participation questioned because of anti-Semitism of Nazi government. German Führer Adolf Hitler's desire to use Games to prove Aryan supremacy partially foiled by three gold medals of U.S.'s Jesse Owens. In broad jump, Owens beat German Lutz Long on final jump. Owens hugged by Long in admiration, but shunned by Hitler.

1940	Tokyo, then Helsinki

Games originally awarded to Japan, but by 1938 Japan already at war with China. Then awarded to Helsinki, but canceled because of World War II.

1944	London

Awarded to London as formality but never held due to war. London given claim to 1948 Games.

1948	London	United States

While defeated Axis powers not invited to 1948 Winter Games, they were allowed to compete in London. International Olympic Committee ruled new state of Israel could not compete because it was not yet member of IOC, averting Arab-bloc walkout.

1952	Helsinki	United States

Soviet Union entered Games (one week after deadline) for first time since 1912. Russians and their satellites had own separate Olympic Village.

1956	Melbourne	Soviet Union

Only Australian and Southern Hemisphere city to host Games, so Summer Games held November 22 to December 8. Equestrian events held in Stockholm because of Australian quarantine regulations.

1960	Rome	Soviet Union

Italians financed Games through weekly pro soccer lottery. Republic of China, forced to compete as Formosa, did so under protest, only political incident of Games. Official song was "Arivederci Roma," popular Italian song by R. Rascal, with added English lyrics by Carl Sigman, 1955.

1964	Tokyo	United States

1968   Mexico City   United States
Noteworthy for altitude of competiton (7,800 ft. above sea level),
which affected distance runners, and for long jumper Bob Beamon
(U.S.), who set World record of 29 ft. 2½ in., which has yet
to be broken.

1972   Munich   Soviet Union
Games marred by massacre of 11 Israeli athletes by Arab terrorists.
Games proceeded, with American swimmer Mark Spitz winning
seven gold medals.

1976   Montreal   Soviet Union
Only Games in Canada (1988 Winter Games scheduled for Calgary),
which became only Summer Games host nation not to capture gold
medal (won five silvers, six bronze). Princess Anne competed as
member of Great Britain equestrian team; only female athlete exempt
from sex test. The princess won no medals.

1980   Moscow   Soviet Union
United States and 62 other nations boycotted to protest Soviet
invasion of Afghanistan.

1984   Los Angeles
Despite 14-nation boycott led by the Soviet Union, record 142
nations confirm intention to participate. 1988 Games planned for
Seoul, Korea.

OLYMPIC GAMES, WINTER

Year	Site	Unofficial Winner
1924	Chamonix, France	Norway
1928	St. Moritz, Switzerland	Norway
1932	Lake Placid, NY	United States
1936	Garmisch-Partenkirchen, Germany	Norway
1940	Not awarded, not held (World War II)	
1944	Not awarded, not held (World War II)	
1948	St. Moritz, Switzerland	Sweden

1952	Oslo, Norway	Norway
1956	Cortina d'Ampezzo, Italy	Soviet Union, Italy
1960	Squaw Valley, CA	Soviet Union

U.S. hockey team beat Czechoslovakia, 9-4, in final game (Canada second, USSR third).

1964	Innsbruck, Austria	Soviet Union
1968	Grenoble, France	Norway
1972	Sapporo, Japan	Soviet Union

Only Winter Games held in Asia, on northernmost Japanese island. Pre-Olympic controversy centered on eligibility of Alpine skiers. Karl Schranz of Austria, considered world's top skier, declared ineligible because of accepting commercial endorsements.

1976	Innsbruck, Austria	Soviet Union

Denver, CO, originally chosen to host Games, but Coloradans, concerned about ecology and finances, voted down necessary bond issue.

1980	Lake Placid, NY	East Germany

Second Winter Olympics staged at Lake Placid. U.S. hockey team upset heavily favored Soviet team 4-3. Won gold medal two days later with 4-2 win over Finland. Team member Mark Johnson famed for exclaiming, "I still can't believe it—we beat the Russians."

1984	Sarajevo, Yugoslavia	Soviet Union (medals) East Germany (points)

1988	Scheduled for Calgary, Alberta, Canada

OLYMPIC MOTTO *Citius, Altius, Fortius*—Latin, meaning "faster, higher, braver" or (modern interpretion) "swifter, higher, stronger." Coined by French monk Father Didon (1895), who had it embroidered on pennants of his school's clubs. Baron Pierre de Coubertin, leading advocate of restoration of ancient Games, suggested its adoption as Olympic motto at advent of modern Games, 1896.

OLYMPIC SWIMMING POOL Olympic-sized pool has

eight lanes 50 m. long (55 yds.). Each lane, numbered one to eight (right to left on starting line), is 2.5 m. wide. Swimmer with fastest entry time assigned lane to right of center. In all races except backstroke (start in water), swimmers dive into pool from blocks 75 cm. (2½ ft.) above water line.

OLYMPIC SYMBOL   Five interlocking rings colored (left to right) blue, yellow, black, green, red. Rings represent five continents; colors represent countries of world. At least one color is found on flag of every country.

OLYMPIC TELECAST   First Olympic telecast aired in summer 1956 from Melbourne, Australia, with limited coverage. ABC began full coverage with anchorman Jim McKay in 1960 at Squaw Valley, CA, and Rome, Italy. Ratings estimate that Olympic telecasts capture 50% of American audience, therefore highly sought by TV networks. ABC paid $225 million for rights to 1984 Los Angeles Games.

ON THE ROAD. See KEROUAC, JACK

ON THE WATERFRONT   1954 film which swept the Oscars, winning Best Picture, Best Actor (Marlon Brando), Best Direction (Elia Kazan) and others. Rod Steiger made his first big impact in the role of Brando's brother. Realistic story of New York's harbor unions. Contains Brando's classic line "I coulda' been a contenda'." Lee J. Cobb portrayed Johnny Friendly.

ONASSIS, JACQUELINE KENNEDY (1929–   ) Former journalist and photographer. Married John F. Kennedy, 1953. Mother of Caroline (1957) and John Fitzgerald, Jr., (1960). First lady during her husband's presidency, 1961–63. After redecorating White House, conducted televised tour of her achievement. Preserved historic homes in Washington, DC. At J. F. Kennedy's funeral, was first to light the eternal flame on her husband's grave. Remarried, 1968, Aristotle Onassis (1906–1975). Went to work in publishing after his death. Jackie's maiden name, Bouvier. Became editor at Doubleday and Co. in 1977.

ONE FLEW OVER THE CUCKOO'S NEST   1975 Oscar-winning Best Picture about misfit who leads revolt of patients in mental ward of state hospital. Jack Nicholson won Oscar for Best Actor; Louise Fletcher won for Best Actress as the unfeeling head nurse. Though based on novel by Ken Kesey, Kesey refuses to see film. (see KESEY, KEN)

ONE O'CLOCK In anonymous nursery rhyme "Hickory Dickory Dock": "Hickory dickory dock,/The mouse ran up the clock./The clock struck one,/The mouse ran down,/Hickory dickory dock."

100 RIFLES Raquel Welch stars in this 1968 film as lover of black actor and former football star Jim Brown.

ONISHCHENKO, BORIS Russian pentathlon competitor disqualified for cheating in 1976 Montreal Summer Olympics. Had illegal electronic device implanted in tip of fencing épée so he did not have to actually touch opponent for electronic scoreboard to record tally. Soviet Union claimed no knowledge of ploy.

OPERATION AVALANCHE Allied invasion of Italy, World War II. Began with large-scale landing at Messina on "toe" of Italian peninsula, September 3, 1943. Followed by landings at Salerno, the "shin," and near port city of Taranto, the "heel."

OPIUM POPPY Flower native to Middle East from which opium is derived. Codeine, morphine and heroin are also made from opium. Most opium is now grown in southwest and southeast Asia.

OPPENHEIMER, J. ROBERT (1904–1967) American physicist. Directed Los Alamos laboratory, 1940s, where first atomic bomb was designed and built. Accused of disloyalty to U.S., 1953, because of opposition to development of hydrogen bomb. Cleared of charges.

OPOSSUMS Marsupials, or mammals without placentas, as are kangaroos, koalas and wombats. Found in North and South America; the only marsupials not located in the Australian region. The common type in North America plays dead when threatened.

OPTIC NERVE Transmits information from retina, the light-sensitive layer at rear of eyeball, to brain. Goes from right half of each eye to right half of brain and similarly with left half.

ORCHID Over six thousand species. Some grow in trees with roots dangling below them. Word from Greek *orkhis* meaning "testicle," so named because of shape of root. Beans from vanilla vine orchid processed to make vanilla extract.

ORCZY, BARONESS EMMUSKA (1865–1947) Hungarian-born English novelist and dramatist. Wrote *The Scarlet Pimpernel* (1905), adventure story about French Revolution. Pimpernel is a plant of primrose family, with small flowers that close in bad weather.

Sequels: *The Elusive Pimpernel* (1908) and *Way of the Scarlet Pimpernel* (1933).

ORDINARY PEOPLE   1980 Oscar-winning Best Picture directed by Robert Redford. Story concerns breakup of a family after death of oldest son. Mary Tyler Moore, Donald Sutherland and Timothy Hutton star. Redford won an Oscar for his directorial debut.

OREGON   State nickname: Beaver State. State bird: Western meadowlark. State flower: Oregon grape. State Tree: Douglas fir.

ORGANIZATION OF AMERICAN STATES   Founded in 1948. Association of 27 Latin American countries and U.S. Functions within UN. Charter states members share belief in international law, social justice, economic cooperation and equality of all people. Act of aggression against one nation regarded as an act of aggression against all nations.

ORIENT EXPRESS   First run, October 4, 1883, went from Paris to Istanbul. Last run was in 1976, when it was no longer the glamorous train it had once been. *Express* was restored May 1982 and now runs from London to Florence.

ORIENTEERING   Sport invented by Swedish Major Ernst Killander, 1918. Competitive cross-country race. Participants can use only map and compass to find way between various checkpoints and finish line. No set course; competitors try to find fastest route.

ORIGIN OF SPECIES, THE   Published by Charles Darwin, 1859. Describes theory of natural selection. Full title of controversial book: *On the Origin of Species by Means of Natural Selection; Or, The Preservation of Favored Races in the Struggle for Life.*

ORION'S BELT   Three bright stars marking belt of constellation Orion. Constellation named after mighty hunter in Greek mythology. Depicts Orion with club in right hand, lion's skin in left hand and sword hilt hanging from belt.

ORKAN   The language of planet Ork, from which emerged character Mork, portrayed by Robin Williams on TV comedy series *Mork and Mindy* (1978–1980). Mindy (played by Pam Dawber) was his companion and earthly guide. Mork would end each episode by saying "goodbye" in Orkan: "Nanoo-Nanoo."

ORR, BOBBY (1948–   )   First defenseman to win National Hockey League scoring title (1969–1970 and 1974–1975). Revolutionized game with offensive-oriented style for defensemen. NHL Rookie of the Year 1966–1967 (at age 18) with Boston Bruins. Named outstanding NHL defenseman eight consecutive years (1968–1975). League MVP, 1970, 1972. *Sports Illustrated* Sportsman of the Year, 1970. Signed five-year contract with Chicago Black Hawks prior to 1976–1977 season, but doctors advised him give up sport due to serious knee injury, so he spent most of season as team's assistant coach.

ORWELL, GEORGE (1903–1950)   English satirist-novelist. Born in India as Eric Blair. Fought with Republicans in Spanish Civil War, basis for *Homage to Catalonia* (1939). Best known for antitotalitarian novels. Wrote *Animal Farm* (1946), satire on Stalinist Russia. Farm animals overthrow farmer and run it themselves. Animals betrayed by pigs, led by Napoleon. Their slogan: "All animals are equal, but some are more equal than others." Author, *1984* (1949), satirical novel. In its totalitarian society, world is divided into Oceania, Eurasia and Eastasia. Propaganda replaces truth; thought and love are punished; privacy impossible. Placards everywhere announce, "Big Brother [the ruler] is watching you."

OSAKA, JAPAN   Third-largest Japanese city. Called "Venice of Japan" because of canals and rivers. World's fastest trains travel from Osaka to Tokyo at 125 m.p.h. (201 km.p.h.). Site of Expo 70, Asia's first world's fair.

OSCAR   Statue awarded by Academy of Motion Picture Arts and Sciences for excellence since 1927. The statue, of a strong man holding a crusader's sword and standing on a reel of film, is ten in. tall, weighs seven lbs. and is gold-plated. During World War II, statue was made of plaster. Two actors refused award for Best Actor during the 1970s: Marlon Brando and George C. Scott. Two actresses tied for 1968 Best Actress Award: Barbra Streisand (*Funny Girl*) and Katharine Hepburn (*The Lion in Winter*).

OSHKOSH STEAMER. See AUTO RACING—FIRST RACE

OSLO   Norway's capital, largest city and leading seaport. Founded in 1048 and destroyed by fire in 1624. Originally named Christiania for King Christian IV, who rebuilt city. Renamed Oslo in 1925. Its folk museum contains famous ships belonging to Norse Vikings, such as the *Fram* used by explorers Fridtjof Nansen and Roald Amundsen, and the *Kon-Tiki* raft used by Thor Heyerdahl.

OSTRICH   Largest living bird. Up to 8 ft. (24 m.) in height, 345 lbs. (156 kg.) in weight, run 40 m.p.h. live up to 70 years, lay 3 lb. eggs (largest bird egg) and have 46-ft.-long small intestines. Polygamous. Mates sit on eggs at night. Only birds raised for hide, used in shoes, wallets and handbags. Their plumes once fashionable.

OSWALD, LEE HARVEY (1939–1963)   Accused assassin of President J. F. Kennedy. On November 22, 1963, Oswald allegedly shot the president from sixth-floor window of Texas School Book Depository, where he was employed. As he left depository, Dallas Patrolman J. D. Tippitt confronted him, whereupon Oswald shot Tippitt four times, killing him. Approximately 90 minutes following assassination, Oswald was arrested inside nearby movie theater. He was charged with Kennedy's murder and killing of policeman while resisting arrest. His booking number was 54018. Two days later, while millions of television viewers watched, he was shot by Jack Ruby, a local nightclub owner, while being transferred between jails. This was the first live murder on national television. While no one actually saw Oswald shoot the president, the gun used, a high-powered Italian rifle, was traced to him through the Chicago mail-order company that supplied it. Ironically, Kennedy, Oswald and Ruby all died at Dallas' Parkland Memorial Hospital. Oswald's brother later wrote biography called *Lee*. Jean Stafford wrote *A Mother in History* (1966), book about Oswald's mother, Marguerite C. Oswald.

OSWALD, MARINA (1942–   )   Russian born. Wife of Lee Harvey Oswald, accused assassin of John F. Kennedy.

OTHELLO. See SHAKESPEARE, WILLIAM

OUIJA BOARD   Board game for two, from French *oui* and German *ja*, both meaning "yes." Patented as toy by William and Isaac Field, 1892. Trademarked name now owned by Parker Brothers. Heart-shaped planchette with three legs and window points to letters of alphabet, numbers zero to nine, and words *yes*, *no*, and *goodbye* to form messages. Parlor game popular with courting couples, who played with board balanced on touching knees. Beginning in 1919, mediums claimed game could be used to communicate with spirit world.

OUR MISS BROOKS   TV and radio comedy series of late 1940s through mid-1950s. Eve Arden starred as Constance Brooks, wise-cracking English teacher at Madison High School. Her principal, Mr. Conklin, was portrayed by Gale Gordon.

OUR TOWN 1940 film based on play by Thornton Wilder. Martha Scott and William Holden star in story of life in small New England town. Music by Aaron Copeland.

OUTSIDER, THE 1961 film biography of American Indian Ira Hayes, one of the marines who raised the flag at Iwo Jima. Tony Curtis stars as Hayes.

OUZO Popular Greek drink made from distilled skin of grapes after wine has been made. Often flavored with anise. Alcohol content is 40–90%.

OVAL OFFICE President's office inside White House. Described as innermost sanctuary of American power. Name derives from its oval shape.

OVER THERE Popular song written to boost morale in World War I by George M. Cohan. Made popular by singer Nora Bayes in 1917. President Woodrow Wilson called it "a genuine inspiration to all American manhood." Popular again during World War II, song earned Cohan a Congressional Medal of Honor.

OWENS, JESSE (1913–1980) Won four gold medals and set three Olympic records in 1936 Berlin Olympics: 100m. run; 200m. run (new record of 20.7 sec.); 400m. relay (anchored team that set record of 39.8 sec.); and broad jump (his record leap of 26 ft. 5⁵/₁₆ in. stood as world record for 24 years). "The Ebony Express" once set six world records in less than one hour in track meet in Michigan, May 25, 1935.

OWL AND THE PUSSYCAT, THE. See LEAR, EDWARD

OWL AND THE PUSSYCAT, THE 1970 film based on Broadway play by Bill Manhoof. Owl is wise, intellectual George Segal, who becomes involved with pussycat, Barbra Streisand, part-time prostitute. Directed by Herbert Ross.

OXFORD/CAMBRIDGE BOAT RACE Rowing race between two English colleges held annually on River Thames from Putney to Mortlake. Known as "The Boat Race." First rowed at Henley, 1829 (Oxford won). Annual competition since 1839. Moved to present 4½ mi. course on outskirts of London, 1845.

OYSTER CATCHER Large black, brown and white long-legged shorebird. Found on both coasts of U.S. Use their sharp bills to open oysters and clams they eat.

OZZIE AND HARRIET   Ozzie and Harriet Nelson, along with their sons David and Ricky, starred in popular TV situation comedy *The Adventures of Ozzie and Harriet* (1952–1966). Ozzie was a bandleader; Ricky became rock-and-roll idol in late 1950s. First married couple to sleep in same bed on primetime TV.

P

PAAR, JACK (1918–   ) Pioneer of talk show as host of *The Tonight Show* (1957–1962) and *Jack Paar Show* (1962–1965, 1973). His autobiography *I Kid You Not* (1960) tells about his early life, career as an entertainer, and stories of *Tonight Show* regulars: announcer Hugh Downs, bandleader Jose Melis, guests Alexander King, Jack Douglas, Zsa Zsa Gabor, Oscar Levant and Cliff Arquette (Charlie Weaver), who regularly read letters from his mama. Also tells of off-color joke NBC censored causing him to walk off show February 11, 1960. Title comes from Paar's trademark aside to audience. Sequel: *My Sabre is Bent* (1961).

PACIFIC OCEAN Bordered by five U.S. states: Alaska, Washington, Oregon, California and Hawaii.

PAGE, PATTI (1927–   ) Popular singer who gained fame with hit song "Tennessee Waltz" (1950). Song was "B" side of single "Boogie Woogie Santa Claus." Other hits include "How Much Is That Doggie in the Window?" Began variety TV series in 1956, and appeared in films, including *Elmer Gantry* (1959).

PAHLAVI, SHAH MOHAMMAD REZA (1919–1980) Shah of Iran. Last of the rulers to occupy the Peacock Throne. Driven into exile by popular dissent, 1979. Succeeded by Ayatollah Ruhollah Khomeini, the extremely orthodox Moslem ruler.

PAIGE, LEROY (SATCHEL) (1906–1982) Oldest rookie ever, 42 when he pitched for Cleveland Indians, 1948. Pitched three innings for Kansas City A's in 1965 at age 59. Sparkling career in

Negro Leagues (pre-1948) won him election to Hall of Fame despite 28-31 major league record. Though Dan Bankhead of Brooklyn Dodgers was first black pitcher in majors (August 26, 1947), Paige was first in American League and first in World Series (Cleveland, 1948).

His six rules for staying youthful: 1. Avoid fried meats, which angry up the blood. 2. If your stomach disputes you, lie down and pacify it with cool thoughts. 3. Keep the juices flowing by jangling around gently as you move. 4. Go very lightly on the vices, such as carrying on in society. 5. Avoid running at all times. 6. Don't look back. Something might be gaining on you.

PAINT BY NUMBERS   Children's hobby. Kit includes pre-drawn picture, carefully outlined, with numbers in each area corresponding to numbered paints included in kit. Kits come with oil, acrylic, watercolor or tempera paints; colored pencils or crayons. Pioneered by Palmer Paint Products of Troy, MI (1957–1968); now manufactured by many toymakers in a wide range of designs.

PALACE OF VERSAILLES, THE   More than one-half mi. (0.8 km.) long. Louis XIV began construction in 1661. Cost $100 million. The extravagance contributed to unrest leading to revolution. Treaty of Versailles, which ended World War I, signed in Hall of Mirrors, a long room walled with elaborate mirrors. J. D. Rockefeller contributed $2,850,000 in 1920s for Versailles restoration.

PALADIN   A knight without armor in a savage land was star of *Have Gun Will Travel* (1957–1963), popular TV Western starring Richard Boone as high-priced gun for hire. Paladin was college-educated, literate man of culture who dressed in black when on assignment.

PALEONTOLOGY   From Greek meaning "ancient life." Study of plant and animal remains preserved in rock (fossils). Aims to trace evolution of life. Runs counter to religious notions that earth was created in six days.

PALMER, ARNOLD (1928–   )   Golfer credited with establishing Professional Golfers tour as major spectator sport. Golf's first superstar. Large gallery that followed him around course called Arnie's Army. One of golf's Big Three of 1960s and early '70s (with Gary Player, Jack Nicklaus). Turned professional 1954. Named Athlete of the Decade for 1960s. Set record as first pro to win more than $100,000 in purses in one year (1963, $128,230). First to win more than $1 million lifetime (1968). Still active on regular and Seniors PGA tours. Has won four Masters, two British Opens. PGA Tournament only major event he has never won.

PALMER, HARRY British criminal turned spy, created by novelist Len Deighton. Portrayed in movies by Michael Caine in three films, *The Ipcress File* (1963), *Funeral in Berlin* (1966), and *The Billion Dollar Brain* (1967). (see DEIGHTON, LEN)

PALMIPED FEET To resemble a hand with the fingers spread. An aquatic bird whose anterior toes are united in a web: webbed feet. From *palm*, the concave part of hand between the bases of the fingers, and *ped*, meaning "foot."

PALMISTRY Also chiromancy. Practice of studying lines and other physical features of hand to predict future and reveal character. Four main lines: life, fate, head and heart. Once considered a science.

PAMPAS Grassy plains in temperate region of South America. Most prevalent in Argentina. Similar to North American prairies. Main economic assets: wheat, corn and grazing lands for cattle.

PAMPLONA Spanish town where bulls are let loose in streets at fiesta of San Fermin held annually in July. The "running of the bulls" lets amateurs try their skill at bullfighting.

PAN Greek god of shepherds and flocks. Has goat feet, horns and prick ears. Gods were earliest musicians: Hermes invented shepherd's pipe and lyre, and Pan invented seven-reed syrinx, type of flute called "Pan's pipe."

PANAMA Small Central American country where Atlantic and Pacific Oceans are 47 mi. (75 km.) apart. Site of the Panama Canal, waterway connecting oceans to enable thousands of ships annually to pass from one to the other. Capital is Panama City.

PANAMA CANAL Man-made waterway which cuts across Isthmus of Panama, linking Atlantic and Pacific Oceans. Built by U.S. in 1914 for U.S. $380 million. Extends 50.72 mi. (81.63 km.) and consists of three sets of locks: Gatun Locks, Pedro Miguel Locks and Miraflores Locks. Pan American Highway crosses canal over the $20-million Thatcher Ferry Bridge.

PANCREAS Gland that lies beneath stomach. Secretes digestive enzymes into the stomach and secretes the hormones insulin and glucagon into bloodstream. These hormones are released from tissue called "islets of Langerhans," and are necessary to metabolize sugar.

PAPER   Matted sheet of cellulose fibers. Invented by the Chinese, A.D. 105. Six hundred and forty pounds of paper are used per person per year in the U.S. Measured in reams, which are 500 25 × 38-inch sheets.

PAPER, STONE, SCISSORS GAME   Ancient game of chance for two players, who thrust hand forward either open (paper), clenched (stone), or with two fingers making a V (scissors). Paper covers stone; stone blunts scissors; scissors cut paper. After each round, loser's wrist is tapped by winner's two extended fingers.

PAPRIKA   Hungarian for "sweet pepper." Red powder made from it has slightly pungent taste. Used as seasoning in goulash, Hungarian national dish.

PAPUA NEW GUINEA   Major languages: English (official), Melanesian Pidgin and Police Motu.

PAPYRUS   Plant whose stem was used in ancient Egypt to make paperlike writing material. Parts of plant also used for sandals, boats, twine, cloth, fuel and food. Word *paper* derived from it. Paper as we know it came from ancient China, reaching Europe around 12th century.

PARALLAX VIEW, THE   1974 film starring Warren Beatty as reporter trying to expose conspiracy involving assassination of presidential candidate. The film, directed by Alan J. Pakula, opens with assassin falling to his death from Seattle Space Needle.

PARASITE   Organism that lives in or on other organisms and is dependent on them. Probably every animal has some type of parasite.

PARENT TRAP, THE   1961 film starring Hayley Mills as two look-alike teenagers who met by chance, discover they are actually twin sisters who were separated shortly after birth and hatch plot to reunite their parents (Brian Keith and Maureen O'Hara).

PARIS   Trojan prince in the *Iliad*, attributed to blind Greek poet Homer. His abduction of Helen from King Menelaus sparked 10-year seige of city of Troy (Illium) by Greeks led by Achilles.

PARIS   Capital and largest city of France. Celtic tribe called Parisii lived in what is now Paris. Roman invaders discovered them in 52 B.C.; hence, city's 2000th anniversary took place 1952. Became known as Paris in A.D. 300. Nicknamed City of Lights because floodlights shine on its many monuments and palaces. Divided by Seine river for 8 mi. (13 km.) from east to west. North of river, called Rive Droite (Right Bank), characterized by fashionable shops, expensive hotels, offices and small factories. South of river, called Rive Gauche (Left Bank) inhabited by many artists and students.

Newspapers: Of many published in Paris, *Le Figaro* and *Le Monde* cover the arts; *L'Aurore*, *France-Soir* and *Le Parisian Libere* are general publications.

Sewer: Historical exhibitions and film shows can be seen in underground galleries. Tours are cancelled in wet weather and when Seine floods. This attraction did not get any "stars" in Michelin's Guide to Paris.

Transportation: Major stops on subway system ("Metro") include Les Halles, Austerlitz and Victor Hugo. Large train stations include Gare de Lyon, Gare de L'est and Gare d'Austerlitz. Served by three airports: Charles de Gaulle, Orly and Le Bourget.

PARIS LIBERATION Occupied since June 1940, freed of Nazi German troops and domination August 1944. A journalist wrote, "I have never seen in any face such joy as radiated from the faces of the people of Paris this morning."

PARKER, SUZY (1933–   ) America's top fashion model, 1950s. Favorite of noted photographer Richard Avedon. Earned over $100,000 annually at her peak. First appeared on national magazine cover at 19.

PARKING METER First installed July 1935, in Oklahoma City, OK. Carl C. Magee, inventor. Designed as a way to provide cities with extra revenue.

PARKLAND HOSPITAL. See OSWALD, LEE HARVEY

PARROTS Member of group of Tropical birds that includes macaws, cockatoos, parakeets and lorikeets. Can be taught to imitate the human voice, sometimes learning whole sentences. All have four toes, two in front and back.

PARSLEY Hardy biennial green herb with grassy taste. Served on side of many dishes as garnish, or dried and sprinkled into recipes for various stocks and sauces to enhance taste. Two main varieties are Italian and Hamburg (turnip-rooted parsley). Both grown in U.S. Hamburg is most available and widely used.

PARTHENON   Ancient Greek temple. Largest building on the Acropolis in Athens. Example of Doric order of architecture. Built with white marble from Mount Pentelicus to honor patron goddess of Athens, Athena Parthenos. Central part blown up when Turks used it as powder house in 1687 and powder exploded. Sculptures called Elgin Marbles relocated to British Museum in London.

PARTRIDGE FAMILY, THE   TV situation comedy, 1970–1973, about a family (a mother, played by Shirley Jones, and her five children) who become rock-and-roll stars. Teen idol David Cassidy co-starred as the song-writing Keith Partridge. Their song, "I Think I Love You," became a number one hit in 1970.

PASCAL, BLAISE (1623–1662)   French philosopher, physicist and mathematician. Made important mathematical discoveries and invented a mechanical calculator. Inspired by an interest in gambling, he also contributed to theories of probability and chance.

PASTERNAK, BORIS LEONIDOVICH (1890–1960)   Russian poet and novelist. Best known for novel *Doctor Zhivago* (1957), about a Russian doctor-poet's reaction to the Revolution. Soviet government repressed its publication as anti-Soviet, but it won international acclaim and Nobel Prize for Literature (1958) when published abroad. Soviet authorities made him decline prize. Became U.S. best seller in 1958. Film (1965) starred Omar Sharif and Julie Christie.

PATAGONIA   Region in southern part of South America. Name is Spanish word for "big feet" because early inhabitants were tall Indians who wore grass-stuffed boots. Area corresponds with territory in Argentina and Chile though the term generally refers to Argentine section of region.

PATE DE FOIE GRAS   French for "paste of fat liver." A delicacy often served as an hors d'oeuvre. Produced by force-feeding geese kept in tiny cages so they can't move, livers become enlarged. Cruelty-to-animal laws prevent its manufacture in U.S.

PATTERSON, FLOYD (1935–   )   Won vacant heavyweight boxing title by knocking out Archie Moore in 1956. Lost to Sweden's Ingemar Johansson, June 26, 1959. Became first to regain heavyweight title by knocking out Johansson, June 20, 1960. KO'd the Swede again in sixth round, March 13, 1961.

PATTON, GEORGE SMITH (1885–1945) American general, World War II. Brilliant tank-warfare strategist. Began first tank school. Nickname, "Old Blood and Guts." General most feared by the Germans. In a 1943 inspection of a field hospital, slapped two men suffering from battle neuroses. Incident received widespread publicity. He was later forced to apologize to the men. Patton died December 10, 1945, when his army jeep collided with a truck. In the 1912 Olympic pentathlon, Patton had placed fifth.

PAUL BUNYAN Legendary hero of lumber camps of northwestern U.S. Feats said to include cutting Grand Canyon by dragging his pick behind him. Babe the Blue Ox was lumberjack Bunyan's constant companion. Beast measured "42 axhandles" long, and had a plug of Star tobacco between its eyes.

PAULSON, PAT (1927–   ) Comedian. Won Emmy for individual achievement on *Smothers Brothers Comedy Hour*, 1967–1968. Began ill-fated presidential campaign on the program. Paulson left the program because of dispute with CBS over censorial practices.

PAVLOV, IVAN (1849–1936) Russian physiologist, Nobel Prize winner, 1904, for research citing that nerves monitor flow of digestive juices. Trained dogs to salivate at sound of bell in place of food; discussed in his book *Conditioned Reflexes*.

PAWNBROKER, THE 1965 film directed by Sidney Lumet. Rod Steiger portrays Sol Nazerman, a pawnbroker whose memories of Nazi Germany haunt his life in New York's Spanish Harlem.

PAY TELEPHONES Busiest pay phones are located in transportation depots. Allegedly, the busiest pay phone is one in Chicago's bus terminal. Others with inordinately heavy use include one in Grand Central Station in New York City, and one in O'Hare Airport in Chicago.

PEA, THE Oldest vegetable known. Used by Chinese in 2000 B.C., mentioned in the Bible. First brought to America in early 1800s. Have nearly as much protein as meat.

PEACH MELBA Dessert named after Nellie Melba (1861–1931), Australian opera soprano. The dessert was created by French chef Escoffier at the turn of the century and was first served to the opera singer at Savoy Hotel in London.

PEACOCK Male peafowl. Females known as peahens. Only male has characteristic train which displays in a fan during courtship. Its feathers are superstitiously believed to bring disaster to a house or theater. Superstition comes from either an Islamic belief that a peacock opened the gate of Paradise and let the devil in, or from ancient Greek and Roman belief that only priests could wear peacock feathers. Wild varieties are found in India, Sri Lanka, Burma, Malaysia and Java, while domesticated peafowl live worldwide.

PEANUTS. See SCHULZ, CHARLES MONROE

PEARL HARBOR On December 7, 1941, site of surprise attack by Japanese on U.S. naval base in Oahu, Hawaii. Forced U.S. into World War II. Led by Admiral Yamamoto, a Japanese task force of six carriers and two battleships crossed the Pacific, and with code words "Climb Mount Niitaka" began the bombing that sank eight U.S. battleships and killed more than 2,400 Americans. Three of the ships destroyed were the *Arizona*, the *Oklahoma* and the *Utah*.

PEARY, ROBERT EDWIN (1856–1920) American Arctic explorer. Reached North Pole April 6, 1909 with assistant Matthew Henson and four Eskimos. As the first to do this, voted rank of U.S. rear admiral.

PECKINPAH, SAM (1926–   ) Director known for his violent action movies. Began in television where he created *The Rifleman* series. Directed many films including *Ride the High Country* (1962), *The Wild Bunch* (1969), *Straw Dogs* (1971) and *The Getaway* (1972).

PEDOMETER Device that records the distance a person has walked. Can have an internal lever that swings with each step, or can have a wheel that measures distance traveled as it rolls along the ground.

PEGASUS Winged horse of Muses in Greek mythology. Born of sea foam and blood of slaughtered Medusa. Caught by Bellerophon, who fell off trying to ascend to heaven. Riderless Pegasus mounted skies to become constellation of same name.

PEKINGESE Breed of very small long-haired dog. In China, where they originated, only royalty could own them. Are usually tan or brown and weigh 6 to 10 lbs.

PELE Brazilian soccer player, born Edson Arantes do Nascimento, 1940. Considered greatest player in history of sport. Led Brazil to World Cup Championships, 1958, 1962, 1970. Played for New York Cosmos in North American Soccer League, 1975–1977. Nicknamed "the Black Pearl."

PENGUIN   Short-legged, stout-bodied flightless bird. Wings resemble flippers. Excellently adapted for underwater swimming— webbed feet and tail used as rudders. Emperor penguin, largest, reaches 4 ft. (1.2 m.) in height and weighs up to 90 lbs. (40 kg.). Return annually to ancestral breeding grounds. May travel 60 mi. (97 km.) to reach the same rookery. Courtship behaviors include pointing their bills to the sky and holding wings extended.

PENICILLIN   Germ killer and antibiotic. Produced by molds. Accidently discovered by Sir Alexander Fleming, 1928. Only effective against germ-caused diseases, especially infections of the blood. Resistance may develop.

PENN, WILLIAM (1644–1718)   English author. Wrote political-religious treatises, 1670s. Founder and proprietor of American territory that bears his name, Pennsylvania.

PENNEY, JAMES CASH (1875–1971)   Businessman. Founder, J. C. Penney, incorporated 1913. Company is unique in that each store manager shares in profits of entire company. Thousands of stores nationwide.

PENNSYLVANIA STATION   Better known as Penn Station. Commuter and long-distance rail station located at West 33rd Street and 7th Avenue in New York City. Name dates back 100 years when Pennsylvania was the main rail center for the East Coast.

PENTAGON   Office building (world's largest) which houses headquarters of the U.S. Department of Defense. Building has five sides, covers 29 acres, has 3,705,397 sq. ft. (344,234 sq. m.) of space, cost U.S. $83,000,000 to construct and houses approximately 26,700 workers. Restaurants and cafeterias serve over 17,500 meals daily. Facilities include radio and television stations and heliport.

PENTAGON PAPERS   Forty-seven-volume secret study of origins of Vietnam War that Daniel Ellsberg gave to the New York *Times* in 1971. Compiled by think-tank experts at RAND Corporation. *Times* began printing summary in June, followed shortly by the Washington *Post*, then other newspapers. Nixon administration Attorney General John Mitchell obtained temporary restraining order to halt publication, but Supreme Court ruled 6-3 that papers could be published because First Amendment prohibited "prior restraint" of publication.

PENTHOUSE   Calling itself "The International Magazine for Men," founded by editor-publisher Bob Guccione, 1965. Similar editorially and pictorially to *Playboy*, with more tongue-in-cheek editorial tone. 1983 circulation approximately 4 million. *Viva* and *Forum* are other *Penthouse* publications. Includes monthly advice column by former madam Xavieria Hollander. (see GUCCIONE, BOB and HOLLANDER, XAVIERIA)

PEOPLE MAGAZINE   Slick, weekly Time-Life Company publication that established a new trend in short human-interest journalism. Spawned many imitators (*Us* Magazine and *Real People*). Actress Mia Farrow, about to star in *The Great Gatsby*, was on first cover, March 4, 1974. Celebrated 10th anniversary, March 1984, with circulation of more than 2.6 million (1982 figure), ranking it in top 20 for general-interest U.S. magazines.

PEOPLE'S TEMPLE COMMUNE   Guyana, South America. Reverend Jim Jones, founder. Several hundred members committed suicide by drinking poison-laced Kool-Aid in 1978 at Jones' request. Mass suicide came hours after some temple members murdered U.S. Congressman Leo Ryan and his staff, who were investigating activities of the commune.

PEPE LE PEW   The romantic French skunk of ze Warner Brothers cartoons. Voiced by Mel Blanc. Pepe's appearance in the cartoon *For Scent-imental Reasons* won Oscar for Best Short Subject in 1949.

PEPPER   Known by cooks as "the master spice." Used in almost all culinary preparations. One of first spices introduced to Europe and India. Hippocrates used pepper, a stimulant, in prescriptions. Black and white varieties come from same berry.

PEPPERMINT LOUNGE, THE   New York nightclub where the twist dance fad was started by Joey Dee and the Starlighters, whose twist records included "Peppermint Twist." During the 1960s, club was located in Knickerbocker Hotel on West 45th Street. Club now located on 5th Avenue and 15th Street.

PEPSI-COLA   America's second-favorite soft drink. First American product mass marketed in Soviet Union, 1974. In exchange, a sister company of Pepsi gained exclusive rights to sell Stolichnaya Russian vodka in this country.

PEPYS, SAMUEL (1633–1703) English diarist. Kept most famous diary in English language. Never intended for publication. Written 1660–1669. Met and wrote about many leading figures of his time. First published 1825.

PERCENT From Latin meaning "from one hundred," is a way of expressing fractions as parts of one hundred. For example, 40% means 40 hundredths or .40. Forty percent of 70 equals 49.

PERELMAN, SIDNEY JOSEPH (S. J.) (1904–1979) American humorist. Noted for mock gentility and unpredictable imagination. His many *New Yorker* magazine humor essays collected into several books, starting with *Strictly from Hunger* (1937). Also wrote movie scripts for Marx Brothers, including *Monkey Business* (1931), and *Horsefeathers* (1932).

PEREZ, MANUEL BENITEZ. See CORDOBES, EL

PERMAFROST Permanently frozen ground. Usually a mass of ice, earth and rock; sometimes pure ice. May reach depth of 3,000 ft. (910 mi.). Occurs in areas with average annual temperature of 32°F (0°C) or less. May contain preserved prehistoric animals.

PERONI BEER. See BEER, FOREIGN

PERPETUAL-MOTION MACHINES Dream of inventors for centuries. With development of First Law of Thermodynamics and Principle of Conservation of Energy, it became clear that such devices could not be built. Perpetual motion is the rule, however, at the atomic level.

PERRAULT, CHARLES (1628–1703) French writer and historian. Most famous work, *History and Tales of Long Ago* (1697), includes first appearance of Mother Goose and definitive versions of tales "Puss-in-Boots," "Little Red Riding Hood" and "Sleeping Beauty," story of magic spell confining beautiful princess to castle where she must sleep 100 years unless awakened by handsome prince. Also, "Cinderella," story of heroine Ella. Title means "little cinder girl." Raised by cruel stepsisters Anastasia and Drizella, who taunt her saying, "Cinderslut... hold this skein of wool for me." Sent by fairy godmother to Prince's Ball. Prince falls in love with her; later locates her by fitting her with glass slipper she left behind.

PERRY MASON Erle Stanley Gardner's fictional defense attorney. *Perry Mason* became popular TV series, 1957–1966, with Raymond Burr in title role. Barbara Hale portrayed secretary Della Street; William Hopper, his personal investigator Paul Drake. (see GARDNER, ERLE STANLEY)

PERRY, FREDERICK JOHN (1909–   ) British tennis player who won all four major championships between 1934 and 1936. First to win three Wimbledon singles titles in succession (1934–1936). Won French Open, 1935, Australia Open, 1934, and U.S. Open, 1934, 1935. Was also world champion table tennis player, 1929. Björn Borg (five) and Rod Laver (four) have eclipsed his Wimbledon record.

PERSIAN GULF, THE   Countries bordering Persian Gulf: Iran, Iraq, Kuwait, Saudi Arabia, Bahrain, Qatar, United Arab Emirates, Oman.

PERSON TO PERSON   Popular interview TV show. Premiered 1953 with Edward R. Murrow as host (until 1959); Charles Collingwood continued to 1961. Host in studio interviewed celebrities in their homes. Interviewees included John F. Kennedy, Humphrey Bogart and Fidel Castro.

PERU   South America's westernmost point. Once center of Inca Empire and most important Spanish Viceroyalty. Now third largest country in South America.

PETER GUNN   TV detective series from 1958, starring Craig Stevens in title role. Picked up clues from favorite nightclub, Mothers. Herschel Bernardi played friend, police lieutenant Jacoby; Lola Albright was his girl, Edie Hart. Jazz theme by Henry Mancini.

PETER PAN. See BARRIE, SIR JAMES MATTHEW

PETER PRINCIPLE, THE   Phrase picked up from Laurence J. Peter's 1969 book *The Peter Principle: Why Things Always Go Wrong*, which states: "In a hierarchy, every employee tends to rise to his level of incompetence." Thus people who perform job well will be promoted until reaching level they cannot cope with, where they will remain.

PETER, PAUL AND MARY   Popular folksingers of 1960s. Group formed in 1961 by Peter Yarrow, Paul Stookey and Mary Travers; hit songs include: "If I Had a Hammer" (1962), "Blowin' in the Wind" (1963), "Puff the Magic Dragon" (1963) and "Leavin' on a Jet Plane" (1969).

PETER, PETER, PUMPKIN-EATER In nursery rhyme: "had a wife and couldn't keep her. He put her in a pumpkin shell, and there he kept her very well."

PETRIFIED FOREST,THE 1936 film based on Robert Sherwood stage play. Leslie Howard stars as writer who wanders into Arizona roadside restaurant, which is taken over by gang of killers. Bette Davis co-stars. Humphrey Bogart, as leader of hoods, established tough-guy image with this film.

PETRIFIED FOREST NATIONAL PARK Located in Painted Desert of northern Arizona. Contains world's highest concentration of petrified wood. Covers 95,000 acres. Trees are about 150 million years old. Rainbow Forest is most colorful area.

PEWTER Alloy of antimony and copper added to tin. Originally, this ancient mixture contained lead, which caused tarnishing and was poisonous.

PEYTON PLACE. See METALIOUS, GRACE

PHALACROSIS Or alopecia. From Greek, meaning "baldness." Absence of hair from skin areas where normally present. May occur over entire body. Hair loss with age is congenital condition.

PHIL SILVERS SHOW, THE TV situation comedy set at Fort Baster, KS, about con man Sergeant Ernie Bilko, played by Phil Silvers. Bilko always pulling off some scheme under nose of his commanding officer, Colonel J. T. Hall, played by Paul Ford, with the help of his men, including Harvey Lembeck as Corporal Rocco Barbella and Maurice Gosfield as Private Doberman.

PHILADELPHIA Name given to several cities by ancient Greeks, meaning "brotherly love." Pennsylvania city founded in 1682 by English Quaker William Penn as religious freedom center. Fourth largest U.S. city, called "City of Brotherly Love" and "Quaker City."

PHILADELPHIA ZOO Philadelphia Zoological Society was chartered in 1859, but zoo's construction delayed 15 years because of Civil War. Finally opened in 1874. Central Park Zoo in New York City opened in 1864 and is oldest zoo in U.S.

PHILBIN, REGIS (1933–   ) Genial TV personality who first came to national prominence on Joey Bishop talk show. After stint as local newscaster, became bona fide celebrity as host (with Cyndi Garvey, former wife of baseball player Steve Garvey) of Los

Angeles–based talk show, which moved to New York in 1983.
Currently also seen on cable TV's Lifetime Network.

**PHILBY, HAROLD ADRIAN (KIM) (1885–
1960)** Head of British Counter-Espionage, 1944–1951. Provided
Russians with Allied secrets. Correspondent, *London Observer*, 1955.
Detected as spy, 1962, by Soviet defector. Forced to flee.

PHILEAS FOGG. See VERNE, JULES

PHILLIPS, MARK (1948–   ) Married 13th cousin, Princess Anne of Great Britain, November 14, 1973. Engaged after
romance that began at 1968 Mexico City Olympics, where he was
on U.K. equestrian team. Now captain of Queen's exclusive Dra-
goon Guards.

PHOBIAS Unreasonable fears:

Androphobia	-	Fear of men
Arachnaphobia	-	Fear of spiders
Autophobia	-	Fear of self
Basophobia	-	Fear of standing
Carcinomaphobia	-	Fear of cancer
Sinophobia	-	Fear of the Chinese
Gallophobia	-	Fear of anything French
Gynephobia	-	Fear of women
Hippophobia	-	Fear of horses
Monophobia	-	Fear of being alone
Panophobia	-	Fear of everything
Phobophobia	-	Fear of fear
Phonophobia	-	Fear of noise
Triskadekaphobia	-	Fear of number 13
Xenophobia	-	Fear of strangers or foreigners

PHOENIX, THE In Arabian myth: bird that consumed itself
in fire, but rose from ashes of its nest to new life that repeated
former one. Has become symbol of immortality.

PHOTO FINISH. See HORSE RACING TERMS

PHOTOSYNTHESIS. See TREES

PHRENOLOGY Nineteenth-century science holding held that
person's character can be told by feeling bumps on head, because
bumps tell which areas of brain are overdeveloped. Abandoned in
20th century.

PI Ratio of circle's circumference to its diameter, roughly

3. 14159265. Ancient Chinese used 3 as estimate of pi. Impossible to represent exact decimal value. Calculated by IBM 7090 computer to more than 100,000 places in 1961.

PIANO Or pianoforte, meaning "soft and loud" in Italian. Musical instrument with keyboard that provides sounds when keys are pressed, causing hammers to strike strings. Most are either upright, baby grand or grand and have 88 keys (52 white, 36 black) and three pedals, which control string vibrations.

PIAZZA SAN MARCO Central square of Venice. Opens on Grand Canal. Covered passageways shelter well-known shops and cafés. Site of St. Mark's Basilica, church embellished with marble and mosaics, built from 1063–1073.

PICASSO, PABLO (1881–1973) Spanish painter, sculptor, graphic artist and ceramist. Leader of School of Paris. Generally considered foremost artist of 20th century. Only living artist displayed in Grand Gallery of Louvre. Painted *Three Musicians* and *Guernica*. Signed paintings with only last name.

PICCADILLY CIRCUS Major intersection in London where six busy downtown streets join. Location of statue of Eros. Center of London shopping and entertainment. Once called "the Hub of the British Empire."

PICKFAIR Legendary home of actor Douglas Fairbanks and actress Mary Pickford. Fairbanks built Beverly Hills, CA, mansion for wife as wedding present, 1920. Site of many Hollywood parties for over 30 years; now a museum and landmark.

PICKFORD, MARY (1893–1979) Canadian-born actress who became "America's Sweetheart" as star of silent movies since 1909. Among her films: *Pollyanna* (1919), *Little Lord Fauntleroy* (1921) and *Little Annie Rooney* (1925). Won Oscar for her first talkie, *Coquette* (1929). Also called "the Girl with a Curl."

PICKUP STICKS Also called jackstraws. Played with 50 wood or plastic sticks or straws, about 6 in. long, colored to signify point value. Players try to remove sticks from pile without disturbing other sticks. Player who does so ends game; winner is player with highest point total for sticks accumulated.

PIED PIPER OF HAMELIN According to German folklore, town of Hamelin hired this magician in 1284 to rid town of rats. Magician lured them out by playing pipe; when town leaders refused to pay, lured town's children away, never to be seen again.

PIERRE   Capital of South Dakota. Two mi. (3.2 km.) from geographical center of North America. Has four palisaded forts. Was capital to Aricara Indians.

PIGASUS. See YOUTH INTERNATIONAL PARTY

PIGEON, CLAY   Thin, saucer-shaped target, 3–4 in. in diameter, used in skeet or trapshooting. Introduced in 1860s. Originally made of clay, but proved too difficult to break with gunfire. Now made of mixture of river silt and pitch or asphalt. Thrown from "trap" at angle unknown to shooter, on trajectory, giving height of 8–12 ft. when 10 yds. from trap. Released on shooter's command, "Pull!" Designed to simulate game birds.

PILGRIMS   Religious reformers. Left Leiden, Holland, on *Mayflower*, September 1620, seeking religious freedom. Landed at Plymouth Rock, MA, November 21, 1620, and established colony.

PILLOW TALK   1959 comedy film starring Rock Hudson and Doris Day as songwriter and interior decorator who become enemies when forced to share party line. Tony Randall and Thelma Ritter co-star.

PILLSBURY BAKE-OFF   Baking/recipe contest sponsored by Pillsbury Company of Minneapolis since 1948. Most winners of $25,000 grand prize (two awarded every year since 1972) have been housewives; no man has won grand prize, though men have won in lesser categories. Among recent winners: Nan Rob's Onion Lover's Twist, 1969; Mrs. Gerald Collins' Chewy Cocoanut Crescent Bars, 1972; Mrs. Leulla E. Maki's Sour Cream Apple Squares, 1975.

PINA COLADA   Cocktail originated at Caribe Hilton Hotel, San Juan, Puerto Rico, 1952. Spanish, meaning "strained pineapple." Mixed by blending 1½ oz. cream of coconut, 3 tbsp. crushed pineapple (or 6 oz. pineapple juice) and 3 oz. light rum with shaved ice. Hit song known as "Piña Colada Song," about placing newspaper personal ads for romance, by Rupert Holmes.

PINEAPPLE   Genus ananas, species A. comosus. Named after pine cone. Hawaii is world's largest producer. Leaflike structures on skin, called floral bracts or "fruitlets," develop from blue-violet flower. Ninety percent of crop is canned. Highest quality achieved when ripened on the plant.

PINK PANTHER, THE   1964 hit comedy film, directed by Blake Edwards, that introduced Inspector Clouseau (Peter Sellers), accident-prone French detective on trail of thieves who stole Pink Panther diamond. Sequel, released same year: *A Shot in the Dark.*

PINKERTON   Private detective and security agency. Motto: "We never sleep." Founded 1850 by Allan Pinkerton. In 1861 guarded President-elect Abraham Lincoln from home state of Illinois to Washington, D.C. Also helped establish Secret Service to guard presidents and combat counterfeiting.

PINOCCHIO   1940 animated film by Walt Disney. Wooden puppet comes alive with help of magical Blue Fairy. If he tells a lie, his nose grows longer. Jiminy Cricket sings "When You Wish upon a Star" and becomes his conscience. In the end, Pinocchio becomes a real boy. (see COLLODI, CARLO)

PINTER, HAROLD (1930–   )   English playwright noted for "comedies of menace": plays of fear, horror and mystery. First stage success, *The Caretaker* (1960; film adaptation, 1962), about devious old tramp Davies. *The Collection* (1961), adaptation of his original TV play, expresses husband's fear of wife's infidelity. Pinter noted for ambiguous dialogue and long silences in plays. Also wrote screenplays for *The Servant* (1962), *Accident* (1967), *The Go-Between* (1971) and *The Homecoming* (1965).

PIPE VOLUME   Given by formula $\pi(\frac{1}{2}D)^2L$, where D is diameter of pipe and L is length. If diameter of pipe is doubled, volume is quadrupled.

PIRATES OF PENZANCE, THE   Comic operetta by Gilbert and Sullivan, performed for first time in 1879. Story involves young orphan, Frederick, raised by pirates but abandoning their ways on 21st birthday. On dry land, Frederick falls in love with Mabel, Major General's youngest daughter.

PISCATOLOGY   Art or science of fishing. From Latin *piscatus,* present participle of *piscari* ("to fish").

PISTACHIO NUTS   Members of cashew family that grow in clusters on pistachio trees. Nuts have pale shells with green kernels inside. Often salted in shell and dyed red. Grown especially in Mediterranean area and southwest Asia.

PITA BREAD   White, whole or cracked wheat bread from

Near East and Greece. Round and flat, can be partially split to form pocket for sandwich fillings. Often called "pocket bread."

PITCAIRN ISLAND   Island in South Pacific Ocean just south of Tropic of Capricorn. Population: 65. Famous as landing spot of nine mutineers from British ship *Bounty*. Unequal proportion of men to women created vicious fighting; of men, only John Adams survived. Island's only village is called Adamstown.

PITTI AND UFFIZI GALLERIES. See FLORENCE

PITTSBURGH   City in southwestern Pennsylvania, located at meeting point of Allegheny and Monongahela rivers. One of world's primary steelmakers. Nicknamed "Iron City," "Steel City," "Hearth of the Nation" and "Arsenal of the World." City grew around military post called Fort Pitt, named after British prime minister William Pitt.

PITUITARY GLAND   Three-lobed structure hanging from base of brain. Manufactures and releases hormones that stimulate thyroid, adrenal and sex glands. Regulates growth; if diseased, growth will be impaired.

PIZARRO, FRANCISCO (c.1478–1541)   Spanish explorer. With Balboa, "discovered" Pacific Ocean, 1513. Conquered Peru, 1533, and ruled there until murdered by group of Incas.

PLACEBO   Preparation devoid of pharmacological effect. Given for suggestive or psychological effect. From Latin, meaning "I will please." Also used as control in evaluating medicines believed to have pharmacological effect; patient and physician may or may not know which is which.

PLAGUE   Epidemic viral disease. Killed one-quarter of Europe's population in 14th century; spread through Asia and Africa as well. Causes black spots of blood to gather under skin; also causes buboes, or swellings in the lymph glands. Called Black Death, Bubonic Plague and Black Plague.

PLAIN DEALER, THE   Cleveland's morning newspaper. Independent daily publication established in 1842. Circulation: 487,672 daily (495,277 on Sundays).

PLAINS OF ABRAHAM   Located in Quebec City, Canada. Site of Battle of Quebec, where French surrendered city to British in 1759. After another defeat in 1760, French lost all possessions

Plaka, The

in North America except islands of St. Pierre and Miquelon, Martinique and Guadeloupe.

PLAKA, THE District in Athens, Greece, dating from years of Turkish control when city was just village. Characterized by winding cobblestoned alleys, cafés, small shops and traces of Turkish influence.

PLANETS—WORLD ORIGINS Planet named after Mercury, Roman messenger god: Mercury. Venus, Roman goddess of love and beauty: Venus. Earth, Indo-European root, *er*, meaning "earth" or "ground." Mars, Roman god of war: Mars. Jupiter, supreme Roman god: Jupiter. Saturn, Roman god of agriculture: Saturn. Uranus, Greek god of the sky: Uranus. Neptune, Roman god of the sea: Neptune. Pluto, Roman god of the dead and ruler of underworld: Pluto.

PLATINUM RECORD Award given by Recording Industry Association of America (RIAA) to performers whose albums have sold one million copies. Conceived in 1976. First winner: Eagles' *Their Greatest Hits LP*.

PLATO (c.427–347 B.C.) Greek philosopher. Called "father of Western philosophy" because his works, or dialogues, touched on virtually every problem subsequently studied by philosophers.

PLAY IT AGAIN, SAM 1972 film written by and starring Woody Allen, based on his Broadway play. Allen plays movie buff, with huge *Across the Pacific* poster on his wall, who has no luck with women despite advice he receives from spirit of Humphrey Bogart (Jerry Lacy).

PLAY MISTY FOR ME 1971 film directed by and starring Clint Eastwood as disk jockey involved with psychopathic fan. Introduced song "The First Time Ever I Saw Your Face."

PLAYBOY Monthly magazine calling itself "Entertainment for Men", founded December 1953 by former *Esquire* staffer Hugh Hefner. Accents sophisticated male interests and associates sex with "girl next door" centerfold Playmates. Art director Art Paul designed rabbit logo for first issue, which cost $.50 and sold 53,991 copies (now brings as much as $400). This issue featured actress Marilyn Monroe on cover and nude inside as first "Sweetheart of the Month" centerfold (name later changed to Playmate of the Month), Hefner bought Monroe photos for $500 from Chicago calendar company and used them without her permission. First man to appear on cover was actor Peter Sellers, April 1964, portrayed as Rudolph Valentino-type sheik, highlighting pictorial feature "Sellers Mimes the Movie Lovers." Magazine now ranks 13th in U.S. circulation, with 4.5 million copies monthly (1983 figures). Besides Playmates, offers monthly interview with leading personality (Jimmy Carter created controversy when interviewed during 1976 presidential campaign), articles and stories by famous writers such as Ian Fleming, Norman Mailer and Alex Haley (see separate entries) and cartoons such as Little Annie Fannie—Little Orphan Annie satire created by *Mad* illustrator/writers Harvey Kurtzman and Will Elder in October 1962; satire features buxom Annie Fannie, Sugardaddy Bigbucks, Annie Fannie's roommate Wanda Homefree and slick press agent Solly Brass. (see HEFNER, HUGH)

PLAYER, GARY (1935–   ) South African golfer. First player not born in U.S. to win Masters Tournament (1961), beating Arnold Palmer by one stroke on final hole. Also won Masters in 1974, 1978; U.S. Open, 1965; PGA Tournament, 1962, 1972; British Open, 1959, 1968, 1974. With Palmer and Jack Nicklaus, one of golf's Big Three of 1960s and early '70s.

PLAYING CARDS   *Aces:* Called "bullets," especially in poker, because card players could not argue with aces any more than they could with bullets; term originated in 1930s. Four aces in standard 52-card deck, one in each of four suits. Odds of cutting ace therefore 1 in 13, or 12–1. Ace of spades considered card of ill omen, malice, misfortune and death, although Napoleon Bonaparte thought eight of spades was unluckiest card in deck. Spades traditionally denote treachery, disappointment and death.

Court cards: Jack, queen and king in each of four suits. Identified by stylized drawings and initial letter of card (J, Q or K). Each has two faces. Profile cards are king of diamonds and jack of hearts (facing right) and jack of spades (facing left). Number of eyes shown in deck is 42: four on each full face card (nine), two on each profile card (three).

Four of clubs: Called "four of bedposts" or "devil's bedposts" in sailors' slang. Playing cards often called invention of devil by religious groups, thus increasing popularity of card games and readings.

Nine of diamonds: Nicknamed "the curse of Scotland," most probably because card is pope in old card game Pope Joan. Scottish feeling of antagonism against papacy led to card's monicker. First written reference in *The British Apollo*, 1710.

Nine of hearts: Fortunetellers and other "guides" to card reading see love in suit of hearts (originally "cups" in tarot deck). Nine symbolizes wish fulfilled or prosperity. Ace of hearts also cited as symbol of love, as is nine of clubs (success in love).

Queen of spades: Referred to in Old West as "Calamity Jane," after real-life Calamity Jane, a.k.a. Mary Jane Canary (1852–1903), South Dakota frontier woman who "dressed, cursed and shot like a man." Card is key in game of hearts, an "avoidance" game in which player tries to avoid taking hearts (one point each) and queen of spades (13 points) if not trying to "shoot the moon" (take all point cards).

King of diamonds: Famous monarchs have graced faces of kings and queens of playing cards for centuries. Roman emperor Julius Caesar first appeared on king of diamonds c. 1490. Others pictured on this card are Charlemagne and Napoleon.

King of hearts: Known as "suicide king" because illustration on card shows him sticking sword into own head with left hand. Right hand holds lapel.

PLAYING CARDS—DECK Jocularly referred to as "California Prayer Book" or "California Bible" c. 1855, after 1849 Gold Rush brought merchants, gamblers and hangers-on to Far West. Marked or fixed deck known as "doped cards" or "cheaters," "coolers," "paper," "readers" and "fishback." "Humps" were cards with slightly raised edges. "Reflectors" were cards with marks on the backs for cheating. Deck consists of four suits: spades and clubs (black symbols); hearts and diamonds (red symbols). Each card carries its suit symbol twice (in upper left and lower right corners), and court cards have an additional two symbols. Numerical cards also have symbols representing their value (e. g., nine diamonds on nine of diamonds). Therefore, 87 of each symbol are contained in standard pack.

PLIMPTON, GEORGE AMES (1927–   ) Editor of literary quarterly *Paris Review*. Wanted readers to get feeling of what it was like to compete with pro athletes and wrote about many of his own exploits. Among them: pitching against baseball All-Stars (*Out of My League*, 1961); joining Detroit Lions of National Football League for training camp (*Paper Lion*, 1966); entering three professional golf tournaments (*Bogey Man*, 1968). All originally appeared

Merkin & Frankel

as *Sports Illustrated* articles. Also braved three rounds with light-heavy-weight boxing champ Archie Moore in 1959.

PLOCK Port town on Vistula River. Situated in east central Poland. On major pipeline from Soviet Union to Poland; major petrochemical center.

PLUTO Planet discovered by Clyde Tombaugh in 1930, although Percival Lowell predicted its existence in 1915. Smallest planet and farthest from sun; however, occasionally its elliptical orbit brings it closer than Neptune. May have moon nearly as large as itself. Cannot be seen without telescope. Takes 248 years to travel once around sun. Temperature: about −300°F (−150°C).

PLUVIOMETER Device to measure rainfall. From Latin *pluvia* ("rain") and *metiri* ("to measure"). Rain falls through funnel into cylinder marked specifically for measurement.

PO RIVER Largest river in Italy. Rises in Cottian Alps and empties into Adriatic Sea. Surrounding land is very fertile. River frequently causes devastating floods.

POCAHONTAS (1595–1617) American Indian princess. Daughter of Chief Powhatan. Saved life of Captain John Smith of Jamestown, VA, 1608, by offering her own head. Later converted to Christianity. Married Englishman John Rolfe, 1614, and moved to London. Buried near Thames River.

POCKET BILLIARDS. See BILLIARDS

POE, EDGAR ALLAN (1808–1849) American poet, critic, editor and short-story writer. Led mysterious, macabre life that was reflected in his works. Among them is "Murders in the Rue Morgue" (1841), considered first modern detective story, in which amateur detective C. Auguste Dupin solves "locked room" murders of mother and daughter that have baffled Parisian police. Dupin also appears in later stories "The Mystery of Marie Roget" and "The Purloined Letter" (1845), about cabinet minister who uses compromising letter for blackmail. Baffled police again turn to Dupin, whose deductive techniques became model for many other literary detectives. In "The Fall of the House of Usher" (1839) narrator receives letter inviting him to visit boyhood friend Roderick Usher, who fears he is beset with some mental disorder. He is, and house comes down, literally as well as figuratively. In "The Pit and the Pendulum" (1842) narrator is condemned to death by Spanish Inquisition but rescued from edge of pit at last second by outstretched arm of General Lasalle as French army captures Toledo. In "The Raven" (1845) poet lost in melancholy memories of dead love is startled by raven knocking on parlor door. Raven's mysterious, unchanging chant "Nevermore" serves as eerie epitaph on Poe's gravestone in Baltimore, MD, where he died at age 40 of consumption induced by alcoholism and depression.

POETRY   Sometimes known as "the gay science" because of its old Provençal name: *gai saber.* Guild formed in Toulouse, France, 1323, to keep alive dying Provençal language and culture called *Gai Saber,* short for "The Very Gay Company of the Seven Troubadors of Toulouse."

POGO   Walt Kelly's newspaper comic strip, 1948–1975, about opposum living in Okefenokee Swamp, GA. Pogo keeps order in society of swamp characters, including Albert the Alligator, P. T. Bridgeport the bear, Beauregard the bloodhound and Churchy la Femme the turtle.

POITIER, SIDNEY (1924–   )   Acclaimed actor, first black man to win Best Actor Oscar (*Lilies of the Field,* 1963). Many popular films include: *The Blackboard Jungle* (1955); *The Defiant Ones* (1958), for which he received first nomination; *In the Heat of the Night* (1967); *Guess Who's Coming to Dinner* (1967).

POKER   Probably originated in Orient. Introduced to U.S. in 19th century by sailors.
Ante: Commonly, stake each player must put into "pot" before receiving cards or drawing new ones to hand. Card experts maintain difference between "blind," stake put up before hand is dealt, and "ante," voluntary bet made before hand is complete but after first cards have been seen.
Dead man's hand: Includes black aces and eights. Named after hand frontier marshal Wild Bill Hickok held when shot in back by Jack McCall in Deadwood, SD, 1876.
Dealer's choice: Option exercised by dealer in choosing type of poker to be played on his deal. May choose any variant, including any he can devise. May not: alter betting limits, add or remove cards from deck, or alter basic poker rules.
Number of possible hands: In five-card poker, 2,598,960 hands are possible. Of these, no-pair hands are most common: 1,302,540. There are twice as many straights as flushes; 36 straight flushes and four royal flushes.

World Series of Poker: World's biggest-money poker tournament, held annually in May since 1970 in Horseshoe Casino, Las Vegas, NV. Competitors play eight hours a day. Main event is game called Hold 'Em, variation of seven-card stud. Johnny Moss first to win more than once.

POKER—RANK OF HANDS Following universally recognized (with no wild cards). Each hand loses to one preceding, defeats those after: royal flush (ace, king, queen, jack, 10, of same suit); straight flush (five cards of same suit in sequence); four of a kind; full house (three cards of one denomination, two of another); flush (five cards of same suit, not in sequence); straight (five cards in sequence, but not of same suit); three of a kind; two pairs; one pair; high card (of five unmatched cards). When hands are of same rank, winning hand is one with highest-ranking cards. Variations of this order usually agreed upon before game begins. Lowest hand: ace, two, three, four and six, provided cards not of same suit (which would create a flush; a five would create a straight).

POKER VARIATIONS Acknowledged standard games are five-card stud, seven-card stud and five-card draw. Numerous variations, with and without wild cards, include lowball (where lowest hand wins), Cincinnati (ten-card game with five in hand and five face-down on table, exposed singly at betting intervals, with player able to use any of table cards to compose final hand) and Chicago (variation of seven-card stud, in which hand with highest spade wins half of pot). In five-card draw (with wild cards) high hand would be five aces, in this case beating royal flush.

POLAR BEAR One of largest meat-eating mammals living. White fur blends with icy landscape of Arctic. Scientific name: *Thalarctos maritimus,* meaning "sea bear." Good swimmer. Called *nanook* in Eskimo. Robert Flaherty's documentary film, *Nanook of the North,* 1922, was about Eskimo life.

POLAR EXPLORATION In 1910 British explorer Robert Scott received message "Heading south, Amundsen" from Roald Amundsen, Norwegian explorer. Race to South Pole began. Amundsen arrived December 14, 1911; Scott, January 18, 1912. All of Scott's crew starved and froze to death on return.

POLISH INVASION. See WORLD WAR II

POLITBURO Soviet Union's agency in control of public policy and government. Part of Communist Party until 1952, when it became part of U.S.S.R.'s direct government.

POLLOCK, PAUL JACKSON (1912–1956) American abstract painter. Earned nickname "Jack the Dripper" in 1940s, when developed technique of spattering paint on canvas using subdued colors, producing overall design with curves and texture. Initiator of op art in 1950s and '60s. Among paintings: *Mural* (1944), *Full Fathom Five* (1947) and *Autumn Rhythm* (1955).

POLO Game played by two teams of four players mounted on horseback. Score by stroking ball with long-handled mallet through goalposts. Helmeted players control ponies with left hand, stick with right hand. Game consists of six chukkers, or periods, with three minutes between. Originated in Persia as early as 500 B.C. Played on largest field of any game: 12.4 acres, or 300 × 200 yds. (without sideboards).

POLO, MARCO (1254?–1324?) Italian adventurer. Traveled to China, 13th century. Guest at court of Kubla Khan. Returned to Italy 24 years later with jewels, silk and pasta.

POLYGONS With number of sides: triangle (3), quadrilateral (4), pentagon (5), hexagon (6), heptagon (7), octagon (8), nonagon (9), decagon (10), dodecagon (12).

POMPIDOU, GEORGES (1911–1974) French premier of Fifth Republic. Appointed by President Charles de Gaulle, 1966. When de Gaulle resigned, 1968, Pompidou was voted in by national election.

PONCE DE LEON, JUAN (c.1460–1591) Spanish explorer. During 1513 search for legendary Fountain of Youth, discovered Bimini in Bahamas; also discovered Florida. Named governor to colonize these finds. Died in attack by Seminole Indians.

PONTIUS PILATE (?–A.D. 39) Roman governor of Judea, appointed A.D. 26. Tried Christ for treason against Rome by claiming to be king of Jews. According to Passover tradition, Pilate offered Jews right to free one prisoner. They chose Barabbas, convicted murderer, over Christ. Pilate sentenced Christ to crucifixion, a common punishment of that time.

PONY EXPRESS Early mail delivery service, on horseback. Began April 1860. Route stretched from St. Joseph, MO, to Sacramento, CA. Riders braved rough terrain and inclement weather conditions. Discontinued October 1861, when first telegraph lines reached across country.

POOL. See BILLIARDS

POPCORN Introduced to English colonists by Quadequina, brother of Massasoit, at first Thanksgiving dinner, February 22, 1630. Kernels found in nearly 7,000-year-old remains of Central American settlements, thought to be earliest variety of corn. Water in kernels causes popping.

POPE Elected by College of Cardinals within 18 days of death of previous pope. Cardinals vote by secret ballot in Sistine Chapel. Ballots burned afterward, causing white smoke if pope has been elected. If no decision reached, straw is added to fire, causing black smoke. Among notable popes is Pius XII (1879–1958), ordained 1899; crowned March 12, 1939. During World War II, criticized for maintaining Vatican neutrality by keeping silent about extermination of Jews. Paul VI (1897–1978), pope 1963–1978, was first to visit North Africa (1964) and U.S. (1965). John Paul I (1912–1978) succeeded Paul VI. Pope August 26– September 29, 1978; shortest papacy since 1605. John Paul II (1920–   ) succeeded John Paul I, October 22, 1978. Former Archbishop of Krakow, Poland. Born Karol Wojtyla, took papal name from predecessor. On May 13, 1981, shot and wounded, St. Peter's Square; afterward, reportedly asked, "Why did they do it?" John has been name of 21 popes and two antipopes. First ruled, 523–526; most recent, Pope John XXIII (born Angelo Giuseppe Roncalli), ruled 1958–1963.

POPEYE Cartoon comic strip sailor created by E. C. Segar in 1929. Trademarks include pipe, anchor tattoos and love of spinach, which gives him great strength. Girlfriend Olive Oyl, rival Bluto and adopted son Swee' Pea are part of legend. First Popeye animated motion-picture cartoon produced in 1933; live action feature (starring Robin Williams) released in 1980.

POPEYE DOYLE Character played by Gene Hackman in Oscar-winning *The French Connection* (1971). Hair-raising automobile chase highlights film, based on exploits of New York narcotics detective. Hackman won Best Actor Oscar for role reprised it in sequel, *French Connection II* (1975).

POPULATION, WORLD Approximate world population is 4,219,000,000. China (1,008,175,288), India (713,000,000), Soviet Union (268,800,000) and U.S.(232,000,000) together contain over half the world's people. World population density is 78 persons per sq. mi. (30 per sq. km.). Most populated continent is Asia, with approximately 2,757,383,000 people; density, 161 people per sq. mi. (62 per sq. km.). Asia's largest ethnic groups are Chinese, Indians and Arabs. Second most populated continent is Europe, with about 669,000,000; highest density of any continent with 166 people per sq. mi. (64 per sq. km.).

PORGY AND BESS   George Gershwin's folk opera about lives of inhabitants of Catfish Row, tenement section of Charleston, SC. 1959 film version starred Sidney Poitier and Dorothy Dandridge, with Sammy Davis, Jr., as Sportin' Life. Lyrics by Ira Gershwin and Dubose Heyward.

PORT SAID   Port city in northeast Egypt at northern entrance to Suez Canal. Administrative headquarters of Suez Canal. Handles large portion of Egypt's export trade. Vacation spot.

PORT SIDE OF BOAT. See BOAT

PORT-OF-SPAIN   Capital and port of Trinidad and Tobago, South American island country off northeast coast of Venezuela. City located on Trinidad's northwest coast. Founded by Spanish in 1560. Famed Belmont Hill overlooks city.

PORTUGUESE   Romance language similar to Spanish. Official language of Portugal and Brazil. Portuguese colonizers brought language to Brazil in 1500s. Spoken by 75 million Brazilians. Galician is dialect of language.

PORTUGUESE MAN-OF-WAR   Floating jellyfish of warm seas. Has poisonous tentacles up to 100 ft. long that paralyze and capture fish. Can be dangerous to humans.

POST, EMILY (1872–1960)   American columnist and author on etiquette. Her definitive book on proper social behavior, *Etiquette, the Blue Book of Social Usage*, 1921, was in 10th edition at time of her death. Rules changed over years; gum chewing, originally not discussed, later all right "whenever formal standards of behavior not in force"; doughnut-dunking likewise acceptable if doughnut broken in half first.

POST, WILEY (1899–1935)   Pioneer in American aviation. First to fly around world alone. Helped prove possibility of high-altitude flights. In 1924, lost eye in mining accident; bought first airplane with compensation money. Died in plane crash with famed American humorist Will Rogers.

POSTSCRIPT   Abbreviated P.S. Means literally "written after." From Latin, combining *post* ("after") with *scribere* ("to write"). In letter writing, note added below writer's signature.

POTATO   Root tuber of potato plant, close relative of tomato, pepper, tobacco and eggplant. Originated in South America. Important varieties are Red Nordland, Kennebec, Russet, Idaho and California Long White. Foreign names for potato include: *patate* (Albania); *pomme de terre* (France); *Kartoffel* (Germany); *pomo di terri* (Italy); *patata* (Spain).

POTATO CHIPS   Invented 1853 by George Crum, in Saratoga Springs, NY. Have become most popular snack food in North America. Of $3.8 billion Americans spent annually on snack foods, $1.7 billion spent on potato chips, $1 billion on nuts, $485 million for corn chips.

POTSDAM CONFERENCE   Held after German surrender, World War II. Churchill, Truman and Stalin agreed upon division, demilitarization, denazification and democratization of Germany. Also issued ultimatum to Japan for unconditional surrender.

POTTER, HELEN (BEATRIX) (1866–1943)   English writer and illustrator of children's stories. Flopsy, Mopsy and Cottontail are rabbit characters in her *Tales of Peter Rabbit*. Collected and published 1902, *Peter Rabbit* began as illustrated stories Potter sent to sick children. Characters based on animals she saw around her Lake District home.

POTTERY   Craft also known as ceramics. Kickwheel (pedal-powered wheel) used to aid artist in forming and molding wet clay. Objects then fired in kiln (special oven) for durability.

POUND, EZRA LOOMIS (1885–1972)   Poet and critic. Left U.S. to live in Italy. Made what were considered anti-American broadcasts on Roman radio's *American Hour*, 1941. Charged with treason by U.S. government. Case never tried.

POWELL, JR., ADAM CLAYTON (1908–1972)   U.S. Congressman from Harlem, 1945–1967 and 1969–1970. Outspoken on civil rights. Declared, "Black power is black responsibility." Published two collections of essays, *Keep the Faith, Baby* (1967) and

Marching Blacks (1945). Barred from Congress for alleged "misuse of funds." Regained seat in special election.

POWER BOATS Most prestigious competitions in this sport are for Gold Cup and Hamsworth Trophy. Boats named *Miss Bardahl* and *Slo-Mo-Shun* each won Gold Cup five times. Others that also dominated sport in 1950s and '60s were *Maverick* and *Miss Supertest.*

PRADO MUSEUM Spanish national museum of painting and sculpture. Located in Madrid; opened 1819. Initially maintained by royal family and called Royal Museum, holding only Spanish paintings. Became national property and renamed, 1868. Includes jewelry, furniture, tapestries and paintings by Titian, Veronese, Rubens, Van Dyke, Brueghel, El Greco, Goya and many others.

PRAGUE Czechoslovakia's capital and largest city. Often called "city of a hundred spires." Home to Wenceslaus Square, wide boulevard of hotels, shops and cafés, and Prague's busiest street. City founded in A.D. 800s. Became capital in 1918. Russians invaded in 1945.

PRAVDA Means "truth." Official U.S.S.R. Communist Party newspaper. Began as underground paper in St. Petersburg, 1912. Lenin was a founder. Paper now published in Moscow. Prints editions in 30 plants around U.S.S.R. Eight million circulation.

PRAYING MANTIS Large insect so called because it rests with forelegs folded as if in prayer. Two to 5 in. long, found nearly worldwide. Voracious eaters; female will often eat smaller male after mating. Bred and distributed in U.S. because it eats harmful insects.

PREAKNESS STAKES. See TRIPLE CROWN

PRESLEY, ELVIS AARON (1935–1977) First true rock-and-roll star, became teen idol and national sensation in the late 1950s. Won second prize in 1945 at Mississippi-Alabama Fair and Dairy Show singing "Old Shep." First hit song, "Heartbreak Hotel," released in 1956. Other songs include: "Hound Dog" (1956), "Don't Be Cruel" (1956), "All Shook Up" (1957), "Are You Lonesome Tonight?" (1960), "Burning Love" (1972). Colonel Tom Parker was manager. Presley served briefly in U.S. Army; discharged, March 5, 1960.

PRIESTLEY, JOSEPH (1733–1804) English chemist and clergyman. Discovered oxygen in 1774; called it delphlogisticated air. Gave rubber its name, 1770, when he discoverd it could "rub out" pencil marks.

PRIMA DONNA, THE   Star or leading singer in an opera. Some of most famous "first ladies" are Lily Pons, Grace Moore and Maria Callas.

PRIMARY COLORS   Red, yellow and blue. Called "primary" because greatest variety of other colors can be made from them. Secondary colors: orange, violet and green, made by mixing primary colors.

PRIME MERIDIAN. See GREENWICH, ENGLAND

PRIME NUMBERS   Numbers that can be divided evenly only by themselves and the number one. One is not considered a prime number. Two is smallest and only even prime number.

PRIMROSE LANE   Hit song by actor/singer Jerry Wallace (1959), in which "life's a holiday on Primrose Lane." Other Wallace hits include "In the Misty Moonlight" and "To Get to You."

PRINCE CHARLES (1948–   )   Eldest son of Queen Elizabeth II. Presently Prince of Wales, heir apparent to throne. First member of royal family to graduate from university. Married Lady Diana Spencer, 1981. In 1982 Diana gave birth to their son, William.

PRINCE VALIANT   Hero of Harold Foster's meticulously drawn and plotted Sunday comic strip about characters in Arthurian legend. First appeared February 13, 1937. Foster stopped drawing it in 1971, but the strip continues. Film version (1953) starred Robert Wagner, with Janet Leigh as his wife, Queen Aleta.

PRINCESS OF WALES. See SPENCER, LADY DIANA

PRINCETON UNIVERSITY   Fourth oldest university in U.S. Founded 1746 as College of New Jersey. Moved from Elizabeth to Newark in 1748. In 1756 moved to Princeton, small town 10 miles from New Jersey's present capital, Trenton. Renamed Princeton University in 1896.

PRIVATE LIFE OF HENRY VIII, THE   Charles Laughton won Best Actor Oscar for portrayal of Henry VIII in 1933 film directed by Alexander Korda. Picture presents life and loves of infamous king.

PRODUCERS, THE   Mel Brooks' 1967 comedy film about has-been theatrical producer (Zero Mostel) and his accountant (Gene Wilder), who figure they can make more profit from a Broadway flop than from a hit. Unfortunately, their play *Springtime for Hitler* is a smash.

PROFUMO, JOHN (1915–   )   British secretary of war. Resigned, 1963, after admitted lying to Parliament about relationship with 21-year-old London model, Christine Keeler. Scandal began after Keeler failed to appear to testify at unrelated trial. Thought her testimony would reveal her relationships with other high-ranking members of government. (see RICE-DAVIES, MANDY)

PROHIBITION   As defined in 1920 18th Amendment to Constitution: forbidding of manufacture, transportation and sale of some or all types of alcoholic beverages. Marked culmination of movement toward temperance. Ironically, "prohibition era" marked by wild living and ganster violence. On December 6, 1933, New York *Daily Mirror* announced repeal of this amendment, (only amendment yet repealed), with words: "Prohibition ends at last." Twenty-first Amendment, repealing 18th, passed in hope that liquor tax money would stimulate economy.

PROJECT MERCURY   First U.S. manned space program. Begun under term of President John F. Kennedy in response to Soviets' having sent first man into space, April 12, 1961. First American in space, Alan B. Shepherd, Jr., May 5, 1961, aboard Project Mercury's Freedom spacecraft. Each flight manned by one astronaut.

PROMETHEUS   Titan of Greek mythology who created men from mud and became their benefactor, stealing fire from heaven for them. Zeus punished him by chaining him to mountain where eagle pecked his liver all day (it grew back at night). Eventually Heracles (Hercules in Latin) rescued him.

PROOF   Standard measurement of alcoholic content. In U.S. 1 proof is one-half percentage by volume; hence 100-proof gin is 50% alcohol by volume. Proof measurement not usually used for wine and beer.

PROVIDENCE STEAMROLLERS   Early team in National Football League, 1925–1931. League champions, 1928.

PROXMIRE, EDWARD WILLIAM (1915–   )   U.S. senator who cuts unnecessary government expenses. Gives out Golden

Fleece Awards for cases of glaringly wasteful government spending. One recipient was $280,000 Pentagon study of effectiveness of Frisbees in carrying flares in combat situations.

PRUNES   Are to plums what raisins are to grapes. Only some plum varieties can be dried to make prunes. California produces 200,000 tons of this vitamin- and iron-rich dried fruit per year.

PSALM 23   Most famous and popular of 150 psalms, known as Psalm of David. Number 23 built around metaphors of shepherd and host. Begins: "The Lord is my shepherd, I shall not want; / he makes me lie down in green pastures."

PSYCHO   Popular 1960 suspense film directed by Alfred Hitchcock. Janet Leigh is Marion Crane, who steals fortune but is stabbed to death at Bates Motel. Martin Balsam is second to die. Anthony Perkins portrays motel proprietor Norman Bates, under spell of domineering mother. Sequel: *Psycho II* (1983).

PTERODACTYL   Prehistoric flying reptile, now extinct. Not an ancestor of birds. Ranged from size of sparrow to about 15 ft. (4.6 meters) long. Batlike wings. Had teeth.

PUFF, THE MAGIC DRAGON   Hit 1963 song by Peter, Paul and Mary, in which Puff's human friend is Jackie Paper.

PULITZER PRIZE   Awarded annually, since 1917, in journalism, letters and music. Established in bequest to Columbia University, New York City, in will of American newspaper publisher Joseph Pulitzer (1847–1911). Since 1947 awarded each spring by university trustees and administered by Columbia University Graduate School of Journalism. Awards in 14 categories made on recommendation of 14-member advisory board.

PULLMAN, GEORGE M. (1831–1897)   American industrialist who developed railroad sleeping car. Trained as cabinetmaker. Built *Pioneer* (1863), first modern sleeping car, attached to President Lincoln's funeral train. In 1867, with Andrew Carnegie, organized Pullman Palace Car Company. Also invented dining car, 1868.

PUN   Play on words using words similar or identical in sound, suggesting more than one meaning. In *Romeo and Juliet*, for example, dying Mercutio says: "Ask me tomorrow, and you shall find me a grave man."

PURSE   Prize money in boxing and horse racing. Originally, purse was pouch (usually leather) containing prize money most often in gold or silver coins.

PUSSY GALORE. See BOND, JAMES

PUZO, MARIO (1920–   ) American novelist and screenwriter best known for novel *The Godfather* (1969), about Mafia and fictional Corleone family. Godfather is Don Vito Corleone. Book ends with line ". . . she said the necessary prayers for the soul of Michael Corleone." In Francis Ford Coppola's 1972 Oscar-winning movie, Al Pacino portrayed Michael. Puzo also wrote *The Fortunate Pilgrim* (1965), *Fool's Die* (1978) and screen adaptations for *The Godfather* (I and II).

PYRENEES, THE Mountain border between Spain and France. Extends 270 mi. (435 km.) between Mediterranean Sea and Bay of Biscay. Average height: 3,500 ft. (1,070 m.). France and Spain traded for years by sea due to natural barrier created by Pyrenees.

PYTHON Constricting snake, closely related to boas. World's longest snake; may exceed 30 ft. (about 10 m.) in length and 450 lb. (200 kg.) in weight. Wraps coils around prey and kills by asphyxiation. Swallows victim whole.

Q Seventeenth letter of English alphabet, corresponding to kappa of Western Greek. English letter developed from Latin, in which it had guttural *k*-like sound. Since it does not exist in Old English and has been transformed in many words into simple *k* sound, it is least used letter in English, where it is now followed by *u* in all but a few cases, making *kw* sound.

QANTAS AIRWAYS Australia's national airline. Founded in 1920 by Lt. Hudsun Fysh and P.J. McGinness. World's second-oldest airline after KLM. Name stands for Queensland And Northern Territorial Aerial Service.

QUAKERS Members of Society of Friends, a Christian sect. Founded, 1648. Shun formal worship characteristic of most other churches. Value simplicity, honesty and nonviolence. Famous Quakers include William Penn, Herbert Hoover and Richard Nixon.

QUANT, MARY (1934–) London boutique owner. Developed mod Chelsea look of 1960s. Designed first above-the-knee skirts, vinyl boots and dresses with strong, colorful patterns.

QUARTIER LATIN Or Latin Quarter in English. Area on Left Bank of Seine River in Paris. Got its name during Middle Ages, when students and teachers at nearby University of Paris conversed in Latin.

QUASAR Or quasi-stellar radio source. A galaxy radiating energy in the form of radio and light waves. Releases approximately

100,000 billion times as much energy as the sun. Center of quasar called a black hole.

QUASIMODO. See HUGO, VICTOR

QUEBEC   Largest and northernmost Canadian province. Nick-named "La Belle Province" (the beautiful province) because of its natural beauty. 80% of residents are French-speaking. Winter temperatures average from 16 to -13°F (-9 to -25°C).

QUEEN ELIZABETH, THE   British Cunard ocean liner. World's largest; 1,031 ft. (314 m.) long, displaces 83,675 tons, carries over 2,000 passengers. Launched, 1938. Used as troop ship, World War II. Returned to commercial service, 1946. Sank in flames, Hong Kong harbor, 1972.

QUEEN MARY THE   British Cunard ocean liner. Sold to city of Long Beach, CA, for $3.4 million, July 26, 1967, where she was turned into a hotel and exhibition ship.

QUEEN NUR (1951–   )   American-born Lisa Halaby. Graduated in Princeton's first coed class, 1969. Became Queen Nur when she married King Hussein of Jordan, 1978.

QUIET MAN, THE   1952 feature film starring John Wayne as boxer who returns to his native Ireland for peace and quiet. John Ford won Oscar for Best Director; Maureen O'Hara co-starred.

QUININE   Alkaloid drug obtained from bark of cinchona trees in South America. Used to relieve fever and arrest progression of malaria. Also used with water in manufacture of tonic water.

QUISLING   A traitor; someone who collaborates with the enemy. From Major Quisling, who ruled as German puppet in Norway during World War II, from 1940 until his ouster and execution, 1945.

QUITO   Capital of Ecuador. Situated on the equator. Every day of the year the sun rises at six A.M. and sets at six P.M. Temperatures usually reach only 55°F (13°C) because of its high elevation.

QUIVER. See ARCHERY

QUO VADIS   Latin for "Where are you going?" or "Whither goest thou?" Question asked by St. Peter of a vision of Christ: *Domine, quo vadis?* (Lord, where go thou?).

R

RA Also Re or Phra. Pyramid Age, considered chief Egyptian deity, sun god and creator of all things. Thought to travel across sky in solar boat each day, through underworld in another boat each night.

RABAT Capital city of Morocco on Atlantic coast of Africa. Mosques scattered throughout old section called Medina. New section designed after European-style buildings. City exports corks, canned fruits and vegetables, and textiles.

RABBITS Can run 18 m.p.h. and leap 10 ft. Live throughout the world and are common farm pests. Popular food in many countries. Should not be lifted by the ears, but instead by the back of the neck. Differ from hares in the following ways: rabbits have shorter ears and legs, and are usually smaller. Newborn hares have fur and can see, while newborn rabbits are naked and blind.

RABIES Latin, meaning "rage." Known as *la rage* in France, this disease is virus-caused and transmitted by the bite of an infected animal. Symptoms are muscle spasms, convulsions and paralysis. Also called hydrophobia because victims cannot swallow.

RADAR O'REILLY Corporal in 4077th Mobile Army Surgical Hospital, featured on the hit series *M*A*S*H*. The shy and bumbling aide to Lt. Col. Henry Blake and Col. Sherman Potter, his favorite drink was a grape Ne-Hi soda pop. Portrayed by Gary Burghoff. (See *M*A*S*H*)

RADIO CITY MUSIC HALL New York City movie theater that sells most tickets, because it has most seats: 6,200. World's largest theater, opened December 22, 1932. Today, features many live productions, world-famous Rockettes, dancing chorus-line girls.

RAGING BULL. See LAMOTTA, JAKE

RAGWEED   Found in U.S. and Canada. Many varieties. Grows rapidly. Produces large amounts of pollen, carried by the wind. Greatest irritant to hay fever sufferers.

RAIDERS OF THE LOST ARK   Blockbuster 1981 feature film directed by Steven Spielberg. Introduced character of Indiana Jones (portrayed by Harrison Ford), archaeologist trying to beat Nazis to ancient artifact. Sequel: *Indiana Jones and the Temple of Doom* (1984).

RAILROAD, GAUGE OF TRACK   Before gauge was standardized, freight was unloaded and reloaded. In 1860s, move to standardized gauge to ensure uninterrupted flow of commerce. Stephenson gauge, 4 ft. 8½ in. wide, became accepted as standard.

RAINBOW   Formed by splitting of sunlight into seven colors of visible spectrum (red, orange, yellow, green, blue, indigo, violet) by water droplets, spray, or mist in the air.

RAINBOW BRIDGE   Crosses Niagara River connecting Niagara Falls, NY with Niagara Falls, Canada. Completed in 1942, replacing Honeymoon Bridge, which was destroyed in 1938 by ice.

RALEIGH, SIR WALTER (1552–1618)   English explorer, soldier and writer. Discovered territory of Virginia naming it after "The Virgin Queen," Elizabeth I. According to many accounts, Raleigh once spread his cape over a puddle in London so that she might walk over it without wetting her feet. Raleigh also founded the "Lost Colony" of Roanoke Island in Virginia. All inhabitants vanished by 1590. After Queen Elizabeth's death, her successor considered Raleigh a political foe. After being imprisoned in Tower of London, he was beheaded, 1618. Buried with pipe and box of tobacco. Raleigh, capital of North Carolina, named after him.

RAND, AYN (1905–1983)   Russian-born American writer. Advanced philosophy she called objectivism, or rational self-interest. Best known for novels *The Fountainhead* (1943) and *Atlas Shrugged* (1957), in which hero John Gault epitomizes Rand's superior, self-made individual.

RASPUTIN, GRIGORI EFIMOVICH (1871–1916)
Russian monk and mystic. Joined religious cult. Gained reputation
as having holy powers. Successfully treated Czar Nicholas II's son
for hemophilia. Became czar's adviser. Unpopular with Russian nobility. Dubbed the "Mad Monk." Assassinated, December 1916.

RATHAUS. See CITY HALL

RATHER, DAN (1931–   ) Current anchor of *CBS Evening
News*, succeeding Walter Cronkite. Co-author of *Sixty Minutes* (1975–
1982). CBS White House correspondent (1964, 1966–1974). Wrote
The Palace Guard (with Gary Gates, 1974), about Nixon's White
House staff. *The Camera Never Blinks* (with Mickey Herskowitz, 1977)
is his autobiography, from Houston boyhood to chief CBS correspondent, giving inside look at TV news.

RATS Destructive pests, destroy stored grain and other foods,
spread diseases such as bubonic plague. Most common in U.S. is
brown rat, brought from Europe by ship. Strychnine is often used
to kill them because they are unable to vomit after eating it.

RATTLESNAKE Poisonous snake of North and South America. The largest ever found was eight ft. nine in. long. Although
sometimes called "a gentleman among snakes," it does not always
rattle before biting.

RAWHIDE TV Western series starring Clint Eastwood (as
Rowdy Yates), right-hand man to trail boss Eric Fleming (as Gil
Favor). Stories told of adventures on cross-country cattle drive.
Frankie Laine sang theme song over opening credits. Wishbone, the
cook, was portrayed by Paul Brinegar.

RAY, JAMES EARL (1928–   ) Serving 99-year sen-
tence for 1968 assassination of civil rights leader Martin Luther King,
Jr. Attempted four escapes, one successful for 54½ hours. Married
in prison, 1978, to TV artist who covered one of his trials. Stabbed
22 times by another inmate, requiring 77 stitches, 1981. Eligible
for parole in 1998. Life story is *The Portrait of an Assassin* by George
McMillan.

RAY, JOHNNIE (1927–   ) Popular singer of the early
and mid-1950s, gained attention with his ballad "Cry" in 1952. Other
hits include "Please, Mr. Sun," "Just Walking in the Rain" and "You
Don't Owe Me a Thing."

RCA—RADIO CORPORATION OF AMERICA

Founded 1919. Parent company of National Broadcasting Company (NBC). Company trademark is of terrier named Nipper listening to "His Master's Voice" coming from an early model phonograph.

READER'S DIGEST According to latest figures (18,035,959) the biggest-selling magazine in America. *Parade* magazine's 21,781,708 tops it, but *Parade* is Sunday newspaper supplement not sold separately. *TV Guide* (17,260,297), once first, now second in U.S. circulation. *Digest*, which condenses articles from other publications and fiction, founded 1922 by DeWitt Wallace and wife Lila Acheson Wallace in a Greenwich Village basement. Now diversified corporation based in Pleasantville, New York.

REAGAN, RONALD WILSON (1911–   ) Fortieth U.S. president (1981–   ). At age 69, oldest president inaugurated. Married actress Jane Wyman, 1940, with whom he had worked at Warner Bros. Divorced, 1948. Remarried, March 1952, to Nancy Davis, his current wife. Nancy, a former actress, appeared with Reagan in 1957 film *Hellcats of the Navy*. The two met when Reagan was president of Screen Actors Guild, 1947–1952 and 1959–1960. Nancy, mistaken for another woman, was listed as a communist sympathizer. Reagan helped clear up confusion. Reagan's involvement in *SAG* made him first union leader to become president. Called himself the Errol Flynn of B movies. Signed Clark Gable's military discharge. Known for many outspoken statements and occasional blunders. In 1975, he said, "The United States has much to offer the Third World War." In 1979 he reflected: "I used to say that politics was the second oldest profession, and I have come to know that it bears a gross similarity to the first."

On March 30, 1981, John W. Hinckley, Jr., attempted to assassinate the President as he was leaving Washington Hilton Hotel. At hospital while being operated on for chest wound, Reagan joked to surgeons, "Please tell me you're Republicans." He later said to his wife, "Honey, I forgot to duck." Reagan was first president to survive gunshot wound while in office.

During his term in office, Reagan provided extensive military and economic assistance to El Salvador in effort to establish democracy and defeat rebel guerrillas. After high voter turnout in 1982 Salvador elections, which guerrillas had threatened to disrupt by violent means, Reagan said, "The ballot is stronger than the bullet."

The President often spends weekends at his Santa Barbara, CA

Rancho Del Cielo, Spanish meaning "Ranch of the sky (or Heaven)." Here he rides horseback and chops wood, escaping "executive fatigue" of presidency. His autobiography *Where's the Rest of Me?* (1965) was co-written with Richard Gibson Hubler.

REAL MCCOYS, THE TV situation comedy about West Virginia mountain family that moves to California. Starred Walter Brennan as Grandpa Amos McCoy and Kathy Nolan as his wife, Kate. Premiered October 1957.

REAR WINDOW 1954 film directed by Alfred Hitchcock. James Stewart stars as photographer confined to his apartment with broken leg, who spies on his neighbors in the apartment building across the yard. Raymond Burr portrays a neighbor Stewart suspects of murdering his wife.

REBECCA 1940 Oscar winner for Best Picture, directed by Alfred Hitchcock. Based on novel by Daphne du Maurier about girl (Joan Fontaine) who marries British nobleman, Max de Winter (Laurence Olivier), who is obsessed with memory of his first wife.

REBOZO, CHARLES GREGORY (1912–   ) Banking millionaire. Nickname "Bebe." Offered to longtime friend President Richard Nixon his Key Biscayne, FL home, where Nixon had his Florida White House.

RED BRIGADES Italian leftist terrorist group. Kidnapped and killed former Premier Aldo Moro (1916–1978), who was expected to become the next president. Moro had facilitated cooperation between Christian Democrats and communists; red brigades opposed all parties.

RED CROSS. See INTERNATIONAL RED CROSS

RED RIVER Classic Western film directed by Howard Hawks. Cattle Baron Thomas Dunson (John Wayne) quarrels with foster son Matt Garth (Montgomery Clift) over cattle drive. Based on novel by Borden Chase.

RED SCHOOLHOUSE Most schoolhouses originally painted red. Red paint was least expensive color available.

RED SEA Arm of Indian Ocean separating Arabian Peninsula from northeastern Africa. Has highest temperature of world's seas, often reaching 100°F (38°C). Named for its red algae, reddish surrounding hills, coral reefs and seaweed.

RED SQUARE Situated in heart of Moscow, just outside

Kremlin walls. Location of military and civilian parades. Russian rulers watch festivities from atop Lenin Mausoleum. Also on the square is *GUM*, Russia's largest department store.

REDGRAVE, MICHAEL (1908–   ) British stage and screen actor, father of actresses Vanessa and Lynn Redgrave. Films include *The Importance of Being Earnest* (1952), *1984* (1956), *The Quiet American* (1958) and *Goodbye Mr. Chips* (1969).

REED, JOHN (1887–1920) American journalist and poet. Covered Eastern Front during World War I, went to Russia, became active supporter of Bolsheviks. Wrote eyewitness account of Russian Revolution, *Ten Days That Shook the World* (1919). Helped start American Communist Party. Life and romance with writer Louise Bryant basis for Warren Beatty film *Reds*.

REFORMATION Sixteenth-century movement to reform the church. Aimed to bring Christianity back to basics of worship as found in Bible. Organized by Martin Luther. October 31, 1517, Luther posted his "Ninety-Five Theses," many of which challenged infallibility of pope and corrupt church practices.

REGICIDE "Killing a king"; from Latin *regi*, form of *rex* (king), and *cide*, from Latin *caedere*, "to kill." Compare: homocide (killing a man); pesticide (killing insects); suicide (killing oneself); genocide (killing a race of people).

REMBRANDT (1606–1669) Born Rembrandt Harmenszoon van Rijn. Greatest of Dutch master painters. Produced 600 paintings, including sixty-four self-portraits, plus more than 300 etchings and 2,000 drawings. *The Night Watch* (1642), also titled *The Shooting Company of Capt. Fran Banning Cocq*, his most famous group portrait. When cleaned in 1946–1947, painting discovered to be daytime scene. Hangs in Rijksmuseum, Amsterdam, the Netherlands.

REMSEN, IRA (1846–1927) American chemist. First professor of chemistry at Johns Hopkins University. Founded first American scientific journal, *American Chemical Journal*, 1879. Discovered saccharin same year. Alleged to have proclaimed "how sweet it is!" upon discovery.

RESISTANCE In electrical circuit, the part that opposes current. Measured in ohms. Materials such as rubber have high resistance and therefore are poor conductors while metals such as copper and silver have low resistance and are good conductors.

RESURRECTION   Concept of being transformed from dead into transcendental state of existence. Associated with Christianity and resurrection of Jesus. One who exhumes graves is sometimes called resurrectionist.

RESURRECTION CITY   In May and June 1968 a "Poor People's March" brought roughly 3,000 people to Washington, DC, where they set up makeshift "Resurrection City" to focus attention on problems of the nation's poor. The city's first manager: Reverend Jesse Jackson.

REVERE, PAUL (1735–1818)   American revolutionary and silversmith. Led Boston Tea Party, 1773. April 18, 1775, made famed "midnight ride" from Boston to Concord, warning colonials of imminent British attack. Also supplied George Washington with false teeth made of wood.

REYKJAVIK   Capital of and only large city in Iceland. Buildings heated by subterraneous hot water springs. Protected from possible German invasion during World War II by British and American troops. Largest city between Ireland and Canada. Northernmost national capital in world.

REYNOLDS, BURT (1936–   )   Film and TV actor and former Florida State football player in mid-1950s (all–Southern Conference halfback before knee injury ended career). Football talent handy in role as pro quarterback in 1974 film *The Longest Yard*. Other films include *Smokey and the Bandit* and *Deliverance;* after this breakthrough role, posed for nude centerfold for *Cosmopolitan* and felt antagonism over it from Hollywood establishment cost him Academy Award.

REYNOLDS, DEBBIE (1932–   )   Musical actress, star of *Singin' in the Rain* (1952), *The Unsinkable Molly Brown* (1964) and *The Singing Nun* (1966). Starred in *Tammy and the Bachelor* (1957) and recorded the hit title tune.

RHETT BUTLER. See MITCHELL, MARGARET

RHINE RIVER. See RIVERS, LONGEST

RHINOCEROS   Huge, horned mammal. Name is from Greek for "horn-nose." Third-largest land animal after elephant and hippopotamus. White Rhino is biggest, 6 or more ft. tall, 15 ft. long, and weighing 3½ tons. Its horn is actually compressed hair. The Indian variety is largest of Asian rhinoceroses. Weighs approximately 2 short tons (1.8 metric tons). Single blue-black horn may measure up to 2 ft. (61 cm.) long. Some rhinoceroses have two horns.

RHODA Mary Richards' friend and neighbor on *The Mary Tyler Moore Show*, portrayed by Valerie Harper. Rhoda Morgenstern moved back to her hometown, New York City, when she starred in her own series *Rhoda* (1974–1978) and married Joe Gerard.

RHODE ISLAND Origins of state's name uncertain. One theory says Italian navigator Giovanni da Verrazano explored Narragansett Bay in 1524 and recorded an island resembling the Island of Rhodes. Historians also believe that Dutch explorer Adrian Block named the state Roodt Eylandt (Red Island) because of its red clay. Official name: The State of Rhode Island and Providence Plantations. U.S. state with longest name and smallest area: 1,214 sq. mi. (3,144 sq. km.).

RHODES, CECIL JOHN (1853–1902) British financier and administrator in South Africa. Became wealthy as diamond miner. Founded DeBeers Mining Company. His will provided for first great financial foundation for education, the Rhodes Trust, for scholarships at England's Oxford University.

RHONE RIVER Commercial waterway of France. Rises in Switzerland's Rhone glacier, picking up its glacial clay in Swiss Alps, which gives it a milky color. Travels through Lake Geneva, loses clay and becomes clear. Upon entering France it flows through Lyon and into Gulf of Lions, an arm of Mediterranean Sea.

RHUMBA Also spelled rumba. Dance of Cuban Negro origin with complex rhythm. Modern ballroom adaptation characterized by pronounced movements of hips and pelvis. Other dances of Cuban derivation are conga and mambo.

RICE Staple food of more than one-half of world's population. Water-loving plant usually grown on flooded fields called paddies. Wild rice is not true rice but type of wild grass.

RICE-DAVIES, MANDY (1946?–   ) Teenage prostitute. Roommate of Christine Keeler in brothel run by Dr. Stephen Ward, English osteopath. Rice-Davies testified in Ward's 1963 trial after Keeler's affairs with British War Minister Profumo and Russian

Naval Attaché "Honeybear" Ivanov brought brothel to public attention. Rice-Davies currently runs Chinese restaurant in Tel Aviv,
called Singing Bamboo.

RICH, CHARLIE (1932–   )   Country-and-blues singer,
songwriter and pianist. Known as "The Silver Fox" because of his
gray hair, had his biggest hit records in 1970s with "Behind Closed
Doors" (1973) and "The Most Beautiful Girl" (1974).

RICHARD DIAMOND   TV detective series starring David
Janssen as ex-New York cop turned private eye. Diamond would
receive important messages via "Sam," his contact at answering service, seen only from waist down, portrayed by Mary Tyler Moore.
Telecast from 1957 through 1960.

RICHARD, MAURICE (1921–   )   "The Rocket" scored
record fifty goals in 50-game season for National Hockey League
Montreal Canadiens, 1944–1945. Tied by Bernie "Boom Boom"
Geofrion of Montreal, 1960–1961, and Bobby Hull of Chicago
Black Hawks, 1961–1962, but both had 70-game season. Hull later
scored 52 goals (1966–1967) to break record. Latest record set in
1981–1982 by Wayne Gretzky of Edmonton Oilers who scored 50
goals in 39-game span.

RICHTER, CHARLES (1900–   )   Known for Richter
scale of earthquake magnitude. Logarithmic. Earthquake that measures 6 is 10 times stronger than one measuring 5. Wrote *Elementary
Seismology*, (1958).

RICKENBACKER, EDDIE (1890–1973)   Top U.S. flying
ace in World War I, became one of America's leading race car
drivers. Never got driver's license. First to wear helmet in Indianapolis 500 auto race. Later president and chairman of Eastern Airlines
(1938–63).

RICKLES, DON (1926–   )   Insult comedian gained fame
with appearances in Las Vegas and *The Tonight Show*. Acted in many
movies, including *X, The Man With the X-Ray Eyes* (1963), *Enter
Laughing* (1967) and *Kelley's Heroes* (1970). Nicknames: "Mr. Warmth"
and "The Merchant of Venom."

RIDDLE OF THE SPHINX, THE   What walks on four
legs, then on two legs, then on three? Answer: man. As infant,
crawls on four; then walks on two; in old age uses cane. Oedipus
gave right answer to sphinx of Greek mythology—not Egyptian

variety. Sphinx devoured people of Thebes when they couldn't answer riddle.

RIDGEWAY, JOHN AND BLYTH, CHARLES First Britains to row across Atlantic, 1966. Traveled from Cape Cod to Inishmore, Ireland, in 91 days. First transatlantic trip by rowboat accomplished by Americans George Harpo and Frank Samuelson, 1896, in 54 days.

RIFLEMAN, THE Popular TV Western starring Chuck Connors as Lucas McCain, who lived with his son Mark on ranch outside North Fork, NM. Paul Fix was Marshall Micah Torrance.

RIGBY, CATHY (1953–   ) First female American gymnast to win medal (silver) in world championship (1970). Although shut out in 1968 Mexico City Olympics at age 15, she impressed spectators with her maturity. Went on to acting, professional exhibitions and commercials.

RIGGS, BOBBY (1918–   ) Tennis player. Won Wimbledon singles and doubles, 1939; U.S. Open singles, 1939, 1941. Professional singles champion, 1946, 1947, 1949. Later a tennis promoter, gained notoriety by losing 1973 exhibition to Billie Jean King at Houston Astrodome after belittling women's tennis. His book, *Court Hustler*, published 1973.

RIGHT ANGLE. See TRIANGLES

RILEY, CHESTER A. Factory worker whose home life was the basis of a popular radio and television series. Created in 1943 for radio with William Bendix in title role, Jackie Gleason portrayed Riley for one season on TV (1949) and Bendix returned to lead role, 1953–1958.

RIN-TIN-TIN A German police dog turned movie star—voted most popular film performer of 1926. Made many silent features and serials, including: *The Night Cry* (1923), *Jaws of Steel* (1927), *The Lone Defender* (1930) and many more. TV series, starring Lee Aaker as Corporal Rusty of Rusty B Company and his dog Rin-Tin-Tin assisting the cavalry, lasted from 1954 through 1958.

RINGLING BROTHERS Of seven original Ruengeling brothers, five of them, after changing spelling of surname, organized Ringling Brothers Circus. Began touring around 1894. Purchased Barnum and Bailey Circus, 1907.

RIO DE JANEIRO Second-largest city of Brazil and South

America. Country's capital until 1960, when former President Juscelino Kubitschek moved capital to Brasilia to promote the 600 mi. (960 km.) inland city's growth. Rio is surrounded by mountains, Atlantic Ocean and Guanabara Bay. Famed for its exclusive beaches including Flamengo, Botafago, Copacabana, Ipanema and Leblon. An 82 ft. (25 m.) statue called "Christ the Redeemer" stands on Corcovado Mountain overlooking city. Most inhabitants are Roman Catholic.

RIO GRANDE RIVER Flows 1,885 mi. (3,034 km.) through southwestern U.S. Forms two-thirds of U.S./Mexican border. Rises on Continental Divide in Colorado, and empties into Gulf of Mexico.

RIOJA WINE. See SPAIN

RIP VAN WINKLE. See IRVING, WASHINGTON

RISK In Parker Brothers board game of world conquest, if attacker's die is higher, defender loses one army from territory under attack. If defender's die is higher, attacker loses one army. In tie, defender always wins. Board has 42 territories grouped into 6 continents. Asian territories are Irkutsk, Yakutsk, Kamchatka, Middle East, Afghanistan, India, China, Siam, Mongolia, Ural, Siberia, Japan. Of six continents, Australia is easiest to defend, because it has only one access route; other continents have more, with Asia having most.

RIVER CITY Setting for Broadway musical (and later feature film) *The Music Man*. Fast-talking salesman, Professor Harold Hill, arrives in River City, Iowa, and after convincing locals that playing pool is trouble, attempts to organize boys' band. Score by Meredith Willson includes: "76 Trombones" and "Till There Was You."

RIVER FLOW Rivers flow from hills or mountains into sea. Current is the direction of flow. Flowing downstream, or with current, left and right banks are on your left and right side respectively.

RIVERS, LONGEST Longest river in: North America—Mississippi, 3,710 mi. (5,936 km.); Western Europe—Rhine, 820 mi. (1,312 km.), Canada—Mackenzie, (to head of Finlay) 2,635 mi. (4,241 km.).

RIYADH Saudi Arabia's capital and largest city. Founded in 1746, became capital city in 1932 when country was formed. Main center for Saudi Arabian oil industry.

ROAD TO SINGAPORE   1940 film, first of Bob Hope–Bing Crosby "Road" series. Two woman-haters, hiding out in Singapore, fall for the same woman. Dorothy Lamour co-stars.

ROARING FORTIES   Areas of ocean between the 40th and 50th degrees latitude, both north and south. Noted for their storms.

ROB ROY   Drink made by combining scotch, sweet vermouth and angostura bitters. Takes name from Rob Roy Macgregor, Scottish "Robin Hood," subject of 1817 Walter Scott novel. Presumably named because it would take hero like Rob Roy to swallow such a concoction.

ROBBINS, HAROLD (1916–   ) Author. Pseudonym, Harold Rubin. Novels include *The Carpetbaggers*, based on reclusive billionaire Howard Hughes (1961), *The Betsy* (1971), *The Pirate* (1974), *Spellbinder* (1982), *Goodbye, Jeanette* (1982) and *Descent from Xanadu* (1983).

ROBERTSON, OSCAR (1938–   ) "The Big O," born 1938, was one of all-time top basketball players. All-American guard at U. of Cincinnati, 1957–1960. Played in National Basketball Association with Cincinnati Royals (1960–1970) and Milwaukee Bucks (1970–1974). Won NBA championship with Milwaukee, 1970–1971 season. A passer as well as a scorer, is all-time NBA assist leader.

ROBIN. See BATMAN AND ROBIN

ROBIN AND THE SEVEN HOODS   1964 film starring Frank Sinatra as kindhearted gangster. Dean Martin, Sammy Davis, Jr., and Peter Falk co-starred. Introduced song "My Kind of Town."

ROBIN HOOD   Legendary 12th-century English outlaw. Lived in Sherwood Forest, Nottinghamshire. His band included Friar Tuck, Little John, Will Scarlet and troubador Alan-a-Dale. Scarlet's name also appears as Scadlock, Scarlock and Scathlock. In one ballad, he is Robin's nephew.

ROBINSON, BILL (1878–1949)   Black tap dancer and entertainer in vaudeville and films. Nicknamed "Bojangles." Films include *The Little Colonel* (1935) and *Stormy Weather* (1943).

ROBINSON, EDWARD G. (1893–1973)   American film actor, born Edward Goldenburg in Hungary. First prominent in 1930s gangster films such as *Little Caesar* (1930), later branched out to more versatile roles. Autobiography *All My Yesterdays* published

1973. Awarded special Academy Award for achievement, 1972. Last film: *Soylent Green* (1973).

ROBINSON, FRANK (1935–   ) After playing career, first man to manage major league baseball team: player-manager of American League Cleveland Indians, 1975. Retired as player, 1976; fired as manager, 1977. Became first black manager in National League with San Francisco Giants, 1981. As player, 1956–1976, only man to win MVP award in both leagues (Cincinnati, 1961; Baltimore, 1966). Won triple crown, 1966. Hit 586 lifetime homers. Elected to Hall of Fame, 1982.

ROCK Divided into three major classes. Igneous rock is solidified molten rock from within earth. Sedimentary is from material deposited on ocean floors millions of years ago. Metamorphic is either igneous or sedimentary rock, altered by heat and pressure.

ROCKEFELLER, JOHN DAVISON (1839–1937) Oil magnate and philanthropist. Made his fortune in oil, railroads, iron and steel. Gained control of several oil producers, refineries and retail outlets. Combined them to form Standard Oil Company. At its height, controlled 90% of the oil refineries' capacity in the country. In 1911, it was broken up under provisions of Sherman Anti-Trust Act. By that time, Rockefeller had amassed an estimated $1 billion, making him country's first billionaire.

ROCKEFELLER, NELSON ALDRICH (1908–1979) American politician. Grandson of John D. Rockefeller, founder of Standard Oil Company. Governor of New York, 1959–1973. Under Gerald Ford, wealthiest vice-president to date, 1974–1979. Michael Kramer and Sam Roberts' 1976 biography entitled *I Never Wanted to be Vice-President of Anything!*, an investigative biography of Nelson Rockefeller.

ROCKNE, KNUTE (1888–1931) Notre Dame University football player and later head football coach, 1918–1930. Teams had overall record 105-12-5, won national championships 1924 (29–30) to establish South Bend, Indiana, campus by "Golden Dome" (campus landmark) as national football power. Popularized forward pass as player and coach. Died in 1930 plane crash. Famous for saying, "When the going gets tough, the tough get going," and "Win it for the Gipper," about dying star George Gipp. Pat O'Brien immortalized movie role, with Ronald Reagan as Gipp (*Knute Rockne, All-American*, 1940).

ROCKWELL, GEORGE LINCOLN (1918–   ) Foun-
der, American Nazi Party, a small group of fanatical Hitler worshipers. Party believes that American blacks should go back to Africa.
Denies that six million Jews were exterminated in World War II.

ROCKWELL, NORMAN (1894–1978) American illustrator. Specialized in warm and humorous scenes of small-town American life. In more than 300 covers for then-weekly *Saturday Evening
Post*, developed realistic style rich in detail.

ROCKY Sylvester Stallone wrote and starred in this low-budget
1976 film, which became popular success and won Best Picture
Oscar. Story of boxer who goes from rags to riches spawned at least
two sequels, *Rocky II* (1979) and *Rocky III* (1982).

ROCKY MOUNTAINS *Passes that cross Rockies:* Yellowhead
Pass, in Banff National Park, Alberta, Canada; Kicking Horse Pass,
Jasper National Park, Alberta, Canada; South Pass, near Wind River
Range, Wyoming, U.S.

ROCKY RACCOON Song by The Beatles from their 1968
album *The Beatles (The White Album)*. Song concerns a boy from the
black hills of South Dakota whose woman runs off with another
man and his desire to get revenge by shooting the legs off of his
enemy. (see *Beatles, The*)

RODEO Competition in cowboy skills. Comes from Spanish
word for roundup. Calgary Stampede in Calgary, Alberta, Canada,
is world's largest; held annually in July with attendance exceeding
one million for 10 days. Record one-day attendance: 141,670 in
1974.
Bronco riding: Bareback bronco riding, rodeo cowboys must ride buck-
ing wild horse for eight seconds, holding on with one hand on
handle attached to strap around horse's chest. Rider may not touch
horse, strap or handle with free hand. In saddle bronco riding,
contestants must stay on for ten seconds.
Bull Dogging: Timed event in which cowboy jumps from back of his
horse onto neck of running steer. Wrestles steer to ground by twisting neck until it falls. Also called steer wrestling.
Calf-Roping: Event in which mounted cowboy attempts to rope running calf, tie rope to horn of saddle, dismount, throw calf to ground,
and tie any three of its legs together in shortest time. If calf is
already down, cowboy must let it rise, then throw it. In team roping,

two cowboys combine to wrestle grown steer to ground and tie its two hind legs.

Clowns: Used in arena to entertain crowds between events and distract wild bulls from thrown riders.

RODGERS, JIMMIE (1897–1933)   Known as the Father of Country Music, gained fame with million-selling record "Blue Yodel" in 1928. His hit "Brakeman's Blues" (1929) earned him nickname of "The Singing Brakeman."

ROENTGEN, WILHELM (1845–1923)   German physicist. Discovered, in 1895, x-rays, a type of electromagnetic radiation, as are light and radio waves. X-rays penetrate some materials but not others, making them useful in medicine, science and industry.

ROGERS, ROY (1912–   )   "The King of the Cowboys," Western star of the 1940s and 1950s. Usually seen with his horse Trigger, dog Bullet, cowgirl Dale Evans, backup singing group The Sons of the Pioneers, and sidekick Gabby Hayes, in countless films, including *Dark Command* (1940), *South of the Santa Fe* (1942), *Out California Way* (1946) and *Son of Paleface* (1952). His theme song: "Happy Trails."

ROGERS, WILL (1879–1935)   Comedian and popular philosopher in the Ziegfeld Follies and on silent screen. Made his first film in 1918; continued into the talkies era with movies including *State Fair* (1933) and *Judge Priest* (1934). Died in a plane crash, August 1935.

ROGERS, WILLIAM PIERCE (1913–   )   Secretary of State under President Richard Nixon. Formerly President Eisenhower's attorney general. Considered a good negotiator.

ROHMER, SAX (1883?–1959)   Pseudonym of Arthur Sarsfield Ward, English mystery writer of series about Dr. Fu Manchu, sinister Chinese criminal genius who seeks to conquer the world. His constant adversary, Sir Denis Nayland Smith, is aided by Dr. Petrie. Wrote 13 Fu Manchu novels between 1913 and his death.

ROLLER DERBY   Sport developed by Leo Seltzer, combining aspects of roller skating, bicycle racing, dance marathons and walkathons of 1920s and 1930s. Competitors on roller skates race around wooden, banked track. Points gained by "lapping" opponents. Pushing and jostling allowed. Jammers are players who break out of pack of skaters and try to pass (lap) players on opposing team. Racquel Welch starred as derby star in 1972 film *Kansas City Bomber*.

ROLLER SKATES   Invented by Belgian Joseph Merlin, 1760. Publicized them by wearing pair to fashionable London masquerade party, where he skated around ballroom playing violin. Crashed into expensive mirror, shattering it and violin, and injuring himself. In 1863, American furniture maker James Leonard Plimpton patented skate with cushioned mountings, allowing skater to steer, and soon opened several roller rinks to popularize his invention.

ROLLER COASTERS: TEXAS CYCLONE AND MISTER TWISTER   Two of world's highest and most exciting roller coasters. Texas Cyclone, at Astroworld, Houston, TX, opened July 12, 1976. Mister Twister, at Elitch's Gardens, Denver, CO, opened 1969 and includes tunnel ride.

ROLLING STONES, THE   English rock-and-roll band formed in 1962 by Mick Jagger, Keith Richards and Brian Jones. On "The Ed Sullivan Show" appearance in 1967, changed words of song "Let's Spend the Night Together" to "Let's Spend Some Time Together." Hits include "Satisfaction" (1965), "Mother's Little Helper" (1966), "Jumping Jack Flash" (1968) and "Brown Sugar" (1971). 1971 album cover, designed by Andy Warhol for *Sticky Fingers*, featured a real metal zipper on the cover.

ROLLS-ROYCE   Classic automobile created by Sir Frederick Royce and partner, Charles Rolls in 1904. Represented the most in luxury that money and technology allowed. Capable of speeds of about 100 m.p.h. or more.

ROMAN CATHOLICS   November 18, 1966, National Conference of Catholic Bishops decreed that practice of abstinence (abstention from eating meat and certain meat products) need be observed only during Lent. This eased Pope Paul VI's February 17 decree that all Roman Catholics above age 14 abstain from meat on Fridays.

ROMAN EMPIRE   At its height in A.D. 120, the empire's border stretched from England, which was annexed in A.D. 43, to what is today Iraq. This period is known as the Pax Romana, or "Roman Peace," when the Empire enjoyed wise emperors and unrivaled military supremacy.

ROMAN NUMERALS

1 = I	100 = C	10,000 = $\bar{X}$
5 = V	500 = D	50,000 = $\bar{L}$
10 = X	1,000 = M	100,000 = $\bar{C}$
50 = L	5,000 = $\bar{V}$	1,000,000 = $\bar{M}$

The number zero cannot be represented.

ROMANOFF, MICHAEL (1892(?)–1971) Born Harry Gerguson. Hollywood personality. Claimed at different times to be newphew, half brother, and son of Czar Nicholas II. Maintained that he murdered Rasputin, a monk who had great influence over czar. Rasputin assassinated, 1916, in court of Nicholas II.

ROMANTIC ENGLISHWOMAN, THE Comedy-drama (1975) directed by Joseph Losey. Glenda Jackson starred in title role as wife of Michael Caine, novelist trying to write screenplay.

ROMBAUER, IRMA (c.1876–1962) American author of cookbook *The Joy of Cooking* (1931). First published at her own expense, became one of best-selling cookbooks of all time. Revised (1951) as *New Joy of Cooking*, co-authored and illustrated by daughter Marion Rombauer Becker. *Little Acorn* (1961) is collection of readers' responses to *Joy of Cooking*, published on book's 30th anniversary.

ROME Capital of Italy. Important throughout more than 2,000 years of history. Called "Eternal City." Ancient story of Romulus and Remus claims that the twin brothers, raised by a wolf, founded city in 753 B.C. Romulus later murdered Remus and became Rome's first king, hence the city's name.
Food: Common items on a modern Roman menu include prosciutto (ham), carciofi (artichokes), gelato (ice cream) and pollo (chicken). *Transportation:* Served by two airports—Fiunicino (also called Leonardo da Vinci Airport) and Ciampina. Its railway station is Termini Station, and subway system is called Metropolitana, which runs southwest from Termini Station to port of Ostia.

ROMEO. See SHAKESPEARE, WILLIAM

ROMMEL, ERWIN JOHANNES EUGENE (1891–1944) German general. Led Germany's North African operations, World War II. Sly and daring, called "The Desert Fox." Said to have taken poison to avoid trial for conspiracy against Hitler.

ROMULUS AND REMUS. See ROME

ROOD, FLOYD SATTERLEE   Only person to drive golf ball across U.S. Hit ball from Pacific to Atlantic Oceans, September 14, 1963, to October 3, 1964. Took 114,737 strokes. Lost 3,511 balls on 3,397.7 mi. trip.

ROOM TEMPERATURE   Temperature at which most people feel comfortable. From 68°F to 78°F (20°C to 26°C). Higher humidity tends to make people feel warmer. Lower temperatures can be tolerated if extra moisture is added to air by humidifier.

ROOSEVELT, ANNA ELEANOR   (1884–1962) American First Lady, writer and lecturer. Second volume of Joseph P. Lash's biography of wife of President Franklin Delano Roosevelt entitled *Eleanor: The Years Alone* (1972). Describes her life after FDR's death in April 1945, serving Truman and Kennedy administrations as diplomat and champion of humanitarian causes.

ROOSEVELT, FRANKLIN DELANO (1882–1945) Thirty-second U.S. president, 1933–1945. Elected an unprecedented four times, after which Republicans in Congress had a law passed limiting the number of presidential terms to two. Fifth cousin of 26th U.S. President Theodore Roosevelt, (1858–1919); seventh cousin once removed of England's Prime Minister Winston Churchill (1874– 1965).

On February 15, 1933, bricklayer Giuseppe Zangara tried to kill the then president-elect in Miami. Zangara missed, killing Chicago's Mayor Anton J. Cermak. Roosevelt inaugurated March 4, and Zangara executed March 20.

Barely one week into his first term, the President began his "fireside chats." During the unfamiliarity, fear and despair of Great Depression, Roosevelt broadcast over the radio, explaining his policies and problems the country faced. He was also first president to appear on television while in office, speaking at opening of New York World's Fair in Flushing, Queens, April 30, 1939, over NBC affiliate station WNBT New York.

To combat the Depression, Roosevelt immediately initiated his New Deal programs, broadening the role of the federal government. This program for economic recovery included relief, loans and jobs administered by host of new "alphabet" agencies, including Tennessee Valley Authority (TVA), Works Progress Administration (WPA) and National Recovery Administration (NRA).

Victim of polio attack in 1921 that left his legs paralyzed, he also established many programs and institutions for the treatment of paralysis, including National Foundation for Infantile Paralysis, and Warm Springs Foundation.

His term in office spanned most of World War II, beginning with December 7, 1941, bombing of Pearl Harbor, "a day," said Roosevelt, "which will live in infamy." Describing the political and and economic climate of the times, he once declared, "this generation of Americans has a rendezvous with destiny." Roosevelt died early in his fourth term, 1945.

ROOSEVELT, THEODORE (1858–1919) Twenty-sixth U.S. president. Fifth cousin of future president Franklin D. Roosevelt, 32nd U.S. president, 1933–1945. Succeeded President William McKinley (1843–1901) who had been assassinated. "Teddy," at age 42, was the youngest man to occupy the post. (President J. F. Kennedy was 43 when he was sworn in.) In 1904, Roosevelt was elected as the incumbent.

On February 14, 1884—Valentine's Day—T. Roosevelt suffered death of both wife Alice and mother Martha Bulloch. This tragedy occurred just after birth of his daughter, also named Alice. During Spanish-American War, he led Rough Riders in charge of San Juan Hill, Cuba, July 1, 1898. Marked beginning of U.S. victory in the war. Became known as "Hero of San Juan Hill."

Frontiersman and ranch owner, he was also called "The Cowboy President." On August 22, 1902, he became first U.S. president to ride in car, the electrically powered Columbia Victoria. He was also first president to ride in submarine, the U.S. Plunger, August 25, 1905; and on plane, October 11, 1910. The Teddy Bear bears his name.

Wrote 37 books. Subjects included history (including four-volume *The Winning of the West*, 1889–1896), hunting, wildlife and politics.

ROOTS   A five-part mini-series that won record-breaking ratings in January 1977. Based on Alex Haley's novel tracing his own roots, series starred LaVar Burton as Kunta Kinte, John Amos as Toby. Leslie Uggams played Kizzy, Ben Vereen portrayed Chicken George and George Standford Brown was Tom. Its sequel, *Roots: The Next Generation* (1979), featured Marlon Brandon as U.S. Nazi leader George Lincoln Rockwell. (see HALEY, ALEX)

ROSE MARIE   1936 motion picture based on Rudolph Friml

operetta. Jeanette MacDonald stars as opera singer trying to help her brother, escaped convict (James Stewart), flee from Royal Canadian Mounted Policeman (Nelson Eddy) sent to capture him. She falls in love with Mountie.

ROSE, PETE (1942–   ) Nicknamed "Charley Hustle" for hard-nosed play. Baseball's number-two all-time hit man, passing 4,000 in April 1984 with Montreal Expos aiming at Ty Cobb's 4,191. Won three batting titles and 1973 National League MVP with Cincinnati Reds. Played on Philadelphia 1981 World Series and 1983 pennant-winning teams. Played five defensive positions during career.

ROSEBUSH The rose is probably the most popular flower. Over 1,000 varieties. Fruit of the rose is called rose hip and is very rich in vitamin C. The rose family of plants includes the apple, peach, pear, raspberry, strawberry, plum and cherry.

ROSEMARY Young woman who gives birth to Satan's child, Andrew John, in *Rosemary's Baby* (1968). Portrayed by Mia Farrow in film based on Ira Levin's novel, directed by Roman Polanski.

ROSENBERG, ETHEL (1916–1953), AND JULIUS (1918–1953) American Jews from Germany. Convicted and sentenced to death for espionage, 1951, in nation's first atomic spy trial. Accused of stealing bomb secret for Russians in 1945. Evidence never verified. Rosenbergs pleaded innocence.

ROSETTA STONE Discovered, 1799, by officer of Napoleon's army. Black basalt surface carved, in both hieroglyphic demotic and Greek, with decree commemorating crowning of King Ptolemy V Epiphanes (reigned 203–181 B.C.). Knowledge of Greek enabled translation of hitherto inaccessible ancient Egyptian language.

ROSSNER, JUDITH LOUISE (1935–   ) Born Judith Louise Perlman. American novelist. Wrote *Attachments* (1977), and *Looking for Mr. Goodbar* (1975) about Theresa Dunn, school teacher who spends nights in singles bars looking for ideal lover ("Mr. Goodbar"). Diane Keaton played Theresa in 1977 movie, introducing Richard Gere.

ROSY CRUCIFIXION, THE. See MILLER, HENRY

ROTH, PHILLIP (1933–   ) American novelist and short-story writer. Frequently writes about middle-class Jewish life in

America. *Goodbye Columbus* (1959), a collection of short stories, including the title novella about a Jewish family in Bronx. Filmed in 1969 with Richard Benjamin in screen debut. Also wrote *Letting Go* (1962), *Portnoy's Complaint* (1969) and *Our Gang* (1971).

ROTTERDAM　Second-largest city in the Netherlands. Developed as medieval fishing village. Its port, Rotterdam-Europort, is world's busiest. Port is located at mouth of Rhine and Meuse rivers, handling approximately 300 million tons (270 million metric tons) per year.

ROULETTE　World's oldest banking game still being played. Said to be invented by French scientist Blaise Pascal, 1655, during a monastic retreat. First popularized in French casinos, now popular in Monte Carlo (called "The Big Wheel"), Las Vegas and Caribbean gambling resorts. Wheel divided into 37 spaces (38 in U.S.). Sectors alternately red and black, numbered 1–36, plus 0 sector (and 00 in U.S.) colored green. Croupier spins wheel. Bets, made against house, can be on single number (pays 35 to 1, highest odds in game), color (even money), odd or even number (even money), low number (1–18, even money), high number (19–36, even money) or various combinations of these.

ROUND ROBIN　Tournament in which every team plays every other team once, with overall won–lost record determining final standing. In five-team round robin, each team would play four games: 1–2, 1–3, 1–4, 1–5, 2–3, 2–4, 2–5, 3–4, 3–5, 4–5. In double round robin, each team plays others twice.

ROUTE 66　Hit TV series of the early 1960s about two young men traveling around America, meeting different people and getting into romantic, dangerous and amusing situations. Martin Milner played Tod Stiles, and George Maharis was his companion, Buz Murdock.

ROWAN AND MARTIN'S LAUGH-IN　Popular TV comedy-variety series from 1968 through 1973, starring comedy team of Dan Rowan and Dick Martin. Zany comedy sketches, blackouts and cameo appearances by famous celebrities were the show's trademarks. Lily Tomlin and Goldie Hawn were among the regulars. Judy Carne was the "Sock-it-to-me" girl. Each episode ended with Dan's line "Say good night, Dick"—to which the reply "Good night, Dick" was sounded by the cast. Each week, Dan and Dick awarded the Flying Fickle Finger of Fate Award on their show.

ROWING   Sport which races in one-, two-, four-, or eight-man shells. With eight-man shell, a ninth person (coxswain) sits in rear, facing forward and barking cadence. Men sit on slides (movable seats that slide on metal track) in shell (sometimes called scull) making fast strokes with oars (also called sculls). Term stroke can also refer to oarsman nearest stern (back of boat), usually crew's strongest. Sport is governed by FISA (*Fédération Internationale des Sociétés d'Aviron*).

ROYAL MONTREAL GOLF CLUB   Oldest golf club in North America, established November 4, 1873. By that date, Canadians had determined need for governing body to lay down rules of golf, and thus formed club for organized play.

RUBBER AND GRAND SLAM   While many games have grand slams and several use term *rubber* (as in deciding or rubber match), only bridge and baseball use both. In baseball, rubber is whitened slab on pitcher's mound which pitcher must touch while delivering ball, and grand slam is home run with bases loaded. In bridge, rubber is three-game match or series, while grand slam is taking all tricks in a particular hand.

RUBENS, PETER PAUL (1577–1640)   Flemish baroque painter, known for exuberant religious themes and paintings of allegories and fables. Used dynamic colors and plump figures. Among his paintings: *The Rape of the Sabine Women* (1635–1640), *Venus and Adonis* (1635) and *Christ on the Cross* (1635–1640).

RUBIK'S CUBE   Multicolored fist-sized puzzle devised by Hungarian design professor Erno Rubik in mid-1970s. Ideal Toy Co. has U.S. rights. Sold 4.5 million units in 1980. Each of six sides has nine squares, with each row able to rotate around its center. When solved, each side is one color. Forty-three quintillion possible positions. Least possible moves to solve: about twenty. Knowledge of group theory and algorithms is helpful.

RUBIN, JERRY (1938–   )   Founder of Youth International Party (Yippies) and defendant in Chicago 8 (later Chicago 7, after Bobby Seale's case was separated) conspiracy trial. His 1970 revolutionary manifesto *Do It: Scenarios of the Revolution* urges action toward social disorder. Introduction by black writer/revolutionary Eldridge Cleaver. Rubin later became Wall Street financial adviser.

RUBLE   Basic monetary unit of Soviet Union. Circulates in denominations of 1, 3, 5, 10, 25, 50 and 100. One ruble equals 100 kopeks. Forbidden to import or export, to protect currency from devaluation on international exchange. Government uses foreign currencies for international transactions.

RUBY, JACK (1911–1967) Born Jack Rubinstein. Dallas nightclub owner and admirer of J. F. Kennedy. Shot Lee Harvey Oswald, accused assassin of President Kennedy, November 24, 1963. Oswald was being transferred between Dallas jails. The shooting was broadcast live on NBC and CBS, the first live murder on television. Ruby was later sentenced to death by Dallas jury. This sentence was commuted one month before his scheduled execution. He died at Parkland Memorial Hospital, January 3, 1967, from blood clot in his lung.

RUDOLPH, WILMA (1940–   ) Black American sprinter, bedridden for four years with polio as child, won three gold medals in 1960 Rome Olympics: 100 and 200 m. dashes, and anchor leg of 400 m. relay. Tennessee State undergraduate. First American woman to win three Olympic gold medals.

RUGBY Invented by student William Ellis of England's Rugby College, 1823. Game derived from soccer, but allows hand contact with ball. Played officially, 1841. Rules standardized 1848, when team leaders from several schools met and named it rugby football.

RUGBY, HOOKER IN A SCRUM Forward who plays in middle of front line in scrum (huddle into which ball is tossed to restart play). Only player permitted to use his foot to hook ball out of scrum.

RUIZ, ROSIE Crossed finish line of 1980 Boston Marathon with third-best marathon time ever for woman, but immediate questions raised: hair not matted with perspiration, and no race-spotters had seen her. When finish-line doctor said she couldn't have run whole race and two spectators said they saw her emerge from crowd one-half mile from finish line, she was disqualified and Jackie Gareau of Montreal declared women's winner.

RUMINANT Grazing animal that chews its cud and has split hoofs. Chews food slightly, swallows, then food is sent back to mouth in form of cud for further chewing. Cow, ox, sheep, llama, deer, goat, antelope and giraffe are cud-chewers.

RUMPELSTILTSKIN Dwarf of German folklore who teaches

miller's daughter (not his own) to spin straw into gold so king will marry her. In return, he is to get her firstborn. When queen, she grieves so bitterly upon birth of child that dwarf agrees to relent if she can guess his name in three days. On third day he is overheard gloating, and he kills himself in a rage at losing bet.

RUN FOR YOUR LIFE   TV adventure series starring Ben Gazzara as Paul Bryan, a lawyer with an incurable disease, with only two years to live. He used his time to see the world; series ran from 1965 to 1968. Featured Bonneville Salt Flats during opening credits.

RUN TO DAYLIGHT   1963 book by Green Bay Packers coach Vince Lombardi (with W. C. Heinz) detailing week of preparation for game against Detroit Lions, climaxing with play-by-play of game. Never adapted to film. ABC network aired one-hour special called "Portrait: Legend in Granite," December 14, 1973, about two years in Lombardi's life leading up to his becoming Packer coach in 1959; Ernest Borgnine played Lombardi, Colleen Dewhurst played his wife, James Olson and John Calvin were players Max McGee and Paul Hornung, respectively.

RUNNING BEAR   Rock novelty song, number one on charts in 1960. Song was recorded by Johnny Preston, written by J. P. "The Big Bopper" Richardson, who also provided backup vocals. Inspired by Dove soap commercial, Indian maiden in song was Little White Dove.

RUNYON, ALFRED (DAMON) (1884–1946)   American journalist and short-story writer, famous for tales about colorful Broadway and racetrack characters. His style (now called Runyonesque), relies heavily on slang, outrageous metaphors, and use of present tense. Wrote *Guys and Dolls* (1931), later a successful Broadway and Hollywood musical; *Blue Plate Special* (1934); *Money from Home* (1935).

RUSK, DEAN DAVID (1909–   )   Secretary of State under presidents Kennedy and Johnson. Began as assistant professor, 1940. Joined state department, 1945. Truman's Undersecretary of State for Eastern affairs, 1949. President of Rockefeller Foundation, 1951. Returned to teaching, Georgetown University, 1960.

RUSSELL, BILL (1934–   )   Basketball player and coach. Led U. of San Francisco to two NCAA titles and won gold medal with 1956 U.S. Olympic team. Six-ft.-nine-in. center for Boston

Celtics revolutionized defensive game with shot blocking and intimidation and led them to eleven NBA titles. Won six MVP awards. Succeeded "Red" Auerbach as Celtics coach, 1966, becoming first black coach of major league pro sports team. Coached Celtics to NBA titles, 1968 and 1969.

RUSSIAN ALPHABET   Or Cyrillic alphabet, has 32 letters; 12 look the same as English, 6 also sound the same including the letter A. Changes made by Peter the Great (1708) and Communists after Russian Revolution brought it closer to Latin. Most nearly phonetic of European languages.

RUSSIAN RULERS   Earliest Russian rulers through the 1500s said to be descendants of Rurik, a 9th-century Viking king. The last house to rule before the revolution was the House of Romanov, from 1613 until Nicholas II's abdication, 1917.

RUSSIAN SPACE PROGRAM   Got off to quick start in Space Race. Launched first satellite (1957), first man (1961), and first woman (1963). Not yet stepped on moon, although U.S.S.R. has landed unmanned craft.

RUTH, GEORGE HERMAN (BABE) (1895–1948)   Also known as "Bambino." Went from Baltimore orphanage to become "Sultan of Swat" for New York Yankees. Started career and excelled as pitcher for Boston Red Sox. First game was Red Sox vs. Cleveland, July 11, 1914. Left game after seven innings with score tied (3-3). Sox won the game. Jack Graney was first batter he faced. As pitcher, lifetime mark was 94-96, plus three World Series wins. Broke own season home run record (59 in 1921) with 60 in 1927; received $70,000 for year. Set career home run record of 714. Season record broken by Roger Maris (61 in 1961); career record broken in 1974 by Hank Aaron (755). Holds major league record for career walks received (2,056; Ted Williams second, Mickey Mantle third). Hit three-run homer in opening game at Yankee Stadium, called "House that Ruth Built." Used 44 oz. bat he called "Black Betsy."

RYAN'S DAUGHTER   1970 film directed by David Lean. Story of girl (Sarah Miles) who marries town schoolteacher (Robert Mitchum), then has an affair with British soldier (Christopher Jones) during 1916 Irish uprising. John Mills earned Oscar as Best Supporting Actor, portraying village idiot.

RYAN, CORNELIUS JOHN (1920–   )   Irish-born

Ryan, Leo Joseph (1925–1978)

American novelist and journalist. *The Longest Day: June 6, 1944* (1959), one of his several World War II novels, looks at events of D-day invasion of Europe from viewpoints of ordinary people involved. He advertised in North American and European newspapers for participants, got 6,300 replies, selected 1,000 for interviews and used 400 in his narrative.

RYAN, LEO JOSEPH (1925–1978) American politician. Congressman representing San Francisco, CA. Murdered by People's Temple cult members while investigating their commune in Guyana, South America.

S

S.N.C.F *Société Nationale des Chemins de Fer Français* (The French National Railway). State-controlled system, 80% electrified. Among fastest trains in world, some travel 125 m.p.h. (200 km.p.h.). First French railroad opened 1828.

SABENA AIRLINES Founded 1923. Based in Brussels, Belgium. Fly 26 aircraft to approximately 70 cities worldwide, including U.S. cities of New York, Atlanta, Chicago, Detroit. First transatlantic flight, 1946.

SABRINA Romantic comedy film, 1954, starring Audrey Hepburn in title role as chauffeur's daughter being pursued by two wealthy socialite brothers (Humphrey Bogart, William Holden). Directed by Billy Wilder.

SACCHARIN Artificial sweetener. Contains no carbohydrates. Used by dieters and diabetics. Four to five hundred times as sweet as natural cane sugar. Possible carcinogen. No food value. Made from petroleum and toluene.

SACKLER, HOWARD (1929–1982) American playwright. Wrote 1969 Pulitzer Prize–winning *The Great White Hope* (1968) about race relations in U.S. Portrayed rise and fall of black world heavyweight champion boxer Jack Jefferson, modeled after real-life boxer Jack Johnson (1878–1946), first black to hold world heavyweight title (1908–1915). James Earl Jones and Jane Alexander won Tony Awards for leading roles, which they repeated in 1970 film version.

SAFFRON   Spice made from dried stamens of cultivated crocus, bulb flower originated in the East, introduced to Spain by Arabs. Cultivated in France since 16th century. Contains volatile oil and coloring substance, indispensible for bouillabaisse. Should be dark orange, without white streaks. Generally costs $15–22 per oz., depending on quantity purchased. Higher priced spice is wild gensing, from Chan Pak Mountains area of China, reported to cost almost $23,000 per oz. in Hong Kong, because of purported aphrodisiacal quality.

SAGAN, CARL (1934–   )   Professor of space, science and astronomy, Cornell University. Popularizer of issues in science, such as the possibility of extraterrestrial life and the evolution of life on Earth. *The Dragons of Eden*(1977) discusses evolution of human brain. Also author of *Cosmos*(1980), *The Cosmic Connection* (1973) and *Broca's Brain*(1979).

SAHARA DESERT   Located in Northern Africa. World's largest desert region. Covers more than three million sq. mi. (seven million sq. km.). Three to four million inhabitants. Called "The Garden of Allah." Contains point that is Earth's sunniest area. Seems to be spreading southward at ½ mi. or more per year because of unwise land use practices. Wind blows sand dunes higher than those in any other desert.

SAILING   Sport in which participants hike out (lean or hang over side of boat in order to use body to counterbalance force of wind) while close-hauled (sailing as close to directly against wind as possible).

SAKE   Also called Japanese rice wine, made from fermented rice. Sweet, colorless, high alcoholic content: 12–16% by volume. Thought to be named after town of Osaka, Japan. Served warm.

SALAD DRESSING   Usually a combination of oil, vinegar (acetic acid) and spices. Word vinegar from French *vinaigre*, meaning "sour wine." Produced by fermentation. Vinegar bacteria, *Mycoderma aceti*, changes alcohols into vinegar.

SALEM   Capital of Oregon. Originally a village called Chemeteka. Named Salem, 1846. Became capital, 1864. Known for processing of wood products.

SALES, SOUPY (1926–   )   TV kiddie-show host of the 1950s and '60s. Known for getting a pie in his face. Soupy's regular adversaries included: White Fang, his giant dog; Hippy the Hippo; Pookie the Lion; and Black Tooth, another dog.

SALINGER, JEROME DAVID (J. D.) (1919–   ) American author. Captivated the nation with 1951 novel *The Catcher in the Rye*. Centers on 16-year-old boy Holden Caulfield, who writes first-person account of his near-breakdown at private boarding school. 1953 collection *Nine Stories* introduced Glass family, including Zooey and older brother Seymour, who commits suicide. Family is also subject of *Franny and Zooey* (1961).

SALINGER, PIERRE (1925–   ) Press Secretary for President Kennedy, 1961–1963. Began as correspondent with San Francisco *Chronicle*. Fought in navy, World War II. Later became correspondent for ABC News. Appointed ABC News Paris Bureau Chief, 1979.

SALISBURY, HARRISON A. (1908–   ) New York *Times* foreign correspondent and author of *The 900 Days*, 1969 book about German siege of Leningrad, 1941–January 1944.

SALIVA Fluid secreted by salivary glands. Moistens food so that it can be tasted and swallowed. Keeps inside of mouth clean. One to two quarts of saliva a day are secreted by salivary glands.

SALK, DR. JONAS EDWARD (1914–   ) Research scientist. Developed vaccine for prevention of polio, 1953. First tested on himself and his family. Officially accepted, 1955. Weakens polio virus without interfering with body's autoimmune response. Salk refused all cash awards.

SALOME Egged on by her mother, Herodias, Salome asked her stepfather, Herod Antipas, for John the Baptist's head. John had denounced mother for adulterous second marriage to Herod, who promised to grant Salome's wish after seeing her dance. Mother thought she could disgrace John and Herod at same time.

SALT NaCl (sodium chloride). Most of table variety is dug from underground mines. Roman soldiers were paid in salt, then very valuable. The word salary comes from the Latin word for salt. Many superstitions involve salt, probably because in ancient times salt was valuable commodity. The custom of throwing spilled salt over left shoulder came from belief that devil looked over one's left shoulder and thrown salt would get into his eyes. Indispensible to Hebrews, not only for use in their food, in animal food, and as antidote to effects of heat, but also as religious offering. For these reasons it is mentioned more than 30 times in Bible. Lot's wife turned into a pillar of salt. Scientifically, in liquid form, it is called brine. Mixed with ice or snow, has freezing point less than 32°F (0°C). Used to freeze ice cream. Used more than any other food seasoning, though only 5% of the world's product is used this way.

S.A.L.T. (STRATEGIC ARMS LIMITATION TREATY) Agreement between U.S. and U.S.S.R. to limit antiballistic missiles. S.A.L.T I signed, 1972. A second S.A.L.T, 1979, never ratified. Even so, both countries have agreed to abide by its terms.

SALT LAKE CITY Utah's capital and largest city. In 1847, under leadership of Brigham Young, it became headquarters of Church of Jesus Christ of Latter-Day Saints, (the Mormon Church). Mormons comprise two-thirds of city's population.

SALVATION ARMY Founded in England, 1865, as the Christian Mission, by William and Catherine Booth. "General" William Booth, a fire-and-brimstone preaching evangelist, renamed it the Salvation Army, 1878. Instituted a semimilitary chain of command. Missions operate in over 86 countries. Came to U.S. 1880; more than 8,000 centers to date. Motto: Blood and Fire. Members believe they are "saved to save." Published newspaper *The War Cry*.

SALZBURG City in western Austria. Named for its salt mining and trading. Mozart's birthplace; home of annual music and theater summer festival.

SAM RAYBURN RESERVOIR Largest lake in Texas. Located in eastern part of state. Named for Sam Rayburn, congressman who held post as Speaker of the House longest. Position held from 1940 until his death in 1961, except during 80th (1947–1949) and 83rd (1953–1955) congresses when Republicans had majority in the House.

SAM THE SHAM AND THE PHAROAHS Rock-and-roll group of the late 1960s. Hit songs include: "Wooly Bully" (1965), "Li'l Red Riding Hood" (1966) and "Oh, That's Good" (1967). Sam the Sham was born Domingo Samudio.

SAN ANDREAS FAULT Large fault that runs 600 mi. (950 km.) through California's coastal regions. Western side moves northward in relation to eastern side.

SAN DIEGO ZOO   Home of over 5,500 animals, 1,600 species and subspecies. One of the largest collections in the world. Located in Balboa Park, CA, covering 1,400 acres. Tropical flowers and trees occupy more than 100 acres.

SAN FRANCISCO   Originally inhabited by Costanoan Indians. Bay was named *Puerto de San Francisco* (Port of St. Francis) in 1595 by a Portuguese explorer. In 1776, Spanish priests opened a mission nearby called Mission San Francisco de Asís in honor of St. Francis of Assisi. Entire region eventually named *Pueblo de San Francisco* (Town of San Francisco). The city is surrounded by water on three sides: Pacific Ocean on west, Golden Gate Strait on north and San Francisco Bay on east. Called "the Queen of the Pacific." Famous streets: World's steepest streets are Filbert Street on Russian Hill and 22nd Street in Dolores Heights. Both rise one ft. (0.3 m.) for every 3.17 ft. (0.95 m.) of length.

SAN FRANCISCO EARTHQUAKE   At 5:13 A.M., April 18, 1906, an earthquake struck. Lasted less than one minute. Started fires that eventually killed 700 people, destroyed 300,000 homes, and caused over five hundred million dollars' worth of damage.

SAN JUAN CAPISTRANO   City 60 mi. (97 km.) southeast of Los Angeles, CA. Built around mission that was founded here, 1776. Famous for regular departure and arrival of migrating swallows, which fly south on October 23 and return, March 19.

SAN JUAN ISLANDS   Located between state of Washington and Vancouver Island. Approximately 170 islands owned by Washington. Noted for farming, fishing, tourism. Named by Spanish explorers.

SAN MARINO   World's oldest republic. Completely surrounded by Italy. Official name: *La Serenissima Republica di San Marino* (The Most Serene Republic of San Marino). Official language: Italian. Founded in the fourth century. Stands mostly on Mount Titano. One of world's smallest republics covering only 24 sq. mi. (61 sq. km.). Famous for its beautiful postage stamps.

SANCHO PANZA. See CERVANTES

SAND PEBBLES, THE   The San Pablo is U.S. battleship anchored off China coast in this taut thriller directed by Robert Wise. Steve McQueen headed cast that included Richard Attenborough, Richard Crenna, Simon Oakland, Candice Bergen.

SANDBURG, CARL (AUGUST) (1878–1967)   American man of letters. Distinguished himself in five fields: poetry, history, fiction, music, biography. His four-volume biography of Abraham Lincoln, *The War Years*, won the 1939 Pulitzer Prize in History. Also wrote *Lincoln: The Prairie Years*, (two volumes, 1926). Best known for poetry celebrating American spirit, and for his unassuming personality. Once asked, "What did the last man on Earth say?" he answered, "Where is everybody?"

SANDERS, HARLAND (THE COLONEL) (1890–1980)   Founder and representative of Kentucky Fried Chicken chain. Developed secret recipe for "Finger-lickin' good" chicken served in buckets. Born in the South, 1890, Sanders "kicked the bucket," 1980.

SANDS OF IWO JIMA, THE   1949 film starring John Wayne as Marine Sergeant John M. Stryker. John Agar co-stars as rebellious recruit whipped into shape by tough sergeant.

SANDSTORMS   Storms in which winds at 10 m.p.h. or more carry sand through the air. Called *haboobs* in Northern Africa and India, occur most often in deserts or on beaches. Can disrupt travel and damage crops.

SANGRIA   Drink made by adding pieces of fresh fruit to red wine. Also called wine cup. Traditional throughout Spanish-speaking world. Usual fruits added are orange, lime, apple. Soda water also added.

SANTA CLAUS' REINDEER   According to Clement Clark Moore's 1823 poem "A Visit from St. Nicholas," eight reindeer pull Santa's sleigh: Dasher, Dancer, Prancer, Vixen, Comet, Cupid, Donner, Blitzen.

SANTIAGO   Chile's capital and largest city. Situated in Central Valley, Chile's agricultural heartland. Founded by Pedro de Valdivia, 1541, as first permanent Spanish settlement in Chile. Became capital, 1818.

SAO PAULO. See BRAZIL

SAPPHIRE   Gem of mineral carundum, as is ruby. Comes in all colors, finest is blue. Largest: Star of India, 563 carats. Second hardest mineral to diamond. Can be made by man, but not gem quality.

SARGASSO SEA   Irregular oval-shaped area of North Atlantic Ocean. Set apart from ocean by presence of seaweed floating on surface. Water is unusually clear and very deep blue. High salt content and temperature. Bermuda is only nearby island. Discovered by Christopher Columbus, 1492.

SARDI'S Broadway restaurant, favorite with members of theatrical profession. Opened, 1921 as The Little Restaurant, by Vincent Sardi. Its reputation for hospitality spread among theater community, has become tradition for Broadway actors to celebrate opening nights there.

SATELLITES Any object that orbits a planet. The moon, 2,160 mi. in diameter, is earth's largest satellite. Other planets have moons. Jupiter, with twelve, including Ganymede, Io and Hades, has more moons than any other planet. The first five countries to launch their own satellites were U.S.S.R. (Sputnik, 1957), U.S. (Vanguard I, 1958), Canada (Alouette I, 1962), France (Asterix I, 1965) and Australia (Oscar 5, 1970). The U.S. currently has the largest number of satellites, followed by U.S.S.R. and France, which has launched 19.

SATURDAY NIGHT FEVER 1977 film starring John Travolta as Brooklyn youth whose only escape is through his dancing at local disco. Bee Gees' hit score included "Staying Alive," which became title of 1983 sequel.

SATURN Planet ranking second in size after Jupiter. Rapid rotation of 10 hours 39 minutes. Temperature: -285°F (-176°C). Surrounded by rings composed of chunks of ice. Photographed by Voyager 2.

SAVAK Secret police force by which Iran's Shah Mohammad Reza Pahlavi is said to have crushed freedom of speech and other freedoms before opposition forced him into self-exile, 1979. (see SHAH OF IRAN)

SAVE THE TIGER 1973 film about businessman who faces choice of going bankrupt or hiring arsonist to burn down one of his factories. Jack Lemmon won a Best Actor Oscar for his performance.

SAVILE ROW London street near Piccadilly Circus. Address of most fashionable London tailors. Synonymous with high quality tailoring. Named for wife of third Earl of Burlington, whose family name was Savile. Street also has many old homes, modern government buildings and a multilevel parking lot.

SAWYER, TOM. See TWAIN, MARK

SCADUTO, ANTHONY   American biographer. His book *Scapegoat: The Lonesome Death of Bruno Richard Hauptmann*(1976) refutes evidence used to convict man executed for 1932 kidnap-murder of Charles A. Lindbergh's baby. Hauptmann convicted, 1935; electrocuted, 1936. (see LINDBERGH, CHARLES A.)

SCALLOPS   Shellfish considered delicacy in many parts of world. Two main varieties: bay scallops and larger, sea scallops. Have 35 blue eyes arranged in rows between two shells.

SCAMPI   Italian for large, greenish prawn (shrimp), considered delicacy in cooking. Scampi is plural; singular is scampo, according to Italian noun declination. Dinner entree shrimp scampi is shrimp broiled in garlic butter.

SCARLET LETTER, THE. See HAWTHORNE, NATHANIEL

SCARLET PIMPERNEL, THE. See ORCZY, BARONESS EMMUSKA

SCARLETT O'HARA. See MITCHELL, MARGARET

SCHICK, COLONEL JACOB (1877–1940)   Patented a shaving implement, November 6, 1928 (No. 1,721,530). Manufactured first electric dry shaver March 18, 1931 by Schick Inc., Stamford, CT.

SCHLITZ   Founded 1849 by August Krug, taken over 1856 by bookkeeper Joseph Schlitz, who renamed brewery, 1874. Slogan, "Beer that made Milwaukee famous" first appeared on labels in 1894, referring to Schlitz shipping beer to Chicago after 1871 fire. Pabst, at time larger and better established, used slogan "Milwaukee beer is famous; Pabst has made it so," and sued Schlitz. Matter settled out of court after marriage between families of two competing breweries.

SCHMELING, MAX (1905–   )   Won world heavyweight boxing championship (only German ever to have title) from Jack Sharkey (on foul), 1930. Handed American heavyweight Joe Louis first professional loss, June 19, 1936, Yankee Stadium, knocking him out in 12th round. In rematch with Louis, then heavyweight champion, Schmeling was ko'd in first round of title fight, June 22, 1938, Yankee Stadium. Hitler's favorite boxer.

SCHOONER   Fore- and aft-rigged sailboat characteristically having two or more masts. Smaller mast is forward of main mast, which is located approximately at center of ship. Other two-masted boats, ketch and yawl, have smaller mizzenmast behind main mast.

SCHORR, DANIEL LOUIS (1916–   ) News correspondent, worked with CBS news for 23 years. Resigned after February 11, 1976 suspension for passing copy of secret Pike Committee report on CIA operations to New York City's *Village Voice*. Refused to name his source, pleading a reporter's First Amendment.

SCHROEDER. See SCHULZ, CHARLES MONROE

SCHULTZ   Most common surname in Germany. Means magistrate or sheriff, or steward or overseer. Several names derived from Schultz: Schulz, Schulze, Schultze, Shult, Sholes.

SCHULZ, CHARLES MONROE (1922–   ) U.S. cartoonist, nicknamed "Sparky," who created the world's most read comic strip *Peanuts* (October 2, 1950), originally called *Li'l Folks*. Schulz author of *Charlie Brown, Snoopy and Me*. Among strip's characters are: Lucy van Pelt: Charlie Brown's chief tormentor, who charges five cents for psychiatric sessions. Linus van Pelt: Lucy's precocious brother who goes to pieces without his flannel blanket. Schroeder: idolizes Beethoven, whose music he plays on his toy piano to the dismay of Lucy, who wishes he were interested in her instead of the composer. Snoopy: beagle who stars at shortstop on Charlie Brown's baseball team and fantasizes he is superhero and author. Woodstock: Snoopy's bird pal. Occasionally serves as Snoopy's secretary when beagle dictates responses to letters in his advice column. *Peanuts* has added such expressions to contemporary usage as "Happiness is a warm puppy."

SCOPES TRIAL   Public school teacher John T. Scopes was tried, 1925, for teaching Darwin's theory of evolution. This was in violation of Tennessee state law. Clarence Darrow (1857–1938) defended Scopes; William Jennings Bryan (1860–1925), a religious fundamentalist and President Wilson's secretary of state, was prosecuting attorney. Scopes was found guilty and fined $100.

SCOTLAND YARD   Detective agency. Created by Sir Robert Peele's 1829 Act of Parliament. Originally built at Whitehall Place, 1890. New quarters erected on Thames Embankment. Moved again in 1960s to what was the scene of an unsolved murder.

SCRABBLE   Crossword board game copyrighted 1948, developed from Criss Cross, a spelling game with wood tiles originated by Alfred M. Butts in 1931. Scrabble produced by Selchow and Righter since 1952.

SCRABBLE LETTERS

	Value	# of tiles		Value	# of tiles		Value	# of tiles
A	1	9	J	8	1	S	1	4
B	3	2	K	5	1	T	1	6
C	3	2	L	1	4	U	1	4
D	2	4	M	3	2	V	4	2
E	1	12	N	1	6	W	4	2
F	4	2	O	1	8	X	8	1
G	2	3	P	3	2	Y	4	2
H	4	2	Q	10	1	Z	10	1
I	1	9	R	1	6	Blank	-	2

SCRABBLE RULES AND PLAY   The game board has 225 squares, 15 by 15, including: 8 triple-word scores; 17 double-word scores (including center square, starting point of game); 12 triple-letter scores; and 24 double-letter scores. Each player selects seven of 100 tiles with letter and numerical value printed on one side. Points are scored from values assigned to letters used in words and from making use of bonus squares. First player must combine two or more letters to form a word making use of center square (double-word score). Player who cannot make word of at least two letters must pass, but may use turn to trade in some or all of his tiles. Game continues by players taking turns, adding on to build new words. Rules provide demonstration game, in which HORN is the first word spelled on board; placed horizontally, with letter *R* on center square, the word scores 14 points.

SCREWDRIVER   Cocktail made by mixing 1½ oz. vodka with 5 oz. orange juice. Reportedly first made by oilmen who didn't like to drink their vodka straight, so they mixed it with juice and stirred it with their tools.

SCRIPPS INSTITUTION OF OCEANOGRAPHY   Graduate research institution in La Jolla, near San Diego, CA, for study of ocean geography and related sciences. Part of University of California, San Diego. Founded, 1903. Conducts studies on: composition of ocean bottom; properties of water, waves, currents and tides; and marine biology.

SCROOGE   Miserly old man who changes his ways due to the spirits of Christmas Past, Present and Future in Charles Dickens' novel *A Christmas Carol*. Has been portrayed in the movies by Reginald Owen in the 1938 film; Alastair Sim in the 1951 remake; and Albert Finney in the 1970 musical film *Scrooge*. (see DICKENS, CHARLES)

SCROOGE MCDUCK (1860–   )   Walt Disney cartoon character whose "biography" was compiled during 1940s by Disney employee Carl Barks. Born in Glasgow, Scotland, Scrooge emigrated to U.S. in 1879. Made first money in copper, then became millionaire after investing in Star of the World diamond mine. Billionaire in 1902, settled in Duckburg but traveled widely. By late '40s had accumulated three cubic acres of money. His fortune, said to exceed J. Paul Getty's, estimated at $1 multiplijillion, 9 obsquatumatillian, making him world's richest duck (by far). (see HUEY, LOUIE AND DEWEY)

SCROUNGE   Slang for "pilfer," added to American vocabulary in World War I. Troops would "scrounge" countryside for supplies.

SCUBA   Stands for Self-Contained Underwater Breathing Apparatus. Tanks hold compressed air for divers, allowing more mobility than diving suit with air pumped from surface through breathing tube. Popularized through TV series *Sea Hunt* with Lloyd Bridges.

SCURVY   Disease caused by lack of vitamin C. Victims bruise easily, have sore bleeding gums, and may lose their teeth. Sailors on long voyages often get it. The British navy gave lime juice to its sailors to prevent scurvy, hence the nickname "Limey" for British sailors.

SEA GULL   Long-winged bird of gull family, laridae. Found near oceans, lakes and other waters. Migratory. Eats any food or garbage that floats; will drink saltwater.

SEA OF SHOWERS   Largest "sea" on the moon, 750 mi. wide. Seas on the moon are actually dry plains, as moon has no water. Nine major lunar seas, which appear as darker areas on surface when seen from Earth.

SEA OF TRANQUILITY   Also called *Mare Tranquillitatis*. Area on the moon's surface composed of volcanic rock. Surface is dark, low-lying, level and smooth with an irregular outline. Completely waterless. Site of Apollo 11's landing on July 20, 1969.

SEAGRAM   Largest distilling business. Began, 1924, when Samuel Bronfman bought out the established Seagram in England. Family-run.

SEARS TOWER   World's tallest building (110 stories). Height: 1,454 ft. (443 m.). Located in downtown Chicago along South Wacker Drive.

SEAS NAMED FOR COLORS   *White Sea*: Southern extension of Barents Sea, off northwest coast of U.S.S.R. Frozen 200 days per year. *Yellow Sea*: Shallow sea between China and Korea. Rivers emptying into it carry large amounts of silt, giving it a yellow color. *Black Sea*: Large, deep sea surrounded by Russia, Romania, Turkey, Bulgaria. Low salinity causes blackish color. *Red Sea*: Long, narrow, landlocked sea between Africa and Arabia. During certain times of year, water contains reddish algae.

SEASONS   Summer in Northern Hemisphere begins when sun is above Tropic of Cancer, about June 21.

SEASONS (STATISTICALLY MOST HAZARD-OUS)   Ranking by number of fatal accidents: 1. Summer 2. Fall 3. Spring 4. Winter

SEAT BELTS   Mandatory car equipment, Illinois, July 1, 1956; mandatory nationally, March 31, 1968. Even so, 45,000 deaths occur each year due to automobile accidents, or 21 people killed per 100,000.

SEATTLE MARINERS   Entered Western Division of American Baseball League in 1977, same year Toronto Blue Jays entered American League's Eastern Division. Seattle previously had American League expansion team in 1969 season (Pilots), but they became Milwaukee Brewers in 1970. Mariners finished sixth in first season, have never won division title. Play in Kingdome.

SEATTLE WORLD'S FAIR   In 1962, Seattle, WA hosted the fair. Also called the Century 21 Exposition. The "Space Needle," a 607-ft. (185-m.) high tower with restaurants as well as viewing decks, still stands as landmark of the event.

SECRET LIFE OF WALTER MITTY, THE   1947 film based on James Thurber character. Danny Kaye starred as nebbish who dreams himself a hero and gets involved with real spy caper.

SECRETARIAT   Winner 1973 Triple Crown; won Belmont Stakes by 31 lengths in track record 2:24 for 1½ mi. Trained by

Lucien Laurin, ridden by Ron Turcotte, owned by Meadow Stable. In 21 races, had 16 wins. Earned $1.3 million while racing. First Triple Crown winner since 1948 (Citation).

SEGAL, ERICH (1937–   ) American novelist and Yale classics professor (1965–1973). Author of *Love Story* (1970), novel about ill-fated romance between wealthy Harvard pre-law student and hockey player Oliver Barrett IV and Radcliffe coed Jenny Cavilleri, daughter of poor Italian widower. Ends with Jenny, dying at age 25, telling husband Oliver, "Love means never having to say you're sorry." Ryan O'Neal and Ali McGraw starred in Arthur Hiller's 1970 film version. *Oliver's Story* (1977), *Love Story* sequel, concerned attorney Barrett's life after wife's death. Ryan O'Neal reprised his role in 1978 film version, falling in love with Candice Bergen.

SEGAL, GEORGE (1934–   ) Successful actor and professional musician (he plays the tenor banjo). Appeared in *Ship of Fools*(1965), played leads in *King Rat* (1965), *Who's Afraid of Virginia Woolf?*(1966) with Sandy Dennis, *The Owl and the Pussycat*(1970) with Barbra Streisand, *Where's Poppa*(1970) and *A Touch of Class*(1973), among others.

SEINE RIVER France's major waterway flowing 475 mi. (764 km.) from Dijon into the English channel near Le Havre. In Paris, it is crossed by more than 30 bridges built over 300 years.

SELASSIE, HAILE (1892–1975) Emperor of Ethiopia, 1930. Upon assuming power, changed name from Ras Taffari to Haile Selassie, meaning "Power of the Trinity." Also called "Lion of Judah." Overthrown, 1974, in military coup.

SENATOR BEAUREGARD CLAGHORN Fictional southern politician portrayed by Kenny Delmar on radio program *The Fred Allen Show*. His catch phrase "That's a joke, son" made him popular character in "Allen's Alley," a segment of the show, which also featured characters Mrs. Nussbaum, Titus Moody and Ajax Cassidy.

SENSES As distinguished by Aristotle: vision, hearing, touch, taste, smell. Smell, first to develop yet least understood. Perception of odor allows us to experience all flavors other than sweet, salty, bitter and sour. Smell is associated with memory, perhaps because the nerve that carries smell information goes to part of brain linked to memory.

SENSUOUS MAN, THE   Nonfiction book of the year, 1971. Written by "M," anonymous author answering previous year's *The Sensuous Woman* by "J." Published by Lyle Stuart. Sales were just over half those of *The Sensuous Woman.*

SENSUOUS WOMAN, THE   Published, 1970. Described itself as the first how-to book for female who yearns to be "all woman." Written under pseudonym "J." Author gave her views and advice on sex and sex relations. Inspired 1971 book *The Sensuous Man* by "M."

SENSURROUND   Universal Pictures' stereophonic sound device that created a frightening rumble in theater, which lent to realism of certain movies. *Earthquake*(1973) was first, soon followed by *Midway*(1976), *Rollercoaster*(1977) and *Battlestar Galactica*(1979).

SEOUL   Largest city and capital of South Korea. Name means "capital." General Yi Songgye, first member of Yi Dynasty, made Seoul his capital, 1394.

SEQUOIA, THE   Presidential yacht. Commissioned, 1931. Used by Presidents Franklin Delano Roosevelt through Gerald Ford. Sold by President Jimmy Carter, 1977, as austerity measure.

SEQUOYA (1770–1843)   Cherokee Indian educator. Invented writing system for Cherokee language. Originally intended to record customs and culture of the ancient tribe. Giant sequoia trees of California named after him.

SERGEANT PRESTON OF THE YUKON   TV adventure series about officer of Royal Northwest Mounted Police who fought crime in Klondike territory at turn of century. Richard Simmons played the title role, confronting outlaws with line, "I arrest you in the name of the Crown!" He was aided by his horse, Rex, and his dog, Yukon King.

SERGEANT SCHULTZ   The inept officer in charge of Stalag 13 on TV series *Hogan's Heroes* (1965–1971). His superior, Col. Klink, was just as incompetent in keeping Col. Hogan and the rest of the POWs in camp. Schultz's reponse to Klink in times of distress: "I see nothing, I know nothing."

SERGEANT YORK   1941 film starring Gary Cooper as Tennessee mountain boy who becomes World War I hero. Cooper won Best Actor Oscar for the role.

SEVEN   Considered by many, including Adolf Hitler, lucky and magical number. Based on Babylonian astrology that recognized seven planets, including sun and moon. From this we get seven day week.

SEVEN DAYS IN MAY   1964 film about a plot by military chiefs to overthrow the U.S. Government. Fredric March plays President Jordan Lyman, who signs agreement with U.S.S.R. that sparks the tensions.

SEVEN DEADLY SINS. See CARDINAL VIRTUES

SEVEN DWARFS, THE   Miners in story that became Walt Disney's first full-length cartoon (1937), *Snow White and the Seven Dwarfs*. Their names: Bashful, Sleepy, Grumpy, Sneezy, Happy, Dopey, Doc.

SEVEN MULES. See NOTRE DAME, FOUR HORSE-MEN OF

SEVEN WONDERS OF THE ANCIENT WORLD Great Pyramids of Khufu (only one still in existence); Hanging Gardens of Babylon (only one ever living); Colossus of Rhodes; Lighthouse (Pharos) at Alexandria; Mausoleum at Halicarnassus; Temple of Diana Ephesus; Statue of Zeus by Phidias at Olympia.

77 SUNSET STRIP   TV detective series, 1958–1964, starring Efrem Zimbalist, Jr., and Roger Smith. Most popular character on show was jive-talking parking lot attendant Gerald Cloyd Kookson III, or "Kookie," portrayed by Edd Byrnes.

SEWING PATTERN   Ellen and Ebenezer Butterick invented first sewing pattern, 1863. An act of entrepeneurship that helped commercialize the textile industry and bring it to industrial age.

SEXTETTE   1978 film written by and starring Mae West. In her last screen appearance, Mae is a Hollywood glamour queen whose many husbands keep popping up at hotel where she is having her latest honeymoon. Co-starring Tony Curtis, Dom DeLuise.

SHADOW, THE   Mysterious crime fighter of pulp magazines, radio and movie serials in 1930s. With the power to "cloud men's minds," criminologist Lamont Cranston would don black cape and mask to become "The Shadow," who knew "what evil lurks in the hearts of men."

SHADOWS   Seasons are result of Earth's 23½° tilt on its axis. In summer, the sun is more directly overhead than in winter; shadows are thus shorter. It is summer in southern hemisphere when it is winter in northern hemisphere.

SHAFFER, LEVIN PETER (1926–   ) Playwright. Wrote *Equus*, psychological thriller about boy who blinds six horses in one night. Acclaimed in London, opened on Broadway October 1974, winning virtually all available dramatic awards given that season.

SHAGGY DOG, THE 1959 film from Walt Disney about a boy with an ancient ring that transforms him into shaggy sheep dog. Tommy Kirk was the boy; Fred MacMurray, Jean Hagen his parents.

SHAH OF IRAN (1919–1980) Mohammed Reza Pahlavi, social reformist, 1960s. Initiated so-called White Revolution. Modernization attempts violated Islamic tradition. Absolute rule enforced by ruthless secret service met by popular opposition. Fled to Egypt, 1979, when Ayatollah Khomeini seized power. (see SAVAK)

SHAKESPEARE, WILLIAM (1564–1616) English dramatist. Wrote 38 plays, including one or two possible collaborations. Many produced at London's Globe Theatre. Also wrote nondramatic poetry, including *Sonnets*(1609). Contemporary Ben Jonson wrote Shakespeare "was not of an age, but for all time." Married Anne Hathaway, seven or eight years older, when he was 18. Daughter Susan born 1583, twins Hamnet and Judith in 1585. Died April 23, 1616, same day as Spanish novelist Miguel de Cervantes. Shakespeare also born on April 23, 52 years before. Among his best-known plays: *A Midsummer Night's Dream*(1594), comedy about star-crossed lovers, set in late spring in Athens and nearby woods. Merry character Puck has magic love-juice that makes person whose eyelids are anointed while asleep fall in love with first object seen upon waking. Used it somewhat indiscriminately, complicating plot; *Romeo and Juliet*(1596), tragedy about ill-fated lovers of feuding Montague (Romeo's) and Capulet (Juliet's) families of Verona ("a plague on both your houses," from Act III). Romeo and then Juliet commit suicide; two houses make sorrowful peace. Basis for many future works, including Broadway musical *West Side Story*. In famous balcony scene (Act II), Romeo says, "But, soft! What light through yonder window breaks? It is the east, and Juliet is the sun!"; *The Merchant of Venice*(1596), about Antonio, merchant of Venice, who borrows from moneylender Shylock to finance Bassanio's voyage to win hand of Portia. When Antonio can't repay, Shylock tries to get his "pound of flesh." Shylock, one of Shakespeare's most controversial characters, now usually played as tragic, dignified figure, enduring persecution because he is Jewish. Has famous "Hath not a Jew eyes?" speech; *Henry the IV*(1597) and *The Merry Wives of Windsor*(1597), feature Sir John Falstaff, Shakespeare's best-known comic character. A braggart and liar, his lust for life is so keen that character has become a favorite. His hangout is the Boar's Head Tavern; *Twelfth Night, or What You Will* (1599) plot hinges on physical likeness of Sebastian and twin sister Viola, separated in shipwreck, each believing the other is dead. Play begins with line, "If music be the food of love, play on!"; *Hamlet, Prince of Denmark*(1601), perhaps Shakespeare's most famous play. Tragedy about murder and revenge. Famed line "rotten in the State of Denmark," refers to King Claudius' murder of Hamlet's father to get the throne. Hamlet has more lines than any other Shakespearian character: 1,422. Results in expression, "It's Hamlet without the prince" when principal person at a function is absent, because play would lose all meaning if Hamlet's lines were omitted. It is Polonius, however, who says (act I, scene 3), "Neither a borrower or lender be / For loan oft loses both itself and friend / And borrowing dulls the edge of husbandry." Minor characters Rosencrantz and Guildenstern, two treacherous courtiers, gained greater fame when playwright Tom Stoppard turned them into leads of *Rosencrantz and Guildenstern Are Dead*(1967); *Othello, The Moor of Venice*(1604), about Moorish general Othello who appoints Cassio as chief lieutenant, arousing jealousy of his ensign Iago, who hints to Othello that his wife Desdemona has had an affair with Cassio. Enraged, Othello strangles Desdemona. Emilia, Iago's wife and Desdemona's servant, discovers Iago's plot and denounces him, but Othello, asking to be remembered as one who "loved not wisely, but too well," commits suicide. Iago condemned to torture; *King Lear*(1605), about old King Lear who decides to divide England among three daughters Goneril, Regan, Cordelia. First two, crafty and insincere, profess love for him in grandiose terms, but Cordelia says she loves him according to her bond, "nor more, nor less." Although she is favorite daughter, she is youngest; Lear divides kingdom equally between two oldest sisters. Cordelia marries king of France, eventually battles with sisters' armies. Defeated, she is taken prisoner and hanged. Lear, broken-hearted, dies soon after; *Macbeth*(1606), set in Scotland. Shakespeare's shortest play, and most bloody, described as a study in fear. Ambitious Macbeth, urged by his wife, murders Duncan to become king. Early performances of *Macbeth* often plagued by calamities, causing the name Macbeth, said in theater, to be bad luck; *The Tempest*(1611), Shakespeare's last play. Opening scene, storm at sea. Magician Prospero rules enchanted island after being ousted from dukedom 12 years earlier. Son of a rival arrives on island, falls in love with Prospero's daughter Miranda, and helps him regain his land.

SHALOM   Hebrew word meaning "peace, hello or good-bye," depending when used. Related to Arabic salaam.

SHAMPOO   1975 comedy directed by Hal Ashby. Warren Beatty produced and starred as Beverly Hills hairdresser having affairs with women customers. Lee Grant won Best Supporting Actress Oscar for her role.

SHANE   1953 Western film starring Alan Ladd as a former gunfighter defending homesteaders. Brandon de Wilde plays idolizing youth who cries film's last line, "Shane, come back!"

SHANGHAI   Most populated city in the world, with about 11,000,000 inhabitants. China's Communist Party founded there, 1921; took over city, 1949. Before 1949, Japan, Britain, U.S., France set up trading businesses in areas called concessions.

SHANNON RIVER, THE   Located in Ireland. Longest river in British Isles. Flows 250 mi. (402 km.). Empties into Atlantic Ocean. Limerick is principal city on river.

SHARIF, OMAR (1932–   )   Egyptian-born actor. Films include *Lawrence of Arabia*, *Dr. Zhivago*, *Funny Girl*. Learned to play bridge between scenes on movie set and became accomplished player. Member of 1964 Egyptian team at Bridge Olympiad, won second place at London Invitational, 1967. Formed his own team, called "The Bridge Circus." Produced feature film about bridge, trying to boost its popularity as spectator sport.

SHARK   Carnivorous fish. Will eat other sharks. Parents do not care for young. Have no bones, only cartilage. Skin once used to manufacture as sandpaper. Served in "fish and chips," Great Britain.

SHAW, CLAY (1913–   )   Prominent New Orleans businessman, once connected with CIA. Two months prior to Lee Harvey

Oswald's assassination of President J. F. Kennedy, a man who looked like Shaw had been seen with Oswald. Shaw was charged with conspiracy in assassination, 1967, later acquitted.

SHAW, GEORGE BERNARD (1856–1950) British dramatist and critic. Wrote "drama of ideas," reflecting passion for social reform. Awarded Nobel Prize for Literature, 1925. Among many well-known plays: *Man and Superman*(1903) about young revolutionist John Tanner, named guardian of Ann Whitfield, who loves him. To avoid her, he flees to Spain where, in a long (and frequently omitted) scene, dreams he is Don Juan in hell. Ann pursues him and eventually breaks his resolve. *Major Barbara*(1905), about Barbara Undershaft, a major in the Salvation Army whose millionaire father owns an armaments company. He and his friend, a whiskey distiller, donate money to Army, but Barbara quits rather than accept "tainted" donation. *Pygmalion*(1913): phonetics professor Henry Higgins transforms Cockney flower girl Eliza Doolittle into a lady. She falls in love with him. Lerner and Lowe adapted it into award-winning 1956 musical *My Fair Lady*.

SHAW, IRWIN (1913–1984) Playwright—short story writer who later gained acclaim for novels *The Young Lions*(1948), about three men in World War II, and *Rich Man, Poor Man*(1970), a 30-year chronicle of fictional Jordache family.

SHEBOYGAN Wisconsin port at mouth of Sheboygan River on Lake Michigan. Called "the city of cheese, chairs, children and churches." Lies in heart of dairy farming country.

SHELLAC Varnish made from lac resic. Lac is produced by scale insects that live in trees in India and Burma. Lac is harvested, purified, dissolved in alcohol to make shellac.

SHELLEY, MARY WOLLSTONECRAFT (1797–1851) English novelist. Daughter of Mary Wollstonecraft Godwin, first radical feminist. Eloped with poet Percy Bysshe Shelley at 18. Author of novel *Frankenstein, or The Modern Prometheus*(1818), about Swiss doctor who creates living monster while seeking elixir of life. Monster ultimately murders doctor in Arctic. Wrote it at age 19 when she, poet husband, and his friend Lord Byron competed to see who could write best ghost story. She claimed she dreamt it.

SHELLS The hard, outer coverings of mollusks such as clams and snails. They are made of the mineral calcium carbonate. Giant clams can have 500 lb. shells. The study of mollusks and shells is conchology.

SHEPARD, ALAN B. JR., (1923–   )   First American to travel in space, American astronaut. May 5, 1961; flew Freedom 7 117 mi. (188 km.) into space. Top speed, 5,180 mi. (8,336 km.) per hour. Splashed down, Atlantic Ocean 15 minutes later. Flight occurred 23 days after U.S.S.R. launched first manned space trip.

SHERIDAN, ANN (1915–1967)   Actress in films since 1934. Known as "The Oomph Girl," starred in *Black Legion*(1936), *Angels With Dirty Faces*(1938), *Kings Row*(1941), *Shine on Harvest Moon*(1944), among others.

SHERLOCK HOLMES. See DOYLE, SIR ARTHUR CONAN

SHIELDS, BROOKE (1965–   )   Child model, first appeared on Ivory Snow box at the age of 11 months. Turned actress with role as 12-year-old prostitute in *Pretty Baby*(1978). Other films include: *Just You and Me, Kid*(1979), *Wanda Nevada*(1979), *The Blue Lagoon*(1980), *Endless Love*(1981) and *Sahara*(1984).

SHIRER, WILLIAM LAWRENCE (1904–   )   American journalist specializing in Nazi Germany. Depicted rise of Nazism in CBS Radio reports from Germany before World War II. Wrote massive history *The Rise and Fall of the Third Reich*(1960), a best seller, *The Rise and Fall of Adolf Hitler*(1961) and *The Collapse of the Third Republic, an Inquiry into the Fall of France in 1940*(1969).

SHIRLEY TEMPLE   Nonalcoholic "cocktail" usually made for children. Named after 1930s child actress Shirley Temple. Mixed by pouring ½ oz. grenadine syrup (or cherry juice) in cocktail or champagne glass, filling with ginger ale and garnishing with maraschino cherry.

SHOEMAKER, WILLIAM LEE (WILLIE) (1931–   )   Nicknamed "Wee Willie" (4'11", 95 lbs.) and "Shoe." First jockey to win more than 8,000 races (now over 8,200). All-time leader in victories and mounts' earnings (more than $90 million). Won record $3,052,146 in 1967 (since broken). Rode three Kentucky Derby winners, four Belmont Stakes winners, and two Preakness winners in racing's three Triple Crown Events.

SHOOTIST, THE   1976 Western film, notable as John Wayne's last film. Story of legendary gunfighter dying of cancer, who cannot escape his past. Lauren Bacall and James Stewart co-star.

SHORE, DINAH (1921–   ) Pop vocalist. Career spanned from the late 1930s–1960s. Her show, *The Dinah Shore Show*, was sponsored by Chevrolet, 1951–1961. Starred in the Chevy show, 1950s, telling her audience "See the U.S.A. in your Chevrolet." Ended each show by blowing audience a kiss.

SHREDDED WHEAT The first ready-to-eat breakfast food. The machine used to make it was patented in 1893. The first packaged ready-to-eat breakfast cereal was Grape Nuts introduced by Charles William Post, 1897.

SHREWS Insectivores, a group of mammals that also includes moles and hedgehogs. Are smallest mammals. Smallest: Savi's white-toothed Pygmy shrew, two inches or less in length, less than one-tenth of an oz. in weight. Most have poisonous saliva, eat their own weight in food every day, and only live about one year.

SHRIVER, ROBERT SARGENT (1915–   ) American lawyer. Appointed Director of Peace Corps, 1961, after its creation by President Kennedy's executive order. Ran for vice-president, 1972, with George McGovern. Thomas Eagleton, original choice for vice-president, removed from race after disclosure that he had undergone psychiatric therapy.

SHROUD OF TURIN Cloth believed to have been wrapped around body of Jesus Christ in tomb. Stains on cloth scientifically proven to bear image of a crucified man. Darkness of stains depended on how close body was to cloth.

SHROVE TUESDAY Or *Mardi Gras* (French for "Fat Tuesday"), the day before Ash Wednesday, the beginning of Lent in the Christian calendar. Day of celebration in many countries.

SHUFFLEBOARD Began as shipboard deck game in 1870s. Two or four players use 52 ft. by 6 ft. flat, smooth surface. Players slide discs with long cue toward triangular target at far end of court. Object: shovel disks into scoring area, and/or knock opponent's disks away. Last player shoots "hammer," intending to hammer opponent's disks off court while remaining in scoring area.

SHUTE, NEVIL (1899–1960) English novelist and aeronautical engineer who settled in Australia. Novels noted for technological detail. Of 26 novels, best-known for *On The Beach* (1957), about Australians awaiting radioactive fallout from nuclear war that has destroyed rest of world. 1959 movie version starred Gregory Peck, Ava Gardner, Fred Astaire.

SHUTTLECOCK   Also called "bird" or "shuttle." Object hit over net with racquets in badminton. Traditionally made of cork and feathers; more recently, nylon or plastic. Weighs 4.73–5.5 gm.; 3⅞ inches from end to end. Object of game to hit shuttle to floor on opponent's side of net. Game derived from ancient "battledore and shuttlecock."

SICILY   Italian island known as "Jewel of the Mediterranean." Largest island in Mediterranean Sea. Separated from toe of Italy's boot-shaped peninsula by Strait of Messina. Mount Etna, active volcano, causes earthquakes on island. Island's inhabitants called Sicilians.

SIDECAR, THE   Cocktail reportedly originated at Harry's New York Bar in Paris. Owner Harry MacElhone claimed it was concocted in 1931 for customer who always arrived in motorcycle sidecar. Mixed by combining ½ oz. lemon juice, ½ oz. Triple Sec or Cointreau and ½ oz. brandy.

SIERRA NEVADA   Huge, tilted mountain range which extends north and south for 400 mi. (640 km.) in eastern California. Highest point is Mt. Whitney, 14,494 ft. (4,418 m.). Also name of steep line of mountains in Spain bordering southern Mediterranean coast. Includes Spain's tallest peak, Mulhacen, 11,424 ft. (3,427 m.).

SIERRE LEONE   Small African country. Diamonds are basis of its industry. Rice is main crop food. Capital is Freetown, founded in 1787 as settlement for freed slaves.

SIESTA   From the Spanish for "sixth (hour)," suggested by Latin *sexta hora*, the sixth hour of the day. Traditionally nap time.

SILENT MOVIE   1976 film directed and starring Mel Brooks. Brooks and his assistants Marty Feldman and Dom DeLuise attempt to recruit stars for new silent movie. Shot silent with music and sound effects. The only word in the film is spoken by Marcel Marceau.

SILKWORMS   Larvae or caterpillars of a kind of moth. Their cocoons are unwound to yield silk. Silkworms will eat only the leaves of mulberry trees. Because of domestication, can no longer fly.

SILLY PUTTY   Mixture of boric acid and silicone oil invented accidentally in General Electric research lab, 1945. Plastic egg served as inexpensive way to hold and ship it. Nonsticky Silly Putty, invented in 1960, given to Apollo VIII astronauts as present, proved useful for holding tools under weightless conditions.

SILVERHEELS, JAY (1920–1980)   Full-blooded Indian actor who portrayed the Lone Ranger's faithful Indian companion Tonto on TV 1949–1956, and in two feature films (1956, 1958).

SIMMONS, RUTH. See MURPHY, BRIDEY

SIMON AND GARFUNKEL   Paul Simon and Art Garfunkel grew up together in Queens, NY. Calling themselves "Tom and Jerry," they had a minor hit, "Hey, Schoolgirl," in 1957. As Simon and Garfunkel, their first hit was "Sounds of Silence" (1965); others followed: "Homeward Bound," "I Am a Rock," etc. Created music for movie *The Graduate*(1967), including the song "Mrs. Robinson," which asked, "Where have you gone, Joe DiMaggio?"

SIMON, CARLY (1945–   )   Folk-pop singer and songwriter. Hit songs include: "Anticipation" (1971) and the theme from the James Bond movie *The Spy Who Loved Me*, "Nobody Does It Better." Also wrote "You're So Vain," number one hit song (1972), supposedly inspired by and sung to actor Warren Beatty. Song says you should travel to Nova Scotia to see the total eclipse of the sun.

SIMON, MARVIN (NEIL) (1927–   )   American playwright, primarily of comedies. Had four shows running simultaneously during 1966–1967 Broadway season (*Barefoot in the Park*, *The Odd Couple*, *Sweet Charity* and *Star-Spangled Girl*), and three during 1969–1970 season. Also wrote *Come Blow Your Horn*, *Plaza Suite*, *Promises, Promises*, *California Suite*, *Chapter Two*, *They're Playing Our Song*, *Only When I Laugh*, and many others. Among them: *The Odd Couple*(1965), about divorced sportswriter Oscar Madison, a slob, and his roommate, photographer Felix Unger, who is meticulous. Humor focuses on their roommate relationship and their date with Pidgeon sisters, Gwendolyn and Cecily, who live in apartment upstairs. Cowritten with Simon's brother Danny, based on his experiences as divorcé. Walter Matthau (Oscar) and Art Carney (Felix) originated roles on Broadway. Later turned into successful film (Matthau and

Jack Lemmon) and TV sitcom (Jack Klugman and Tony Randall). *The Sunshine Boys*, (1972) play about two veteran vaudevillians who have shared love-hate relationship for decades, and efforts to reunite them for TV special. George Burns won an Oscar opposite Walter Matthau in the 1975 screen version.

SIMPLE SIMON In third verse of nursery rhyme, "Simple Simon went a-fishing / For to catch a whale / All the water he had got / was in his mother's pail." He also "met a pie man, going to the fair," and asked him to taste his "ware." Pie man wants a penny first, to which Simon replies, "Indeed, I have not any."

SIMPSON, ORENTHAL JAMES (O.J.) (1947–) All-American and All-Pro running back. Led University of Southern California Trojans to 1967 National Championship and '68 Rose Bowl win over Indiana (14-3). Won 1968 Heisman Trophy. Led National Football League in rushing four times, including single-season record 2,003 yds. in 1973. Broke league record in touchdowns with 23 in 1975 season. After knee surgery (1977), "Juice" was traded from Buffalo Bills to San Francisco '49ers (1978). Retired, 1979. Now actor, sports commentator and TV commercial representative for Hertz Rent-a-Car

SINATRA, FRANK (1915–) One of the most popular singers of the 1940s, started with "The Hoboken Four," starred on radio's *Your Hit Parade*. His first nonsinging role in the film *From Here to Eternity* won him the 1953 Oscar for Best Supporting Actor and rescued his career. On December 8, 1963, his son Frank, Jr., was kidnapped from a Nevada hotel. He was released unharmed two days later after his father paid $240,000 ransom. Two men were arrested and convicted; most of ransom was recovered. In 1966, married actress Mia Farrow, later divorced. Calls Chicago "my kind of town in a popular song.

SINBAD. See ARABIAN NIGHTS

SING SING Name of state prison in Ossining, NY, until 1971 when it was renamed Ossining Correctional Facility. Still commonly referred to as Sing Sing. Has schools and factories. Only houses male prisoners.

SINGAPORE, REPUBLIC OF Asian Island located on tip of Malay Peninsula. Formerly a British Crown colony. Became state of Federation of Malaysia, 1963–1965, and has since been an independent republic in the British Commonwealth. Population density:

10,700 per sq. mi., greatest in Asia. Area only 239 sq. mi. (621 sq. km.), with approximately 2.5 million inhabitants.

SIRHAN, SIRHAN (1944–   ) Assassinated Senator Robert F. Kennedy, June 5, 1968. Sirhan, an Arab, disagreed with Kennedy's support of Israel. Sentenced to death, 1969. Sentence later reduced to life in prison. Scheduled for parole release, February 28, 1986.

SIRICA, JOHN JOSEPH (1904–   ) Chief judge of U.S. District Court for Washington, DC, 1971–1974. Presided over trial of seven original Watergate break-in defendants. Explained it all in book *To Set the Record Straight.*

SIRIUS Brightest star in the night sky. Located in Canis Major, a southern hemisphere constellation. About nine light-years away (53 trillion mi.). Also known as Dog Star.

SIROCCO Warm, southeasterly wind. Two types: 1) damp wind preceding rain, and 2) dry wind carrying Saharan desert dust. Dry sirocco parches the throat and burns the skin. Common in areas north of Mediterranean Sea.

SISTINE CHAPEL. See MICHELANGELO

SIX DAY WAR On June 5, 1967, Israel made surprise air attack, crippling Egypt. By the time of cease-fire on the sixth day of the war, June 10, 1967, Israel had taken Sinai Peninsula, Gaza Strip, part of Syria, Golan Heights, Jerusalem and the West Bank of Jordan River.

SIX DAYS OF THE CONDOR. See GRADY, JAMES

$64,000 QUESTION, THE TV quiz show of 1950s that popularized big-money giveaways. Hosted by Hal March, 1955–1958. Dr. Joyce Brothers gained fame and $64,000 by answering questions about boxing. Jack Benny appeared and won $64. Show canceled amid scandal that this and other quiz shows were rigged.

SKATEBOARDING Riding on board attached to rolling wheels like those on roller skates, using surfing-type maneuvers. Originated in California c. 1960. Stunts include tick-tacking, series of 30° kick turns performed while board is moving, and walking the dog, series of 180° spins first on back wheels, then on front. Latter also known as ro-lo or endover.

SKELTON, RED (1910–   ) Radio and movie star of the 1940s who became a fixture of TV with a variety show lasting 20 years (1951–1971). Characters he portrayed included the hobo Freddie the

Freeloader, hayseed Clem Kadiddlehopper, and Sheriff Deadeye. Told jokes from the point of view of two seagulls, Gertrude and Heathcliff.

SKIING, ALPINE   Three Olympic events:

Downhill:	Course for speed. Fastest time wins.
Slalom:	Twisting course marked by flags (gates). Skier takes two runs on different courses. Fastest aggregate time wins.
Giant Slalom:	Same as slalom, but course longer and gates further apart. Men usually have two runs, women one.

SKIING, HERRINGBONING   In skiing, method of climbing hill or slope. With ski tips pointed outward, skier steps forward with alternating feet, weight on inside edges of skis, creating herringbone pattern in snow as skier moves uphill.

SKIING, NORDIC   Cross-country skiing and ski jumping. "Nordic Combined" events include both; competitor with highest total score wins, regardless of placement in individual events.

SKIN   Largest human organ. Surface area: 18 sq. ft. Approximately six lbs. in weight. Thickest type found on back and heels; eyelids have the thinnest. Controls body temperature, protects body, defines location for sense of touch. Epidermis: outermost layer. Contains dying skin cells. Also contains protein keratin that toughens skin and makes it waterproof. Dermis: middle layer. Primarily blood vessels, nerve endings and fingertips. Subcutaneous Tissue: deepest layer. Also connective tissue and blood cells, plus fat cells. Acts as body's shock absorber. Fat also keeps body warm. Shedding of dead skin cells called desquamation.

SKINNER, B. F. (1904–)   American psychologist. Ph.D. Harvard, 1931. Developed the Skinner Box to control and measure animal behavior. By delivering electrical shocks to rats, concluded that behavior could be modified by rewarding or reinforcing correct responses.

SKIP TO MY LOU   Popular folk song dating back to early 1800s. In song, flies are in the buttermilk. Gained new popularity in film *Meet Me in St. Louis* (1944).

SKITTLES. See BOWLING, VARIATIONS

SKUNK   Member weasel family, Mustelidae. Foul-smelling liquid, called musk, sprayed from pair of glands at base of tail. Will give warning first by stamping front feet and growling or hissing. Aim accurate up to 12 ft. (4 m.).

SKY KING   1951 adventure TV series about "America's Favorite Flying Cowboy," starring Kirby Grant as Arizona pilot-rancher, who used airplane to maintain law and order in his area. With him on Flying Crown Ranch were his teenage niece Penny and nephew Clipper. His Twin Cessna plane named "The Songbird."

SKYDIVING   Speed of 185 m. p. h. achieved in headdown, free-falling position; highest speed in any nonmechanical sport. In delayed drops at rarified altitudes, speed of 614 m. p. h. recorded. Highest speed in moving ball game is 188 m. p. h. in pelota (jai alai); golf ball driven off tee at 170 m. p. h.

SKYLAB   Manned space laboratory, launched May 14, 1973. Observations of sun, comet Kohoutek, auroras, hurricanes, ocean currents, volcanoes and other physical phenomenon. Medical information as to human adaption to space conditions. Fell, 655 days later, in desert of western Australia.

SKYSCRAPER   World's first skyscraper: the Home Insurance Building. Built in Chicago by William Le Baron Jenney, 1884; destroyed in 1931. Had iron frame. City nicknamed "Birthplace of the Skyscraper."

SLAVERY   Introduced to the "New World" by English sea captain, John Hawkins, 1562. By 1860, over four million slaves in U.S. alone.

SLED DOG RACING   World championship race held annually in February through streets of Anchorage, AL, as part of winter carnival called Fur Rendezvous. Run in heats of 12–30 mi.; best cumulative time wins. Longest sled race is annual Iditarod, run on winter mail route from Anchorage to Nome: 1,049 mi. Run first weekend in March. Record: 14 days, 14 hr., 43 min., 15 sec.

SLEEP   Most people spend about eight hours a day, or one-third of their lives, asleep. Only two to four hours are spent dreaming. Newborn babies sleep about 16 hours per day. Scientists are unsure why sleep is necessary. On average, people take about seven minutes to fall asleep.

SLEEPER   1973 film, starring and directed by Woody Allen. Woody awakens 200 years in the future and tries to overthrow evil dictatorship. Futuristic devices encountered include a robot dog and the "orgasmatron."

SLEEPING BEAUTY 1959 animated film by Walt Disney, based on the fairy tale of Princess Aurora, put under a sleeping spell by the evil fairy Maleficent. Aurora can wake only to love's first kiss, delivered by Prince Phillip.

SLEUTH Laurence Olivier and Michael Caine starred in 1972 film based on Anthony Shaffer's two-man play. Joseph L. Mankiewicz directed story of a game-playing mystery writer who leads wife's lover into diabolical trap.

SLIDE RULE Ruler-shaped device for mathematical calculations. Most have middle section that slides, enabling proper arrangement of numbers chosen for calculation. For multiplication, two logarithmic scales are used. Made obsolete by the calculator.

SLOOP Small, one-masted sailboat, rigged fore and aft (front and back) with triangular mainsail and smaller, triangular jib sail. Mast usually located about two-fifths of way from bow (toward stern) of boat.

SLOT MACHINE "One-armed bandit" mechanical gambling device. Invented by immigrant Charles Fey, San Francisco, 1895. First machine used nickels. Today certain machines take pennies, but others take up to a silver dollar. In Las Vegas, NV, where machines are prevalent, women often play them because of their convenience, accessibility, easy rules and frequent payback. Largest slot machine, Super Bertha, covers 555 cu. ft. and was installed at Four Queens Casino, Las Vegas, September 1973. Once in every 25 billion players, Super Bertha may yield $1 million for a $10 play.

SMIRNOFF Distillery began vodka production, Moscow, 1818. Selected as "Purveyors to the Imperial Russian Court," 1886, after being sampled by Czar Nicholas III. After 1917 revolution, Smirnoff re-established in America, currently the country's best-selling vodka.

SMITH. See U.S. SURNAMES

SMITH, KATE (1909–) Popular singer since early 1930s, on radio and in movies. Known as "Songbird of the South"; her theme song is "When the Moon Comes Over the Mountain." She is most famous for her rendition of Irving Berlin's 1938 song "God Bless America."

SMITH, TOMMIE, AND CARLOS, JOHN U.S. sprinters, first and third in 200-m. run at 1968 Mexico City Olympics. Raised black-gloved, clenched fists and bowed heads on victory stand during national anthem when receiving medals, protesting treatment of blacks and minorities in U.S. and all over world. Created controversy that saw them denounced, expelled from Olympic Village and sent home.

SMITHSON, FORREST (1885– ?) American hurdler won 110-m. hurdles on closing day of 1908 London Olympics. U.S. swept event, with J. C. Garrels second and A. B. Shaw third. Winning time, then-record 15 seconds. Smithson, a divinity student, carried Bible during race to protest Sunday competition.

SMITHSONIAN INSTITUTION, THE Vast museum complex, educational and research center, Washington, DC. Known as "America's Attic" because it houses America's cultural, historical and scientific collections. Englishman James Smithson gave U.S. $508,318.46 in 1846 to found "an Establishment for the increase and diffusion of knowledge among men."

SMOKING Controversy over health effects of tobacco since early 16th century. Surgeon general declared it health hazard, January 1964. Since then, advertising for tobacco products has been restricted; warnings printed on cigarette packages.

SNAIL Univalve (one-shelled) mollusk. Reproductive organs in head, and anus behind and above head. Escargot is a dish made from garden snails.

SNAKES AND LADDERS English children's game played on square board, subdivided into eight to ten squares to a side, for total of 64 to 100 squares. Forerunner of trademarked Chutes and Ladders game. Certain squares connected by "ladders" and "snakes." Player landing at foot of ladder square moves to top; player landing at top of snake square slides back to bottom. Normal moves determined by throw of dice.

SNEEZING Rids nose of irritating objects. Occurs when sensitive nerve endings are stimulated. May occur in bright sunlight due to proximity of eye and nose nerve endings. Eyes close involuntarily, and germs are released through nose and mouth. Inhalation of pepper into proboscis (nose) also causes sneezing. During a sneeze, air can be ejected at 200 m.p.h.

SNICKERS Candy bar produced by Mars, Inc., also makers of Milky Way. Two bars differ in that Snickers has peanuts, and Milky

Way has a more caramel flavor and lighter malted-milk filling. Snickers has often been referred to as a Milky Way with peanuts.

SNIDER, EDWIN (DUKE) (1926–   ) "Duke of Flatbush," named after Flatbush Avenue, Brooklyn. Hit 407 homers in 18 seasons with Brooklyn and Los Angeles Dodgers, New York Mets (one year) and San Francisco Giants (one year). Immortalized in Terry Cashman song, "Talkin' Baseball (Willie, Mickey and the Duke)."

SNOOKER. See BILLIARDS VARIATIONS

SNOOPY. See SCHULZ, CHARLES MONROE

SNOW WHITE AND THE SEVEN DWARFS Walt Disney's first animated film had its world premiere in December 1937. Seven dwarfs named Grumpy, Sleepy, Happy, Sneezy, Bashful, Doc and Dopey (only one with no beard). Contains classic songs "Whistle While You Work" and "Someday My Prince Will Come."

SNOWFLAKE Six-sided mass of ice crystals. Platelike (star-shaped) and columnar (needlelike) types. Crystal shape depends on temperature and humidity. First artificial snow produced in Japan, 1936.

SNOWSHOES Beavertail-shaped frames of wood fitted with cross pieces and criss-crossed with strips of leather. Worn on feet to prevent sinking in deep snow.

SNUFF Powdered tobacco. Called snuff because originally taken into the nose; now it is usually chewed. At one time snuff was very popular, but now most tobacco is smoked.

SNYDER, JIMMY (THE GREEK) (1919–   ) American odds-maker, born Dimitrios George Synodios. Began as midwest gambler in 1930s, moved to Las Vegas in '50s. Claims to be co-inventor of point spread for sports betting. Now writes newspaper column and appears as CBS commentator on *NFL Today* football telecasts.

SOAP BOX DERBY (ALL-AMERICAN) Annual national contest for gravity-powered coasting cars. Finals held in Akron, OH, after local competition nationally. Youths 11–15 construct racers from wooden crates. Cost strictly limited by rules. Cars allowed no propulsion system or brakes. Race on sloping course. Car must be designed and built by driver. Race for scholarship funds.

SOCCER Also known as association football. Played competitively in more countries than any other game. Regulation play lasts 90 minutes with two 45-minute halves. Played by two teams of 11 each on rectangular field 50–100 yds. wide by 100–130 yds. long. Goals are 8 ft. high and 24 ft. wide. Goalkeeper is only player allowed to touch ball with hands, and only within own penalty area (44 yds. by 18 yds. in front of goal); cannot take more than four steps while holding ball. Feet, head, thighs and torso used to direct ball. Game has one referee, who also acts as time-keeper, stopping clock for injuries and infringements; assisted by two linesmen.

SOCCER, EUROPEAN TEAMS Real Madrid (Spain) founded 1889, A. C. Milan (Italy) founded 1889 and Ajax (Netherlands) founded 1900, are a few of many European soccer teams. League champions of each European country have met annually since 1956 for European Cup. Real Madrid has dominated.

SOCRATES (469–399 B.C.) Athenian philosopher and teacher. Known for concepts of moderation and "Socratic method" of questioning. Controversial views of religion led to his being tried and sentenced to death. Carried out his own sentence by drinking hemlock poison in the company of his followers.

SODA WATER Carbonated, bubbling beverage. Invented, 1767, by English scientist Joseph Priestly, discoverer of oxygen. In 1807, Townsend Speakman of Philadelphia mixed fruit flavor with carbonated water. Marketed world's first soda pop, called Nephite Julep.

SODOM AND GOMORRAH Two biblical cities destroyed because of their wickedness. Some sources say their crime was what is now known as sodomy, but others contend it was their ill treatment of poor and needy that marked them for destruction. Story in Book of Genesis, 19:24.

SOFIA Capital and largest city in Bulgaria. Characterized by high-rise apartment buildings that contrast with city's ancient houses of worship. Country's chief economic and cultural center.

SOFTBALL Regulation game consists of seven innings, while baseball game (major league and most leagues of high school level and above) has nine. Softball played in both slow-pitch (10 fielders) and fast-pitch (9 fielders) styles. In both, ball larger and heavier than baseball is pitched with underhand motion.

SOLITAIRE   Card game played more than any other card game worldwide. Also called Patience. General name for any game for one player. Hundreds of variations exist including Canfield (named for 19th-century American gambler and art collector Richard A. Canfield), Klondike (named for destination of 1898–1899 Alaskan Gold Rush) and Spider (two-deck game reputed to be favorite of former President Franklin D. Roosevelt). Other solitaire fanatics included Napoleon Bonaparte, who played constantly while in exile on St. Helena; financier J. P. Morgan (who favored the two-deck game Miss Milligan) and Russian novelist Leo Tolstoy.

SOLOMON GRUNDY   Anonymous nursery rhyme goes: "Solomon Grundy / Born on a Monday / Christened on Tuesday / Married on Wednesday / Took ill on Thursday / Worse on Friday / Died on Saturday / Buried on Sunday / This is the end of Solomon Grundy." 1945 parody by Britain's National Savings Committee went: "Solomon Grundy / Rich on a Monday / Spent some on Tuesday / More on Wednesday / Poor on Thursday / Worse on Friday / Broke on Sunday / Where will he end / Old Solomon Grundy?"

SOLOMON'S TEMPLE   In Book of Kings I, Chapters 5–6 King Solomon has 80,000 men cut stone in hill country and 70,000 men haul it to site of temple on Mt. Zion. Cedars of Lebanon, also used in its construction (1006 B.C.), were provided by King Hiram of Tyre. Temple site now occupied by mosque. Wailing Wall in Jerusalem is only remaining portion of this principal temple of Israelites, destroyed several times by conquerors.

SOLZHENITSYN, ALEXANDER (1918–   )   Soviet novelist and historian. Exiled 1974 for actions incompatible with Soviet citizenship. His account of Stalin's prison camps in *One Day in the Life of Ivan Denisovich* (1962), based on his own imprisonment for writing anti-Stalin letter in 1945, published in accordance with then-Premier Krushchev's 1964 ouster, and subsequent novels, *First Circle* (1964); *August 1914* (1972); and *Gulag Archipelago* (1974) were not published in U.S.S.R. although published abroad and widely circulated. Won 1970 Nobel Prize for Literature. Arrested and deported, 1974. Now lives in U.S.

SOME LIKE IT HOT   1959 comedy by Billy Wilder. Tony Curtis and Jack Lemmon star as musicians on the lam from Chicago gangsters. They join all-girl band disguised as women. Marilyn Monroe co-stars as the group's singer.

SOMNAMBULISM Or sleepwalking. More common among children. Frequency increases during periods of worry or stress. Rarely occurs while sleeper is dreaming. From Latin *somnus* meaning "sleep," and *ambulare*, "to walk."

SOMOZA, ANASTASIO PORTO CARRERO (1925–1980) Dictator of Nicaragua. Succeeded his father who was assassinated, 1956. Defeated by Sandanistas in bloody civil war. Fled to Paraguay, where he was assassinated.

SON Male person related to either or both parents. Word *son* of Indo-European origin, perhaps from *su-ius*, meaning "birth" or "to give birth."

SON OF A GUN Slightly derogatory epithet, euphemistic substitute for "son of a bitch." First used to describe boys born at sea. An admiral once described how he was "literally thus cradled under the breast of a gun."

SONIC BOOM Noise caused by airplanes flying faster than speed of sound. Change in air-flow pattern around plane causes a pressure disturbance or shock wave. Results in thunderous noise. Sonic barrier first crossed October 14, 1947, by U.S. Air Force Captain Charles E. (Chuck) Yeager.

SONNET A 14-line poem of set rhyming scheme and movement. In English, written in iambic pentameter (e.g., Shakespeare's *Sonnets*, 1609). Earliest form was Italian.

SORBONNE Liberal arts and sciences division of University of Paris until 1970. Entire university often called "The Sorbonne." No longer a separate college, its buildings are being used by three of the university's 13 units. Founded as theological school by theologian Robert of Sorbon in 1200s.

SOUND OF MUSIC, THE Hit Rodgers and Hammerstein musical show (their last) which became Oscar-winning Best Picture of 1965. Robert Wise directed film starring Julie Andrews as Maria Von Trapp, an aspiring nun who became the governess, then mother to the Von Trapp family singing troupe.

SOUSA, JOHN PHILIP (1854–1932) Musical composer, known as "the March King," was the subject of 1952 film biography; *Stars and Stripes Forever* portrayed by Clifton Webb. Film focused on years when he served as leader of Marine Corps Band. Started his own band in the late 1800s.

SOUTH AFRICA   Comprised of four provinces: Cape Province (Cape of Good Hope Province), Naral, Orange Free State and Transvaal. Official languages are Afrikaans and English; African languages such as Xhosa, Zulu and Sesotho are also spoken.

SOUTH AMERICA   Bolivia and Paraguay are only noncoastal countries in South America. Paraguay is bordered by Argentina, Bolivia and Brazil; Bolivia is bordered by Peru, Chile, Paraguay, Argentina and Brazil. All other countries on the continent are bordered by the Atlantic or Pacific oceans, or Caribbean Sea. The elevation extremes of the continent are both located in Argentina; highest point is Mt. Aconoagua at 22,831 ft. (6,959 m.), and lowest point is Peninsula Vales at 131 ft. (40 m.).

SOUTH PACIFIC   Hit Broadway musical, later 1958 film starring Mitzi Gaynor and Rossano Brazzi. Story about the romance of a young American navy nurse who falls for a Frenchman during World War II. Contains Rodgers and Hammerstein songs including "Some Enchanted Evening."

SOUTH POLE, THE   Located near center of Antarctica at point where all the Earth's lines of longitude meet. Norwegian explorer Roald Amundsen beat Robert Scott of England there by one month, 1911. Scientific base called Amundsen Scott South Pole Station set up there by U.S., 1956. Temperatures are colder than in the North Pole.

SOUTHERN LIGHTS   Or Aurora Australis. Caused by collisions between particles from sun and atmosphere. Usually seen close to earth's poles and often appear as waving curtains of greenish light. Northern Lights called Aurora Borealis.

SOVIET UNION   Official name in English is Union of Soviet Socialist Republics. Russian name is Soyuz Sovetskikh Sotsialisticheskikh Respublik. Russian alphabet initials of these words are C.C.C.P.

Flag: Red background with a gold hammer, sickle and star. Red symbolizes revolution, the hammer and sickle stand for united peasants and workers and the star represents the Communist Party.

Time Zones: More than any other country. Eleven zones are labeled internationally as C, D, E, F, G, H, I, J, K, L and M, each one hour apart. Moscow is in C, which is 12 hours ahead of New York City (EST).

Climate: Minimum temperature (degrees F) of 10 chief Soviet cities: Minsk -27°; Saratov, -27°; Moscow, -27°; Lvov, -29°; Stalingrad, -30°; Leningrad, -36°; Ufy, -42°; Kirov, -43°; Arkangelsk, -49° and Vst'Shchugor, -67°.

Borders: World's largest country; has borders with greatest number of other countries. Eleven bordering countries are Finland, Poland, Czechoslovakia, Hungary, Romania, Turkey, Iran, Afghanistan, China, Mongolia and North Korea. Russia includes 11 of the 24 time zones, and covers one-seventh of the Earth's land mass.

SOWETO City in South Africa, southwest of Johannesburg. White authorities introduced Afrikaans as language of instruction at schools for blacks in 1976, spurring black residents to riot in nearby towns and cities. About 600 people were killed. Government, however made no changes in policy.

SPACEBALL. See TRAMPOLINING

SPAGHETTI WESTERNS The collective name given to Italian-made Western films. *A Fistful of Dollars* (1964), directed by Sergio Leone and starring Clint Eastwood, was first internationally successful "spaghetti western" and generated numerous imitations.

SPAIN One of world's leading producers of citrus fruits, olives and wines, including well-known Rioja wines. For centuries, income came from exporting these products, as well as silk and raisins. Recent exorbitant taxes have damaged productivity. Tourism is now the country's main source of income, with approximately 38 million people per year visiting its sunny beaches, bullfights and many festivals. Spain's Cape Tarifa is Europe's southernmost point.

SPAM Processed canned meat product. Combination of pork shoulder and SPiced hAM, thus SPAM. Introduced by George Hormel and Company, Austin, MN, 1937. Approximately 100 million pounds sold annually.

SPANISH ARMADA (1588) Fleet of ships dispatched by Spain's King Phillip II to invade England. Phillip II was angered by England's support of rebels in certain Spanish-controlled territories. Main battle fought in English Channel. Armada ran out of ammunition; forced to retreat with heavy losses.

SPANISH CIVIL WAR (1936–1939) Fought between polarized elements of Spain's Second Republic. Nationalists, the fascist right wing, led by Generalissimo Franco. Represented landowners, church and army. Received military aid from fascist Germany and Italy. Defeated the Republicans, or Loyalists, comprised of workers, landless peasants and intellectuals.

SPANISH STEPS   Monumental staircase in Rome (138 steps) connecting Piazza di Spagna with French Church of Santi Trinita dei Monti. Constructed 1723, partly financed by French funds. Steps overlook Via Condotti, home of Gucci, Ferragamo and other of Rome's most expensive shops.

SPANISH-AMERICAN WAR   Sparked by explosion of U.S.S. *Maine* in Cuba's Havana Harbor, 1898. Spain accused of the bombing. Slogan "Remember the Maine" served to justify U.S. involvement in the war.

SPARTACUS   1960 gladiator epic film directed by Stanley Kubrick. Kirk Douglas stars as rebel escaping from slavery and challenging the might of Imperial Rome. Peter Ustinov won Best Supporting Oscar.

SPARTACUS (?–71 B.C.)   Greek herdsman. Made a slave after trying to desert Roman Army. As a gladiator, he organized a revolt of his fellow slaves, 73 B.C. His army of 70,000 escaped slaves controlled large region of southern Italy until defeated in 71 B.C. when Spartacus died in battle.

SPASIBO. See THANK YOU

SPASSKY, BORIS (1937–   )   Russian World Chess Champion, 1969–1972. Lost to American Bobby Fischer, September 1, 1972 in Reykjavik, Iceland. Spassky lost in 21st game of 24-game series. First time in 25 years title passed out of Russian hands.

SPEAR, SAMMY (1910–1975)   Orchestra leader on *The Jackie Gleason Show* (1962–1966). Gleason called him "The Flower of the Music World."

SPECTRUM   Continuous band of colors of different wavelengths. Colors, from longest to shortest wavelengths, are red, orange, yellow, green, blue, indigo and violet. Easily remembered by acronym ROY G BIV. Visible when white light is passed through prism.

SPEED OF SOUND   Varies with material the sound is traveling through. It is 16,600 ft. per second in steel and 1,125 ft. per second in sea-level air. An airplane flying at speed of sound is said to be at Mach 1.

SPEEDY GONZALES   The Fastest Mouse in All of Mexico first appeared in the Warner Bros. cartoon *Cat-Tails for Two* (1953). His second appearance in *Speedy Gonzales* (1955) won Oscar for Best Short Subject (cartoon).

SPEER, ALBERT (1905–1981)   German architect and Nazi administrator who directed German economic production during World War II. Tried by Nuremberg tribunal for war crimes, sentenced to 20 years at Spandau Prison, Berlin. Kept diaries there, published as *Spandau, The Secret Diaries*, after his release in 1966.

SPELUNKER   One whose hobby is speleology, the science of exploring caves. From the Latin *spelaeum* and Greek *spelaion*, meaning "cave."

SPENCER, LADY DIANA (1961–   )   Princess of Wales. Married Charles, the Prince of Wales and heir to the British Crown, July 29, 1981, in St. Paul's Cathedral. Before marriage, "Lady Di" was a nursery school teacher.

SPERMOLOGY   Literally, branch of science that investigates sperm or seeds; figuratively, babbling or trifling talk. Spermologer is gatherer of gossip or trivia.

SPHINX, THE   Huge rock monument that has stood in front of Egypt's Great Pyramids for about 4,500 years. Measures 240 ft. (73 m.) long, 66 ft. (20 m.) high. Its face is said to be a portrait of Egyptian king who built it but his identity is uncertain.

SPICE ISLANDS   Former name of East Indies, often called Moluccas. Located in eastern Indonesia. Explored by Magellan, 1511–1512, settled by Portuguese, controlled by Dutch from 1600s until Japanese occupation in 1942. After World War II, part of newly formed Republic of Indonesia. Contains valuable spice plants.

SPIDER   Small, eight-legged animal that spins silk. Differs from insects in that it has two more legs and does not have antennae or wings. Eats only liquids. Solids sprayed with powerful digestive liquids to dissolve the tissue; process called predigestion.

SPIDERMAN   Superhero who gained powers and strength of spider multiplied to size of man after being bitten by radioactive spider. Alter-ego Peter Parker is sometimes student, sometimes photographer for New York *Daily Bugle*. Created by Stan Lee for Marvel

Comics, 1962. Appears in both comic books and newspaper comic strip.

SPILLANE, MICKEY (1918–) American mystery novelist. Created Mike Hammer, tough-guy New York detective, in 1947; wrote *I, The Jury* and more than a dozen succeeding books. Played Hammer in *The Girl Hunters* movie (1953). Appears in Lite Beer commercials.

SPIRIT OF ST. LOUIS, THE 1957 film drama directed by Billy Wilder. James Stewart starred as Charles Lindbergh, first man to fly solo nonstop across Atlantic.

SPITZ, MARK (1950–) American swimmer who predicted he would win a record six gold medals at 1968 Mexico City Olympics. Was on two winning relay teams, but finished second, third and last in individual events. Redeemed himself at 1972 Munich Olympics with record seven golds in: 100 m. freestyle; 200 m. freestyle; 100 m. butterfly; 200 m. butterfly; 400 m. medley relay (team); 400 m. freestyle relay (team); and 800 m. freestyle relay.

SPLENECTOMY Surgical removal of spleen. The spleen helps filter blood and also stores extra blood. When enlarged because of disease, it is removed, usually without serious side effects.

SPOCK, DR. BENJAMIN MCLANE (1903–) American pediatrician, author and peace advocate. His famous "baby book," *The Common Sense Book of Baby and Child Care* (1946) has sold more than 24 million copies, became major influence on American child-rearing. Said, "Feed 'em, love 'em and leave 'em alone." Encouraged parents to understand child as individual and develop warm relationship. After retiring, 1967, became active in anti–Vietnam War movement, running for president, 1972 on Peace and Freedom Party ticket.

SPORTS ILLUSTRATED America's first and leading national sports weekly magazine with largest circulation (2.3 million in 1982). Appeared August 16, 1954, with baseball on the cover during stretch drive of New York Giants and Cleveland Indians for 1954 pennants. Issue sold for 25¢. Cover price now $1.95. Ranks 23rd in circulation among all U.S. magazines. Closest competitor, *Sport*, has less than half *SI's* circulation. Published by Time-Life.

SPUR Critical riding tool. Attaches to back of each boot. Used for guiding, speeding up and stopping horse. Includes rowel, a wheel with spikes, jinglebobs, and heel chains. Cowboys considered it a disgrace to be seen without their spurs.

SPUTNIK I   First orbiting satellite. Launched by Russians October 4, 1957. Circled earth approximately once every 95 minutes. Traveled at speed of 18,000 m.p.h. (29,000 km.p.h.). Fell to earth three months later. *Sputnik* means "traveler" in Russian.

SPY WHO LOVED ME, THE. See SIMON, CARLY

SPYRI, JOHANNA (1827–1901)   Author of *Heidi*, children's story about little girl living in Swiss Alps. Shirley Temple played title role in 1937 film version.

SQUARE ROOT   Number that, when multiplied with itself, equals a second number. For example, the square root of four is two, since $2 \times 2 = 4$. The square root of 25 is five; of one-quarter, one-half. The square root of 121 is 11, and the square root of 900 is 30.

SQUARES   The square of a number is the product of that number multiplied by itself. For example, 12 squared is 144. The squares of zero and one are zero and one, respectively. Squares cannot be negative.

SQUASH   Also called squash racquets. Game played on four-wall court. Players on each side alternately hit small black ball to front wall of court, trying to make a shot opponent cannot return to front wall. Ball made of rubber, built to rebound with resiliency and "squash" into deformed state under pressure.

SQUID   Sea mollusk having two eyes, set of jaws, tongue and ten tentacles. Tentacles covered with rows of suction cups used for catching prey. Can change color to blend with surroundings.

SRI LANKA   Island nation in Indian Ocean. Famous for spices and precious stones. Name means "resplendent land" and comes from Hindu epic. Called Ceylon until 1972. Sirimavo Bandaranaike governed country in 1959, as world's first woman prime minister. Country now governed by president.

ST. ANDREW   One of Christ's 12 Apostles. Preached in Scythia. Crucified on $\times$-shaped cross. Patron saint for Greece, Scotland and Russia. Feast day: November 30.

ST. ANDREWS   Scotland golf course that is first and most famous in world. "Old Course," 6,883 yds. long, founded c.1552 during reign of Mary, Queen of Scots, first woman golfer. Prior to her reign, attempts made to outlaw golf because it interfered with archery practice. St. Andrews Royal and Ancient Golf Club, organized c. 1754, wrote original game rules, since adopted faithfully around world. An 800-year-old bridge leads to one of the holes on the course.

ST. AUGUSTINE, FL   City on Atlantic coast in northeastern Florida. Oldest city in U.S., founded 1565 by Spaniard Pedro Menendez de Aviles. Area first visited in 1513 by explorer Juan Ponce de Leon as he searched for Fountain of Youth.

ST. CHRISTOPHER   Giant man who carried travelers across river. Legend states that one traveler revealed himself to be Christ, carrying the weight of the world. Christopher means "Christ-bearer." Has become saint of travelers.

ST. GEORGE   Also called George the Great. Martyr who suffered in Palestine, probably under Diocletian. Considered one of 14 Holy Helpers in East, model of knighthood and avenger of women. Patron Saint of England, Aragon, Portugal, Germany, Venice, Genoa.

ST. JOHN'S VISION   In Revelations 1:14, last book of Bible, John relates his vision of Jesus in letter to seven churches. Says His head and hair were "white as white wool, white as snow; His eyes were like a flame of fire."

ST. LOUIS   Largest city in Missouri. Situated on west bank of Mississippi River just south of its junction with Missouri River. Largest inland port in U.S. Directly across the Mississippi River from East St. Louis, IL.

ST. MORITZ   Resort town in Switzerland. Visitors come to ski and see its 16th-century baths. Lies 6,037 ft. (1,840 m.) above sea level, one of highest villages in Inn River Valley.

ST. NICHOLAS   Patron saint of sailors and children. Fourth century bishop of Myra in Asia Minor. In Netherlands, his feast day is children's holiday. English settlers in New York adopted him from Dutch, calling him Santa Claus.

ST. PATRICK (c.389–461)   Apostle of Ireland. Lived in British province of Rome. Kidnapped, age 16, and sold into slavery in Ireland. Underwent conversion during six years of sheep herding. Escaped and became priest. Returned to preach and convert the Irish to Christianity. Used three-leaf clover (Irish shamrock) to explain concept of Trinity. Honored every March 17, St. Patrick's Day.

ST. PAUL'S CATHEDRAL   Center of Church of England in London. Built by Christopher Wren between 1675 and 1710 to replace original, destroyed in Great Fire of 1666. Largest cathedral in London. Dome reaches 365 ft. (111 m.) above ground. Royal wedding vows exchanged here by Prince Charles and Lady Diana on July 29, 1981.

ST. PETER'S. See VATICAN CITY

ST. VALENTINE (?–270)   Catholic bishop and martyr. Beheaded in Rome, 270 A.D., during rule of Claudius of Goth, a descendant of Visigoths who brought down Roman Empire. Date of death believed to be February 14, now remembered as Valentine's Day.

STAGE COACH   1939 Western film directed by John Ford. John Wayne stars as "The Ringo Kid," who saves passengers from Indian attack.

STAIRCASE   1969 film directed by Stanley Donen. Richard Burton and Rex Harrison starred as homosexual lovers. Film concerns their homelife above the barbershop they run.

STALAG 17   1953 World War II drama directed by Billy Wilder. William Holden won Oscar for his portrayal of pessimistic sergeant suspected of being German spy. Also starred Don Taylor and Robert Strauss, with Otto Preminger appearing as commandant of POW camp.

STALAGMITE   Calcium carbonate deposit. Rises in columnar structure from floor of limestone caverns beneath stalactites, icicle-shaped drippings of same mineral deposits. Stalactite, from Greek meaning "to fall in drops"; stalagmite, from Greek meaning "that which drops."

STALIN, JOSEPH (1879–1953)   Russian communist leader. Born Joseph Vissarionvich Djugashvilli. Adopted name "Stalin," meaning "man of steel," 1912. Succeeded Lenin as premier, 1924. Carried out industrialization and collectivization of U.S.S.R. Authorized Great Purges, 1936–1938, which killed perhaps millions of political prisoners.

STAMP COLLECTING   Also called philately. Hobby began soon after first stamp (Penny Black) issued by Great Britain, 1840.

Today, Canadian Twelve-Penny Black, first stamp issued by Canada after gaining independence from Britain, is a most valuable collector's item. Printed catalogs and albums first appeared in 1860s. Collectors usually concentrate on a particular country or subject (animals, birds, presidents, etc.). Among other varieties collected:

Commemorative: Stamp on sale for limited period, usually linked to specific event.

Corner block: Four stamps at corner of fresh sheet, having serial number. Rarer than single specimen of stamp.

Definitive: Stamp intended for everyday use, put on sale for indefinite period.

First-day cover: Commemorative envelope postmarked at place of dedication of first day of stamp's release.

Overprint: Stamp bearing any printed inscription applied after stamp originally printed.

Tete-beche: Pair of stamps in which design of one is upside-down in relation to the other, due to printing error.

STANLEY CUP Trophy won by National Hockey League playoff champions. Oldest trophy for professional athletes in North America. Originally presented in 1893 by Lord Stanley of Preston, Governor-General of Dominion of Canada, to Canadian champions Montreal Amateur Athletic Association. Exclusively given to NHL champion since 1926. Montreal Canadians have won it 20 times (including five in a row, 1956–1960), more than any other team. Nicknamed "The Big Mug."

STANLEY STEAMER Steam-powered automobiles built in U.S. 1897–1927 by twin brothers F. E. and F. O. Stanley. Could out-accelerate contemporary gasoline-powered cars. Once clocked at 127.66 m.p.h. in 1906. Also called "The Flying Teapot."

STANLEY, HENRY MORTON. See LIVINGSTONE, DR. DAVID

STAR IS BORN, A Story of self-destructive actor and the young movie hopeful he marries is Hollywood classic. Filmed three times: 1937, starring Fredric March and Janet Gaynor; 1954, as musical with James Mason and Judy Garland (with famed tearful ending line: "This is Mrs. Norman Maine"); 1976, refitted to world of rock music, with Kris Kristofferson and Barbra Streisand.

STAR TREK Science fiction TV series which gained popularity after its cancellation. Set in 23rd century. Crew of starship *Enterprise*

(I.D. number NCC 1701), on a five-year mission through deep space, explores "where no man has gone before." William Shatner portrayed ship's commander, Captain James T. Kirk. Premiered in 1966; canceled in 1969. Produced spin-off animated cartoon show in 1973 and three hit feature films in early 1980s. Scotty was in charge of *Enterprise*'s engineering.

STARBOARD TACK. See TACK

STARBOARD SIDE OF BOAT. See BOAT

STARR, BART (1934–   )   Green Bay Packer quarterback, MVP in Super Bowl I, 1967, and Super Bowl II, 1968. Completed 16 of 27 passes vs. Kansas City in Super Bowl I and 13 of 24 passes in Super Bowl II vs. Oakland (Packers, 33-14). Had led team to three previous National Football League titles. Later coached Packers, 1975–1983.

STARR, RINGO (1940–   )   Replaced Pete Best in 1962 as drummer for Beatles. After breakup of group in 1970, established acting career while continuing his success in music. Hit records include "It Don't Come Easy" (1971), "Photograph" (1973), "You're Sixteen" (1973) and "No No Song" (1974). Films include *The Magic Christian* (1969) and *Caveman* (1981). (see BEATLES, THE)

STARS AND STRIPES FOREVER   1952 film biography of John Phillip Sousa, portrayed by Clifton Webb, focusing on years when he served as leader of Marine Corps Band and started his own, in late 1800s.

STARS AND STRIPES, THE   U.S. military newspaper, created in bombed-out London, 1942. Independent of official military control. Headquarters, Darmstadt, Germany. Staff mostly civilians. Circulation 111,000. Pacific edition, based in Tokyo, serves 50,000.

STATES OF THE UNION   In August 1959, Hawaii became 50th and most recent state admitted to the Union. This followed by just seven months admission of Alaska in January 1959. The 49th state, Arizona, joined in 1912.

STATUE OF LIBERTY   Large copper statue standing on Liberty Island, New York Harbor. Gift to U.S. from France in 1884 as symbol of friendship and freedom. Depicts proud woman who holds torch in her extended right hand and tablet with date of Declaration of Independence, July 4, 1776, in her left. She stands with sandals on her feet. Largest statue ever made, standing 151 ft. tall, about 20 times life-size. There are 168 steps on stairway to her seven-pointed crown. Originally stood in Paris, where model of it now stands. Closed in May 1984 for extended renovation.

STEIN, GERTRUDE (1874–1946) American author. Lived primarily in Paris after 1903. Center of American expatriate artist-writer colony there. Wrote "Rose is a rose is a rose is a rose" (*Sacred Emily*, 1913) and *Autobiography of Alice B. Toklas* (as though it were written by her secretary). Her statement, "You are all a lost generation," used by Hemingway as epigraph to novel *The Sun Also Rises* (1926).

STEINBECK, JOHN (1902–1968) American novelist. Born in Salinas, CA. Grew up in fruit-farming area, setting for *The Grapes of Wrath* (1940), Pulitzer Prize–winning novel describing hardships of Joad family as they move from Oklahoma dust bowl to California, "land of milk and honey." Title derived from "The Battle Hymn of the Republic." Wrote *East of Eden* (1956), *Cannery Row* and other novels also set in California. Also wrote *Travels with Charley* (1962), account of 58-year-old Steinbeck's three-month drive across U.S. in pickup truck named Rocinante (name of Don Quixote's horse) with his 10-year-old French poodle, Charley. His 1937 novelette, *Of Mice and Men* is about feeble-minded but strong Lenny Small and his protector, George Milton, who work in Salinas Valley fruit farms.

STEINEM, GLORIA (1934–) American editor, journalist and feminist. Began journalism career 1962, freelancing for *Esquire*, *Vogue*, *Glamour*, *McCalls* and others. Became contributing editor of *New York* magazine, 1968, gaining notoriety for article describing experiences as Playboy Club bunny. Co-founder of Women's Active Alliance, 1970 and Women's Political Caucus, 1971. Founder and editor of *Ms.* magazine, 1972.

STENGEL, CHARLES DILLON (CASEY) (1890–1975) Baseball player and manager. After managing New York Yankees to seven World Series victories (1949–1960), had to ask, "Can't anybody here play this game?" while managing 1962 New York Mets, expansion team of cast-offs from other National League teams. Mets went 40–120, worst record in major league history. "Casey" managed 25 years overall. Elected to Hall of Fame, 1966.

STERN West German illustrated news magazine, roughly equivalent to America's *Time.* Its competitors are *Bunte Illustrierte, Neue Revue* and *Quick.*

STEVENSON, ADLAI EWING (1900–1965)   American lawyer and diplomat. Elected governor of Illinois, 1948. Democratic nominee for president, 1952 and 1956. Defeated, both times, by Dwight D. Eisenhower. Ambassador to UN during Kennedy and Johnson administrations. Key U.S. spokesman in UN during Cuban Missile Crisis, 1961.

STEVENSON, ROBERT LOUIS BALFOUR (1859– 1894)   Scottish author. Best known for adventure and mystery novels and short stories. In ill health most of his life, traveled widely to warm climates. Lived last five years in Samoa. Among his works: *New Arabian Nights* (1882), *A Child's Garden of Verses* (1885) and *Treasure Island* (1883), about peg-legged pirate Long John Silver (with talking parrot Captain Kidd), whose men masquerade as crew members on ship *Hispaniola,* carrying young Jim Hawkins and his allies to find buried treasure. Cabin boy, with help of hermit Ben Gunn, discovers plot, which he and loyal members of crew thwart, winning treasure. Introduced pirate chant, "Yo-ho-ho and a bottle of rum." *The Strange Case of Dr. Jekyll and Mr. Hyde* (1886) has good Dr. Henry Jekyll taking drug that changes him into evil Mr. Edward Hyde. Although change is temporary, Hyde personality gradually takes over. *Kidnapped* (1886) tells adventures of David Balfour. In 1751, his uncle has him kidnapped and shipped aboard brig *Covenant* so he can claim Balfour's inheritance. On board ship, Balfour befriends Alan Brech, and together they overthrow ship's crew. *Covenant* later strikes a reef and sinks.

STING, THE   1973 Best Picture Oscar winner directed by George Roy Hill. Paul Newman and Robert Redford star as pair of con artists in 1930s Chicago, who set out to fleece a big-time racketeer (portrayed by Robert Shaw).

STINGER   Cocktail made with ¾ oz. brandy (which provides sting) and ¾ oz. white crème de menthe. Served in cocktail glass with lemon twist.

STIVIC, MICHAEL   Rob Reiner played Michael Stivic (also known as "Meathead," according to father-in-law Archie Bunker) on TV's *All in the Family.* Originally conceived as foil for Archie's reactionary pyrotechnics, liberal Mike was allowed in later seasons to mature as character, and some of show's best moments were built around him.

STOKER, ABRAHAM (BRAM) (1847–1912)   Irish novelist. Created Dracula, 1897, bloodthirsty Transylvanian count who was vampire. First played on screen by Max Schreck in German silent film *Nosferatu*, 1923. Since played by Bela Lugosi, Christopher Lee and George Hamilton.

STONE MOUNTAIN   Located in northwest Georgia. World's largest mountain of exposed granite. Has carvings of figures on horseback: Jefferson Davis, president of Confederate States of America; General Robert E. Lee; General Thomas J. (Stonewall) Jackson; and other Civil War Confederate heroes.

STONE SKIPPING   Sport in which small, flat stones are flipped by hand against surface of lake or other flat body of water. Origins in Greek game *epostrakimos* and English children's game Ducks and Drakes. Players try to get most touches of stone on water before stone sinks. In English version, one hop called a duck; two hops is duck and drake; three times called a duck, a drake and half a cake; four times called penny to pay old patch; etc. In other terminology, long initial bounds called plinkers; short hops at end called pittypats, variation of sound made (pit-a-pat).

STONE, IRVING (1903–1984)   American novelist specializing in fictionalized biography, starting with his second book *Lust for Life* (1934), about Dutch painter Vincent van Gogh. Also wrote about Charles Darwin (*The Origin*), Jack London (*Sailor on Horseback*), Eugene V. Debs (*Adversary in the House*) and Michelangelo (*The Agony and the Ecstacy*).

STONEHENGE   Monument, estimated 3,000 years old, on Salisbury Plain in Wiltshire, England. Group of huge, rough-cut stones erected by unknown people may have served as astronomical calendar predicting seasons, solar and lunar eclipses. If so, it is the first known observatory.

STONEY BURKE   1962 Western TV series, starring Jack Lord as professional rodeo rider seeking "The Golden Buckle," trophy awarded to best bronco buster. Bruce Dern co-starred as E.J. Stocker, a fellow rodeo performer.

STOUT, REX (1886–1975)   American writer, primarily of detective fiction. Created Nero Wolfe, America's largest detective, who weighed "a seventh of a ton." Wolfe, a big eater, drinks beer brought to his New York City brownstone office by chef Brenner or confidential assistant (and narrator) Archie Goodwin.

STOWE, HARRIET (ELIZABETH) BEECHER (1811–1896)   American novelist and contributor to *Atlantic Monthly*. Wrote *Uncle Tom's Cabin* (1852), novel about slavery in Louisiana and Kentucky, which greatly influenced Northern pre–Civil War attitudes on the issue. Was all-time best-selling American novel until *Gone with the Wind* (1937) surpassed it.

STRAITS OF FLORIDA   Channel at southern tip of Florida. Connects Gulf of Mexico with Atlantic Ocean. Separates southeast Florida and Florida Keys from Bahamas and Cuba.

STRANGERS IN THE NIGHT   1966 number-one hit song recorded by Frank Sinatra. Record ends with Sinatra ad-libbing "dooby-dooby-doo."

STRATEMEYER, EDWARD L. (1862–1930)   American author. Under pseudonym Franklin W. Dixon, wrote first nine books in *Hardy Boys* series; writing syndicate churned out others. Books about teenage detectives Frank and Joe Hardy, who solve *Viking Symbol Mystery*, *Mystery at Devil's Paw* and more than 50 others.

STRAUSS, JOHANN (1825–1899)   Classical composer known as "the Waltz King." Lived in Vienna, Austria. Compositions include "The Blue Danube" and "Tales from the Vienna Woods."

STREET NAMES, AMERICAN   Five most common names (in order): Park, Washington, Maple, Oak, Lincoln. (Main Street is ranked 32nd.)

STREISAND, BARBRA (1942–   )   Actress, singer and filmmaker. Only person to win Oscars both for Best Actress (in her debut film, *Funny Girl*, 1968 (tied with Katharine Hepburn), and for Best Song ("Evergreen" from *A Star is Born*, 1976). Also appeared in *Hello Dolly* (1969), *What's Up, Doc?* (1972) and *The Main Event* (1979). Produced, starred in and directed *Yentl* (1983).

STROUD, ROBERT F. (1890–1963)   Prisoner and author. While in prison for murdering man who had beaten his girlfriend, Stroud wrote definitive work on bird diseases and cures. Earned title "Birdman of Alcatraz." Stroud later killed prison guard. President Wilson changed his death sentence to life in prison.

STUDENTS FOR A DEMOCRATIC SOCIETY   Abbreviated SDS. Founded early 1960s, Port Huron, MI, by anti-war activist Tom Hayden. Largest anti-war, anti-establishment group of 1960s. Organized massive 1968 Democratic Convention protest in Chicago.

STUDIO 54 New York discotheque. Popular in late 1970s. Carter's White House chief of staff, Hamilton Jordan, accused of using cocaine here, 1978; cleared by grand jury, 1980.

STUTZ BEARCAT Luxury car built during 1920s by Stutz Motor Car Company. Stutz and other companies (e.g. Packard, Pierce-Arrow) produced fancy cars for rich and near-rich, a market cut back significantly by 1929 stock market crash.

STYRON, WILLIAM (1925–   ) American novelist. Author of *Lie Down in Darkness* (1951) and *Sophie's Choice* (1979). Best known for 1967 Pulitzer Prize–winning *Confessions of Nat Turner*, based on Virginia slave who led brief 1831 slave rebellion in Tidewater district. Controversial book in racially sensitive 1960s.

SUBWAY SYSTEMS

City	Year Opened	Length of Route Mi./Km.
London	1863	270/435
Boston	1897	17/ 27
Paris	1900	157/253
New York	1904	237/390
Madrid	1919	35/ 56
Moscow	1935	100/161
Toronto	1954	26/ 42
Milan	1964	22/ 35
San Francisco	1974	71/114

SUCCOTASH American Indian dish made by combining corn, lima or shredded green beans, butter, salt, paprika, parsley. Ingredients heated together in double boiler.

SUDAN Northeast African nation, largest on continent. Located directly south of Egypt. One-fourth size of U.S. Covers 967,000 sq. mi. (2,514,200 sq. km.). Almost half the country is desert or semi-desert.

SUEZ CANAL, THE Artificial waterway in Egypt, opened 1869, joining Mediterranean and Red seas. Extends approximately 100 mi. (160 km.). Shortened route between England and India by 6,000 mi. (9,700 km.). Closed during border clashes between Israel and Egypt. Egypt lifted ban against Israeli use of canal, 1979. Name spells Zeus (Greek god) backwards.

SUGAR   Food sweetener. Known in India, 3000 B.C. Produced from sugar beet and sugarcane. In raw form, called demerara or turbinado; light brown, 97% sucrose. Refined or white sugar, 99.96% sucrose.

SUGAR BOWL. See FOOTBALL, COLLEGE BOWL GAMES

SUICIDE   Approximately 70 per day in U.S.; 1,000 per day worldwide. Frequency rising since at least 1960. More common among males, though proportion of female suicides in relation to males has risen. Firearms most common method chosen by young males; for females, poison.

SULLIVAN, EDWARD VINCENT (ED) (1902– 1974)   New York *Daily News* columnist, then variety-show host. Wife's name, Sylvia. Series began, 1948, as *The Toast of the Town*. Orchestra leader Ray Bloch was with Sullivan from beginning until serie's end, 1971. Brought Beatles and Elvis Presley to national attention.

SULLIVAN, JOHN L. (1858–1918)   Last heavyweight boxing champion to fight without gloves. Stopped challenger Jake Kilrain, 1889, in 75 rounds in last bare-knuckle title fight. Never defeated as London Prize Ring (bare-knuckle) champ. First boxer to fight under Queensbury Rules (using gloves and three-minute rounds). Knocked out by James J. Corbett in 21st round of first championship fight using gloves.

SULLIVAN, SIR ARTHUR (1842–1900)   Composer, most famous for collaborations with lyricist William Gilbert, with whom he pioneered English light opera. Their works include *H.M.S. Pinafore* (1878), *The Mikado* (1885) and *The Pirates of Penzance* (1879).

SULTANA   Word for sultan's wife. *Sultan* is French adaptation of Arab *sultan*, "ruler." Italian version is *sultano*; feminine of Italian nouns ending in *-o* is *-a*—thus, *sultana*.

SUMMER OF LOVE   Began on weekend in March 1967 when tens of thousands of youth gathered in New York City's Central Park to celebrate love. At end of summer, coffin marked "Summer Love" was burned in Golden Gate Park, San Francisco.

SUMMER OF '42   1971 film about coming-of-age of three 15-

year-olds during World War II, one of whom has affair with war widow portrayed by Jennifer O'Neill. Gary Grimes (Hermie), Jerry Houser (Oscy) and Oliver Conant (Benjie) repeated their roles in 1973 sequel *Class of '44*.

SUMMER SOLSTICE   Falls on June 21 or 22 in Northern Hemisphere. First day of summer and longest day (and shortest night) of year. Summer solstice in Southern Hemisphere occurs on December 21 or 22.

SUMO WRESTLING   Quasi-religious ritualistic national sport of Japan. Potential wrestlers undergo long apprenticeships beginning at early age. Trained to gain strength, agility and weight (wrestlers usually weigh 300–400 lbs.).

SUN   Our nearest star, approximately 93 million mi. (150 million km.) away. Light takes about 8 min., 20 sec., to reach earth. About 75% hydrogen, 25% helium. Nuclear fusion produces sunshine. Diameter: roughly 864,000 mi. (1,390,180 km.); almost 110 times that of earth. Sun's atmosphere may be divided into three regions: 1) photosphere, roughly 10,000°F (5,500°C); 2) chromosphere, roughly 50,000°F (27,800°C), containing shooting streams of gas called spicules; 3) Corona: 2,000,000–3,000,000°F (1,100,000–1,670,000° C). Outermost region. Easily studied during solar eclipse.

SUN ALSO RISES, THE   1957 film based on novel by Ernest Hemingway. Tyrone Power stars as Jake Barnes, member of "lost generation" of 1920s. Ava Gardner and Errol Flynn co-star.

SUNDIAL. See HOROLOGY

SUNRISE AT CAMPOBELLO   1960 film based on Broadway play. Ralph Bellamy portrayed Franklin Roosevelt during time of paralysis in 1921 until Democratic Convention in 1924. Greer Garson portrayed wife Eleanor.

SUPER BALL   Bounces six times higher than regular ball, with 95% rebound. Chemist Norman Stingley discovered highly resilient material while doing synthetics research; sold it to Wham-O Co., whose Frisbee and Hula Hoop are among other best-selling toys of all time. Wham-O founded by Richard Knerr and Arthur "Spud" Melin, 1948.

SUPER BERTHA. See SLOT MACHINES

SUPER BOWL   National Football League championship, usually played on third Sunday in January. Called "Super Bowl Sunday" and "Super Sunday." Most watched annual TV sporting event.

SUPER BOWL I Played January 15, 1967, at Los Angeles Coliseum. Green Bay Packers of National Football League defeated Kansas City Chiefs of American Football League, 35—10, in first game resulting from merger. Green Bay quarterback Bart Starr was game MVP. Game televised nationally by NBC and CBS simultaneously (because of individual league contract obligations). Super Bowl trophy later named for Vince Lombardi, coach of Packers.

SUPERMAN Created by two 17-year-olds, writer Jerry Siegel and artist Joe Shuster. Debuted in Action Comics No. 1 (June 1938). First costumed superhero, prototype of all comic book superhero features, and impetus for comic book boom of 1940—1945. Came to Earth from planet Krypton. Born Kal-El, son of scientist Jor-El and his wife Lara. Jor-El predicted Krypton's explosion and sent infant to Earth in rocket; later found by John and Martha Kent, who adopted him. Grew up in Smallville, IL, as Clark Kent; later moved to Metropolis as mild-mannered reporter for *The Daily Planet*, edited by Perry White. Most common initials of Superman's friends and enemies are L.L.: high school chum Lana Lang, fellow reporter Lois Lane, arch-enemy Lex Luthor, and cousin Linda Lee (Supergirl). Another character from Krypton is Superman's dog Krypto, who appears in Superboy and Supergirl stories. George Reeves portrayed on 1950s TV series, sponsored by Kellogg's. Big-budget, all-star 1978 film starred Marlon Brando as Jor-El and Gene Hackman as Lex Luthor. Christopher Reeve became star in title role; Margot Kidder was Lois Lane. Sequels: *Superman II* (1981) and *Superman III* (1983).

SUPERSTITIONS—WAKING Historical tendency to regard left side of bed as wrong side to wake up on, since left has been linked with evil. (Word *sinister* is from Latin for "left side.") Also believed that upon rising, right foot must touch ground first.

SURFING Sport of riding flat, crafted board in ocean waves. Requires great technical skill, daring, balance. Surfers who ride with left foot forward on board called naturals or standard- or regular-footed; surfers who put right foot forward called goofy-footed. Among oldest sports in U.S. Hawaiians surfed more than 500 years ago. World's best surfing beaches face west.

SURFSIDE SIX   Detective series broadcast from 1960–1962. Van Williams starred as Ken Madison, continuing his role from *Bourbon Street Beat*. Located on houseboat in Miami Beach, Ken, along with fellow detectives Dave (Lee Patterson) and Sandy (Troy Donahue), kept eye on criminal activity and girls.

SURIBACHI, MOUNT. See IWO JIMA

SUSANN, JACQUELINE (1921–1974)   In *Valley of the Dolls* (1966) and *The Love Machine* (1969) had two number-one best sellers in two tries; also wrote *Once Is not Enough* (1973)."Dolls" are pills show-biz celebrities in first book depend on. Critics despised Susann's trashy tales of sex, drugs and despair in Hollywood.

SWALLOWING   Process of taking food and saliva from mouth to stomach via esophagus. Muscles of esophagus contract, producing downward wave toward stomach; called peristalsis. Average person swallows 295 times while dining.

SWANS   Large, stately waterbirds that mate for life. Male swans are called cobs; females pens. Their young are called cygnets. Heaviest flying birds in North America. Black swan is native to Australia.

SWAYZE, JOHN CAMERON (1906–   )   One of first TV network newscasters. Anchored NBC's 15 *Camel News Caravan* from 1948–1956. Became spokesman for Timex watch company.

SWAZILAND   National anthem: "Ingoma Yesive," beginning "Oh God, Bestower of the blessings of the Swazi." Flag: blue, yellow, crimson; yellow and blue stripes with shield and spears of Emasotsha regiment superimposed on crimson stripe. Independence Day: September 6. Languages: English (official), Siswat.

SWEDEN   Europe's fourth-largest country. Prosperous industrial nation. Largest country in Scandinavia. Way of life called "middle way" because country combines Socialist government with private enterprise. Swedes have one of highest standards of living in Europe; spend more money on holidays than any other Europeans. Country bordered by Norway for 1.030 mi. (1,648 km.), Finland for approximately 340 mi. (544 km.). East coast runs into Baltic Sea and Gulf of Bothnia.

SWIFT, JONATHAN (1667–1745)   Irish-English poet, satirist, pamphleteer, clergyman. Leading conservative writer, became Irish hero for writing *Drapier Letters* (1724) and *A Modest Proposal* (1729). Best known for four-part satire *Gulliver's Travels* (1726). Ship's surgeon Lemuel Gulliver shipwrecked on island of Lilliput, whose inhabitants are no more than six inches high.

SWIMMING *Breaststroke*: Oldest stroke in swimming. Executed in prone position. Combines frog kick, glide with arms outstretched overhead, and double-arm pull downward and to side of body. After foundation of first swimming clubs (first national swimming federation formed in Great Britain, 1874), additional strokes tried and developed.
Freestyle: Refers to swimmer using stroke of choice in race—usually front crawl, fastest stroke. Each arm alternately brought overhead, then into water while legs kick. Swimmer breathes on one side in trough made by arm pull.

SWISS FAMILY ROBINSON. See WYSS, JOHANN DAVID

SWITZERLAND Former name: Helvetian Republic, used when Celtic tribe called Helvetians lived here before Christ. Julius Caesar's Roman army conquered tribe, 58 B.C. Today French-speaking people of western Switzerland sometimes call their land Helvetia. Central European country; has remained neutral in European wars, including two world wars, since early 16th century. Because of neutrality and stability, has become international banking center. Twenty-three political divisions are called cantons, of which three are divided into half cantons (bringing total to 26). From Italian *contone* ("corner" or "angle"). In five of these divisions, voting is done by show of hands at open meeting called Landsgemeinde. Letters CH appear on vehicles as abbreviation for Confederation Helvetique. Four official languages: German (65%), French (18%), Italian (9%) and Romansch (1%). Sixty percent of country covered by Swiss Alp; and 10% by Jura (series of limestone ridges). Remaining 30% called Swiss Plateau, also very hilly. Europe's most mountainous country.

SYMBIONESE LIBERATION ARMY Violent extremist organization led by Donald DeFreeze. Kidnapped Patricia Hearst, daughter of famed newspaper publisher, February 4, 1974. Demanded that Hearsts open free food program for poor. Patricia surfaced months later during bank robbery; DeFreeze was present.

T

T.I.D. Phrase often found on doctor's prescription, abbreviation for Latin *ter in die*, meaning "three times a day." Reveals medicine's roots in Latin, formerly the language of scholars.

TABASCO State of southeastern Mexico on Gulf of Mexico. Name derived from Indian word for "damp earth." Area covered with swamps, lakes, dense tropical forests.

TABEL, JUNKO (1939–   ) Mountain climber. First woman to reach summit of Mount Everest, world's highest peak. Climbed with an all-female Japanese expedition, 1975.

TABLE TENNIS Indoor game, played singles or doubles. Players use small wooden racquet to hit hollow celluloid ball over net stretched across table. Parlor craze in Europe and U.S. in early 20th century under trademarked name Ping-Pong. Japanese and Chinese have dominated international competition. Players wear black shirts so swiftly traveling white ball is not hidden against light background.

TACK In sailing, direction boat is heading with respect to direction of wind. If wind comes from starboard (right) side of boat, boat said to be on starboard tack; when wind comes from left, boat on port tack. In common usage, refers to heading toward direction of wind; act of tacking refers to changing direction by changing sail position with respect to wind direction.

TAGUS RIVER Longest river of Iberian Peninsula. Runs 550 mi. (165 km.) through Spain and Portugal. Empties into Atlantic Ocean at Lisbon, capital and largest city in Portugal.

TAIPEI   Capital and largest city in Taiwan, seat of Chinese Nationalist Government since 1949. Lies on Hsintien, Keelung and Tanshui rivers. Founded, 1708. Grew in three separate settlements: Wanhwa, Tataocheng and Chenghei. Merged into one city, 1920.

TAIWAN   Island in South China Sea also called Formosa. Mountains cover two-thirds of area. Tropic of Cancer runs through it. Temperatures average 80°F (27°C) in summer and 65°F (18°C) in winter.

TAJ MAHAL, THE   Architecturally striking tomb built by Mogul Shah Jahan in memory of his favorite wife. Her title, Mumtaz-i-Mahal, which means "Pride of the Palace," gave the building its name. Built by 20,000 workmen in Agra, India between 1632–1653. Made of marble. No airplanes permitted to fly over this sacred tomb.

TAKING OF PELHAM ONE TWO THREE, THE. See GODEY, JOHN

TALES OF PETER RABBIT. See POTTER, HELEN (BEATRIX)

TALLAHASSEE   Capital city of Florida, located in northwestern part of state. Old State Capitol, completed in 1845, and capitol building in Austin, TX were only confederate capitols not captured by Union Troops during Civil War. New capitol opened, 1977.

TALLYHO   Cry from huntsman when sighting fox breaking from cover. Fox hunting is sport in which mounted horsemen follow and observe pack of hounds that search for and pursue fox. Steeped in tradition, primary appeal is advanced horsemanship, including hard riding and jumping.

TANGIER   Atlantic coastal region of Morocco which includes city of Tangier. Inhabitants are Muslims, Arabs and Berbers, and called "Tangerines," (*Tangerois* in French). Owned by Portugal, Spain, and England at different times between 1400 and 1600. Moors took over until 1924. Tangier became part of Morocco in 1956.

TANK   Developed, World War II, by British. Also called "cistern" or "reservoir." Mailed to France in huge crates marked "tank" so German agents would not realize what they were.

TANZANIA   East African country. Consists of Tanganyika, on the mainland, and Zanzibar, a group of offshore islands. After gaining independence from Britain, 1964, Tanganyika and Zanzibar joined to form United Republic of Tanzania.

TAP AIRLINE *Transportes Aereos Portugueses*. Portugal's national airline. Began regular passenger service, 1946. Its 32 aircraft fly to four continents.

TARESTHESIA Word from Greek *tarsos*, meaning "flat surface," "sole of foot," or "edge of eyelid"; suffix —aesthesia from Greek *aisthes(is)*, meaning "feeling"; and —ia, frequently used in medical terminology to denote condition of sensation, perception or feeling. Tarsoptosia: condition of flat foot. Tarsitis: inflammation of instep or ankle.

TARLETON TWINS, THE. See MITCHELL, MARGARET

TAROT CARDS Pictorial cards used in fortune-telling. Origins in ancient Babylonian and Assyrian culture. Sequence in which card is picked from deck, placed on table, and its placement upon table affects reading. Deck of 78 includes the moon, the sun, the juggler, the devil.

TARTS What Knave of Hearts stole from Queen of Hearts in nursery rhyme, *The Queen of Hearts*. In second verse King of Hearts beats Knave, who returns tarts and vows to steal no more.

TARZAN Fictional English Lord lost in Africa as a child and raised by apes, becomes jungle hero as adult. Created in 1912 by Edgar Rice Burroughs. Johnny Weissmuller played character the most times in film. Elmo Lincoln was first screen Tarzan (1918); Christopher Lambert the latest (1984).

TASMAN SEA Section of Pacific Ocean. Situated between Australia, Tasmania and New Zealand. First reached by Dutch navigator Abel Janszoon Tasman in the mid-1600s. Submarine cable which provides communication between Sydney, Australia and Cape Farewell, New Zealand lies on sea bed.

TASMANIA Island state of the Australian Commonwealth. Vacation spot. Formerly southeastern corner of Australian mainland, but rough waters of Bass strait split it off. Home of Tasmanian Devil, a fierce marsupial; and the Tasmanian Tiger, believed extinct.

TASTE Sense that allows us to discern substances in mouth. There are four tastes: salty, sweet, sour and bitter, which are detected by taste buds on the tongue. Sense of smell is also involved in taste.

TAYLOR, ELIZABETH (1932–   ) Actress. London born. Danced before Princess Elizabeth, 1935. Came to America at outbreak of World War II. Film debut in *Lassie Come Home*, 1943. Married: Conrad Nicholas Hilton, Jr. (1950), Michael Wilding (1952), Mike Todd (1957), Eddie Fisher (1959), Richard Burton (1964, again in 1975), John William Warner (1976).

TAYLOR, JAMES (1948–   ) Singer-songwriter who gained fame with hit song "Fire and Rain" (1970). Married Carly Simon in 1972. Other popular records include: "You've Got a Friend" (1971) and "How Sweet It Is" (1975).

TCHAIKOVSKY, PETER ILYICH (1840–1893) Russian composer. Known for six symphonies, 11 operas, orchestral works like *1812 Overture* (1880), and classic ballet scores, including *Swan Lake* (1877), *The Nutcracker* (1892) and *Sleeping Beauty* (1890). Latter ballet in three acts based on Perrault fairy tale, features "Procession of Fairy Tales" in Act III, with appearances by Puss-in-Boots, Cinderella, Little Red Riding Hood and several others.

TEASPOON. See LIQUID MEASURE VOLUME EQUIVALENTS

TEETH Normal mouth contains 32 permanent teeth. Eight incisors (from Latin *incidere*, "to cut"), 4 canines, 8 bicuspids and 12 molars. Last four molars are often called wisdom teeth because they appear in early adulthood.

TELEPHONE Rotary Dial telephone was invented in 1891, 15 years after Alexander Graham Bell invented telephone itself. Standard dial, with three leters above each number (beginning with two), was first used by the Bell System in 1920. U.S. patent No. 174,465, granted to Alexander Graham Bell for telephone on March 7, 1876. All letters of alphabet, except Q and Z, are divided among numbers two through nine. First transcontinental telephone conversation, January 25, 1915 between Alexander Graham Bell in New York City and Thomas Augustus Watson in San Francisco. Service began April 7, 1915 at cost of $20.70 for first three minutes.

TELEPHONE AREA CODES. See AREA CODES (U.S.)

TELEPHONE OPERATORS *Blake, Amanda* (1931–   ),

actress. Wife of Frank Gilbert. Played Kitty, the saloonkeeper, on the television show *Gunsmoke*.

Nixon, Patricia Ryan (1912–   ). Wife of President Richard Nixon. College jobs included department store clerk, telephone operator and library aide.

Onassis, Aristotle Socrates (1906–1975). Greek shipping tycoon. Telephone operator in Buenos Aires before beginning the tobacco import business that started off his fortune.

TELEVISION   Invented by Vladimir Zworykin and Philo T. Farnsworth in 1922. First two licensed stations were WNBT and WCBN in New York, 1941. Franklin D. Roosevelt was first president to appear on TV; Eisenhower, first in color.

TELLER, EDWARD (1908–   )   American nuclear physicist. Worked on atom bomb project at Los Alamos, NM during World War II. Called Father of the Hydrogen Bomb for contributions to development of weapon.

TELSTAR   First U.S. communications satellite launched in 1962. Inspired hit single by the Tornadoes, a British rock-and-roll band.

TEMPELHOF AIRPORT. See WEST BERLIN, AIRPORTS

TEMPERATURE: FAHRENHEIT/CENTIGRADE-
Most commonly used temperature scales.
One common value: 40°F equals 40°C
Centigrade Fahrenheit Steam point 100° 212°
Ice point 0° 32°
Centigrade scale succeeded by Celsius; differs only by hundreths of a degree.

TEMPEST, THE. See SHAKESPEARE, WILLIAM

TEMPLAR, SIMON. See CHARTERIS, LESLIE

TEMPLE OF KARNAK   Amon-Re Temple at Karnak honoring chief god of ancient Egypt. Built in 1200 B.C. by King Ramses II. Largest columned hall ever built. Remaining column stands 78 ft. (24 m.). Situated on Nile River.

TEMPLE-BLACK, SHIRLEY (1928–   )   Child actress turned politician. Began acting in movies at age of three in 1932 and made her first starring film in 1934, *Little Miss Marker*. In 1935, voted top box-office attraction. Introduced her theme song "On the Good Ship Lollypop" in *Bright Eyes* (1934). Youngest person ever listed in *Who's Who in America*, 1934, at age eight. By the age of 10, she had earned a million dollars, seventh highest income in country. Continued in films through 1940s as a teenager, most notably in *That Hagen Girl* (1947) with Ronald Reagan.

TEN COMMANDMENTS, THE   God bestows them to Moses on Mount Sinai in Exodus, XX, 3 – 17; 1: 1) Thou shall have no other god before Me. 2) Thou shall worship no false idols. 3) Thou shall not take the name of the Lord in vain. 4) Thou shall observe the Sabbath. 5) Honor thy father and mother. 6) Thou shall not murder. 7) Thou shall not commit adultery. 8) Thou shall not steal. 9) Thou shall not bear false witness. 10) Thou shall not covet thy neighbor's house, wife or possessions.

TEN COMMANDMENTS, THE   1956 epic film directed by Cecil B. DeMille (remaking his silent 1923 version). Biblical tale of Moses (portrayed by Charlton Heston) leading the children of Israel to Promised Land. Won Oscar for special effects, including parting of Red Sea.

TENERIFE   March 27, 1977, KLM 747 collided with Pan Am 747, killing 574 and seriously injuring 11; 70 persons survived. Occurred in thick fog at Tenerife, Canary Islands. KLM had not been given proper take-off permission.

TENNIS   Currently played form of game is lawn tennis, invented in 1873 by Major Walter Wingfield of England. Originally played on grass, now also played on clay, asphalt and synthetic surfaces. Match usually consists of best of three sets (women), or best of five sets (men).
Ball: Fuzzy, cloth-covered hollow rubber sphere, approximately 2½ in. diameter and 2 oz. in weight. Usually white or yellow. No stitches in seam. Pressurized to bounce 53 – 58 in. when dropped 100 in. onto concrete.
Court: Net to service line, 21 ft.; Service line to base line (back boundary), 18 ft.; Net to base line, 39 ft.; Base line to base line, 78 ft.; Center line to singles sideline, 13½; Sideline to sideline (singles), 27 ft.; Sideline to sideline (doubles), 36 ft.
Grand Slam: Includes Wimbledon or All-England Tennis Championships (began 1877), U.S. Open (began 1900), French Open (began 1891), and Australian Open (began 1905). Only players to win all four in same year: Don Budge of U.S. (1938), Rod Laver of

Australia (1962 and 1969), Maureen Connolly (1953) and Maragaret Court Smith (1970).

Love: Term for zero (no points in game or no games in set), probably corruption of French, *l'oeuf,* the egg. Game in which player does not score called "love game"; set in which player doesn't win "love set."

Net: Three feet high at center court, 3½ ft. high at fastening posts. 36 ft. long, kept taut by vertical strap fastened to ground at center. Height adjusted by handle attached to one of posts.

Service: Server gets two tries to hit ball over net into opponent's service court. Serves from alternate sides of center line, first from behind baseline of his right court, and then his left court. Good serve that is not returned called an ace; bad serve a fault. Double fault results if both serves do not land within service court's boundaries, and awards point to opponent.

TENNIS, SCORING Games scored as follows: love, no points; 15, one point won; 30, two points won; 40, three points won; deuce, tie score, once both sides have reached 40; advantage, point won after deuce (if server wins, called "ad-in"; if receiver wins, called "ad-out"); winning two consecutive points past deuce wins game, 45. Set won by side that wins at least six games by margin of two games, or wins tiebreaker game after sixth game won. Match usually consists of best of three sets (women) or best of five sets (men).

TEQUILA National alcoholic drink of Mexico. Takes name from settlement near Guadalajara, where Spanish *conquistadors* set up first distillery. True tequila made from fermented juice of the maguey, cactuslike flower. Basic ingredient of cocktails Aztec Punch, Margarita and Tequila Sunrise (made with orange juice and grenadine, and sometimes Galliano and/or banana liqueur). Submerged in beer, it forms submarino, (Mexican equivalent of a boilermaker). Also drunk in traditional manner: salt is poured on thumb and licked off, tequila is gulped and citrus fruit (usually a lemon) is immediately chewed.

TERESHKOVA, VALENTINA (1937–) Russian cosmonaut. First woman to travel in space, 1963. Orbited earth once every 88 min. Operated ship by manual controls. Made more than 125 parachute jumps before beginning training in space flight school.

TERKEL, STUDS (1912–) American author. Spent

three years traveling around U.S. interviewing people about their jobs for book, *Working*. Other books (*Division Street: America, Hard Times*) compiled and written in same style.

TEST-TUBE BABIES   Children conceived outside of womb, in laboratories, then placed in womb and born in usual manner. Louise Joy Brown, a five-lb., 12-oz. girl born July 25, 1978 to an American couple, was first.

TESTICLES   Or testes (plural of testis). Sperm-producing organs of male animals. Also produce male hormone, testosterone. Polyorchidism, term for rare condition of male with more than two testicles.

TETANUS   Disease caused by a type of bacteria. Causes severe muscle spasms; called lockjaw because victims often cannot open their mouths. Bacteria enter the body through breaks in skin. Tetanus vaccine has been developed.

TEXAS   Second largest state in U.S. Became Independent Republic of Texas after defeating Mexico in Battle of San Jacinto, 1836. Sam Houston was first president. Independent for 10 years. Called "Lone Star State" because of single star on its flag representing independence. Became U.S. state, 1845. Six flags have flown over the state: those of U.S., Spain, France, Mexico, The Republic of Texas and The Confederate States of America. State hosts over 500 annual fairs, festivals, and expositions including Texas Citrus Festival (winter), Watermelon Thump (spring), Texas Cowboy Reunion and Rodeo (summer) and World Champion Chili Cookoff (fall).

THACKERAY, WILLIAM MAKEPEACE (1811–1863)   English novelist noted for satirical novels about upper-class life in 19th-century London like *Vanity Fair* (1848). *Barry Lyndon* (1844) about scoundrel who lets success go to his head. Stanley Kubrick's 1975 three-hour adaptation starred Ryan O'Neal as Lyndon, and Michael Hordern as the book's Irish narrator Redmond Barry.

THAILAND   Country in Southeast Asia. Name in Thai language is *Muang Thai*, meaning "Land of the Free." Name changed in 1939 from Siam reflecting its intentions to extend frontiers to all Thai people in neighboring countries.

THANK GOD IT'S FRIDAY   1978 comedy film about typical night at disco. Starring Donna Summer, who sings Oscar-winning song, "Last Dance."

THANK YOU Translated in seven languages: Finnish, *Kiitos*; Korean, *Kam Sam Ni Da*; Mohawk, *Nia: Wen*; Portuguese, *Obrigado*; Russian *Spasibo*; Serbo-Croatian, *Hvala*; Swahili, *Asante*

THANT, U (1909–1974) Burmese statesman. Secretary General of United Nations, 1961– 1972. Succeeded by Kurt Waldheim, Austrian statesman. Born Thant, he later added the "U," meaning "Mister." Initiated negotiations between Americans and Soviets during Cuban Missile Crisis, 1962.

THAT WAS THE WEEK THAT WAS TV comedy series which satirized week's news events in revue style. Affectionately known as TW3. Series regulars included Nancy Ames, David Frost and Buck Henry.

THATCHER FERRY BRIDGE. See PANAMA CANAL

THATCHER, MARGARET HILDA (1925–   ) British stateswoman and Britain's first woman prime minister, elected 1979. Leader of Conservative Party. Known as "Iron Lady" for her determination and strict dealings with opposition, especially labor unions. Successful campaign to retake Falkland Islands from Argentina helped her win 1983 general election. Former Secretary of State for Education and Science.

THAYER, ERNEST LAWRENCE (1863–1940) American journalist, editor and poet. Most famous for classic baseball poem, "Casey at the Bat" (1888). In poem, at beginning of last inning, the score stands "two to four," and it ends that way as Mighty Casey, the home team's slugger, strikes out, leaving no joy in Mudville. Poet James Wilson redeemed fallen slugger in "Casey's Revenge" (1906).

THE English language's most used written word. Next 11 most popular written words in order are: of, and, a, to, in, is, you, that, it, he and for.

THEY CALL THE WIND MARIA Popular song from Broadway musical *Paint Your Wagon*, by Lerner and Loewe. In song, which was sung by Harve Presnell in the 1969 feature film version, the rain's name is Tess.

THIRD MAN, THE 1950 mystery film starring Joseph Cotten

as pulp writer seeking murderer in Vienna. Orson Welles portrayed Harry Lime, the murder victim. Based on story by Graham Greene.

THIRD REICH   Name used to symbolize strength of Germany's National Socialist party of 1920s. Led by Adolph Hitler. Later known as Nazism. Name derives from treatise by Moeller Van Den Bruck.

THIRD WAVE, THE   Alvin Toffler's 1980 sequel to *Future Shock*. Offers more on effects of technological revolution. The book states technology determines patterns in every other phase of society.

THIRD WORLD WAR, THE. See HACKETT, SIR JOHN WINTHROP

THIRTEEN   Superstitions about number have existed since early Roman days. Thirteen attended Last Supper making a 13-seat table unlucky; 13 is traditional number of coven of witches, and 13th tarot card is death. Unreasonable fear of 13 is called triskaidekaphobia.

THIRTY   Numeral "30" means "end of story" in newspaper industry. "30" signified end of telegraph message, thus end of correspondent's dispatch or article. Other numerical wire jargon includes "95" for urgent message and "73" for best regards.

THOR   Norse god of thunder and war, yet benevolent character. Symbols are magic hammer, thunderbolt, belt of strength and iron gloves. Thursday comes from his name.

THOREAU, HENRY DAVID (1817–1862)   American naturalist, essayist and poet. With Ralph Waldo Emerson and others, member of mid-1800s Transcendentalist movement. Best known for 1849 essay "Civil Disobedience," which attacked what he considered imperialistic war against Mexico, slavery and government mistreatment of native Indians. Also wrote *Walden* (1854), description of his two years in solitude in shack on Walden Pond, outside Concord, MA. Subtitled *Life in the Woods*, urges life be simplified so its meaning may become clear. Wrote, "the mass of men lead lives of quiet desperation."

THORPE, JIM (1888–1953)   Greatest U.S. athlete of first half of 20th century according to Associated Press Poll of sportswriters and broadcasters. Part Algonquin Indian, part Irish. All-American college halfback at Carlisle (PA) Indian School. Played professional football 1921–1925 after professional baseball career with New York Giants (1913–1920). Best known for winning pentathlon (5 events) and decathlon (10 events) for U.S. in 1912 Stockholm Olympics. Medals later rescinded when discovered Thorpe had played semi-pro baseball in 1909, voiding amateur status. Medals restored posthumously, 1982.

THREE BLIND MICE   Mother Goose rhyme: "They all ran after the farmer's wife, / who cut off their tails with a carving knife. / Did you ever see such a sight in your life? / As three blind mice." Can be sung as a round.

THREE LITTLE KITTENS   In 19th-century nursery rhyme: "Three little kittens lost their mittens / And they began to cry." Mother tells them they get no pie, but then they find mittens and get some.

THREE LITTLE PIGS   Traditional English folktale, believed to have been first published by Joseph Jacobs (1854–1916), Jewish scholar and folklorist. Story concerns three pigs pursued by wolf, who destroys first their straw house, then their stick house by "huffing and puffing" and blowing them down. Pigs ultimately find safety in brick house.

THREE MEN IN THE TUB   Anonymous nursery rhyme entitled "Rub-a-Dub-Dub": "Rub-a-dub-dub / Three men in a tub / And who do you think they be? / The butcher, the baker / The candlestick-maker, / Turn 'em out, knaves all three!"

THREE MUSKETEERS, THE. See DUMAS, ALEXANDRE

THREE RIVERS STADIUM   Pittsburgh stadium. Home to Pirates of National Baseball League, Steelers of National Football League, and Maulers of United States Football League. Capacity 54,598 for baseball; 50,350 for football. Artificial turf. Located at junction of Allegheny, Monongahela and Ohio rivers.

THREE STOOGES, THE   There were actually six. Moe, Larry and Curly, the most familiar version of the comedy trio, were originally teamed with vaudevillian Ted Healy before striking out on their own in 1934. Curly, who died in 1946, was replaced by Shemp Howard, Moe's brother, who in turn was succeeded by Joe Besser and Curly Joe DeRita. Altogether, the Stooges made 190 short films and several full-length features.

THREE WISE MEN   Also known as the Magi or the Three Kings of the Orient. Brought gold, frankincense and myrrh to Jesus Christ on Epiphany, the 12th day of Christmas (January 6). Their names were Gaspar (or Casper), an Indian king; Melchior (or Melkon), a Persian king; and Balthasar (or Bithisarea), an Arabian King.

THRESHER   One of new line of nuclear attack submarines. Never surfaced after making a deep-dive test off Massachusetts coast, April 10, 1963. All 129 U.S. crewman killed. Accident blamed on piping problems.

THRILLA IN MANILA. See FRAZIER, JOE

THROUGH THE LOOKING GLASS. See CARROLL, LEWIS

THUMB   Generally considered one of the five fingers of the hand, although it contains two bones instead of three as in the other fingers. Man has an opposable thumb, making it possible to use tools.

THURBER, JAMES GROVER (1894–1961)   American humorist and cartoonist. Frequent contributor to *New Yorker*, where "The Secret Life of Walter Mitty" originally appeared, March 18, 1939. Two-thousand-five-hundred-word short story about henpecked man who daydreams about heroic deeds. Movie version (1947) starred Danny Kaye. Thurber also known for *Is Sex Necessary?* (1929, written with E.B. White), *My Life and Hard Times* (1933) and *Fables for Our Time* (1940).

THYROID GLAND   Endocrine or ductless gland located in the throat of most vertebrates, including man. Produces thyroxine, a hormone involved in regulation of metabolism, and calcitonin, a hormone necessary to regulate calcium levels. Goiter is an enlarged thyroid gland.

TIBER RIVER   Italy's third largest river. Flows 252 mi. (403 km.) through the Sabine Mountains in Rome, Italy and finally into the Tyrrhenian Sea.

TICK-TACK-TOE   Game played by two people with pencil and paper. Also called "Naughts and Crosses" (for Os and Xs). Two vertical lines, crossed by two horizontal lines, form nine spaces. First player marks X in any space, second marks O in any remaining space. Continue in turn, with first player to get three marks in a row—horizontally, vertically or diagonally—the winner. Most games end in a draw but since X goes first, that player has better chance of winning.

TIDDLYWINKS   Game in which each player tries to flip small discs, called "winks" into cup by shooting them with larger disc called "shooter." Players shoot in turn, getting extra shot each time wink lands in cup. First to get all winks in cup wins.

TIDE   Periodic motion of waters of sea. Caused by attractive gravitational forces of moon and sun. In most places, two high tides and two low tides every day; called semidiurnal. Also diurnal and mixed tides. Inland flow of water called flood current; seaward flow, ebb current. Flood and ebb currents result in high and low tides, respectively.

TIERRA DEL FUEGO   Group of islands off southern tip of South America. Name meaning "Land of Fire" given by Ferdinand Magellan, who sighted large blazes there made by Indians to keep warm. Argentina owns eastern part and Chile owns western part.

TIGERS   Largest members of cat family. Largest variety is Siberian tiger which can be more than 10 ft. long and weigh 550 or more lbs. Live in Asia.

TIJUANA, MEXICO   City on Mexican-U.S. border, 16 mi. (26 km.) south of San Diego, CA. American tourists visit here more than any other foreign city. Restaurants, shops, bullfights and night-clubs attract vacationers.

TIMBUKTU   Small trading town in central Mali. Once, one of Africa's richest commercial cities and center of Muslim learning. Close to Sahara Desert and Nile River. Therefore, known as "meeting point of camel and canoe."

TIME MAGAZINE   Former Yale classmates and Baltimore *News* reporters Henry R. Luce and Briton Hadden founded weekly news-magazine in 1923. Conceived for "the busy man." Invented "Time-style" characterized by inverted sentences, compound adjectives, puns and neologisms, coining such words as cinemaddict, pufflicity, sexational. Hadden died 1929; Luce built *Time* (later joined by *Life, Sports Illustrated, Fortune, People* and other interests) into empire before his death in 1967. Time's "Presidency" column started in pre-1972 weekly *Life*, written by Hugh Sidey. Virgin Mary has been woman appearing most frequently on cover—10 times. Eleanor Roosevelt second.

Time Man-of-the-Year:

1927 Charles Lindbergh

1928 Walter P. Chrysler

1929 Owen D. Young

1930 Mohandas K. Gandhi

1931 Pierre Laval

1932 Franklin D. Roosevelt

1933 Hugh S. Johnson

1934 Franklin D. Roosevelt

1935 Haile Selassie

1936 Wallis Warfield Simpson

1937 Gen./Mme. Chiang Kai-Shek

1938 Adolf Hitler

1939 Joseph Stalin

1940 Winston Churchill

1941 Franklin D. Roosevelt

1942 Joseph Stalin

1943 George C. Marshall

1944 Dwight D. Eisenhower

1945 Harry S. Truman

1946 James F. Byrnes

1947 George C. Marshall

1948 Harry S. Truman

1949 Winston Churchill

1950 The American Fighting Man

1951 Mohammed Mossadegh

1952 Queen Elizabeth II

1953 Konrad Adenauer

1954 John Foster Dulles

1955 Harlow Curtice

1956 Hungarian Freedom Fighter

1957 Nikita Krushchev

1958 Charles DeGaulle

1959 Dwight D. Eisenhower

1960 U.S. Scientists

1961 John F. Kennedy

1962 Pope John XXIII

1963 Martin Luther King, Jr.

1964 Lyndon B. Johnson

1965 Gen. William C. Westmoreland

1966 The 25—and—Under Generation

1967 Lyndon B. Johnson

1968 Anders, Borman and Lovell

1969 The Middle Americans

1970 Willy Brandt

1971 Richard M. Nixon

1972 Kissinger and Nixon

1973 John J. Sirica

1974 King Faisal

1975 Women of the Year

1976 Jimmy Carter

1977 Anwar Sadat

1978 Teng Hsiao-ping

1979 Ayatollah Khomeini

1980 Lech Walesa

1982 The Computer

1983 Ronald Reagan and Yuri Andropov

TIME PERIODS   Biennial, two years; decennial, 10 years; vicennial, 20 years; centennial, 100 years; sesquicentennial, 150 years; bicentennial 200 years; millenium, 1,000 years.

TIMES SQUARE   Area in Manhattan bounded by intersection of Broadway and Seventh Avenue between 42nd and 47th Streets. Corner of 42nd Street and Broadway, the hub. Theater district of

New York. Office buildings are interspersed with striptease parlors and movie houses.

TIMOTHY Grass named for Timothy Hanson. Introduced to U.S., 1770. It is the most important type grown for hay in North America. Called cat's-tail in England.

TINY TIM (1925–) Born Herbert Khaury. As "Tiny Tim," known for strange, high voice, ukelele and unusual appearance (big nose, long stringy hair, old clothes). Gained fame from guest spots on "Laugh-In" and "Johnny Carson" shows of late 1960s. Had hit record "Tiptoe Through the Tulips" in 1968. Married Victoria May Budinger (Miss Vicky) on *The Tonight Show*, December 17, 1969.

TIRANA Capital city and industrial center of Albania. Population est. 174,800. Founded by Turkish General, 1600. Farm products, olives, almonds cultivated in outskirts.

TITANIC Luxury ocean liner. Sister ship of the *Olympic*. Reputedly unsinkable. Went down after hitting iceberg near Newfoundland, night of April 14, 1912. This was ship's maiden voyage, from England to New York. Approximately 1,500 of the 2,200 on board died, including Captain E. S. Smith. Liner had insufficient emergency provisions for number of passengers. After this incident, a rule was passed requiring all ships to provide emergency equipment for every passenger on board.

TITZLING, OTTO (1884–1942) Invented brassiere, 1912. Did not patent. 1929, Frenchman Philippe de Brassiere stylized Titzling's original design. First padded bra designed by D. J. Kennedy, 1929, to protect breasts from injury.

TO CATCH A THIEF 1955 film directed by Alfred Hitchcock. Cary Grant stars as "the Cat," an ex-jewel thief who falls in love with American girl played by Grace Kelly. Kelly met future husband Prince Ranier while on location in Monaco.

TO ERR IS HUMAN In Latin, *errare humanum est*. "To err is human, to forgive, divine," written by Alexander Pope (1688–1744), English writer, in *An Essay on Criticism*.

TOAD, HORNED Actually a lizard that lives in deserts of Mexico and U.S. Small, harmless, spiny with unusual defense: can shoot a stream of blood from their eyes up to three ft. away when antagonized.

TODAY SHOW, THE Popular NBC-TV morning series began broadcasting January 14, 1952. Dave Garroway was original host through 1961; would sign off each show by saying, "Peace." Other hosts followed, among them: John Chancellor (1961), Hugh Downs (1962), Frank McGee (1971) and Jim Hartz (1974).

TOFFLER, ALVIN (1928–) American social critic and author. His *Future Shock* (1970) says change is happening so fast that people can't keep up with changing values, leaving millions without direction or purpose. Sequel *The Third Wave*(1980) offers more on psychological effects of technological revolution, saying technology determines patterns in every phase of society.

TOILET PAPER Invented by Joseph Gayetty, 1857. Originally, sold as "Gayetty's Medicated paper—a perfect article for the toilet and for the prevention of piles." Gayetty's name was printed on each sheet.

TOKYO Capital of Japan. Business center and national government headquarters. Western-influenced city. Its inhabitants shop at department stores and go to nightclubs on busy street called The Ginza. Tokyo has more neon lights than any other city in world. Connected to other world cities by three airports: Tokyo International Airport (Haneda); New Tokyo International Airport (Narita); and Kagoshima Airport.

TOKYO ROSE Alias of Iva Toguri d'Aquino. American citizen. Graduate, UCLA. Visiting Japan at outbreak of World War II. Not allowed to return to U.S. Notorious World War II radio-propaganda broadcaster for Japan's "Radio Tokyo'" program popular for music and other nonpropaganda. Heard nightly by U.S. forces in South Pacific. Convicted and imprisoned by U.S. for treason. Pardoned, 1977, by President Ford.

TOLKIEN, JOHN RONALD REUEL (J. R. R.) (1892–1973) Oxford University philologist and author. His adult fairy tales—introductory book *The Hobbit*(1938), the *Lord of the Rings Trilogy*(1954–1956) and *The Simarillion*(1977)—created the mythical kingdom of Middle Earth, which had its own language, history and magical inhabitants, human and otherwise. Central character of *The Hobbit* is Bilbo Baggins, gnomelike creature with passion for food and tobacco, as all hobbits have. Three individual books in Trilogy (in chronological order): *The Fellowship of the Ring*, *The Two Towers* and *The Return of the King*.

TOLSTOY, LEO NIKOLAYEVICH, COUNT (1828–

1910) Russian novelist-philosopher. Born of nobility, had 13 children, then became Christian anarchist, abandoning worldly goods and devoting himself to social reform. Noted for epic novels *Anna Karenina* (1875–1877); *War and Peace* (1865–1869), about Napoleon's 1812 invasion of Russia, includes more than 500 characters, each individually developed, representing every level of life from emperors to peasants.

TOM BROWN'S SCHOOL DAYS. See HUGHES, THOMAS

TOM JONES Oscar-winning Best Picture of 1963, directed by Tony Richardson. Albert Finney stars as Tom Jones, a playboy in 18th-century England, chasing girls, sucking lobster claws and swallowing oysters. Based on novel by Henry Fielding.

TOM, TOM, THE PIPER'S SON In the nursery rhyme, piper's son Tom "stole a pig / And away he run / The pig was eat / And Tom was beat / And Tom went howling down the street." In another verse, the only song Tom can play is "over the hills and far away."

TOMATOES Fruits of the tomato plant. Rich in vitamins A and C. Native to Central America. When first brought to Europe, grown for decoration and as supposed aphrodisiac, called Love Apples. Did not become popular food until after Civil War.

TOMBSTONE, ARIZONA Famous silver-mining town of 1880s. Named by its founder, prospector Ed Schieffilin. Friends told him he'd only found a tombstone, not silver. Tourists visit O.K. Corral and Boot Hill, a cemetery for gunmen.

TOMMY 1975 film by Ken Russell based on 1969 rock opera by The Who. Film starred band's lead singer Roger Daltry as a deaf-dumb-blind boy who becomes a pinball champ and cult leader. Elton John co-starred as "Pinball Wizard," who plays Bally's Wizard pinball machine.

TONGUE Organ of taste and speech. Taste buds covering one-third of the back of tongue. Impulses travel via glossopharyngeal nerve to taste areas in brain. Almost completely muscle; strongest muscle in the body.

TONIGHT SHOW, THE The popular, late-night talk show premiered September 1954, with Steve Allen as host. Jack Paar hosted between 1957–1962. Johnny Carson took over in 1962 and continues today. Carson's bandleader Doc Severinsen replaced Parr's Skitch Henderson. Highlights during Johnny's stretch include the marriage of Tiny Tim on December 17, 1969; and actor Ed Ames (at the time playing an Indian on *Daniel Boone* TV series) demonstrating his skill with the tomahawk—unintentionally hitting a dummy in the crotch. Theme music, "Johnny's Theme," written by Paul Anka.

TONSIL PAINT Old West cowboy term for whiskey. Other terms used: tonsil varnish, nose paint, joy juice, red dynamite, red disturbance, tongue oil, stump puller, tiger spit, dust cutter.

TONTO Friend of The Lone Ranger, played on TV by Jay Silverheels. Would ride with his *kemo sabe* (faithful friend) on his horse, Scout.

TOOTH DECAY Dental decay, caries or cavities. Result of acid-producing action of bacteria in the mouth. Acid dissolves protective enamel, resulting in decay. Affects 98% of the world's population. Noncommunicable.

TOPAZ Transparent mineral. Hardness rating of eight; will scratch quartz. Gem or precious topaz, November's birthstone, most often yellow or golden. Very rare. Less valuable topaz, white or blue crystals, more abundant.

TOPKAPI Popular 1964 caper film starring Melina Mercouri as mastermind of scheme to rob a museum. Peter Ustinov, Maximilian Schell co-starred as her accomplices in the jewel theft.

TOPO GIGIO The little Italian mouse, created by puppeteer Mario Perego, whose appearance on *The Ed Sullivan Show* in early 1960s became a favorite feature of program. When Ed would put Topo to bed, he'd say, "Hey Eddie, kees me goodnight." Appeared in feature film *The Magic World of Topo Gigio* (1965).

TOPPER Thorne Smith's novel of a henpecked businessman and his ghostly friends became a popular movie starring Cary Grant in 1937, with Roland Young as Cosmo B. Topper. A 1953 TV series starred Leo G. Carroll in the title role. Neal is the martini-drinking St. Bernard. Jack Warden played lead in a 1979 made-for-TV movie.

TORN CURTAIN 1966 film directed by Alfred Hitchcock. Paul Newman stars as American scientist who pretends defection to East Germany to learn secrets. "Curtain" of title is, of course, the Iron Curtain.

TORNADO   Twisting wind storm. Most violent winds on earth. Can travel up to 60 m.p.h. (99 km.p.h.), covering a distance of 200 mi. (322 km.). Usually lasts less than one hour. Occurs throughout world but mostly in midwestern and southern U.S.

TORONTO   Capital of Canada and its second-largest city. Largest metropolitan population in Canada, although entire city of Montreal has more people. Chief manufacturing center of Canada. Major industries include food processing, printing, publishing. Home of world's tallest building outside U.S.: Canadian National Tower, 1,815 ft. (544 m.).

TORONTO BLUE JAYS   Entered Eastern Division of American Baseball League in 1977, same year Seattle Mariners entered Western Division. Toronto one of three major league teams with bird nicknames (St. Louis Cardinals and Baltimore Orioles are others). Finished last in first season, but by 1983 had become pennant contender under manager Bobby Cox. Play in Exhibition Stadium on grounds of Canadian National Exhibition.

TORTOISE   Besides man, longest living animal. Record held by black seychelles tortoise, over 152 years old. Species now extinct. Giant tortoise lives more than 100 years.

TOUCH   Fifth sense. Actually four senses of touch: hot, cold, pressure, pain. Tongue and lips, the fingertips, specifically the index fingers, and the tip of the nose have most sensitivity to touch, while the head and the back have the least.

TOULOUSE-LAUTREC, HENRI DE (1864–1901) French painter-lithographer. Broke both legs as child, permanently stunting growth. His technical innovations in color lithography created new freedom and immediacy in poster design. Created posters of dancers at Moulin Rouge.

TOUR DE FRANCE, THE   World Series of bicycle racing. World's longest-lasting unmotored sports event; 3,000 mi. race through five nations takes 25 to 30 days to complete. Began 1903.

TOWER BRIDGE   Spans the River Thames in London, England just below Tower of London. Designed by Sir Horace Jones and Sir John Wolfe Barry. Built, 1886–1894. Lattice-work footbridges connect two tall towers that rise from the piers.

TOWER OF LONDON   In the heart of London's East End. The first building, the "White Tower," was built by William the

Conqueror, c. 1070. Originally designed as a fortress. Used as a prison, royal palace, place of coin manufacture, barracks and observatory. Site of Anne Boleyn's execution. Now a museum, housing the Crown Jewels and a display of Henry VIII's armor collection.

TRACK AND FIELD *Bell Lap*: Also called "gun lap," because sound of bell or gun signals competitors that one lap remains. Sounded as leader begins last lap. Used in distance running races, bicycle races, swimming. Allows competitors to modify rhythm for sprint to finish.

Break the Tape: Win footrace. Tape is piece of string stretched across track above finish line. Aids officials in determining winner. Competitors placed in order in which any part of their torso reaches finish line.

Decathlon: Olympic event consisting of ten parts: 100 m. run; 40 m. run; 1,500 m. run; 110 m. high hurdles; high jump; long jump; pole vault; shot put; discus; and javelin. Final event is 1,500 m. run, with tired competitors often sprawling across finish line. Events held on two consecutive days. Scoring done according to tables giving points commensurate with performance in each event. Winner considered to be world's best all-around athlete. Olympic record currently held by Bruce Jenner of U.S.— 8,618 points, 1976 Montreal Olympics.

High Jump: Competitors must clear round, horizontal bar 4 m. long. May start at whatever height they choose, with three attempts allowed at each height. No one style of jumping obligatory. Among most popular methods used is scissors, in which jumper leads leg nearest bar, crosses bar in sitting position, then brings trailing leg up over bar as lead leg is brought down on other side. Other methods include western roll, eastern cut-off and Fosbury Flop. (see FOSBURY, DICK)

Javelin: Event in which pointed wooden shaft, about 8½ ft. long, is thrown for distance. If fewer than eight competitors, each gets six attempts; if more than eight, each gets three attempts, and then best eight get another three tries. Winner is one with farthest single throw. Javelin is longest of four throwing events; world record is 327'2". Other attempts are 16-lb. hammer (275'11"), discus (235'9") and 16-lb. shotput (72'10 3/4").

Metric Mile: The 1,500 m. run, so called because it is metric race that is closest to mile run. One mile is 1,760 yds.; 1,500 m. is 1,650

yds. Therefore, 1,500 m. run is only 110 yds. less than a mile.
On Your Marks: First instruction race starter gives runners. Means to
assume position in starting blocks. Followed by "set," which means
to get in starting position and ready for start signal. When all
competitors steady in position, starter fires pistol or shouts, "Go!"

TRACY, SPENCER (1900–1967) Distinguished film actor, who starred in many famous Hollywood films including *Stanley
and Livingston*(1939) and the title roles in *Edison, The Man*(1940), *Father
of the Bride*(1950). Received Best Actor Oscars for *Captains Courageous*(1937) (the award was engraved to "Dick Tracy") and *Boy's
Town*(1938). Co-starred with Katharine Hepburn in many comedies,
including *Woman of the Year*(1942) and *Adam's Rib*(1949). Last film,
Guess Who's Coming to Dinner?(1967).

TRAFALGAR GRAVEYARD. See GIBRALTAR

TRAFALGAR SQUARE Famous square marking center of
London. Paved area with statue of Admiral Horatio Nelson, hero
of Battle of Trafalgar, 1805. Statue stands on 167 ft. (50 m.) victory
column.

TRAMPOLINING Individual acrobatic sport consisting of
various maneuvers in air performed with aid of trampoline, a raised
canvas springboard. Among them: kaboom, a backward somersault
in tuck position from back drop position; swivel hips seat drop,
half-twist to seat drop (i.e., landing on seat with legs fully extended
in front of body). Spaceball, invented 1962 by Nissen (inventor of
trampoline), is played singles or doubles with 8 oz. ball on trampoline with backstops at both ends and net erected vertically across
center. Played competitively only in U.S. and England.

TRANS-SIBERIAN RAILROAD, THE First railroad
built across Siberia in U.S.S.R. World's largest railroad when built,
1916. Extended 5,799 mi. (9,278 km.) and had 97 stops. At present,
no official railroad named Trans-Siberian Railroad. Trans-Siberian
Express now makes trip from Moscow to Vladivostok in seven days.

TRANSYLVANIA Geographical region of Romania near
Hungarian border. Separated from rest of Romania by Carpathian
Mountains and Transylvanian Alps. Popularized in Bram Stoker's
famous horror story of Count Dracula.

**TRAP (AND SKEET) SHOOTING TARGETS. See
PIGEON, CLAY**

TRAVERS, PAMELA (P. L.) (1906–   ) Australian author of books about mythical nanny Mary Poppins. Walt Disney's 1964 film version starred Julie Andrews (in Oscar-winning role) and Dick Van Dyke.

TREASURE OF THE SIERRA MADRE, THE Hit 1949 film starring Humphrey Bogart (as Dobbsy), Walter Huston and Tim Holt, as a trio of prospectors who lust for gold. Father Walter Huston won an Oscar for Best Supporting Actor, while son John Huston took Oscars for Direction and Screenplay. Walter Huston performed in movie without his teeth.

TREES Like most plants, use energy of sun to convert carbon dioxide in air to living material. This process, known as photosynthesis, occurs when leaves are exposed to light. Up to 90% of a tree is made of air. The rest is minerals from the soil.

TREVI FOUNTAIN Located in Rome, Italy. Created in 1762 by Niccolo Salvi. Exhibits Neptune, the sea god, in chariot of shells, being pulled by seahorses and tritons. Visitors throw coins into fountain as a promise that they will return to Rome. Featured in 1954 movie *Three Coins in the Fountain*.

TREVINO, LEE (1939–   ) Mexican-born pro golfer, dubbed himself "Super Mexkin," shortened to "Super Mex," after winning 1968 U.S. Open. Repeated Open win, 1971. Won British Open 1971–1972, Professional Golfers Association Championship, 1974. PGA Player-of-the-Year, 1971. Won Varden Trophy (low stroke average) 1970–1972, 1974.

TRIANGLES

Acute	—All angles less than 90°
Equilateral	—All sides and angles equal
Isosceles	—Two sides and two angles equal
Obtuse	—One angle larger than 90°
Right	—One angle of 90°
Scalene	—No sides or angles equal

TRINIDAD AND TOBAGO Languages spoken in Trinidad and Tobago include English (the official language), Hindi, French and Spanish.

TRIPE Is the netlike or honeycomblike layer of the stomach of sheep, goats and especially oxen. It is an ingredient in many dishes. It can also mean something worthless or offensive.

TRIPLE CROWN   Comprised of three classic races ("jewels") for three-year-old horses.

Race	Run	At	Length	First Run	Official Flower	Official Song
Kentucky Derby*	First Saturday in May	Churchill Downs, Louisville, KY	1¼ mi.	1875	Roses	"My Old Kentucky Home"
Preakness Stakes	Third Saturday in May	Pimlico Race Course, Baltimore, MD	1³⁄₁₆ mi.	1873	Black-Eyed Susans	"Maryland My Maryland"
Belmont Stakes	Third Saturday After Preakness	Belmont Park, Elmont, NY	1½ mi.	1867	White Carnations	"The Sidewalks of New York"

*Known as "The Run for the Roses." Considered "The most exciting two minutes in sports."

TRIPOLI   Libya's capital and largest city. Went to war with U.S. in 1801, when Barbary pirates attacked American ships. Gave its name to a glass, metal and the marble polishing powder first used here.

TRIVIAL PURSUIT   Trivia board game craze that swept U.S. and Canada, 1983. Trademarked game copyright 1981 by Canadian firm Horn Abbot Ltd. Distributed in U.S. by Selchow and Righter, makers of Scrabble. There are 19 cherub drawings on game board: two next to each of six colored wedges, six in center and pink one next to blue wedge.

TROILISM   Sex with three people. Sometimes referred to as *ménage à trois*, from the French, meaning a "household of three." Consists of either a man, his wife and his mistress, or a woman, her husband and her lover.

Merkin & Frankel

TROPIC OF CAPRICORN   Imaginary line marking southern boundary of tropical zone. 23°27′ south of the equator; farthest limit south where sun can shine directly overhead. This occurs noon of December 21 or 22, the winter solstice. Passes through northern Chili, southern Brazil, South Africa, Madagascar and Australia.

TROPICAL ZONE, THE   Area between Tropic of Cancer and Tropic of Capricorn. Also called "The Tropics." Region of Earth lying 1,600 mi. (2,560 km.) north and 1,600 mi. south of equator. Sun shines directly over head only in this zone.

TROTSKY, LEON (1879–1940)   Lenin's chief aide. Helped plan Bolshevik Revolution. Defeated in the power struggle that followed Lenin's death. Exiled by Joseph Stalin, who had him assassinated, August 20, 1940, in Mexico City.

TROUBLE WITH HARRY, THE   1955 film directed by Alfred Hitchcock. Black comedy about group of locals trying to dispose of a body found in Vermont woods. Edmund Gwenn, John Forsythe star; Shirley MacLaine makes screen debut.

TROY   City whose siege is subject of Homer's *Illiad* and Virgil's *Aeneid*. In 12th century B.C., Greeks under Agamemnon (with hero Achilles) used giant wooden Trojan Horse to recapture hostage Helen. Troy's location Asia Minor, now Turkey, gave it a strategic position in history, controlling major east-west trade routes.

TRUCK FLEETS   Private truck fleets comprise over 50% of all U.S. trucking. Though private fleets are not required to report total vehicle numbers, 1983 figures indicate that Quality Bakers Corp. of America is largest in food category, and Honeywell, Inc. is largest in general industry category.

TRUDEAU, GERRITSON BEEKMAN (GARRY) (1948–   )   American cartoonist. Created Doonesbury comic strip as "Bull Tales" in Yale *Record* while undergraduate student. Strip moved to Yale *Daily News*, 1969. United Feature Syndicate renamed it after character Michael ("Mike") Doonesbury and distributed it, 1970. Appeared in more than 400 newspapers. Won Pulitzer Prize, 1975.

TRUDEAU, MARGARET (1945–   )   Canadian. Married future Prime Minister Pierre Trudeau, March 1971. They had three children before separating, 1977. She reportedly remarked that Cuba's Fidel Castro was "the sexiest man I ever met."

TRUE GRIT John Wayne won his only Oscar for this 1969 Western directed by Henry Hathaway and also starring Kim Darby, Glen Campbell. Wayne played Rooster Cogburn, an irascible old gunfighter, a role he reprised in *Rooster Cogburn*, 1976.

TRUFFLES Certain fungi that live underground. These expensive delicacies are harvested in France and Italy by use of dogs or pigs who have been trained to hunt their scent. They are found four ft. or less below ground, are up to four in. in diameter.

TRUMAN, HARRY S. (1884–1972) Thirty-third U.S. president, 1945–1953. Named Harry after one of his uncles. Given only middle initial "S" so both grandfathers, Solomon Young and Anderson Shippe Truman, could say he was named after them. Assumed office after Franklin Delano Roosevelt's death, 1945. Famous for motto "The Buck Stops Here." Authorized bombing of Hiroshima, Japan, August 6, 1945, and Nagasaki, three days later. Addressed joint session of Congress, April 16, 1945, pledging to carry out policies of his predecessor. Truman said: "In the memory of our fallen president, we shall not fail." In 1948 presidential election, he unexpectedly carried 28 states vs. 16 by Republican Thomas E. Dewey. On the eve of the election Truman was photographed holding a copy of the Chicago *Daily Tribune* which erroneously printed: "Dewey defeats Truman."

TRUMAN, MARGARET. See DANIEL, MARGARET TRUMAN

TRUTH OR CONSEQUENCES Town in New Mexico. Formerly called Hot Springs for its warm mineral springs. Changed its name during 1950 tenth anniversary celebration of Ralph Edwards radio program. Edwards returns each year for fiesta.

TUBERCULOSIS From Latin *tuberculum*, meaning "lump." Infectious disease usually involving the lungs. Once known as "The White Plague," leading cause of death, U.S., 1900—200 per 100,000 population. In 1978, reduced to 1.3 deaths per 100,000, reflecting general improvement in living conditions, health and treatment, especially chemotherapy.

TUCK, RICHARD (1924?–   ) Democrat opposed to Richard Nixon. Actively harrassed Nixon on several occasions. One of Tuck's more imaginative pranks was to have the train from which Nixon was giving a campaign speech pull away from the station.

TUCKER, SOPHIE (1884–1967)   Singer, famous for risqué, honkytonk songs. Was known as "The Last of the Red Hot Mamas." Began in burlesque and vaudeville at the turn of the century, gained fame with her 1911 performance of song "Some of These Days." Appeared in every part of show business, from Broadway to movies, radio and TV.

TUG-OF-WAR   Contest of strength between two teams pulling against each other from opposite ends of long, thick rope. Longtime rural pastime in England. Anchor man, at end of rope, is commonly heaviest member of team.

TUMBLEWEEDS   Humorous Western comic strip by Tom K. Ryan. Began 1965. Set in town of Grimy Gulch. Slow-witted Tumbleweeds is West's most inept cowboy. Rides anemic horse Epic. Constantly pursued by town spinster Hildegard Hamhocker.

TUNISIA   Northernmost African country. Its northern tip is 85 mi. (137 km.) from island of Sicily. Bordered by Mediterranean Sea on north and east.

TUNNEY, GENE (1897–1978)   American boxer who won world heavyweight championship from Jack Dempsey, 1926, and retired undefeated two years later. Noted for that fight and second victory over Dempsey on September 23, 1927, the "long count" bout in which Dempsey knocked Tunney down in seventh round, but referee delayed in starting ten-count. Tunney, down for about 14 seconds altogether, survived to win on points. Lost only once (to Harry Greb in non-title fight) in career.

TURCOTTE, RON (1950–   )   Canadian jockey. Won 1965 Preakness on Tom Rolfe, 1972 Kentucky Derby on Riva Ridge and 1973 Triple Crown on Secretariat. Mounts won career total of $28,844,203, with 3,033 winners. Confined to wheelchair after being paralyzed from waist down in July 13, 1978 spill aboard Flag of Leyte Gulf in eighth race at Belmont Park. Sued New York Racing Association and others for $100 million, 1979 (still pending). His brother Rudy, also a jockey, had been hurt in Pimlico accident three months before. Ron elected to Racing Hall of Fame, 1979.

TURKEYS   Large game fowl and important agricultural product native to Western Hemisphere. Americans consume nine pounds of it per person per year, much of it during Thanksgiving and Christmas. California produces more turkeys than any other state. Turkey meat is either dark or light. Dark meat comes from the legs and thighs, and white from the breast. Different colors arise from differences in muscle types. Dark meat has slightly more fat, and therefore more calories, than white meat. Thought to be the least intelligent domesticated animal.

TURNER, LANA (1920–) Actress, known as "The Sweater Girl" during World War II. Films include *Ziegfield Girl* (1941), *Somewhere I'll Find You* (1942), *The Postman Always Rings Twice* (1945) and *Peyton Place* (1957).

TURNER, TED (1938–) Owner Atlanta Braves (baseball) and Hawks (basketball), "superstation" WTBS (Atlanta) and Cable News Network. Skippered America's Cup–winning yacht *Courageous*, 1977. Managed Braves for one game in 1977, during which team extended its losing streak to 17. For that and other outspoken actions and comments, known as "the Mouth of the South."

TUTANKHAMEN (HAMON OR HAMUN) (c.1371– c.1352 B.C.) Pharoah of Egypt from approximately age ten until his death. Gained recent fame after the discovery of his magnificent, nearly undisturbed tomb. Opened by Howard Carter and Lord Carnarvon, 1922.

TV COMMERCIAL, ALKA-SELTZER Popular Alka-Seltzer commercial in which ailing husband says, "I can't believe I ate the whole thing," to which his helpful wife responds, "You ate it, Ralph."

TV DINNER Introduced nationally, 1954, by L.A. Swanson and Sons Company. Box depicted a TV set. Dinner included sliced turkey, gravy, buttered peas and sweet potatoes. Cost approximately $1.00. Current annual sales exceed $300 million.

TV GUIDE First published 1953 with cover price of $.15. Desi Arnaz, Jr., son of TV star Lucille Ball, appeared on first cover. Now costs $.50. Seventeen million–plus circulation makes it top-selling weekly magazine. Covers all aspects of TV. Gives listings in 108 separate editions.

TWAIN, MARK (1835–1910) American novelist, short story writer and humorist. Real name Samuel Langhorne Clemens; took pen name from phrase "mark twain," meaning two fathoms (12 ft.) deep, used on Mississippi riverboats to call out water levels. Spent boyhood on Mississippi in Hannibal, MO, and worked as river pilot (1857–1861), both described in autobiography *Life on the Mississippi* (1883), which was first manuscript presented to publisher in typewritten form (Twain had bought Remington Model No. 1 in 1874, but could type only 19 words a minute).

Mark Twain's death: After Associated Press carried his obituary in 1897, Twain cabled from London, "The report of my death was an exaggeration." (Another story has Twain saying line to startled reporter coming to his door.) Born day Halley's Comet appeared in 1835 (first observed by Edmund Halley in 1682, it returned in 1759 and 1835), he often vowed he would live until it reappeared. Sure enough, it showed up April 21, 1910—the day he died.

Mark Twain's list of 27 things to save from boardinghouse fire: The top items on his list included fiancées, first and second cousins, sisters and step-sisters, and invalids. Near the bottom of his to-be-rescued list were firemen, landladies and landlords, and furniture. The last thing to save, according to Twain, was one's mother-in-law.

Mark Twain Tonight!: One-man show starring actor Hal Holbrook (1925–   ) as mustachioed Twain. Opened April 6, 1959 on Broadway; ran 174 performances, then toured internationally. Holbrook has performed Twain since late 1940s, doing it on *Ed Sullivan* and *Wide, Wide World* TV shows before Broadway. Did extensive research to perfect impersonation.

Mark Twain's works include *The Adventures of Tom Sawyer* (1876), story which introduces Tom Sawyer and Huckleberry Finn. Based on Twain's boyhood experiences along Mississippi. Orphan Tom lives with his Aunt Polly, courts pretty Becky Thatcher, and convinces his pals to whitewash fence for him. In *The Adventures of Huckleberry Finn* (1884), Huck and runaway slave Jim float down the Mississippi River on a raft, stopping for adventures. Jim teaches Huck about dignity and the value of life. *The Prince and the Pauper* (1882) is Twain's novel about two boys who are doubles: Edward, Prince of Wales (later King Edward VI), and pauper Tom Canty. They trade places, and the Prince is jailed when he tries to reclaim his identity. Truth discovered just as Tom is about to be crowned King. "The Celebrated Jumping Frog of Calaveras County" (1865), is Twain's first short story, about Dan'l the jumping frog. *New York Saturday Press* published it after it had been rejected elsewhere. Its popularity established his first fame as humorist. Based on actual event reported in California papers (Twain was reporter on San Francisco *Call* at the time), inspired frog jumping contest now held annually.

TWEED   Textured woolen fabric. Originally hand-woven by people near Tweed in Scotland and England. Name "tweed" derives from misprint of word "tweel" (Scottish for twill, which is a weave of the cloth). Harris Tweed, still hand-woven. Also Saxony, Donegal and Lewis types.

TWELVE DAYS OF CHRISTMAS   Popular Christmas carol based on the twelve days between Christmas (December 25) and Epiphany (January 6). Gifts given in song include a partridge in a pear tree, five gold rings, seven swans a-swimming, ten lords a-leaping.

24 SUSSEX DRIVE   Official residence of Canada's prime minister, overlooking Ottawa River in Ottawa, Ontario. House completed, 1951. Maintained by Canadian government. Popular tourist attraction, along with House of Commons and Peace Tower.

TWIGGY (1949–   )   London-born Leslie Hornby. Famous model, 1960s. Began new look in fashion. According to Mary Quant, owner of the boutique where many fashion fads began, she was the "knock-out beauty" of the time.

TWIN CITIES   Name for Minneapolis and St. Paul, Minnesota's largest city and capital city, respectively. Mississippi River flows between the cities. St. Paul originally called "Pig's Eye," nickname of its founder, Pierre Parrant.

TWINS   One of two offspring born at one birth. Five main types:
1. Allantiodoangiopagous: Fusion at allantoic vessels.
2. Conjoined: Fusion may occur at various bodily regions. Symetrical and assymetrical types. Includes Siamese.
3. Dizygotic: Two separate zygotes. Fraternal.
4. Monozygotic: Single fertilized ovum. Identical.
5. Monamniotic: Common amnion.

TWIST, THE   A dance craze and hit song of early 1960s. Record by Chubby Checker (written by Hank Ballard) became number one hit in September 1960, stayed on the chart for four months, dropped off, and later returned to number one early in 1962.

2001: A SPACE ODYSSEY   1968 science-fiction film directed by Stanley Kubrick. Spectacular special effects used in showing life in year 2001. Pan Am space shuttles and Howard Johnson's restaurant in space station lend to authenticity. Richard Strauss' "Also Sprach Zarathustra" was film's theme music. Story concerns manned space trip to moon of Jupiter, though en route ship's computer, HAL 9000, takes over. Keir Dullea stars as surviving astronaut who orders, "Open the pod bay doors, HAL," dismantles the computer and later encounters a "time warp" on Jupiter. Filmed in Cinerama. (See CLARKE, ARTHUR C.)

TWO WOMEN   1961 film starring Sophia Loren as a mother coping with life after she and her daughter are raped by German soldiers during World War II. Loren won Oscar for Best Actress.

TYPEWRITER   Universal keyboard in use today dates from 1872. It is based on the arrangement of type in a printer's case as follows:

Q W E R T Y U I O P
A S D F G H J K L
Z X C V B N M

TYPHOID FEVER   Generalized infection due to bacillus *salmonella typhi*. Associated with unsanitary conditions and carriers (approximately 3% of persons infected). Mary Mallon, or Typhoid Mary, a carrier who did not suffer from the disease, was confined by health authorities until her death, 1929. Fever is spread by excreta of persons infected.

TYROLEANS   Inhabitants of Tyrol, a mountainous region in northern Italy and western Austria. Covered mostly by Alps, which attract climbers in summer and skiers in winter. Austria controls Northern Tyrol; Italy controls Southern Tyrol.

U

U-2 INCIDENT   May 1960, American U-2 spy plane piloted by Francis Gary Powers shot down over Russia. Eisenhower accepted responsibility but refused to apologize to Khrushchev, who then canceled a planned summit conference.

U-BOAT   Nickname for German submarines in World War I and II. *U* stands for undersea. As many as 235 operated at once. Highly successful against convoys in Atlantic bringing supplies to our European allies.

U.N.C.L.E.   United Network Command for Law and Enforcement was setting for secret agent TV series *The Man From U.N.C.L.E.* (1964–1968). Mr. Waverly (portrayed by Leo G. Carroll) sent agents Napoleon Solo (Robert Vaughn) and Illya Kuryakin (David McCallum) on dangerous missions against agents of THRUSH.

U.S. BORDERS   U.S. borders Canada to north, Mexico to south. Western Alaska is separated from Russia by Bering Strait, at which point Russia (third closest country to U.S., and closest Communist country) is only 50 mi. (80 km.) from U.S.

U.S. CIVIL WAR (1861–1865)   Fought between gray-uniformed "Johnny Rebs" of the South (Confederacy) and blue-uniformed "Billy Yanks" of the North (Union). Conflicts centered on slavery and industrial development. More Americans died, by battle wounds and disease, than in any other war to date. Death toll, 618,000, more than one-fifth of soldiers in the war. (World War II saw 300,000 American soldiers die; World War I, 115,000; Vietnam, 56,000.) Due to unlikelihood of Confederate victory, Britain and France, who relied heavily on Southern cotton imports for textile industries, reluctant to back them. Dealings between Confederacy and these two countries became known as "Cotton Diplomacy." In 1860, Confederacy adopted Daniel D. Emmet's song, "I Wish I Was in Dixie Land" (1859) in anti-Lincoln campaign. Became South's "unofficial national anthem." After Confederate defeat, reunited Congress abolished slavery.

U.S. COASTLINES Three states with longest coastlines:
Alaska   :   6,640 mi. (10,686 km.)
Florida   :   1,350 mi. (2,173 km.)
California :   840 mi. (1,350 km.)

U.S. DAMS Has more dams than any other country. Orville is highest U.S. dam at 771 ft. (235 m.), constructed across Feather River in California, 1968. U.S. is home to New Cornelia Tailings, world's largest dam at 274,016,000 cu. yd. (209,500,000 cu. m.).

U.S. EXTREMITIES Outermost points of 48 contiguous states:

	State	Points	State Capital
North:	Minnesota	Northwest Angle	Olympia, WA
South:	Florida	Key West	Austin, TX
East:	Maine	West Quoddy Head	Augusta, ME
West:	Washington	Cape Alava	Salem, OR

Outermost of all 50 U.S. states:
North	Alaska
South	Hawaii
East	Maine
West	Alaska

Greatest distance between points within U.S. is approximately 7,200 mi. (11,520 km.) between Key West, FL and Lihue on island of Kauai, HI.

U.S. FLAG Seven U.S. flags in order of usage:
Name of flag	Number of stars
The Continental Colors	0
Flag of 1777	13
Flag of 1795	15

Flag of 1818	20
Flag of 1861	34
The 48-Star Flag (1912–1959)	48
50-Star Flag (1960–present)	50

Present flag's 50 stars (one for each state) are laid out in 9 rows (5 rows of 6 alternating with 4 rows of 5). Thirteen stripes represent original 13 colonies, 7 red, 6 white. During War of 1812, Francis Scott Key penned "The Star-Spangled Banner," which gave the 15 star, 15-stripe flag that nickname. Today, flag is called "Stars and Stripes."

U.S. GEOGRAPHIC CENTERS U.S. (including Alaska and Hawaii): Butte County, west of Castle Rock, South Dakota. Approx. lat. 44° 58′ N, long. 103° 46′ W.

Contiguous U.S. (48 states): near Lebannon, Smith Co., KS. Lat. 39° 50′ N, long. 98° 35′ W.

North American continent: Pierce County, ND, 6 mi. (9.6 km.) west of Balta. Lat. 48° 10′ N, long. 100° 10′ W.

U.S.–MEXICO BORDER Crossed more than any other international border. More immigrants come to U.S. from Mexico than from any other country. About 55,000 entered U.S. legally in 1983. Hundreds of thousands cross border into U.S. illegally every year.

U.S. NATIONAL SYMBOL The bald eagle. Chosen by John Adams, war hawk. Other proposals, unaccepted, were Benjamin Franklin's argument in favor of the turkey and Thomas Jefferson's advocacy of the dove, for peace.

U.S. PAPER MONEY Printed on special paper 25% linen, 75% cotton, containing red and blue strands. Bills are printed with black (front) and green (back) inks. A one dollar bill, on average, lasts 17 months.

U.S. PRESIDENT *Eligibility:* natural-born citizen, at least 14 years U.S. residence, 35 years of age. Theodore Roosevelt, 42 in 1901, was the youngest president inaugurated; Ronald Reagan, 69 in 1980, the oldest. Exact meaning of natural-born remains disputed. President and vice-president not permitted to travel together. Restriction designed to guard against them both being killed in travel mishap.

Presidential surnames—Four names have been surname of more than one president:

Adams, John	Johnson, Andrew
Adams, John Quincy	Johnson, Lyndon Baines
Harrison, William H.	Roosevelt, Theodore
Harrison, Benjamin	Roosevelt, Franklin D.

Presidents' most common Christian name—James:

James Madison	James Buchanan
James Monroe	James Garfield
James Polk	James Carter

Second most common Christian name—John.

Presidents assassinated:

Lincoln, Abraham	April 14, 1865, by actor John Wilkes Booth
Garfield, James A.	July 2, 1881, by Charles Guiteau, frustrated politician
McKinley, William	September 6, 1901, by Leon Czolgosz, anarchist
Kennedy, John F.	November 22, 1963, by Lee Harvey Oswald

Presidents to die on same day and month—July 4:

Adams, John	July 4, 1826
Jefferson, Thomas	July 4, 1826
Monroe, James	July 4, 1831

U.S. STATES

Alabama	Hawaii	Massachusetts	New Mexico	South Dakota
Alaska	Idaho	Michigan	New York	Tennessee
Arizona	Illinois	Minnesota	North Carolina	Texas
Arkansas	Indiana	Mississippi	North Dakota	Utah
California	Iowa	Missouri	Ohio	Vermont
Colorado	Kansas	Montana	Oklahoma	Virginia
Connecticut	Kentucky	Nebraska	Oregon	Washington
Delaware	Louisiana	Nevada	Pennsylvania	West Virginia

| Florida | Maine | New Hampshire | Rhode Island | Wisconsin |
| Georgia | Maryland | New Jersey | South Carolina | Wyoming |

Borders: Missouri and Tennessee each border eight states, more than any other U.S. state. Missouri borders Nebraska, Iowa, Kentucky, Tennessee, Arkansas, Oklahoma, Illinois and Kansas. Tennessee borders Kentucky, Virginia, North and South Carolina, Georgia, Alabama, Mississippi, Arkansas and Missouri.

Capitals: Four state capitals are named for U.S. presidents—Jackson, MS; Jefferson City, MO; Lincoln, NE; Madison, WI.

Flags: Blue is the most common field color on state flags (26). White is next most common (8).

Population: Alaska is the least populated (4,318,000); California is the most populated (23,677,902).

Size: Three largest are Alaska (591,004 sq. mi./1,536,610 sq. km.); Texas (267,338 sq. mi./695,078 sq. km.); and California (158,693 sq. mi./412,601 sq. km.).

U.S. SURNAMES Five most common names: Smith, Johnson, Williams, Jones, Brown.

U.S. TRADE Three biggest trading partners:

	Import to U.S.	*Export from U.S.*
Canada	Passenger cars ($7.3 billion)	Passenger cars ($3.9 billion)
Japan	Cars ($10.8 billion)	Corn ($1.8 billion)
U.K.	Crude petroleum ($3.9 billion)	Office machinery and computers ($1.7 billion)

U.S. VOLCANOES Active volcanoes in the United States are: Mt. Shasta and Lassen Peak in California, Mauna Loa and Kilauea in Hawaii, Mt. Katmai in Alaska, and Mt. St. Helens and Mt. Rainier in Washington.

U.S.S. PUEBLO Intelligence-gathering ship. Captured, January 23, 1968, 25 mi. east of North Korea. Eighty-three crewmen, including Commander Lloyd M. Bucher, taken prisoner when, according to U.S. accounts, ship was seized in international waters. Prisoners released, December 22, 1968.

U.S.S.R. See SOVIET UNION

ULAN BATOR   Capital of Outer Mongolia. Established in 1649. Once called Urga. Produces woolen cloth, felt and saddles.

ULSTER   Name of one of Ireland's original five provinces. Included what is now Northern Ireland and counties of Cavan, Donegal and Monaghan. Today, it refers to country of Northern Ireland.

ULYSSES   Homer called him Odysseus in *The Odyssey*; king of Ithaca and Greek leader in Trojan War. Romans called him Ulysses in *The Iliad*. Called Ulysses in most English poetry, including earlier translations of Homer. Tennyson's 1842 poem "Ulysses" has him still longing for adventure in his old age; Leopold Bloom in Joyce's *Ulysses* is modern incarnation.

UNCLE TOM'S CABIN. See STOWE, HARRIET (ELIZABETH) BEECHER

UNION PACIFIC RAILROAD   Founded, 1862. President Lincoln's 1863 executive order fixed its eastern border at Omaha, NE. May 10, 1869, its tracks joined recently created Central Pacific RR at Promontory in Utah, creating continent's first coast-to-coast railroad network.

UNION STOCKYARDS   Chicago's meat stockyards. Before closing in 1971, they processed about 18 million head of livestock a year. Chicago was once world's largest livestock market. When regional meat-packing centers developed, Chicago's stockyards declined.

UNITED ARTISTS   Movie distributor formed in 1919 by Mary Pickford, Douglas Fairbanks, Charlie Chaplin and D. W. Griffith. Many famous films had their origin at UA: *The General* (1925), *Scarface* (1932), *Red River* (1948), *Twelve Angry Men* (1957), *The Pink Panther* (1964) and *Rocky* (1976). In 1982, MGM bought United Artists and is now MGM/UA.

UNITED KINGDOM EMBLEMS   Unofficial national emblems of the four regions of United Kingdom:
Wales: leek
Ireland: shamrock
Britain: rose
Scotland: thistle

UNITED NATIONS, THE   Organization of 158 nations whose goal is world peace. Established, 1945, after World War II ended. Headquarters on East River in New York City between 42nd and 48th Streets. UN building is an international zone.

UNITED NATIONS SECURITY COUNCIL Upon founding of UN, 1945, permanent membership was granted to Britain, China, France, U.S. and U.S.S.R. in effort to balance their powers. Each has veto power. At present there are six additional members, serving two-year terms each.

UNIVAC-1 Stands for Universal Automatic Computer. One of first advanced computers. Completed in 1951, for U.S. Bureau of the Census, it used vacuum tubes and could perform thousands of computations a second.

UNSER, AL (1939–) AND BOBBY (1934–) Only brothers to win Indianapolis 500 auto race. Al won 1970, 1971 and 1978; U.S. Auto Club overall champion, 1970. Bobby won Indy in 1968, 1975 and 1981; USAC champ 1968, 1974. Bobby, who holds Indy record for fastest pit stop (four seconds to refuel, 1976). Al finished second to Tom Sneva in 1983.

UNTOUCHABLES, THE Premiering October 1959 on ABC-TV network, Robert Stack starred as Eliot Ness (agent for Treasury Dept.) who fought against crime bosses of Chicago during Prohibition in early 1930s. Each episode narrated by Walter Winchell (who received $25,000 per episode fee).

URAL MOUNTAINS Situated in western Soviet Union. Run for 1,500 mi. (2,410 km.) from Arctic Circle to close to Aral Sea. Form boundary between Europe and Asia. During WWII provided Russian armies with minerals. Contain one of world's largest asbestos reserves.

URANUS First planet discovered by telescope and seventh in order from sun; surrounded by a band of light (aurora) which results from large-scale electrical discharges.

URIS, LEON MARCUS (1924–) American novelist has string of best sellers. Also collaborates on photo-text books with photographer-wife Jill. Among his books are spy novel *Topaz* (1972), *The Haj* (1984) and *Battle Cry* (1953), his first novel. Lengthy story about Marines in World War II. Uris dropped out of school at 17 to join Marines. Also wrote screenplay for 1955 film version. *Exodus* (1958), story of Jewish resettlement of Palestine and creation of Israel in 1948. Otto Preminger brought it to screen (1961) with Paul

Newman and Eva Marie Saint. Wrote *Mila 18* (1961), novel about Jewish uprising in Poland's Warsaw Ghetto during World War II. Its popularity caused title of first novel by Joseph Heller to be changed to *Catch-22* from *Catch-18*. Uris' title refers to command post of resistance movement organized by Warsaw Jews. *Armageddon* (1964) covers Berlin from close of World War II to end of Berlin Airlift. American captain Sean O'Sullivan, responsible for military government of nearby city of Rombaden, hates Germans, but falls in love with German woman. *QB VII* (1970) centers on trial held at London's Queen's Bench (QB VII), a courtroom. Surgeon Adam Kelno sues American novelist Abraham Cady for writing that Kelno performed experimental sterilizations on Jewish inmates in World War II concentration camp. Uris' book, *Ireland, a Terrible Beauty: The Story of Ireland Today* (1975), is an extremely sympathetic portrait of Ireland in text and photos, done in collaboration with wife Jill.

URSA MAJOR   Or the Great Bear. North polar constellation. Contains Big Dipper. Named after nymph Callisto in Greek mythology. Zeus loved Callisto and changed her into a bear to protect her from his jealous wife, Hera.

UTAH   Five bordering states: Arizona to the south; Colorado to the east; Nevada to the west; Idaho to the north; Wyoming to the northeast.

UVULA   Soft muscular tissue hanging from roof of mouth. Part of soft palate. When one swallows, soft palate prevents food from entering nasal passage. Lies behind hard palate, which is bone.

V-E DAY   May 8, 1945, the day of Germany's surrender, World War II. Marked end of war. Stands for "Victory in Europe."

VACUUM   Technically, a space which contains no matter. True vacuums do not exist on Earth, but areas of very low pressure are often called vacuums. They do not carry sound or conduct heat.

VALENTINO, RUDOLPH (1895–1926)   Screen actor of 1920s. Born Rodolfo Alfonzo Raffaelo Pierre Filibert Guglielmi di Valentina D'Antongoulla. Nickname, "The Great Lover." When he died, an 11-block-long crowd of over 100,000 gathered at New York City funeral. There were riots and suicides.

VALHALLA   In Norse mythology, dead heroes were brought to Valhalla. Odin, the most important god, held court and feasted with fallen warriors on food served by supernatural battle maidens, the Valkyries.

VALIUM   Brand name for one of the benzodiazepines. Manufactured by Roche Products, Inc. Most widely used tranquilizer; taken to relieve nervousness. Tolerance may develop rapidly. To discontinue use, dosage must be decreased gradually.

VALLEE, RUDY (1901–   )   Crooning idol of the late 1920s known as "The Vagabond Lover," turned character actor. Movies include *The Palm Beach Story* (1942), *The Bachelor and the Bobbysoxer* (1947) and *How to Succeed in Business Without Really Trying* (1967), recreating stage role.

VAMPIRE   A corpse that supposedly comes back to life. Superstition has it that 1) they require fresh blood which they obtain by biting necks of sleeping victims, 2) they abhor smell of garlic and 3) they have no reflection or shadow.

VAN DYCK, SIR ANTHONY (1599–1641) Flemish painter and etcher. After Charles I of England appointed him Painter-in-Ordinary to English Court, his work set style in English portraiture for the next century.

VAN GOGH, VINCENT (1843–1890) Dutch Post-Impressionist painter. Signed paintings "Vincent." Best known for swirling colors of work painted during last two years of life (*Starry Night, Cypress Road*), foreshadowing Expressionist movement. *Potato Eaters* (1885) an earlier masterpiece. Epilepsy and depression drove him to suicide during painting of *Wheatfield with Crows*. Two years earlier, had cut off part of left ear after argument with friend and French painter Paul Gauguin, hence painting titled *Self-Portrait with Bandaged Ear*. Tempestuous life inspired Irving Stone's novel *Lust for Life*, later 1953 film with Kirk Douglas as Van Gogh and Anthony Quinn as Gauguin.

VAN PELT, LUCY AND LINUS. See SCHULZ, CHARLES MONROE

VARIETY Official newspaper of show business. Founded 1905. Unique language used in stories and headlines. "Nix pix in stix" means audiences in secondary markets aren't attending movies.

VARIG AIRLINES Founded 1927 in Porto Alegra, Brazil. Largest private airline outside U.S. Owned by employees of Ruben Berta Foundation, not government. Flies 60 aircraft to 50 cities around world.

VATICAN CITY Smallest independent state in world. Located entirely within commune of Rome, Italy. Spiritual and governmental center of Roman Catholic Church. Covers only 1/6 sq. mi. (.4 sq. km.). Contains St. Peter's Basilica, world's largest Christian church, which stands over tomb believed to contain body of Saint Peter, first Pope. City's armed forces are Swiss Guards who protect Pope, Vatican City's absolute ruler. Has own mail, telephone, telegraph systems, bank and rarely occupied jail. The Vatican, in which the Pope lives, is world's largest residence occupied by one person.

VEGETABLES The edible parts of plants, not including fruits and grains. Except for perennial crops asparagus and rhubarb, all vegetables must be replanted every year. Technically, tomatoes, peppers, eggplants and squashes are fruits. Scientific name for the beet is *beta vulgaris.*

VENETIAN BLIND   Window blind made of slats. Developed by Japanese who used bamboo rods. Named for their popularity in Venice in 1600s.

VENI, VIDI, VICI   Latin phrase meaning, "I came, I saw, I conquered." Written by Julius Caesar in his *Commentaries* on Gallic Wars. Starting in 58 B.C., Caesar conquered Gaul (France) and added to Roman Empire.

VENICE   Italian city made of 120 islands in Adriatic Sea. Nicknamed "Bride of the Sea." Has canals instead of streets, and boats instead of cars, buses, taxis and trucks. Today, motorboats have replaced most of the gondolas (black, flat-bottomed boats that were previously chief means of transportation). The Grand Canal is main waterway of city, and is spanned by Rialto Bridge in city's center.

VENUS   The second planet from the sun and only slightly smaller than Earth in size and mass. Surrounded by light-reflecting clouds, making it the most visible planet. Often brightest object in sky, it is called both evening and morning star. Earth's twin, reflecting similarity in size. Rotates once every 243 days, making it planet with longest day. Only planet to rotate in retrograde (opposite) direction from its orbit around sun.

VENUS DE MILO   Greek marble statue of Venus, Roman goddess of vegetation (later equated with Aphrodite, Greek goddess of love, beauty and fertility). Sculpted between 5th and 2nd century B.C. Found on island of Melos, 1820. Presented to the Louvre, Paris, by French King Louis XVIII. Statue's arms destroyed while buried for centuries. Artist unknown.

VERMONT   Only New England state not on Atlantic coastline. Half of state, however, is bordered by water: the Connecticut River forms eastern border, Lake Champlain extends half the length of western border. Known for Green Mountains.

VERNAL EQUINOX   March 21, or March 20 in leap years. Poles are equidistant from sun. Duration of day and night, equal. Term from Latin *ver* meaning "spring," *aequus* meaning "equal" and *nox* meaning "night." Marks first day of spring.

VERNE, JULES (1828–1905)   French novelist. More than 50 of his adventure and science fiction books—frequently adapted into modern films—predicted such 20th-century inventions as submarines, aqualungs, television and space travel. Among his works: *Five Weeks in a Balloon* (1863), *A Journey to the Center of the Earth* (1864), *Twenty Thousand Leagues Under the Sea* (1870) and *Around the World in Eighty Days* (1873). Best known characters include: Phileas Fogg, hero of *Around the World in Eighty Days*. Undertakes and wins bet made in London club that he can go around world in 80 days. Trip begins and ends there. David Niven won Oscar as Fogg in Todd A-O Best Picture of 1956. Total winner, five Oscars. Captain Nemo, commander of *Nautilus*, electricity-powered submarine that cruises world terrorizing shipping in *Twenty Thousand Leagues Under the Sea*.

VERRAZANO-NARROWS   BRIDGE   Longest suspension bridge in world. Crosses Narrows Channel between Brooklyn and Staten Island in New York City. Center span is 4,260 ft. (1,2968 m.).

VERSAILLES, TREATY OF   Marked end of World War I. Signed by allied nations and Germany, November 11, 1918 at 11 A.M. U.S. helped write treaty but never signed. Stipulated Germany would compensate Allies for war expenses and damages. Limited Germany's armed forces to 100,000 men, confiscated Germany's overseas possessions and redrew its borders. Germany considered the treaty unfair. Violated by Adolf Hitler, 1935, when he expanded his army to 600,000 men.

VESPUCCI, AMERIGO (1454?–1512)   Italian explorer claiming discovery of American continent, 1497. Christopher Columbus explored islands in western hemisphere in 1492, but thought he was in Indies, and did not dispute Vespucci's claim. Name was given to South America and came into use for North America as well. Historians no longer believe he was actual discoverer.

VIA DOLOROSA or THE WAY OF SORROWS   Path to Mt. Golgotha, or Calvary, along which Jesus of Nazareth walked to his crucifixion.

VIA VENETO   Street in Rome lined with cafés, tea rooms and fashionable shops. Address of Santa Maria della Concezione (church built in 1624), and U.S. Embassy and Consulate.

VICHYSSOISE   Potato-and-leek cream soup, served cold, created by chef Louis Diat at Ritz-Carlton Hotel, New York City, c. 1910. Named after Vichy, France, near where he grew up. During and after World War II, chefs in New York tried to change soup's name to *crème gauloise* because of animosity to Nazi puppet regime established in Vichy during war.

VICTORIA CROSS English medal for great heroism at war. Granted only to members of armed forces. First given by Queen Victoria, 1856. Reads "For Valour." Second highest medal, George Cross, available to civilians as well.

VICTORIA STATION London's chief train station. Provides transport to major cities of Continent such as Paris with Sealink service. Two million passengers travel to and from Continent through this station annually.

VICTORIA, QUEEN ALEXANDRINA (1819–1901) Queen of England, 1837– 1901, longest rule of any British monarch. Born of German Royal House of Hanover. Fluent in both English and her native German. After proposing to Prince Albert of Saxe-Coburg-Gotha, October 15, 1839, she married him February 10, 1840. Her rule during height of British Empire spanned years including two assassinations in U.S.: Abraham Lincoln, 1865, and James A. Garfield, 1881. Had she lived a few months longer, assassination of President William McKinley (1901) would have been added to list. Known for her personal austerity, Victorian Age bears her name. Adjective *Victorian* has come to mean stuffy, prudish and hypocritical.

VIDAL, GORE (1925–   ) American novelist, playwright and critic. Wrote *Myra Breckenridge* (1962) about transsexual. Myra (once Myron) seduces both Rusty Goodowski and his girlfriend Mary-Ann Pringle. Raquel Welch starred in 1970 film version. Also wrote *1876* (1976), second volume of trilogy, with *Burr* (1973) and *Washington, D.C.* (1967), published during U.S. Bicentennial. Traces U.S. history from break with British Empire to U.S. ascendancy as imperial power. Aaron Burr's son Charlie Schuyler (also narrator of *Burr*) narrates. He returns to U.S. after four decades in Europe, hoping to marry his widowed daughter into New York aristocracy.

VIDEO CASSETTE RECORDER or VCR Machine commonly used for recording television programs for future viewing. Hooks directly into TV. Addition of video camera enables produc-

tion of videotapes. VCR translates taped material into picture on
TV screen.

VIDEO DISPLAY TERMINAL   Abbreviated VDT, is
where most computers display information. VDTs are similar to
television sets and sometimes called cathode ray tubes (CRT).

VIENNA   Capital and largest city of Austria. Famous for opera
houses and art galleries. Home of Beethoven, Brahms, Mozart. Called
Wien in German. Lent name to Wiener schnitzel (Vienna cutlet), a
breaded veal cutlet.

VIETNAM WAR   Conflict in Indochinese peninsula of Southeast Asia. Began as guerilla civil war, late 1950s. U.S. involvement,
1964–1975, the longest commitment of U.S. troops to war in history. Combat action instantly transmitted via satellite to thousands
of U.S. households nightly. The conflict soon became known as
the "living room war." Peace talks beginning in Paris, 1973, frequently encountered obstacles. At one point talks broke off in a
disagreement over the shape of table.

VIKING I   Along with Viking II, most complex unmanned spacecraft yet developed. Designed to withstand 20 to 30 hours of dry
heat (125°C, 257°F) necessary to meet international guidelines on
planetary quarantine. Soft-landed on Mars, July 20, 1976.

VILLA, PANCHO (1877–1923)   Radical revolutionary leader
of Mexican War, 1910. Helped to overthrow President Diaz. Controlled portions of northern Mexico until he was killed in ambush.

VINCE LOMBARDI TROPHY   Silver football sitting atop
spike, given to winner of annual Super Bowl football game pitting
American Conference Champion vs. National Conference Cham-
pion, held in mid-January. Trophy named after late coach of Green
Bay Packers and Washington Redskins before Super Bowl V, 1971.
Lombardi died September 3, 1970.

VIRGIN ISLANDS   Two groups of small islands lying between Caribbean Sea and Atlantic Ocean. One group (St. Croix,
St. John, St. Thomas) is called the Virgin Islands of the U.S.; was
sold to U.S. for $25 million by Denmark, 1917. Other group (British
Virgin Islands) includes Anegada, Jost van Dyke, Tortola and Virgin
Gorda Islands; Islands named for St. Ursula, a British martyr, and
her 11,000 maidens.

VIRGIN MARY   Virgin mother of Christ. Popular subject for artists since death of Christ. Depicted more often than any other woman. Usually in red tunic with blue mantle. Often shown in one of "Five Joyful Mysteries" or "Seven Sorrows."

VIRGINIAN, THE Popular TV Western from 1962–1971. James Drury played "The Virginian," who fought for law and order in Wyoming territory. First ninety-minute Western series.

VISIT FROM ST. NICHOLAS, A. See MOORE, CLEMENT CLARKE.

VITAMIN B Like vitamin C, is water-soluble vitamin, as opposed to fat-soluble vitamins A, D, E and K. Includes thiamine (B1), necessary to prevent the disease beriberi; riboflavin (B2), important to derive energy from food; and niacin, which prevents the disease pellagra. Also, pyridoxine (B6), pantothenic acid, biotin, folic acid and others.

VITAMIN C Or ascorbic acid. Best sources: citrus fruits, fresh vegetables and potatoes. Deficiency affects joints, bones, mouth and capillaries; may result in scurvy. May play role in wound-healing, infectious disease, and stress reactions.

VOCAL CORDS Two bands of elastic tissue located in larynx or voice box. Their vibration produces human voice. Men's are longer than women's, therefore men's voices are deeper.

VOLCANO NATIONAL PARK One of Hawaii's two national parks, on island of Hawaii. Contains state's only active volcanoes: Mauna Loa and Kilauea. Highway passing near crater of Kilauea led to nickname, "drive-in volcano."

VOLGA RIVER Europe's longest river. Flows for 2,194 mi. (3,531 km.). Located entirely within Russia. Drains into Caspian Sea, which is approximately ⅓ of the European Soviet Union.

VOLLEYBALL Team game with six players on each side. After server hits ball with hand into opponents' court, receiving team may touch it up to three times before sending it back over net. If two or more teammates touch ball at same moment, counts as two touches, except when front-line players are attempting to block ball coming over net. If ball not returned after three touches, or return falls out of bounds, point is over. Only serving team can score points, however. If serving team loses point, it loses serve.

VON BRAUN, WERNHER (1912–1977) Leading rocket

engineer. Directed building of rockets which sent Americans into space and to moon. Born in Germany, he helped develop V-2 rocket which Nazis used against Allies in World War II.

VON RICHTHOFEN, BARON MANFRED (1892– 1918) German aviator. Leading air ace, World War I. Flew red Fokker triplane. Became known as "Red Baron" or "Red Knight." To become an ace, a term originating in World War I, pilot must down five enemy aircraft during war. The Red Baron shot down 80. He died when his own plane was shot down by Captain Roy Brown of Royal Viking Corps.

VONNEGUT, KURT (1922–   ) American novelist and short story writer. One of 1960s' most popular writers among young adults. Novels reflect disenchantment with modern society. *Slaughterhouse-Five* (1969), based on personal experiences in World War II prisoner-of-war camp. About Billy Pilgrim, American soldier who witnesses firebombing of Dresden while prisoner. Other novels: *Cat's Cradle* (1963), *Player Piano* (1951), *Slapstick* (1976), and *Breakfast of Champions* (1973).

VOODOO Religious and magical beliefs of certain tribes in West Africa. Includes belief that enemies may be injured by sticking pins into wax figures of their images. Also practiced in Haiti.

VOSGES MOUNTAINS Mountain range in northeastern France. Separated on south from Juca Mountains by Belfort Gap. Highest point is Ballon de Guebweiller, at 4,672 ft. (1,401 m.).

VSOP Abbreviation for "Very Superior Old Pale" found on many bottles of brandy. Quality brandies classified by letters: C = cognac; E = extra or especial; F = fine; O = old; P = pale; S = superior; V = very; X = extra. Combinations of these letters have significance; V.O., V.S.O.P. (or the word Reserve) indicate cognac has been aged in wood at least 4½ years. V.S.O.P. cognacs usually aged seven to ten years. (see BRANDY; COGNAC).

VTOL Type of aircraft that can only take off and land vertically. Unlike a helicopter, has fixed wings and can travel more rapidly. First model, U.S. Navy Convair XFY-1, or "Pogo Stick," test-flown 1954.

WAGGA WAGGA   Town in New South Wales, Australia, on Murrumbidgee River. Grows wheat and fruit.

WAILING WALL   Wall in Jerusalem that formed western wall of Jews' holy Temple in Biblical times. In 1700s, Arabs permitted Jews to gather at the wall, where they bewailed their lost city. In 1948, Jordanians prohibited new state of Israel from using it. Jews regained access in 1967 after Arab–Israeli War.

WAKE ISLAND   U.S. possession in Pacific Ocean. Triangular atoll made of three small coral islands: Wake, Peale and Wilkes. U.S. claimed it in 1899 because it lay on cable route from San Francisco to Manila, Philippines.

WAKE UP, LITTLE SUSIE   Song by Everly Brothers (Don and Phil) banned in Boston because of suggestive lyrics. Other hit songs by the Everlys: "Bye, Bye, Love," "All I Have to Do is Dream" and "Bird Dog."

WALCOTT, JOSEPH (JERSEY JOE) (1914–   )   Born Arnold Cream. Became at 37 oldest man in modern ring history to win heavyweight boxing title by knocking out Ezzard Charles, July 18, 1951. Made one successful title defense (against Charles in 1952). Fought for, and lost title on record six other occasions: vs. Joe Louis (1947 and 1948); vs. Charles (1949 and 1951); vs. Rocky Marciano (1952 and 1953). Floyd Patterson and Charles each lost four title fights.

WALESA, LECH (1943–   )   Polish union leader. Originally an electrician, fired for organizing a strike. Founded Solidarity, first legally sanctioned union in a Soviet bloc country, on September 1, 1980. Government dissolved union when it declared martial law, December 13, 1981.

WALKER, MOSES FLEETWOOD (1857–1924) First black baseball player to play in major leagues, in Toledo with American Association (then considered a major league) in 1884. After season, group headed by Chicago White Sox star Cap Anson sought to have blacks banned. Brother Welday Walker also played for Toledo, 1884. Blacks didn't appear again in major league baseball until Jackie Robinson played with Brooklyn Dodgers, 1947.

WALKING TALL Popular 1973 feature film starring Joe Don Baker as Tennessee Sheriff Buford Pusser, who wages a one-man war against crime in his area. Based on a true story.

WALL STREET Short, narrow street in New York City which forms financial district along with Broad and New Streets. In 1653, was northern limits of town Nieuw Amsterdam, when Governor Peter Stuyvesant ordered a protective wall to be built to keep out the English.

WALLACE, GEORGE CORLEY (1919–   ) American politician. Democratic governor of Alabama, 1963–1967, 1970–1979, 1982–present. At his inauguration he promised, "segregation now, segregation tomorrow and segregation forever." Considered public school integration a state matter; opposed federal intervention. Ran for presidential election 1964, 1968, 1972. Most successful in 1968, finishing third behind Nixon and Humphrey. Shot by Arthur Bremer campaigning for 1972 presidential election in Laurel, MD. Left partially paralyzed.

WALLACE, IRVING (1916–   ) American novelist whose works include *The Chapman Report* (1960); *The Prize* (1962); *The Man* (1964), about the first black president, U.S. Senator Douglas Dilman, who becomes president after the president, vice-president, and Speaker of the House die; book climaxes in impeachment proceeding. With his son, David Wallechinsky, created "entertainment reference books." *The People's Almanac* (1975); *The People's Almanac II* (1978); *The People's Almanac III*. With son, daughter, and wife Sylvia, wrote *The Intimate Sex Lives of Famous People* (1981), 250 sketches of the idiosyncracies of the well-known.

WALLACE, LURLEEN BURNS (1926–1968) American

politician. Governor of Alabama, 1967–1968. Succeeded husband George Wallace, becoming Alabama's first female chief executive. Third female governor in U.S. history. Died of cancer, May 7, while still in office.

WALLACES, THE. See WALLACE, IRVING

WALRUS, THE. See CARROLL, LEWIS

WALSTON, RAY (1917–　　) Comedic character actor of stage and screen. Portrayed the devil in Broadway and movie versions of *Damn Yankees*. Other films include *South Pacific* (1958) and *The Apartment* (1961). Starred as Uncle Martin on TV's *My Favorite Martian* (1963).

WALTERS, BARBARA (1931–　　) Former *Today Show* co-host, made news when she signed a $5 million, five-year contract with ABC-TV as co-anchor with Harry Reasoner (and as the first woman anchorperson) on the *ABC Evening News* in 1976.

WAMBAUGH, JOSEPH (1937–　　) Member Los Angeles Police Department, 1960–1974. Published first novel, *The New Centurions* (1971). Also wrote police novels *The Blue Knight*, *The Onion Field* and *The Choirboys*. Created TV series *Police Story* (1973).

WAMBSGANSS, BILL (1894–　　) Cleveland Indians second baseman who turned unassisted triple play in 1920 baseball World Series. Caught line drive, stepped on second base and tagged runner coming to second from first. Cleveland beat Brooklyn Dodgers in game and Series.

WAR AND PEACE. See TOLSTOY, LEO NIKOLAY-EVICH, COUNT

WAR LOVER, THE 1962 feature film starring Steve McQueen as the captain of a Flying Fortress during World War II. Conflict arises when he and his copilot (Robert Wagner) are attracted to the same girl. Based on John Hersey's novel.

WAR OF THE ROSES (1455–1485) Power struggle between English royal houses of York and Lancaster. York used a white rose as its emblem and Lancaster, headed by Henry VI, a red rose. Occurred near end of Hundred Years' War between England and France.

WAR OF THE WORLDS, THE H.G. Wells' 1898 novel about a Martian invasion of earth has been the basis for historic radio program and spectacular motion picture. Orson Welles and his Mercury Theatre performed radio play of the story Halloween night, 1938, which created a national panic. George Pal's 1953 feature film starring Gene Barry won an Oscar for special effects. Radio version was performed at the Hotel Park Plaza.

WARHOL, ANDY (1930–   ) American artist, TV producer, and filmmaker. Leading exponent of Pop Art movement, emerging at end of 1950s. Painted comic strip heroes, Campbell soup cans, Brillo boxes and Heinz ketchup bottles, heightening color and changing scale to make them larger than life. Also did multi-image, mass-produced silk screen prints of celebrities like Marilyn Monroe and Jacqueline Kennedy, employing newspaper photographs for their likenesses. Seriously injured, June 1968, when he was shot with a .32 caliber pistol by actress Valerie Solanis; she had worked for him.

WARLOCK Also sorcerer or wizard. Male who possesses supernatural powers. Term "witch" originally used to describe men and women; now used exclusively for women. *Warlock* from Old English meaning "one that breaks oath"; "the devil."

WARM-BLOODED ANIMALS Birds and mammals. Maintain a body temperature that varies by no more than a few degrees. Insulated by fur or by layer of fatty tissue beneath skin. In humans, body temperature regulated by sweating and shivering.

WARREN REPORT. See WARREN, EARL

WARREN, EARL (1891–1974) American politician and lawyer. Chief Justice of U.S. Supreme Court, 1953–1969. Governor of California 1942, 1946, and 1950. Chaired commission later known as the Warren Commission on assassination of President John F. Kennedy. 26-volume Warren Report, 1964, concluded that assassin Oswald had not acted alone. As public property, there were no book rights. First book in history put out by five different publishers. Sold in some places for $76.00.

WARREN, ROBERT PENN (1905–   ) American author and educator. Wrote 1946 novel *All The King's Men* about rise and fall of Southern demagogue Willie Stark, based on Louisiana Senator Huey Long. Broderick Crawford won Oscar, 1949 film version.

WASHINGTON Name of more places in U.S. than any other name, all honoring George Washington. First location named for him was Fort Washington, NY, in 1776. Washington, DC was named in 1791.

WASHINGTON: BEHIND CLOSED DOORS 1977 TV mini-series on ABC based in part on John Ehrlichman's novel *The Company.* Illustrating the corruption in politics was President Monckton, portrayed by Jason Robards. Others in the cast included John Houseman, Cliff Robertson and Robert Vaughn.

WASHINGTON, GEORGE (1732–1799) Revolutionary War commander. First U.S. president, 1789–1797. Elected February 4; first inaugural address, April 30, New York City. U.S. government officially transferred from New York City to site selected by Washington, for whom it was named. In 1793, he laid cornerstone of the new capitol. Since 1800, White House has been official presidential residence. All presidents except Washington have lived there. Washington created the Purple Heart award for soldiers demonstrating great bravery. Originally, medal was a triangular piece of white cloth; today it bears his likeness. In later life he wore false teeth designed by Boston silversmith Paul Revere. They were made of wood.

WASHINGTON POST, THE 1981 Pulitzer Prize winner, feature writing awarded to reporter Janet Cooke for "Jimmy's World," description of eight-year-old heroin addict. Two days later Cooke confessed story was fabrication. 1973, *Post* won Pulitzer for "meritorious public service" for Watergate investigation. *Post* city desk reporters Bob Woodward and Carl Bernstein, aided by source "Deep Throat" and using old-fashioned legwork reporting, linked arrest of burglars who broke into Democratic headquarters in Watergate Hotel to Nixon administration and ultimately to Nixon himself. Recounted process in their book *All the President's Men.*

WASHINGTON SENATORS Became Minnesota Twins after 1960 season. Original member of American League, 1901. To replace franchise, Washington got expansion team for 1961 season, also called Senators, who moved to Arlington, TX (outside Fort Worth) after 1971 season. Washington franchises combined won only one World Series, 1924.

WASHINGTON SQUARE Center of New York City's Greenwich Village. Named for George Washington. Land was originally given to slaves. Later became the site of public hanging.

Fashionable residential district grew around it in 1820s. Arch at entrance first constructed of wood in 1889 to honor centennial of George Washington's inauguration.

WASHINGTON STATE   Only U.S. state named after a president (George Washington). His portrait appears on the state seal and flag. Original name, Territory of Columbia, was changed to Washington due to existence of District of Columbia.

WASSERMANN, AUGUST VON (1866-1925)   German bacteriologist. Discovered the Wasserman Reaction, 1906, led to development of blood test for venereal disease syphillis. Still used.

WATER   Called universal solvent because so many substances will dissolve in it. Molecular compound of two parts hydrogen, one part oxygen. Chemical bond holds hydrogen atoms together; hydrogen bond links water molecules together. Called H_2O or hydrogen hydroxide. Most common substance on earth. Only substance naturally present in three forms: liquid, solid (ice) and gas (water vapor). Satisfies thirst better than any other liquid. Average person consumes 16,000 gal. (60,600 l.) in a lifetime. Cannot be digested for energy, as it contains no calories.

WATER POLO   Two teams of seven players each, including a goalie, try to maneuver ball through net at either end of rectangular swimming pool. Started in Britain in 1870s. Olympic sport since 1900.

WATER TAPS   France: Hot—Chaud (C), Cold—Froid (F); Spain: Hot—Caliente (C), Cold—Frio (F).

WATERFALLS   World's three highest waterfalls: 1. Angel Falls, Venezuela 3,213 ft. (964 m.); 2. Yosemite, California 2,425 ft. (728 m.); 3. Mardalsfossen (southern), Norway 2,149 ft. (645 m.).

WATERFORD   Seaport on southern coast of Ireland. Known for fine crystal since 1700s.

WATERLOO BATTLEFIELD   Site of Battle of Waterloo where Napolean Bonaparte was finally defeated, 1815. Waterloo is small town south of Brussels, Belgium. Today, town has over 21,000 residents.

WATERMAN, LEWIS E. (1837-1901)   Invented fountain pen, New York City, 1884. Technically, term describes any pen with its own ink supply. Usually refers to pens with slit nibs (points). Refillable rubber bladder which held ink supply has been replaced by disposable cartridge.

WATERMELON SEED SPITTING World Championship Watermelon Seed Spitting Association (WCWSSA) holds annual contest in Paul's Valley, OK. Current record: 65 ft. 4 in., by John Wiltinson, 1980. Spitters wear twelve-inch, block-ended boots, so practice and competition spits can be measured easily without tape.

WAVES Created by wind blowing across water, causing it to vibrate at a particular rhythm. Water in a wave does not actually move forward but rather oscillates up and down.

WAY WE WERE, THE Barbra Streisand and Robert Redford starred in this 1973 love story about two people with totally different lifestyles (she a political activist, he a Waspish screenwriter) who marry and separate between the late 1930s and mid-'50s. New York's Plaza Hotel is the scene of their reunion.

WAYNE AND SHUSTER Canadian comedy team who gained fame from numerous appearances on *The Ed Sullivan Show*. They hosted a documentary series on comedy performers titled *Wayne and Shuster Take an Affectionate Look At...* (1966).

WAYNE FONTANA AND THE MINDBENDERS British rock-and-roll group of the 1960s. Had number one hit, "Game of Love" (1965), then Mindbenders went solo and songs included "A Groovy Kind of Love" (1966) and "Ashes to Ashes" (1967).

WAYNE, JOHN (1907–1979) Born Marion Michael Morrison, B-Western actor turned Hollywood star and American legend. John Ford's *Stage Coach* (1939) was Wayne's (playing "The Ringo Kid") classic role. Followed by *Red River* (1948), *The Sands of Iwo Jima* (1949) as Sgt. John Stryker, *The Searchers* (1956), *The Alamo* (1960) and *True Grit* (1969) as Rooster Cogburn, among many other films. Before lengthy acting career, attended University of Southern California on football scholarship (1925–1927). Maurice Zolotow's biography, *Shooting Star*, traces the career of "the Duke." Last film, *The Shootist* (1976).

WEAVING Craft in which weaver interlaces warp and weft. Warp are foundation threads stretched taut and lengthwise in loom; weft are those laid through warp threads in various ways to produce different kinds of cloth. Weft also called woof, filler or weaving threads.

WEBB, JACK (1920–1982)   Actor turned television producer. Gained fame portraying Sergeant Joe Friday on TV's *Dragnet*. His production company, Mark VII Ltd., has created *Adam-12* (1968), *Emergency* (1972) and *The D.A.* (1971).

WEBER,   RICHARD   ANTHONY   (DICK) (1929–   )   Bowler of the Year, 1961, 1963, 1965. Won more than 24 Professional Bowlers Association titles. Known for ability to adjust delivery before release of ball. Member of St. Louis Budweisers, holder of record for all-time highest team score.

WEBSTER, NOAH (1758–1843)   American lexicographer. Wrote extensively on language and spelling, including proposals for spelling reform. Published *A Compendious Dictionary of the English Language* (1806), first American dictionary. His crowning achievement was *An American Dictionary of the English Language* (1828). Also "Father of American copyright."

WEDDING ANNIVERSARY. See ANNIVERSARIES

WEE WILLIE WINKIE   Scottish children's poem by William Miller (1810–1872). Willie runs through town in his nightgown (at ten o'clock, not eight), peeking at the window, crying at the lock.

WEED, STEVEN. See HEARST, PATRICIA

WEIGHT MEASUREMENTS

14 pounds =	1 Stone
27$\frac{1}{32}$ grains =	1 Dram (dr.)
16 Drams =	1 Ounce (oz.)
16 Ounces =	1 Pound (lb.)
100 Pounds =	1 Hundred Weight (cwt.)
20 Hundred Weights =	1 Ton

WEIGHTLIFTING   Sport in which competitors attempt to lift weighted bar by one of two methods: snatch or clean jerk (also called jerk). In snatch, lifter pulls bar in single movement from ground to full extent of both arms vertically above head. Clean jerk has two steps: lifter brings bar to shoulders in a single movement and rests it on chest (clean); lifter then straightens bent legs and extends legs and arms, lifting bar to full extent of both arms vertically above head (jerk).

WEIMAR REPUBLIC Governed Germany from end of World War I until Hitler's Nazi takeover, 1933. So named because the German constitution was drafted in city of Weimar.

WEISSMULLER, JOHNNY (1908–1984) American Olympic swimming champion and actor. Won metals in 1924 and 1928 Olympics for 100 m. event, a race in which he held world record (under one minute), 1922. Also won 400 m. free-style, 1924. Made more Tarzan movies than any other actor. Played Jungle Jim in movies and on TV. First inductee, U.S. Swimming Hall of Fame.

WELCOME BACK, KOTTER Comedy series of late 1970s which made a star of actor John Travolta. Gabriel Kaplan starred as Gabe Kotter, teacher in Brooklyn High School assigned to academic outcasts "The Sweathogs." Program's theme song, "Welcome Back," became hit single for singer/composer John Sebastian.

WELK, LAWRENCE (1903–   ) Orchestra leader and host of long-running TV music series. Played accordian and introduced The Lennon Sisters to America. His automobile license plate reads "A1ANA2."

WELLINGTON Capital of New Zealand since 1865, when government seat moved from Auckland, due to Wellington's central location. Major seaport and one of country's most populated regions. Southernmost of all world's national capitals.

WELLS, H.G. (1866–1946) First great science fiction writer. Father was professional cricket player. Wells saw himself as more of a prophet than novelist. His 1898 book, *War of the Worlds* caused public panic in 1938 when Orson Welles broadcast his adaptation on radio as though real life. Also wrote futuristic novels. *The Time Machine*, his first novel, set at the turn of century. Machine's inventor travels into future, witnessing degeneration of life on earth. Wrote *The Invisible Man*.

WELSH NATIONAL EMBLEM. See UNITED KINGDOM EMBLEMS

WEMBLEY STADIUM Located in London suburb Middlesex. Built for British Empire Exhibition, 1924–1925. Decision to build not made until agreement reached with English Football Association for stadium's use for annual F.A. Cup final. Work completed on 100,000-seat stadium four days before 1923 F.A. Cup final. Cup symbolizes championship of amateur soccer in England and is played at stadium each May.

WENDY. See CASPER, THE FRIENDLY GHOST

WEST BERLIN In 1945, Berlin, Germany's capital, was divided into four zones among World War II's major Allied Countries. After war, the eastern half of Germany, which included Berlin, was given to Russia by Allied Forces. However, non-Communist forces gave their section of city to new, free West Germany. Although West Berlin is now West Germany's capital, it has no voting rights, and most government offices are in Bonn. West Berlin is served by Tegel, Tempelhof and Gatow airports.

WEST GERMAN BANKS Three largest (in order): Deutsche Bank, Dresdner Bank, Commerz Bank.

WEST QUODDY HEAD, MAINE. See U.S. EXTREMITIES

WEST SIDE STORY Oscar-winning Best Picture of 1961, based on hit Broadway musical. A modern-day *Romeo and Juliet*, set in New York, as two rival gangs, the Jets from the West Side, and the Sharks, a Puerto Rican group, battle for the streets. Movie starred Natalie Wood as Maria, opposite Richard Beymer as Tony.

WEST, MAE (1892–1980) Playwright, actress and comedienne, the original larger-than-life sex symbol of 1930s Hollywood. Witty lines, such as "When I'm good, I'm very good, but when I'm bad I'm even better," and "It's not the men in my life, it's the life in my men," she wrote herself; said "Come up and see me sometime" to Cary Grant in *She Done Him Wrong* (1933). Films include *I'm No Angel* (1933), *Klondike Annie* (1936) and *Myra Breckinridge* (1969). Last film, *Sextette* (1978).

WEST, MORRIS L. (1916–   ) Australian novelist. Wrote best-sellers *The Devils Advocate* (1959) and *The Shoes of the Fisherman* (1963) which reflect his background as a Christian Brother. In *Shoes*, 50-year-old Russian bishop who spent 17 years in labor camps is elected Pope Kiril I, then tries to settle tensions between Russia and the U.S. Anthony Quinn starred in 1968 film version.

WESTERN WHITE HOUSE Nixon's house in San Clemente, CA. Dubbed Western White House because he often used it for "working vacations."

WESTMINSTER ABBEY   National church of England. Located in London near Houses of Parliament. Except for Edward V and Edward VIII, all English rulers were crowned here. Burial place of honored Britons. Great English poets buried in Poets' Corner.

WESTMORELAND, WILLIAM CHILDS (1914–)   American general. Headed U.S. Military Assistance Command, Vietnam, 1964–1968. Presided over build-up of U.S. troop involvement from roughly 25,000 men to several hundred thousand by time he left.

WHALES   Mammals uniquely geared for life in the oceans. They have little hair, no sense of smell, no back limbs, and front limbs that have become flippers. Blue whale is largest animal on earth, measuring over 100 ft. and weighing nearly 200 tons.

WHAT'S MY LINE?   The longest-running nighttime game show. Premiered February 16, 1950 on CBS and lasted until 1967. Hosted by John Daly, Arlene Francis was only permanent panelist; she was joined throughout the years by Dorothy Kilgallen, Bennett Cerf, Steve Allen and Hal Block. Contestants were quizzed by panel members who tried to determine what contestants did for a living.

WHAT'S NEW, PUSSYCAT?   Popular 1965 comedy film starring Peter O'Toole as a fiancé reluctant to give up his girlfriends. Peter Sellers plays his psychiatrist; Woody Allen wrote the screenplay and appears as a wardrobe man in a strip club.

WHAT'S UP, TIGER LILY?   Woody Allen's 1966 film, in which he took a Japanese "secret agent vs. gangsters" film and re-dubbed it into a comedy about an international plot to steal recipe for best egg salad in world.

WHATEVER HAPPENED TO BABY JANE?   1962 film starring Bette Davis and Joan Crawford. Story concerns the psychopathic relationship between two sisters, one a former child vaudeville star, the other a crippled ex–silent movie star. Davis torments Crawford by serving her a dead rat for dinner.

WHEAT   The largest food crop in the world. One of the first agricultural products, having been cultivated since prehistoric times. More than 300 million tons of wheat grown yearly in the world.

WHIP   Politcal party member in U.S. Congress. Enforces attendance and discipline. Office formally initiated into the House, 1899, and into the Senate, 1913. Origins in British Parliament, where not voting with "whip" is tantamount to withdrawing from the party.

WHISKERS AND HAIR   Grows on all mammals, although whales and hippos have very little. Humans have hair on all parts of the body except palms and soles. Human scalp has average of 100,000 hairs and an average man's face has 13,000 whiskers. Average eyebrow has 550 hairs.

WHISKEY-A-GO-GO   First discotheque in America. Opened by Elmer Valentine, 1963, on Sunset Boulevard, Hollywood, CA. Remains one of the best rock/dancing clubs.

WHISTLER, JAMES (1834–1903)   American painter. The model for *The Artist's Mother*, Whistler's most famous painting, was his real mother. Excelled as etcher, lithographer and watercolorist as well.

WHITE HOUSE, THE   Located at 1600 Pennsylvania Avenue, Washington DC. Residence of all presidents since John Adams lived there in 1800. One-half million tourists visit annually and are only permitted to see five of the 132 rooms. They are: State Dining Room, Red Room, Blue Room, Green Room, East Room. Telephone number: (202) 456-1414.

WHITE NILE. See LAKE VICTORIA

WHITE, EDWARD H. II (1930–1967)   U.S. astronaut. 1965, first American to walk in space. Walk lasted 21 min. Died, 1967, aboard Apollo spacecraft being tested at what was then called Cape Kennedy.

WHITE-WALLED TIRES   To a "hot-rodder," "snowballs" or "marshmallows," are slang expressions used derogatorily, since hot rods (cars whose motors have been supercharged for high speed) always use black tires called "slicks," wide, smooth-tread tires shaved on bevel for asphalt track racing. Tires also called "baloneys," "doughnuts," "gums," "hoops," "rubbers," "skins," "sneakers" and "wheels."

WHITEMAN, PAUL (1890–1967)   Bandleader known as "King of Jazz," popular since 1920s. Many famous musicians and performers first appeared with his orchestra, including Bing Crosby, and Tommy and Jimmy Dorsey. Premiered George Gershwin's *Rhapsody in Blue* at New York's Aeolian Hall.

WHITER SHADE OF PALE, A hit 1967 song by British rock group Procol Harum. Song is combination of rock, classical Bach and mystical lyrics that mention sixteen vestal virgins.

WHITNEY, ELI (1765–1825) American inventor. Created cotton gin, machine for cleaning cotton. Revolutionized the industry, making it profitable. Also invented machine for producing standardized gun parts. Father of mass production.

WHITWORTH, KATHY (1939–   ) First woman golfer to win $1 million, passing mark in 1981 (JoAnne Carner and Donna Caponi also passed $1 million later in 1981). Leading woman money winner of Ladies Professional Golfers Association tour eight times; LPGA Player of the Year, seven times; twice Associated Press Woman Athlete of the Year.

WHO'S AFRAID OF VIRGINIA WOOLF? 1966 film based on Edward Albee hit Broadway play. A middle-aged history professor and his wife, portrayed by Richard Burton and Elizabeth Taylor, get together with a younger couple, George Segal and Sandy Dennis, for an evening of bitter conversation. Taylor won Oscar for Best Actress. (see ALBEE, EDWARD FRANKLIN)

WICKED WITCH OF THE WEST. See WIZARD OF OZ, THE

WIESENTHAL, SIMON (1908–   ) Austrian Jew. Founded Jewish Documentation Center in Vienna, 1961. Serves as information-clearing house on the World War II holocaust. Helped catch more than 1,100 suspected Nazi war criminals.

WILD ONE, THE 1954 film starring Marlon Brando as Johnny, leader of motorcycle gang terrorizing small town. Co-starring Lee Marvin and Robert Keith.

WILDE, OSCAR (1854–1900) Irish playwright. Wrote *The Importance of Being Earnest* (1895) and *The Picture of Dorian Gray* (1891). Served two years at hard labor (1895–1897) for homosexual offenses, inspiring two of his poems, "The Ballad of Reading Gaol" (1898) and "De Profundis" (1905).

WILDER, THORNTON NIVEN (1897–1975) American novelist and playwright. His novel, *The Bridge of San Luis Rey* (1927), based on life stories of five victims in 1714 Peru bridge disaster, won 1928 Pulitzer Prize for Fiction. Also won Pulitzer for play *Our*

Town (1938). Play *The Merchant of Yonkers* (1938), revised as *The Matchmaker* (1954), adapted into 1960s musical *Hello Dolly!*

WILHELM, HOYT (1923-   ) Major league pitcher, 1952-1972. Specialized in knuckleball (knuckler), an unpredictable, slow pitch thrown with no rotation on ball. Appeared in record 1,070 games for NY Giants, Baltimore Orioles, Chicago White Sox, others. Lifetime: 143-122. Low 2.52 Earned Run Average. Saves as relief pitcher numbered 277.

WILLIAM TELL Legendary 14century Swiss hero. Austrian tyrant forced him to shoot arrow through apple on his son's head. Used second arrow to kill tyrant and start rebellion. Story used by Schiller in play *Wilhelm Tell* (1804) and in Rossini opera of same name (1829), which yielded overture used as theme for *The Lone Ranger* TV series.

WILLIAMS, THOMAS LANIER (TENNESSEE) (1911-1983) American playwright. Often deals with controversial themes like homosexuality, cannabalism and castration. Major works include *The Glass Menagerie* (1945), his first Broadway play, about crippled girl Laura who retreats into fantasy world with her collection of glass animals. *A Streetcar Named Desire* (1947), story of neurotic Blanche Dubois who lives with her sister Stella and Stella's brutish husband Stanley. Won 1947 Pulitzer Prize in Drama. Vivien Leigh (Blanche), Kim Hunter and Karl Malden all won Oscars in 1951 film version, but T-shirted Marlon Brando's Stanley was his breakthrough role. *Cat on a Hot Tin Roof* (1955), about family of "Big Daddy" Pollitt, won Williams his second Pulitzer. Son's wife Maggie is "Cat." *The Rose Tattoo* (1951), contained uncharacteristic humor. Williams tells story of widowed Sicilian dressmaker who falls in love with young truckdriver who, like her husband, has rose tattoo on his chest. *The Night of the Iguana* (1959), first produced in Italy, opened in New York, 1961. Concerns Shannon and Hannah, down on their luck in Mexico. John Huston's 1964 film version starred Richard Burton, Ava Gardner and Deborah Kerr.

WILLIAMS, TED (1918-   ) Baseball outfielder with Boston Red Sox, 1939-1960. "Splendid Splinter" or "The Thumper." One of best batters of all time. Last major leaguer to hit .400 for season (.406, 1941). Won six batting titles. Won Triple Crown 1942, 1947. Won batting crown at age 40 and homered in last at-bat. Hall of Fame, 1966.

WILLIG, GEORGE (1949–)   Arrested for climbing the south tower of the Word Trade Center, May 26, 1977. Sued by the city for $250,000.00. Case settled when Mayor Abraham Beame accepted $1.10—or one cent for each floor of building.

WILLS, FRANK (1946–)   Night watchman, Watergate apartment complex. Discovered burglary of Democratic headquarters, triggering investigation of Watergate scandal, which culminated in Nixon's 1974 resignation.

WILSON, WOODROW (1856–1924)   Twenty-eighth U.S. president, 1913–1921. Defeated in 1920 by Republican Warren Harding. After attempting neutrality, eventually entered World War I, 1917. Strong force in League of Nations. Formerly, New Jersey governor, and president of Princeton University. Died and buried in Washington DC. Only president buried there.

WIMBLEDON   Town on southwestern outskirts of London which has hosted the All-England Lawn Tennis Club Championships (commonly called Wimbledon championships) since 1877. World's oldest tennis tournament. Still played exclusively on grass courts. Town's stability, rich tradition, dignity and style create atmosphere making it tennis' premiere event. Traditions include serving of strawberries and cream, and after-tournament formal ball honoring winner.

WIMPY   J. Wellington Wimpy was introduced in the Popeye comic strip as fight referee, but stayed around to become Popeye's famous hamburger-eating pal. His famous line: "I will gladly pay you on Tuesday for a hamburger today."

WINCHELL, PAUL (1924–)   TV ventriloquist who shared the spotlight with most popular of his dummies, Jerry Mahoney. Since 1947, Winchell and Mahoney were seen regularly through early 1970s. Other Winchell dummies include Knucklehead Smith and Ozwald.

WINDSHIELD WIPERS   Invented in 1920 by W.M. Folberth. Operated by suction. First electric windshield wipers appeared in U.S. in 1923 and became standard equipment by late 1920s, along with electric starters, safety glass, all-steel bodies and low pressure tires, as drivers became more safety conscious.

WINDSOR. See BRITISH ROYAL FAMILY

WINDSOR CASTLE   Located in Windsor, England. Chief

residence of Great Britain's royal family. Built by William the Conqueror. Consists of several chapels, towers and lawns. Lies near the River Thames. Largest inhabited castle.

WINE   Fermented juice of grape (can also be made from other berries). Usually classified according to color—red, white or rose (pink)—and other species characteristics of grape it is made from. White wines have more subtle flavor than reds and go best with meats that are also subtle: fish, chicken, veal. Factors governing appreciation of wine are bouquet, body and taste. Bouquet applies to wine's aroma, coming from perfume emitted in form of esters. More than three-fourths of wine's taste actually stems from its smell. Wine said to have body when it produces sensation in mouth resulting from harmonious combination of strength, flavor and content of essence and tannin. Color gives first indication of wine's body: deeper the color, fuller the wine.

Glass placement: Should be set to the upper right of the plate (viewed from above). Water glass goes closest to plate, then sherry glass (for soup course) to its right, then wine glass. Glasses go on same side of plate as knives.

Tastevin: French word, from *taster* meaning "to touch or taste" plus *vin* meaning "wine." Shallow silver cup often worn hung around neck, used by *sommelier* (wine steward) for tasting wine. Steward will present wine, uncork it, pour a little into *tastevin* and sip it to ensure it has not turned to vinegar.

WINE CONSUMPTION   Wine consumption per capita (latest available data, 1982) by country in gallons consumed per person in one year: Argentina, 19.4; France, 22.7; Italy, 21.9; Portugal, 20.7; Spain, 15.1.

WINE TYPES   *Bordeaux:* Wines of Bordeaux region of France, aged in oak barrels, called "the queens of wines." Red Bordeaux, called claret, more delicate than heavier-bodied Burgundies. Bordeaux area considered greatest wine district of world. Varieties include Medoc, Graves and St. Emilion.

Chablis: Considered a white wine, its color should be pale straw-yellow. Driest and palest of table wines. Traditionally comes from northernmost part of Burgundy, France, although varieties developed in other areas. Its distinguishing characteristic, not found in every vintage, is austere, flinty quality.

Port: Known as "Englishman's Drink" because British controlled its export from Oporto in Portugal, and actually changed it from a natural wine to the rich, fortified and sweet wine it is today.

Rhine: German wine bottles are tall and tapered; brown bottles are used for wines of Rhine River region; green bottles are used for wines of Moselle region. All Germany's great wines are white, because country is too far north for fine reds.

WINGS 1927 film, first winner of Academy Award for Best Picture, and only silent film to achieve that honor. Story concerns two buddies who join the Air Force, their battles against the enemy, and their loves. Charles "Buddy" Rogers, Richard Arlen and Clara Bow star.

WINTER Northern Hemisphere: coldest season, from winter solstice (December 22) to vernal equinox (March 20). Probably from Indo-European root meaning "to be wet." Southern Hemisphere: winter corresponds to summer in Northern Hemisphere, June through August.

WINTER SOLSTICE December 22. Marks last day of fall. Earth positioned in its orbit such that polar axis is tilted towards sun. Also occurs June 21, summer solstice. On these two days, sun is farthest from equator and appears to stand still. From Latin *sol,* meaning "sun," and *sistere,* "to stand still."

WINTER WHEAT Grown in mild climates. Planted in fall. Growth begins before cold weather sets in. Resumes growth in spring. Will not produce a crop if planted in spring. Varieties include Cheyenne, Commanche, Triump, Pannee and Seneca.

WINTERS, JONATHAN (1925–   ) Nightclub and TV comedian. Created many popular comic personas: Maudie Frickert, Chester Hunihugger, Elwood P. Suggins, etc. Appeared in films *The Loved One* (1965), and *Viva Max* (1969).

WINTERS, SHELLEY (1922–   ) American actress. Born Shirley Schrift in Brooklyn, NY. In her autobiography *Shelley: Also Known as Shirley* (1980), she described her climb to Oscar-winning success: Best Supporting Actress for *Diary of Anne Frank* (1958) and *A Patch of Blue* (1965). Book stops in mid-1950s with her bitter divorce from Vittorio Gassman. Much of her best-known work (*The Poseidon Adventure, Lolita, A Patch of Blue* and *Alfie*) came after that.

WITCH TRIALS Salem MA, 1692. Colonial court found 20 women guilty of being witches and ordered their executions. Nineteen were hanged; one pressed to death. Popular notion that accused were burned at the stake is erroneous.

WITNESS FOR THE PROSECUTION   Film drama from 1957 directed by Billy Wilder. Tyrone Power as young man on trial for murder of wealthy woman friend. Marlene Dietrich plays his wife, Charles Laughton his defense attorney. Based on Agatha Christie's novel.

WIZARD OF ID, THE   Johnny Hart, creator of B.C. comic strip, collaborated with artist Brant Parker on this daily comic strip. Debuted 1964. Kingdom of Id has grouchy midget monarch whose sorcerer's spells often backfire. Wizard's wife Blanch is huge, nagging battleax. Bung, always-inebriated jester, often plays tricks on the king and gets away with them.

WIZARD OF OZ, THE   1939 musical film based on book by Frank L. Baum. Judy Garland starred as Dorothy of Kansas who is whisked over the rainbow by a tornado. Her house comes crashing down on Wicked Witch of the East, making Dorothy a heroine in wonderful land of Oz. Helping her to find the way home are The Scarecrow (Ray Bolger), The Tin Man (Jack Haley) and The Cowardly Lion (Bert Lahr). Billie Burke played Glinda, the Good Witch of the North. En route to Emerald City, the Wicked Witch of the West (Margaret Hamilton) sky-writes "Surrender, Dorothy." Ultimately, the witch is destroyed by her weakness, water. (see BAUM, LYMON FRANK)

WODEHOUSE, PELHAM GRANVILLE. See JEEVES

WOLF   Scientific name *canis lupus*. Wild relative of dog. Can weigh over 100 lbs. Rarely attack humans in spite of reputation. In danger of extinction in continental U.S.

WOLFE, TOM (1931–   )   Author-essayist. Wrote *The Pump House Gang* (1968) about tribal nature of surfing California youth. In essay "The Me Decade and the Third Great Awakening" from 1976 collection *Mauve Gloves & Madmen, Clutter & Vine*, described "Me Decade" as reaction to togetherness of 1960s; in '70s, people cared more about themselves. Also wrote *The Right Stuff*, 1980 book about first NASA Mercury astronauts. Film version (1983) won four Oscars.

WOLFMAN JACK (1938–   )   Legendary radio disc jockey of the late 1950s. Born in Brooklyn as Robert Smith, the Wolfman gained fame from his appearance in film *American Graffiti* (1973). Has since hosted many TV shows and appeared in films.

WOLVERTON MOUNTAIN Hit song recorded by Claude King, 1962. In song, Clifton Clowers lives with his daughter at top of mountain and will prevent any suitors from taking her hand. Song was written by King and Merle Kilgore.

WOMAN SCORNED, A. See CONGREVE, WILLIAM

WONDER WOMAN Wearing star-spangled costume, Amazon princess (calling herself Diana Prince) debuted as comicbook character in December 1941. Came to America to help fight World War II. Created by writer William Moulton Marston, pen name Charles Moulton, inventor of lie detector.

WOOD, GRANT (1892–1942) American painter, primarily of midwestern farm life. Best known for *American Gothic* (1930), picturing tight-lipped farm couple in front of home, with man holding pitchfork. Wood posed his sister and her dentist friend against Gothic-style house. Sold painting to Chicago Art Institute for $300.

WOODSTOCK Music festival, August 15–18, 1969. Held on Max Yasgur's dairy farm, Bethel, NY. Originally planned for nearby village of Woodstock but legal actions interfered. Drew estimated crowd of 250,000–400,000. Performers included Jimi Hendrix, The Who, C.S.N.Y. and Arlo Guthrie, who reported that, due to massive traffic jams, "The New York Thruway is closed, man!"

WOODWARD, ROBERT UPSHUR (BOB) (1943–) One of Washington Post's Watergate reporters. With Scott Armstrong, wrote *The Brethren: Inside the Supreme Court* (1979), account of Court from 1969–1976, when it made landmark decisions on busing, abortion and Pentagon Papers. Based on interviews with several justices, 170 former clerks and other Court employees. With Carl Bernstein, earlier wrote Watergate books *All The President's Men* (1974) and *The Final Days* (1976). Also wrote *Wired: The Short Life and Fast Times of John Belushi* (1984).

WOOFER One of two speakers contained in most high fidelity loudspeakers. Reproduces low frequency, bass sounds. Other speaker, tweeter, reproduces high frequency, treble sounds. Sound loudspeakers have additional third, midrange speaker which reproduces intermediate frequency sounds.

WORLD TRADE CENTER Consists of two towers that

house offices of New York City trading firms. Controlled and owned by Port Authority of New York and New Jersey. Has 110 stories, 208 elevators and 43,600 windows. World's third tallest skyscraper, rising 1,804 ft. (550 m.) to tip of its television antenna.

WORLD WAR I (1914–1918) Called the "Great War" or "The War to End All Wars." Began on June 28, 1914 with assassination of Archduke Francis Ferdinand, event later known as "The shot heard round the world." The Archduke was heir to the crown of the Austro-Hungarian Empire. The Empire went to war against Serbia, suspecting a plot, and the rest of Europe followed because of a series of alliances. Austro-Hungary, overcome early on, was divided at the close of war into Austria, Czechoslovakia, Hungary, Yugoslavia and Rumania. Over 100 million troops were involved in the war, of which about 13 million died. The cost was estimated at $282 billion. Mustard gas, the tank, the airplane and the machine gun were introduced as weapons of modern warfare. U.S. became involved in 1916 with the hope, in the words of President Wilson, to "make the world safe for democracy". On November 11, 1918, at 11:00 A.M., the Treaty of Versailles was signed between Germany and the allied nations (except U.S.) ending the five-year conflict. Due to the delay in bringing troops home, "Wanna-Go-Home" riots allegedly occurred.

WORLD WAR II (1939–1945) German invasion of Poland, September 1, 1939 triggered a series of alliances eventually bringing total number of countries involved to 57. War cost estimated at $1.154 trillion. Soviet Union lost 7.5 million soldiers in combat, more than any other country. China lost 2.2 million; Germany, 3.5 million; Japan, 1.2 million; and U.S., 300,000. All told, approximately 55 million civilian and military deaths. First U.S. destroyer sunk, Reuben James, October 31, 1941, by German U-boat (undersea boat, i.e., submarine) on patrol. U-boats' effectiveness accounted for Allied shipping losses of approximately 23 million tons. World War II was the first war in which a black man was given rank of general in U.S. Army. (As of 1942, there were two black Army officers and no black Navy officers). Brigadier General Benjamin O. Davis was the first, and his son, by the same name, the second. (The first war during which combat forces were not segregated was the Korean War). After World War II, Germany was split into four occupation zones. Eastern zone was administered by

U.S.S.R.; is now East Germany. Rest of country and parts of Berlin divided among England, France and U.S.

WORLD'S FAIR Held twice in New York City. First in 1939 with theme "The World of Tomorrow." Promoted television, nylon and air conditioning. Second in 1964 with theme "Peace Through Understanding." Displayed color television, picture telephones and computers.

WOUK, HERMAN (1915–   ) American novelist and playwright. Consistent writer of best sellers. Among his books: *The Caine Mutiny* (1951). Captain Queeg is mentally disturbed captain of fictional U.S. Navy minesweeper in this Pulitzer Prize-winning novel, which Wouk adapted into successful Broadway play *The Caine Mutiny Court Martial*, with Lloyd Nolan as Queeg. 1954 film version starred Humphrey Bogart as the captain who revealed his anxiety by rolling two steel ball bearings in his palm. *Youngblood Hawke* (1962) is a novel about career of aspiring author, modeled partially on novelist Thomas Wolfe. James Franciscus starred in 1964 film version. *Marjorie Morningstar* (1955) is a novel about middle-class Jewish girl who falls in love with show business but ends up a suburban housewife. Natalie Wood starred in 1958 film version. *Winds of War* (1972) and *War and Remembrance* (1978) are novels centering on fictional Henry family before and during World War II. First culminates with Pearl Harbor; second traces war in Pacific and Europe through experiences of various family members. Became 1983 TV mini-series.

WREN, CHRISTOPHER (1632–1723) Seventeenth century English architect, designer, astronomer and mathematician. Helped rebuild London after the Great Fire of 1666. St. Paul's Cathedral is considered his masterpiece.

WREN, PERCIVAL CHRISTOPHER (P.C.) (1885–1941) English novelist, soldier and traveler. Known for adventure stories about life in French Foreign Legion, including bestselling *Beau Geste* (1924), about rigors endured by uppity Englishman serving in Legion in Sahara. Filmed in 1926, 1939 (with Gary Cooper) and in 1966.

WRESTLING, HALF NELSON Hold applied by placing one arm under corresponding arm of opponent and with same hand reaching up to push against back of opponent's head. Full nelson, done with both arms, is dangerous and banned in amateur competition.

WRESTLING, PROFESSIONAL   Originally serious sport of freestyle wrestling but by end of 1930s became feigned competitions and performances. Popularized through TV, matches sellout New York's Madison Square Garden and other large arenas. Pro wrestlers must hold opponents' shoulders to mat for three seconds for a pin, as opposed to two seconds in legitimate amateur bouts. Well-known professional wrestlers include Mr. Moto, who teamed with the Great Togo to form one of the top tag-teams (two-man wrestling team) of the 1950s; Lou Thesz, legendary champion of the 1940s and '50s; Gene "Big Daddy" Lipscomb, National Football League star defensive lineman with Los Angeles Rams, Baltimore Colts, Pittsburgh Steelers, 1953–1962, who pro-wrestled in off-season and after NFL retirement; and Georgeous George, George Wagner, who wrestled in 1940s and '50s, an ordinary wrestler until he decided to dye his hair blond and set it. Hired a valet to spray Chanel No. 5 perfume around ring before match. Refused to be touched by anyone outside ring. Routine made him wrestling's number one box office attraction.

WRIGHT BROTHERS, THE   Orville and Wilbur invented, built and flew first successful airplane called Kitty Hawk Flyer. First flight, December 17, 1903 at Kitty Hawk, NC with Orville at controls, lasted 120 ft. and 12 sec. Orville flew for 43 years without license. First members of the U.S. Aviation Hall of Fame: Wilber elected 1955; Orville elected 1965. September 17, 1908, Orville's passenger Thomas E. Selfridge died in world's first fatal plane crash. Orville suffered broken bones. Man joined bats as the only other flying mammals when Wilbur and Orville made their first flight.

WRIST WRESTLING   Version of arm wrestling. Instead of gripping hands, opponents interlock right thunbs, rest right elbows on high table, forming arch. Fingers of left hands are hooked on table under arch. Winner forces opponent's right arm to table, left arm to lift off table, or release grip with either hand. World championships held annually in October in Petaluma CA, north of San Francisco.

WRONG BOX, THE   1966 black comedy film about a large inheritance sought by two brothers of large British family. John

Mills and Ralph Richardson are the siblings. Peter Sellers plays an oddball doctor who uses a cat as ink blotter.

WYNDAM, JOHN (1903–1969)   English science fiction writer whose *Midwitch Cuckoos* (1957) was filmed as *Village of the Damned.* Novel *Day of the Triffids* (1951) about survivors of world struck down with blindness and plague. Menaced by hostile giant plants called Triffids that humans had developed in search of new source of vegetable oil. Film version (1963) starred Howard Keel.

WYNETTE, TAMMY (1952–   )   Country singer, songwriter and musician, popular since mid-1960s, with hits including "Apartment No. 9," "Your Good Girl's Gonna Go Bad" and "I Don't Wanna Play House." Had her biggest record in 1969 with "Stand By Your Man," and has been a regular of "Grand Ole Opry" since that time.

WYNKEN, BLYNKEN AND NOD   Children's poem by American poet-journalist Eugene Field (1850–1995). "Wynken, Blynken and Nod one night / Sailed off in a wooden shoe / Sailed on a river of crystal light / Into a sea of dew."

WYNN, ED (1886–1966)   Vaudeville, radio and television comedian, nicknamed "The Perfect Fool." Movie appearances include *Cinderfella* (1960), *Mary Poppins* (1964) and *The Greatest Story Ever Told* (1965).

WYSS, JOHANN DAVID (1743–1818)   Author of *Swiss Family Robinson* (1813), novel subtitled *Adventures on a Desert Island,* about Swiss clergyman, wife and four sons wrecked on desert island. Theatrical movie versions, 1940, 1960 (by Disney), and 1975 TV movie. Novel actually published and popularized by son Johann Rudolf Wyss (1781–1830).

X Twenty-fourth letter of English alphabet, standing for consonant combinations *KS* or sound of *Z*. Evolved from Greek letter *X*
(chi). Begins fewest words of all letters in English, with only 3 pages
in *Webster's New Third World International Dictionary*; compared to 7
pages of *Z*, 12 of *Q* and 154 of *T* (most used as initial letter).

Y

YAHTZEE Commercial and copyrighted version of dice game "yacht." Object is to score most points by throwing five dice. Scoring is in various categories, most of which conform to poker hands (e.g., three of a kind, full house, straight). Highest points (50) scored for all five dice with same number, called a "yahtzee."

YAK Ox of Asia. Relative of American bison. Inhabits cold plateaus of Tibet. Agile despite bulk of up to 1,200 lbs.(544 kg.). Domestic yak used to carry travelers and mail. Provides rich, pink milk. Lives at higher altitude than any other mammal, occasionally foraging at 20,000 ft. above sea level.

YALE UNIVERSITY One of the U.S.'s oldest schools. Located in New Haven, CT, on an arm of Long Island Sound. Its stadium, Yale Bowl, seats 70,896. Sixteen-story Payne-Whitney Gymnasium is one of the world's largest sports buildings.

YALE, LINUS JR. (1821–1868) Unsuccessful portrait painter. Invented cylinder lock, 1861. Until that time any lock could be opened simply with skeleton key.

YALTA CONFERENCE February 1945 meeting of Joseph Stalin, Franklin Roosevelt and Winston Churchill. Completed plans for final defeat of Germany, its occupation and control. Also arranged for collection of postwar reparations.

YANGSTZE RIVER Asia's longest river, third-largest in the world. Most important river in China. Known to Chinese as *Ch'ang Chiang*, meaning "long river." Also called "the child of the ocean."

City of Shanghai is on banks. Begins in T'ang-ku-la Mountains of Tsinghai Province; ends in East China Sea, 3,915 mi. (6,300 km.) from its source.

YANKEE DOODLE DANDY 1942   Film starring former vaudeville performer and Broadway actor, James Cagney, Hollywood star of 1930's, '40s and '50s who won Oscar for performance as George M. Cohan.

YANKEE STADIUM   Opened 1927. Nicknamed "House that Ruth Built" after Yankee slugger Babe Ruth who hit three-run homer on stadium's opening day. Monuments to Ruth, Lou Gehrig and 1920s Yankee manager Miller Huggins in center field; used to be in playing area, but now beyond outfield fence.

YASTRZEMSKI, CARL (1939–   )   Won American League Triple Crown in 1967 (44 homers, 121 r.b.i., .326 avg.) to lead Boston Red Sox to pennant. Red Sox lost to St. Louis Cardinals, 4-3. Retired in 1983 after 22 years with Sox.

YEAST   Microscopic single-celled fungi. Used to convert sugar into carbon dioxide and alcohol in production of bread, beer and wine. Some kinds can cause disease.

YELLOW FEVER   Viral disease. Carried by certain mosquitoes. Damages body tissues, especially liver. Liver malfunction results in yellow bile pigments gathering in skin, making it look yellow, thus name Yellow Fever.

YELLOW PERIL   Term given to rise in immigration of Japanese and Chinese, mid-19th century. Immigrants brought as laborers to build U.S. railroads. Laws passed by Congress, 1882, expressly excluded immigration.

YELLOW RIVER   Second-longest river in China. Called Huang Ho ("yellow river") because its waters carry soft, yellow earth. Known for its flooding, which brings death and hunger, hence called "China's sorrow." Worst flood killed almost one million people in 1887.

YELLOW ROSE OF TEXAS, THE   1955 hit song for musical arranger Mitch Miller. In song, Yellow Rose "beat the belles" of Texas. Miller's success with this tune led to TV series *Sing Along with Mitch* (1961–1964).

YELLOW SUBMARINE   1968 animated film featuring the music and cartoon likenesses of The Beatles. The Beatles come to aid of Pepperland by battling the Blue Meanies, who have turned everything to stone and eliminated music, love and happiness. Songs include "Nowhere Man" and "All You Need Is Love."

YELLOW-SHAFTED FLICKER Large woodpecker. Wooded regions, Canada and U.S. Gets name from loud call which sounds like word *flicker.* Also known as golden-winged woodpecker or yellowhammer.

YELLOWSTONE NATIONAL PARK Oldest national park in U.S. Has more geysers and hot springs than any other area in world. Covers area in Wyoming and spreads slightly into Idaho and Montana. Attractions include Fairy Falls, Firehole River and Minerva Terrace. Most famous attraction is Old Faithful Geyser in park's upper geyser basin. Old Faithful erupts approximately every 65 min. with boiling water, shooting up more than 100 ft. (30 m.) into air. Roosevelt Arch stands at entrance.

YEN Japan's basic unit of currency. Five coin denominations: 1, 5, 10, 50, 1,000. Paper money is printed in denominations of 100, 500, 1,000 and 10,000. Considered most difficult currency to counterfeit.

YEW Evergreen tree or shrub. Many near English Channel and in English churchyards. Branches used as funeral decorations, made into wreaths for heads of mourners. Often symbolizes sadness.

YIDDISH Yiddish words commonly used in America:
Klutz: a clod, a slow-witted person.
Gesundheit: health, said after someone sneezes.
Schlock: cheaply made article.
Kvetch: to complain, gripe.

YO-YO Toy thought to have originated in China. Became popular in 18th-century Europe. Consists of top on a string made to perform tricks like "sleeping," making yo-yo spin at end of its string until slight jerk pulls it up. Other tricks include "walking the dog" and "around the world."

YOGI BEAR Smarter than the average bear, Yogi, with his pal Boo-Boo, lived in Jellystone National Park and ate from picnickers' lunch baskets. This Hanna-Barbera cartoon TV series (1961–63) spawned a theatrical feature film, *Hey There, It's Yogi Bear* in 1964. Yogi's nemesis was Park Ranger Smith; Yogi was voiced by actor Daws Butler.

YOGI, MAHARISHI MAHESH (1911–   ) Indian spiritual leader. Best known for his association with The Beatles in the late 1960s. Through him, The Beatles learned transcendental meditation, a relaxation and enlightenment method.

YOGURT Semisolid, fermented, slightly acidic dairy product. Produced by adding *lactobacillus bulgaricus* and *streptococcus thermophilus* to whole and skimmed milk. Fermentation, a form of respiration without oxygen, produces lactic acid. Also spelled yoghurt.

YOM KIPPUR Jewish Day of Atonement. Celebrated 10 days after Rosh Hashanah, the New Year. Traditionally observed by fasting, confession and prayers for forgiveness.

YORK, ALVIN CULLUM (1887–1964) American soldier. Hero during Battle of the Argonne (Forest), World War I. Killed over 20 Germans and captured 132 others, October 8, 1918. Though widely known as Sergeant York, he was corporal at time of feat.

YORKSHIRE RIPPER, THE (1945?–   ) Or Peter Sutcliffe, a 34-year-old British truck driver. Murdered 13 women in and around Yorkshire, England (1980–1981). Pleaded temporary insanity. Claimed he had been on a divine mission to kill prostitutes. Found guilty, May, 1981. Sentenced to life in prison.

YOU BET YOUR LIFE Popular game show hosted by Groucho Marx. Players won money by answering questions, including extra $100 by saying secret word, but highlight of each show was Groucho's ad-libbed interviews with each contestant.

YOU ONLY LIVE TWICE. See FLEMING, IAN

YOUNG TOM EDISON 1940 film biography of Thomas Edison, portrayed as young man by Mickey Rooney. Edison's early childhood, first inventions and time he saved a train from being wrecked are dramatically re-created.

YOUNG, ANDREW (1932–   ) American politician. Former assistant to Martin Luther King, Jr. Early supporter of Jimmy Carter. First black American to become UN ambassador. Lost credibility for dealings with Palestinian Liberation Organization, which although it has observer status at the UN, is not recognized by U.S. Resigned, 1979. Currently mayor of Atlanta, GA.

YOUNG, BRIGHAM (1801–1877) Second president of Mormon Church. Succeeded founder Joseph Smith. Led Mormon migration to Salt Lake City, UT, reputedly with 27 wives. Fathered estimated 56 children.

YOUTH INTERNATIONAL PARTY Organization opposed to Vietnam War. Members referred to as Yippies. Nominated a pig, "Pigasus," as presidential candidate at Democratic National Convention in Chicago, August 23, 1968. Seven Yippies arrested for disorderly conduct at postconvention celebration. Tension between Yippies and police culminated in riot, August 28, 1968.

YUCATAN PENINSULA Located in southeastern Mexico separating Gulf of Mexico from Caribbean Sea. Inhabitants called Yucatehos, the descendants of Maya Indians who lived there before Spaniards settled. One of world's chief henequen-raising (material used in making rope) areas.

YUGOSLAVIA Located in southeastern Europe. Mountains cover most of country's area. Coastal region is strip of land on Adriatic Sea. Dubrovnik, a medieval seaport; Split and Rijeka are three coastal cities. Coast is made up of karst, a type of limestone. Country organized into six socialist republics corresponding to historic boundaries of its major nationality groups. They are Bosnia and Hercegovina, Croatia, Macedonia, Montenegro, Serbia and Slovenia. Established 1918 as Kingdom of the Serbs, Croats and Slovenes. Became federal republic in 1945.

YUKON RIVER Runs through Alaska and Canada's Yukon Territory. Starts in British Columbia and empties into Bering Sea.

Z

ZAIRE Large country in central Africa. King Leopold II of Belgium took control of area as personal colony in 1885, calling it Congo Free State. Taken over by Belgian government in 1908, calling it Belgian Congo. Gained independence from Belgium, 1960, renamed Congo. Country's President Mobutu changed name to Zaire, 1971, to encourage pride in African heritage.

ZAMBEZI RIVER Africa's fourth-largest river. Follows winding 600 mi. (2,570 km.) course, traveling over Victoria Falls, and emptying into Indian Ocean. First European to explore it was David Livingston, 1850s–1860s.

ZANZIBAR Largest island of group of offshore islands (also called Zanzibar) in Indian Ocean that make up part of Tanzania. Noted for cloves, coconuts and chili peppers. Formerly known as Spice Island.

ZAPRUDER, ABRAHAM (1904?–1970) Amateur moviemaker. Filmed 15-sec. close-up sequence of President Kennedy's assassination. Purchased by *Time-Life* for approximately $40,000.

ZERO HOUR "Time set for beginning of military operation." Added to English and American vocabulary during World War I.

ZIEGLER, RONALD L. (1939–   ) American political aide. Nixon's press secretary during Watergate scandal. After 1973 break-in, said: "Certain elements may try to stretch this beyond what it is." Called the break-in "a third-rate burglary attempt."

ZIPPER Or hookless fastener. Whitcomb L. Judson, inventor, obtained Patent No. 504,038, August 29, 1893, for a model designed for shoes. First manufactured, 1893, by Automatic Hook and Eye Company, Meadville, PA. Allegedly derived its name from 1926 advertisement: "Zip, it's open, zip, it's closed."

ZODIAC SIGNS

Sign	Symbol	Date of Birth
Aries	Ram	March 21–April 20
Taurus	Bull	April 21– May 22
Gemini	Twins	May 23–June 21
Cancer	Crab	June 22–July 22
Leo	Lion	July 23– August 22
Virgo	Virgin	August 23–September 22
Libra	Scales	September 23–October 22
Scorpio	Scorpion	October 23–November 21
Sagittarius	Archer	November 22–December 22
Capricorn	Goat	December 23–January 20
Aquarius	Water Carrier	January 21–February 19
Pisces	Fishes	February 20–March 20

ZODIAC, THE HOUSES Astrology. The division of horoscope into twelve parts, called houses. Each house has 30° representing the 12 characteristics in individual's life:

1) appearance and personality
2) possessions
3) family relations
4) parents
5) children
6) health
7) friends and marriage
8) death
9) travel
10) career
11) ideals
12) illness and sorrow

ZOMBIE Cocktail containing several different kinds of rum. Commonly contains lime juice, pineapple juice, syrup, apricot liqueur and light rum, medium rum, Jamaican rum and 151 proof Demeraran rum.

ZOONOSE DISEASE Or Zoonosis. Animal disease, such as malaria or rabies, that is communicable to man. Word from Greek meaning "animal," plus suffix nosos, meaning "disease."

ZOOT SUIT A style of coat and pants worn by "hep cats," jazz artists and fans of the 1940s. Pants were full-legged and tight-cuffed; coat was long with flared lapels and padded shoulders.

ZORRO Black-garbed, masked swordsman, a Robin Hood of

Spanish California, was created in 1919 by Johnston McCulley. Many actors have performed role on screen, including Douglas Fairbanks in *The Mark of Zorro*(1920), Reed Haley in *Zorro's Fighting Legion*(1939), Guy Williams in TV's *Zorro*(1959) and George Hamilton as *Zorro, The Gay Blade* (1981).

ZURICH   Switzerland's largest city and capital of state of Zurich. Country's manufacturing, commercial and banking center. One of world's major financial centers and core of international trade. Located at north end of Lake Zurich. Divided into Little City and Great City by Limmat River. City settled as early as 100 B.C. State joined Swiss Confederation in 1351, which later became Switzerland.